THE MODERN
EARLY MI

MW01027613

The Early Middle Ages, which marked the end of the Roman Empire and the creation of the kingdoms of Western Europe, was a period central to the formation of modern Europe. This period has often been drawn into a series of discourses that are more concerned with the eighteenth, nineteenth, and twentieth centuries than with the distant past.

In *The Modern Origins of the Early Middle Ages*, Ian Wood explores how Western Europeans have looked back to the Middle Ages to discover their origins and the origins of their society. Using historical records and writings about the Fall of Rome and the Early Middle Ages, Wood reveals how these influenced modern Europe and the way in which the continent thought about itself. He asks, and answers, the important question: why is early-medieval history, or indeed any pre-modern history, important? This volume promises to add to the debate on the significance of medieval history in the modern world.

The Modern Origins of the Early Middle Ages

IAN WOOD

OXFORD
UNIVERSITY PRESS

OXFORD
UNIVERSITY PRESS

Great Clarendon Street, Oxford, OX2 6DP,
United Kingdom

Oxford University Press is a department of the University of Oxford.
It furthers the University's objective of excellence in research, scholarship,
and education by publishing worldwide. Oxford is a registered trade mark of
Oxford University Press in the UK and in certain other countries

© Ian Wood 2013

The moral rights of the author have been asserted

First published 2013
First published in paperback 2016

All rights reserved. No part of this publication may be reproduced, stored in
a retrieval system, or transmitted, in any form or by any means, without the
prior permission in writing of Oxford University Press, or as expressly permitted
by law, by licence or under terms agreed with the appropriate reprographics
rights organization. Enquiries concerning reproduction outside the scope of the
above should be sent to the Rights Department, Oxford University Press, at the
address above

You must not circulate this work in any other form
and you must impose this same condition on any acquirer

Published in the United States of America by Oxford University Press
198 Madison Avenue, New York, NY 10016, United States of America

British Library Cataloguing in Publication Data
Data available

Library of Congress Cataloging in Publication Data
Data available

ISBN 978–0–19–965048–4 (Hbk.)
ISBN 978–0–19–876749–7 (Pbk.)

Links to third party websites are provided by Oxford in good faith and
for information only. Oxford disclaims any responsibility for the materials
contained in any third party website referenced in this work.

For Ann, Jinty, Pauline, and Wendy

Preface

All books have specific contexts, and this one is no exception. Its subject matter is the changing interpretation within Europe of the end of the Roman Empire and the early Middle Ages from the eighteenth century to the present and how individual interpretations influenced and were influenced by the circumstances in which they were written. The underlying question of the book, however, is a related but slightly different one: why is early medieval history, or indeed any pre-modern history, important? This question was raised in a very sharp way by the then education secretary, Charles Clarke, in May 2003 when he allegedly stated 'I don't mind there being some medievalists around for ornamental purposes but there is no reason for the state to pay for them.'[1] A similar vision seems to underlie the Coalition Government's views of the place of the Humanities in Higher Education since 2010.

Modern historians can claim that they have a function in policing the use and abuse of the immediate past, some of which impinges unquestionably on the present.[2] Certainly history can and sometimes has to be a fact-checking exercise: but facts, particularly those relating to the distant past are often not amenable to strict verification. Moreover, interpretation is frequently an issue that is not black and white, and uncertainty is even more likely to affect our reading of the Middle Ages than of the modern period. Nevertheless, the issue of use and abuse is as relevant to interpreting the sixth as the twentieth century.[3] The Middle Ages are used and abused all the time.[4] Part of a response to Charles Clarke must therefore be that Medieval History is often exploited improperly, and this should not be allowed to pass without comment. At first sight, however, the misuse of Medieval History is insignificant: it is most obvious in the tendency of journalists and politicians to describe as 'medieval' or 'dark age' an atrocity that could only have happened in the nineteenth, twentieth, or twenty-first century: that is, when the word 'modern' would be more accurate.[5] It is easy to dismiss political rhetoric as nothing other than words. Yet rhetoric does matter, and the use of words like 'medieval' in modern discourse involves the exploitation of the past.

The use of the distant past, however, even of the early Middle Ages, is more than a matter of rhetorical colouring. The period from 300 to 700 has often been at the

[1] For what Charles Clarke may or may not have said, see Nelson, *Leadership in Society and the Academy*, pp. 4–5.

[2] Macmillan, *The uses and abuses of history*. For a medievalist such a response seems over-simple.

[3] Wood, 'The use and abuse of the Early Middle Ages, 1750–2000'.

[4] A particularly startling abuse of the supposed barbarian involvement in the Fall of the Roman Empire dominates a speech 'On the failure of multiculturalism and how to turn the tide' delivered in Rome by the right-wing Dutch politician Geert Wilders on 25th March 2011.

[5] Simon Jenkins of the *Guardian* is a regular offender, even though, as a lover of medieval parish churches he should know better.

heart of arguments about the modern world. It was central to debates about aristocratic privilege and about despotism in the eighteenth century; about class conflict, exploitation by foreign powers, and nationalism in the nineteenth; about the limits of Germany and the nature of Europe in the twentieth. Naturally, the circumstances in which they were discussed led the Fall of Rome and the early Middle Ages to be interpreted in particular ways. Historical argument is not just about the past: it is about the present. While the present determines how we see the past, the past is often used to validate or attack current circumstances—and that use may be accurate, mistaken, or fraudulent. In short, to use a concept developed by Michel Foucault, the interpretation of the early Middle Ages belongs to a modern historico-political discourse.[6]

We tend to use the past without thinking, above all about where our understanding of it has come from and why that might matter. Yet if we address the question of why certain historical events are and have been interpreted in particular ways, we start to understand why they have significance for the present, and we begin to have a more sophisticated response to Charles Clarke than a simple call for getting facts right. This book is thus a response to the notion that medieval history is purely ornamental.

That such a book needs to be written is a reflection of the tendency of historians, perhaps particularly historians trained in Britain, to have little interest in historiography—and those historians who do think a great deal about historiography, even those who are aware of the intellectual origins of the interpretations that concern them, rarely think hard about the political, social, economic, and cultural contexts in which those ideas were formulated. The Oxford History School, where I was trained in the early 1970s, was little interested in historiographical questions. Certainly there were historians who knew and appreciated their Gibbon, Kemble, Stubbs, Maitland, Brunner, and Pirenne. Yet the intellectual and social histories to which these authors themselves belonged were not made integral to our understanding of the past. In part this was because of a very Whiggish sense that historical interpretation was steadily improving. Indeed, I can remember being told, when embarking on research on fifth- and sixth-century Gaul that there was no point in reading anything on the Franks earlier than Wallace-Hadrill's *The Long-haired Kings*.[7] I hasten to add that it was not Wallace-Hadrill himself, who was my supervisor, nor indeed any of my tutors, who said this.[8] Among early medievalists, it would be Walter Goffart in the 1980s and 90s who first made me, and no doubt many of my generation, realize the quality of work written in the nineteenth century.[9]

---

[6] Foucault, *Society Must be Defended* (originally published as *Il faut défendre la société: cours au Collège de France 1975–6*).

[7] Wallace-Hadrill, *The Long-haired Kings and Other Studies in Frankish History.*

[8] Nor was it said by any of my undergraduate tutors, the early medievalists among them being Thomas Charles-Edwards, Henry Mayr-Harting, Peter Brown, Sabine McCormack, James Howard-Johnston, and John Matthews.

[9] Goffart, *Barbarians and Romans A.D. 418–584: The Techniques of Accommodation.*

I was, however, made aware of the relationship between the past and the context in which it has been interpreted on moving to London in 1974 and working in the Institute of Historical Research under the watchful eye of the librarian, Bill Kellaway. There was a certain frisson in opening volumes of the *Monumenta Germaniae Historica*, perhaps the greatest collection of early medieval sources, and seeing the bookplate 'Geschenk des Deutschen Reiches' ('Gift of the German Reich'), in seeing, just along the shelf, with the same bookplate, Adolf Hitler's *Mein Kampf*, and knowing that the students of the University of London had prevented von Ribbentrop from presenting them in person in 1937.[10] This was clearly medieval history that mattered.

That frisson certainly sensitized me to look for a relationship between past and present, but it scarcely brought home quite how important interpretations of the Early Middle Ages might be for an understanding of the present. No medievalist living at the time of the break-up of Yugoslavia in the 1990s, however, could have failed to realize quite how dangerous a reading of the past might be, especially after reading a work like Branimir Anzulovic's *Heavenly Serbia: From Myth to Genocide*.[11] It was as a result of this growing sensitivity to the relation between past and present that I first attempted to write about the development of historiography, in response to a request from Henk Wesseling at the Netherlands Institute for Advanced Study.

The significance of individual historians in interpreting the past was also borne in upon me as I came to appreciate the recollections of individuals I knew. Peter Sawyer's fund of anecdotes brought to life the intellectual milieux in which the Viking Age and Late Anglo-Saxon England had been debated in the 1950s and 60s—in Manchester, Birmingham, and in Scandinavia. Most students who studied the Early Middle Ages in Oxford in the late 1960s and early 1970s were equally aware of belonging to a period of intellectual ferment surrounding the lectures of Peter Brown and exemplified in the publication of *The World of Late Antiquity* in 1971.[12] Twenty-five years later I was fortunate enough to be invited to contribute to a volume reflecting on the significance of the book. The introductory article was Brown's own reconsideration of the work's genesis.[13] Here was a level of self-reflection that was then uncommon among historians, at least in print.

I had already started to consider historiography of a more distant period, as a result of a conference held in Oxford to mark the bicentenary of Gibbon's death[14]—centenaries of Gibbon have been among the rare moments over the last decades when specialists in Antiquity and the Early Middle Ages have thought hard about the development of their subject.[15] For me, the discovery in preparing a paper was not the value of Gibbon, which was less than I had expected, but rather the

---

[10] I should add that they are no longer on the open shelves.
[11] Anzulovic, *Heavenly Serbia: From Myth to Genocide*.
[12] Brown, *The World of Late Antiquity*.
[13] 'SO Debate: Peter Brown, *The World of Late Antiquity*'.
[14] McKitterick and Quinault (eds), *Edward Gibbon and Empire*.
[15] See Bowersock, Clive, and Graubard, *Edward Gibbon and the Decline and Fall of the Roman Empire*.

x Preface

importance of Mably—and that without Mably on the Merovingians Gibbon's attempt to deal with the Franks would have looked very different.[16]

One other circumstance led me to think hard about the relationship between the present and interpretation of the past. Michael Wallace-Hadrill died in 1985. Fifteen years later I was asked to write an obituary for the *Proceedings of the British Academy*. I settled down to read all Wallace-Hadrill's works in chronological order, so as to be able to describe the development of his thought.[17] It was in so doing that I found myself increasingly faced with the problem of understanding the relationship between his wartime experiences and his views of the early medieval past and its Germanic barbarians—and extrapolating from that the relationship between the Second World War and the interpretations developed by some of those who lived through that conflict. I was thinking about this in 2003, when Charles Clarke claimed that medieval history was ornamental.

A clear awareness of the importance of ideas and illusions about the Middle Ages for understanding current events in Yugoslavia, and a sense of the interrelation between Wallace-Hadrill's wartime experiences and his historical writing, fused to suggest the possibility of a response to the recurrent question of the value of early medieval history. A study of the historiography of the Early Middle Ages could provide something of an answer. To write about early medieval history is not just to solve a series of problems relating to the distant past: it is to engage in a complex (and often unrecognized) dialogue between past and present, in which the past is called upon as validation and critique of the here and now, and in which the present is, therefore, as much the subject of consideration as the past.

At the time that I embarked on the study of the interpretation of the late Roman and early medieval periods a number of continental historians were engaged in similar work. There was Claude Nicolet's study of the historiography of early Merovingian Gaul,[18] and François Hartog's intellectual biography of Fustel de Coulanges.[19] Even more exciting was Cinzio Violante's examination of the origins of Pirenne's *Histoire de l'Europe*,[20] lent to me by Girolamo Arnaldi. The liveliness of the subject has been confirmed most recently by Agnès Graceffa's study of French and German research on the Merovingians[21] and Hubert Fehr's analysis of archaeological work on Franks and Romans.[22]

The heritage industry would no doubt offer a different justification for work on the past, but its justification would be one of visitor numbers and hence of marketing and finance. Not that visiting museums and ruins can be entirely divorced from the question of the relationship between past and present: alongside films and historical novels, they are the part of the discourse that the general public

---

[16] Wood. 'Gibbon on the Merovingians'.   [17] Wood, 'John Michael Wallace-Hadrill'.
[18] Nicolet, *La Fabrique d'une nation.*   [19] Hartog, *Le XIXe siècle et l'histoire.*
[20] Violante, *La fine della 'grande illusione': uno storico europeo tra guerra e dopoguerra, Henri Pirenne (1914–1923): Per una rilettuta della 'Histoire de l'Europe'.*
[21] Graceffa, *Les Historiens et la question franque: le peuplement franc et les Mérovingiens dans l'historiographie française et allemande des XIXe–XXe siècles.*
[22] Fehr, *Germanen und Romanen im Merowingerreich. Frühgeschichtliche Archäologie zwischen Wissenschaft und Zeitgeschehen.*

experiences most frequently. In what follows I have not stretched my material to
cover film,[23] but I have occasionally turned to novels, notably those written by
historians who also wrote 'scholarly' history, and I have looked at the role of exhibitions of the early Middle Ages in presenting the period to the general public over
the last twenty years. The simple point is that the past matters, and not just because
of what happened, but also because of how we read it. Because the period from 300
to 700 saw some of the greatest changes in the history of Europe,[24] that past matters a great deal. It is at the heart of European identity—or at least of the identity
of French, Italians, Austrians, Germans, and Britons. To call the study of the early
Middle Ages ornamental seems to me to fundamentally misunderstand our own
situation in the modern world.

A few points need to be made about the references. For the sake of brevity I have
not provided full citations in the footnotes: the reader will find the information in
the bibliography. Where I have given a title in the text, and the comment is a
general one, I have not provided a footnote, but again the information is in the
bibliography.

With regard to references to works that ran through numerous editions, I have,
inevitably had to cite the edition to which I have had access, even if it is not the
first or the most scholarly. No doubt on occasion this will cause problems. In the
case of Gibbon's *Decline and Fall*, faced with an embarrassment of riches I have
simply cited by chapter number. So too, I have cited both Montesquieu's *De l'esprit
des loix*, Felix Dahn's *Ein Kampf um Rom*, and Thomas Hodgkin's *Italy and her
Invaders*, by volume/book and chapter number.

In addition, there is a question of terminology. Although on intellectual grounds
I would prefer to use the phrase 'Germanic people' rather than 'German' when
talking about the ancient people, I have not always done so. In English we do not
have the convenient distinction of 'allemand' and 'germain' that one finds in French
or 'Deutsch' and 'Germanen' in German, though in the nineteenth century I could
reasonably have used the word 'Teuton'. Sometimes writing 'Germanic people' is
simply too cumbersome: sometimes 'German' is a reflection of what is in the work
I am discussing.

In writing this book I have been extremely fortunate to hold a British Academy
Research Readership in 2004–6, the Balsdon Fellowship at tbe British School at
Rome in 2005–6, an AHRC Research Leave Award in 2009, and a fellowship at
Collegium Budapest in the same year. The awards made possible extensive research
way outside the normal field of competence of an early medievalist: certainly the
range of reading I have covered would have been impossible within the normal
pattern of teaching and study leave. In addition I was fortunate to have study leave
from the School of History at the University of Leeds in 2012 in order to complete

---

[23] On films of the Middle Ages, Airlie, 'Strange eventful histories: the Middle Ages in the
cinema'.

[24] It is, of course, a period of massive change globally, but that is not the theme of this book. The
global change can be glimpsed in Keys, *Catastrophe: An Investigation into the Origins of the Modern
World*.

the project. In many ways Leeds has been an excellent base for my work: the eighteenth-century collections in the Brotherton Collection are truly remarkable; the same cannot be said of the late nineteenth- and early twentieth-century holdings, some of which were simply thrown into skips on the librarian's instructions in the 1990s. Fortunately, interlibrary loan, the web, and also holdings at and in collections accessible from the British School at Rome and Collegium Budapest more than compensated. The staff at the British School and at the Collegium could not have been more helpful in supporting my research.

My intellectual debts are far too great to be listed in full, and no doubt there are some that I have forgotten, inexcusably. There are certainly many to whom I owe thanks. Jinty Nelson and Wendy Davies supported the project from the start. Jinty, Peter Brown, Ann Christys, Helmut Reimitz, and Pauline Stafford read drafts of every chapter, and Mayke de Jong and Martial Staub read all but two. Individual chapters (in some cases several of them) have been read by Simon Dixon, Moritz Foellmer, Alan Forrest, Pat Geary, Wolfgang Haubrichs, Joep Leerssen, Bill Stafford, Robert Tombs, and Mark Vessey. Girolamo Arnaldi, Enrico Artifoni, Janos Bak, David Ganz, Rafe Isserlin, Gabor Klaniczay, Cristina La Rocca, David Laven, Stéphane Lebecq, Regine Le Jan, Dáibhí Ó Cróinín, Meritxell Pérez Martínez, Walter Pohl, Pavlina Richterova, Hedwig Röckelein, Barbara Rosenwein, Felicitas Schmieder, and Peter Stamatov, have all provided me with information, answering questions, or supplying or lending copies of articles or books. I have benefitted from those present at seminars at Aberystwyth, Birmingham, Budapest, Cambridge, Leeds, Liverpool, London, Rome, and Vienna, when I presented early versions of various chapters. To everyone who has provided comment on or criticism of my work I owe a great debt of thanks.

This book has taken an interminable length of time to write, with the result that two people who I would have wished to thank did not live to see its appearance, much to my regret, given how much I owe them: Robert Markus, and Alberto Tarquini, who taught Italian to generations of scholars and students at the British School at Rome, and provided me with the skills to read the language with some ease.

Contents

1
300–700

1.1 INTRODUCTION

The period of transition from the end of classical Antiquity to the Middle Ages is regarded as one of the most important in history—at least from a European viewpoint. In political terms it has been seen as marking the break-up of the Roman Empire and the establishment of the so-called barbarian kingdoms. It is, therefore, the period to which several Western European states have traced their origins. France emerged from the Frankish kingdom and England from the kingdoms of the Anglo-Saxons. It has also been understood as marking a major socio-economic watershed: for Marx it saw the establishment of the feudal mode of production.[1] And it was the age of the triumph of Christianity in Western Europe.

Being a period of such rich importance, it is scarcely surprising that it has been interpreted in many ways, and that its significance has come to be variously understood. There are three dominant lines of interpretation: one is to see the period essentially in terms of the Fall of the Roman Empire; a second is to see it as the history of barbarian migration (the so-called *Völkerwanderung*) and the establishment of the barbarian kingdoms; the third is a religious reading. To a large extent these three interpretations deal with the same chronological period, although they have remained distinct in a number of ways: above all the first two are distinguished because the Fall of Rome is often seen from the perspective of a classicist, while the barbarian migration from that of a medievalist. What follows, however, will move between the historiographies of the Fall of the Empire, of the *Völkerwanderung*, and of the Church. The question of how the interpretations of the period have shifted, why, and in what contexts those shifts took place provides the subject matter of this book.

Certainly the *Völkerwanderung* has been treated within the broader framework of the historiography of the early Middle Ages, and it has been seen as the prelude to the creation of feudal society—especially within the French tradition, as it developed in the eighteenth century. One might, therefore, argue that to treat interpretations of the barbarian migration without continuing to the end of the millennium is to leave half the story untold. There are, however, distinct differences between the historiography of the period before

---

[1] Wickham, 'The other transition: from the ancient world to feudalism'.

the end of the seventh century and that which follows. While the origins of feudalism have been a point of discussion within the historiography of the *Völkerwanderungzeit*, they have not been a dominant issue since the nineteenth century, except perhaps in Spain, where protofeudalism has been a major theme.[2] By contrast, feudalism is a central issue in discussions of the period from the end of the seventh century onwards. Moreover, discussions about feudalism are usually discussions about society and social structure: discussions about the Fall of Rome and about the settlement of the barbarians have been much more focused on the idea of Western Europe and its constituent nations. From the beginning of the nineteenth century the dominant discourse underlying discussion of the period from 300 to 700 has often been the nature of Europe itself.

To make clear the extent of the changes that took place between 300 and 700, this chapter begins by sketching the start and end points of the period. What was the Mediterranean World like in 300? What was it like in 700? Having set out the beginning and the end, for the sake of orientation the chapter goes on to present a brief, essentially conventional narrative, of events between the two poles. This is by no means the only possible narrative, but the facts at least are not likely to be wrong—whether they are the most important ones is a different matter.

The facts are one thing, their interpretation another. The chapters that follow deal with the evolving interpretation of the period, in a predominantly chronological sequence, albeit one that initially sticks largely within national boundaries: France, Italy, Germany, and England. Historians in the eighteenth, nineteenth, and early twentieth centuries, however, were not insular, and we will often and increasingly consider debates that were not confined to any single country. In this chapter I will merely indicate the main schools of interpretation, their origins, and the basic discourses, that is, the major socio-political debates, to which they belong.

1.2 THE FOURTH AND THE SEVENTH CENTURIES

Between the beginning of the fourth and the end of the seventh century, the lands surrounding the Mediterranean and stretching up to the North Sea—in short, the lands of the Roman World—were transformed, politically, economically, culturally, and in their religious adherence. Although any period of four centuries will see considerable change, the developments in this region in this particular time-span were remarkable for their scale and for the extent to which they affected the future map of the region.

In 300, Southern and Western Europe (Ireland and Scotland excepted) was simply a part of the Roman Empire, whose focus was the Mediterranean, and the

---

[2] See now Hidalgo, Pérez, and Gervás (eds), *'Romanización' y 'Reconquista' en la península Ibérica: Nuevas perspectivas*.

Empire itself was still a major force.[3] It may not have been as peaceful and secure as it had been in the heyday of the second century, but it had just come through a long period of political unrest, when it had been subject to major onslaughts from alien peoples—both from the barbarian tribes that lived to the east of the Rhine and the north of the Danube, and also from the exotic and dangerous Persians of Mesopotamia. Diocletian (284–305) and his colleagues, and in the next generation Constantine (306–37), seemed to have put the Roman State back on the road to recovery. Its governmental institutions were reformed, and, while they may have been oppressive, they were functioning.[4] So too, its armies were reorganized, and they were now more than a match for their enemies to the North and East. And if the early fourth century was no Gold or Silver Age of Latin or Greek literature, there would nevertheless be a number of great prose and poetry writers over the next two hundred and fifty years, whose style and language gains grudging approval even from classicists.[5]

Four hundred years later the Mediterranean was no longer central. The Roman Empire still existed, but had been transformed into the Byzantine State, based on the great city of Constantinople. In size it was much smaller than the eastern half of the Roman Empire had been, although it still had substantial possessions in the Balkans immediately to the north and west of the city, and in Asia Minor, Greece, the Greek islands, together with a small amount of territory in southern Italy. In what had been the Roman province of Syria there was now a major new force: the Umayyad caliphate, whose power also encompassed Egypt and North Africa, as well as Persia and Arabia. In 711 it would start to expand into Spain.

In Western Europe, in place of the power of Rome, there were a number of what modern writers have called successor states. The Frankish kingdom, which occupied what had been the Roman provinces of Gaul and Germany, and whose power also stretched east beyond the Rhine, was potentially a force to be reckoned with, but in the late seventh and early eighth centuries it was in the doldrums. So too, the Visigothic kingdom in Spain had been of some influence and importance, but was entering a period of crisis, which would culminate in the Muslim invasion of 711. The kingdom of the Lombards by contrast was in its heyday, but, limited to the north and middle of the Italian peninsula, with two outliers in the duchies of Spoleto and Benevento, the latter of which was largely independent, it was never a superpower. Ultimately it would be crushed by an alliance between the papacy and the revived Frankish State under the Carolingians. Britain was divided into a series of petty kingdoms, some of which would amalgamate and would come in time to form the elements that would develop into the modern units of England, Wales,

---

[3] For a recent assessment, Cameron, *The Later Roman Empire: AD 284–430*, and id., *The Mediterranean World in Late Antiquity: AD 395–600*. For the centrality of the Mediterranean, Pirenne, *Mahomet et Charlemagne*; Wallace-Hadrill, *The Barbarian West*, 3rd edn, pp. 21–42; Brown, *The World of Late Antiquity*, pp. 11–21.

[4] For the functioning of the Roman State, Jones, *The Later Roman Empire, 284–601: A Social, Economic and Administrative Survey*. For its oppression, M. Rostovtzeff, *The Social and Economic History of the Roman Empire*; see Brown, 'Report', pp. 5–7, 13–14.

[5] See, for instance, Binns (ed.), *Latin Literature of the Fourth Century*.

and Scotland. Beyond what had been the Roman frontiers there had been significant changes, and not just in Scotland. New peoples had emerged to the north of
the Danube, most notably the Avars, a tribe of steppe nomads, and various Slav
groups, which were beginning to make their presence felt in areas that had previously been associated with those Goths and Lombards who had established successor states within the old Empire.

The economy of the Mediterranean was naturally affected by this political fragmentation. In the fourth century there had been an empire-wide economy, whose
chief motors were the demands of the State, and also those of the senatorial aristocracy, which had estates scattered through the whole of the Mediterranean
world as well as Rome's more northerly provinces: their holdings even stretched
to Britain.[6] With the collapse of the Western Empire these forces for economic
unity were gone. Not that there was no long-distance trade: amphorae from the
southern Mediterranean continued to reach western Britain into the sixth century, while ceramic and glass was imported from south-west Francia in the seventh.[7] After the First World War Henri Pirenne famously thought that the
expansion of Islam following Muhammad's death led to the collapse of the export
of papyrus from Egypt, and he saw this as indicative of the ending of Mediterranean trade, but we know that papyrus continued to reach Rome through to the
eleventh century.[8] And the recent discovery of an eighth-century rubbish dump
in the *Crypta Balbi* has revealed that Rome itself was involved in a rather more
vibrant economy than anyone had suspected.[9] Even so, the economy of the lands
to the north of the Mediterranean in the seventh century was more local and
poorer than it had been four hundred years earlier.[10] The southern shore belonged
to the different political world of the Islamic caliphate and hence to another,
albeit overlapping, economy.

While there was political, social, and economic fragmentation in the territory of
the Roman world during the fifth, sixth, and seventh centuries, religious change
followed a different trajectory, not that it ended in absolute unity. The spread of
Christianity, which was still the religion of a persecuted minority in 300, and was
only officially recognized as a State religion by Constantine after 312, is perhaps
the most significant feature of the ensuing centuries.[11] Before its western half collapsed, the Roman Empire had been christianized, despite divisions within the
Church caused by disputes over key tenets of belief, notably concerning the nature
of Christ. Divisions in doctrine and in cult made this an age of 'micro-Christen-
doms'.[12] By the early sixth century the incoming barbarians had been converted,
and the eighth century would see the beginnings of missionary activity way to the

---

[6] For an example of the scale of aristocratic estate holdings, see *Vie de sainte Mélanie*, ed. Gorce,
p. 147, with n. 1.
[7] Campbell, *Continental and Mediterranean Imports to Atlantic Britain and Ireland, AD 400–800*.
[8] Wickham, *Framing the Early Middle Ages*, p. 701.
[9] Manacorda, *Museo Nationale Romano: Crypta Balbi*.
[10] Wickham, *Framing the Early Middle Ages*.   [11] Brown, *The Rise of Western Christendom*.
[12] Brown, *The Rise of Western Christendom*.

east of the Rhine. In the East, however, Christianity was challenged by Islam from the 630s onwards.

The institution of a new religion meant more than a change in belief and the substitution of one (trinitarian) God for the pagan pantheon. Despite its great temples, Roman paganism, divided as it was among numerous cults, never exercised the same influence as that built up by the early medieval Christian Church, for it was nothing like as coherent an institution: indeed it was not an institution.

The Church impacted upon everything that contributed to its upkeep, which involved vast transfers of land and wealth (in Francia perhaps up to a third of the kingdom).[13] It left its mark on the landscape with the erection of churches and monasteries: in so far as any major stone building was set up in the seventh century, it was commissioned by or for the Church.[14] But even the greatest of the churches built after the mid-sixth century were on a smaller scale than that of the major buildings of the late Roman world.[15] The most impressive of the monuments set up in the late seventh and early eighth centuries were the great mosques of the Middle East: the al-Aqsa and the Dome of the Rock in Jerusalem, and the Umayyad Mosque in Damascus.

In cultural terms, as in economic, the late seventh century looks a good deal poorer than the fourth, although one can point to individual artistic masterpieces—particular pieces of goldwork and jewellery and certain outstanding manuscripts.[16] It is possible to defend the written language of the period, by saying that it reflected change and was closer to the spoken word than what had been written down before, but it certainly does not conform to the standards of grammar and style that an educated Roman would have understood.[17] One can also say that texts of this period, other than inscriptions, survive from more centres, and from a far larger social range, than is the case in classical Antiquity. That may be largely a matter of survival: but it is also a reflection of the fact that the majority of written texts from late seventh-century Western Europe are in some way or other connected to the Christian churches, whether composed by churchmen or preserved within Church archives—some of which had a continuous history up to modern times. That, however, only reinforces the sense to which the seventh century differs from the fourth.

1.3 NARRATING THE CHANGE

It is easy to contrast the two periods. It is not difficult to offer a basic narrative of events linking them. Even so, any narrative sketch is inevitably an act of

[13] Wood, 'Landscapes compared', p. 236; id., 'Entrusting Western Europe to the Church, 400–750'.
[14] Ward-Perkins, *The Fall of Rome and the End of Civilization*, pp. 148–50.
[15] Ward-Perkins, *The Fall of Rome and the End of Civilization*, pp. 148–50.
[16] For an assessment of cultural change see Wood, 'Culture'; Ward-Perkins, 'Art and architecture of Western Europe'.
[17] Banniard, *Viva voce: communication écrite et communication orale du IVe au XIe siècle en occident latin*; Wright, *Late Latin and early Romance in Spain and Carolingian France*.

interpretation—or rather the product of generations of scholarship influenced by the social, political, and religious debates that will concern us later. And while its basic line may be generally accepted, what follows involves omissions that some would see as leading to substantial misrepresentation, especially as it leaves to one side a good deal of ecclesiastical history: above all it bypasses the detailed religious narrative, with its tortuous theological conflicts. To do so begs an important question relating to the extent to which religious debate impinged on contemporary social and political developments.[18] As a brief introduction to a sequence of stories that we will revisit on a number of occasions throughout this book, the following sketch may, however, be useful.

Following his seizure of power, a process that began in 306 and concluded in 324, Constantine completed a series of military and administrative reforms that had been initiated by the emperor Diocletian.[19] As a result, the Empire seemed to have been restored to its former glory. At the same time, his acceptance of Christianity made possible the christianization of the Empire, which proceeded steadily through the fourth century, despite a brief period of pagan revival under the emperor Julian (355–63).

In 376 a new crisis confronted the Roman world, when Goths, themselves under attack from Hunnic nomads, begged to be allowed to cross the Danube frontier. At roughly the same time, and perhaps partly in negotiation with the Empire, they accepted Christianity, thus making them the first barbarian group to be converted.[20] In other respects their entry was mishandled, leading to open war, and the defeat of a Roman army and the death of an emperor, Valens, at the Battle of Adrianople in 378. Although the Romans did regain the upper hand militarily during the reign of Theodosius (379–95), they did not solve the problem posed by the Visigoths, with rival eastern and western administrations in Constantinople and Rome failing to unite to deal with the danger for once and for all.

This disunity between East and West and incompetence on the part of the western government led the Visigoths to sack Rome in 410. Meanwhile, the rivalry with the East and the presence in Italy of the Goths, distracted the western government, by now based in Ravenna, and gave other barbarian invaders (above all Vandals, Alans, and Sueves) the opportunity to cross the Rhine in 406. This in turn prompted local leaders in Britain and Gaul to take matters into their own hands and to rebel against the Western Roman imperial court. Continuing rivalries between Roman generals prevented any unified response to the barbarians, with the result that the Vandals were able to establish themselves in North Africa after 429. A decade later they took Carthage and thus deprived the city of Rome of its vital grain supplies. On top of this crisis, a renewed Hunnic threat under the leadership of Attila further exposed the weakness of the Western Empire, despite a Roman victory at the battle of the Catalaunian Plains, to the east of Paris, in 451.

---

[18] Frend, 'Heresy and schism as social and national movements'; Markus, 'Christianity and dissent in Roman North Africa'.

[19] Cameron, *The Later Roman Empire*.

[20] Heather, 'The crossing of the Danube and the Gothic conversion'.

Given the divisions at court, and the fact that Rome's generals became increasingly dependent on barbarian troops, it is not surprising that Germanic leaders took matters into their own hands: one barbarian general, Odoacer deposed the last western emperor to be appointed, Romulus Augustulus, in 476, and by 500, new kingdoms had been established in Gaul, Spain, Africa, and Italy. The government of these 'successor states' was essentially Roman, as indeed was the religion, for the new barbarian elite quickly accepted Christianity, albeit often in its heretical, Arian, form, which led to occasional conflict with the indigenous Catholic hierarchy. The establishment of Germanic kingdoms in what had been the Roman province of Britain is rather harder to trace: it is only from the late sixth and early seventh century that we can be sure that dynasties described as either Anglian or Saxon actually constituted the main political power in what would become England,[21] and it was only in the century beginning in 597 that the new Anglo-Saxon regimes were converted.

From the early 530s onwards, the Byzantine emperor Justinian (527–65) attempted to reverse the collapse of Roman power in the western Mediterranean, launching campaigns against Vandal Africa and against Ostrogothic Italy, while also meddling in Visigothic Spain. For all Justinian's success, Byzantine Africa was left open to Berber incursions and would, in the second half of the seventh century, fall to Islamic invaders. The wars in Italy, which were drawn out over almost two decades (535–54), devastated the region and did more to destroy Roman society than did any of the preceding barbarian settlements—indeed the Ostrogothic State had been notable for the extent to which it marked a continuation of Roman, even imperial, tradition in the peninsula. The result was that Italy was powerless to cope with a new Lombard invasion in 568, which resulted in the creation of a kingdom based on Pavia and Milan in the North, with dependent duchies in Spoleto and Benevento—leaving a much reduced area of Byzantine control that was essentially limited to Ravenna, Rome, and the far south, with Rome itself increasingly looking to the popes for leadership. The Lombards, when they moved into Italy, abandoned the territory they held in what had been the Roman province of Pannonia (essentially western Hungary), supposedly gifting it to the Avars—a nomadic force that in many ways revived the Hunnic threat. Expanding alongside them were the newly emergent Slavs, whose origins still remain obscure.[22] The Avars and Slavs effectively broke Byzantine control of the western Balkans.

Crisis in the Balkans, culminating in the overthrow of the emperor Maurice (582–602), encouraged the renewal of Persian aggression against the Roman provinces of the Near East, which had already been somewhat alienated from Constantinople as a result of a series of doctrinal conflicts.[23] Although Heraclius (610–41) was able to reassert Byzantine control in 627, a further threat emerged in the following decade, when the successors of Muhammad began to expand their activities

[21] Bassett (ed.) *The Origins of Anglo-Saxon Kingdoms*.
[22] Curta, *The Making of the Slavs*; Barford, *The Early Slavs*.
[23] Frend, *The Rise of the Monophysite Movement*.

outside the Arabian Peninsula, destroying the Persian Empire and taking over the provinces of Syria and Egypt.[24] By 670 Umayyad power had expanded as far as Kairouan in eastern Tunisia, and in 698 Carthage fell to what was by then a largely Berber, rather than Arab, force. Thirteen years later a Berber army crossed the Straits of Gibraltar. The expansion of Islam radically reduced the scale of Byzantine power. It also broke the unity of the eastern Mediterranean: that of the West had been upset already by the Vandal seizure of Africa, and had never really been re-established, despite Justinian's attempts at conquest. Thus, the expansion of Islamic power effectively brought to a conclusion the developments that began with the Gothic entry into the Empire in 376.

1.4 INTERPRETING THE CHANGE

Interpretations of the developments of these centuries have tended to emphasize one of three major perspectives: the internal history of the Roman Empire itself (a reading often referred to as Romanist), the contribution of the barbarians (the Germanist reading),[25] and the triumph of Christianity.[26] Few historians apart from Edward Gibbon have attempted to consider all three issues, although a larger number have looked at the first two, and tried to balance the significance of internal weakness against the destruction brought by the barbarian incomers.

Those who have concentrated on the internal problems of the Empire have often stressed the tendency of imperial power to degenerate into despotism, which, it was thought, led to a steady weakening of civic virtue.[27] As the power of the emperors grew, so the commitment of the citizens towards the state was undermined. The senatorial aristocracy, largely exempt from tax and able to avoid the burdens of administrative duty, may have become less interested in contributing to serving the state. Moreover, although some aristocrats still retained a sense of public duty and beautified their cities through acts of public munificence, this happened much less frequently than had been the case in the second century.[28] Lower down the social scale, the burdens imposed by the administration and the weight of taxation led to growing social discontent.[29]

Alongside these arguments, stress has been laid on the problem of the Empire's size and the difficulty of governing it.[30] The administrative division of East and West, which occurred from the late third century onwards in an attempt to render

---

[24] Kennedy, *The Prophet and the Age of the Caliphates*; id., *The Great Arab Conquests*.
[25] The extent to which recent discussion has been polarized around these two lines of interpretation is well brought out by Halsall, 'Movers and Shakers', p. 133.
[26] Brown, *The Rise of Western Christendom*; Markus, *The End of Ancient Christianity*.
[27] Montesquieu, *Considérations sur la grandeur des romains*, ch. 17, ed. Charvat, pp. 195–207; trans. Lowenthal, pp. 156–65; Gibbon, *Decline and Fall*, ch. 38, 'General observations on the Fall of the Roman Empire in the West', II.
[28] Brown, *Poverty and Leadership in the Later Roman Empire*, p. 28.
[29] Van Dam, *Leadership and Community in Late Antique Gaul*, pp. 42–5.
[30] Cameron, *The Later Roman Empire*, pp. 99–112.

the Empire more manageable, has been seen as a major weakness, not least because of the emergence of rival courts, whose leading politicians were frequently unwilling to work in the common interest. The eastern court encouraged the Visigoths to move west, thus relieving the Balkans of a threat, but radically destabilizing Italy, and subsequently Gaul and Spain. Although Justinian in the sixth century made an attempt to reunite the Mediterranean, the role previously played by Constantinople had been a factor in the failure of the Western Empire.

Other explanations for imperial decline have concentrated on the role of the army, which was required to defend the frontiers, but was liable to become too powerful for its political masters—a danger that was already apparent in 69 AD, following the death of Nero, when four emperors were put on the imperial throne, each backed by different forces. Despite the importance of the legions, by the beginning of the fourth century there were increasing problems in military recruitment.[31] As a result of the shortfall in numbers, the army had to rely more and more on the contribution of barbarians, long before the Visigoths crossed the Rhine.

Rather than see the internal weaknesses of the Empire as carrying the key to its disintegration, other historians have presented the barbarians as playing the chief role in its destruction.[32] Here the emphasis has usually been on the scale of the fourth- and fifth-century invasions (something which is itself hotly debated, with those historians inclined to stress internal factors tending to present the barbarians as relatively few in number).[33] In addition to the question of the scale of the barbarian invasions, there has been a debate about the extent to which the barbarians deliberately set out to destroy the Empire. Some have seen the incomers as being intent on finding a place within the Roman world, and only breaking it by accident:[34] others, especially those writing in the period immediately after 1945, saw the barbarians as much more destructive.[35]

Instead of concentrating on either the internal problems of the Empire or the threat posed by the barbarians, historians of the Church have looked at the extraordinary triumph of Christianity, following the failure of the Great Persecution (303–11).[36] Alongside the establishment of Christianity as the State religion, which occurred decisively under Theodosius I, this was the age of the great oecumenical councils of the Church. It was also that of the Church Fathers—Ambrose (d.397), Jerome (d.420), Augustine (d.430), and Gregory the Great (pope, 590–604)—whose writings, taken all together, are often seen as marking a cultural and intellectual highpoint in religious history. But, in addition, it was a period of religious division: the writings of the Fathers were essentially salvos in the theological

[31] Ferrill, *The Fall of the Roman Empire: The Military Explanation*.
[32] Ward-Perkins, *The Fall of Rome and the End of Civilization*.
[33] Goffart, *Barbarian Tides*.
[34] The classic statement is Pirenne, *Mahomet et Charlemagne*.
[35] See the comments in Ward-Perkins, *The Fall of Rome and the End of Civilization*, p. 173–4. Thompson, 'The Visigoths from Fritigern to Euric', stressed the existence of factions hostile to the Empire among the Visigoths. Id., 'Economic Warfare', also stresses antagonism between Romans and barbarians.
[36] Markus, *Christianity in the Roman World*; id., *The End of Ancient Christianity*.

arguments of the period. The ensuing doctrinal divisions, as various theological parties battled for dominance, led to the establishment of an orthodoxy, and the condemnation of those who lost out as heretics—Arians, Donatists, Priscillians, Pelagians, Nestorians, Monophysites, and Monotheletes, to name only the most significant of the losers.

In addition to theological debates of the period, some historians have stressed its ascetic spirituality, placing particular emphasis on the development of monasticism.[37] Also seen as indications both of the spirituality of the age and of its superstition, the cult of saints and of relics had their origins in the fourth century.[38] The cult of icons appears to have developed slightly later, but certainly by the end of the sixth.[39] Relics and icons have, like monasticism, been interpreted both as an indication of the decadence of the age and of its spiritual vitality.

1.5 THE ORIGINS OF THE DEBATES

Although much discussion of the decline of the Empire has ignored the rise of the Christian Church, the ecclesiastical history of the late Roman and early medieval periods was placed at the centre of debate by Reformation apologists in England and Germany. Already in the reign of Henry VIII, the ex-Carmelite John Bale put the early history of the Church to use in defence of Protestantism, arguing that corruption set in during Constantine's reign.[40] Not all the English protestants placed the decline of the Church so early: in the second half of the sixteenth century Archbishop Parker was concerned to find antecedents for the ideas of the Anglican Church in the writings of Anglo-Saxon churchmen, and it was largely to this end that he collected the earliest English manuscripts.[41]

At the same time a group of Lutheran scholars, known from their place of study as the Magdeburg Centuriators, produced a history of the first thirteen centuries of Christianity, progressing century by century, hence the name under which they are known. Their work appeared between 1559 and 1574: the fourth volume of the history was dedicated to queen Elizabeth. Like Parker, the centuriators were happy to accept Gregory the Great as orthodox. Rather than identify a single period at which the Church degenerated, they assessed each author according to his theological works.[42] The work of the Magdeburg Centuriators prompted the Italian cardinal Cesare Baronio (usually known to later historians as Baronius) to produce his *Annales Ecclesiastici* (1588–1607), which traced the history of the Church

[37] Dawson, *The Making of Europe*.
[38] Brown, *The Cult of the Saints*.
[39] For a discussion of the early history of images, see Noble, *Images, Iconoclasm, and the Carolingians*, pp. 10–45.
[40] Frantzen, 'Bede and Bawdy Bale: Gregory the Great, Angels, and the "Angli"'; also id., *Desire for Origins*, pp. 37–42; MacDougall, *Racial Myth in English History*, pp. 33–4.
[41] Frantzen, *Desire for Origins*, pp. 43–4; on other contributors to the debates, see pp. 130–67. Also MacDougall, *Racial Myth in English History*, pp. 38–40.
[42] On the Centuriators, see Scheible, *Die Entstehung der Magdeburger Zenturien*.

up to the end of the twelfth century, providing a Catholic response to the Lutheran reading. This was a good deal more than a simple work of polemic: having access to the Vatican archives, Baronio was able to consult material that had long been forgotten.[43] As a result, his work constituted a major contribution to Church history.

Churchmen were also the first to direct attention to the early history of the barbarians. At the Council of Basel, which lasted from 1431 to 1449, the Swedish bishops insisted on the importance of the *Historia Getica*, the *Gothic History* by the sixth-century historian Jordanes, claiming that it revealed the Swedes to be the oldest nation in Europe, and therefore that they should have precedence at the council. The bishops of Habsburg Austria disagreed with their conclusions.[44] The idea that the Goths originated in Sweden was picked up again by the last Catholic bishop of Uppsala, Johannes Magnus, in his *Historia de omnibus Gothorum Sueonumque Regibus* ('History of all the kings of the Goths and Swedes'), which was published by his brother Olaus in Rome in 1554.[45] Olaus followed this up a year later with own *Historia de gentibus septentrionalibus* ('History of the Northern Peoples').[46] Although Johannes wrote in exile, following his country's adoption of Lutheranism, his argument was not a religious one, but rather an assertion of Swedish nationalism against the Danish crown, which had ruled Sweden up until 1523.

Equally important was another political argument, but this time one initially confined to France.[47] The thesis of François Hotman in his *Franco-Gallia* of 1573/4 is abundantly clear from the sub-title of the English translation, published in 1711: 'An account of the Ancient Free State of France and most other parts of Europe, before the loss of their liberties'.[48] Hotman was, as it so happened, a Protestant, but his arguments about early medieval history were secular, amounting to an essay in political theory. He traced the history of the land of France from the time that it was held by the Gauls, before the Roman conquest, down to the end of the Capetian dynasty. The Gauls he saw as a free people, whose rulers were not hereditary. Their freedom was ended by the Roman occupation, which introduced a period of servitude. This they challenged, according to Hotman, by hiring colonies of German auxiliaries to help them.[49] For Hotman the Roman period was a time of great oppression.[50] The Franks he regarded by contrast as freedom-loving: indeed he

---

[43] See Falco, 'La questione longobarda e la moderna storiografia italiana', pp. 154–6; Jedin, *Kardinal Caesar Baronius*. Also Tabacco, 'Latinità e germanesimo nella tradizione medievistica italiana', pp. 699–700.

[44] Christensen, *Cassiodorus, Jordanes and the History of the Goths*, pp. 7–8. For the Austrian response, Wolfram, *History of the Goths*, p. 2. For the conciliar context, Hirschi, *Wettkampf der Nationen*, pp. 135–43.

[45] Magnus, *Historia de omnibus Gothorum Sueonumque Regibus*; see Beck, *Northern Antiquities*, vol. 1, p. 46.

[46] Magnus, *Historia de gentibus septentrionalibus*.

[47] See Bloch, 'Sur les grandes invasions: quelques positions de problèmes', in id., *Mélanges historiques*, p. 92.

[48] Hotman, *Franco-Gallia*.

[49] Hotman, *Franco-Gallia* (1711), p. 18.   [50] Hotman, *Franco-Gallia* (1711), p. 19.

took their name to mean 'freemen'.[51] Although they had kings, they were not tyrants, 'but keepers of their Liberties, Protectors, Governors and Tutors.'[52] They were, moreover, elective rather than hereditary.[53] The elective nature of the monarchy was even apparent in the appointment of the first Carolingian ruler, Pippin III, who, Hotman was particularly concerned to demonstrate, was not appointed by the pope.[54] He regarded the constitution of the Franks as being an ideal one that blended the kingly, the noble, and the popular, seeing therein the origin of the Three Estates, a pattern that he found echoed throughout Europe.[55] In the Merovingian and Carolingian periods the Frankish constitution was dominated by the public assembly,[56] and, according to Hotman, this remained the case under the Capetians.[57]

Hotman's analysis of government, with its insistence on the ideal balance of the Three Estates, was not the only appeal to the early medieval past made by political commentators of the sixteenth and seventeenth centuries. The English Parliamentarians, and Sir Edward Coke in particular, made a great deal of Anglo-Saxon law in their attack on the powers of the monarchy: here were the origins of English liberty, before the imposition of the Norman yoke.[58] Thus, the early development of Anglo-Saxon studies was divided between the Church tradition, which concentrated on discovering origins for the Anglican settlement, and that of the lawyers, who used the pre-Norman past to argue against royal absolutism, much as Hotman had used the Merovingian and Carolingian periods to criticize the growing power of the French monarchy. Hotman in France and the likes of Coke in England initiated a set of political arguments in which the early medieval past, whether Frankish or Anglo-Saxon, was central to an analysis of royal authority through the seventeenth and into the early eighteenth century.[59]

Feeding into the debates about liberty was a further text that came to be regarded as central to an understanding of the early Middle Ages: the *Germania* of Tacitus, the sole manuscript of which was discovered in 1425,[60] shortly before the Swedish bishops produced their copy of Jordanes. Although written at the end of the first century AD, it provided one of the most extensive accounts of the Germanic peoples and was thus cited to provide descriptions of the barbarians of the Migration Period of the fourth and fifth centuries. It would come to play a role in defining the German nation in the decades running up to unification in the nineteenth century, but a hundred years earlier it was seen by the likes of Montesquieu as a key text in the association of the barbarians with the notion of liberty.

---

[51] Hotman, *Franco-Gallia* (1711), p. 29.   [52] Hotman, *Franco-Gallia* (1711), p. 31.
[53] Hotman, *Franco-Gallia* (1711), pp. 42–3.   [54] Hotman, *Franco-Gallia* (1711), pp. 90–7.
[55] Hotman, *Franco-Gallia* (1711), pp. 63–77.
[56] Hotman, *Franco-Gallia* (1711), pp. 77–85, 104–10.
[57] Hotman, *Franco-Gallia* (1711), pp. 114–24.
[58] Murphy, 'Antiquary to academic: the progress of Anglo-Saxon scholarship', p. 5; MacDougall, *Racial Myth in English History*, pp. 54–64.
[59] On the English debate, MacDougall, *Racial Myth in English History*, pp. 73–86; for the French, Leffler, 'French historians and the challenge to Louis XIV's absolutism'.
[60] Schama, *Landscape and Memory*, pp. 76–7. See now Krebs, *A Most Dangerous Book*.

The division between ecclesiastical and secular history was, therefore, not created by modern historians, but rather grew out of the way that different groups in the sixteenth and seventeenth centuries used the past for their own ends. The two types of history had effectively already been separated during the early modern period. There were exceptional historians who worked across the divide. In the second half of the seventeenth century Louis-Sébastien Le Nain de Tillemont wrote impressively on both the secular and ecclesiastical histories of the first Christian centuries in his *Mémoires pour servir à l'histoire ecclésiastique* and his *Histoire des empereurs et autres princes qui ont regné pendant les six premiers siècles de l'Église.*[61] Not surprisingly, on a number of occasions he is cited by Gibbon, whose explanation for the Fall of the Empire combined notions of the decline of Roman civic virtue, imperial despotism, Christian superstition, and Germanic barbarism.

The Italian tradition also tended to combine aspects of secular and ecclesiastical history, and has continued to do so, perhaps because of the central position of the papacy within the peninsula. Thus, Machiavelli's analysis of post-Roman Italy saw hostility between the papacy and the Lombards as being a central factor in the region's weakness. Although Baronius countered with a more providential, Catholic reading, Muratori, who also edited many of the major sources for the history of medieval Italy, went some way towards reinstating Machiavelli's anti-papal approach, and this became the norm among eighteenth-century Italian historians.[62] As we shall see, in the nineteenth century Manzoni rejected Machiavelli's sympathetic interpretation of the Lombards, presenting them rather as heretical conquerors, who oppressed the population of northern and central Italy. Like Machiavelli, however, Manzoni did put relations between the papacy and the Lombards at the heart of his interpretation.

1.6 POLITICO-HISTORICAL DISCOURSES OF THE MODERN PERIOD

Manzoni was engaging in a long-established Italian debate about the division of the Italian peninsula and its resulting weakness. He was also tapping into a new set of debates in which the history of Rome's fall and the establishment of the barbarian kingdoms came increasingly to move away from discussion of government and to emphasize instead issues of privilege and class, and subsequently of nation and state. It is these debates that really form the starting point of the current study.

In the early eighteenth century Henri comte de Boulainvilliers presented the Frankish invasion as justification of the privileges of the French aristocracy. This Michel Foucault saw as the beginning of a new politico-historical discourse.[63] By

---

[61] Le Nain de Tillemont, *Mémoires pour servir à l'histoire ecclésiastique des six premiers siècles*; id., *Histoire des empereurs et autres princes qui ont regné pendant les six premiers siècles de l'Église.*

[62] Falco, 'La questione longobarda e la moderna storiografia italiana', pp. 153–9.

[63] Among Michel Foucault's works I have been particularly influenced by *Society Must be Defended*, which deals with a number of the figures who are central to my own enquiry, most particularly Henri, comte de Boulainvilliers.

the end of the century the argument had been turned inside out, with the revolutionaries determined to destroy the privileges supposedly derived from the Frankish conquest of the fifth century. In the early nineteenth century Augustin Thierry portrayed the conquest overtly in terms of class conflict. Manzoni drew on this interpretation in his depiction of the Lombards, and in his suggestion that the period of Lombard rule presented a model for understanding the political divisions of an Italy still subject to the authority of foreign powers.

Not everyone, however, saw the early Germans in a negative light. Within Germany itself there was increasing emphasis on Germanic ancestors, who came to play a significant role in the sense of national unity that underlay the drive towards unification. And here it was not just the historical narrative that provided material for interpretation: the vernacular languages, as elucidated by the developing science of philology,[64] shed light on the heroic culture of the early medieval world, while the emergence of scientific archaeology allowed study of the material culture of the Germanic peoples and, if not their settlements, at least their cemeteries.[65]

Thus, interpretations of the early Middle Ages came to be dominated in the nineteenth century by nationalist discourse, which took the place of the previous political and social readings current in the *Ancien Régime* and which had originated in the Renaissance and Reformation. As a result, from the middle of the century, the Germanic reading of the period from 300 to 700 tended to overshadow that which stressed the internal history of the Empire. The heroic Germans, as revealed by history, philology, and archaeology, were given a role in the creation of a new Germany, and they would be used as a justification for expansion beyond the frontiers of the Reich. They thus came to dominate discourse about the Fall of Rome in the first half of the twentieth century. There was, however, always a body of active Romanists, formed through the ever-thriving study of Classics,[66] who looked on the period in a different way and who contributed greatly to debates about Empire, which fed into the ideology of late Victorian Britain. The Christian significance of the age, meanwhile, was stressed by a handful of authors whose prime concern was the religious and spiritual regeneration of Europe.[67]

1.7 HISTORICAL DISCOURSE AND THE PROFESSION OF HISTORY

Despite the Italian historiographical tradition, the history of the Church has rarely been integrated into works that have dealt with the political, economic, and social changes of Western Europe. The end of the Roman Empire and the rise of Western

---

[64] Leerssen, *National Thought in Europe*, esp. pp. 122–6.
[65] Effros, *Merovingian Mortuary Archaeology and the Making of the Early Middle Ages*.
[66] Marchand, *Down from Olympus*.
[67] Ozanam, *La Civilisation au cinquième siècle*; Montalembert, *Les Moines d'Occident*; Dawson, *The Making of Europe*.

Christendom, although to a large extent coterminous, have largely been the subject of different historiographies. There is clearly a case for integrating the two lines of enquiry.[68] That, however, is not my purpose in what follows. My concern is rather to trace the developing interpretations of the end of the Western Empire and the emergence of the successor states from the fourth through to the beginning of the eighth century, and to look at the interplay between the contexts—political, social, cultural and religious—in which historians were working, on the one hand, and at their interpretations of the past, on the other.

To follow every interpreter and interpretation would make for a very dense study. Rather, I have followed Michel Foucault's model in trying to identify a dominant discourse,[69] or, better, discourses in the plural. The major areas of debate and the types of arguments deployed naturally reflect dominant concerns of the period in which they were set down. This is not simply a matter of spin or bias, although both are frequently, but not always, present. Choices were, and are often, made unconsciously, but they are no less important, and no less visible in hindsight, for that.

The English historian Edward Augustus Freeman, writing in 1860, remarked that

> The past and the present are for ever connected; but the kind of connexion which exists between them differs widely in different cases. Past history and modern politics are always influencing one another; but the forms which their mutual influence takes are infinitely varied. Sometimes the business of the historian is to point out real connexions and real analogies which the world at large does not perceive. This is most conspicuously his duty in dealing with what is called the 'ancient' history of Greece and Italy, and to a large extent also, in dealing with the early and mediæval history of our own island. Sometimes, on the other hand, it is his duty to upset false connexions and false analogies, which have not only misled historical students, but have often exercised a most baneful influence on public affairs. This is his primary duty when dealing with the history of Gaul and France.

Freeman could see that use was always being made of the past: he could see its dangers, but he also felt that comparison between past and present did have its place.

> It is worth our while to show that Queen Victoria is in every sense the true successor of Cerdic and Ælfred and Edward the First, it is no less worth our while to show that Louis Napoleon Buonaparte is in no conceivable sense the successor of Clovis and of Charles the Great.[70]

Thus, for all his admirable sentiments, Freeman himself descends into patriotism and Francophobia, by denigrating the French and elevating the English: in short, into bias.

---

[68] Brown, *The Rise of Western Christendom* goes some way towards doing so.
[69] Foucault, *Society Must be Defended*.
[70] Freeman, 'The Franks and the Gauls', *Select Historical Essays*, pp. 49–50.

In fact, Freeman both points to the interplay between past and present, and illustrates how difficult it is to keep an appropriate distance between them. One should remember that he was writing relatively soon after History had become a fully established university subject in Britain. Although Regius Professorships had been established in Oxford and Cambridge in 1724, it was not until 1851 that History was firmly established as a subject in the Cambridge curriculum, while the first History degree-scheme was only introduced in the University of Oxford in 1872, under the guidance of Bishop Stubbs.[71] Freeman was his successor in the Regius Chair. In other words, he was writing when the professionalization of history in Britain was in its infancy. Although France and Germany were a little further advanced,[72] many of the interpreters of the early Middle Ages who we will meet in the following chapters received their intellectual formation before History was truly professionalized.

It would be wrong, however, to think that professionalization has led to historians being immune from the circumstances in which they write, or to think that, as a result of improved training, they are any less likely to suffer from bias. The professional historian is caught up in the discourses of his or her age—just as much as is the amateur—and we will meet twentieth-century professionals who have abused their subject matter every bit as much as writers with less formal academic training.[73] It is, however, precisely the interplay between scholarship and the world in which the scholar is working that concerns me in this book, for it sheds considerable light on the question of why certain issues have been privileged in the debate about the period from 300 to 700, and why others have drifted from view.

1.8 LIMITING THE FIELD

In opting to begin my investigation of the historical discourses that dominate the reading of Late Antiquity and the early Middle Ages with the writings of a French aristocrat, Henri comte de Boulainvilliers, I have no intention of denying the interest and value of scholarship set down in the course of the sixteenth and seventeenth centuries.[74] Yet, as Foucault noted, Boulainvilliers can be described as initiating a

---

[71] Harrison, Jones, and Lambert, 'The institutionalisation and organisation of history', pp. 15–19.

[72] For a brief discussion of matters in Germany, see Harrison, Jones, and Lambert, 'The institutionalisation and organisation of history', pp. 9–14; for an exhaustive examination of the French evidence, see den Boer, *History as a Profession*.

[73] The distinction between professional and amateur historians implied by Macmillan, *The Uses and Abuses of History* is problematic: before the mid-nineteenth century it did not exist. In recent years universities have produced many properly trained historians who have gone on to gain their main employment in other fields. And in the late nineteenth and early twentieth centuries when there might have been a meaningful distinction between amateur and professional, many professional historians did not distinguish themselves by their objectivity.

[74] Leffler, 'French Historians and the challenge to Louis XIV's absolutism'. On one aspect of the crucial contribution of the de Valois brothers, see Kelly, 'Adrien de Valois and the chapter headings in Ammianus Marcellinus'.

new historico-political discourse about 'the theory of races or race war', or more simply about racial division.[75] This debate can be seen as the trigger for a whole sequence of discussions that dominate the interpretation of the period of the end of the Roman Empire and the establishment of the successor states. The triad of nationalism, race, and geopolitics that it engendered meant that early medieval studies had a role to play in, and were influenced by, German aggression in two World Wars. Since then, Late Antiquity and the early medieval kingdoms have been exploited, albeit rather less dangerously, in debates over the nature of Europe.

Of course there are significant debates that do not fit neatly into this pattern, and some readers may conclude that I have privileged as dominant interpetations that were less important than others that I have neglected. There is certainly material enough for that to be true. The work of some of the major historians I cover (including Gibbon, Fustel de Coulanges, Hodgkin, Bury, and Dopsch) does not fit neatly into the dominant discourse of their day, which may help explain why their work has lasted better than that of their contemporaries. Although their ideas sometimes stand outside the common debates of their generation, I have, of course, paid full attention to them. However, I have left much out, not least by concentrating largely on work written in France, Italy, Germany, England, and Belgium. This limitation to some extent reflects the fact that the first four of those countries have often been portrayed as having their origins in the post-Roman period, while the last of them has suffered aggression at the hands of those who wished to make it fit a map of early medieval settlement. A search for origins has given a particular twist to their historiographical traditions. American scholarship inevitably does not share the same emotional commitment, with the result that some scholars have placed themselves deliberately apart from European debates.

Spain is a clear omission. Certainly, the kingdom of the Visigoths, and especially its seventh-century Church, has been central to the self-definition of the Spaniards. So too, there have been extensive debates about proto-feudalism, that have looked back to the Visigothic period. However, Spanish historiography has had little to say about the end of the Roman World or the creation of the Visigothic state. It has been much more concerned with the collapse of the Gothic kingdom in 711. Indeed, debates about the Muslim Conquest and about the subsequent Reconquista are far more important in Spanish historiography than is the arrival of the Visigoths in the fifth and sixth centuries.[76] Although there is a notable Spanish tradition of studies of individual Roman and Visigothic sites, and of religious, and especially conciliar history, Spanish historiography has been largely absent from the major European debates of the Fall of the Roman Empire and of the barbarian

---

[75] Foucault, *Society Must be Defended*, pp. 127–33. Nicolet, *La Fabrique d'une nation*, p. 67, also sees a new debate beginning with Boulainvilliers.

[76] e.g. *Claudio Sánchez-Albornoz, Atti dei Convegni Lincei* and *Al-Andalus/España, Historiografías en contraste*. See also Hillgarth, 'Spanish historiography and Iberian reality', esp. pp. 32–5.

migrations until the last thirty years.[77] So too, while there has been significant debate about the history of early Christian Ireland, because it has rarely been integrated into debates about the Fall of the Roman Empire and the *Völkerwanderung*, Irish historiography has remained for the most part outside my purview.

Despite such limitation of my field I have been able to do no more than sketch the major arguments of the scholars I discuss, although I have tried to draw attention to individual insights that have been forgotten for one reason or another. My overriding aim, however, has been to explain why interpretations of the period from 300 to 700 have developed as they have, through the consideration of a whole tradition of historiography, or rather three great historiographical streams (Romanist, Germanist, and Ecclesiastical), much of which has been forgotten, but which, as I hope to show, deserves to be remembered. It deserves to be remembered not just because it includes a great deal that is intellectually distinguished, but above all because it has been integral to way the modern Western European world has come to understand itself. Early medieval history is important not just as a branch of learning, but because it is used, again and again, deliberately and unconsciously, as we consider our position in the present.

---

[77] Hidalgo, Pérez, and Gervás (eds), *'Romanización' y 'Reconquista' en la península Ibérica*. A good indication of the relative lack of interest in the late and post-Roman periods among Spanish historians until recently can be seen from the bibliography of works by Arce, e.g. *El último siglo de la España romana (284–409)*, *España entre el mundo antiguo y el mundo medieval*, and *Bárbaros y romanos en Hispania (400–507 A.D.)*. For a survey of recent developments in the study of post-Roman Spain, Stocking, 'Review article: Continuity, culture and the state in late antique and early medieval Iberia'.

2

The Franks and the State of France

2.1 BOULAINVILLIERS AND THE *ÉTAT DE LA FRANCE*

Our story begins in France, and French scholarship will dominate much of our discussion of the eighteenth and early nineteenth century. Whilst the Italians tended to look back to a Roman past, and the Germans and English to a Germanic one, the French found it less easy to decide whether to see themselves as heirs of Rome or of *Germania*, with the result that they invested rather more in debates about the end of the Roman World and the coming of the barbarians, than did other peoples, at least until the mid-nineteenth century.

Although the barbarian invasions of Europe had been the subject of debate from the sixteenth century onwards, argument about them took a new turn in the 1720s, largely because of the writings of Henri comte de Boulainvilliers (1658–1722).[1] His interpretation of early Frankish history, and the response of the abbé Jean-Baptiste Du Bos, transformed discussion of the subject and raised a significant number of the issues that would dominate readings of the late- and post-Roman periods in the centuries to come. Effectively their writings foreshadowed what would be called the Germanist and Romanist readings of the Fall of Rome.[2] These two major lines of interpretation, the one emphasizing the Germanic origins of Western Europe, the other the Roman, were to become the two traditions of interpretation that dominated scholarship concerned with the end of the Roman World through the second half of the eighteenth, nineteenth, and twentieth centuries. It is with the contributions of Boulainvilliers and Du Bos that this chapter is concerned.

For Michel Foucault the work of Boulainvilliers marked the emergence in France of a new historico-political discourse, a discussion of the nature of society through the medium of history.[3] It had its parallels in English political debate of the seventeenth century.[4] Du Bos' work also marked a departure from the established interpretations of the Merovingians, which for the most part can be seen as discussions of monarchy derived ultimately from Hotman. The chief influences on Du Bos as a historian were the Englishman John Locke,[5] and the dissident Frenchman, Pierre

---

[1] For the importance of Boulainvilliers in France: Foucault, *Society Must be Defended*, pp. 128–97; Nicolet, *La Fabrique d'une nation*, pp. 67–85.

[2] Nicolet, *La Fabrique d'une nation*, p. 58.

[3] See Bloch, 'Sur les grandes invasions: quelques positions de problèmes', pp. 92–4, for the debates before Boulainvilliers.

[4] Foucault, *Society Must be Defended*, pp. 49–50.   [5] Lombard, *Du Bos*, p. 73.

Bayle.[6] With such influences it is no surprise that the theses of the two historians were not simply arguments about the interpretation of the minutiae of early medieval history. The historical writings of Boulainvilliers cannot be separated from his broader analysis of the development of the French state, while the output of Du Bos also encompassed aesthetics, numismatics, and science. The two men began to write at the end of Louis XIV's reign. They thus belong to the early phases of the French Enlightenment.[7] Boulainvilliers was a full generation older than Montesquieu, who would seem to have lodged with him during his early years in Paris:[8] Du Bos was to influence the compilers of the *Encyclopédie*.[9]

Boulainvilliers was a minor aristocrat who claimed descent from the French-Burgundian house of Croy, and beyond that from Hungarian royalty.[10] His noble origins were important to him: he pursued them in his genealogical research, but they also underlay many of the *nobiliaire* ideas, championing traditional rights of the aristocracy that he would advance in his historical writings. Born in 1658, he was educated at the Oratorian College of Juilly. Thereafter, he intended to embark on a military career, an ambition that he soon abandoned, apparently because of the lack of adequate financial support from his father.[11] At home he dedicated himself to the education and, after the death of his wife, to the general upbringing of his two sons, prior to their entry to Juilly, where one of them overlapped with the young Montesquieu.[12] The education of his sons would seem to have prompted Boulainvilliers' first attempts at writing history.[13] However, he continued his historical pursuits even after (and perhaps in response to) their early deaths.[14] He was subsequently taken up as a researcher and writer by a series of court patrons: initially by the circle of Louis XIV's grandson, the Duc de Bourgogne, and then by the Duc d'Orléans. Although he wrote extensively for such political patrons—and indeed they seem to have largely provided him with his means of livelihood—only one of his works was published in his lifetime: the *Justification de la naissance légitime de Bernard, roy d'Italie, petit-fils de Charlemagne*—a work of early medieval history that was intended to contribute to current debates about the succession to Louis XIV.[15] Boulainvilliers' other works were all published posthumously, although some of his writings were already in circulation in manuscript form before his death.[16] When he died, in 1722, his papers were collected by the Duc d'Orléans:

[6] Lombard, *Du Bos*, pp. 79, 96.

[7] For a useful and succinct study of the context, Jones, *The Great Nation: France from Louis XV to Napoleon*, pp. 171–225.

[8] Shackleton, *Montesquieu, a critical biography*, pp. 12–13.

[9] Lombard, *Du Bos*, pp. 339–42.

[10] Ellis, *Boulainvilliers and the French Monarchy*, p. 23. There is also a biography by Simon, *Henry de Boulainviller*, though it is a rather uncritical work.

[11] Ellis, *Boulainvilliers*, p. 23.

[12] Montesquieu, *De l'esprit des Loix*, ed. Brethe de la Gressaye, vol. 4, p. 359.

[13] Ellis, *Boulainvilliers*, pp. 17, 23. The importance of writing for his sons is mentioned in *État de la France*, vol. 1, p. III.

[14] *État de la France*, vol. 1, p. VII.

[15] Boulainvilliers, *Justification de la naissance légitime de Bernard, roy d'Italie, petit-fils de Charlemagne*; Ellis, *Boulainvilliers*, p. 169.

[16] Ellis, *Boulainvilliers*, p. 2.

his contribution to the *État de la France* was published in 1727, followed by many of his essays, most notably the *Essais sur la noblesse de France*, which appeared in 1732. These works caused a considerable stir. That he was not published in his lifetime probably reflects the extent to which his stance was critical of the monarchy and current administration. At the same time, the fact that his works were published after his death, but not in their order of composition, has meant that it is difficult to trace the development of his thought.[17] And he did change his mind on a number of issues, for example, over the merits or otherwise of Carolingian feudalism.[18] His views on the coming of the Franks, however, and their establishment in Gaul, remained reasonably constant.

The *État de la France* as published in 1727–8 is a lavish three-volume work, the bulk of which is a collection of regional reports drawn up by *intendants* for the Duc de Bourgogne in 1698.[19] Boulainvilliers compiled his introductory essay to the reports while working in the Burgundy circle in 1711, probably at the request of the Duc de Beauvillier.[20] He seems to have prepared two versions of the introduction, which were edited after his death into a single text by Philippe Mercier.[21] Boulainvilliers' comments on the work done by the *intendants* are scathing, both because of his disapproval of their office, which he thought smacked of despotism, and also because he thought they had not carried it out well.[22] He believed that a survey of France could only be understood against the background of French history, which explained the 'génie des Princes et du gouvernement de la Nation'. His introduction to the *État de la France* thus included an interpretation of early French history, which, while drawing on previous scholarship, also broke new ground.

There was a well-established discourse on the origins of feudalism that went back at least two centuries.[23] Many of the ideas Boulainvilliers expressed in the *État de la France* were taken from Jean Le Laboureur, and a substantial proportion of his text derived from François-Eudes de Mézeray and Louis Dufort de Longuerue.[24] Boulainvilliers also explicitly addressed arguments set out by his older contemporary, the Jesuit Père Daniel.[25] He did, however, see himself as doing something new. In a letter addressed to Mlle Cousinot in 1707 he attacked the established tradition of monarchical history, arguing in favour of a history of government, manners (*mœurs*), and passions: in short, the history of the nation.[26]

Before providing a study of the kings of France up to the death of Hugh Capet, Boulainvilliers sets out his basic premises. He begins by arguing that the name Frank

---

[17] Ellis' account is thus crucial to an understanding of the development of Boulainvilliers' thought.

[18] Ellis, *Boulainvilliers*, pp. 105, 153, 167.   [19] See 'The Intendants' Mémoires of 1698'.

[20] Ellis, *Boulainvilliers*, pp. 55, 64.   [21] Ellis, *Boulainvilliers*, p. 66.

[22] *État de la France*, vol. 1, pp. I–XVI. Ellis, *Boulainvilliers*, p. 70; see 'The Intendants' Mémoires of 1698'.

[23] Ellis, *Boulainvilliers*, pp. 31–51.   [24] Ellis, *Boulainvilliers*, pp. 73–4.

[25] *État de la France*, vol. 1, pp. 6, 74. On Daniel, Leffler, 'French Historians and the challenge to Louis XIV's absolutism'.

[26] Ellis, *Boulainvilliers*, pp. 207–8.

applies not to a single people, but to all those who came from the land between the Rhine and the Elbe.[27] Thus, they originated not in Troy, as ancient tradition asserted (on account of a confusion, according to Boulainvilliers, between Frisia and Phrygia), but in *Germania*.[28] They were natural warriors who often fought successfully against the Romans. As a result the Romans decided to employ them to defend the frontier. Thus, the emperor Julian granted them the region of *Toxandria*. This process, Boulainvilliers thought, began in the reign of Constantius Chlorus, the father of Constantine. The panegyrists who praised Constantius presented these *laeti*, or 'Happy Ones' in Boulainvilliers' understanding of the word, as simply working for the Empire.[29] They failed to realize that they would eventually destroy it. Initially the *laeti* did indeed fight for Rome, despite maltreatment, about which they complained. After the defeat of Attila, however, the Franks pursued their own interests and turned against the Romans. With these preliminaries out of the way, Boulainvilliers then turned to a reign-by-reign analysis of Frankish history, beginning with Mellobaudes, who appears in the pages of the fourth-century historian Ammianus Marcellinus.

Although the narrative supplied by Boulainvilliers scarcely stands up to modern scrutiny, it is in fact marked by hard-headed commonsense, as can be seen in his discussion of the first Frankish kings. He denies the existence of Pharamond—a founding father in earlier monarchical traditions, and he does so by pointing out that he does not appear in the genuine chronicle of Prosper of Aquitaine, but rather in a compilation which he ascribes to 'Prosper Tiro'. He could have gone further, as the abbé Du Bos would,[30] since Pharamond's name is actually an interpolation into what is now called the Chronicle of 452. Boulainvilliers was, however, prepared to accept the existence of Chlodio, which had been questioned by the yet more sceptical Père Daniel,[31] and he supported his case by marshalling evidence from such authors as (the real) Prosper, Sidonius Apollinaris, and Cassiodorus, as well as the Byzantine Priscus.[32] Chlodio was succeeded by his son Merovech, and then by his grandson Childeric, evidence for whom, as Boulainvilliers rightly remarks, largely comes from the seventh-century Fredegar, and not from Gregory of Tours. In addition, there was the fact of the king's tomb, unearthed at Tournai in 1653, the grave-goods from which were preserved in the *Bibliothèque du roi*. Despite their military exploits, Boulainvilliers concluded that Chlodio, Merovech, and Childeric had never ruled in Gaul.[33] In his view matters changed radically with the reign of Clovis, and it is this that sparks off a major set of considerations about the Frankish kingdom and its origins.

---

[27] *État de la France*, vol. 1, p. XXIII.   [28] *État de la France*, vol. 1, p. XXVII.

[29] The term *laetus* is of uncertain meaning. In the fourth century *laeti* would appear to be groups of barbarians settled within the Empire by the agents of the emperor, perhaps as tied recruits, who received land on semi-servile terms. The institution somehow lasted into the Merovingian period, when the *laeti* seem to have been rather better regarded. For a recent discussion, Drinkwater, *The Alamanni and Rome 213–496*, pp. 166–9.

[30] Du Bos, *Histoire critique de l'établissement de la monarchie françoise*, vol. 1, bk 2, pp. 360–1.

[31] *État de la France*, vol. 1, p. 5.

[32] *État de la France*, vol. 1, pp. 4–6. His reference to Priscus does, however, seem to be inaccurate.

[33] *État de la France*, vol. 1, p. 9.

Boulainvilliers presents Clovis as a conqueror who exacted tribute from other kings. He was a heroic figure, though not a particularly likeable one.[34] He then provides an account of Clovis' conversion to Catholic Christianity, which combines the account of Gregory of Tours with that to be found in the seventh-century Life of St Vedast. Following his conversion Clovis took over Roman territory between the Loire, the Seine, and the sea. As a result of his successes, Catholicism rather than the heretical doctrine of Arianism, triumphed. He was opposed in Gaul by the Burgundians, whom Boulainvilliers saw as the softest of the barbarians, and who had initially converted to Catholicism, before becoming Arian. They subsequently reverted to their previous religious allegiance, and their kingdom became, in Boulainvilliers' eyes, a retreat for the wise and for saints—though it is unclear whether this should be read as a positive comment: the churchmen who were so influential in Burgundy knew only Roman law, which for Boulainvilliers was the creation of a despotic empire, whereas the illiterate, but libertarian, Franks, by contrast, had *Lex Salica*, in his view the only governmental text to have survived from this period in their early history.

According to Boulainvilliers what followed Clovis' war with the Burgundians was central to French history, although he admitted that it was desperately obscure.[35] In asserting this, he was deliberately downplaying the importance of Clovis' conversion. What interested him was the new order established by the Frankish conquest of Gaul, during which many of the Gallo-Romans lost their possessions and their liberty.[36] The conquest of the South began with Romans fleeing to the Visigoths: Clovis demanded their return. The Ostrogothic ruler Theodoric tried to prevent open conflict, but the Franks attacked, defeating and killing the Visigothic king Alaric at Vouillé. Clovis thereafter took over the South-West of Gaul. His position was recognized by the Byzantine emperor Anastasius, who (in Boulainvilliers' interpretation) elevated Clovis to the consulship. The king then decided to eliminate his rivals, even his old allies. This, says Boulainvilliers with a wry sense of *Realpolitik*, was the only way to lay solid foundations for a great monarchy, even though such a policy had its opponents.[37] He even speculates that Clovis may have been poisoned: after all, the king died relatively young. This closing swipe at Clovis marks an interesting modification of the previously established and standard picture of the first Christian monarch of the Franks and, by extension, of France.

Having reached the death of Clovis in his narrative, Boulainvilliers interrupts the strict regnal organization of his account with a number of excursus. He turns first to the *État de la Nation Françoise*. For him the conquest of the Gauls by the Franks

[34] *État de la France*, vol. 1, p. 10: 'Clovis was an ambitious, ferocious, bold, cruel, and very cunning young man. That is to say that he possessed the true qualities of a barbarian hero. On the other hand, the Romans of his time were in the final stages of the decline of their power.'

[35] *État de la France*, vol. 1, p. 13: 'It is the most essential, although the most defective and the least illuminated part of our history.'

[36] *État de la France*, vol. 1, p. 13: 'Many there lost a part of their goods, and everything in general that they called their liberty.'

[37] *État de la France*, vol. 1, p. 15: 'It is true that it was the only way of giving a great monarchy firm foundations, but such a bloodthirsty policy has as yet not found any supporters.'

constituted the foundation of the state. From it followed the nation and the rights of all its ministers.[38] He goes on to argue that within this scheme the king's role was limited—he was no more than a general of a free army that elected him as leader, and he was expected to act for the glory and profit of his followers.[39] The relationship between the king and the army is central to the second excursus: on the *Liberté des François*.[40] In Boulainvilliers' reading (and in the opinion of many who followed him) all Franks were free and equal. Their kings were no more than elected civil magistrates. In addition there were military leaders. Boulainvilliers knew his Tacitus, and he cites the famous maxim from the *Germania*: 'Reges ex nobilitate, Duces ex virtute sumunt.' ('They take kings for their nobility, generals for their prowess.')[41] Kings, in Tacitus, had less authority than generals, who Boulainvilliers equated with the *maiores*, in other words the mayors of the palace. Thus, in origin, the king was not superior to the people. Indeed, all Franks were his companions; they were his *leudes*, or in Latin, his *fideles*. The Franks themselves appointed the king, whose sole duty was to sustain and defend the people. The Gauls, that is, the Gallo-Romans, on the other hand, had been conquered by the Franks, and as a result they were subject to the lord on whose land they lived: only those living on royal estates were subject to the king. This meant, in Boulainvilliers' view, that when the *Tiers État* put itself directly under the monarch in later centuries it was acting illegally. Although there were some Gallo-Roman freemen (*ingenui*) who retained property, they were in fact slaves, subject not to the king, but to the Frankish state.

Boulainvilliers follows his analysis of Frankish liberty with a discussion of the *Noblesse des François*.[42] For him the words *Salic* and *noble* are synonymous. The real division was between Salians and Romans: between conquerors and conquered. The former held Salian land and were subject to Salic law; the latter were subject to Roman law. The Salians were soldiers; by contrast the Romans were excluded from military service, but had to pay taxes. The Franks thus constituted a noble military elite. Boulainvilliers then sets out their privileges: the *Avantages des François après la Conquête*. They were exempt from all obligations except military service. Everything they acquired was shared. They could only be judged by their peers at the general assembly, or *Champ de Mars*.[43] They had the right to defend themselves, their goods, and their friends. Of this Boulainvilliers clearly approved, for he subsequently laments the attempt of lawyers in his own day to end the tradition of duelling, arguing that it would lead to a decline in virtue and courage.[44]

---

[38] *État de la France*, vol. 1, p. 15: 'The conquest of the Gauls...the foundation of the French State...it is to this period that we should ascribe the political order, followed thereafter by the nation, and the essential and primordial right of all its ministers.'

[39] *État de la France*, vol. 1, p. 15: 'Clovis was only the general of a free army, which had elected him to lead its undertakings, the glory and profit of which ought to have been common to all.'

[40] *État de la France*, vol. 1, pp. 16–18.

[41] On the difficulties of translating Tacitus' words see Wallace-Hadrill, *Early Germanic Kingship and on the Continent*, p. 3.

[42] *État de la France*, vol. 1, pp. 18–21.

[43] For his discussion of the Champ de Mars, *État de la France*, vol. 1, pp. 46–7.

[44] *État de la France*, vol. 1, p. 28. See also the discussion of 'Guerres Particulières des Francs', *État de la France*, vol. 1, p. 45.

Crucially, the Franks understood that peace could only be achieved by war. At the same time they saw that the military system of the Roman Empire had failed: the Roman army, which had been made up largely of outsiders, had no interest in its wars, while the taxes which had been required to keep it in being had bankrupted the provinces, leading to the abandonment of land, and resulting in famine and plague. This state of affairs was avoided by the Franks who were all soldiers, but were unpaid and received only what they conquered. At the same time the conquered Gauls, who were not allowed to fight, found the manual labour which they had to perform to be a lighter burden than the Roman tax system. Surprisingly, then, being a Frankish slave was better than being a free Roman.[45] Cultivation improved, and the Frankish state avoided the faults that had ruined Rome. Boulainvilliers was thus mindful of the weakness of the Roman Empire when he considered the success of the Franks.

He continues his analysis with consideration of the Frankish tradition of equal division: *partage égal entre les françois*.[46] His discussion begins with a story recounted by Gregory of Tours, the interpretation of which was in many ways central to debates on the structure of Frankish society. According to Gregory, in the course of the conflict between Clovis and the Roman general Syagrius a good deal of booty was taken, including a large vase that had been stolen from a church (in later versions identified as the church of Rheims). The bishop asked for its restitution, and Clovis promised that he would hand it back if it were allotted to him. At Soissons, where all the loot was piled up, Clovis asked the Franks if he might take the vase over and above his share. All agreed, except for one warrior, who smashed the object with his axe. Clovis took the battered vase and handed it back to its owner. The next year at the annual assembly, while he was inspecting the army, he came across the warrior who had opposed him. He threw the man's axe to the ground, and as the warrior stooped to pick it up, Clovis smashed his own axe into the offender's skull. In discussions of Frankish society the story could either be used to indicate equality—the booty was to be divided equally, and the king went out of his way to petition for one specific piece—or tyranny—the king took his revenge in public the following year. Boulainvilliers more than most saw the ambiguities: the story reveals both the absolute power of Clovis, and also the fact that he was constantly acting under restraint.

Boulainvilliers addressed the tale of the vase of Soissons because it was already well known, but he was more interested in the changing relationship between Franks and Romans. After the take-over of Gaul the Franks could no longer treat the Romans as enemies; instead they had to allocate them and their lands as booty. Boulainvilliers admitted that we have no idea how this division took place, noting only possible parallels in the Burgundian settlement. He recognized, however, that there were too few Franks for them to take over all their conquests, and he assumed

---

[45] *État de la France*, vol. 1, p. 20: 'And therefore the conquest by the Franks had a completely different effect than one would have expected. The provinces were keen to call them in to help, and to submit to their government, finding themselves happier in this new slavery, than they had been when they enjoyed the false liberty which the Romans gratified them with.' See also *État de la France*, vol. 1, pp. 37–8, 41, 44.

[46] *État de la France*, vol. 1, pp. 21–5.

that there was regional variation. In his view the Franks must have taken over all of Flanders and Picardy (this question of settlement would turn out to be a dominant issue in the twentieth century); at the other extreme in Aquitaine, apart from distributing a few choice estates to magistrates, dukes and counts, they only exacted tribute.[47] Their concern was to remain as a military force, living from the booty they took. Boulainvilliers assumes that taxes and tribute were gathered together in large 'magazins' for distribution,[48] but saw this and the income from property as providing no more than subsistence for the conquerors.

At this stage the Franks were still theoretically equal, at least according to Boulainvilliers. Of course, on campaign a Frank was subordinate to his commander. But otherwise all Franks were organized into hundreds: they were all *seniores, centenarii*, or *seigneurs*. Law was supposedly exercised in common.[49] The king might preside as the *premier magistrat civil*. Already, however, under Clovis one can see the origins of despotism, as for instance in the story of the vase of Soissons. Had the king lived longer, in Boulainvilliers' opinion, he would have reduced the Franks to slavery alongside the Gauls. His death stopped that, and the general assembly continued to be important. Indeed, the Gauls started to imitate it.

For Boulainvilliers Frankish law had traditionally been simple. He thought that it was only written down in the first instance by Clovis, and that it was written for the benefit of the Church. Indeed, he argued that it had been translated into Latin by bishop Remigius of Rheims.[50] He noted the absence of any reference to a general assembly in *Lex Salica*, but took that as an indication that the laws were ancient customs, the simplicity of which he admired.[51] The only new legislation concerned the Church. More important was the clause in *Lex Salica* that ruled against female inheritance.[52] According to Boulainvillers the reason for excluding women from inheriting land was to prevent them from transferring property to Gallo-Romans through marriage. Boulainvilliers' view of the role allotted to women by the Frankish constitution is strikingly unmodern: they existed to please their husbands and to bring up children to serve the fatherland.[53] Far too liberal was a text in the Formulary of Marculf allowing female inheritance: Boulainvilliers concluded that clerical prejudice had ruined Marculf's judgment. From the Church's point of view, female inheritance was to be encouraged, because women were more likely to give donations and alms.[54] This notion of a deliberate manipulation of the laws of property by the Church would resurface in the twentieth century.[55]

[47] *État de la France*, vol. 1, pp. 38–40.
[48] He seems to have deduced the existence of these warehouses from place-names. See his discussion of Malines/Mecbelen in Flanders: *État de la France*, vol. 1, pp. 32, 39.
[49] *État de la France*, vol. 1, pp. 25–7.   [50] *État de la France*, vol. 1, pp. 28–9.
[51] On judicial organization see *État de la France*, vol. 1, pp. 41–4.
[52] *État de la France*, vol. 1, pp. 29–31.
[53] *État de la France*, vol. 1, p. 30: 'The constitution of the government and the genius of the nation gave the sex no other ambition that to please their husbands and to bring up children for the service of the fatherland.'
[54] *État de la France*, vol. 1, p. 31.
[55] Goody, *The Development of the Family and Marriage in Europe*.

Boulainvilliers was extremely sensitive to threats to the social and political structures that he saw as having been established with the conquest of Gaul. The Franks,
for him, initially constituted an exemplary over-class: heroic, militaristic, and
equal. The ideal Frankish leader was both a soldier and a magistrate.[56] One threat
to this ideal lay in the distribution of offices. Clovis needed to establish officials in
his newly conquered territory, and he did so by filling established Roman posts, to
the delight of the indigenous population. In Boulainvilliers' eyes the Franks should
have objected, but out of ambition, individuals warmed to the opportunities
offered by holding office.[57] Everywhere there was a danger that men might abuse
their position, though for a while, at least, Boulainvilliers felt that Frankish traditions remained strong.

Having examined the structure of the Frankish kingdom in some detail, Boul-
ainvilliers returned to a reign by reign narrative, drawing largely on Gregory of
Tours, but with additions from other historians and chroniclers, both western and
Byzantine. He shows a familiarity with major Byzantine writers such as Procopius,
Agathias, and Theophanes (all of whom he probably read in Latin translation), as
well as Visigothic chroniclers such as Isidore, Victor of Tunnuna, and John of
Biclaro, and minor Frankish figures, like Marius of Avenches. For the most part his
narrative is terse, though he occasionally pauses to praise a king, such as Theude-
bert I and Sigibert I.[58] So too he notes evidence of what he regards as Frankish
decline. Thus, in his discussion of the bid for the throne made by Gundovald in
the 580s he draws attention to Gregory's reference to the presence of Gallo-Roman
troops led by Frankish officers, which he thought marked a diminution in the
Frankish armies.[59] More important in his eyes were the civil wars around the year
600, when he thought that the Franks were doing no more than fight over which
tyrant to follow, without realizing the implications of their actions.[60] He presented
the final emergence of Chlothar II as sole ruler in 614 as an extraordinary set of
events, many of them criminal.[61] For him it was at this point that the real *décadence*
of the Merovingians began,[62] though he found some virtue in Chlothar himself:
indeed, his chief criticism of the king concerned his decision to remit the tribute
owed by the Lombards. Boulainvilliers continued his reign-by-reign analysis up
until the death of Hugh Capet, but the basic outline of his approach is already
apparent. Once he reached the late Merovingians his interpretation was focused
not on the end of the Roman Empire and the establishment of the successor states,
but rather on the origins and development of feudalism.

In short, for Boulainvilliers the Roman Empire was an oppressive institution, above all because of its system of taxation. This burden on the provincials

---

[56] *État de la France*, vol. 1, pp. 38, 40.   [57] *État de la France*, vol. 1, p. 34.
[58] *État de la France*, vol. 1, pp. 54, 57.
[59] *État de la France*, vol. 1, p. 59: 'Troops of Gaulish nationality...under the leadership of Frankish
officers...evident mark of the corruption of Frankish discipline...or indication of the great diminution of the Frankish armies, caused by the decline of the monarchy.'
[60] *État de la France*, vol. 1, p. 63.   [61] *État de la France*, vol. 1, p. 66.
[62] *État de la France*, vol. 1, p. 66.

was necessary in order to pay the army, but it created a form of servility. As for the army, because it was largely made up of foreigners, it was not committed to the good of the state. By contrast, the Franks were free, equal, and militaristic (one needs to remember here Boulainvilliers' personal enthusiasm for the military). Although initially settled within the Empire, as part of a policy for defending the frontiers, they were not well treated, and eventually, after the invasions of Attila, turned against the Romans. They took Gaul by conquest, creating a state in which there were two groups, the Franks, or conquerors, and the Gauls, or conquered. The Gauls, despite their servile position, found life less oppressive than it had been under the Roman Empire. The Franks, who constituted an upper military class, theoretically remained equal: the king was merely a *primus inter pares*. The main institution of government was the annual assembly. Nevertheless, the seeds of despotism already existed. One can see them in Clovis' behaviour over the vase at Soissons. And he had opportunity to develop royal power through the appointment of officers needed to govern his expanded kingdom. The ambitions of individual Franks played into his hands, undermining equality. At the same time there are indications that the Gallo-Romans were being used in a military capacity, thus eroding their non-military, servile, status. In the distant future the king would ally with the *Tiers État*, and as a result undermine the position of the Frankish nobility—this unholy alliance was at the heart of eighteenth-century debates about the evils of feudalism.

It is not difficult to see that Boulainvilliers' interpretation essentially reflects his political position, and that it belongs to a strand in the *nobiliaire* thinking of those aristocrats who felt that their traditional rights had been reduced by the last years of Louis XIV and throughout the reign of Louis XV. Some of the nobility saw themselves as the victims of collaboration between the monarchy and the *Tiers État*, and wished for a restoration of their position and their supposed rights. Above all, the role of the *Parlement*, which Boulainvilliers saw as derived from the *Champ de Mars*, or *Assemblé général*, was being undermined.[63] He and his fellows disapproved of heavy taxation and of governmental intervention (represented by the *intendants*): they disapproved too of the growing power of lawyers and of the wealth of the Church. They also held rather romantic notions of the army and military service, which were all the more poignant in the period following the French failure in the War of the Spanish Succession. All this is blatantly reflected in Boulainvilliers' interpretation. And yet one would be wrong to reject his arguments out-of-hand: first, because his work prompted considerable debate, which showed that his ideas could not be dismissed with ease; and second, because his arguments are underpinned by a commendable knowledge of the sources. He did not have all the editions that are now available to us, and at times he did not read particularly accurately, but read he did, and he found in his sources enough to give support, however spurious, to his *nobiliaire* ideas.

[63] Ellis, *Boulainvilliers*, p. 76.

2.2 DU BOS AND THE *HISTOIRE CRITIQUE DE L'ÉTABLISSEMENT DE LA MONARCHIE FRANÇOISE DANS LES GAULES*

Only seven years after the publication of Boulainvilliers' contribution to the *État de la France*, his ideas were challenged by one of the most remarkable works of history to be written in the eighteenth century: the *Histoire critique de l'établissement de la monarchie françoise dans les Gaules* of the abbé Jean-Baptiste Du Bos (1670–1742). Whilst Boulainvilliers had been well read, Du Bos was formidably so, and he was blessed with a prodigious memory.[64] He prefaced his account with a *discours préliminaire*, in which he discussed his sources,[65] showing a thorough knowledge of almost all the texts then available—and one should remember that scholars such as Sirmond, Valesius, Bolland, and Mabillon had already put most of the relevant material into print. In fact, Du Bos' work so impressed Martin Bouquet, the editor of the *Recueil des historiens des Gaules et de la France*, that he invited him to participate in preparing his collection of texts.[66] For Gibbon the first eleven volumes of Bouquet's *Recueil* would be an invaluable resource when he came to write his account of the early Franks.[67] Quite apart from his knowledge, Du Bos also had a rare sense of historical methodology, which is apparent both in his source criticism, which surfaces throughout his text, and in his development of the notion of critical history—which goes some way towards combining the traditions of the *érudits* and the *philosophes*, a combination that Momigliano ascribed to Gibbon.[68] According to Du Bos *une histoire critique* 'allows one to interrupt the narrative whenever there is an opportunity to make remarks appropriate to prove a point that one has been able to advance there'.[69] One might think that here he was following in the footsteps of Boulainvilliers, the regnal organization of whose work is interrupted with excursus on specific issues. But Du Bos' argument was not constructed as a reign-by-reign narrative. In fact, his constant assessment of detail tends to get in the way of the broad outlines of his account.

Book 1 of the *Histoire critique* deals first with Gaul and then with the barbarians.[70] It establishes the extent to which the framework of his account is Roman rather than barbarian. When he turns to the barbarians Du Bos refuses to discuss their origins, concentrating instead on the extent to which a rather mongrel group of peoples worked alongside the Empire from the third century onwards. According to Du Bos, Clovis and the Franks brought little change to the Roman world. In fact, in so far as there was a Frankish invasion, it was the settlement of the *laeti*, under Constantine and his successors. Boulainvilliers had noted the use of *laeti*, but unlike Du Bos he saw a major change in Frankish activity in the late fifth

---

[64] Lombard, *Du Bos*, p. 172. [65] Du Bos, *Histoire critique*, vol. 1, pp. 1–65.
[66] Lombard, *Du Bos*, p. 167. [67] Gibbon, *Decline and Fall*, ch. 38, footnote.
[68] Momigliano, 'Gibbon's contribution to historical method'; see Bullough, *Italy and her Invaders*, p. 14.
[69] Du Bos, *Histoire critique*, vol. 3, bk 5, pp. 202–3.
[70] Du Bos, *Histoire critique*, vol. 1, bk 1, pp. 1–257.

century. For the latter, by contrast, there was no invasion in Clovis' time—though he did admit that there were individual raids. Rather, when Clovis came to power, he did little more than take over the imperial patrimony.

Having set out his view of the Empire and the extent to which it survived under Clovis, Du Bos retraces his steps, turning his attention in Book Two to the fifty years following 407.[71] He begins with the politics of the corrupt and despotic court of Honorius: indeed, he provides a history of the whole of the Western Empire, Britain included, which he underpins with a detailed discussion of individual annals and events. Because of the weakness of the surviving evidence he has little to say on the Franks, concentrating rather on the Visigoths and Burgundians, and their settlement—which he presents very much in terms of a Roman allocation of quarters in return for military service already performed.[72] Rather more fanciful is his ensuing discussion of Armorica, a region of the north-west of Gaul,[73] whose size he overextends, though perhaps rather less than his critics have assumed, since in the fourth century the name could apparently be applied not just to Brittany, but to an area as far south as the Garonne, and as far east as Auxerre.[74] For Du Bos, Armorica was a centre of Gallo-Roman resistance, which contributed greatly to continuity between the Roman and Frankish periods. He also discusses the power of Syagrius, the Roman general who fought against Clovis, rightly presenting him as merely one leader among several in late fifth-century Gaul. Against this background he sets the expansion of Frankish power. He presents the Franks as allies of Rome, and even argues that the Ripuarians were Roman soldiers who had joined the barbarians. He notes the campaigns of Chlodio but sees them as having little impact, emphasizing rather the extent to which the arrival of Attila brought the Romans and barbarians together.[75] His account of events at this point covers not just Gaul, but also Italy, and indeed he carefully establishes a chronology for events throughout the Western Empire.

Book Three opens with the startling question: what rights did the eastern emperor have over the Western Empire? For Du Bos this was crucial for understanding *notre Histoire*.[76] He immediately provides the answer: not only did the emperor have rights, but these were also recognized by the barbarians, because they were confederates. These rights were, however, ceded to the sons of Clovis by Justinian, and thus provided the foundations of the French monarchy.[77] The full significance of this argument he only expounds later on in his work. Du Bos then considers relations between East and West, especially as they affected imperial succession, throughout the fifth century.

---

[71] Du Bos, *Histoire critique*, vol. 1, bk 2, pp. 258–627.
[72] Du Bos, *Histoire critique*, vol. 1, bk 2, p. 363.
[73] Du Bos, *Histoire critique*, vol. 1, bk 2, pp. 300, 308. There is a summary in Larrere, '"La République des Armoriques", une fiction politique de l'abbé Dubos'.
[74] Borius, *Constance de Lyon: vie de saint Germain d'Auxerre*, p. 99.
[75] Du Bos, *Histoire critique*, vol. 1, bk 2, pp. 531–2.
[76] Du Bos, *Histoire critique*, vol. 2, bk 3, p. 1.
[77] Du Bos, *Histoire critique*, vol. 2, bk 3, p. 2.

Gradually he returns to the politics of the Western Empire following the failure of Attila. His narrative ranges over the whole of the West, with substantial passages dedicated to the Vandals in Africa. His account of Childeric's career, which involves a good deal of discussion of how best to interpret points of detail, is integrated into this larger picture. Indeed, Du Bos is careful to cut Childeric down to size: his kingdom was not very important—a point with which Boulainvilliers would have agreed. In his discussion of the early part of the Frankish king's career Du Bos has as much to say about the Roman Ægidius as he does about Childeric himself.[78] And he raises some important questions in his consideration of the period of Childeric's exile when the Franks accepted Ægidius as their leader. What language was used? Did religious difference cause any problems? These are questions that he answers by considering the polyglot armies of his own day.[79] After Childeric's return from exile in Thuringia, Du Bos is careful to treat his actions in the widest possible context.[80] Indeed, Childeric is seen as a man constantly changing sides in an extremely confused political world.[81] Pretty well every piece of information is examined to reveal the complexities of the last decades of the Western Empire.

When he finally reaches Childeric's death, Du Bos pauses to provide an extraordinary account of the treasure that was found in his tomb in 1653, and of its history following its excavation. He traces its discovery in Tournai, then in the hands of Philip IV of Spain, and its transfer to Leopold of Austria. From him the grave-goods passed to Maximilian Henry of Bavaria, archbishop of Cologne and bishop of Liège, who had the objects copied, before giving the originals to Louis XIV.[82] The subsequent history of the treasure would be of some importance in the nineteenth century. That Du Bos was so well informed might be due to his association with Maximilian II of Bavaria, to whom he had been introduced as a numismatist in 1699.[83]

Clovis is initially treated much as Childeric had been: Du Bos narrates the early part of his reign very much in the context of what is known of the other kingdoms of Gaul, notably that of the Burgundians. When Clovis came to the throne, the Frankish kingdom was still small.[84] Du Bos prefers to see him as a Roman official rather than a barbarian king: his kingdom was still part of the Empire.[85] He presents Clovis (probably incorrectly) as taking over the office of *magister militum* that he assumes (on rather thin evidence) that the king's father had held.[86] Indeed, Du Bos emphasizes the Roman office of several of the barbarian leaders of the period: there were Burgundian *magistri militum*, and Clovis would become consul.[87] He is insistent that barbarian

---

[78] Du Bos, *Histoire critique*, vol. 2, bk 3, pp. 59–72.
[79] Du Bos, *Histoire critique*, vol. 1, bk 2, pp. 65–7.
[80] Du Bos, *Histoire critique*, vol. 2, bk 3, pp. 102–7.
[81] Du Bos, *Histoire critique*, vol. 2, bk 3, p. 186.
[82] Du Bos, *Histoire critique*, vol. 2, bk 3, pp. 301–5.
[83] Lombard, *Du Bos*, p. 22.
[84] Du Bos, *Histoire critique*, vol. 2, bk 3, p. 305.
[85] Du Bos, *Histoire critique*, vol. 2, bk 3, p. 342.
[86] Du Bos, *Histoire critique*, vol. 2, bk 3, pp. 307, 323, 330.
[87] Du Bos, *Histoire critique*, vol. 2, bk 3, p. 225.

kings did not regard Roman office as degrading, and he points to a modern parallel: William III of England was also captain and general of the United Provinces, while the king of Sardinia was a general in both the Spanish and French armies.[88]

The structure of Du Bos' discussion of Clovis is scarcely clear, and it is not helped by the fact that it is divided between the third and fourth books of his *Histoire*. Rather than follow his case, with all its digressions, along its rather tortuous path, it will be enough to draw out some of the central issues. Inevitably he addresses Clovis' conversion and baptism, though his stance on the significance of the event is complex, both because at one moment or another he discusses every significant piece of evidence, but also because there is a conflict within his approach. On the one hand, he was sceptical about religion in general, despite his being ordained. Indeed, his biographer compared his objectivity on the matter to that of Voltaire.[89] On the other hand, he is remarkably uncritical when it comes to Hincmar's account of the king's baptism and the legend of the Ste Ampoule, in which a dove miraculously descends carrying the chrism for the ritual.[90] Here, Du Bos' understanding of the importance of the story for the position of the monarchy in France is clearly in conflict with his scholarship. Moreover, throughout what is in many ways a rigorous discussion of the evidence, Du Bos finds himself unable to avoid drawing parallels with more recent history, notably the conversion of Henri IV to Catholicism.[91]

A second of the themes that recurs throughout the discussion of Clovis' reign is that of the king's dealings with the Armoricans. Indeed, it is only in the context of this part of his analysis that the significance of his interpretation of them becomes clear. For Du Bos the Armoricans were representative of the Gallo-Roman population in general. The Frankish take-over of their territory is thus indicative of the nature of the Frankish expansion. Following comments in Procopius, to which he added the evidence of a charter of 497 (which is unfortunately a forgery),[92] Du Bos noted, first, that the Franks were unable to defeat the Armoricans, and, second, as a result, that they concluded an alliance and thus became one people.[93] This flies directly in the face of the argument of Boulainvilliers, that the Franks had conquered the Gallo-Romans.

A third theme, which we have already touched on, both adds to the overall interpretation, and indeed helps to explain why that interpretation was to be rejected by the end of the eighteenth century, and that is the relationship of the barbarians to the Empire in the East. The Roman offices held by Burgundian and Ostrogothic kings are carefully enumerated by Du Bos.[94] Alongside these, and related to them, he envisages a series of treaties between the barbarians and the Empire, few of which

---

[88] Du Bos, *Histoire critique*, vol. 2, bk 3, p. 226.   [89] Lombard, *Du Bos*, pp. 30–2.

[90] Du Bos, *Histoire critique*, vol. 2, bk 4, pp. 506–7.

[91] Du Bos, *Histoire critique*, vol. 2, bk 3, p. 438; see also p. 469.

[92] Du Bos, *Histoire critique*, vol. 2, bk 4, pp. 547–58.

[93] Du Bos, *Histoire critique*, vol. 2, bk 4, pp. 542–7, 561–6. In certain respects this prefigures Michelet's understanding of the formation of the French, though Du Bos places the combination of races rather earlier.

[94] Du Bos, *Histoire critique*, vol. 2, bk 4, pp. 581–5.

are actually listed in the evidence.[95] What Du Bos regarded as Clovis' consulship opens the fifth book of his *Histoire*: in his view this effectively made the Frankish king the emperor of the Gauls, placing him over all the other Roman office-holders in the region,[96] but still leaving him as a subordinate to the emperor in Constantinople.[97] The culmination of this developing relationship between the Byzantines and the Franks comes not in Clovis' reign, but in that of his sons, and very specifically in the context of the Frankish take-over of Provence.

Throughout his analysis of events Du Bos tackles developments not just in Gaul, but also in Italy and elsewhere in the West. He is careful to note that the emperor Zeno had conceded jurisdiction over Provence to the Ostrogoths ruling in Italy.[98] In the course of the war against Justinian, the Ostrogothic king Wittigis decided to give up his claims to Provence, in order to win Frankish support.[99] Subsequently, and crucially, Justinian, who also sought a Frankish alliance, confirmed the concession. Up until this point the Romans in Gaul could have regarded the emperor as their sovereign, but no longer: they now had to recognize 'our kings as their legitimate and sole masters. The full Sovereignty of the Gauls belongs henceforth to these princes in its entirety'.[100] It must be admitted that Justinian's cession of Gaul to the Franks is not clearly stated in the sources, and that Du Bos has to gather together a number of fragments of information to make his case, and even he finds it hard to work out the exact diplomatic narrative, which in his eyes involved more than one treaty—though there are enough pieces of information to mean that one cannot dismiss the basic outline of his reconstruction out of hand.[101] What one might object to, and what later generations clearly found difficult, was his conclusion:

> This right of obedience over the provinces, which is peculiar to the French monarchy, is the authentic concession of these provinces made by the Roman Empire, which held them for nearly six centuries by right of conquest. They were ceded to the French monarchy by one of the successors of Julius Caesar and Augustus, but one of the successors of Tiberius, whom Jesus Christ himself recognized as the legitimate sovereign of Judaea, over which this emperor had no rights other than those which he held over the Gauls and part of Germany.[102]

This statement tends to be seen as central to Du Bos' monarchist stance, but the real target here surely were the Habsburgs, as becomes apparent when he explains that only the French monarchy could claim that its rights came from the Roman Empire, and that those of the German Empire derived from Charlemagne.[103]

Book Five ends with this explosive set of claims. The ensuing and last book investigates *la forme de la première Constitution of the Monarchie Françoise*. It

[95] Du Bos, *Histoire critique*, vol. 2, bk 4, pp. 579, 581.
[96] Du Bos, *Histoire critique*, vol. 3, bk 5, pp. 1–12.
[97] Du Bos, *Histoire critique*, vol. 3, bk 5, p. 20.
[98] Du Bos, *Histoire critique*, vol. 3, bk 5, pp. 194–5.
[99] Du Bos, *Histoire critique*, vol. 3, bk 5, pp. 211–20.
[100] Du Bos, *Histoire critique*, vol. 3, bk 5, pp. 233–4.
[101] Du Bos, *Histoire critique*, vol. 3, bk 5, pp. 243–7.
[102] Du Bos, *Histoire critique*, vol. 3, bk 5, p. 252.
[103] Du Bos, *Histoire critique*, vol. 3, bk 5, pp. 252–4.

emphasizes the Franks' initial position as confederates and guests of the Roman Empire.[104] It deals with the nature of monarchy, asserting that under the Merovingians it was hereditary[105]—thus contradicting the interpretation of Boulainvilliers, and before him of Hotman. It then turns to questions of class, and especially of servile[106] and noble status.[107] Again his target, by implication, is Boulainvilliers, and he denies both the equality of all Franks and the idea that they originally had particular rights and privileges. Although every Frank bore arms, they were not a separate military caste, but became farmers: not that Roman land was simply distributed to them,[108] though Du Bos claims that different arrangements were made by the Burgundians, Goths, and Vandals.[109] He even notes that Franks could become merchants.[110] Meanwhile, Roman militias had survived, so that it was quite wrong to think that the Franks alone performed military service.[111]

All this is a clear attack on Boulainvilliers' interpretation, and indeed, Du Bos addresses his notion of a Frankish conquest directly.[112] Only Tongres and the territory of Syagrius round Soissons was conquered by the Franks,[113] and the population was certainly not reduced to slavery.[114] There was little difference between Franks and Romans: they both claimed Trojan origins.[115] Du Bos also notes that Sidonius had claimed that Romans and Goths were related.[116] Intermarriage between Franks and Gauls is explored in a number of luminous pages.[117] In considering the workings of government, Du Bos denies the survival of the *Champ de Mars* as a regular institution, arguing that it was no longer practicable once the Franks had been dispersed throughout Gaul, and that it was, therefore, only summoned before military campaigns.[118] Rather, Roman patterns of administration continued: he discusses the survival of senates,[119] of taxation,[120] and of Roman law.[121] Indeed his discussion of Roman Law is particularly acute. In addition, and again in opposition to Boulainvilliers, he stresses the importance of the Church.[122]

Given the diversity within the Merovingian kingdom, what surprised Du Bos was not its collapse, but its survival.[123] For him the great caesura in history was not

---

[104] Du Bos, *Histoire critique*, vol. 3, bk 6, p. 274.
[105] Du Bos, *Histoire critique*, vol. 3, bk 6, pp. 279–87.
[106] Du Bos, *Histoire critique*, vol. 3, bk 6, pp. 318–27.
[107] Du Bos, *Histoire critique*, vol. 3, bk 6, pp. 328–32.
[108] Du Bos, *Histoire critique*, vol. 3, bk 6, pp. 383, 535.
[109] Du Bos, *Histoire critique*, vol. 3, bk 6, pp. 542–50.
[110] Du Bos, *Histoire critique*, vol. 3, bk 6, p. 384.
[111] Du Bos, *Histoire critique*, vol. 3, bk 6, p. 527.
[112] Du Bos, *Histoire critique*, vol. 3, bk 6, pp. 414, 523.
[113] Du Bos, *Histoire critique*, vol. 3, bk 6, pp. 414–15.
[114] Du Bos, *Histoire critique*, vol. 3, bk 6, pp. 426, 479.
[115] Du Bos, *Histoire critique*, vol. 3, bk 6, pp. 416–19.
[116] Du Bos, *Histoire critique*, vol. 3, bk 6, p. 420.
[117] Du Bos, *Histoire critique*, vol. 3, bk 6, pp. 481–3.
[118] Du Bos, *Histoire critique*, vol. 3, bk 6, pp. 359–60.
[119] Du Bos, *Histoire critique*, vol. 3, bk 6, pp. 501–2.
[120] Du Bos, *Histoire critique*, vol. 3, bk 6, pp. 553–602.
[121] Du Bos, *Histoire critique*, vol. 3, bk 6, pp. 433–45.
[122] Du Bos, *Histoire critique*, vol. 3, bk 6, pp. 426–30.
[123] Du Bos, *Histoire critique*, vol. 3, bk 6, p. 445.

the end of the Roman period, but the Capetian age. That was when the last of the Roman senates vanished (here he was certainly optimistic), and it was when the dukes and counts created *seigneuries*, usurping the rights of the people.[124] The Capetians themselves, however, countered this usurpation in restoring communal rights.[125] Where Boulainvilliers had seen a conspiracy of the monarchy and the *Tiers État* against the privileges of the nobility legitimately acquired through conquest, Du Bos denied the supposed conquest and argued rather for a restitution of rights that had been seized in the early Capetian period.

Just as one can easily see how his *nobiliaire* views determine Boulainvilliers' understanding of the Fall of the Roman Empire and the Merovingian period, it is easy to show how the interpretation offered by Du Bos is dependent on his position as a monarchist and a member of the *bourgeoisie*. Born into a *bourgeois* family in Beauvais in 1670,[126] he expected to find Church preferment in his hometown, but when his expectations were blocked he decided on a more literary career. He moved to Paris, where he became involved in the Opéra, and he also travelled, not least to England, where he became acquainted with Locke,[127] Amsterdam, where he met the Huguenot exile Pierre Bayle,[128] and Italy.[129] He was employed by a number of leading French politicians and diplomats, not least the Duc d'Orléans (one of Boulainvilliers' patrons, and the man who ensured the publication of his works) and the Maréchaux de Matignon[130] and d'Huxelles.[131] For the latter he acted as secretary in the run up to the Peace of Utrecht, which concluded the War of the Spanish Succession, and he was widely regarded as having played a role in the negotiations.[132] When he returned to Paris he attracted considerable praise for the first of his major intellectual works, the *Réflexions critiques sur la poésie et sur la peinture*, published in 1719, and destined to become a cornerstone of aesthetic theory. Its publication was enough to ensure that Du Bos was elected to the Académie française, which he entered in 1719/20,[133] He became *secrétaire perpétuel* three years later,[134] in which post he was to play a crucial role in the election of Montesquieu in 1727.[135] So firmly was he associated in the minds of his contemporaries with the theory of aesthetics that his *Histoire critique* came as a surprise when it was published in 1734.[136]

His career explains many of the strengths and weaknesses of his history. Apart from his political position, as a bourgeois and a monarchist, which can be neatly set alongside his reading of the constitutional position of the Merovingians, there is his role in the negotiations preceding the Peace of Utrecht, which no doubt explains his sensitivity to questions of diplomacy, and his desire to see treaties as

[124] Du Bos, *Histoire critique*, vol. 3, bk 6, p. 502.
[125] Du Bos, *Histoire critique*, vol. 3, bk 6, p. 503.   [126] Lombard, *Du Bos*, p. 4.
[127] Lombard, *Du Bos*, pp. 73, 194.
[128] Lombard, *Du Bos*, pp. 79, 96. Bayle, one might note, wrote a short biography of Hotman: see 'A Short extract of the life of Francis Hotoman, taken out of Monsieur Bayle's Hist. Dict. and other authors', in Hotman, *Franco-Gallia* (1711), pp. 1–9.
[129] Lombard, *Du Bos*, pp. 85–6.   [130] Lombard, *Du Bos*, p. 194.
[131] Lombard, *Du Bos*, p. 123.   [132] Lombard, *Du Bos*, p. 130.
[133] Lombard, *Du Bos*, pp. 145, 158.   [134] Lombard, *Du Bos*, p. 160.
[135] Lombard, *Du Bos*, p. 165.   [136] Lombard, *Du Bos*, p. 166.

underpinning many of the events of the fifth and early sixth centuries. As his biographer Alfred Lombard noted:

> He transposes into the past the diplomatic behaviour of his own times, and presents the barbarians of the fifth century as sitting around the gaming table of a European congress. He had been a diplomat, and he remained one. He gave much emphasis, among his sources, to collections of laws and to treaties. For him the historian's gospel was the Codex of Leibnitz and the work of Grotius, about which he delivered his *discours* at the Académie....[137]

It should be said, however, that his sensitivity to diplomacy might not have been entirely ill-founded. It is likely that embassies and treaties were rather more important than our sources admit.[138] In fact, despite the excesses of some aspects of his interpretation, his work is distinguished by its learning—many of the sources he cited had not been used in previous discussions of the period[139]—and by his concern for accuracy. In this he was probably most deeply influenced by Bayle,[140] the French Calvinist who spend much of his life in Amsterdam, and whose critical approach to the handling of information would later influence Gibbon.[141] Indeed, the tendency to present Du Bos simply as a monarchist opponent of Boulainvilliers[142] completely underestimates his qualities as a historian, which outshine those of almost all, if not all, his contemporaries.

The *Histoire critique* was an instant success, although there were those who did not accept every aspect of the argument.[143] While it does occasionally lapse into Bourbon propaganda, and certainly reflects a debate about the French constitution, those moments are few and far between: indeed, Du Bos's *Histoire critique* was very much less propagandist than were Boulainvilliers' historical works. For the most part it offers an extraordinarily scholarly reading of the sources. By any standards it is a major work of historical writing. And in setting out the 'Romanist' reading of the establishment of the Frankish kingdom, in opposition to Boulainvilliers' 'Germanist' case, Du Bos essentially created the second great model for the interpretation of the period from the fourth to the seventh centuries. Between them the two models would dominate subsequent scholarship.

---

[137] Lombard, *Du Bos*, p. 399. I have followed Peter Brown in seeing the *tapis vert* as the green baize of a gaming table.

[138] See now Gillett, *Envoys and Political Communication in the Late Antique West, 411–533*; and Chrysos, 'Die Amaler-Herrschaft in Italien und das Imperium Romanum'.

[139] Lombard, *Du Bos*, p. 432.   [140] Lombard, *Du Bos*, pp. 53–68, 391.

[141] Pocock, *Barbarism and Religion*, vol. 1, pp. 74–5.

[142] E.g. Jones, *The Great Nation*, pp. 217–18.

[143] On its reception, Lombard, *Du Bos*, pp. 465–9.

3

The Old German Constitution

3.1 MONTESQUIEU AND *L'ESPRIT DES LOIX*

Du Bos' *Histoire critique* was an immediate success, but in 1748, six years after the author's death, the work's reputation suffered the first of a number of responses which were thought to undermine its credibility. Indeed, so supposedly devastating was the attack launched by Montesquieu in the closing chapters of *De l'esprit des loix* that the *Histoire critique* came to be remembered chiefly for *la brilliante réfutation de Montesquieu*.[1] This was not the view of Voltaire, who thought that, one or two points of detail apart, Montesquieu had failed to deal with the case put forward by Du Bos.[2] Voltaire's position, however, was not a common one. Such is the criticism expressed in *De l'esprit des loix* that it used to be thought that there was some bad blood between the two men regarding Montesquieu's election to the *Académie*.[3] This interpretation is no longer accepted, and indeed, Du Bos is known to have supported Montesquieu's candidature. In fact, the latter goes out of his way to praise other of Du Bos' works in *De l'esprit des loix*.[4] But, as he comments of the *Histoire critique*, 'Nothing hinders the progress of knowledge more than a bad work by a well-regarded author.'[5]

Montesquieu's response to Du Bos' history takes up a good part of the last two books, 30 and 31, of *De l'esprit des loix*. These were apparently an afterthought, and certainly differ from the previous books, in style, form, and length.[6] Unlike Du Bos, Montesquieu begins his analysis of *l'établissement de la monarchie* with an examination of the evidence of Caesar and Tacitus[7]—sources that had appealed rather more to Hotman and to Boulainvilliers. Montesquieu, however, appears to have paid unusual attention to Tacitus,[8] and he was to place the Roman author's

---

[1] Lombard, *Du Bos*, p. 469.

[2] Voltaire. 'Lois (Esprit des)', pp. 11–13. For a general assessment of Montesquieu's critique, Lombard, *Du Bos*, pp. 469–74.

[3] Lombard, *Du Bos*, pp. 165, 326.

[4] Lombard, *Du Bos*, p. 326. Montesquieu, *De l'esprit des loix*, bk XXX, ch. 25, ed. Brethe de la Gressaye, vol. 4, p. 217.

[5] Montesquieu, *De l'esprit des loix*, bk XXX, ch. 15, vol. 4, p. 179.

[6] Shackleton, *Montesquieu*, pp. 328–9. I am indebted to Simon Dixon for reminding me of the extent to which books 30 and 31 differ from what has come before.

[7] Montesquieu, *De l'esprit des loix*, bk XXX, chapters 2–4, vol. 4, pp. 154–7.

[8] Volpilhac-Auger, *Tacite et Montesquieu*. Montesquieu used the *Annals* as well as the *Germania*, the former serving him more for his study of the Roman Empire. However, as is noted in Shackleton, *Montesquieu*, p. 158, Camille Jullian pointed out that for each chapter he only relied on one or two authorities, adding that this made him less reliable than Tillemont.

reading of the early Germanic peoples very firmly at the centre of discussion. In this chapter, therefore, we will look first at Montesquieu's attack on Du Bos, and then at some of the ramifications of his use of Tacitus and the ancient Germans, an investigation that will take us to Denmark. We will return to France with the abbé de Mably, and his reconsideration of early Frankish history. Montesquieu's analysis of the decline of the Roman Empire, which he set out in another, earlier work, the *Considérations sur la grandeur des romains et de leur décadence* of 1734, and revised by him in 1748, will concern us in the next chapter.

Montequieu's *De l'esprit des loix* is, of course, very much more than an essay on early French history. It has recently been characterized as 'not just a legal-anthropological disquisition on the relations between laws, *mores* and societies, but also, importantly, an argument proving that concentrated authority does not necessarily make a state strong'.[9] It is a commentary on the reign of Louis XIV (and indeed on what followed), much as Boulainvilliers' writings had been. Montesquieu's comments on the ancient history of the Franks are, thus, no more objective than those of Boulainvilliers or of Du Bos: indeed *De l'esprit des loix* is a much more politically engaged work than is Du Bos' *Histoire critique*—as are the *Considérations sur les causes de la grandeur des Romains et de leur décadence.*

Montesquieu begins his discussion of the Frankish monarchy before the establishment of the Merovingian kingdom. From his reading of Tacitus he envisaged a society dominated by princes, who had to persuade men to follow them in their various warlike projects. They granted out land to their followers, but only for a year. In the pre-Migration Period there were thus vassals, but no fiefs. Turning to the fifth century, Montesquieu accepted that the Franks conquered the Gallo-Romans, but he also believed that the emperors made treaties with the incoming barbarians, and his understanding of the partition of land is based on a detailed examination of the evidence of the Gothic and Burgundian law codes (which had also been discussed by Du Bos).[10] His interpretation, thus, lay midway between those of Boulainvilliers and Du Bos, and in acknowledging this himself, he stressed their political affiliations: as he saw it, the former created a model that attacked the *Tiers État*, the latter one that attacked the nobility.[11]

For Montesquieu, unlike Boulainvilliers, the indigenous population as a whole was not reduced to servitude—a point of some importance for his reading of the subsequent social and political history of France. He noted the presence of free Romans in both the Burgundian and the Frankish law codes,[12] and accepted that Roman institutions and rights remained in place during the Merovingian period.[13] Yet, at the same time, there was a conquest, and there was some initial looting (which again prompts an allusion to the story about the vase at Soissons), and indeed the continuing Frankish civil wars meant that individuals were still being

[9] Leerssen, *National Thought in Europe*, p. 74.
[10] Montesquieu, *De l'esprit des loix*, bk XXX, ch. 7–9, vol. 4, pp. 159–62.
[11] Montesquieu, *De l'esprit des loix*, bk XXX, ch. 10, vol. 4, p. 163. Shackleton, *Montesquieu*, pp. 330–2.
[12] Montesquieu, *De l'esprit des loix*, bk XXX, ch. 10, vol. 4, pp. 162–3.
[13] Montesquieu, *De l'esprit des loix*, bk XXX, ch. 11, vol. 4, p. 164.

enslaved after the period of conquest.[14] There was thus a rise in serfdom. Despite his insistence on Roman continuity, Montesquieu noted that the barbarians did not pay taxes, and that the Romans and Gauls soon commuted tax into military service.[15] His discussion of military service, however, takes him quickly into the evidence for the ninth century. He is particularly interested in the origins of the fief, which he discusses largely in Carolingian terms, though he does trace *leudes* (a particular type of military following) and vassals back into the pre-Migration Period and notes the examples of fiefs in the Merovingian sources.[16] In discussing law, he pauses on the courts of the count, *graphio,* and *centenarius,* stressing their origins in the forests of Germany,[17] to which he had already attributed the representative traditions of England.[18] Once again, what he has in mind is the model of Tacitus' *Germania.*

Although a large portion of Montesquieu's argument is directed as much against Boulainvilliers as against Du Bos, it is the latter whose basic case is subject to a much more direct attack, particularly in a chapter entitled 'Idée générale du livre de l'Établissement de la monarchie françoise dans les Gaules, par M. l'abbé Dubos'.[19] There he denounces the book as a colossus with feet of clay, attacking what he sees as conjecture piled on conjecture, as well as its lack of evidence.[20] This last point is remarkably far from the mark, as Voltaire was to note.[21] Montesquieu begins the chapter by rejecting Du Bos' argument that the Franks did not come in as conquerors, emphasizing instead that Clovis and his followers conquered and pillaged.[22] He then turns to Du Bos' theories about the Armoricans, claiming with a certain amount of justification, that there was no evidence to underpin them,[23] and suggesting that this meant that there was no evidence for the Gauls calling in the Franks. Thereafter he considers Clovis' position: did he hold any Roman office?[24] Although the evidence is not clear, Montesquieu goes further in dismissing it than would most scholars. Justinian's concession of Provence to the Franks is also rejected.[25] Again, there is more to support Du Bos than Montesquieu allows. Turning to the Franks, he rejects Du Bos' notion that they had no hereditary noble class.[26] This is in fact an issue that has continued to be debated, because of the

---

[14] Montesquieu, *De l'esprit des loix*, bk XXX, ch. 11, vol. 4, pp. 164–7.

[15] Montesquieu, *De l'esprit des loix*, bk XXX, ch. 12, vol. 4, pp. 168–71.

[16] Montesquieu, *De l'esprit des loix*, bk XXX, ch. 16, vol. 4, pp. 180–1. See Shackleton, *Montesquieu,* pp. 328–33.

[17] Montesquieu, *De l'esprit des loix*, bk XXX, ch. 18, vol. 4, p. 188. For a recent consideration of these offices, Murray, 'The position of the grafio in the constitutional history of Merovingian Gaul'; Murray, 'From Roman to Frankish Gaul: "Centenarii" and "Centenae" in the administration of the Frankish kingdom'.

[18] Montesquieu, *De l'esprit des loix*, bk XI, ch. 6, vol. 2, pp. 63–77.

[19] Montesquieu, *De l'esprit des loix*, bk XXX, chapters 23–25, vol. 4, pp. 204–17. Shackleton, *Montesquieu*, pp. 330–2.

[20] Montesquieu, *De l'esprit des loix*, bk XXX, ch. 23, vol. 4, p. 204.

[21] Voltaire, 'Lois (Esprit des)'.

[22] Montesquieu, *De l'esprit des loix*, bk XXX, ch. 23, vol. 4, p. 204.

[23] Montesquieu, *De l'esprit des loix*, bk XXX, ch. 24, vol. 4, p. 206.

[24] Montesquieu, *De l'esprit des loix*, bk XXX, ch. 24, vol. 4, p. 207.

[25] Montesquieu, *De l'esprit des loix*, bk XXX, ch. 24, vol. 4, pp. 207–8.

[26] Montesquieu, *De l'esprit des loix*, bk XXX, ch. 25, vol. 4, pp. 209–17.

silence of *Lex Salica* on the matter.[27] Du Bos, however, was much more willing to see social distinction among the Franks than was Boulainvilliers, who believed that they were all members of a single class. For Boulainvilliers that class was noble: obviously this was a more acceptable position for Montesquieu, who seems to have taken Du Bos' dismissal of a hereditary Frankish noble class personally, talking of 'a slight on our nobility'[28]—and thus betraying his own *nobiliaire* sympathies, which here took him closer to Boulainvilliers than the bourgeois Du Bos.

Book 30 of *De l'esprit des loix* concludes with this outburst. Book 31 embarks on a chronological survey of French history, from Clovis to Hugh Capet. It begins with a discussion of offices and fiefs. According to Montesquieu, again extrapolating from Tacitus, offices were originally granted for no more than a year; fiefs, by contrast, were given for longer, although they were theoretically recoverable.[29] This led to abuse, the queens Brunhild and Fredegund being particularly arbitrary in their confiscations. As a result there was a major reform following Brunhild's death. Montesquieu rightly attributes the Edict of Chlothar to the second king of that name, seeing it as a reaction to the injustices of the preceding years.[30] In so doing he rejected the earlier ascription of the edict to Chlothar I.[31] With the reign of Chlothar II Montesquieu turns to the rise of the mayors of the palace, and thus increasingly to issues associated with the Carolingians and with the history of feudalism.

Just as the arguments of Boulainvilliers and Du Bos can be associated with their social and political positions, the same is true of those of Montesquieu. Born in 1689, like Boulainvilliers he came from the nobility, and like him he was educated at Juilly: indeed, as we have seen, he was a contemporary of one of Boulainvilliers' sons at the school. In 1716 he succeeded to his uncle's position as *Président à Mortier* in the *Parlement* of Bordeaux: not surprisingly, like Boulainvilliers, he saw the *Parlements* as originating in the ancient constitution of the Franks.[32] He resigned his hereditary office in 1725, by which time he was to be found mainly in Paris, where he sometimes lodged with Boulainvilliers, and as a result had access to his works before they were published.[33] He was elected to the Académie, with the support of Du Bos in 1727. However, as a critic of despotism, he found Du Bos' arguments rather too favourable to the monarchy, and as a member of the nobility he disliked the abbé's rejection of the existence of a Frankish noble class.[34] In his desire for checks and balances on the monarchy, he followed Boulainvilliers in looking back to Tacitus and to the ideal world of the *Germania*. It was there that

[27] See especially Irsigler, *Untersuchungen zur Geschichte des frühfränkischen Adels*; Grahn-Hoek, *Die fränkische Oberschicht im 6. Jahrhundert: Studien zu ihrer rechtlichen und politischen Stellung*.

[28] Montesquieu, *De l'esprit des loix*, bk XXX, ch. 25, vol. 4, p. 210.

[29] Montesquieu, *De l'esprit des loix*, bk XXXI, ch. 1, vol. 4, pp. 225–9. Montesquieu's interpretation of the fief is more fully set out in book 30.

[30] Montesquieu, *De l'esprit des loix*, bk XXXI, ch. 2, vol. 4, pp. 229–33. On this see Shackleton, *Montesquieu*, p. 335.

[31] For a full study of the edict and its historiography, Esders, *Römische Rechtstradition und merowingisches Königtum*.

[32] Jones, *The Great Nation*, p. 217.

[33] Shackleton, *Montesquieu*, pp. 12–13, 50, 64, 330.   [34] Shackleton, *Montesquieu*, pp. 330–2.

he located the origins both of the French *parlements*[35] and also of the representative traditions of the English political system.[36] He, therefore, found rather more to admire in the Germanic law codes than did Du Bos, who had concentrated instead on the Roman. As we shall see, Rome itself had already attracted Montequieu's attention in the *Considérations sur la grandeur des romains et de leur décadence*, but in the closing chapters of the *De l'esprit des loix* it is the Frankish and Germanic past that concerned him. There he saw the Franks as conquerors, and he was happy to talk of 'nos pères, les anciens Germains'.[37]

It was not only in his discussion of early Merovingian history that Montesquieu emphasized the role of the early Germans. In fact, they play a significant role throughout *De l'esprit des loix* and had already made their entry in his *Lettres persanes* of 1721.[38] As a result of his reading of Tacitus, he accepted that liberty and democracy were to be associated with the Germanic peoples, and above all with Scandinavia.[39] This he attributed to the climate. Montesquieu had probably taken the idea from the *Viaggio settentrionale* of Francesco Negri,[40] although it had its antecedents in numerous medieval and early modern writers, including Paul the Deacon, Machiavelli, Rudbeck, Montaigne, Bossuet, and Bodin,[41] and indeed in Du Bos. It was from the North as the home of Liberty, according to Montesquieu, that the barbarians came to destroy 'the tyrants and slaves of the South'.[42] For not only did he accept Tacitus' view of Germanic liberty; he also combined it with the idea of Scandinavia as the *vagina gentium*, which he, like others, derived from Jordanes (who had talked not of Scandinavia but of Scandza) and Paul the Deacon. He, therefore, accepted that there had been a very substantial migration of peoples from the North. Thus, whilst for Jordanes, Scandza was a womb of peoples, for Montesquieu Scandinavia became the factory that produced the tools (i.e. Liberty) to break the chains of the South.[43]

3.2 PAUL-HENRI MALLET AND THE DANES

Montesquieu associated the notions of Liberty, Democracy, and Equality, as expressed by Tacitus in the *Germania*, firmly with Scandinavia, which he identified as the *vagina gentium* of Jordanes. These ideals he combined with his own sense

[35] Jones, *The Great Nation*, p. 217.
[36] Montesquieu, *De l'esprit des loix*, bk XI, ch. 6, vol. 2, pp. 63–77; see vol. 4, p. 368.
[37] Montesquieu, *De l'esprit des loix*, bk VI ch. 18; bk X, ch. 3; bk XIV, ch. 14: vol. 1, p. 171; vol. 2, pp. 19–22, 205.
[38] Montequieu, *Lettres persanes*, lettres 131, 136, ed. Adam, pp. 333–5, 345–7.
[39] Montesquieu, *De l'esprit des loix*, Bk XVII, ch. 5, vol. 2, pp. 270–2; Beck, *Northern Antiquities*, vol. 1, pp. 22–3.
[40] Beck, *Northern Antiquities*, vol. 1, p. 56. For Negri, *Viaggio settentrionale*, see Beck, op. cit, p. 42, n. 139.
[41] Beck, *Northern Antiquities*, vol. 1, p. 60; Shackleton, *Montesquieu*, p. 304. For Du Bos' views on climate, Lombard, *Du Bos*, pp. 67, 94, 248–54.
[42] Montesquieu, *De l'esprit des loix*, bk XVII, ch. 5, vol. 2, p. 272; Beck, *Northern Antiquities*, vol. 1, pp. 21, 63.
[43] Montequieu, *De l'esprit des loix*, bk XVII, ch. 5, vol. 2, p. 272; Beck, *Northern Antiquities*, vol. 1, p. 22.

that the nobility had a valuable role to play. This was a balance that was picked up almost immediately by a young Swiss scholar, Paul-Henri Mallet (1730–1807), who on the one hand championed the notions of liberty and democracy, but at the same time believed that unfettered democracy was dangerous, and that it required the protective authority that could be provided by an active aristocracy: in other words, he looked to a free and mixed constitution.[44]

Mallet made his name as tutor to the son of the Count of Calemberg, and as a result found himself preferred at the early age of 22 to the post of *Professeur Royal des belles-lettres françoises* at Copenhagen in 1752. Having very little to do in the post, he devoted himself to the study of Scandinavian languages and history. In this he was encouraged by a Danish government still smarting from the attack levelled by Robert Molesworth, in *An Account of Denmark as it was in the year 1692*, which had appeared in print two years later.[45] This was essentially a critique of Danish absolutism as it developed after its adoption of a French model of government in 1660. Molesworth's account was translated into a number of languages, and hence was extremely influential, and was drawn on, for example, by both Voltaire in his *Charles XII* and by Montesquieu, in his *Lettres persanes*, his *Considérations sur la grandeur des romains*, and in *De l'esprit des loix*.[46] Not surprisingly, the Danish authorities were looking for someone who could counter its influence, and to this end Count Moltke and Prime Minister Bernstorff turned to Mallet.[47] The result was his *Introduction à l'histoire de Dannemarc*, of which the first prefatory volume appeared in 1755,[48] to be followed a year later by a French translation of Snorri Sturlasson's *Edda*. This appeared in a work entitled *Monuments de la mythologie et de la poésie des Celtes et particulièrement des anciens Scandinaves*.[49] Mallet followed Philipp Clüver and Simon Pelloutier in thinking that the Teutons and Celts were one and the same group of peoples.[50] This was an error that was denounced in no uncertain terms by Bishop Henry Percy, who otherwise admired Mallet's work, and produced an English translation of the two books in 1770.[51] It was, however, not until 1787 that the distinction between the Teutons and Celts was firmly set out, by John Pinkerton in his *Dissertation on the Origin and Progress of the Scythians or Goths*.[52]

[44] Sismondi, *De la vie et des écrits de P.H. Mallet*, p. 38.
[45] Molesworth, *An Account of Denmark as it was in the year 1692*. On the relation between the works of Molesworth and Mallet, Beck, *Northern Antiquities*, vol. 1, pp. 12–14.
[46] Beck, *Northern Antiquities*, vol. 1, pp. 13–15.
[47] Beck, *Northern Antiquities*, vol. 1, p. 15.
[48] Mallet, *Introduction à l'histoire de Dannemarc*.
[49] Mallet, *Monuments de la mythologie de de la poésie des Celtes*.
[50] Clüver, *Germania Antiqua*: S. Pelloutier, *Histoire des Celtes*.
[51] Mallet, *Northern Antiquities*. Most of the following references to Mallet are to Percy's 1770 translation, despite the fact that it does not always adhere closely to the original. Mallet himself made a number of changes in the 3rd (1787) edition of his *Introduction*; see Beck, *Northern Antiqutities*, vol, 1, pp. 41, 63, 75. Contrast with p. 16, where Beck downplays the changes. On the importance of the changes, see also Clunies Ross and Lönnroth, 'The Norse Muse', p. 15. Percy's attack on Mallet's erroneous identification of Teutons as Celts can be found in pp. pp. i–xlvii, 'Translator's Preface: proofs that the Teutonic and Celtic nations were ab origine two distinct peoples'.
[52] For Pinkerton, *Dissertation on the Origin and Progress of the Scythians or Goths*, see Horsman, 'Origins of racial Anglo-Saxonism in Great Britain before 1850', pp. 391–2.

Despite this mistake, Mallet made a major contribution to scholarship by including among his *monuments* a French translation of Snorri's *Edda*, which until then had only really been studied within Scandinavia.[53] Yet the first volume of the *Introduction à l'histoire de Dannemarc* was just as significant as the translation of Snorri for the development of early medieval history.[54] Mallet already knew Montesquieu's *De l'esprit des loix*,[55] and he therefore combined the evidence of Tacitus with that of Adam of Bremen, Snorri, Saxo Grammaticus, and Olaus Worm, to create a dramatic image of the Northern peoples in the early Middle Ages.

After a brief account of the extent of the eighteenth-century Danish kingdom, including Norway, Iceland, and Greenland, Mallet turned to what the classical sources had to say of the Cimbri, who for him were the first inhabitants of Denmark.[56] Their history he thought could only be traced back to the arrival of Odin, an event that he dated to around 70 BC.[57] Odin he understood to have been a warrior and a religious reformer, and his religious reforms and their impact on Scandinavia take up three of the ensuing chapters.[58] It should be noted that although this idea may now seem somewhat outlandish, it was taken seriously in the eighteenth century (and a version of the idea was revived by Kenneth Harrison in 1976).[59] It was accepted by Gibbon, though he thought that Mallet was mistaken in his chronology, and that Odin's arrival should be seen as contemporary with the reign of Trajan.[60] Moreover, Mallet did distance himself from other ideas that were circulating, including Olaus Rudbeck's notion that Sweden should be identified with Atlantis[61]—an idea that would be revived in Nazi circles in the 1930s.[62]

Having dealt with the religion of the early Danes, Mallet turned to their earliest forms of government. Here Tacitus' *Germania* was his chief source.[63] Gibbon was less inclined to accept Mallet on this point, arguing that Tacitus was not trustworthy when it came to his description of the early Germans, and that there was certainly no reason to think that his account held true for the peoples who did not live in proximity to the Roman frontier.[64] Mallet, however, having claimed that Tacitus provided evidence that vassalage and feudal tenure were already in existence at the start of the second century AD, went on to ask how notions of liberty survived in the North. He found his answer in Montesquieu's association

[53] Sismondi, *De la vie et des écrits de P. H. Mallet*, p. 19. For an unbroken tradition of interest in the past within Iceland, Clunies Ross and Lönnroth, 'The Norse Muse', pp. 7, 8–14.
[54] On the importance of Mallet, see Beck, *Northern Antiquities*, vol. 1. For a more recent assessment, Clunies Ross and Lönnroth, 'The Norse Muse', pp. 6–7, 14–18,
[55] See, for instance, the citation in Mallet, *Introduction à l'histoire de Dannemarc*, p. 110.
[56] Mallet, *Northern Antiquities*, vol. 1, pp. 20–40.
[57] Mallet, *Northern Antiquities*, vol. 1, pp. 21–2, 68. On the Odin legend, Beck, *Northern Antiquities, Vol. 2, The Odin legend and the oriental fascination*.
[58] Mallet, *Northern Antiquities*, vol. 1, pp. 78–155.
[59] Harrison, 'Woden'.
[60] Gibbon, 'An examination of Mallet's Introduction to the History of Denmark'.
[61] Rudbeck, *Atland eller Manheim*.
[62] See the discussion of Herman Wirth in Pringle, *The Master Plan*, pp. 60–1.
[63] Mallet, *Northern Antiquities*, vol. 1, p. 161; see also pp. 306–404.
[64] Gibbon, 'An examination of Mallet's Introduction to the History of Denmark', p. 232.

of certain constitutional forms with particular climatic zones.[65] For Mallet, as for Montesquieu, it was climate that helped develop and preserve Germanic notions of liberty, which were spread by the Teutons as they settled throughout northern Europe.[66]

Mallet then turned his attention to the representative assemblies of the North, including the Icelandic *Althing*, the Anglo-Saxon *Wittena-gemot*, and the Frankish *Champ de Mars*,[67] before looking at law, and especially at the ordeal and compurgation. In discussing these he showed considerable knowledge of the early law codes.[68] He next considered war, which he presented in the context of expansion from the *vagina gentium* of Scandinavia.[69] And he concluded his *Introduction* with a look at the 'customs and manners of northern nations', drawn mostly from Tacitus and Caesar, with some additional observations from the fifth-century moralist Salvian, who was concerned to present the barbarians as being more virtuous than the Romans.[70]

The first of Mallet's volumes on Denmark thus used classical and early medieval accounts of *Germania*, the Goths and of *Scandza*, to create a picture of Denmark as the original home of democracy.[71] As an answer to Molesworth, this was a rather peculiar offering. Even if one accepted that one could extract democratic and egalitarian ideas from Tacitus, Jordanes, and the Icelandic sagas, and that one could apply them to early medieval Scandinavia, this scarcely amounted to a defence of Danish absolutism. There is, in fact, a good deal of evidence to suggest that Mallet was not particularly happy with his brief. His earliest biographer, the Swiss economist and historian Sismondi, to whom we will return in a later chapter, while admitting that Mallet did see aristocratic authority as a useful element in a mixed and free constitution,[72] also noted that his subject found himself constrained by the requirements of his patrons, first the Danish government, and then, among others, the Princes of Brunswick and Hesse.[73]

There are also some indications that Mallet did not quite see eye to eye with Montesquieu. He was actually a good deal less committed to the notion of Scandinavia as the *vagina gentium* than was the French *philosophe*—though he was infinitely less sceptical than the Scots philosopher, David Hume, who in 1752 cast a withering eye over the whole issue in his essay 'Of the populousness of Ancient Nations'.[74] Unlike Montesquieu, Mallet certainly did not accept Rudbeck's identification of Scandinavia as Atlantis.[75] He saw the Scythians, rather than the Scandinavians, as the first of the peoples of Europe,[76] and he doubted, especially in later

---

[65] Mallet, *Northern Antiquities*, vol. 1, pp. 162–7. For the relevant passages in Montesquieu, *De l'esprit des loix*, bk XVII, vol. 2, pp. 265–74.
[66] Mallet, *Northern Antiquities*, vol. 1, pp. 165–6.
[67] Mallet, *Northern Antiquities*, vol. 1, pp. 174–80.
[68] Mallet, *Northern Antiquities*, vol. 1, pp. 188–90.
[69] Mallet, *Northern Antiquities*, vol. 1, p. 226.
[70] Mallet, *Northern Antiquities*, vol. 1, pp. 306–404.
[71] Beck, *Northern Antiquities*, vol. 1, p. 72.
[72] Sismondi, *De la vie et des écrits de P.H. Mallet*, p. 36.
[73] Sismondi,, *De la vie et des écrits de P.H. Mallet*, p. 22; Beck, *Northern Antiquities*, vol. 1, p. 113.
[74] Hume, 'Of the populousness of Ancient Nations'.
[75] Beck, *Northern Antiquities*, vol, 1, p. 28.   [76] Beck, *Northern Antiquities*, vol, 1, pp. 23–4.

editions of his work, that overpopulation in Scandinavia was the cause of mass migration.[77] He also came increasingly to talk about the North rather than Denmark.[78] Despite these *caveats*, Mallet's *Introduction* was read as a major statement that Scandinavia was the womb of nations, as well as the birthplace of democracy, which was supposedly spread by the migrating barbarians throughout Western Europe. To a large extent it was through Mallet that the French in particular discovered the North.[79] The image of the noble savage that he presented was perfectly in tune with the new aesthetic and political ideology of Jean-Jacques Rousseau.[80]

3.3 MABLY'S *OBSERVATIONS SUR L'HISTOIRE DE LA FRANCE*

Interestingly, Mallet, in the 1763 edition of his *Introduction* to the history of Denmark paused to note Du Bos' disagreement with Boulainvilliers. Twenty-four years later, he removed the comment, in his 1787 edition.[81] Indeed, initially Du Bos' *Histoire critique* weathered the storm roused by *De l'esprit des loix*.[82] What sealed its fate were not only the writings of Montesquieu, but also those of the likes of Louis-Gabriel du Buat-Nançay,[83] and especially of the abbé Gabriel Bonnot de Mably. To understand the triumph of the latter, one has to remember the esteem in which he, like Montesquieu, was held during the French Revolution.

Mably, who was born in Lyons in 1709, was a generation younger than Montesquieu, and twenty years older than Mallet.[84] His family was associated with that of de Tencin, and through the circle of Mme de Tencin he met Montesquieu.[85] Mme de Tencin also recommended him to her brother, the cardinal, for whom he prepared translations of texts in advance of the meetings that culminated in the Treaty of Westphalia.[86] In certain respects, he shared Du Bos' experiences of diplomacy. But Mably fell out with his patron, though he continued to write for members of the government, and indeed for the royal family. His *De l'étude de l'histoire* was written for Louis XV's grandson, the Duc de Parme et de Plaisance, in 1765.[87] Despite these connections with the Bourbons, he was remembered as a radical and a forerunner of the French Revolution. He planned to write a history of the American Revolution, but was persuaded by John Adams to write instead a commentary on the American Constitution, which he did in *Four Letters*.[88] He died in 1785, the same year that the Letters were published, and before crisis erupted in France.

---

[77] Beck, *Northern Antiquities*, vol, 1, pp. 30, 40–3.   [78] Beck, *Northern Antiquities*, vol. 1, p. 63.
[79] Beck, *Northern Antiquities*, vol. 1, p. 9.
[80] Clunies Ross and Lönnroth, 'The Norse Muse', p. 15.
[81] Beck, *Northern Antiquities*, vol. 1, p. 75.   [82] Lombard, *Du Bos*, pp. 475–85.
[83] Buat-Nançay, *Les Origines ou l'ancienne gouvernement de la France, de l'Italie et de l'Allemagne*. Not that Buat-Nançay was in agreement with Montesquieu; see the comments in Foucault, *Society Must be Defended*, pp. 129, 197, 221.
[84] Brizard, *Eloge historique de l'Abbé de Mably*, p. 4.
[85] Brizard, *Eloge historique de l'Abbé de Mably*, p. 93.
[86] Brizard, *Eloge historique de l'Abbé de Mably*, pp. 94–5.
[87] Brizard, *Eloge historique de l'Abbé de Mably*, p. 110.
[88] Hancock and Lambert (eds), *The legacy of the French Revolution*, p. 144, n. 9.

Mably's chief work on the history of the Franks is to be found in his *Observa-tions sur l'histoire de la France*, which appeared in 1765.[89] Like Boulainvilliers, Montesquieu, and Mallet, he began not in Roman Gaul, but in the forests of Ger-many, or perhaps even further to the east.[90] Despite Roman attempts to destroy the Franks, they regarded Gaul as a place to plunder.[91] Before their move across the Rhine they were a free and equal people: the story of the vase at Soissons was pressed into service to demonstrate their egalitarianism.[92] As yet their legal system was primitive, and, remarkably, Mably insisted that there was no evidence for the existence of the *Champ de Mars* at this stage.[93]

The Frankish move into Gaul Mably placed firmly in the context of the Hunnic invasions, and he argued that it was unsurprising that the Franks should wish to move into the Empire, given the deserted state of the Rhineland provinces.[94] He found little to say about their establishment in the region, turning quickly to Clovis, and to a demolition of Du Bos' presentation of him as a Roman officer:

> The abbé Du Bos, presents Clovis as no more than an officer of the Empire, a *magister militum* who held his power from Zeno and Anastasius. He imagines an Armorican republic, confederacies, and treaties. He indulges in conjectures which are never appropriate to the customs of habits of the time about which he is speaking...He supposes that the French (*Français*), as patient and docile as mercenaries, only con-quered for the gain of their captain, and did not regard the conquest as their own, or the right to command there as part of their booty.[95]

Mably then turned to the question of the *condition des Gaulois et des autres peu-ples soumis à la domination des Francs*.[96] He rightly stressed the lack of evidence, but remarked that it was likely that they seized land in a disorderly and illegal way. Yet he was insistent that the Romans were not enslaved, but merely valued at a lower rate than the Franks—thus adopting a position closer to Montesquieu than Boulainvilliers. Like both of them, however, he insisted that the Gauls had effectively been in a state of slavery under the Empire, given the avaricious nature of the Roman government. By comparison the Franks were more egalitarian:

> Their government initially suffered no change in its most important principles. The nation, still free and forming a true republic, of which the prince was only the first magistrate, ruled as a body over the different peoples in the lands they had conquered. There was still [by this time] an assembly at the *Champ de Mars*: the magnates still constituted the prince's council, and the cities of the Gauls were governed as the strongholds of *Germania* had been.[97]

[89] Mably, *Oeuvres*, vol. 1, pp. 129–214.
[90] Mably, *Observations sur l'histoire de la France*, p. 142.
[91] Mably, *Observations sur l'histoire de la France*, pp. 130, 135.
[92] Mably, *Observations sur l'histoire de la France*, p. 134.
[93] Mably, *Observations sur l'histoire de la France*, p. 133.
[94] Mably, *Observations sur l'histoire de la France*, p. 136.
[95] Mably, *Observations sur l'histoire de la France*, p. 141.
[96] Mably, *Observations sur l'histoire de la France*, pp. 143–52.
[97] Mably, *Observations sur l'histoire de la France*, p. 145.

In this context, it is not surprising that the Gauls took advantage of the new state of affairs to throw off their tax burden—thus again Mably followed Montesquieu and rejected the arguments of Du Bos.

The old legal customs of the forest, however, were not adequate for the new state of affairs, and as a result the Franks gradually took on Roman laws.[98] At the same time they began to abandon their principles of liberty,[99] becoming more interested in property, and thus in private interest rather than the public good. In time the *Champ de Mars*, which had been introduced by Clovis' day, was abandoned. Power fell into the hands of the king and the great men. The bishops, who ought to have protected the people, and indeed who may initially have done so,[100] were too used to subservience, and thought the state should be run by the monarchy.[101] Thus, wealth took over from merit. The king's *leudes* started to usurp rights, exacting tolls and dues.[102] Moreover, during the civil wars under the successors of Clovis, people had to look for protection, and as a result they became indebted to *seigneurs*, who grew ever more powerful.[103] There was thus an increasing abuse of authority. Members of the royal *leudes* sought to make hereditary their benefices—estates granted by the king[104]—and those in the provinces sought to establish themselves as *seigneurs*. Others attempted to become *leudes*, and the king had to alienate more property.[105] Avarice was the driving force even for the Church: 'During these rough centuries there was a belief that avarice was the first attribute of God, and that the saints traded their credit and protection.'[106] Thus, the king gradually found himself without property and devoid of power.[107]

At this point, and even more extensively in the relevant *remarques et preuves* which are appended to the text,[108] Mably addressed the question of *l'origine de la noblesse parmi les Français*.[109] Here he is critical of Boulainvilliers, Du Bos, and Montesquieu, in turn. He did agree with Du Bos that there was originally no hereditary nobility among the Franks, and was forthright in his condemnation of Montesquieu's contrary stance[110]—not surprisingly, given his firm view that the States General, rather than the *Parlements*, were representative of the nation.[111] However, he also saw a steady move towards class distinctions as benefices became hereditary. Those who had allods (hereditary land) pushed for them to be changed into benefices. On the one hand this made the tenure less secure, but on the other

---

[98] Mably, *Observations sur l'histoire de la France*, p. 154.

[99] Mably, *Observations sur l'histoire de la France*, p. 155.

[100] Mably, *Observations sur l'histoire de la France*, p. 150.

[101] Mably, *Observations sur l'histoire de la France*, p. 159.

[102] Mably, *Observations sur l'histoire de la France*, p. 165.

[103] Mably, *Observations sur l'histoire de la France*, pp. 165–6.

[104] For his definition of benefices (which involves a distinction between Roman and Frankish benefices, and which he differentiates from the fief), Mably, *Observations sur l'histoire de la France*, pp. 365–6. Unlike Montesquieu, Mably did not think that benefices went with military service, because he thought that everyone was liable to that anyway, p. 409.

[105] Mably, *Observations sur l'histoire de la France*, pp. 169–80.

[106] Mably, *Observations sur l'histoire de la France*, p. 172.

[107] Mably, *Observations sur l'histoire de la France*, pp. 179–80.

[108] Mably, *Observations sur l'histoire de la France*, pp. 389–99.

[109] Mably, *Observations sur l'histoire de la France*, pp. 181–9.

[110] Mably, *Observations sur l'histoire de la France*, pp. 396–8.

[111] Baker, 'Representation', p. 476.

it brought seigneurial rights. The scene was thus set for a discussion of the decline of the Merovingians and the rise of the Carolingians, which involved an elaborate discussion of the distinction between *seigneurie* (or lordship), the benefice, and the fief. In a final chapter, in which he tried to explain why it was that the Merovingian kingdom survived when others failed, Mably argued that it was simply luck: they were among the last of the barbarian groups to enter the Empire, and by the time of their arrival the Gauls were already used to Germanic customs and traditions.[112] Furthermore, they remained militarized and thus had no need to create a mercenary army to fight the peoples on the east of the Rhine or the Saracens, who threatened them from the eighth century.[113]

3.4 GIBBON ON MABLY

Since the mid-nineteenth century Mably has not had a good press as a historian. Lombard, the biographer of Du Bos, described his book on the *Manière d'écrire l'histoire*, as a 'book where it transpires that a lack of accuracy is the first duty of the historian'.[114] Moral concerns were more important that accuracy. As for his *Observations*, Lombard called them 'the worst book ever written on the history of France', presenting the work as no more than a republican version of Boulainvilliers.[115] This is not quite fair. Writing in 1809, the Regius Professor of History at Cambridge, William Smyth had nothing but praise for Mably: talking about the early history of France he wrote, 'in all and every part of these subjects, and of all this history, the work of the Abbé de Mably is inestimable'.[116] Equally significantly, Gibbon felt that Mably's arguments had to be addressed.

This he did both in *Decline and Fall*, and yet more directly in an essay 'Du gouvernement féodal surtout en France' which was not published until after his death.[117] The essay was essentially a review of Mably's *Observations*. Although he had become more critical of Mably by the time he wrote chapter 38 of *Decline and Fall*, even there he still followed the structure of Mably's argument in his own account of the early Franks.[118] Like Mably, Gibbon begins his thirty-eighth chapter with Tacitus, but significantly he chooses the *Annals* and not the *Germania* as his starting point: the equality of the German forests was not for him.[119] He quickly reaches Clovis, about whom he is remarkably complimentary, noting his mixture of valour and 'cool and consummate prudence'. The picture he presents is largely derived from Gregory of Tours, even to some extent with regard to his emphasis on the king's conversion and commitment to Catholicism. Unlike Du Bos, Gibbon notes of the legend of the Ste Ampoule that it was no more than a fable, 'whose slight foundations

---

[112] Mably, *Observations sur l'histoire de la France*, p. 210.

[113] Mably, *Observations sur l'histoire de la France*, pp. 213–14.

[114] Lombard, *Du Bos*, p. 390. *De la manière d'écrire l'Histoire* is published in vol. 12 of the *Collection complète des Oeuvres de l'Abbé de Mably*.

[115] Lombard, *Du Bos*, p. 487.   [116] Smyth, *Lectures on Modern History*, vol. 1, p. 42.

[117] Gibbon, 'Du gouvernement féodal, surtout en France'.

[118] Wood, 'Gibbon and the Merovingians', pp. 128–31.   [119] Gibbon, *Decline and Fall*, ch. 38.

the Abbé de Vertot [1655–1735] has undermined with profound respect and consummate dexterity.'[120] In addition, however, Gibbon discusses the matter of the Armoricans, following in the footsteps of Du Bos and his critics—and concluding with a reading reasonably close to that of Du Bos. Having related the histories of Clovis' wars against the Burgundians and Visigoths, he comes to Gregory's tale of the consulship conferred on the Frankish king by the emperor Anastasius, and while he dismisses it as 'a name, a shadow, an empty dignity', he does go on to accept Du Bos' reading of the Byzantine concession to the Franks of jurisdiction over Provence. He even states that 'The Franks, or French, are the only people of Europe who can deduce a perpetual succession from the conquerors of the Western Empire.' Thereafter he turns, as had Mably, to the question of the seizure of land by the barbarians and the subsequent status of the population. Here he notes,

> In the space of thirty years [1728–1765] this interesting subject has been agitated by the free spirit of the Count de Boulainvilliers [*Mémoires Historiques sur l'Etat de la France*], the learned ingenuity of the Abbé Dubos [*Histoire Critique de l'Etablissement de la Monarchie Françoise dans les Gaules*], the comprehensive genius of the President de Montesquieu [*Esprit des Loix*], and the good sense and diligence of the Abbé de Mably [*Observations sur l'Histoire de France*].[121]

His own stance is rather closer to that of Du Bos than to those of Boulainvilliers, Montesquieu, or Mably. Having noted the fact that each indigenous group retained its own law, he continues:

> The silence of ancient and authentic testimony has encouraged an opinion that the rapine of the Franks was not moderated, or disguised by the forms of a legal division; that they dispersed themselves over the provinces of Gaul without order or control; and that each victorious robber, according to his wants, his avarice, and his strength, measured with his sword the extent of his new inheritance.

Montesquieu and Mably are clearly within his sights. Against this vision he sets 'the firm and artful policy of Clovis', giving as illustration the tale of the vase of Soissons, and arguing that he 'might lawfully acquire the Imperial patrimony, vacant lands, and Gothic usurpations'. Like Du Bos, Gibbon makes more of Roman law than had either Montesquieu or Mably, though he follows the latter in pursuing the history of the benefice.

Gibbon claimed in his *Memoirs* that 'I have followed the judicious precept of the Abbé de Mably... who advises the historian not to dwell too minutely on the decay of the eastern empire; but to consider the barbarian conquerors as a more worthy subject of his narrative'.[122] But chapter 38 of *Decline and Fall* shows that he also followed Mably in structuring his account, and that he worked carefully through the conflicting arguments of Boulainvilliers, Montesquieu, Du Bos, and Mably. Indeed, it is not really possible to understand Gibbon's position without having read the works on which he was dependent. Mably was not impressed by

---

[120] Gibbon, *Decline and Fall*, ch. 38, note.   [121] Gibbon, *Decline and Fall*, ch. 38, note.
[122] Gibbon, *Memoirs of my Life and Writings*, p. 204, n. 71; see Bryer, 'Gibbon and the later Byzantine Empire', p. 103.

the result. In *De la manière d'écrire l'histoire* he wrote 'You must have observed Historians (Mr Gibbon, for example) who get entangled within their subject; are at a loss how either to open or to conclude it, and, as it were, turn perpetually on themselves.'[123] Gibbon was of the opinion that Mably was unable to understand him, because he could not read English.[124] In fact, not being able to read *Decline and Fall* in English would not have proved a barrier for long, for in 1777 the work appeared in a French translation, in part by Louis XVI himself.[125]

3.5 THE TRIUMPH OF MABLY

Despite the more balanced judgement of Gibbon, his reading of the end of Roman Gaul and the establishment of the Merovingians did not hold sway. In *Qu'est-ce le Tiers-état* of 1789 the abbé comte Joseph Emmanuel Sieyès stated:

> In truth, if one really wants to distinguish birth from birth, couldn't one tell our poor fellow citizens that what one derives from the Gauls and the Romans is worth at least as much as what comes from the *Sicambri*, the Welches, and other savages who came out of the woods and the marshes of ancient Germany? Yes, they say, but the conquest destroyed all relations, and nobility of birth passed to the conquerors. Well, it must be made to pass back to the other side: the *Tiers État* will become noble in becoming the conqueror in its turn.[126]

Here was a deformed version of Mably's interpretation, in itself a deformation of the arguments of Montesquieu and of Boulainvilliers. The French nobility, descended from the Frankish conquerors of Gaul, had its origins in the forests to the east of the Rhine, and should therefore return there.

Sieyès was not concerned primarily with the nobility, but with the *Tiers État*, and in this he parted company with Montesquieu and Mably. For him it was the Third Estate, and not the clergy or the nobility, that constituted the nation: it alone could be defined as society, and the other two orders were mere parasites.[127] This grounding of French identity in a particular reading of history was to have a huge impact on the debates of the States General in 1789. And, indeed, it was following Sieyès' proposal that what was left of the *États généraux* redesignated itself as the *Assemblée nationale*. Sieyès' invocation of the *Sicambri* and the forests of Germany is not only an indication of which version of events had triumphed—that of the critics of Du Bos; it is also a clear indication of the importance of the Barbarian Invasions to French politicians in 1789. And not just in 1789: Sieyès was one of the leading theorists of the ensuing decade, down to the establishment

[123] Mably, *De la manère d'écrire l'histoire*, in *Two Dialogues: Concerning the Manner of Writing of History*, p. 289.
[124] Gibbon, *Memoirs*, ed, Bonnard, p. 158; Wood, 'Gibbon and the Merovingians', p. 127.
[125] Gibbon, *Histoire de la décadence et de la chute de l'Empire romain*, trans. M. Leclerq de Septchênes. Wood, 'The fall of the Roman Empire in the eighteenth and nineteenth centuries', p. 329.
[126] Sieyès, *Qu'est-ce que le Tiers-état*, pp. 17–18. On the centrality of Sieyès' work, Jones, *The Great Nation*, pp. 400–1.
[127] See the comments in Leerssen, *National Thought in Europe*, pp. 86–9.

of Napoleon.[128] Nor was he the only speaker in 1789 to invoke the early Middle Ages: a certain Dacalle suggested that the word *Franc* should be dropped in favour of *Gaulois*[129]—and in doing so he was challenging the tradition, which included both Montesquieu and Mably, that privileged the Franks.

The early Middle Ages featured once again in 1794, when the Abbé Grégoire presented his *Rapport sur les destructions opérées par le vandalisme, et sur les moyens de le réprimer* to the National Convention.[130] It was a attempt to stop wanton destruction that, for the time being, fell on deaf ears. The word 'vandalism', however, would soon pass into common parlance. Although the Vandals had previously been seen as destructive—and indeed, Du Bos had contrasted their path through Gaul with the very much more civilized Frankish take-over[131]—it was Grégoire's work that made them rather than the Goths (who were the byword for violence for Gibbon), the epitome of a barbaric force.[132]

Given the political climate, it is not difficult to see how it was Mably rather than Du Bos (whose works were tainted with their support for Bourbon rule) that won out. Mably's radical credentials included being invited by Adams to comment on the American Constitution. Yet his reading was not only accepted in radical France or America. Smyth, writing in Cambridge, in 1809, remarked, 'Gibbon and Montesquieu, through all this period of history, you will refer to. But the Abbé de Mably is the writer, who will afford you the best assistance, given neither in the distant, obscure manner of Gibbon, nor with the affectation and paradox of Montesquieu.'[133]

One should not underestimate the amount of the historical scholarship that had poured into the debates on the establishment of the French monarchy, which is impressive for its quality as well as its quantity. Its neglect is symptomatic of the amnesia which has drawn a veil over past history-writing, and which even afflicted an appreciation of Gibbon as a historian in the years before the celebration of the bicentenary of *Decline and Fall* in 1976.[134] It may be easy to pick holes in the arguments of the likes of Boulainvilliers, Du Bos, and Mably, but the scholars themselves were formidably learned, and the protagonists essentially laid down the lines along which the Fall of the Roman Empire would be debated, down to the early twenty-first century. What was the state of the Empire itself? How happy were its inhabitants? How much did the barbarians contribute to its fall? How much survived in the way of Roman administration? And how much of what followed had its origins in the world of the Germanic peoples? These fundamentally important questions were debated in the long eighteenth century, and above all in France. Admittedly they were asked because they had contemporary relevance: but that is an issue that will recur in the chapters that follow.

---

[128] Jones, *The Great Nation*, pp. 399–401, 570–80.
[129] Bloch, 'Sur les grandes invasions. Quelques positions de problèmes', p. 95.
[130] Merrills, 'The Origins of "Vandalism"', pp. 155–6.
[131] Merrills, 'The Origins of "Vandalism"', p. 163.
[132] Merrills, 'The Origins of "Vandalism"', p. 163. See also Merrills and Miles, *The Vandals*, p. 9.
[133] Smyth, *Lectures on Modern History*, vol. 1, pp. 60–1.   [134] Brown, 'Report', pp. 5–6.

4

The Barbarians and the Fall of Rome

4.1 GIBBON AND THE HISTORIANS

Modern historiography of the end of Rome, especially since 1976, has tended to present Gibbon as the seminal figure. This, however, has not always been the prevailing view. Even in the 1960s he was regarded as being a writer of literary rather than historical importance.[1] The idea that he was not to be categorized primarily as a historian was already in circulation in the early nineteenth century. As William Smyth, Regius Professor of History at Cambridge, explained in his 1809 lectures, '[i]f his work be not always history, it is often something more than history, and above it; it is philosophy, it is theology, it is wit and eloquence, it is criticism the most masterly upon every subject with which literature can be connected'.[2] The extent to which *Decline and Fall* is much more than a work of history has been extensively studied in recent years, not least by J. G. A. Pocock. What follows here is an attempt to set some aspects of Gibbon's work rather more firmly within their historiographical context.

The modern elevation of Gibbon as a historian has tended to ignore the extent to which he was writing within a well-trodden field[3]—and indeed, on the Fall of Rome itself and the immediately succeeding period, he added remarkably little. A more accurate impression might be gained from what Smyth had to say in his Cambridge lectures:

> ...the dark ages are almost the first subject that is to be encountered by the student of history.
>
> This is unfortunate—unfortunate more especially for the youthful student. Look at the writers that undertake the history of these times. They oppress you by their tediousness; they repel you by their very appearance, by the antiquarian nature of their researches, and the very size of their volumes.[4]

---

[1] Brown, 'Report', p. 5.

[2] Smyth, *Lectures on Modern History*, vol. 1, p. 85. In some ways this assessment concurs with the approach of Pocock, *Barbarism and Religion*, which concentrates more on Gibbon as an enlightenment thinker than it does on Gibbon as historian.

[3] Pocock's *Barbarism and Religion* has relatively few references to works written about the period from 350 to 650.

[4] Smyth, *Lectures on Modern History*, vol. 1, p. 36. See also p. 87: 'In other words, you must acquire some proper knowledge of the French and German histories: these histories are, for a long time, very tedious and repulsive.'

Among those Smyth found nearly unreadable were Voltaire and Bolingbroke, but it is clear that the observations were also intended to include Gibbon, whom, despite his earlier paean of praise, Smyth regarded as little more than a repository of fact from a historical point of view: 'Let the detail be studied, whenever it is thought necessary, in Gibbon.'[5] Even then 'the reader will be often reminded, but too painfully of the simplicity of Hume and the perspicuous though somewhat laboured elegance of Robertson'.[6] Of course, neither Hume nor Robertson was a specialist in the Fall of Rome and the Barbarian Migrations, although Smyth did recommend Hume's essay 'On the populousness of ancient nations'.[7]

One might note that many found the Regius Professor himself somewhat tedious: the caricaturist Gillray wrote:

> All Granta's Nobs,
> By sundry Jobs,
> —Were brought to hear a Lecture;
> But set at naught
> Their Lesson taught
> —And yawn'd beyond conjecture![8]

Harriet Martineau described Smyth's appointment to the Regius chair as 'an act of kindness to the individual but scarcely so to the public'.[9]

One indication of the range of eighteenth-century scholarship to which Gibbon had access, though a partial one, is to be found in the footnotes of *Decline and Fall*. We have already met a number of the scholars cited in the work, including Montesquieu, to whose *Considérations sur la grandeur des romains et de leur décadence* we will return before considering Gibbon's own assessment of the role of the barbarians in the collapse of the West Roman Empire. First, however, we will turn to some of the other authors cited in *Decline and Fall*.

Among Italian scholars Gibbon cites no specialist on the Fall of Rome, but there are the obvious old masters, Machiavelli and Guicciardini. Indeed, they were still being cited well into the nineteenth century. Then there were the ecclesiastical historians: there are references to Cesare Baronio (1538–1607), above all his *Annales ecclesiastici*, which were corrected by the Frenchman Antoine Pagi (1624–99), and to the more nearly contemporary Ludovico Antonio Muratori (1672–1750), whose editions of texts were among the greatest contributions to scholarship in the period. In addition there was Francesco Scipione Maffei (1675–1755), a noted antiquarian, who worked in both Italy, most notably Verona, and also France, describing its monuments and inscriptions in *Galliae antiquitates quaedam selectae*.

---

[5] Smyth, *Lectures on Modern History*, vol. 1, p. 37.
[6] Smyth, *Lectures on Modern History*, vol. 1, p. 33. For a longer analysis of Gibbon's faults, pp. 82–6.
[7] Smyth, *Lectures on Modern History*, vol. 1, p. 30.
[8] Butler, 'A "Petty" Professor of Modern History', p. 217.
[9] Butler, 'A "Petty" Professor of Modern History', p. 218.

4.2 MASCOV

Gibbon, not being able to read German,[10] inevitably cited few German historians. A notable exception is Johann Jacob Mascov (1689–1761), whose *Geschichte der Teutschen bis zu Anfang der Fränckischen Monarchie* of 1726–37 was translated into English almost immediately by Thomas Lediard (1685–1743), as *The History of the Ancient Germans, including that of the Cimbri, Celtæ, Teutones, Alemanni, Saxons, and other Northern Nations, who overthrew the Roman Empire and established that of the Germans, and most of the Kingdoms of Europe.*[11] The English title gives an accurate indication of the extent to which it is concerned with the Fall of Rome. In its English translation this was a work of considerable popularity: in Britain it was admired by Sharon Turner, historian of the Anglo-Saxons,[12] and by Smyth, who noted Gibbon's dependence on it.[13] In America it seems to have been known more often by the title used by Lediard in his letter of dedication addressed to Walpole in volume 2, *The History of our Great Ancestors.*[14] That the Founding Fathers saw themselves as descended from the early Germans is clear from Thomas Jefferson's 1776 proposal that Hengest and Horsa should feature on the reverse of the Great Seal of the United States.[15]

Lediard, the translator, is a figure of some interest: he describes himself as 'Late Secretary to his Majesty's Envoy Extraordinary in Lower Germany', a post he held from 1713 to 1732. He was also an author in his own right, numbering among his works *The German Spy* (1738), which he described as

> [f]amiliar letters from a gentleman on his travels thro' Germany, to his friend in England. Containing an exact and entertaining description of the principal cities and towns…An account of the customs and manners of the people. Remarks on their language, interests and policies…Interspersed with the secret history and characters of the several princes and princesses, and other the most considerable personages in the empire of Germany.

His interest in customs, manners, and language, at least, overlapped with that of Mascov.

Johann Jacob Mascov was born in Danzig in 1689. He moved to Leipzig, where he studied at the university, and where he subsequently became Professor of Law: in Leipzig he also held the posts of Ratsherr, Proconsul, Rats-, and Stadtrichter. He died in 1761. As professor of law he wrote the *Principia juris publici romano-*

---

[10] *The Letters of Edward Gibbon*, ed. Norton, vol. 2, pp. 202–6.

[11] Mascov, *Geschichte der Teutschen*: Mascou (*sic*), *The History of the Ancient Germans*.

[12] Turner, *The History of the Anglo-Saxons*, pp. 80, 129.

[13] Smyth, *Lectures on Modern History*, vol. 1, p. 32: 'There is likewise an history of the Germans, written originally in German, by Mascou, and an English translation by Lediard, where the facts are told more simply and intelligibly; and to the learning and merit of this author, Mr Gibbon bears ample testimony.'

[14] Mascov, *The History of the Ancient Germans*, p. i.

[15] Frantzen, *Desire for Origins*, pp. 15–17.

germanici, and his interests stretched into the period of the Holy Roman Empire with his *De jure feudorum in Imperio Romano-Germanico*, and his *Commentarii de Rebus Imperii Romano-Germanici a Conrado Primo usque ad obitum Henrici Tertii*. In addition, he was a Latinist of note, producing a commentary on Horace.[16] His linguistic and legal skills would serve him well in his *History of the Ancient Germans*, which combines literary and legal sources, together with the evidence of linguistics, as well as coins, medals, and inscriptions, into a clear and coherent narrative. The Germanic law-codes, in particular, are handled admirably. His use of linguistics is perhaps more significant, even though his work in this area has been superseded. Following Leibniz, some of whose researches he was deliberately extending,[17] he understood that language could be a clue to the classification of racial groups and to the study of migration. This was an approach that would come into vogue in the nineteenth century. What he could not easily fit into his basic narrative, he placed in thirty-seven scholarly annotations, appended to the second volume of the history. While Mascov is somewhat self-deprecating about his work, hoping that it would do well because there was something of a vogue for 'works on Antiquities of Germany',[18] Lediard's comments in the translator's preface are perfectly justified:

> In how great Obscurity the History of the Ancient German and other Northern Nations has been hitherto involv'd, is but too well known to those who have been conversant in Antiquity. We find indeed some Fragments of it scatter'd, at Random, in other Histories; but these are only like so many Particles of a Chaos, which want a skilful Hand to unite and digest them into Form.[19]

Even if Gibbon had little access to German scholarship, he was well served in having Lediard's translation of Mascov.

Given his skills as a Latinist and as a lawyer, it is perhaps not surprising that Mascov's assessment of earlier writers is consistently judicious—and he was well read in French, Spanish, Italian, and English, as well as German: he cites Du Bos' *Histoire critique*, even though it had only been published three years earlier.[20] As a man in public life he was more than aware of the political uses to which history might be put, commenting, for instance, on the way in which the conflict between France and Spain in the late seventeenth century had impinged on assessments of the Visigoths:

> There have been great Debates, concerning the Antiquity and Power of the Kingdom of the Wisi-Goths, especially in the foregoing Century, on Occasion of the warm

[16] Mascov, *In Q. Horatii Flacci satiras*.
[17] Mascov, *The History of the Ancient Germans*, vol. 2, Lediard's dedication to Walpole, p. ii. On Leibniz' work on linguistics, Schulenburg, *Leibniz als Sprachforscher*.
[18] Mascov, *The History of the Ancient Germans*, vol. 1, Author's Preface, p. i.
[19] Mascov, *The History of the Ancient Germans*, vol. 1, Translator's Preface. All the quotations from Mascov that follow are from Lediard, whose translation is a work of historiographical significance in its own right.
[20] Mascov, *The History of the Ancient Germans*, vol. 2, p. 375.

Dispute between France and Spain, in the Point of Precedency, and principally between Chiflet and Blondel. The Spaniards pretended to ground the Preference of their Kingdom, on the Antiquity and Power of that of the Goths.[21]

It was Chiflet, working for Archduke Leopold of Austria, who published the grave finds from Childeric's tomb at Tournai. The 1653 discovery and its publication were important to both the Habsburgs and the Bourbons[22] in their claims to be the heirs of the Frankish monarchy.

Mascov's work was not without its own agenda, as he himself explained in his preface:

> My Design is to lay a Foundation, as well for a general History of Germany, as for those, in particular, of the Countries and Nations appertaining thereto; and to reduce, into some Order, whatever is to be found dispers'd in Ancient History of the Origin of the German People, their Habitations, Migrations, Inroads on the Roman Provinces, Civil Wars; and, at the same Time, of their Form of Government, Genius, Religion, Manners, Arms, etc.[23]

What he does not emphasize, however, is the fact that no ancient source categorized all the peoples to whom he refers as a single group, and that the Germans were essentially a scholarly construct.[24] Mascov was essentially giving a history to an invented German nation, and he was doing so from the Kingdom of Saxony nearly a century and a half before German unification. Indeed, his history might be seen as belonging to the pre-history of German nationalism.

> The particular Reasons Germany has, to be thoroughly acquainted with the Origin of its Constitution, frequently leads the Curious back into the most obscure Times: And for those who will be truly inform'd of the Foundation of their National Laws and Customs, they must be no less conversant in German Antiquity, than those who apply themselves to the Study of the Roman Laws, ought to be in that of Ancient Rome. There are many Countries, to this Day, belonging to the German Empire, which were formerly subject to the Romans; and many others, that were inhabited by Germans, are fallen to the Share of Foreign Nations...As most Nations in Europe find an Account of their most Ancient State, in the Roman History; so, on the other Hand, it is the German History, they must apply to, for the Occurences of the IV, V, and following Centuries, and, in many Points, even for the Origins of their Present Constitutions....
>
> In particular, it cannot but be agreable to Germans, to consider, that their Ancestors could set Bounds to the immense Power of the Romans, and at Length wholly subdue it; and that at a Time, when perhaps even their Descendants look upon them to have been Barbarians.[25]

[21] Mascov, *The History of the Ancient Germans*, vol. 2, p. 553. On Chiflet's political importance, Effros, *Merovingian Mortuary Archaeology*, p. 31.
[22] Effros, *Merovingian Mortuary Archaeology*, pp. 31–5.
[23] Mascov, *The History of the Ancient Germans*, vol. 1, Author's Preface, p. ii.
[24] See Pohl, *Die Germanen*, p. 1.
[25] Mascov, *The History of the Ancient Germans*, vol. 1, Author's Preface, pp. ii–iii.

For Mascov it was important that Germans, and he had in mind the Germany of the last centuries of the Habsburg Empire, should understand their origins and the origins of their constitution—and here one should remember that he was a lawyer and a civic dignitary. However, he thought it equally important that others outside Germany should recognize their own German origins. His emphasis on language and customs thus served to emphasize the extent of German expansion and settlement. It is, perhaps, not surprising that he had a notion of a *Völkerwanderung*, talking of *die große Wanderung der Völker*, or in Lediard's translation a 'Grand Transmigration of a Swarm of Nations'.[26] He thought the numbers involved were considerable.[27]

In all this Mascov was ahead of the field: he was, after all, writing before the publication of Montesquieu's *Considérations sur la grandeur des romains* or his *De l'esprit des Loix* or Mallet's *Introduction*. Mascov's view that one should look as much at the Germanic law-codes as at the Roman would be echoed in the development of the study of the barbarian laws by the *germanische Rechtsschule* (scholarship on Germanic law) as it developed in the nineteenth century.[28] His interpretation of language and settlement would come to be transformed by Jacob Grimm and subsequently by his twentieth-century successors, and, through the study of place names, would ultimately come to underpin a policy of Nazi expansion. The fact that Mascov's history was known in English as that 'of our great Ancestors' is also a mark of its success in encouraging those in the Anglo-Saxon world in the search for their German origins.

Yet, while Mascov's approach was to have dangerous repercussions, the scholarly achievement of *The History of the Ancient Germans* still deserves recognition. As Lediard noted, Mascov had gathered fragments 'scatter'd, at Random', and transformed them into a coherent whole. He begins his narrative with the Cimbri and their wars against the Romans. Indeed, the first six books of his account are taken up with the wars between the Romans and those peoples he identifies as Germans, defined by geographical origin, 'Language, Religion, natural Dispositions, Stature and Custom'.[29] Although one can, and indeed should, argue with these criteria for identification, his actual narrative is hard-headed and sceptical. He was careful to avoid what he regarded as fables.[30] With the seventh book he reaches the 'Grand Transmigration of a Swarm of Nations', and this essentially provides the focus for the next four books, down to the end of the first volume. Here he manages to provide an account not just of the Goths, Vandals, Burgundians, Franks, and Huns, but also of other minor groups.

Into the course of his narrative he provides descriptions of these various peoples, as well as commentary on the policy failures of the Romans. Reflecting on the

[26] Mascov, *The History of the Ancient Germans*, vol. 1, Author's Preface, pp. v, 316. On Mascov's early position within the development of the notion of the *Völkerwanderung*, Goffart, *Historical Atlases*, p. 283, n. 11.

[27] Mascov, *The History of the Ancient Germans*, vol. 1, p. 601.

[28] Wormald, *The Making of English Law*, pp. 11–12.

[29] Mascov, *The History of the Ancient Germans*, vol. 1, p. 4.

[30] Mascov, *The History of the Ancient Germans*, vol. 1, p. 3.

events of 476 he notes that while Rome had previously managed to integrate the barbarians it accepted into the Empire, in the case of the Goths it made the mistake of not dispersing them or setting them under Roman officers.[31] Equally, when he reaches the reign of Honorius he comments that 'the Vanity of the Romans was to prepare them for the Gothick Yoke'.[32] Honorius' death prompts a short analysis of the end of the Empire, and an uncomplimentary comparison of the emperor and the Gothic leaders of the time, and of their respective peoples:

> If it should be objected, that they were yet, in some Measure, savage and ungovernable, I reply, that so many Vices, then unknown to the Germans, were in Vogue among the Romans, that it would not be an improper Question, which of the two Nations were properly the Barbarians? The ancient Inhabitants of the conquer'd Countries ridicul'd sometimes, among themselves, the Manner of Speech, Habits, and Open-heartedness of their new Lords; but when it came to the Point, the Roman embroider'd Cloaths were oblig'd to truckle to the German Skins.[33]

This was an approach drawn from Tacitus and Salvian, which would soon be pursued by Montesquieu.

Later, Mascov offered a further insight into why he thought the Roman Empire collapsed—and in doing so in some respects cut a path for Gibbon to follow:

> Many of the brightest Genius's devoted themselves to the Church; many others chose rather to spend, in Indolence, the Riches, amass'd by their Ancestors. The Debility of the Government, under Honorius and Valentinian III, the frequent Revolutions after the Death of the latter; the mutual Jealousies of the Nations, which appear'd on those Occasions; the bad Understanding with the Grecian Court, and the Dissentions among the Great, hastened, at last, the Subversion of the Empire; which appears the less surprizing in History, as it had been long foreseen.[34]

The comments on the Church should not be read as indicating that Mascov was hostile to the institution, despite their similarity to what Gibbon would subsequently write. He did express critical views on Christianity, as when he wrote of the theological disputes of Justinian's reign: 'The Cloak of Religion was often made Use of, to palliate an Inclination for another's Property.'[35] Yet he was a committed Christian, who was involved in the debates between Pietists and Orthodox Lutherans. He discussed the Christianization of the Germanic peoples, and particularly the work of Boniface and the Anglo-Saxons, with approval,[36] and he also offered strikingly acute comments on early monasticism: 'Each Monastery had its particular

---

[31] Mascov, *The History of the Ancient Germans*, vol. 1, p. 364.
[32] Mascov, *The History of the Ancient Germans*, vol. 1, p. 388.
[33] Mascov, *The History of the Ancient Germans*, vol. 1, pp. 461–2.
[34] Mascov, *The History of the Ancient Germans*, vol. 1, p. 604.
[35] Mascov, *The History of the Ancient Germans*, vol. 2, p. 87.
[36] Most succinctly in Mascov, *The History of the Ancient Germans*, vol. 2, Author's Preface, p. xi: 'The Conversion of the Anglo-Saxons furnishes us with an Opportunity to take Notice of the State of the Saxon Kingdoms, and, at the same Time, of their Religion, in Britain. What the Franks then contributed to their Conversion, the Anglo-Saxons afterwards richly requited, by a like Endeavour with the German Nations in Germania.'

Rules, and the Abbot govern'd the Brethren according either to the Dictates of his own Zeal, or the Rules left by his Predecessor.'[37]

Although he states that his intention was to write about the German people rather than their kings, Mascov's narrative is dominated by individuals, but he does discuss their virtues and vices and their actions in such a way as to provide an insight into his own constitutional views. Thus, he presents Euric as prescribing 'the Goths a written and perpetual Law; whereas they had, 'till then, been only directed by their Customs, and the arbitrary Decision of their Judges'.[38]

The second volume of *The History of the Ancient Germans* pursues the various barbarian groups down to the mid-eighth century, dealing not just with Franks, Burgundians, Goths, and Lombards, but also with Alans, Gepids, Herules, Swabians, Thuringians, Anglo-Saxons, and others, including the peoples of the southern Baltic: each being carefully characterized. Despite his emphasis on the Germans, Mascov explained their relations with the surviving emperor in the East, noting in particular the granting of titles to the rulers of the newly established Germanic kingdoms, in order to preserve the appearance of the supremacy of the Empire. Yet he was careful not to imply that this amounted to much in reality, rather

> the German Prince vouchsafed to accept of this Pomp, which still captivated the Eyes of a People, accustom'd to the Roman Splendor, without making the least Concession of a superior Power, to the Emperor, on the Account; almost in the same Manner, as we at present see one King accepting an order of Knighthood from another, without any Derogation to his Dignity.[39]

One should note that by the time he wrote this he had already read Du Bos (who had used a similar modern analogy to a rather different end),[40] and that he was, therefore, offering a firm put-down to the Romanist school.

A significant part of Mascov's narrative of the sixth century is dominated by an account of Justinian's wars in Africa[41] and in Italy.[42] Like Gibbon and others he relished the opportunity to repeat the stories told by the Byzantine historians Procopius and Agathias. Yet Byzantine success prompts a further moment of analysis:[43]

> Valour may reduce Countries and Dominions, and the Conquerors may, by their Experience, for a Time, maintain them; but Religion and wholsom Laws, Manners, Arts and Sciences must have their Share in establishing a constant Duration. A State, whose Basis is the Constitution of a whole Nation, rises gradually like a Pyramid, and stands the more firmly...[44]

---

[37] Mascov, *The History of the Ancient Germans*, vol. 2, pp. 175–6; see also p. 271.
[38] Mascov, *The History of the Ancient Germans*, vol. 1, p. 584.
[39] Mascov, *The History of the Ancient Germans*, vol. 2, p. 30.
[40] Du Bos, *Histoire critique*, vol. 3, bk 5, p. 252. See this volume, chapter 2, footnote 102, where the passage is given.
[41] Mascov, *The History of the Ancient Germans*, vol. 2, pp. 76–86.
[42] Mascov, *The History of the Ancient Germans*, vol. 2, pp. 89–133.
[43] Mascov, *The History of the Ancient Germans*, vol. 2, p. 165.
[44] Mascov, *The History of the Ancient Germans*, vol. 2, p. 166.

Even so, Byzantine success did not last. The expense of Justinian's wars was such that it left the Balkans open to a sequence of barbarians.[45]

Mascov follows his account of the Gothic Wars with a history of events among the Franks, Visigoths, Lombards, and Anglo-Saxons. The end of the Lombard interregnum and the re-establishment of the monarchy again prompts commentary: the transfer of half their estates by the dukes allowed the king to establish a system of feudal tenure that gave him access to an army that was always ready to fight and was committed to the defence of the kingdom.[46] The nature of the army and its commitment is an issue that surfaces on a number of occasions throughout Mascov's *History*. Like his French counterparts, he noted the problems of an army which was not committed to the cause for which it was fighting: 'Justinian's Army consisted chiefly of Foreigners, who were indifferent, by whom they were paid.'[47]

Again, like his French counterparts, Mascov noted the importance of the Germanic assembly, seeing there 'the first Foundation of the German Laws'.[48] He was, however, more cautious than Boulainvilliers before him, and Montesquieu and Mably after: he firmly downgraded the significance of the Frankish *Campus Martius*, which he saw as being re-established by Pippin II.[49] He had more to say of the Conventions of the Lombards, which issued laws that compared well with that of the Romans, which in his view were 'now hardly intelligible'.[50] The assemblies and laws of the Germans ensured their liberty. By contrast the Saracens lost theirs after the time of Mohammed,[51] and it was something that the Byzantines lacked after Justinian: indeed his tyranny was a cause of the Fall of Byzantium.[52]

Mascov took his narrative down to the eighth century; to the fall of Visigothic Spain, and the emergence of a new Gothic power in Galicia, to the conflicts between the Lombards and the Papacy, and to the end of the Merovingians. The story was to have been continued with a history running from Charlemagne to Charles V, which according to Lediard was more or less complete in 1738.[53] This later account appears never to have been published, although the work for it may well have been integrated into Mascov's later publications on the German Empire. The story of the Germanic migrations and of the Fall of the Roman Empire is, however, covered impressively in the two volumes of the *History of the Ancient Germans*. There, Mascov had provided not only a narrative, but also an analysis of Roman weakness and barbarian strength, and, in addition, he had put the Germans firmly on the map as a group of peoples, united by language and custom, who had a single, coherent history. The Germans, in his view, had contributed as much as the Romans to the Nations of Europe. In particular, their political legacy,

[45] Mascov, *The History of the Ancient Germans*, vol. 2, p. 183.
[46] Mascov, *The History of the Ancient Germans*, vol. 2, pp. 213–14.
[47] Mascov, *The History of the Ancient Germans*, vol. 2, p. 127.
[48] Mascov, *The History of the Ancient Germans*, vol. 2, p. 243.
[49] Mascov, *The History of the Ancient Germans*, vol. 2, p. 269.
[50] Mascov, *The History of the Ancient Germans*, vol. 2, p. 260.
[51] Mascov, *The History of the Ancient Germans*, vol. 2, pp. 253–4.
[52] Mascov, *The History of the Ancient Germans*, vol. 2, pp. 258–9.
[53] Mascov, *The History of the Ancient Germans*, vol. 1, Translator's Preface, p. xix.

of assemblies, conventions, and law, had eclipsed the increasingly tyrannical constitution of the Byzantine Empire.

4.3 MONTESQUIEU'S *CONSIDÉRATIONS*

Despite William Smyth's insistence on Gibbon's debt to Mascov, it has been little explored in recent years. Rather more attention has been paid to some, though not all, of the French scholars who appear in the footnotes of *Decline and Fall*, and not merely in the context of the debate over the origins of the Franks.[54] We have already noted Gibbon's awareness of the French tradition. Boulainvilliers, Du Bos, and Mably he knew well. He was also thoroughly acquainted with Mallet's work: not only had he reviewed it, he had also met the Swiss scholar in Italy.[55]

Like the Italians, the French provided Gibbon with a great deal of information on the history of the Church. The names of Louis Thomassin (1619–95), Jean Mabillon (1632–1707), Thierry Ruinart (1657–1709), Louis-Sébastien Le Nain de Tillemont (1637–98), Bernard de Montfaucon (1655–1741), Martin Bouquet (1685–1754) recur: Mabillon and Bouquet in particular for their editions of texts, Tillemont for his *Mémoires pour servir à l'histoire ecclésiastique des six premiers siècles*, and his *Histoire des empereurs et des autres princes qui ont régné pendent les six premiers siècles de l'Église*. By contrast Gibbon appears to have made little use of Charles le Beau's *Histoire du Bas-Empire, en commençant à Constantin le Grand*, which appeared in twenty-two volumes between 1756 and 1779, though since Le Beau's main virtue is simply to repeat his source material, it would be hard to determine what Gibbon might have derived from him rather than directly from an ancient author. Le Beau might, however, have been another of the researchers on the period who repelled Smyth by 'the very size of their volumes'.[56]

One work from which Gibbon derived ideas, though not facts, on the Fall of the Roman Empire was Montesquieu's *Considérations sur la grandeur des romains et de leur décadence*.[57] As Guizot, who himself translated *Decline and Fall*, remarked, 'Less vigorous, less profound, less elevated than Montesquieu, Gibbon appropriated for himself the subject, of which his predecessor had pointed out the extent and rich stores.'[58] Although Montesquieu's book is relatively short, it covers a period not dissimilar to that dealt with by Gibbon, beginning with the original expansion of Rome and ending after the Fourth Crusade in 1204. Far and away the largest part of this concerns the early history of Rome. For Montesquieu, the military was central: Rome was built on war, rather than commerce. Initially the spoils of war were shared, but increasingly wealth became concentrated in the

---

[54] Not that Du Bos' *Histoire critique* had limited itself to the Franks or to France.
[55] Pocock, *Barbarism and Religion*, vol. 1, pp. 280–1.
[56] Smyth, *Lectures on Modern History*, vol. 1, p. 36.
[57] For an assessment of the *Considérations*, Shackleton, *Montesquieu*, pp. 157–70.
[58] Guizot, 'Preface to the second edition of his translation', in Gibbon, *Decline and Fall, with variorum notes including those of Guizot, Wenck, Schreiter, and Hugo*, vol. 1, p. viii.

hands of the few. 'In the countries conquered by the Germanic nations, power was in the hands of the vassals and only legal authority in the hands of the prince. The exact opposite was true with the Romans.'[59] The wealth and avarice that played a crucial role in the ruin of Rome were already visible in the republican period. The extension of the citizenship meant that not everyone was loyal to the city, and the extension of the army's activities meant that troops looked to their generals. The emperors had to treat their soldiers well, while, at the same time, what Augustus created for the citizenry was a 'durable servitude'.[60] Montesquieu's emphasis on the military continues even in his coverage of the 'good' emperors—though given the terseness of that coverage they scarcely emerge into the limelight as they do in the early chapters of *Decline and Fall*. Trajan, however, is described as

> the most accomplished prince in the annals of history…He was a great statesman and a great general.[61]
> The wisdom of Nerva, the glory of Trajan, the valor of Hadrian, and the virtue of the two Antonines commanded the respect of the soldiers. But, when new monsters took their place, the abuses of military government appeared in all their excesses; and the soldiers, who had sold the empire, assassinated the emperors in order to obtain a new price for it.[62]

Although Diocletian and Constantine introduced reform, which made the emperors more secure, 'another kind of tyranny followed'.[63] The court became increasingly isolated and corrupt, with reputations destroyed by insinuation. At the same time, Constantine's military reforms left the frontiers unguarded, and the barbarians entered. Julian tried to drive them back, and Valentinian I understood the importance of the frontiers, but after the entry of the Goths in Valens' reign, disaster followed. The Empire could not afford to pay for the army, and as a result there was too much dependence on barbarian auxiliary troops. Even so, the tax burden was too heavy: following the critique of the fifth-century Gallic moralist Salvian, Montesquieu remarked that '[i]n making so many citizens serfs—that is, slaves of the field to which they were attached—the barbarians scarcely introduced anything which had not been more cruelly practiced before them.'[64]

---

[59] Montesquieu, *Considérations sur la grandeur des romains*, trans. Lowenthal, p. 76. This is the reading of the 1748, revised version. The original 1734 version, as printed in Montesquieu, ed. Charvet, p. 78, differs in certain crucial respects: 'dans les Etats Gothiques le pouvoir étoit dans la main des Vassaux, le droit seulement dans la main du Prince; c'étoit tout le contraire chez les Romains.'

[60] Montesquieu, *Considérations sur la grandeur des romains*, ed. Charvet, p. 145, trans. Lowenthal, p. 121.

[61] Montesquieu, *Considérations sur la grandeur des romains*, ed. Charvet, p. 173, trans. Lowenthal, p. 141.

[62] Montesquieu, *Considérations sur la grandeur des romains*, ed. Charvet, p. 180, trans. Lowenthal, pp. 145–6.

[63] Montesquieu, *Considérations sur la grandeur des romains*, ed. Charvet, p. 196, trans. Lowenthal, p. 158.

[64] Montesquieu, *Considérations sur la grandeur des romains*, trans. Lowenthal, p. 172: again the 1734 version differs: 'une Nation qui se réservoit la Liberté et l'exercice des armes, et une autre destinée par la loi de sa servitude à cultiver les champs, auxquels chaque Particulier devoit être attaché pour jamais', ed. Charvet, p. 218.

Montesquieu was, however, impressed by Attila. As presented by Priscus, he 'was one of the great monarchs of history'.[65] Following 'the ways of his nation' he subjugated, rather than conquered, peoples. 'He was feared by his subjects, but it does not appear he was hated by them.' He was a model ruler. At his death, however, the barbarian nations, which had been united, were divided again.

Looking back on the Fall of the West, Montesquieu did not attribute it to one invasion, but to an accumulation of many. He stressed both the position of Constantinople in protecting the Asian provinces, and the division between the Eastern and Western Empires, which failed to help each other during the crises. The leaders of the West were not 'impolitic' in deciding to abandon the other provinces in order to save Italy.

> But this whole scheme was upset by a revolution more fatal than all the others. The army of Italy, composed of foreigners, exacted what had been accorded to nations that were more foreign still. Under Odoacer, it formed an aristocracy that gave itself a third of the lands of Italy, thus delivering the mortal blow to this empire.[66]

Montesquieu continued his narrative, but looked to Byzantium rather than the new kingdoms of the West. In this, he obviously foreshadowed Gibbon, whose focus moves largely, though not entirely, eastwards. Montesquieu recounts Justinian's successes against the Vandals, but notes the weaknesses within Constantinople itself: the dominance of women, the role of the circus factions, together with Justinian's attempt to enforce religious uniformity.[67] The emperor Maurice was momentarily successful in defending the Empire against the Avars, but he was too avaricious. Thereafter the emperors could not cope with the expansion of the Arabs, whose cavalry was the best in the world[68]—and whose fanaticism Montesquieu likened to that of Cromwell's troops.[69] By comparison the Byzantines were merely superstitious. They did, however, manage to survive, largely because of their possession of the secret of Greek fire, which gave them control of the sea, and because the Arabs were themselves divided. Although Montesquieu did not pursue his story down to 1453 and the fall of Constantinople to the Turks, he effectively closed with the arrival of this last group on the scene, having observed that Manuel Comnenos allowed the navy to decay.

---

[65] Montesquieu, *Considérations sur la grandeur des romains*, ed. Charvet, p. 223, trans. Lowenthal, p. 177.

[66] Montesquieu, *Considérations sur la grandeur des romains*, trans. Lowenthal, p. 181. The 1734 edition, ed. Charvet, pp. 180–1, differs.

[67] Christianity in general plays a minor role in Montesquieu's account, an absence which may be ascribed to the precise circumstances in which the book was written, and in its author's concern to avoid unnecessary criticism: Shackleton, *Montesquieu*, pp. 160–2.

[68] Montesquieu, *Considérations sur la grandeur des romains*, ed. Charvet, p. 257, trans. Lowenthal, p. 202.

[69] Montesquieu, *Considérations sur la grandeur des romains*, ed. Charvet, p. 259, trans. Lowenthal, p. 203. Smyth, *Lectures on Modern History*, vol. 1, p. 109, draws a similar comparison, but between the forces of Islam, those of early Rome, and those of France in his own day (i.e. Napoleon's troops).

Montesquieu's reading has been seen both as Machiavellian,[70] and as a work that would have surprised Machiavelli.[71] Certainly, in its criticism of a '*despotisme* whose *principe* was *crainte*',[72] it offers a comment on the *Ancien Régime*, and on the threat of the Bastille. The fact that the first edition of the work was anonymous and published in Holland, may be an indication of Montesquieu's awareness of how critical a work it was. It is also an essay on the military. Time and again it points to matters of military organization and recruitment, to explain the success and failure of Rome and its Empire. Montesquieu had perhaps learnt this from Boulainvilliers' views of the armies of the early Franks. It is scarcely surprising that the *Considérations* was a work that attracted the attention of Frederick the Great.[73]

4.4 MARMONTEL'S *BÉLISAIRE* (1767)

The twin themes of military commitment and governmental despotism, which echo throughout Montesquieu's *Considérations*, were certainly picked up by contemporaries, not least by Jean-François Marmontel in his novel *Bélisaire*, published in 1767.[74] The inspiration for the work came from an engraving by Abraham Bosse of a picture by Van Dyck.[75] The image of the blind Belisarius begging was an illustration of the apocryphal story that held that the Byzantine general had been blinded on the orders of the emperor Justinian after his fall from grace. The idea that it might be turned into a work of literature seems to have been suggested to Marmontel by Diderot. The engraving had attracted the interest of the *Encyclopédiste* in 1762, both for its composition and for its sentiment and moral.[76] For Marmontel the underlying story was an ideal illustration of the dangers of despotism, very much as described by Montesquieu in his description of the Roman court following the reforms of Diocletian and Constantine:

> As the court became more isolated, its poisonous influence became more powerful. Nothing was said, everything insinuated. All great reputations were attacked, and the ministers and military officers were constantly placed at the mercy of the sort of person who can neither serve the state nor endure others serving it with glory.[77]

---

[70] Lowenthal, *Considerations of the Causes of the Greatness of the Romans*, pp. 1–20.

[71] Pocock, *Barbarism and Religion*, vol. 3, p. 343. For Montesquieu as the antithesis of Machiavelli, see the satirical attack on Napoleon III, by Joly, *Dialogue aux enfers entre Machiavel et Montesquieu*.

[72] Pocock, *Barbarism and Religion*, vol. 3, p. 343.

[73] Montesquieu, *Considérations sur la grandeur des romains*, ed. Charvet, pp. xii–xv. On Montesquieu and Prussia, see Volpilhac-Auger, 'Les rois de Prusse sous le regard de Montesquieu', pp. 55–65.

[74] Marmontel, *Bélisaire*.

[75] For the inspiration of the story, see Granderout's introduction to Marmontel, *Bélisaire*, p. vi. Also Fried, *Absorption and Theatricality: Painting and Beholder in the Age of Diderot*, p. 151, with p. 237, n. 91.

[76] Fried, *Absorption and Theatricality*, pp. 144–60.

[77] Montesquieu, *Considérations sur la grandeur des romains*, ed. Charvet, p. 197, trans. Lowenthal, p. 158.

Marmontel's novel, or *conte moral*,[78] is set in the last years of Justinian's reign. A group of generals dining in a castle in Thrace are interrupted by the arrival of a blind old man, led by a young boy. The old man reveals himself as Belisarius, hero of Justinian's early wars against the Vandals and Ostrogoths. One of the generals, Tiberius, is so impressed by what he hears that he goes off to tell Justinian about the encounter. The emperor decides to hear for himself, but to do so incognito. Meanwhile Belisarius continues on his journey towards the castle where his wife and daughter are waiting. He stops at an inn where he encounters a man who turns out to be Gelimer, the Vandal king in exile. Before setting off the next day, Belisarius reveals his identity to his old opponent. Back on the road he is intercepted by a group of Bulgars, who having heard his story want to avenge the wrongs done to him. They execute Bessas, whose avarice had caused the failure of Belisarius' attempt to relieve Totila's siege of Rome. Belisarius, however, refuses to betray the Empire when the Bulgar king offers to exact vengeance on Justinian himself for his treatment of the great general. The Bulgars cannot understand the old man's virtue. Yet, as Belisarius explains to them, in terms derived largely from a contrast Montesquieu had drawn between the Roman Republic and the Empire,[79] they have a different view of war from the Byzantines: for the Bulgars war is an end in itself, for the Byzantines it is intended to secure peace. At the next stop, Belisarius is greeted as a hero, for he had once saved the village from the Huns. When he asked how they knew who he was, he was told that a nobleman had been looking for him the previous day. Moreover, the son of his host in the village had once fought with him—the scene is that of the Bosse engraving. This moody ex-soldier wanted to accompany him, abandoning his wife and child. Belisarius told him instead to bring up children to fight for the Empire. Meanwhile, Tiberius had reached Belisarius' castle, where his wife Antonina and daughter (given the name Eudoxia) were waiting. The nobleman told them that Belisarius was free. He also noted the virtuous nature of the girl. When Belisarius himself arrived, his servant Anselm quickly realized that he had been blinded. Antonina, who rushed to greet him, was overcome with emotion and died. One commentator wickedly remarked that Marmontel killed her off so that she would not interrupt ' "les longues et fastidieuses dissertations" de Bélisaire et de ses deux voisins...' (the long and tedious dissertations of Belisarius and his two neighbours).[80]

It is true that the rest of the novel is taken up with discussions between the old blind general, Tiberius, and the incognito Justinian, who make regular visits to see him. These discussions are essentially a critique of despotism, as Belisarius explains how the emperor has been misled by his courtiers.[81] They are also a commentary on military policy, as the general tells the disguised emperor how he

---

[78] Marmontel, *Bélisaire*, ed. Granderout, p. xxv.

[79] Montesquieu, *Considérations sur la grandeur des romains*, ed. Charvet, pp. 149–50, trans. Lowenthal, p. 123: 'In the days of the republic, the principle was to make war continually: under the emperors, the maxim was to maintain peace.'

[80] Marmontel, *Bélisaire*, p. 52, n. 1 (the page references are to Grandrout's edition).

[81] Marmontel, *Bélisaire*, p. 99.

failed to support his armies properly or to reform the tax system.[82] Instead of a standing army, he advocates a civilian militia responsible for defence: expansionist campaigns should be forgotten.[83] He criticizes religious fanaticism, and does so in terms that are effectively Deist, that is, accepting the existence of a God, without clearly identifying him as the Christian God.[84] En route to visit Belisarius the day after his religious discourse, Tiberius and Justinian are captured by the Bulgars, and they appeal to Belisarius to ransom them, which he does. This leads the old general to relate stories from his life, justifying various of his actions. Finally Justinian breaks down, revealing his identity, and asking Tiberius how he might repay him. The young general naturally claims the hand of the virtuous Eudoxia.

The story is a farrago of nonsense in historical terms. The tale of blind Belisarius may have been a fantasy, as Mascov, among others, had pointed out,[85] and as Marmontel himself was well aware. Indeed, he rather disarmingly states in the preface that the notion that Belisarius was blind and a beggar is popular rather than historical, but that in every other way his account follows historical fact![86] The story is a scarcely disguised critique of Bourbon absolutism: which Marmontel himself had experienced, having been imprisoned in the Bastille on the mistaken charge that he had lampooned the Duc d'Aumont.[87] It was not the work's politics, however, but its religion that caused problems, with the Sorbonne attempting to forestall its publication.[88]

Yet, despite the fact that its basic premise is a fiction, and that it is in essence a critique of France under Louis XV, it remains a work based on a serious reading of sixth-century sources. In the *préface* the author announces his dependence on Procopius and Agathias, but argues, against Montesquieu, that the former's *Secret History* should be ignored.[89] Montesquieu, in justifying his belief in the value of the *Secret History*, had argued that the picture it conveys properly reflects the weakness of the Byzantine Empire at the end of Justinian's reign, and that it coincides with the impression given by the emperor's legislation.[90] More striking than Marmontel's use of Procopius and Agathias (to whom anyone writing a novel about Belisarius would obviously turn) is his detailed citation of law.[91] Marmontel had done his homework.

He had initially established himself as a literary figure, and it was as such that he was elected to the *Académie française* in 1763. He became *secrétaire perpétuel* twenty

---

[82] Marmontel, *Bélisaire*, p. 120.   [83] Marmontel, *Bélisaire*, pp. 166–7.
[84] Marmontel, *Bélisaire*, pp. 175–98.
[85] Mascov, *The History of the Ancient Germans*, vol. 1, pp. 511–12. Stanhope, *The Life of Belisarius*, pp. 441–73, in what remains one of the most extensive examinations of the legend of the blinding and beggary of Belisarius, was inclined to accept that the story was authentic.
[86] Marmontel, *Bélisaire*, p. 5.   [87] Marmontel, *Bélisaire*, p. iii.
[88] Marmontel, *Bélisaire*, pp. viii–xx.   [89] Marmontel, *Bélisaire*, pp. 5–6.
[90] Montesquieu, *Considérations sur la grandeur des romains*, ed. Charvet, p. 240, trans. Lowenthal, p. 190.
[91] Marmontel, *Bélisaire*, pp.105–6, 127.

years later.[92] His historical skills were also recognized. In 1772 he was appointed *historiographe du Roi*, and in 1785 *historiographe des Bâtiments*—a post to which he was well suited, having been *secrétaire des bâtiments* on the recommendation of Mme de Pompadour.[93] Also in 1785 he was appointed to a *chaire d'histoire* at the *Lycée*. Despite his close links with the court, and despite his opposition both to the freedom of the press and to the Terror, during the Revolution he was able to retire to Normandy, where he became *président de l'Assemblée électorale de l'Eure* in 1795. Two years later he was elected to the *Conseil des Anciens*, and campaigned for freedom of religious cult—an idea firmly advocated by *Bélisaire*.

Marmontel's novel was a striking success, in part, perhaps, because of the attempts of the Sorbonne to ban its publication. It prompted further representations of the legend of Belisarius, in literature[94] and in painting, most notably David's version of the image painted by Van Dyck, and subsequently Benjamin West's depiction of the same scene.[95] The legend also attracted the interest of Philip Henry Stanhope, Lord Mahon, who made it the subject of a lengthy appendix to his remarkably scholarly study of Belisarius, where he concluded that the Byzantine general probably was reduced to beggary, and may well have been blinded.[96]

Marmontel's novel was read with pleasure by Gibbon,[97] despite an ironic footnote on the retirement of Gelimer:

> In the *Bélisaire* of Marmontel the king and the conqueror of Africa meet, sup, and converse, without recollecting each other. It is surely a fault of that romance, that not only the hero, but all to whom he had been so conspicuously known, appear to have lost their eyes or their memory.[98]

There is a further allusion to the legend of Belisarius in Gibbon's comments on the general's death.[99]

By the time that Marmontel's *Bélisaire* was published, in 1767, Gibbon already had the theme of *Decline and Fall* firmly in mind. Like Marmontel, he chose a subject that had not hitherto been neglected. Smyth, in his brief discussion of Gibbon, claimed, with unusual generosity:

> Hints were to be caught, a narrative was to be gathered up, from documents broken and suspicious, from every barbarous relic of a barbarous age; and, on the whole, the historian was to be left to the most unceasing and unexampled exercise of criticism, comparison, and conjecture.[100]

---

[92] Marmontel, *Bélisaire*, pp. iii–iv.   [93] Marmontel, *Bélisaire*, pp. ii–iv.
[94] Marmontel, *Bélisaire*, pp. lv–lix.
[95] Crow, *Painters and Public Life in Eighteenth-Century Paris*, pp. 204–8; Boime, 'Marmontel's *Bélisaire* and the pre-revolutionary progressivism of David'; McKitterick, 'Edward Gibbon and the early Middle Ages in eighteenth-century Europe', p. 172–3, n. 33.
[96] Stanhope, *The Life of Belisarius*, pp. 441–73.
[97] Ghosh, 'The conception of Gibbon's History', p. 308.
[98] Gibbon, *Decline and Fall*, ch. 41, n.
[99] Gibbon, *Decline and Fall*, ch. 43.
[100] Smyth, *Lectures on Modern History*, vol. 1, pp. 85–6.

For the period of the fall of the Western Empire and the establishment of the successor states, all of that had already been done before Gibbon put pen to paper, as Smyth knew well.

4.5 DECLINE AND FALL

Gibbon was born in 1737, the year in which the second volume of Mascov's history was published. Having disgraced himself at Oxford by converting to Roman Catholicism, he was sent by his father to live under the eye of a Protestant pastor in Lausanne, where he soon abandoned his new faith.[101] He returned to England in 1758, and a year later accepted a commission in the Hampshire grenadiers, which he held until 1763. The experience of civic duty, together with his reading of James Harrington's *Oceana* contributed to his enthusiasm for the notion of an armed citizenry, which he came to see as one of the strengths of Rome before its decline.[102] The value of a citizen army had also struck both Montesquieu and Boulainvilliers.

On the disbanding of the militia Gibbon set out on the Grand Tour. 'It was in Rome, on the 15th October 1764, as I sat musing amidst the ruins of the Capitol, while the barefooted friars were singing vespers in the temple of Jupiter, that the idea of writing the decline and fall of the city first started to my mind.'[103] Having returned to London, he settled down to write his great work, despite the distraction of being MP initially for Liskeard, and later for Lymington. The first volume appeared in 1776. This contained chapters 1 to 16, and thus concluded with two chapters on early Christianity, about which Gibbon was notably critical, and its persecution, which were to prompt a stormy debate over his attitude to religion.[104] Three years later he joined Lord North's government, accepting a post on the Board of Trade.[105] Nevertheless, the second and third volumes appeared in 1781. These concluded, in chapter 37 with a renewed diatribe against the impact of Christianity, and especially of monasticism, and in chapter 38, with an account of Clovis together with the 'General Observations of the Fall of the Roman Empire in the West'. A year later Gibbon's political fortunes suffered a rebuff with the fall of Lord North's government. Moreover, he failed to secure appointment as ambassador to Paris. In 1783 he moved back to Lausanne. Volume 4, which dealt largely with the sixth century, was completed a year later, but it would not appear in print until 1788, when the last three volumes were all published at the same time. Gibbon died in 1796.

---

[101] Wootton, 'Narrative, Irony, and Faith in Gibbon's Decline and Fall', pp. 101–5.

[102] Pocock, *Barbarism and Religion*, vol. 1, pp. 94–134, esp. p. 99 for the influence of Harrington. Also Burrow, *Gibbon*, p. 45.

[103] E. Gibbon, *Memoirs of my life*, Bonnard, p. 136, n. 7.

[104] See now Pocock, *Barbarism and Religion*, vol. 5. See also Noonkester, 'Gibbon and the clergy'; and Young, ' "Scepticism in excess" '.

[105] Seed, ' "The deadly principles of fanaticism" ', pp. 98–9.

Like Montesquieu, Gibbon set the fall of the Roman Empire in a long time frame. Unlike his predecessor, however, he presented a more favourable impression of the Empire, at least during the rule of the Antonines.[106] The arrival of the Goths on the banks of the Danube does not occur until chapter 26, and the following ten chapters chart the disasters from then until the deposition of Romulus Augustulus. After consideration of the Church and the barbarians at the end of book 3, Gibbon turned his attention increasingly to the East. Although book 4 covers both the Ostrogoths and the Lombards, it is dominated rather by Justinian and his successors.

Famously, in the 'General observations on the Fall of the Roman Empire in the West', Gibbon presents the decline of Rome as the 'inevitable effect of immoderate greatness', arguing that the real question to be asked was not why it collapsed, but why it lasted so long. Gibbon notes how the legions, 'in distant wars, acquired the vices of strangers and mercenaries'. For their own safety the emperors, most especially Constantine, undermined military discipline, leaving the Empire to be overwhelmed by the barbarians. Gibbon looks at the significance of Constantinople, downplaying its role in the decay of Rome, but admitting that rivalry between the courts of Arcadius and Honorius was disastrous, and that although relations between Eastern and Western emperors were subsequently better, Byzantium was slow to help the West. In addition, the effect of Christianization was both to weaken the Empire and to soften the barbarians, for whom it came to act as a civilizing influence.[107] Gibbon also emphasizes the significance of the barbarian threat, its scale and the failure of the Romans to recognize it, together with the fact that the Roman provinces had lost any sense of freedom or national spirit under the despotism of the imperial court, and especially of the descendants of Theodosius. Finally he points to the decline of the Roman military, allied to the fact that 'Constantine and his successors armed and instructed, for the ruin of the empire, the rude valour of the barbarian mercenaries'.[108]

Gibbon's analyses of the tendency of empires to become corrupt and of the destruction caused by the barbarians had been anticipated by earlier writers, as had his critique of Christianity. The notion that over-mighty empires carried the seeds of their own destruction had been in circulation since Antiquity and had been forcibly restated by Montesquieu.[109] On the barbarians Gibbon was less sympathetic than many. He appreciated their valour, but unlike Boulainvilliers, Mascov, Montesquieu, and Mably he ignored their supposed egalitarian traditions and their equally supposed enthusiasm for liberty, though he did admit that '[t]he political society of the ancient Germans has the appearance of a voluntary alliance of independent warriors.'[110] His chief discussion of the Germans and their society is to be

---

[106] Gibbon, *Decline and Fall*, ch. 7.

[107] Gibbon, *Decline and Fall*, ch. 37. Pocock, 'Gibbon's *Decline and Fall* and the World View of the Late Enlightenment', p. 300.

[108] Gibbon, *Decline and Fall*, ch. 38, 'General observations on the Fall of the Roman Empire in the West', III.

[109] See Shackleton, *Montesquieu*, p. 163.

[110] Gibbon, *Decline and Fall*, ch. 26, vol. 3, p. 241.

found long before he gets to their arrival in the Roman Empire, in chapter 9, on 'The State of Germany till the invasion of the Barbarians, in the time of the Emperor Decius'. He begins by noting the geography and climate, and the impact these factors had on the physique of the early Germans. Having dismissed all accounts of their origins, on the grounds that they could be no more than fables given the lack of literacy among the Germanic peoples, he turns to their lifestyle, which he categorizes as savage. He notes their enthusiasm for gambling, for drink, and for hunting, portraying them as a people with little interest in agriculture or landed property—finding it difficult, as a result, to accept Tacitus' account of riches and despotism among the *Suinones*. In so far as there was landed property, it was allocated every year by magistrates. More important than the magistrates were the chiefs, especially because everyone strove to follow a successful military leader. Crucially, he regarded Germanic society at this stage as being essentially nomadic, thus seeing the Germans as having achieved a lower state of civilization than if they had been agriculturalists.[111] What others had seen as a praiseworthy egalitarian system, encouraging martial valour, Gibbon portrayed as barbarous. He had a little more sympathy for the reputation of German women for chastity, but was totally dismissive of the people's subjection to superstition (something that he makes rather more of than does his chief source, Tacitus, by exaggerating the role of the priesthood).[112] In the spasmodic references to Germans that follow in the course of the narrative, the tone softens slightly when he reaches the Anglo-Saxons, whom he praises for their valour and maritime skill.[113]

When in chapter 38 Gibbon deals with the barbarian law-codes, in the context of Clovis' reign, he again finds little to praise.[114] Whereas Mascov, a professor of Law, contrasted the Germanic codes favourably with those of the Later Roman Empire,[115] Gibbon has nothing but scorn:

> by a singular coincidence, the Germans framed their artless institutions at a time when the elaborate system of Roman jurisprudence was finally consummated. In the Salic laws, and the Pandects of Justinian, we may compare the first rudiments, and the full maturity, of civil wisdom; and whatever prejudices may be suggested in favour of barbarism [and here he is dismissing a whole raft of earlier scholarship], our calmer reflections will ascribe to the Romans the superior advantages, not only of science and reason, but of humanity and justice. Yet the laws of the barbarians were adapted to their wants and desires, their occupations and their capacity; and they all contributed to preserve the peace and promote the improvements, of the society for whose use they were originally established.[116]

---

[111] Gibbon, *Decline and Fall*, chs 37–8. Pocock, 'Gibbon's *Decline and Fall* and the World View of the Late Enlightenment', pp. 296–7, citing Gibbon's dependence on Guignet's *Histoire des Huns*.
[112] Gibbon, *Decline and Fall*, ch. 9; see Tacitus, *Germania*, 7, 10, 11, 40.
[113] Gibbon, *Decline and Fall*, ch. 25.
[114] Gibbon, *Decline and Fall*, ch. 38.
[115] Mascov, *The History of the Ancient Germans*, vol. 2, p. 260.
[116] Gibbon, *Decline and Fall*, ch. 38.

He goes on to emphasize the importance of vengeance, blood-price, and trial by combat.

For his reading of Christianity Gibbon had access to rather more scholarship than he did for the early Germans: above all he turned to Tillemont's *Mémoires pour server à l'histoire écclésiastique*[117]—though this does not constitute a narrative history but rather a series of studies set out in chronological order—and to a lesser extent to Johann Mosheim's *Insitutionum historiae ecclesiasticae* of 1726.[118] For his interpretation, however, he was dependent not so much on the Church historians as on a British tradition of religious scepticism, which was epitomized by David Hume, in his analysis of the Puritans in the volume of his *History of Great Britain containing the reigns of James I and Charles I*.[119] Gibbon's attack was directed less against superstition, which could be found among the pagans, and which he thought could be compatible with civilized society, than against fanaticism and enthusiasm, vices which likewise were not confined to the Christians.[120]

In the course of writing *Decline and Fall* Gibbon's views of the barbarians and of Christianity shifted, and as a result he modified his initial emphasis on the internal decay of Rome. While the 'General Observations on the Fall of the Roman Empire in the West' stressed that '[t]he story of its ruin is simple and obvious . . . the natural and inevitable effect of immoderate greatness', and 'the empire had absorbed the city and destroyed its virtue',[121] the attention paid both to the barbarians and to the monks seems to point in slightly different directions, as he acknowledged at the very end of his work, when he stated that what he had described was 'the triumph of barbarism and religion'.[122] Although both barbarians and religious fanatics appear in volume one, it is striking that Gibbon puts greater emphasis on them when looking back over the totality of his work than had been his original intention.

Attempts to explain Gibbon's changing explanation for the Fall of Rome have naturally looked to the context in which he was writing. Pocock drew attention to the fact that the first volume of *Decline and Fall* appeared in 1776 and the last in 1788: thus publication fell between the American and French Revolutions. Even

---

[117] Tillemont, *Mémoires pour server à l'histoire écclésiastique des six premier siècles*. Chadwick, 'Gibbon and the Church historians'.

[118] Wootton, 'Narrative, irony, and faith in Gibbon's Decline and Fall', pp. 85–6.

[119] Hume, *History of England from the Invasion of Julius Caesar to the Revolution in 1688*, vol. 1; Pocock, 'Gibbon's Decline and Fall and the world view of the late Enlightenment', p. 301; Wootton, 'Narrative, irony, and faith in Gibbon's *Decline and Fall*'; Seed, ' "The deadly principles of fanaticism" '.

[120] In France the idea that religion could be justified on the grounds of utility was relatively widespread: Jones, *The Great Nation*, p. 199.

[121] Gibbon, *Decline and Fall*, ch. 38, 'General observations on the fall of the Roman Empire in the West'; cited in Pocock, 'Gibbon's *Decline and Fall* and the world view of the late Enlightenment', p. 290.

[122] Gibbon, *Decline and Fall*, ch. 71, II; Pocock, 'Gibbon's *Decline and Fall* and the world view of the late Enlightenment', pp. 290–1. The argument is expanded considerably in the 4 vols of id., *Barbarism and Religion*.

so, Gibbon's narrative seems almost oblivious of events in the New World.[123] Yet, as a placeman in Lord North's administration he had some reason to be sensitive to questions of governmental corruption. That he lampooned the corruption of Rome while making no connection with his own career was noted by an anonymous satirist, possibly Charles James Fox.[124]

> His book well describes
> How corruption and bribes
> O'erthrew the great empire of Rome;
> And his writings declare
> A degen'racy there
> Which his conduct exhibits at home.

In considering Gibbon's increasing concern with barbarism and with religious fanaticism in *Decline and Fall* Pocock has also pointed to his exchanges with Joseph Priestley, who, as a Unitarian with millenarian interests could be portrayed as a modern-day enthusiast, in a line that went back to the Arians and other Christian fanatics.[125] In fact, rather than being a fanatic himself, Priestley was the butt of fanaticism, his house in Birmingham being burned down in 1791—after the appearance of the last volume of *Decline and Fall*. More serious were the Gordon Riots of 1780, launched against Catholics by the Protestant Association, one of the centres of which raged only a short distance from Bentinck Street, where Gibbon was living. Commenting on the disturbances, he wrote 'forty thousand Puritans, such as they might be in the time of Cromwell, have started out of their graves'.[126] While his views on religious enthusiasm had already been set out in chapters 15 and 16 of *Decline and Fall*, published before the Gordon Riots, the events may well have prompted Gibbon to shift the emphasis of his interpretation from corruption to religion and barbarism. His philosophic reading, which can seem in its detachment an archetypical statement of Enlightenment philosophy, may be more closely tied to immediate experiences than sometimes appears.

In considering Gibbon as a historian Smyth was not so wide of the mark. One could usefully read him for all the detail gathered in one place. Others had, however, discussed those details, often with critical skills as considerable as Gibbon's—though, at least in the case of French scholars, with rather more obvious political concerns. As regards the period up to the reign of Justinian, they had offered historical analyses of equal depth, even with regard to the impact of the Church, though without his 'raillery and sarcasm'.[127] What distinguished *Decline and Fall*,

---

[123] Pocock, 'Gibbon's *Decline and Fall* and the world view of the late Enlightenment', pp. 287, 294–5. Pocock rightly rejects (p. 295, n. 20) the contention that Gibbon means America when he says Armorican: the importance of Armorica would be apparent to anyone who had read Du Bos.

[124] Pocock, 'Gibbon's *Decline and Fall* and the world view of the late Enlightenment', p. 294.

[125] Pocock, 'Gibbon's *Decline and Fall* and the world view of the late Enlightenment', pp. 301–2; Seed, 'The deadly principles of fanaticism'.

[126] Seed, 'The deadly principles of fanaticism', p. 96.

[127] Smyth, *Lectures on Modern History*, vol. 1, p. 83. See Mascov, *The History of the Ancient Germans*, vol. 1, p. 604 and vol. 2, p. 87. But see also the reactions of the Sorbonne to Marmontel's supposed Deism: Marmontel, *Bélisaire*, ed. Granderout, pp. viii–xx.

as Smyth noted, was not its historical qualities, but its philosophy and theology, its wit and eloquence.[128] The theology would continue to be discussed through the nineteenth century.[129] As history, however, it would be rather less dominant in the discourse than one might have expected, despite being translated into French and German, and despite its reissue in an expurgated edition by Bowdler in 1826 and in rather more scholarly form by Milman in 1838. Gibbon's reading was that of the Enlightenment, but published between the American and French Revolutions it appeared at the start of a revolutionary age, and as such could rapidly appear old-fashioned.

Even in England this mattered. The historian of the early medieval West Smyth most admired was not Gibbon but Mably. Despite the inferior quality of his work, Mably's political interests were more closely in tune with those of the Revolution and its aftermath. Unlike Boulainvilliers, Mascov, Montesquieu, and Mably, Gibbon had not put Germanic liberty at the heart of his interpretation. Although he did not entirely neglect the issue,[130] this set him outside the main stream of the historical debates over the End of the Western Empire and the Barbarian Invasions, especially as they developed in the early nineteenth century. He was read, and was appreciated by intellectuals and by *literati*, but *Decline and Fall* did not initially dominate debates over the fourth, fifth and sixth centuries, despite the interest shown in it by such historians as Milman, Sismondi, Guizot, and Ozanam. The real change in Gibbon's status among early medieval scholars would have to wait until the work of Thomas Hodgkin in the last quarter of the nineteenth century.

[128] Smyth, *Lectures on Modern History*, vol. 1, p. 85.

[129] For a nineteenth-century reaction, see the preface by Milman to his edition of *Decline and Fall*, vol. 1, pp. iii–xv; Young, ' "Scepticism in excess" ', p. 199. In Italy, however, the tendency was to ignore Gibbon's religious comments: Momigliano, 'Gibbon from an Italian point of view', pp. 75–85.

[130] Brown, 'Gibbon, Hodgkin, and the Invaders of Italy', p. 139.

5

Empire and Aftermath

5.1 MONTLOSIER

Louis XVI seems to have held *Decline and Fall* in high regard. He has been identified with M. de Septchênes who was responsible for the opening fifteen or sixteen chapters of the first French translation of Gibbon's work, the initial volume of which appeared in 1777.[1] The king would no doubt have approved of the Englishman's avoidance of the Germanic virtues of Liberty and Equality. It would be another eighteen years before the translation was complete, by which time the French king had died on the scaffold. Following the upheaval of the Revolution and the Napoleonic period, Gibbon's approach to the Fall of Rome and the establishment of the Germanic successor states was less obviously relevant to current concerns than that espoused by the French scholars who had contributed to the intellectual origins of the Revolution itself. While the image of Rome, especially the Republic, had been central to much Revolutionary ideology and debate,[2] the post-Roman period was to take on increasing significance in the early nineteenth century. It is, therefore, necessary to return to French scholarship to see how debates about the Fall of Rome and the establishment of the barbarian kingdoms were influenced by the creation of a new French Empire. This will take us not just to works of history, but also, in the writings of the circle of Mme de Staël to works of literature and literary criticism.

Napoleon certainly showed an interest in Montesquieu's *Considérations*. Following his victory at Jena in 1806 he stopped for two days at Frederick the Great's palace of Sans-Souci, outside Potsdam. While he was there his secretary, baron Claude François de Meneval, discovered a copy of Montesquieu's work, complete with the Prussian king's annotations. The emperor took it for his own library, from whence Talleyrand borrowed it.[3] Napoleon probably valued the book for its association with the Prussian king as much as for its historical content. Yet he would most certainly have been interested in the content: he was keenly aware of the value of history, even of history of the distant past. The Egyptian campaign was

---

[1] Duckworth, 'Louis XVI and English History', p. 395.
[2] The impact of the Revolution on interpretations of Roman History is explored in detail in Thom, *Republics, Nations and Tribes* (London, 1995). Thom portrays the end of the eighteenth century as marking a radical shift from the notion of city-nation to tribe-nation, and places interpretations of Roman History at the heart of that shift.
[3] Montesquieu, *Considérations sur la grandeur des romains*, ed. Charvet, pp. xii–xv.

notable for its concern with ancient monuments and for its extraordinarily high-quality publication of them.[4] The same period witnessed a major step forward in historical cartography, with Malte-Brun's *Précis de géographie universelle*.[5]

With an eye on the French past in 1804 Napoleon commissioned François Dominique de Reynaud, comte de Montlosier, to write an account which was, according to the author, to address:

'1: the ancient state of France and its institutions; 2: how the Revolution developed out of this state of affairs; 3: attempts made to reverse it; 4: the successes of the Premier Consul in this respect, and his various restorations.' This should be ready and published at the time of the declaration of the Empire.[6]

Here, then, was a work of history commissioned to appear at one of the great moments of Napoleon's career. In the event Montlosier did not meet the deadline, only completing the work in 1807, and then Napoleon, or those who read the text for him, did not like what was submitted. It was returned, and its publication had to wait until Napoleon's fall. In 1814 it was duly published, with a preface outlining the history of the commission and rejection of the work. Perhaps inevitably it caused a good deal of comment.[7]

Montlosier was an interesting choice of author. Belonging to the lesser nobility, he had been a member of the States General for Clermont in 1789, and a monarchist member of the national constituent assembly in 1791. Not surprisingly, during the Revolution he fled from France, first to Germany, and then to London—although he turned out to be violently anti-English. Already in contact with Napoleon's minister of police, Fouché, while in England, he took a conciliatory stance in urging French exiles to adopt a moderate position vis-à-vis the new regime as it was emerging under Napoleon. He returned to France in 1801.[8] Thus, he might have been expected to produce an account of French history that brought together the opposing traditions that had been so sharply debated in the run-up to the Revolution. In the opening pages of *De la monarchie française* this is at times, indeed, what he seems to be doing, but his overall argument runs directly counter to any idea that he might offer an interpretation of French history that was acceptable to both monarchists and Republicans.[9]

There are indications from very early on in Montlosier's text that it would be a divisive work. Among the questions that constituted the object of his research he lists:

---

[4] Reid, *Whose Pharoahs?*, pp. 31–7.

[5] Goffart, *Historical Atlases*, pp. 386–91. On Malte-Brun see also Beck, *Northern Antiquities*, vol. 1, pp. 130–41.

[6] Montlosier, *De la monarchie française*, vol. 1, p. iv.

[7] Montlosier, *De la monarchie française*, vol. 1, pp. iv–v; Gruner, 'Political historiography in Restoration France', pp. 346–7.

[8] For Montlosier, Brugerette, *Le Comte de Montlosier et son temps*; Gruner, 'Political historiography in Restoration France', p. 346.

[9] Gruner, 'Political historiography in Restoration France', pp. 347–9, while giving a useful overview of Montlosier's position, misses some of its nuance.

How did Germanic customs (*mœurs*) come to be associated with what remained of Gaulish customs? What was the reaction (*mouvement*) of these Germanic customs, which were entirely energetic, when faced with entirely debased (*avilies*) Gaulish customs?[10]

The word 'avilies' makes clear his disdain for the Gaulish element in the make-up of France. But a mere four pages later he offers a much less offensive reading:

> But first of all we ought to note that the Franks followed Roman example in almost everything. This is a point that has been very well illuminated by M. l'abbé Du Bos.
>
> Clovis continued to govern the Gauls according to Gaulish law. He maintained the particular administration of the lands that were distributed to seigneurs and to *coloni*: he even maintained the particular government of cities, their senate, their *curiae*, their militias. Neither the law nor the title of conqueror appeared. He who was a king of the Franks was no more to the Gauls than a patrician or a Roman consul. This prince enthusiastically accepted both these titles, which were conferred on him by the Emperor Anastasius: it seems that he valued them more than his title of king.[11]

An author so clearly accepting Du Bos would not seem a likely enthusiast for an interpretation that divided Franks and Gauls into two different camps of victor and vanquished. And Montlosier continues in an apparently similar vein:

> It seems, after what has just been said, that the Franks preserved the *ancien régime* of the Gauls in its entirety when they established themselves. Nevertheless we will see this regime modify itself and alter, little by little, in various ways.
>
> One must not forget that arriving in Gaul, the Franks brought with them their own laws, customs, and even language. So, while respecting the *ancien régime* of the Gauls, since they did not wish to abandon their own, there must have been a period when there were in many respects two separate regimes: one following the ancient constitution of the Gauls, and the other belonging to the new nation which had established itself. These two regimes, when they came into contact with each other, must sometimes have been put in an awkward position. But little by little they mixed, and they finished by fusing.[12]

Montlosier's picture of the various peoples of Gaul living side by side, each following its own traditions has much to commend it. He himself saw very clearly the weaknesses in the positions taken up on the one hand by Boulainvilliers and those who derived their interpretation from him, and by Du Bos on the other. There is something to be said for both a Germanist and a Romanist reading: it depends which block of information one looks at. In this respect, Montlosier was acknowledging the value of each of the main historiographical traditions of the eighteenth century. The actual manner of the fusion of the two races as he presented it, however, was rather less likely to win the support either of those who approved of Du Bos's interpretation or of those inclined to Mably's formulation.

---

[10] Montlosier, *De la monarchie française*, vol. 1, p. 9.
[11] Montlosier, *De la monarchie française*, vol. 1, pp. 13–14.
[12] Montlosier, *De la monarchie française*, vol. 1, pp. 15–16.

In Montlosier's view, although the Gauls and Franks lived side by side, there were irreconcilable differences between them. The first of them looks, initially, to be rather petty. Unlike the Gauls, the Franks had an aversion for domestic slaves. This, however, was to have an extremely significant outcome: 'The effect of this attitude was to move these wretches whom the Gauls and the Romans had forced to serve inside their houses, into trade or the cultivation of land.'[13] And 'this great innovation, which led to the slow abolition of personal slavery, shifted all household slaves, little by little into the class of *roturiers* (commoners) or of tributaries'.[14] Slavery, and its abolition was, of course, a topical issue in the early nineteenth century: Sismondi, to whom we shall turn shortly, was in contact with William Wilberforce.[15] The word 'roturier' would come to be extremely important for the next generation of historians. Effectively the rejection of domestic service, and the movement of domestic slaves into trade and, less significantly, agricultural work, created a working class. And this working class tended to be associated with towns. Thus far, Montlosier's reading might be thought to prefigure that of Engels in 'The origins of the family, private property and the state'.[16] Yet Montlosier's aristocratic leanings soon dominate: the Franks were country dwellers, an opinion he derived from Tacitus.[17] Thus, they preferred to live outside the towns, and the upper levels of Gaulish society tended to follow suit—for Montlosier's distinction is not a simple one between two racial groups: it is explicitly class-based. 'There were already more and more *châteaux* in France in the seventh century. Subsequently their number became infinite.'[18] The members of this upper class, whether from Frankish or Gaulish stock, adopted Germanic values. Montlosier offers an analysis of clientship among the Romans, the Gauls, and the Germanic peoples: in the Roman case it was basically a civil institution; for the Gauls, it was servile; and for the Germanic peoples it was military and noble.[19] It was this military ethic that was the hallmark of the aristocracy—this emphasis on the military looked back, of course, to Boulainvilliers and his followers, as well as to Montesquieu.

Turning from the origins of the French class structure to the position of the monarchy, Montlosier adopts a similar line of approach. The king could be seen from a Roman or a Frankish viewpoint.

> When père Daniel or the abbé Du Bos worked through our ancient charters, they only stopped when they saw something ecclesiastical or Roman. Everything else seemed problematic to them. M. de Boulainvilliers, on the other hand, saw only Franks and *leudes*. In this respect there are two rules to which one must pay attention.[20]

---

[13] Montlosier, *De la monarchie française*, vol. 1, p. 23.

[14] Montlosier, *De la monarchie française*, vol. 1, p. 24.

[15] The copy of Wilberforce's 'A Letter on the Abolition of the Slave Trade, Addressed to the Freeholders and Other Inhabitants of Yorkshire (1807)' in the Library of Senate House, London, was given by the author to Sismondi.

[16] Engels, 'The origins of the family, private property and the state'.

[17] Montlosier, *De la monarchie française*, vol. 1, p. 23.

[18] Montlosier, *De la monarchie française*, vol. 1, p. 24.

[19] Montlosier, *De la monarchie française*, vol. 1, pp. 35–8.

[20] Montlosier, *De la monarchie française*, vol. 1, p. 48. On Daniel see Leffler, 'French historians and the challenge to Louis XIV's absolutism', pp. 5–8.

Each of these viewpoints was valid, but was only held by one segment of society: 'royal authority wavered for some while as if being undecided'.[21] The Gauls and the clergy saw Clovis as the successor to Constantine and Theodosius, and the king himself received a title from Anastasius.[22] By contrast, the king in Frankish tradition had little authority. In Montlosier's view, one can see the division of opinion even in the story of the vase of Soissons, where the majority of the Franks thought the king could do as he wanted, but one man disagreed.[23] These different attitudes influenced royal power: in religious matters, the king governed with the clergy; in military matters with his *leudes*. As for the law, this was enacted at the *Champ de Mars* or *Mai*.[24] The king's authority was, supposedly, further limited by the fact that his office was elective and not hereditary. Montlosier acknowledged that kings were drawn from a single family, first Merovingian then Carolingian: but he seized on every indication that individual kings were chosen by the people of a particular kingdom.[25] Of course, women could not be elected, because they could neither inherit (a point on which Montlosier is simply wrong, except with regard to Salic land), nor could they command.[26] As for the failure of the Merovingians, Montlosier put it down to two factors: the first, excessive alienation of the fisc by the kings, and the second, the growth in the power of lords, who, through the development of the Frankish system of clientship, gained more and more vassals.[27] Further, the emergence of the Saracen threat, helped put Pippin III in a position to make a bid for the crown. Even though he had to despoil the Church to support his followers, the papacy decided to back him.[28]

In his reading of the Merovingian period, Montlosier had thus come close to taking Boulainvilliers' stance, while at the same time acknowledging the merits of Du Bos' research. What would come to be seen as most divisive in his reading was his view of the lower class: the word 'aviles' is a clear indication of his views. He was to go further, calling the Third Estate, in a phrase that would register in the annals of racism, though strictly speaking it is a comment on class rather than on race, 'this new people born of slaves…mixture of all races and of all times'.[29] From Napoleon's point of view the insistence on a hereditary monarchy advised by the nobility was equally unwelcome. So too, Montlosier's anti-clericalism, more apparent in his failure to comment on Clovis' baptism than in any open attack on the Church in his opening chapters, may also have made his reading unwelcome.

[21] Montlosier, *De la monarchie française*, vol. 1, p. 45.
[22] Montlosier, *De la monarchie française*, vol. 1, p. 45.
[23] Montlosier, *De la monarchie française*, vol. 1, p. 46.
[24] Montlosier, *De la monarchie française*, vol. 1, p. 50.
[25] Montlosier, *De la monarchie française*, vol. 1, pp. 54–6.
[26] Montlosier, *De la monarchie française*, vol. 1, pp. 58–61.
[27] Montlosier, *De la monarchie française*, vol. 1, pp. 64–6.
[28] Montlosier, *De la monarchie française*, vol. 1, pp. 66–7.
[29] Simar, *Etude critique sur la formation de la doctrine des races au XVIIIe siècle et son expansion au XIXe siècle*, p. 20.

5.2 NAPOLEON AND THE MEROVINGIANS

If we want to find out what Napoleon hoped to hear about the early Middle Ages, we may get rather closer if we turn from historical writing to matters of ritual and representation. A place to begin is the ceremony with which the publication of Montlosier's book was supposed to coincide: the imperial coronation of 1804. The master of ceremonies, one might note, was Louis-Philippe, comte de Ségur, who subsequently wrote a history of the later Roman Empire.[30] The setting was the church of Notre Dame in Paris, which boasted statues of Clovis and Charlemagne on its principal pillars.[31] The rite deliberately drew on Carolingian ritual and used Carolingian regalia.[32] Charlemagne was perhaps Napoleon's greatest predecessor and his Empire was a model to be emulated. The scene was famously immortalized by Jacques-Louis David in a painting finally completed in 1807. Napoleon himself had various sections of that work repainted, to ensure that it conformed to the image that he wished to have preserved. From the point of view of a historian of the end of the Migration Period it is the regalia and Napoleon's robes that are crucial: sewn onto them were hundreds of little gold bees in imitation of the treasure of Childeric that had been found in Tournai in 1653.[33] Napoleon would show a similar interest in using ancient regalia in Italy, where he had himself crowned with the iron crown of the Lombards.[34]

As we have already seen, Childeric's treasure had been a point of political interest since its discovery. At the time Tournai was part of the Spanish Netherlands, the finds were therefore sent to the then governor, the archduke Leopold of Austria. Leopold subsequently gave them to Maximilian Henry of Bavaria, elector of Cologne, who had them copied, and then gave the originals to Louis XIV, who placed them in the *Bibliothèque du Roi*.[35] Thereafter they were regarded as part of the regalia of France. Having survived the Revolution, they were used by Napoleon as models for details of his coronation garments. In 1831, however, the majority of the objects were stolen from the *Cabinet des éstampes*, and melted down for their gold content.[36]

Childeric's grave supplied Napoleon with the inspiration for some parts of his regalia, but, the Merovingian king, being pagan, was not an ideal inspiration for the new emperor. Clovis was obviously a more luminous predecessor, and not surprisingly Napoleon interested himself in the first Catholic king of the Franks. Clovis had been buried, along with his wife Chrotechildis, or Clothilde in French

---

[30] Ségur, *Histoire du Bas-Empire*.

[31] Lamargue, *Le Sacre de S.M. l'Empereur Napoléon*, p. 5.

[32] Lamargue, *Le Sacre de S.M. l'Empereur Napoléon*.

[33] Effros, *Merovingian Mortuary Archaeology*, pp. 34–5; Wagner, *Die politische Bedeutung des Childerich-Grabfundes von 1653*, p. 26; Tulard, 'Qui a fait coudre les abeilles de Childéric sur le manteau du sacre de Napoléon?'.

[34] See below, chapter 7.

[35] The story is fully recounted by Du Bos, *Histoire critique*, vol. 2, bk 3, pp. 302–5. See also Wagner, *Die politische Bedeutung des Childerich-Grabfundes von 1653*; Werner, 'Childerichgrab', pp. 1819–20.

[36] Effros, *Merovingian Mortuary Archaeology*, p. 35.

tradition, in the church of the Holy Apostles, later to be called Ste Geneviève. Curiously, the exact whereabouts of his tomb was unknown. A number of Merovingian royal graves had been dug up at Saint-Germain-des-Prés in 1656,[37] while the remains of those Merovingian kings from Dagobert I onwards who had been buried at Saint-Denis, just to the north of Paris, were caught up in the destruction of the royal tombs and mausolea, which took place in July 1793, to mark the first anniversary of the overthrow of the monarchy.[38] The tombs of Clovis and Clothilde at Sainte-Geneviève, however, were thought to await discovery. An opportunity to search for them arose with the decision to pull down the old church of Ste Geneviève in 1807. A new church had already been erected on an adjacent site: the building designed by Soufflot, and now known as the Panthéon. The church had been built in 1744, following a vow offered by Louis XV, although its dome was only completed in 1790. A year after its completion it was transformed by the new revolutionary government into a mausoleum of the great men of France, beginning with Mirabeau and Voltaire. In 1806, however, Napoleon ordered that it should have a dual function as church and mausoleum.[39] With the Panthéon in use as a church once more, the old church of Geneviève could, therefore, be pulled down, but, the emperor insisted, a search for the tombs of Clovis and Clothilde should be carried out before the demolition.[40] Some early sarcophagi were indeed discovered in the crypt, and they were initially proclaimed as belonging to the Frankish king and his family, though this view was soon rejected, and they are now thought to have come from a slightly later period.[41]

While Napoleon could not associate himself with the actual earthly remains of Clovis and his saintly queen, he could make a clear connection in the iconography of the re-consecrated Panthéon. In particular, at the beginning of the nineteenth century the interior of the dome remained to be decorated. In 1811 a design was commissioned from the painter Antoine-Jean Gros, showing 'A group (*gloire*) of angels carrying heavenwards the reliquary of Saint Geneviève, Clovis, and his wife Clothilde, founders of the church, Charlemagne, St Louis, their majesties the emperor and empress, consecrating the new church to the cult of the saint (Geneviève).'[42] In the event, because the painting was not finished until after 1815, the image was modified to present Louis XVIII, the duchesse d'Angoulême, and the duc de Bordeaux in place of Napoleon and his empress.

Geneviève was, of course, almost as important as Clovis and Clothilde in all this. A Gallo-Roman, who had supposedly organized the defence of the city of Paris against the Huns, and later against Clovis' father, Childeric, she had been the focus of a major cult from the early sixth century onwards. Indeed it may well have been her burial at the church of the Holy Apostles that led to Clovis' decision to

[37] Effros, *Merovingian Mortuary Archaeology*, pp. 36–42.
[38] Lindsay, 'Mummies and tombs: Turenne, Napoléon, and Death Ritual', p. 476.
[39] Wood, 'The Panthéon in Paris'.
[40] Périn, 'The undiscovered grave of king Clovis', p. 260.
[41] Périn, 'The undiscovered grave of king Clovis', p. 260.
[42] Macé de Lépinay, *Peintures et sculptures du Panthéon*, pp. 27–8.

adopt Paris as his capital and to be buried in the same church.[43] Although she was almost certainly from the upper classes, her image became confused with that of Jeanne d'Arc and by the end of the Middle Ages she was thought of as a shepherd-ess. The cult of Geneviève was a popular one in Paris, but it was also closely associated with the Bourbons, as can be seen in Louis XV's vow to rebuild her church. It is not, therefore, surprising that her remains suffered the same fate as those of the members of the royal family in Saint-Denis, despite the fact that Voltaire himself had been devoted to her, calling her 'this good Gauloise...my shepherdess...my own virgin'.[44] Her shrine was broken up, her bones arraigned, and on 3rd December 1793 they were burned and thrown into the Seine. Ten years later, however, the Bonapartist authorities reinstituted her cult in the church of Saint-Etienne-du-Mont, directly adjacent both to the old church of Ste Geneviève and to the new Panthéon.[45]

Napoleon's interest in the early Middle Ages was not, then, merely confined to the opening chapters of Montlosier's rejected history, but was publicly displayed in his search for the tombs of Clovis and Clothilde, his resurrection of the cult of Geneviève, and his commission for the decoration of the dome of the Panthéon, as well as in the detailed iconography of his coronation robes. Association with the period of the 'premier race', the first royal dynasty of France, was a matter of significance.

5.3 MADAME DE STAËL, ZACHARIAS WERNER, AND THE *PORTRAIT D'ATTILA*

His leading critics, however, did not envisage Napoleon as a new Clovis. Mme de Staël identified him not with the great Merovingian, but with Attila, the Hunnic invader against whom Geneviève organized the first defence of Paris. In 1810 an excerpt from her work *De l'Allemagne* was printed under the title *Portrait d'Attila*. This so angered the emperor that he had all copies of the *De l'Allemagne* pulped.[46] One might note, however, that Napoleon had described himself as 'the Attila of the Venetian people' in 1797.[47]

Mme de Staël, or Anne-Louise-Germaine, baroness of Staël-Holstein, was the daughter of Louis XVI's popular finance minister Necker, whose exile led directly to the revolutionary assault on the Bastille, and of his wife Suzanne Curchod, one-time friend of Gibbon, who had also maintained one of the most glittering salons in pre-revolutionary France. Mme de Staël maintained the family tradition, being very much at the heart of French society and politics through the 1790s. Her lover,

[43] Périn, 'The undiscovered grave of king Clovis', p. 256.
[44] Sluhovsky, *Patroness of Paris*, p. 206.
[45] Sluhovsky, *Patroness of Paris*, pp. 207–8.
[46] Isbell, *The Birth of European Romanticism*, pp. 5, 7, 91. The offending section is contained in de Staël, *De L'Allemagne*, vol 3, 141–9.
[47] Brown, 'Gibbon, Hodgkin, and the invaders of Italy', p. 140.

Narbonne, became minister for war in 1791, and in the same year members of her own salon played a major role in the formulation of the constitution. Four years later she was exiled, but with the establishment of the *Directoire* she was able to return to Paris. She was again exiled, by Napoleon, from 1803. Much of her exile was spent in her chateau at Coppet, outside Geneva, where members of her circle included the aged Mallet,[48] who had been a childhood friend of her father,[49] as well as Mallet's first biographer, Sismondi,[50] to whom we shall return.

De Staël's earliest significant comments on the period of the Fall of the Roman Empire come in *De la littérature*, published in 1800. Chapter eight of the first book is dedicated to 'the invasion of the Northern Peoples, the Christian religion, and the Renaissance of Letters'.[51] There she argued that the barbarians, despite the destruction they wrought, revivified the tired world of Rome, as, simultaneously, did Christianity. This interpretation, which would come to increasing prominence in the course of the nineteenth century through the work of the likes of August-Wilhelm Schlegel[52] and above all Frédéric Ozanam, was effectively an inversion of Gibbon's argument. It also met with immediate criticism from Fauriel and Cabanis.[53]

De l'Allemagne, the work that contained the comparison between Napoleon and Attila, and that caused such offense that it had to be pulped, was originally published in 1810. An English version appeared in 1813, at the same time as the French text was put into circulation once again. These were followed, in 1814, by an Italian version, and then a year later by a German one.[54] In *De l'Allemagne* de Staël set out a description of Germany that was intended, among other things, to act as a critique of Napoleon's France.[55] Since Germany did not exist as a single political unit, de Staël defined it largely in cultural terms, and not least through an analysis of its drama. Among the dramatists she discussed at some length was Zacharias Werner.[56]

Werner was a Prussian, born in Königsberg. Prior to Napoleon's invasion of Germany he held an official post in Berlin. In 1807, as a result of losing his job he travelled south to Weimar, where for a short time he was a protégé of Goethe. His religious leanings quickly led to a breach between the two men, and he travelled to Switzerland, where he became a member of de Staël's circle, before moving to Rome. There he converted to Catholicism and became a priest. As such he moved to Austria, where his sermons attracted a great deal of attention, particularly during

[48] Beck, *Northern Antiquities*, vol. 1, p. 128 calls Mallet one of her friends. Sismondi, in his biography, notes Mallet's friendship with her father, Necker: Sismondi, *De la vie et des écrits de P.H. Mallet*, pp. 4, 9.

[49] Sismondi, *De la vie et des écrits de P. H. Mallet*, pp. 4, 9.

[50] Candaux, 'L'hommage de Sismondi à Paul-Henri Mallet', pp. 331–8.

[51] de Staël, *De la littérature*, vol. 1, pp. 130–48; see Thom, *Republics, Nations and Tribes*, pp. 206–8, 246.

[52] Thom, *Republics, Nations and Tribes*, pp. 227, 261.

[53] Thom, *Republics, Nations and Tribes*, pp. 246, 341, n. 27.

[54] Isbell, *The Birth of European Romanticism*, p. 2.

[55] Isbell, *The Birth of European Romanticism*.

[56] de Staël, *De L'Allemagne*, vol. 3, 141–9.

the period of the Congress of Vienna, where he was an honorary canon of the cathedral of St Stephen.[57] As a preacher he inveighed against his old works, among them *Attila, König der Hunnen*, which was produced with great success at the Theater an der Wien, being performed twenty-nine times between 1809 and 1825.[58] Werner died in 1823.

De Staël discusses five of his plays, *Martin Luther oder die Weihe der Kraft*, *Die Söhne des Tals*, *Das Kreuz an der Ostsee*, *Der vierundzwanzigste Februar*, and, especially, *Attila*.[59] It is the protagonist of Werner's play, rather than the historical Attila, who is compared to Napoleon, or rather, it is Mme de Staël's view of Werner's character, for some of her comments come from her imagination rather than from anything one finds in the text or sees on stage. In one draft on *De l'Allemagne* she describes Attila, saying that '[h]e did nothing other than wage war: however, luxury and fine art pleased him as much as his conquests'.[60] There are no words in the play that indicate this, but it is quite clearly a statement of de Staël's view of Napoleon. Indeed, there is a considerable gulf between Werner's *Attila* and de Staël's account of it, not least because for her the Hunnic king is a villain, while for the playwright he is unquestionably the hero and is a good deal more noble than anyone else on stage apart from pope Leo.

Werner's play scarcely amounts to an accurate rendering of the story of Attila's 451 invasion of Italy, his decision not to attack Rome, and his subsequent death.[61] Some historical details are simply wrong: the old empress Galla Placidia is presented as still being alive at the time, although she had died a year previously; in the course of the drama the general Aetius is killed while Rome is under siege, although he survived for another three years; and the siege itself never took place; Attila's son Irnak dies at the hands of the king's bride and murderer—whereas Ernac, as he is known to history, lived on for some while on the borders of the Roman Empire.[62] Some historical details are fanciful at best: Attila's killer, his new wife Hildegunde, is presented as being a Burgundian intent on avenging her lover, Walther. In one early source Attila was indeed killed by an unnamed bride, but the reasons are not specified.[63] Not that the Viennese audiences of *Attila* would have been troubled by the inaccuracies: Gluck (like Handel before him) had set Metastasio's even more fanciful account of Valentinian III's court in his *Ezio*, the revised version of which was premiered in the Burgtheatre in 1763.[64] Indeed, Metastasio's libretto spawned around forty settings, some of which achieved considerable popularity.[65] Despite such fictions, it is clear that Werner knew his sources, or at least

[57] On Werner in Vienna, Zamoyski, *Rites of Peace*, pp. 400–1; Jackson, ed. Lady Jackson, *The Bath Archives: a further selection from the diaries and letters of Sir George Jackson, K.C.H. from 1809 to 1816*, vol. 2, p. 465.
[58] Porter, 'Verdi's *Attila*', p. 46.
[59] For Werner's *Attila*, see Wood, '"Adelchi" and "Attila": the barbarians and the Risorgimento'.
[60] de Staël, *De L'Allemagne*, III, 144, n. L. 14; Isbell, *The Birth of European Romanticism*, 70.
[61] On Werner, Carlà, 'Il modello di ogni caduta', pp. 83–90.
[62] Thompson, *The Huns*, pp. 171–3.
[63] Marcellinus *comes*, *Chronicle*, *sub anno* 454.
[64] Gluck's first version dates to 1750.
[65] Feldman, *Opera and Sovereignty*, p. 265–8.

had access to some study of them, and much of what is included in the play does have some relationship to the history of the mid-fifth century. The *Attila* is no plausible reconstruction of events, though it is rather less fanciful than Marmontel's *Bélisaire*, but like the regalia used in Napoleon's coronation, it rested on a raft of genuine historical scholarship. Werner, the pious romantic, however, was more interested in the spiritual development of his characters than in factual accuracy. Yet it was the political implications of his play that attracted attention, and not just from Mme de Staël. As we shall see, Werner's *Attila* would have a great impact in the very different milieu of Risorgimento Italy.

5.4 SISMONDI

De Staël's interest in the early Middle Ages was essentially that of a dilettante. The same could not be said of one member of her coterie at Coppet, and indeed her companion on her 1805 tour of Italy, Jean Charles Leonard Simonde de Sismondi, whom we have already met as the first biographer of Mallet. Sismondi was, of course, not only a historian: indeed he is now best remembered as a political economist.[66] His two greatest contributions to the writing of history, the sixteen-volume *Histoire des républiques italiennes du Moyen Age* and the twenty-nine volume *Histoire des Français* have relatively little to say about the Fall of Rome, but they do not sidestep it entirely. Yet the *Histoire de la chute de l'empire romain et du déclin de la civilisation*, which appeared simultaneously in English as the *History of the Fall of the Roman Empire, Comprising a View of the Invasion and Settlement of the Barbarians*, is a significant work, which modified Gibbon's reading in crucial ways.

Sismondi, whose original name was Simonde, was born in Geneva in 1773.[67] A century earlier his family, who were Huguenots, had moved from the Dauphiné to the Swiss city, following the Revocation of the Edict of Nantes.[68] Sismondi himself traced the family origins rightly or wrongly back to the Pisan aristocracy—these supposed links to the world of the Italian republics would resonate throughout his intellectual career.[69] His father was a pastor, who gave up the ministry and was subsequently elected to the Genevan *Conseil des Deux-Cents*, which put the family very much at the centre of the city's politics at a time of political upheaval.[70] Unfortunate investments by his father meant that the young Charles was sent to work in the Lyons branch of the bankers Eynard et Compagnie, and there he learnt the basics of economics and bookkeeping.[71] In

[66] For two relatively recent assessments which prompted renewed interest in his work: Stowell, 'Sismondi: a neglected pioneer'; Stewart, 'Sismondi's forgotten ethical critique of early capitalism'.

[67] The major biographical study of Sismondi remains de Salis, *Sismondi*. There are several short accounts in English, among them T. Roscoe, 'Life of M. Simonde de Sismondi', which provides an introduction to his translation of Sismondi, *Historical View of the Literature of the South of Europe*, pp. 9–24.

[68] De Salis, *Sismondi*, pp. 6–7.

[69] De Salis, *Sismondi*, pp. 7–9.

[70] De Salis, *Sismondi*, pp. 11–12; Papp; 'Sismondi's system of Liberty', p. 253.

[71] De Salis, *Sismondi*, pp. 18–20.

1792, as the Revolution became more threatening, he returned to Geneva, though the memories of the Terror never left him.[72] Geneva, itself, however, with the Montagnards as its own version of the Jacobins, was not much safer than Lyons, and the whole family migrated to England, where Charles threw himself into perfecting his knowledge of the language and the country's constitution, law, and literature.[73] A year later, however, Mme Sismondi insisted on returning home, though once again Geneva proved too dangerous, and the family moved instead to Tuscany, where they purchased an estate, of which the young Sismondi took charge. This experience gave him a sense of agriculture and production, which he combined with the basic economics he had learnt in Lyons. At the same time, residence in Italy, combined with family fantasies about its origins, fired him with a desire to understand the history of the peninsula. His first Tuscan idyll, however, was shattered by Napoleon's seizure of the Grand Duchy of Tuscany, and the young Sismondi returned to Geneva, by now in French hands. There the publication of his experiences of Tuscan agriculture helped to secure him employment in the *Conseil du Commerce* and then in the *Chambre de Commerce* of the department of Léman. His economic reputation he enhanced with the publication in 1803 of *De la richesse commerciale, ou principes d'économie politique appliqués à la législation du commerce*—a work largely restating Adam Smith's views on the virtues of laissez-faire.

At the same time Sismondi started to frequent Mme de Staël's salon, and from 1805 he became her preferred travelling companion. In that year the two of them visited Italy, a tour which de Staël used as the basis for her novel *Corinne*, while Sismondi gathered material for his *Histoire des Républiques italiennes du Moyen Age*, the first two volumes of which were published in Zurich in 1807, simultaneously in French and German, to be followed by the third and fourth a year later. His main concern was with the Italy of the twelfth to sixteenth centuries, and he did little more than sketch in the prehistory of that period. He briefly presented a history of Etruscan austerity, followed by the Roman Republic falling prey to imperial despotism. This in turn was followed by barbarian chaos, which was only reversed in the twelfth century with the revival of civic democracy that was subsequently destroyed in the fifteenth as a result of a return to despotism and foreign intervention.[74] His underlying idea he expressed at the start of the work: 'The virtues and vices of nations, their enlightened state or their ignorance are scarcely ever the effects of climate or of a particular race, but of legislation (l'ouvrage des lois).'[75] The reference to climate concerns an idea beloved of Du Bos, Montesquieu, and also de Staël, that the character of a people is influenced by the weather to which they are subjected. Sismondi's views were more purely constitutional, and his central concern the golden age of the Italian city states. The *Histoire*, with its celebration of the cities in their independent

[72] De Salis, *Sismondi*, p. 20.
[73] De Salis, *Sismondi*, p. 24; Pappé, 'Sismondi's system of Liberty', p. 254.
[74] De Salis, *Sismondi*, pp. 342–3.
[75] Sismondi, *Histoire des Républiques italiennes*, vol. 1, p. v; de Salis, *Sismondi*, p. 342; Pappé, 'Sismondi's system of Liberty', pp. 262–3.

heyday, would become a key work for Risorgimento historians (though he didn't share their Catholicism).[76]

Sismondi's concerns with liberty and democracy, and his dislike of despotism and foreign intervention, were strengthened by his experiences from 1810 to 1815. He witnessed first hand the constant harassment of de Staël by Napoleon's agents[77]—which would eventually force her to flee to Stockholm in 1812. But the triumph of the allies left him in a quandary: for the Swiss, the Austrians threatened a return to the *Ancien Régime*, while France saw a Bourbon restoration.[78] Sismondi happened to be in Paris, seeing volumes of his *Républiques italiennes* through the press in 1815, at the moment of Napoleon's return. He was much taken by the promise of the 100 days, and wrote in enthusiastic support of the new constitution (*la Benjamine*) drawn up by his friend Benjamin Constant. He also had lengthy conversations with Napoleon himself.[79] The defeat of Napoleon and the subsequent decisions of the Congress of Vienna left him both disappointed and isolated.[80] His apparent volte-face, from hostility towards Napoleon to enthusiastic support, was also heavily criticized, though, interestingly, not by de Staël.

As a result he retired to Italy, where in 1817 he finished the *Histoire des Républiques italiennes*. This was followed by the second of his major works of political economics, the ground-breaking *Nouveaux principes d'économie politique* of 1819. Deeply disturbed by what he had seen of developing industrialization, and above all by the hardships caused by the economic crises of 1815 and 1818, he abjured his previous laissez-faire stance and put forward a radical programme intended to balance wealth and the needs of the labour force—a programme that Marx and Engels would see as an example of *petty-bourgeois* socialism.[81] Indeed Engels would draw a good deal from the *Nouveaux principes* in his *Conditions of the Working Class in England*.[82]

At exactly the same time Sismondi turned his hand to writing a history of the French. He may initially have thought of the idea in 1816.[83] What is certain is that the first three volumes appeared in 1821.[84] Here, by contrast with his *Histoire des Républiques italiennes*, he devoted a good deal of space to the early Middle Ages, allocating one entire volume to the Merovingians and another to the Carolingians. In so doing he was very firmly taking up the debates initiated by Boulainvilliers, Du Bos, Montesquieu, and Mably.[85] His own position looked back to Montesquieu

---

[76] Lyttelton, 'Sismondi's *Histoire des Républiques italiennes* and the Risorgimento', pp. 351–66.

[77] De Salis, *Sismondi*, pp. 168–72. On Sismondi as a critic of Napoleon, Lyttelton, 'Creating a national past: History, myth and image in the Risorgimento', p. 44.

[78] De Salis, *Sismondi*, p. 220.

[79] Villari, 'Conversation de Napoléon Ier et de Sismondi'; Villari and Monod, 'Lettres inédites de Sismondi écrites pendant les Cent-Jours'; Villari and Monod, 'Notes de Sismondi sur l'empire et les cent jours'; Villari, 'La storia dei centi Giorni narrata del S. (epistolario inedito)'.

[80] De Salis, *Sismondi*, pp. 256–325.

[81] Marx and Engels, *The Communist Manifesto*, p. 29; de Salis, *Sismondi*, p. 429.

[82] De Salis, *Sismondi*, p. 428.   [83] De Salis, *Sismondi*, p. 430.

[84] De Salis, *Sismondi*, p. 431.   [85] De Salis, *Sismondi*, p. 431.

for its critique of Rome, and to Mably for its reading of the Germanic invaders. In his view, the despotism of both the Roman and the early barbarian regimes was grim. Roman peace brought neither security for the rich nor an honest wage for the poor.[86] Life under the Merovingians was no better, though Sismondi's account is essentially a narrative. Like that of his predecessors, his reading was not just an antiquarian exercise, even the distant past with its examples of exploitation had lessons for the social sciences of his own day.[87] Society ought to exist for universal advantage,[88] but under the Romans and the Franks this had not been the case.

Alongside his historical treatment of the Merovingian period he produced a novel, *Julia Sévéra ou l'an quatre cent quatre-vingt-douze*—a strange romance, in which the heroine narrowly misses being betrothed to Clovis and only succeeds in marrying her Gallo-Roman suitor after a period of imprisonment engineered by the Church.[89] Churchmen often get short shrift in Sismondi, which is no doubt a reflexion of his Genevan Protestantism and his deep suspicion of anything that could be seen as Catholic.[90]

Julia Sévéra is not regarded as one of the Sismondi's more successful works. Indeed, its American reviewer was convinced it would never be translated into English—a conviction that was proved wrong immediately. Sismondi wrote the novel shortly after his marriage to Jessie Allen. Jessie was one of a very large family. Two of her sisters married Wedgwoods, and she was therefore aunt to Charles Darwin. Another sister married the MP and political writer Sir James Mackintosh.[91] Although Sismondi never felt at ease in England among his English in-laws, as a result of his marriage he was extremely well connected, and his later work was written with an eye on an English audience as much as a French, Italian, or even German one. Perhaps *Julia Sévéra* was written for Jessie's pleasure and that of her visitors in Tuscany.[92] Clearly Sismondi had Walter Scott very much in mind:[93] the historical novel was a way to make the distant past accessible.

Shortly before the appearance of *Julia Sévéra* Sismondi, who had been appointed to a chair at the university of Geneva, delivered a series of lectures on the Fall of the Roman Empire. These would appear in print thirteen years later, in 1835, in both English and French. The fact of their simultaneous appearance in the two languages is a mark both of the regard in which Sismondi was held in the Francophone and Anglophone worlds, and also, one suspects, of the fact that he was very

---

[86] Sismondi, *Histoire des Français*, vol. 1, p. 43.
[87] De Salis, *Sismondi*, p. 396; Sismondi, *Histoire des Français*, vol. 1, p. 7. (De Salis' reference is to an earlier edition.)
[88] Sismondi, *Histoire des Français*, vol. 1, p. 9.
[89] Sismondi, *Julia Sévéra ou l'an quatre cent quatre-vingt-douze*, trans., *Julia Sévéra, or, the year four hundred and ninety-two*. See the highly critical, anonymous, review in *The North American Review* 15, 36 (1822), pp. 163–77. A much more sympathetic approach is Déruelle, '*Julia Sévéra* ou pour une autre écriture de l'histoire'.
[90] On Sismondi's anti-catholicism, Patriaca, 'Indolence and regeneration: tropes and tensions of Risorgimento Patriotism', pp. 397–9.
[91] De Salis, *Sismondi*, p. 378–80; Pappé, 'Sismondi's system of Liberty', p. 252.
[92] De Salis, *Sismondi*, pp. 377, and 382 for the circumstances in which he wrote *Julia Sévéra*, as recorded by Villari, 'Une conversation inédite entre Napoléon Ier et Sismondi', p. 238.
[93] De Salis, *Sismondi*, p. 439; Déruelle, '*Julia Sévéra* ou pour une autre écriture de l'histoire'.

deliberately taking on Gibbon. The intellectual shadow of the Englishman was no doubt all the stronger for a man who had been the travelling companion of the daughter of Suzanne Curchod, the woman whom Gibbon has wished to marry. In his *History of the Fall of the Roman Empire* Sismondi gathered and elaborated ideas already expressed in the histories of the Italian Republics and of the French. Once again he insisted on the 'value of history as illustrative of the moral and political sciences',[94] remarking also that 'History is the general storehouse of the experiments which have been made in all the social sciences.'[95] And, of course, he had two declining empires, the French and the Austrian, with which to compare. In surveying the whole period of the Fall of the Roman Empire, he claimed that the first two centuries of the Christian era apparently marked a high point in civilization, but that the germs of its collapse were already present. The barbarians delivered the Empire's *coup de grace*, and then, in trying to reconstruct it, they caused its further dissolution. By the end of the tenth century 'human society had resolved itself into its primary elements—associations of citizens in towns and cities'.[96] It was at this moment that modern history began. This chronological point and the emphasis on towns and cities had already been central to his work on medieval Italy.[97]

Although Sismondi accepted that the arrival of the barbarians led to the death of millions,[98] he did not see the incomers as being the major cause of the ruin of the Empire. More important (and closer to some strands of pre-Revolutionary thinking) was the destruction of patriotism, caused by the extension of citizenship, particularly by Caracalla.[99] He also looked at the class structure of the Roman Empire and argued that, whilst the wealthiest survived, the small proprietors were squeezed out, and the lower classes were either corrupt or oppressed.[100] This essentially follows the model set out in his *Nouveaux principes*, while its emphasis on the small proprietor reflects his own experience as a Tuscan farmer. The so-called Golden Age of Rome was nothing of the sort for the majority of the population. In addition to the collapse of patriotism there was decline in military discipline, which prompted the barbarian invasions of the third century.[101] Although a number of great leaders turned the tide,[102] their success was temporary. At a military level they stored up problems for the future, recruiting barbarians into the army and forbidding the senatorial class from serving.[103] Diocletian recognized that more change was needed, but being himself of servile birth, he did not understand the virtues of liberty and instead founded a despotism.[104]

[94] Sismondi, *Fall of the Roman Empire*, vol. 1, p. 1.
[95] Sismondi, *Fall of the Roman Empire*, vol. 1, p. 7.
[96] Sismondi, *Fall of the Roman Empire*, vol. 1, p. 11.
[97] It is worth noting parallels between the ideas of Sismondi and Condorcet: Thom, *Republics, Nations and Tribes*, p. 202.
[98] Sismondi, *Fall of the Roman Empire*, vol. 1, p. 18.
[99] Sismondi, *Fall of the Roman Empire*, vol. 1, p. 19.
[100] Sismondi, *Fall of the Roman Empire*, vol. 1, pp. 21–5.
[101] Sismondi, *Fall of the Roman Empire*, vol. 1, p. 38.
[102] Sismondi, *Fall of the Roman Empire*, vol. 1, p. 40.
[103] Sismondi, *Fall of the Roman Empire*, vol. 1, p. 42.
[104] Sismondi, *Fall of the Roman Empire*, vol. 1, p. 43.

Having analysed the Empire, Sismondi turned to the barbarians, noting that they played as much of a role in the creation of Europe as did the Romans:

> The intermixture of the two races was not accomplished till after long sufferings, nor without the destruction of a great part of that progress towards improvement which mankind had made during a course of ages. It was, however, this intermixture which made us what we are: we are heirs of the double inheritance of the Romans and the barbarians; we have engrafted the laws, institutions, manners, and opinions of the one race on those of the other. If we would know ourselves, we must go back to the study of our progenitors; of those who transmitted to us their culture, no less than of those who sought to destroy it.[105]

He describes each of the neighbours of the Romans in turn, coming finally to the Germans, who he portrays as independent agriculturalists.[106] His view of their social structure is derived from Tacitus and Caesar;[107] his interpretation of their religion depends somewhat on a mixture of early and late evidence, combining classical sources with accounts of the Valkyries.[108] Here, of course, one should remember his enthusiasm for Mallet's work.

Having set the scene, he provides a narrative, stressing the weakness of the Empire, with its class divisions and its despotic political structure,[109] in the face of which many preferred the barbarians to the Roman tax collectors and magistrates.[110] From the Empire's point of view the greatest disaster was the loss of Africa to the Vandals, because it had been the granary of Rome and Italy.[111] This was followed by the arrival of Attila, and by Aetius' success in defeating him—not that the Catalaunian Plains, the battle at which the Hunnic attack on Gaul was halted, saved the Empire from ruin, but it did save Western Europe from 'Tartar barbarism' and 'Russian civilization'.[112] The most positive outcome of Attila's onslaught was the foundation of Venice, about which Sismondi waxes poetic:

> The extent of his ravages, and the certainty of having no mercy from the barbarian, produced an effect upon the people of Italy that led to the erection of a splendid monument, which has perpetuated to our days the memory of the terror he inspired. All the inhabitants of that part of Italy which is situated at the mouths of the great rivers, and called Venetia, took refuge in the low lands, upon the islands, almost covered with water, which choke the mouths of the Adige, the Po, the Brenta, and the Tagliamento. There they sheltered themselves under huts made of branches, and transported thither a small part of their wealth. In a short time they constructed more commodious habitations, and several cities were seen to rise as it were out of the waters. Such was the origin of Venice; and that haughty republic justly called herself the eldest daughter of the Roman empire. She was founded by the Romans while the

---

[105] Sismondi, *Fall of the Roman Empire*, vol. 1, p. 48.
[106] Sismondi, *Fall of the Roman Empire*, vol. 1, p. 65.
[107] Sismondi, *Fall of the Roman Empire*, vol. 1, p. 66.
[108] Sismondi, *Fall of the Roman Empire*, vol. 1, pp. 66–7.
[109] Sismondi, *Fall of the Roman Empire*, vol. 1, pp. 119, 142.
[110] Sismondi, *Fall of the Roman Empire*, vol. 1, pp. 147–8.
[111] Sismondi, *Fall of the Roman Empire*, vol. 1, p. 156.
[112] Sismondi, *Fall of the Roman Empire*, vol. 1, p. 162.

empire was yet standing, and the independence which characterised her early years was still inviolate to our own time.[113]

And he goes on to spell out the importance of this in his overall historical interpretation:

> The revolution which overthrew the Roman empire, and swept away the ancient forms of civilisation from the earth, made room for new combinations and new social institutions, and led to progress of another kind. It was, perhaps, the most important of all the convulsions which have agitated the human race. It was time for this great change to take place; it was time that the universal languor and feebleness of the soul which lowered the character of humanity should give place to a new principle of virtue, or, at least, to a new principle of action.[114]

For Sismondi, the Western Empire might have survived, but for the stupidity of its last rulers.[115] Turning to their successors, he paints a very varied picture. He begins with the Franks, whom he had already dealt with in much greater detail in the first volume of his *Histoire des Français*. Clovis is presented as a mere captain of the army, like the 'dey of Algiers'.[116] Sismondi notes the *Champ de Mars*, but does not see it as a truly representative institution.[117] In assessing the impact of the Franks, he does not present them as a major force for change—thus, in the division of French historiography he did not side particularly with the Germanists, but his critical view of the social structure of the Roman Empire meant that he was no true Romanist either. For him, the long period of war had naturally ruined many, but '[i]n the rural districts the people remained slaves, as they were before the conquest. They laboured for the proprietor of the estate upon which they happened to work, whether he were Frank or Roman.'[118]

Theodoric in Italy gets a rather better press:

> He consolidated the entire structure of the Germanic liberties of the Goths: their popular judicial proceedings; their laws of Scandinavian origin; their institutions, at once civil and military, which assembled the citizens of the same districts, to deliberate or to judge in time of peace, and to take the field together in time of war.[119]

He attempted to revive Ostrogothic interest in agriculture, giving out land on 'the ancient German tenure of military service'. This did not entail the oppression of the Romans, since the land in question was empty. The Goths, however, proved unable to bring it back into productivity, and therefore Roman estates were divided, or perhaps the Romans gave a third of their crops: as Sismondi notes, this is a point on which Procopius is ambiguous. In general Theodoric preserved Roman liberties,

---

[113] Sismondi, *Fall of the Roman Empire*, vol. 1, pp. 163–4.
[114] Sismondi, *Fall of the Roman Empire*, vol. 1, p. 166.
[115] Sismondi, *Fall of the Roman Empire*, vol. 1, p. 168.
[116] Sismondi, *Fall of the Roman Empire*, vol. 1, p. 186.
[117] Sismondi, *Fall of the Roman Empire*, vol. 1, p. 187.
[118] Sismondi, *Fall of the Roman Empire*, vol. 1, p. 187.
[119] Sismondi, *Fall of the Roman Empire*, vol. 1, p. 194.

leaving much as it had been.[120] Sismondi's favourite political and economic themes are never far from the surface.

As in the *History of the Italian Republics*, law is a central issue.[121] Sismondi notes the Visigothic use of the Theodosian Code. The Ostrogoths

> had promulgated laws of their own, which were not entirely dissimilar from those of the Roman republic…The Burgundians, more rude than the Goths, had retained their national laws, which were certainly less polished than the preceding codes, but equitable in spirit, and equally just to the conquerors and the conquered. The Franks published their laws, which were the most barbarous of all.[122]

By contrast Justinian's Digest is seen as a great flood of light.[123]

Indeed Justinian's reign is seen as one of the most brilliant of periods. Procopius is its worthy historian, and Belisarius (perhaps with an eye to Marmontel or to the growing number of painters who had depicted the Byzantine general) as 'one of the greatest men who ever adorned the annals of the world'.[124] Moreover, because of his encouragement of silk production 'Justinian was the protector of commerce. For the first time in the history of antiquity, we find a government paying some attention to the science of economy…'[125] One is reminded of Sismondi's knowledge of Lyons, with its silk manufacture, and his personal involvement in the organization of trade in Geneva. Yet overall, Justinian's reign is compared to that of Louis XIV, 'which exceeded it in length, and equalled it in glory and disaster'[126]— and this despite the fact that both rulers were wise in their choice of ministers. The cost of Justinian's enthusiasm for building was exorbitant, and did nothing to hold back the barbarians,[127] and his own reconquests led to further destruction.[128] Indeed, the Italians fell under a worse yoke than before.[129] Despite the value of Justinian's legislation, the long-term effect of despotism was such that the citizens no longer possessed enough virtue to defend their rights.[130]

Meanwhile, the Lombards having come to an agreement with the Avars to destroy the Gepids, abandoned their lands on the Danube to their allies and moved into Italy. The Byzantines did nothing to protect the Italian cities, although they did allow the towns to use tax revenue for their own defences. Here Sismondi saw further hints of the origins of the Italian city-state: the *curiae* emerged as the kernels of republican government under the leadership of a local duke or doge. This was the start of a 'happy revolution' unnoticed by the Byzantines.[131] It was a development not just confined to Italy: Sismondi somewhat fancifully traced the origins

[120] Sismondi, *Fall of the Roman Empire*, vol. 1, p. 195.
[121] De Salis, *Sismondi*, p. 342.
[122] Sismondi, *Fall of the Roman Empire*, vol. 1, p. 200.
[123] Sismondi, *Fall of the Roman Empire*, vol. 1, p. 211.
[124] Sismondi, *Fall of the Roman Empire*, vol. 1, p. 212.
[125] Sismondi, *Fall of the Roman Empire*, vol. 1, p. 213.
[126] Sismondi, *Fall of the Roman Empire*, vol. 1, p. 212.
[127] Sismondi, *Fall of the Roman Empire*, vol. 1, p. 213.
[128] Sismondi, *Fall of the Roman Empire*, vol. 1, p. 214.
[129] Sismondi, *Fall of the Roman Empire*, vol. 1, p. 225.
[130] Sismondi, *Fall of the Roman Empire*, vol. 1, p, 232.
[131] Sismondi, *Fall of the Roman Empire*, vol. 1, p. 241.

of the free cities of Catalonia and Aragon to the period of the Byzantine intervention in Spain.[132] He also thought there were equivalent developments in Dalmatia, in North Africa (where they were soon snuffed out by the Arab expansion), and in the Frankish cities of Arles, Marseilles, and Montpellier.[133]

The Lombards themselves entered Italy intending to rule over a land worked by slaves.[134] In the event, however, Sismondi thought that their rule also had the effect of reviving the spirit of social liberty.[135]

> The Lombard kings, who were at first elective, and afterwards hereditary, showed some respect for the liberty of their subjects, whether of Roman or Teutonic origin. Their laws, considered as the laws of a barbarous people, were wise and equal: their dukes, or provincial rulers, early acquired a sentiment of pride and independence, which made them seek support in the affection of their subjects.[136]

Latin remained the language of the kingdom, rural cultivation started again, there was an increase in population, and towns were rebuilt.[137] The equivalent ideas, expressed in Sismondi's *History of the Italian Republics*, would have great resonance within Risorgimento Italy.

His assessment of the Frankish kingdom in the late sixth and seventh centuries was rather more dour. What sense of equality the Frankish warriors once had was eroded when they gained landed possessions, cultivated by slaves, *laeti*, or fiscal dependents. While the Franks did not actually rob the wealthy Romans or reduce them to slavery, what emerged was the rule of the strongest, with weak Franks as well as Romans losing out. The rich became richer and the poor poorer—a pre-industrial application of his *Nouveaux principes*, where he had analysed the tendency of capitalism to put more wealth in the hands of the rich, while impoverishing the worker.[138] 'In less than a century the turbulent democracy of the Franks was transformed into a landed aristocracy of the most oppressive kind.'[139] As for their kings, after Dagobert they were *rois fainéants*, do-nothing kings: 'There was not a Merovingian king that was not a father before the age of fifteen, and decrepit at thirty.'[140] They lived in a state of constant intoxication and were known only for their vices.

On that note, Sismondi closes Book One of his account of the Fall of the Roman Empire. Book Two continues the story up to the tenth century, beginning with the Arab expansion, although it also takes in the history of post-Roman Britain, 'severed from the rest of mankind',[141] but only to provide an introduction to the Viking onslaught on England and the reign of Alfred.

[132] Sismondi, *Fall of the Roman Empire*, vol. 1, p. 242.
[133] Sismondi, *Fall of the Roman Empire*, vol. 1, p. 242.
[134] Sismondi, *Fall of the Roman Empire*, vol. 1, p. 239.
[135] Sismondi, *Fall of the Roman Empire*, vol. 1, p. 242.
[136] Sismondi, *Fall of the Roman Empire*, vol. 1, pp. 258–9.
[137] Sismondi, *Fall of the Roman Empire*, vol. 1, p. 259.
[138] Stewart, 'Sismondi's forgotten ethical critique of early capitalism', pp. 229–31.
[139] Sismondi, *Fall of the Roman Empire*, vol. 1, p. 244.
[140] Sismondi, *Fall of the Roman Empire*, vol. 1, p. 263.
[141] Sismondi, *Fall of the Roman Empire*, vol. 2, p. 176.

As we shall see, Sismondi's interpretation of Merovingian degeneracy has its links with those of the interpretation of another writer, Augustin Thierry, who will concern us in the next chapter. The image of the seventh-century Merovingians apart, Sismondi's interpretation of the Merovingians treads a careful path between the Romanists and Germanists. His general reading of the Fall of Rome, however, is rather more original. Of course, he knew earlier literature on the subject, and he was fully aware of the readings of Montesquieu and Gibbon. As a Swiss republican, he shared many of the former's views of liberty and despotism, but his own political stance differed in his emphasis on economics and social structure—and here one has, of course, to note his own importance as an economic theorist. Like Montesquieu and Mably he saw oppression as an issue, but he went further in seeing it in terms of class—and again there are links with Thierry. So too, Sismondi's views of the development of urban republics may be hopelessly optimistic, but they impress because of his determination to set out the socio-economic underpinning of ancient and early medieval history.

The significance of Sismondi's economic and political theories have increasingly attracted attention in recent decades: outside Italy, however, where the *Histoire des Républiques italiennes* has always held a place of honour, the same cannot be said of his historical writing.[142] Yet in the nineteenth century he was regarded as a titan. His main historical works appeared in German, English, Italian, and Spanish, as well as French, some of them appearing simultaneously in two languages.[143] For Camille Jullian writing at the end of the century, the publication of the first volumes of the *Histoire des Français* was the great historical event of 1821.[144] And de Salis, Sismondi's biographer, estimated that around 1814 he was regarded in England as the leading historian of his age.[145]

In his emphasis on economics and class Sismondi moved the historiography of the Fall of the Roman Empire forward. The subject had not stopped dead with Gibbon. Indeed, Gibbon's impact on the interpretations of the fourth, fifth, and sixth centuries propounded in the generations after the publication of *The Decline and Fall* was remarkably slight. Much of Gibbon's field had already been explored, by the historians of France and by Montesquieu; and much was done in the century after Gibbon's death, not least by Sismondi and subsequently by Fustel de Coulanges. The role played by the Germanic peoples had yet to be come fully to the fore, and yet even there the work of Mascov had covered many of the central questions. We will return to the German contribution to the debates about the Fall of Roman and the period of Germanic migration in due course, but first we need to consider more fully the French and Italian contexts in which Sismondi was writing.

---

[142] One notes the slight attention paid to Sismondi in Nicolet, *La Fabrique d'une nation* and Graceffa, *Les Historiens et la question franque*.

[143] There is an incomplete list of translations in Salis, *Sismondi. Lettres et documents inédits*, pp. 65–7.

[144] De Salis, *Sismondi*, p. 435.   [145] De Salis, *Sismondi*, p. 234.

6

Nation, Class, and Race

6.1 GUIZOT AND GIBBON

The defeat of Napoleon in 1814 saw the initial restoration of the Bourbons, who were every bit as aware of the importance of history as the emperor had been. The constitutional settlement itself looked back to the Frankish past. In the *Charte de 1814*, Louis XVIII, whose image would come to occupy the spot that Napoleon had earmarked for his own in the Panthéon, made clear reference to the old Germanic assemblies: 'We have replaced the ancient Assemblies of the Fields of March and of May and the Chambers of the *Tiers État*, which so often gave proof of their zeal for the interests of the people and of fidelity and respect for the authority of kings, with the Chamber of Deputies.' The Bourbons, however, could not put the clock back. The politico-historical discourse of the eighteenth century, which had revolved around aristocracy and monarchy, came to be reformulated in terms of nation, class and race.[1] The growing emphasis on these issues, and especially the last two of them, in interpretations of the early Middle Ages will occupy us in what follows.

The Restoration, in the eyes of one significant intellectual, François Guizot, marked the reestablishment of constitutional monarchy following a long period in which it had been squeezed out by feudalism and absolutism, a period which had ended in the Revolution and the victory of the *Tiers État* over the nobility and the clergy.[2] Guizot is one of the key voices of the Restoration,[3] reacting against the excesses of the Revolution and of the Empire. His was not the most significant reading of the last years of Rome or beginnings of the Middle Ages, but, as a major political player, he provides an *entrée* into a still-divided intellectual world, which would see major shifts in the reading of the distant past.

Guizot was born in Nîmes in 1787. His father, a lawyer, albeit a liberal, was guillotined in 1794.[4] As a result his mother took the young François to Geneva to be educated. Inspired by Jean-Jacques Rousseau, she insisted on the boy learning a craft (in Guizot's case, carpentry). He also read a good deal, including works by

---

[1] Foucault, *Society Must be Defended*, pp. 215–37.
[2] Nicolet, *La fabrique d'une nation*, pp. 112–13.
[3] Bloch, 'Sur les grandes invasions: quelques positions de problèmes', pp. 99–100.
[4] There is a short and convenient biographical introduction by Hazlitt to his translation of Guizot, *The History of Civilization from the Fall of the Roman Empire to the French Revolution*, vol. 1, pp. vi–vii. The fullest account is Guizot, *Mémoires pour servir à l'histoire de mon temps*. See also Nicolet, *La fabrique d'une nation*, pp. 111–12.

Thucydides, Demosthenes, Cicero, Tacitus, Dante, Alfieri, Schiller, and Goethe, as well as Gibbon.[5] In 1805 he moved to Paris to study law. Four years later, however, he attracted attention by his review, rather more favourable than most,[6] of Chateaubriand's novel, *Les martyrs*—a work to which we will return.

Guizot gained yet further notice with a new translation of Gibbon's *Decline and Fall*, although it appears that a good deal of the work was done by Pauline de Meulan, whom he later married.[7] The translation appeared in 1812—the year in which Guizot was appointed to the chair of Modern History at the Sorbonne. Despite his academic appointment, he was to become rather more of a politician. He served briefly in Louis XVIII's 1814 government before Napoleon's return from Elba: he was thus very much in the opposite camp to that which Sismondi joined. After Waterloo, in 1815–16, he held the post of secretary general of the Ministry of Justice, and in 1819–20 he was *directeur* in the *ministre de l'Intérieure*, a ministry he would enter again in 1830. He lost political office in the reaction following the assassination of the Duc de Berry, the king's nephew, in 1820. For most of the next decade he held no political post, but instead, despite being suspended from teaching at the Sorbonne, he concentrated on his work as a historian. He returned to politics in the 1830s, following the overthrow of the autocratic Charles X, who was in the process of revoking the liberties granted by the *Charte* of 1814. Guizot held a number of offices under the much more liberal 'July monarchy' of Louis-Philippe, including that of *ministre de l'Instruction publique* from 1832 to 1837, and as such he had a major influence on the development of French education. He also played a central role in the physical preservation of France's past, above all in the creation of the *Service des monuments historiques*: in 1834 he appointed Prosper Merimée as general inspector of ancient monuments.[8] Effectively he transformed history into a national institution.[9] Two years later he was elected to the *Académie française*. He was a dominant figure in the government from 1840 to 1848 as *ministre des Affaires étrangères* and subsequently as *président du Conseil*. Despite his liberal credentials, his attempt to ban political meetings was an immediate cause of the 1848 Revolution, and this in turn led to his fall from office, and a short period of exile in England. After his return to France he concentrated on writing. That he was not the easiest of men can be seen in a few devastating lines written by Georg Heinrich Pertz, the editor of the *Monumenta Germaniae Historica*:

> Guizot gave me the impression of a dry, calvinistic professor, who valued learning by its political results. I had before been informed of his character, and succeeding years have exposed his defects. In 1848, in reference to his assumed integrity, he received the appellation in the Chamber of Deputies of "le Tartuffe de l'honnêteté". The sum total

---

[5] Guizot, *History of Civilization*, trans. Hazlitt, vol. 1, p. viii.

[6] For an account of the initial reaction to Chateaubriand's work and of Guizot's review, see de Broglie, *Guizot*, pp. 30–1.

[7] De Salis, *Sismondi*, p. 91, n. 1, and p. 213, attributes the translation entirely to her. See also Johnson, *Guizot*, p. 3.

[8] Den Boer, *History as a Profession*, pp. 61–75.

[9] Gooch, *History and Historians in the Nineteenth Century*, p. 191.

of his philosophy of history was professedly the constant progress of mankind up to the present time, placing himself at the top of the ladder.[10]

Guizot's interest in the Fall of Rome is most apparent in his translation of Gibbon. His notes to *Decline and Fall*, like those of Wenck and Hugo, were incorporated into Milman's new English edition in 1838–9. However, in the preface to the revised edition of his own translation, published in 1828, he compared Gibbon's interpretation of the Fall of Rome unfavourably to Montesquieu's.[11] In all probability, he held a lower opinion of Gibbon in the late 1820s than he had fifteen years earlier.[12]

His own views on the Fall of Rome and the successor states can be found most easily in two books:[13] the *Essais sur l'Histoire de France (pour servir de complèment aux Observations de l'Histoire de France de l'abbé de Mably)* of 1823, and the *Histoire générale de la civilisation en Europe: depuis la chute de l'Empire romain jusqu'à la Révolution* of 1828.[14] The *Essais* were particularly influential in France being adopted *par le conseil royal de l'instruction publique*, as the title page of the seventh edition of 1847 notes—though one should bear in mind the fact that Guizot himself held the office of minister of public instruction. The *History of Civilization* was also read with enthusiasm in England, first appearing in translation in 1837, and again nine years later in a new version by William Hazlitt the younger.[15]

Although these works have a chronological sweep as great, indeed greater than Gibbon's, their format is completely different. They lack any discussion of detail, concentrating instead on what Guizot saw as the major themes. The subtitle of the *Essais sur l'Histoire de France* makes quite clear what are the central issues. Since they were intended to complement Mably, they inevitably focus on political and constitutional matters. An initial essay 'On the municipal government of the Roman Empire in the fifth century AD, at the time of the great invasion of the Germans in the West' presents the very *bourgeois* argument that the Roman Empire collapsed because of the oppression of the Middle Class[16]—an interpretation that has echoes of Sismondi's arguments of the same period. Thereafter, Guizot turns to the origin and establishment of the Franks in Gaul. After a brief discussion of the debates, he presents what is essentially Mably's interpretation, though in Guizot's view eighteenth-century historians had failed to present a balanced picture.[17] He himself thought that the Franks, *Franci*, or, as he interpreted the name, 'free men', emerged

[10] Pertz, *Autobiography*, p. 61.
[11] Guizot, 'Preface to the second edition of his translation', in Gibbon, *Decline and Fall, with Variorum Notes Including Those of Guizot, Wenck, Schreiter, and Hugo*, vol. 1, p. viii.
[12] For the historiographical context in which Guizot was writing, in the 1830s, see Gruner, 'Political historiography in Restoration France', pp. 359–61, 364.
[13] On Guizot as historian, Johnson, *Guizot*, pp. 320–76.
[14] See the comments of Gooch, *History and Historians in the Nineteenth Century*, pp. 188–9.
[15] Guizot, *History of Civilization in Europe*, trans. Hazlitt. The earlier translation (London, 1837) was by Priscilla Maria Beckwith.
[16] Guizot, *Essais sur l'histoire de France*, pp. 1–36. Page references are to the 7th edition (Paris, 1847).
[17] Nicolet, *La fabrique d'une nation*, p. 119.

in the third century. Although some of them served as *laeti* in the Roman army, the majority were raiders. From the reign of Clovis onwards they achieved dominance through their indefatigable energy. Even so, while Clovis himself was 'a barbarian endowed with superior intelligence',[18] Frankish expansion was basically slow and incoherent. After discussing in a third essay the reasons for the fall of the Merovingians and the Carolingians, in the fourth, which constitutes by far the longest section of the book, he embarks on an extended discussion 'Concerning society and political institutions in France under the Merovingians and Carolingians'. The concluding essays are on the nature of the feudal regime and on the origins of representative government in England. A final *résumé* sets out his basic interpretation of what happened at the end of the Roman Empire: the conquered did not have the means to resist, while the conquerors did not have the means to enforce ordered subjection. The resulting need for multiple associations led to the development of feudalism, though this proved to be a weak basis for true government.[19]

Guizot's concerns in his *Histoire générale de la civilisation en Europe* are very different from those expressed in the *Essais*, at least as regards the period of the end of the Roman Empire—even though the geographical region covered is still largely limited to the territory of France. Here he balances three factors: the residual traces of the Roman Empire, which he presents as a largely urban institution,[20] the independence and egotism of the barbarians,[21] which again leads to the institution of feudalism, and the civilizing influence of the Church.[22] We shall return to the subject of early medieval Christianity, and its relation to the Catholic Revival of the nineteenth century. Equally important for Guizot's notion of civilization, however, were questions of liberty and government: above all constitutional monarchy.[23]

6.2 AUGUSTIN THIERRY AND FRANKISH TYRANNY

Despite the popularity of Guizot's works, it can hardly be claimed that he radically altered the understanding of the fall of the Empire and the barbarian invasions, although, like Smyth, his near-contemporary in Cambridge, he did place the period very much at the beginning of the history of modern Europe. Much more dramatic was the impact of Augustin Thierry. Born into a working-class family in Blois in 1795,[24] Thierry established himself entirely through his own abilities. He

---

[18] Guizot, *Essais sur l'histoire de France*, p. 43.
[19] Guizot, *Essais sur l'histoire de France*, p. 348.
[20] Guizot, *History of Civilization in Europe*, p. 29.
[21] Guizot, *History of Civilization in Europe*, p. 41.
[22] Guizot, *History of Civilization in Europe*, pp. 33–9.
[23] Nicolet, *La fabrique d'une nation*, p. 112.
[24] Hazlitt, 'Biographical notice of M. Augustin Thierry', in Thierry, *History of the Conquest of England by the Normans; its Causes, and its Consequences, in England, Scotland, Ireland, and on the Continent*, vol. 1, pp. vii–xvi, speaks of 'poor and humble parents'. For his biography I have followed Hazlitt's account, together with Thierry's 'Autobiographical preface'; Thierry, 'History of my historical works and theories', in Thierry, *The Historical Essays*, pp. vii–xix. For an overview of his role in the debates about the early Franks, see Nicolet, *La fabrique d'une nation*, pp. 115–19, 123–36.

briefly held a post at a college in Compiègne at the age of eighteen, before becoming secretary of the radical political philosopher Saint-Simon. In 1817 he left Saint-Simon to write for *Le Censeur européen*, one of a group of new radical journals that appeared after 1814, and when that was closed down two years later he transferred to *Le Courrier français*.

In 1817 *Le Censeur* published a number of angry responses to Montlosier's onslaught on the 'roturier' class.[25] Some of the earliest of these responses were concerned not with what Montlosier had argued about the Migration Period, but rather with the twelfth century, which for him (as for Boulainvilliers) had been a period of disaster for the old nobility. In Montlosier's view, the Crusades were a time of mass enfranchisement, and since the newly enfranchised were more inclined to subservience, the monarchy used them to further its own power. At the same time, interest in trade and commerce came to overshadow any commitment to agriculture and war. The growing urban classes began to criticize the nobility as tyrants, and set in motion the developments that would culminate in the French Revolution.[26]

This interpretation was quickly challenged by Charles Comte. His 'Considérations sur l'état moral de la nation française' was published in *Le Censeur européen* in 1817, followed quickly, the same year, with 'De l'organisation sociale'.[27] At the same time Augustin Thierry contributed a volume to Saint-Simon's *L'industrie littéraire et scientifique liguée avec l'industrie commerciale et manufacturière*.[28] There Thierry accepted Montlosier's emphasis on the twelfth century, but he saw the liberation of the communes—which he placed in a broader European context—in a positive light, since it benefitted the working man:

> The character of the peoples of antiquity was essentially military. What peaceable work there was was rejected by the members of the tribe (*nation*) and given over to slaves. The great industry was war: the sword was a means of production, and the riches of the state and of the individual were increased by the sword.
>
> This order of things ought to have come to an end with the moral state that produced and maintained it: another should have succeeded it, in accordance with the change in self-conduct that replaced the old tendency that a man had to throw his weight around. The change took place in the twelfth century.
>
> Through the general liberation of communes throughout Europe, peaceable industry, which among the Ancients had been outside the state, entered the state and became an active part, from having previously been passive.
>
> Associated with this change were, at one and the same time, the era of the liberty of services and that of peace, which became a political objective: two changes from which

---

[25] Gruner, 'Political historiography in Restoration France', p. 350. Since the word *roturier* is central to Thierry's writing, I have tended to leave it in French. Nineteenth-century English translations use the word 'plebeian'. A modern translation might be 'commoner'.

[26] Montlosier's argument is summarized by Gruner, 'Political historiography in Restoration France', pp. 348–9.

[27] Gruner, 'Political historiography in Restoration France', p. 353.

[28] Drolet, 'Industry, class and society', p. 1245.

came all the revolutions that have occurred in Europe, and from this will come those which have not yet taken place.[29]

The broader European picture of a communal revolution referred to by Thierry was already appearing in Sismondi's work on the Italian city-states, the first volumes of which had been published in 1807.[30]

Thierry would soon turn his attention more firmly to the early Merovingian period. In the 'Autobiographical preface' to his *Historical Essays*, which appeared in 1834, he described the new direction taken by his research in 1819:

> My attention, hitherto absorbed by theories of social order, by questions of government and political economy, was directed with great curiosity to the disorder which, in the sixth century, succeeded Roman civilization in a great portion of Europe. I thought I perceived in that remote subversion, the roots of some of the evil belonging to modern society; it appeared to me that, notwithstanding the distance of time, some remains of the barbarian conquest still weighed upon our country, and that the present sufferings might be traced back, step by step, to the intrusion of a foreign race into the centre of Gaul, and its violent dominion over the natives.[31]

Thierry then sets out the steps he took to uncover the sixth-century past. He read as much as he could on the French monarchy and the institutions of the Middle Ages, 'from the researches of Pasquier, Fauchet, and other learned men of the sixteenth century, down to the work of Mably, and that of M. de Montlosier, the most recent one, at that time, on the subject'.[32] He read all the legal texts, and then found relief in Ducange's *Glossary*, and was enthused 'to trace this semi-Roman, semi-barbarous language to its root'. As a result 'I studied the ancient Germanic and Scandinavian idioms, aided by my knowledge of German and modern English'.[33] At the same time he was working on the history of England, and especially on the Restoration of 1660 and the Revolution of 1688. The work that he produced on these showed, to his mind, the initial results of his new researches, in that, for the first time he attempted 'to leave to every epoch its originality'.[34] That is, he intended to describe each period in its own terms, giving it its own flavour. This would have its greatest impact on the extraordinary narrative writing of the *Récits mérovingiens*.[35]

Meanwhile, his studies of English history took him back to the Anglo-Saxon period, and especially to the work of Sharon Turner, where once again he came across a history of Germanic conquest[36]—a subject that in fact takes up very little of Turner's narrative, since the Migration Period attracted less interest in

[29] Thierry, *L'industrie littéraire et scientifique*, pp. 27–30.
[30] de Lollis, *Alessandro Manzoni e gli storici liberali francesi della restaurazione*, p. 15.
[31] Thierry, 'Autobiographical preface', in Thierry, *The Historical Essays*, p. ix.
[32] Thierry, 'Autobiographical preface', p. ix.
[33] Thierry, 'Autobiographical preface', p. ix.
[34] Thierry, 'Autobiographical preface', p. x.
[35] See Rigney, *Imperfect Histories*, pp. 82–8, on the *Récits*.
[36] Thierry, 'Autobiographical preface', p. x.

England than did either the conversion of the Anglo-Saxons or the Norman Conquest.[37] On the other hand, in giving space to literary texts like *Beowulf*, Turner had attempted to present the Anglo-Saxons on their own terms. Thierry next directed his attention to Irish history, and to another tale of 'two inimical nations on the same soil', and from Ireland he turned to Scotland. What inspired him most there was not straightforward books of history, but the narratives of Walter Scott, and above all—moving back to English history—Scott's picture of England after the Norman Conquest as set out in *Ivanhoe*.[38] Alongside *Ivanhoe*, and for its image of early Frankish history perhaps more important, there was Chateaubriand's *Les martyrs*—a work that had entranced Thierry in 1810[39]—in which the uncouth Franks have a role to play.[40] With all this ammunition he turned to Bouquet's great collection of medieval sources, the *Recueil des historiens des Gaules et de la France*, and then set out, in his own words, 'to plant for France in the nineteenth century the standard of historical reform'.[41] A footnote points out that 'No portion of the *Histoire des Français*, by M. de Sismondi had then appeared'—although his work on the Italian republics was already in full flow.

Thierry set out his new ideas in a series of 'Letters' on French history, which he sent to *Le Courrier français*, since by this time *Le Censeur européen* had fallen victim to the wave of censorship which followed the assassination of the Duc de Berry. Not only were these letters intended to illustrate the most up-to-date standards of historical writing: they also claimed history for the working class:

> Born a plebeian [*roturier*], I demanded that the common people should have their share in the glory of our annals; that the memory of plebeian honour, of the energy and liberty of citizens, should be preserved with respectful care; in a word, that, by the help of science, joined to patriotism, narratives capable of moving the popular fibre should be made from our old chronicles.[42]

Nothing could be further from Montlosier's reading of French history, even though, in his adherence to a Germanist, rather than a Romanist interpretation of early medieval history, Thierry's views were closer to those of Montlosier and, before him, Boulainvilliers, than to those of Du Bos.

Perhaps not surprisingly, his work instantly fell foul of the censor. His 'True history of Jacques Bonhomme', an account of the whole history of France condensed into a few pages, told through the eyes of a *roturier*, was censored in its entirety, though Thierry insisted on the inked-out pages appearing in print. It was not long,

---

[37] Turner, *The History of the Anglo-Saxons*; Turner, *The History of the Manners, Landed Property, Laws, Poetry, Literature, Religion, and Language of the Anglo-Saxons*. On the conversion period see also Lingard, *The Antiquities of the Anglo-Saxon Church*.

[38] Thierry, 'Autobiographical preface', p. xi. On Thierry and Scott, see Banti, 'Le invasioni barbariche e l'origine delle nazione', pp. 28–32; Leerssen, *National Thought in Europe*, p. 206.

[39] Thierry, 'Preface to the narratives', in Thierry, *The Historical Essays*, pp. 111–12.

[40] Thom, *Republics, Nations and Tribes*, p. 254.

[41] Thierry, 'Autobiographical preface', p. xii.

[42] Thierry, 'Autobiographical preface', p. xii.

however, before *Le Courrier* took fright at the length of some of his submissions, and as a result, after only a year, he stopped publishing in its pages.[43]

Initially he turned to writing a history of the Norman conquest of England, and his *Histoire de la Conquête de l'Angleterre par les Normands* appeared to great acclaim in 1825.[44] It combined the imaginative style that Thierry had learnt from Scott, with a careful reading of Anglo-Saxon and Anglo-Norman sources, developed under the watchful eye of Claude Charles Fauriel. The latter, who was the lover of Mme de Condorcet, had been secretary to Fouché, Napoleon's minister of police and an old acquaintance of Montlosier's, but he had also been drawn into Mme de Staël's circle. In 1830, following the July Revolution, he was appointed Professor of Foreign Literature at the Sorbonne. Six years later he published four volumes on the *Histoire de la Gaule méridionale sous la domination des conquérants germains*. These provided a remarkably detailed study of the South of France from the fifth century to the ninth. Fauriel did not have a positive view of the barbarians. First they destroyed the Roman Empire and then they persecuted the population, even though the clergy had initially thought well of them.[45] What is most striking about his reading, however, is not Fauriel's historical reconstruction, but his emphasis on language and literature. In his emphasis on linguistics he was following the new methodological approaches of Wilhelm von Humbolt.[46]

Given Thierry's political affiliations, the *History of the Norman Conquest* inevitably offered an interpretation that prioritizes ideas of liberty and democracy. In the course of writing, however, his eyesight started to fail: it would not be long before he was both blind and crippled.[47] It is hard not to be moved by his own description of his physical condition. Despite his illness, with the help of an amanuensis he revised his *History of the English Conquest*, and gathered together a collection of essays under the title *Dix Ans d'Études Historiques*. At the same time, though blind, he was producing a set of articles for the *Revue des Deux Mondes*. First appearing in 1829, the journal was to publish some of the most important essays on early medieval history in the course of the nineteenth century. Thierry's articles were gathered together under the title *Récits des Temps Mérovingiens* in 1840.[48] Meanwhile, in 1835, Guizot appointed him to head a project aimed at editing the charters granted to towns and communes by kings and nobles: four volumes of the *Recueil des monuments inédits de l'histoire du Tiers État* appeared.[49]

The *Récits mérovingiens* are scarcely the most sophisticated of Thierry's writings, though their Scott-like narratives are underpinned by an extremely learned set of notes, compiled despite the author's blindness. His adoption of a format close to that of a novel may have derived from Volney, who had argued for the presentation

---

[43] Thierry, 'Autobiographical preface', p. xiii.
[44] Thierry, 'Autobiographical preface', p. xvi.
[45] Fauriel, *Histoire de la Gaule méridionale sous la domination des conquérants Germains*, vol. 1, pp. 442–3, 581–2.
[46] Espagne, 'Claude Fauriel et l'Allemagne', p. 16.
[47] Thierry, 'Autobiographical preface', p. xvi.
[48] Both sets of essays are collected in the English translation under the title *The Historical Essays*.
[49] Den Boer, *History as a Profession*, p. 68.

of textbooks in such a form in the 1790s,[50] as much as from Scott. The result was that their message was widely accessible. They make rather less of the question of class than had his earlier works,[51] but that was an inevitable result of concentrating on the evidence provided by Gregory of Tours, whose narrative, concentrating as it does on the deeds of kings, queens, and bishops, does not afford much opportunity for a full description of the *roturiers*. The tales of Sigebert and Brunhild, and more especially of Chilperic and Fredegund did, however, allow Thierry to set out an image of the barbarous Frank: here, for a wide audience, was a depiction of the class of conquerors, seen at their most brutish. His vision of them was much like Fauriel's. This reading of the Franks would have a huge impact, not just because of Thierry's words: the *Récits* were reissued in the 1880s with illustrations by the artist Jean-Paul Laurens.[52] Laurens was among those who were involved in the decoration of the Panthéon under the Second Empire.[53] He, like others, was inspired by Thierry's writings to paint the Merovingians—and his images were by no means the most barbarous.

Marx recognized the importance of the historiography of the 1820s and 30s: writing to his friend Weydemeyer in 1852 he stated that democratic gentlemen 'should study the historical works of Thierry, Guizot, John Wade, and others in order to enlighten themselves as to the past "history of classes".'[54] Wade was the author of a *History of the Middle and Working Classes*, an obvious source of inspiration, which was published in 1833. Yet Marx also recognized the importance of the historical work of Thierry and Guizot, much of which focused on the French Middle Ages. The issue of class, which had, of course, been implicit in the eighteenth-century debates about conquerors and conquered, had been made central by those reacting to Montlosier.

6.3 AMÉDÉE THIERRY AND HIS GAULISH ANCESTORS

In 1844 Augustin Thierry's wife, who had come to play a major role in organizing her husband's life, died: four years later the Revolution of 1848 led to the collapse of the July monarchy, of which Thierry had been a great supporter. He died in 1856, though his major works had been written some twenty years earlier. He was survived by his brother Amédée, who was also a significant historian, and a local and national politician of note, becoming *préfet de la Haute-Saône* under the July monarchy in 1830, a post he continued to hold until 1838. From then until 1860

---

[50] Thom, *Republics, Nations and Tribes*, p. 43.

[51] A point noted by de Lollis, *Alessandro Manzoni e gli storici liberali francesi*, p. 145: 'Ma, insomma, dai Récits lasciò fuori—lui, l'Omero dei proletari—proprio Jacques Bonhomme.'

[52] Many of them are conveniently reproduced in Murray, *Gregory of Tours: the Merovingians*.

[53] Wood, 'The Panthéon in Paris.'

[54] *Karl Marx-Friedrich Engels Gesamtausgabe, Dritte Abteilung, Briefwechsel*, vol. 5, p. 75, trans. in Foucault, *Society must be defended*, p. 85, n.6. Foucault himself misquotes on p. 79. See also Nicolet, *La fabrique d'une nation*, p. 119.

he was *maître des requêtes* at the *Conseil d'État*. Based in Paris he was able to help his ailing brother, and was indeed present when the younger Hazlitt visited.

Augustin refers to his brother's work in his 'Autobiographical preface'. Writing of the year 1828, he says: 'My brother Amédée Thierry was then finishing his history of the Gauls, one of those works of great and conscientious erudition, in which original documents are exhausted and which remain the last result of science. He was going to give the public one half of the *prologomena* of the history of France, the Celtic origin, the picture of Gallic migrations and that of Gaul under the Roman administration. I undertook for my share the other half, that is, the German origin, and the picture of the great invasions which caused the downfall of the Roman empire in the west.'[55] As it was, Augustin's blindness prevented him from fulfilling his part of the scheme.

Amédée is best known for his half of this intended diptych: his *Histoire des Gaulois, depuis les temps les plus reculés jusqu'à l'entière soumission de la Gaule à la dominance romaine*, published initially in 1828, was a massive success, running to ten editions by 1877.[56] It played a major role in spreading the notion of 'nos ancêtres les Gaulois'. As the title suggests, Thierry's interest in the Gauls was focused on the period up to the Roman domination—many of those who had worked on the subject up until his day had likewise concentrated on the period before and up to the Roman conquest.[57] Amédée also took up one part of the portion of the material that his brother had intended to cover: in 1856 he published his *Histoire d'Attila et de ses successeurs*, a work which shows an extraordinary knowledge of eastern Europe, and especially of Hungary. It attracted the attention of, among others, Napoleon III, who consulted him over the site of the battle of the Catalaunian Plains[58]—one might guess with an eye to some monument equivalent to that erected at Alésia in 1865, commemorating Vercingetorix. For all his posturing, Louis Napoleon made a sincere attempt to underpin his monumental projects with scientific research. He even handed over the palace of Saint-Germain-en-Laye to house a national archaeological museum.[59]

Thierry's *Attila* was a major historical work, which drew not just on the sources of the fourth, fifth, and sixth centuries, but which also followed the presentation of the Huns in later legend. Although now totally superseded, it marks a significant step in the interpretation of the impact of nomadic peoples on the history of Europe, covering not just the Huns, but also the Avars, and indeed the other peoples of the western steppes. In many ways, however, it was not as important for the development of the historiography of the early Middle Ages, or indeed of historiography in general, as his *Histoire des Gaulois*,[60] for it was this work that lay at the heart of the association between physiology and history.[61]

---

[55] Thierry, 'Autobiographical preface', p. xviii.
[56] Lacoste, 'Les Gaulois d'Amédée Thierry', p. 204.
[57] See Volpilhac, 'Les Gaulois à l'Académie des Inscriptions et Belles-Lettres de 1701 à 1793', and Balcou, 'La Tour d'Auvergne, théoricien breton du mythe gaulois'.
[58] The correspondence is printed in Thierry, *Histoire d'Attila*, 5th edn, vol. 2, pp. 428–37.
[59] Nicolet, *La fabrique d'une nation*, pp. 162, 173; den Boer, *History as a Profession*, pp. 78–85.
[60] Thierry, *Histoire des Gaulois*.
[61] Piguet, 'Race chez Amédée Thierry et William F. Edwards', p. 93.

In 1829 William F. Edwards wrote his *Des caractères physiologiques des races considérés dans leurs rapports avec l'histoire: lettre à M. Amédée Thierry auteur de l'histoire des Gaulois*. Edwards had been born to English parents in Jamaica in 1776, but following the slave revolts on the island his family moved first to England, then to Belgium and finally France, where he became a naturalized citizen in 1828. This somewhat traumatic early life had an impact on him. His personal experience in the Caribbean left him sensitized to issues of race. He was, however, also a scientist, and perhaps not surprisingly he came to study race from a scientific point of view.[62] Edwards picked up on the notion of race as expressed by the Thierry brothers. As we have seen, because the model of a race of conquerors and a race of conquered was so widely diffused, the concept of race in French historiography overlapped considerably with that of class.[63] For Amédée Thierry this overlap was less historically important than it was for his brother. Because he was interested primarily in the Gauls before they were subjected to the rule of the invading Franks, he had little to offer to the debate on the end of Roman Gaul. He was more concerned to define the Gauls as a race and to place them within his scheme of Celtic peoples. To do this he resorted to a combination of the historical narratives and philology.[64] Edwards took up this model, and recast it from the perspective of the natural sciences, drawing especially on the science of physiology. He thus opened up a Pandora's box, in which physical characteristics could be linked to the historical evidence for tribes or nations. Edwards' idea that the history of the distant past could be combined with physiology within the scientific study of race was potentially extremely dangerous. Nor was the 'scientific' study of race confined to France: there was a growing body of thought in England and America which was attempting to place the interpretation of race on a 'scientific' footing, and which was also looking back to the Migration Period, and was finding there evidence of Teutonic superiority.[65]

6.4 GAULS AND GERMANS: MICHELET AND *LA NATION*

While the Thierry brothers had hoped to write parallel accounts of the Gauls and Franks, which were intended to be a *prologomenon* to the history of France, Jules Michelet succeeded in not only writing that prologue, but also in taking the history right down to the Revolution. Michelet, who was born in 1798, was the son

---

[62] Blanckaert, 'On the origins of French ethnology: William Edwards and the Doctrine of Race', pp. 18–55.

[63] On the related terminology of class and race, Piguet, 'Race chez Amédée Thierry et William F. Edwards', pp. 94–6. Also, on the importance of Amédée Thierry for the distinction between nation and race, Seliger, 'Race-thinking during the Restoration', p. 281, with n. 56.

[64] Piguet, 'Race chez Amédée Thierry et William F. Edwards', pp. 97–9. See also Seliger, 'Race-thinking during the Restoration', p. 278.

[65] For the development of ideas of race in Britain and America prior to Gobineau, Horsman, 'Origins of Racial Anglo-Saxonism in Great Britain before 1850'. For the development of those ideas in the mid-nineteenth century see below, chapter 11.

of a printer, but received a fine education at the Lycée Charlemagne. In 1830 he was appointed to a chair of history, as a deputy to Guizot, at the Sorbonne. In 1838 he became professor at the Collège de France, but his hostility to the imperial ideals of Napoleon III lost him his post in 1851, and he thereafter made his living as a writer.[66]

Volume one of Michelet's *Histoire de France* is very much an introduction to his overall interpretation, for he only placed the fusion of what he saw as the country's two dominant races, the Gauls and the Germans, in the tenth century. For him the cause of that fusion was the land of France itself. As he explained in the preface to the 1869 edition of his *Histoire*, 'Less selective than Thierry, and downplaying the issue of race, I have especially stressed the geographical element of local influences, and, at the same time, the general labour of the nation which was in the process of creating, of making itself.'[67] *La France* itself was thus central to Michelet. As we shall see, at much the same time the geography of Germany was also at the heart of historical argument—in fact rather more so, not least because of the changing nature of the *Reich*, and the need to establish its boundaries.

In placing the creation of the French nation in the Capetian period, Michelet effectively minimized the importance of the end of the Roman Empire and its aftermath, though he did pause to explain that the chief cause of the fall of the Empire was slavery. The Roman conquest had led to the destruction of the class of small landowners, and to their replacement with slaves: and since the slaves themselves died as a result of their labours, they had to be replaced with yet more.[68] This view of the evils of the Roman social structure was not particularly new—it is a variant of the interpretation offered by, among others, both Sismondi and Guizot—although the precise emphasis on slavery is striking. When it came to describing the Frankish take-over of Gaul, Michelet was content simply to quote large hunks of Guizot.[69]

He was rather more concerned to describe the national genius of both the Celts (who he saw as warlike)[70] and the Germans (lovers of sport and drink, as well as being inclined to acts of vengeance).[71] As he explained, his view of the Germanic peoples was inspired primarily by his reading of Jacob Grimm's *Deutsche Rechts-altertümer* of 1828.[72] Michelet's view of the Celts, or more specifically that of the Gauls, was derived largely from Amédée Thierry, though for the late and post Roman periods he had to turn to Sismondi.[73] He did, however, take a rather different line from Sismondi, who saw only decadence, emphasizing instead what he

[66] Den Boer, *History as a Profession*, p. 115.
[67] Michelet, *Histoire de France*: new edition, vol. 1 (Paris, 1881), p. 21. For Michelet's view of race, Graceffa, 'Race mérovingienne et nation française: les paradoxes du moment romantique dans l'historiographie française de 1815 à 1860', pp. 65–9.
[68] Michelet, *Histoire de France*, vol. 1, pp. 146–7.
[69] Michelet, *Histoire de France*, vol. 1, pp. 260–3.
[70] Michelet, *Histoire de France*, vol. 1, p. 48; Croisille, 'Michelet et les Gaulois ou les séductions de la patrie celtique', p. 212.
[71] Michelet, *Histoire de France*, vol. 1, p. 277.
[72] Michelet, *Histoire de France*, vol. 1, p. 21.
[73] Croisille, 'Michelet et les Gaulois ou les séductions de la patrie celtique', p. 214.

regarded as the continuing creativity of the Gauls, even in the Roman and post-Roman periods.[74] Above all, he pointed to the influence of the Church—and here, despite his hostility to Catholic rightwing historiography, Michelet was no doubt following Chateaubriand.[75] Indeed, for Michelet the Church's primacy substituted for that of the Empire.[76] He saw it as having an improving influence on the Germanic peoples after their arrival—though in time it became contaminated.[77] He even argued that in the Rule of St Benedict the free labour of monks took the place of slavery.[78] In his view there was something especially notable about the role of Celts in the Church: he stressed the free personality of Pelagius, and later of John Scottus Eriugena.[79] Rather more fancifully, he also attributed what he saw as the special quality of Celtic Christianity to its supposed preservation of traits of druidism.[80] The significance of the role of the Irish would be dealt in a rather more scholarly manner by Frédéric Ozanam and by Montalembert, as we shall see.

6.5 *LES RACES HUMAINES*: GOBINEAU

Many of the issues raised by the debates over the Gauls and their Frankish conquerors would be drawn into what proved to be a singularly dangerous work published between 1853 and 1856: the *Essai sur l'inégalité des races humaines* by Joseph Arthur comte de Gobineau.[81] Indeed Hannah Arendt described the author as the 'last heir of Boulainviller [*sic*]'.[82] The historical content of his work has been placed in the intellectual line that runs through Boulainvilliers, Du Bos, Montesquieu, Sieyès, Montlosier, Chateaubriand, and Augustin Thierry.[83] Gobineau's concept of the aristocratic Aryan race draws on a reformulation of the presentation of the Frankish conquest in terms of conquering and conquered classes.[84] In his emphasis on race he has been seen as the heir to the Thierry brothers, Edwards, and to Victor Courtet de l'Isle,[85] though their politics differed radically from his, and unlike Gobineau they were largely in favour of racial mixing or miscegenation. Not that Gobineau was unique in his view of the superiority of pure blood.[86]

---

[74] Croisille, 'Michelet et les Gaulois ou les séductions de la patrie celtique', p. 214.
[75] Graceffa, *Les Historiens et la question franque*, p. 67.
[76] Michelet, *Histoire de France*, vol. 1, p. 161.
[77] Michelet, *Histoire de France*, vol. 1, p. 312.
[78] Michelet, *Histoire de France*, vol. 1, pp. 161–2.
[79] Michelet, *Histoire de France*, vol. 1, p. 162; Croisille, 'Michelet et les Gaulois ou les séductions de la patrie celtique', p. 215.
[80] Michelet, *Histoire de France*, vol. 1, p 164; Croisille, 'Michelet et les Gaulois ou les séductions de la patrie celtique', p. 215.
[81] On Gobineau's dependence on the debates about French history, Biddiss, *Father of Racist Ideology*, pp. 105–6.
[82] Arendt, *The Origins of Totalitarianism*, 2nd edn, pp. 171–2.
[83] Biddiss, *Father of racist ideology*, p. 106.
[84] Biddiss, *Father of racist ideology*, p. 164.
[85] See Lorcin's review of White, *Children of the French Empire*, p. 1508.
[86] See Horsman, 'Origins of racial Anglo-Saxonism in Great Britain before 1850', pp. 405–7, on the views of Robert Knox, whose *Races of Men* appeared in 1850.

Like many of the reactionaries whose writings covered early medieval history, Gobineau was a minor aristocrat, from a family that opposed both the Revolution and Napoleon.[87] He entered political life with the backing of Alexis de Tocqueville, and had some experience as a diplomat in Switzerland before he wrote the *Essai sur l'inégalité des races humaines*. He would subsequently hold diplomatic posts in Persia, Greece, Newfoundland, Brazil, and Sweden.[88] His experiences led him to modify his ideas on certain points of detail, but not his overall interpretation.[89] Yet even the views expressed in the *Essai* were not those of a xenophobe. Rather, he was a 'social pessimist', who had a fatalistic view of the development of society, which in his opinion was in an advanced state of decay, which he sought to explain in terms of racial degeneration caused above all by miscegenation.[90] Gobineau's awareness of decay, like that possessed by Boulainvilliers, derived from his sense of the denial of proper status to the nobility.[91] It was also influenced by his views of the French Revolution and his personal observation of the Revolutions of 1848 in Switzerland and Germany as well as France.[92] In the aftermath of the disasters of 1870 he would describe the ruling bourgeoisie, also within the framework laid down by Boulainvilliers, as the descendents of Gallo-Roman slaves.[93] The opinions that he formed he underpinned with his considerable knowledge, especially of ancient and medieval history, as well as oriental studies.[94] Gobineau certainly had a considerable amount of information at his disposal. On the other hand, despite his claim to be attempting to create scientific history, his knowledge of science seems to have been largely second hand.[95]

His racial theory, which is set out in the opening book of the *Essai sur l'inégalité des races humaines* is supported by his view that human history saw a succession of great civilizations, each of which had been initiated by a white, Aryan, race. Here he adopted the linguistic term that had been introduced in the late eighteenth century by the philologist Sir William Jones, who had been the first to argue for the existence of a family of languages related to Sanskrit. Among the groups that Gobineau saw as Aryan were the Hindus, Iranians, Hellenes, Celts, Slavs, and the

---

[87] For Gobineau's family, Biddiss, *Father of Racist Ideology*, pp. 11–13, 45. For a brief narrative of his life, Richard, 'Arthur de Gobineau'. There is also a useful introduction to his life and thought in Gobineau, *Mademoiselle Irnois and Other Stories*, trans. and ed. Smith and Smith, pp. 1–34, On the assertion that his mother and wife were both créole, see Biddiss, *Father of Racist Ideology*, p. 45, who questions the likelihood that this was the case, and suggests it derives from Gobineau's alienation from both women.

[88] On Gobineau as diplomat, Biddiss, *Father of Racist Ideology*, pp. 181–206, 225–33.

[89] Biddiss, *Father of Racist Ideology*, pp. 181, 247.

[90] Biddiss, *Father of Racist Ideology*, *passim*, but esp. pp. 173–7. On the point that his main concerns were social and political as much as racial, pp. 132, 154–5, 172.

[91] Biddiss, *Father of Racist Ideology*, p. 165.

[92] Biddiss, *Father of Racist Ideology*, p. 92: pp. 139–50 on the more general issue of Gobineau's alienation from the modern world.

[93] Biddiss, *Father of Racist Ideology*, p. 214.

[94] For his views of the Hindu caste system, Biddiss, *Father of Racist Ideology*, p. 165.

[95] Gobineau, *Madame Irnois*, p. 17. For Gobineau's later reading of Darwin, Biddiss, *Father of Racist Ideology*, pp. 246–8.

Germans.[96] Of these the last to dominate Europe was the Aryan-German race, which came to the fore with the Fall of the Roman Empire.[97]

The sixth book of the *Essai sur l'inégalité des races humaines* is made up of a series of chapters examining the peoples of 'la civilisation occidentale'. Gobineau begins with the Slavs, taking their history way back into the prehistoric past.[98] He then looks at the arrival of the Germanic Aryans. He tries to trace the movement of the Aryan Germans to Scandinavia and that of Kymbri to Gaul.[99] Having reached the Migration Period, he describes the Goths,[100] the slightly less 'pure' Vandals,[101] and the 'purer' Lombards and Burgundians.[102] Of the Aryans who migrated from Scandinavia, it was the Anglo-Saxons in his view who had best preserved their purity.[103] Looking back on the period as a whole he noted that 'from this deployment of ethnic principles the whole organization of modern history must have resulted'.[104]

At this point Gobineau provides a description of the 'capacité des nations germaniques', where he explains that the physiognomy or capacity of a people is more important than its vices or virtues: for him a nation's capacity to act, which he describes elsewhere in terms of its vigour or energy, was what mattered. He explains that while the Aryan is not always the best of men, he is the most enlightened with regard to what he is doing, being superior to others in intelligence and energy.[105] He explains how an Aryan, once he saw someone with the right qualities, was happy to offer himself *in commendatio* (essentially to provide military service)[106]— a clear indication that he understood Germanic commendation in much the same positive way as did Montlosier.[107] However, he made a distinction between Germanic social structure outside and inside the Roman Empire. Once inside the Empire the position of the *jarl* (the word he uses for warleader) and the *arimann* (warrior) declined as a result of the development of a military kingship.[108] Gobineau insists on using these terms, the former Scandinavian and the latter Germanic, regardless of the appropriateness of the context. The *arimann* became nothing more than a rural landowner, preferring to live in the country than in a town[109]—again much in line with Montlosier's interpretation.

[96] Biddiss, *Father of Racist Ideology*, p. 120.   [97] Biddiss, *Father of Racist Ideology*, p. 122.

[98] Gobineau, *Essai sur l'inégalité des races humaines*, 4th edn, vol. 2, pp. 311–42.

[99] Gobineau, *Essai sur l'inégalité des races humaines*, vol. 2, pp. 343–6.

[100] Gobineau, *Essai sur l'inégalité des races humaines*, vol. 2, pp. 354–6.

[101] Gobineau, *Essai sur l'inégalité des races humaines*, vol. 2, p. 356.

[102] Gobineau, *Essai sur l'inégalité des races humaines*, vol. 2, p. 357.

[103] Gobineau, *Essai sur l'inégalité des races humaines*, vol. 2, p. 358.

[104] Gobineau, *Essai sur l'inégalité des races humaines*, vol. 2, p. 362.

[105] Gobineau, *Essai sur l'inégalité des races humaines*, vol. 2, pp. 363–34.

[106] Gobineau, *Essai sur l'inégalité des races humaines*, vol. 2, p. 376. On Gobineau's admiration for the Germanic, and the Roman, army, and on the influence of the existing French debates on the impact of the armies at the end of the Roman period, Biddiss, *Father of racist ideology*, pp. 162–3, but on his sense that modern warfare was no longer admirable, ibid. p 210.

[107] Montlosier, *De la monarchie française*, vol. 1, pp. 35–8.

[108] Gobineau, *Essai sur l'inégalité des races humaines*, vol. 2, p. 383. He would later claim that his family descended from that of Ottar *jarl*: Biddiss, *Father of Racist Theory*, pp. 229–30.

[109] Gobineau, *Essai sur l'inégalité des races humaines*, vol. 2, p. 386.

Having described the 'capacité' of the Aryans, Gobineau returns to a rough narrative of the Later Roman Empire. Whereas Montesquieu, among other interpreters of Rome's decline, had decried the Germanization of the army in the third century, Gobineau saw it as a positive development, which he linked to the appointment of the son of a Goth, Maximinus, as emperor:

> From this moment the Germanic essence eclipses all others in Romanity. It animates the legions, takes over high military office, makes decisions in sovereign counsels.... The spirit of *jarls*, war-leaders, takes hold of practical government, and one can already say with justification that Rome is germanised.[110]

For Gobineau the Germans did everything than had been done before, but more intensely, even persecute. (He perhaps had Fauriel's views in mind.) One result of this Germanization in the third century was that the invasions of the fourth occurred when the Empire was already German.[111] This meant that there had already been a mixture of races. It would have been better if the Goths had not entered the Empire, but had remained pure in order to conquer it later, and exploit it, much as the French were exploiting Algeria.[112] This, it might be noted, is one of the few moments when Gobineau presents the France of his own day as not being in decline.

As it was, Germanic groups entered the Empire and were offered land, which in turn led to those still outside wanting to come in. It also led to growing levels of suspicion between Germans and Romans.[113] Despite this, the Germans did not destroy the Empire: rather there was a coincidence of Roman and Germanic tradition.[114] The Germanic *konungr*, as Gobineau insisted on calling the king using the Old Norse term, developed into a perpetual war-leader, who was at the same time recognized by the Romans as a magistrate.[115] Meanwhile, from having had no land, since Germanic tradition did not recognize such ownership, the Merovingians now had imperial estates, which they could distribute, creating a new system of tenure in the *beneficium* (benefice).[116]

The Germans thus came to protect Roman civilization, but not Roman unity.[117] They regularized their own laws, in parallel with those of Rome.[118] As a result of all this, they upheld the Roman Empire for four centuries, until the seventh, while at the same time eliminating the office of emperor. The existence of a despotic state

---

[110] Gobineau, *Essai sur l'inégalité des races humaines*, vol. 2, pp. 408–9. He is citing Amédée Thierry, *Revue des Deux-Mondes*, 15 July 1854: 'La Pannonie et la Mœsie romaines..., furent, aux IIIe et IVe siècles, la pépinière des légions, et par les légions, celle des Césars.'

[111] Gobineau, *Essai sur l'inégalité des races humaines*, vol. 2, p. 410.

[112] Gobineau, *Essai sur l'inégalité des races humaines*, vol. 2, p. 414.

[113] Gobineau, *Essai sur l'inégalité des races humaines*, vol. 2, pp. 415–6.

[114] Gobineau, *Essai sur l'inégalité des races humaines*, vol. 2, p. 421.

[115] Gobineau, *Essai sur l'inégalité des races humaines*, vol. 2, p. 421.

[116] Gobineau, *Essai sur l'inégalité des races humaines*, vol. 2, pp. 421–2. For the meaning of *beneficium* in the post-Roman period, see Fouracre, 'The use of the term *beneficium* in Frankish sources: a society based on favours?'

[117] Gobineau, *Essai sur l'inégalité des races humaines*, vol. 2, p. 423.

[118] Gobineau, *Essai sur l'inégalité des races humaines*, vol. 2, p. 424.

without a head (*un État despotique subsistant sans avoir de tête*)[119] was not, Gobineau insisted, so strange: the Empire had never been hereditary, so regularity of succession was not important for the survival of the body politic or civil society. In deposing Romulus Augustulus 'Odoacer had only accomplished a simple palace revolution'.[120] Rulers simply adopted titles that their followers could understand.[121] After four centuries, however, most barbarian groups had grown weak. In Spain the Goths and Romans had mixed together, the Lombards were a little more distinct, but only the Franks, and more particularly the Austrasian Franks of the North-East, retained any energy.[122]

In general the old Germanic traditions faded, and the kings were not unhappy at the development, being particularly attracted to Roman notions of reverence for authority.[123] Mixed marriage led to a softening of the Germans.[124] Miscegenation was, of course, for Gobineau, the chief factor in the weakening of the Aryans. The old gods fell out of favour, but Christianity spread, especially in the towns, and Germans themselves saw the attraction of episcopal office.[125] Gobineau, who was personally critical of Christianity, was not usually complimentary about the impact of the Church on the Germanic peoples, although he did allow it a leading role alongside the Germans in the regeneration of the post-Roman world.[126] Despite this admission, he largely rejected the line of argument developed by the likes of Chateaubriand, that the Church saved civilization.[127]

In his examination of the social impact of the barbarians, Gobineau noted change at the bottom end of society: the servile classes rose in status to the extent that ex-*coloni* (the *colonus* being a tied peasant-farmer) started to have their own serfs, and that some slaves became officials, while slavery itself was steadily abolished.[128] On the one hand, Gobineau was here reflecting the line of argument that saw the Germanic incomers ending the oppressive systems of the Roman state—and no doubt, given his approval of the social structures of the early Germans as well as his own dislike of American slavery,[129] this was a positive development. At the same time, he disliked any egalitarian trend:[130] hence the somewhat ambivalent tone.

There was variety in the new societies that were established within Roman territory, much of which Gobineau attributed to the extent to which races had remained

---

[119] Gobineau, *Essai sur l'inégalité des races humaines*, vol. 2, p. 427.
[120] Gobineau, *Essai sur l'inégalité des races humaines*, vol. 2, p. 428.
[121] Gobineau, *Essai sur l'inégalité des races humaines*, vol. 2, p. 429.
[122] Gobineau, *Essai sur l'inégalité des races humaines*, vol. 2, pp. 430, 437–8.
[123] Gobineau, *Essai sur l'inégalité des races humaines*, vol. 2, p. 436.
[124] Gobineau, *Essai sur l'inégalité des races humaines*, vol. 2, pp. 436–7.
[125] Gobineau, *Essai sur l'inégalité des races humaines*, vol. 2, pp. 438–40.
[126] Biddiss, *Father of Racist Ideology*, pp. 49–50, 55, 231.
[127] Biddiss, *Father of Racist Ideology*, pp. 151–2, 157, for his hostility to world religions in general and his argument that Christianity did not play a major role in civilization in particular.
[128] Gobineau, *Essai sur l'inégalité des races humaines*, vol. 2, pp. 441–3.
[129] Biddiss, *Father of Racist Ideology*, p. 146. For his reaction to Brazilian slavery, and his view that it harmed the slaveholders more than the slaves, see pp. 201–3, but see pp. 169–70 for his approval of slavery in other contexts.
[130] Biddiss, *Father of Racist Ideology*, p. 141.

pure. The peoples of the South of Italy in particular were lacking in energy, being a mixture of Romans, Greeks, Germans, and, later, Saracens. The Lombards in the North had remained more distinct, but they were not numerous enough to defeat Charlemagne.[131] Thereafter, Gobineau turns to the final migrations: those of the 'ariane-scandinaves' (the Scandinavian Aryans, as he calls the Vikings),[132] though he suddenly leaps back in time to discuss Britain in the pre-Viking period, albeit in a markedly confused way—and this despite his awareness of the writings of John Mitchell Kemble, the English scholar who, as we shall see, had steadily been revolutionizing understanding of the early Anglo-Saxons as a result of his application of the ideas of Jacob Grimm.[133] The Britons, being already heavily Germanized, according to Gobineau, were more active in their own defence than most peoples—as proof of which he notes the number of emperors they produced.[134] As a result they put up significant resistance against the Saxons.[135] Even in those areas that were subjugated by the incomers, the Germanic kings included Romano-Britons among their *leudes* (military followers), who taught them traditions of Roman law and administration. The result was a type of government that would only emerge later elsewhere.[136] As for the Romano-Britons, they in turn became more German, and less 'southern'.[137] This 'Germanness' would be further reinforced by the Norman Conquest. And it was for this reason that Great Britain, while not the most brilliant, human, or noble European state, was the most vigorous.[138]

Given Gobineau's views of race and racial purity it is not surprising that he spends so long on the Migration Period and its immediate aftermath: indeed the period was central to his understanding.[139] It would also feature in a later work, on the *Histoire des Perses*, where he analysed what he saw as the disastrous policy of centralization pursued by the Sassanid state.[140] He intended to write *L'Histoire des Mérovingiens*, but left only a fragment of the work at the time of his death in 1882. The fragment presents the unlucky Merovingians as living in a world of decadent Gallo-Romans, whose descendents were the current supporters of Gambetta.[141]

Despite their modern notoriety, it is important not to attribute too much immediate influence to Gobineau's views: before the 1880s they seem to have had little impact. The publication history of the *Essai* is interesting. It has been estimated that in the first years following its appearance it was only read by around four hundred people in France and a hundred and fifty in Germany: and certainly in so

[131] Gobineau, *Essai sur l'inégalité des races humaines*, vol. 2, pp. 443–4.
[132] Towards the end of his career, while he was the French Minister to Sweden and Norway he revisited various aspects of Viking history: Biddiss, *Father of racist ideology*, p. 229.
[133] Gobineau, *Essai sur l'inégalité des races humaines*, vol. 2, p. 456.
[134] Gobineau, *Essai sur l'inégalité des races humaines*, vol. 2, pp. 458–9.
[135] Gobineau, *Essai sur l'inégalité des races humaines*, vol. 2, p. 460.
[136] Gobineau, *Essai sur l'inégalité des races humaines*, vol. 2, pp. 460–1.
[137] Gobineau, *Essai sur l'inégalité des races humaines*, vol. 2, pp. 462–4.
[138] Gobineau, *Essai sur l'inégalité des races humaines*, vol. 2, pp. 465–7.
[139] Biddiss, *Father of Racist Ideology*, p. 55.
[140] Biddiss, *Father of Racist Ideology*, p. 188.
[141] Biddiss, *Father of Racist Ideology*, pp. 245–6.

far as it was reviewed, the reception was poor.[142] There was a second edition in 1884, supported by a subvention from Wagner's Bayreuth, and a German edition followed.[143] Four further editions appeared in France up to, and including, 1940.[144] Other than that there was an American translation of the first part of the *Essai* in 1856, where the text was manipulated into being a defence of slavery, a change to which Gobineau objected.[145] A full American translation appeared in 1915. There was a German translation in 1902–3, and a substantial study by the translator in 1910.[146] Given this relative lack of interest in Gobineau's *Essai* immediately after its publication, it is not surprising that he had little impact on interpretations of the Fall of the Roman Empire, although his general ideas would have a malign influence in the twentieth century.

In the mid-nineteenth century racial ideas were current: Gobineau's voice was one among many, and initially it was not an influential one. Far more widely read were a number of historians, including Amédée Thierry and, as we shall see, the Englishman Edward Augustus Freeman.[147] Although the physiological approach to the subject was becoming increasingly significant, not least because of scholars such as Edwards, the topic of race had emerged directly out of older historical debates about the barbarian invasions of Western Europe. Nation, class, and race were a new configuration of old ideas. Confusingly the French word *race* itself had been used primarily under the *Ancien Régime* to mean 'dynasty': thus *la première race* described the Merovingian family. In producing a reading of the Frankish invasion of Gaul and of the Norman invasion of England from the point of view of the oppressed classes, Augustin Thierry had developed a model that could be read variously in terms of class or of race.[148] Even in Gobineau's writing the Aryan-German race can effectively be read as an aristocratic class.[149] Crucially, however, the discourse was no longer that of the late eighteenth century. And some aspects of Thierry's interpretation would be transferred to Italy in the second and third decades of the nineteenth century, where they would undergo a major transformation, to become central to the Risorgimento.

[142] Gobineau, *Mademoiselle Irnois*, ed. Smith and Smith, p. 12, with p. 292 n. 13, where the citation is to Lémonon's thesis, *Gobineau et l'Allemagne*. See also Biddiss, *Father of racist ideology*, pp. 147–8.
[143] Biddiss, *Father of Racist Ideology*, p. 247, 257–8.
[144] 2nd edn, Paris, 1884: 5th edn, Paris, 1940.
[145] Biddiss, *Father of Racist Ideology*, pp. 146–7. The translations are listed below, in the bibliography.
[146] On Schemann and Gobineau, see Biddiss, *Father of Racist Ideology*, esp. pp. 256–7.
[147] Seliger, 'Race-thinking during the Restoration'.
[148] For a racial reading, de Lollis, *Alessandro Manzoni e gli storici liberali francesi*, pp. 5–44.
[149] Biddiss, *Father of Racist Ideology*, p. 164.

7

The Lombards and the Risorgimento

7.1 ITALIAN DISCOURSES

Throughout the eighteenth century, and into the early years of the nineteenth, the dominant debates on the Fall of Rome and the establishment of the successor states had taken place in France. That is not to say that all the major contributions had come from French scholars: clearly Mascov and Gibbon prove otherwise. If one distinguishes between French and Swiss scholars, Mallet and Sismondi add to the list. In addition to Mascov, German scholars raised issues of significance in writing about such matters as language, nationality, and law, even if, for the most part, like Leibniz and Herder, they were not historians whose concern was with the last years of Antiquity and the first of the Middle Ages. In the 1820s, however, discussion outside France became very much more important, both in Germany, to which we will turn in a later chapter, and also in Italy, where the introduction of Augustin Thierry's ideas altered the way in which the Fall of Rome and the establishment of the Lombard kingdom were seen. Not that the barbarian invasions were a new topic of discussion in the Italian peninsula. Quite apart from the long-running discussions of the histories of the Goths and Lombards, which go back at least to Machiavelli, there was a more recent tradition of scholarship dealing with the Germanic peoples.

Already in the seventeenth-century the friar Francesco Negri, whose work was published posthumously in 1700, had questioned the supposed Scandinavian origins of the Germanic invaders.[1] Nevertheless, the idea that the barbarians who destroyed Rome originated in Scandinavia was still circulating freely in Italy when it was challenged again in 1822 by Jacob Gråberg di Hemsø, who was the Swedish vice-consul in Genoa and general consul in Morocco. He published his refutation of the notion in *La Scandinavie vengée de l'accusation d'avoir produit les peuples barbares qui détruisirent l'Empire de Rome*.[2] Gråberg's argument, however, seems to have remained unnoticed. In the same year two much more influential works were published: the *Adelchi* and the *Discorso sopra alcuni punti della storia longobardica in Italia*, both by Alessandro Manzoni. Manzoni is best known as the author of *I promessi sposi*, perhaps the greatest Italian novel of the century. In addition, his linguistic work was central to the creation of a standardized Italian language, which

[1] Beck, *Northern Antiquities*, vol. 1, pp. 42–3.
[2] Gråberg di Hemsø, *La Scandinavie vengée de l'accusation d'avoir produit les peuples barbares*; Beck, *Northern Antiquities*, vol 1, pp. 42, 137–9, 144–55.

played an important role in the development of national unity. Alberto Mario Banti has recently included the *Adelchi* in his list of the *canone risorgimentale*— works that were fundamental to the Risorgimento.[3] It will, therefore, be with the *Adelchi* and its related *Discorso* that we begin, before looking at the influence of Manzoni on the writings of Cesare Balbo and Carlo Troya.[4] All three men played a significant role in the formulation of the ideology of the Risorgimento, and indeed their discussion of Lombard history cannot be dissociated from the movement for Italian independence. Having looked briefly at the most famous opera of the period to take as its subject events of the fifth century, Verdi's *Attila*, another of Banti's canonical works,[5] we will look at a younger contemporary of Troya, Pasquale Villari, whose history of the barbarian invasions takes us forward into the opening years of the twentieth century.

7.2 MANZONI'S *DISCORSO*

In October 1822 Alessandro Manzoni published his tragedy *Adelchi*.[6] This tells the story of the last days of the Lombard kingdom in Italy. The play begins with the return of Ermengarda to her father Desiderio, or Desiderius, the last king of the Lombards, following her rejection by her husband, Charlemagne. (Ermengarda is the name given by Manzoni and has no historical justification.) The Lombard king decides to avenge the insult, despite the more conciliatory position adopted by his son, Adelchi. Charlemagne invades Italy and besieges Pavia. Adelchi attempts to escape to Constantinople, so as to organize resistance from outside the peninsula, but is mortally wounded in the attempt. He recognizes the injustices of Lombard rule over the people of Italy and dies.[7] The denouement, it should be said, is the product of Manzoni's imagination, for the historical Adelchis succeeded in reaching Constantinople, and indeed returned to Italy with Byzantine support in 787, but was driven back to Byzantium, where he died.

To write a drama about the Lombard past was nothing new. A number of Handel's libretti, for instance, had been concerned with early medieval Italy,[8] though none of them provide a remotely accurate presentation of events—the *Adelchi* sticks somewhat closer to what was known to have happened, even if certain major aspects of the story, not least the death of the hero, were invented. What was new was not the period, but the emphasis. Although the leading characters, like Handel's, are royal or aristocratic, the people of Italy themselves are given a voice in two long choral odes which express their oppressed situation.

---

[3] Banti, *La nazione del Risorgimento*, p. 45.

[4] For a general comment, see King, *A History of Italian Unity*, vol. 1, p. 113.

[5] Banti, *La nazione del Risorgimento*, p. 45; see also pp. 68–9 and 86–7.

[6] For a convenient study of the context of writing, Deigan, *Alessandro Manzoni's The Count of Carmagnola and Adelchis*, p. 19.

[7] For a discussion of the play and its historiographical significance, Wood, ' "Adelchi" and "Attila" '.

[8] McKitterick, 'Edward Gibbon and the early Middle Ages in eighteenth-century Europe'.

The *Adelchi* was accompanied by a historical study, the *Discorso sopra alcuni punti della storia longobardica in Italia*, published initially in the same year as the drama, but reissued in revised form in 1847, with a number of significant appendices.[9] In the *Discorso*, having briefly described the historical events on which his play was based, Manzoni turned to the major questions that it was intended to address. The first of these is perfectly captured in the title of chapter 2: 'Whether, at the time of Charlemagne's invasion, the Lombards and the Italians constituted a single people.'[10] Manzoni then looked at the implications of the survival of Roman law.[11] There follows a discussion of the supposed virtues of the Lombards, to which a lengthy analysis of two sentences to be found in the *History* of Paul the Deacon was appended in the 1847 edition.[12] According to Paul, '[i]n these days [i.e. 574–84] many of the noble Romans were killed from love of gain, and the remainder were divided among their "guests" and made tributaries, that they should pay the third part of their products to the Lombards'.[13] And 'the oppressed people were parcelled out among their guests'.[14] The closing chapters of the *Discorso* deal with the role of the papacy in the fall of the Lombards,[15] and the reasons for the speed of the Carolingian conquest.[16] Thus, they address the immediate background to the *Adelchi*. For the modern historian of the barbarian invasions it is Manzoni's preceding discussions of the relationship between the Lombards and the Romans that are crucial.

Manzoni's view was that the Lombards and the Italians did not integrate, and indeed he saw non-integration as being the norm throughout Europe:

> Two peoples living in the same country, divided by name, language, clothing, interests, and, in part, laws: such was the state in which for an undefined and indefinable time, almost the whole of Europe found itself, after the invasions and settlements of the barbarians.[17]

This was in direct contradiction to the arguments that had been put forward in the past by Villani and Machiavelli, as well as Muratori, who wrote that the Lombards

---

[9] The most accessible text is to be found in Manzoni, *Tutte le opere*, ed. Martelli, but this has now been totally superseded by the new edition of I. Becherucci, which provides both versions of the *Discorso*, and which is the version cited below.

[10] Manzoni, *Discorso sopra alcuni punti della storia longobardica in Italia*, ch. 2, (1822), pp. 39–79; (1847), pp. 185–217.

[11] Manzoni, *Discorso*, ch. 3, (1822), pp. 80–107; (1847), pp. 218–92.

[12] Manzoni, *Discorso*, ch. 4, (1822), pp. 107–28; (1847), pp. 293–342.

[13] Paul, *Historia Langobardorum*, II 32: 'His diebus, multi nobilium romanorum ob cupiditatem interfecti sunt; reliqui vero per hostes divisi, ut tertiam partem suarum frugum langobardis persolverentm tributarii efficiuntur.' The translation is Foulke, *Paul the Deacon, History of the Langobards*, pp. 87–91. Foulke, pp. 91–3, n. 1, provides an extensive commentary on the problems of translating the sentence, with some reference to the various interpretations offered in the nineteenth century, though he does not mention Manzoni.

[14] Paul, *Historia Langobardorum*, III 16: 'Populi tamen aggravati per Langobardos hospites partiuntur.' Again the translation is by Foulke, p. 114, who provides a lengthy comment on the translation on pp. 114–16, n. 2.

[15] Manzoni, *Discorso*, ch. 5, (1822), pp. 128–51; (1847), pp. 342–58.

[16] Manzoni, *Discorso*, ch. 6, (1822), pp. 151–66; (1847), pp. 358–65.

[17] Manzoni, *Discorso* (1847), p. 185.

and Italians had become 'a single civic body and a single republic'.[18] In Macchiavelli's words, '[t]hey changed into people of the country: they retained only the name of foreigners (*forestieri*)'.

To these arguments Manzoni replied: occupation does not necessarily involve the agreement of the indigenous population if the invaders are armed. The Lombards could be compared to the Moors in Spain or—a much more immediate comparison— the Turks in Greece.[19] As for the argument that, being born inside Italy, they ceased to be outsiders, *forestieri*: that did not make them Italians.[20] The opinion of the native population also mattered. Manzoni denied that conversion, or indeed inter-marriage, necessarily led to integration: in the case of intermarriage, any offspring simply belonged to the race of the father.[21]

He then turned to the title held by Lombard kings: *rex gentis langobardorum*. Did that mean that they were only kings of the Lombards? Or did it mean that the two peoples of Italy had been integrated? In the latter case, why were there still two legal systems?[22] In Manzoni's view, the existence of two legal systems disproved the unity of the two populations. He noted the absence of Roman names among the lists of Lombard office holders.[23] He also used the papal view of the Lombards as a perfidious race of lepers to back up their separateness,[24] as well as Liutprand of Cremona's account of his legation to Constantinople: 'But we Lombards, Saxons, Franks, Lotharingians, Bavarians, Swabians, and Burgundians, so despise these fellows that when we are angered against our enemies we can find nothing more insulting to say than—"You Roman!" '[25]

If the Lombards did not become Italians, did Italians become Lombards? Here Manzoni turned to the interpretation of events in Gaul given by Du Bos.[26] Yet, while for Du Bos there was no conquest, it was not like that in Italy. Manzoni took issue with Muratori's views that the tribute owed to the state by Lombards and Ital-ians came to be the same,[27] and also that military needs would have contributed towards integration in that Italians would be drawn into the army.[28] On the other hand, Manzoni also challenged the position of Maffei: that the Italians were *in vera servitù* ('true servitude'), questioning what this actually meant. He pointed to the absence of information on the subject peoples.[29] Even on the matter of the continu-ance of Roman law he noted the difficulty of determining what this amounted to.[30]

---

[18] Manzoni, *Discorso* (1822), pp. 43–5 (where there is no reference to Villani); (1847), pp. 186–7.
[19] Manzoni, *Discorso* (1822), pp. 46–7; (1847), pp. 188–9.
[20] Manzoni, *Discorso* (1847), p. 189; see also p. 199.
[21] Manzoni, *Discorso* (1822), pp. 47–8; (1847), pp. 192–4.
[22] Manzoni, *Discorso* (1822), p. 50; (1847), p. 194.
[23] Manzoni, *Discorso* (1822), pp. 52–4; (1847), p. 196.
[24] Manzoni, *Discorso* (1822), pp. 54–5; (1847), pp. 196–7.
[25] Manzoni, *Discorso* (1847), p. 198. Liutprand, *Relatio de Legatione Constantinopolitana*, 12. The translation is adapted from that by Wright, ed. Norwich, *Liudprand of Cremona, The Embassy to Con-stantinople*, p. 183.
[26] Manzoni, *Discorso* (1822), pp. 57–8; (1847), pp. 202–3.
[27] Manzoni, *Discorso* (1822), p. 62; (1847), pp. 205, 307–42.
[28] Manzoni, *Discorso* (1822), p. 63; (1847), pp. 206–10.
[29] Manzoni, *Discorso* (1847), p. 211.
[30] Manzoni, *Discorso* (1822), pp. 89–90; (1847), p. 223.

Manzoni then addressed the current opinion that the Lombards possessed *bontà morale* ('moral goodness'). He dealt with this initially by returning to the nature of the Lombard take-over. Paul the Deacon followed his statement about the oppressed population being divided between its Lombard 'guests' with a remarkably upbeat sentence: 'This was indeed admirable in the Lombard kingdom: there was no violence, no ambushes were laid, no one was illegally oppressed, no one was despoiled, there were no thefts, no robberies, everyone proceeded wherever he wished without fear.'[31] Baronius had already noted that this was difficult to square with the evidence of Gregory the Great. Moreover, Paul himself had come near to presenting exactly the opposite image in an earlier passage: 'In these days many of the noble Romans were killed from love of gain…By these dukes of the Lombards…the churches were despoiled, the priests killed, the cities overthrown, the people, who had grown up like crops, annihilated, and besides those regions which Alboin had taken, the greater part of Italy was seized and subjugated by the Lombards.'[32]

Manzoni was fully aware of the long tradition of Italian scholarship that preceded his intervention: he cited Machiavelli and Muratori, Giannone, Fumagalli, as well as Baronius, Maffei, and Tiraboschi. Machiavelli, in his *Istorie fiorentine* had praised Theodoric. Despite the impression given of his interpretation by Manzoni, Machiavelli had been critical of the Lombard kingdom, but he had reserved his chief criticism for the popes, who had prevented the Lombards from uniting the peninsula and had called in the Franks.[33] Like almost all Italian historians who wrote about the early Middle Ages, Machiavelli was directly concerned with the parallels between the barbarian invasions of Italy, and the subsequent interventions by French monarchs and German emperors.[34] Rather closer to the position that Manzoni would subsequently adopt, Baronius took the opposite line to Machiavelli on the role of the papacy: the Church had been the chief focus of opposition to the barbarians: Stilicho he condemned as a traitor, and while Theodoric, again, received some favourable comment, he presented the Lombards in Gregory the Great's terms: as 'pagani crudeliores'.[35]

Muratori, by contrast with Baronius, adopted a position that had more in common with that of Machiavelli. The Fall of the Western Empire had been a disaster, but Theodoric deserved praise. Moreover, Italy was a medieval creation. Although

---

[31] Manzoni, *Discorso* (1822), pp. 109–10; (1847), p. 294, citing Paul, *Historia Langobardorum*, III, 16: 'Erat sane hoc mirabile in regno Langobardorum: nulla erat violentia, nullae struebantur insidiae, nemo aliquem injuste angariabat, nemo spoliabat, non erant furta, non latronicinia, unusquisque quo libebat, securus sine timore pergebat.' The translation is adapted from Foulke, pp. 114–17. See below for Balbo's discussion of the same passage.

[32] 'His diebus multi nobilium romanorum ob cupiditatem interfecti sunt…Per hos Langobardorum duces…spoliatis ecclesiis, sacerdotibus interfectis, civitatibus subrutis, populisque, qui more segetum excreverant, extinctis, exceptis his regionibus quas Alboin ceperat, Italia ex maxima parte capta et a Langobardis subjugata est.' Paul, *Historia Langobardorum*, II, 32, trans. Foulke, pp. 87–93. See Manzoni, *Discorso* (1822), p. 122; (1847), p. 295.

[33] Tabacco, 'Latinità e germanesimo nella tradizione medievistica italiana', p. 695; Falco, 'La questione longobarda e la moderna storiografia italiana', pp. 153–5.

[34] Toppan, 'Evolution du concept de "barbare" en Italie', p. 120.

[35] Falco, 'La questione longobarda e la moderna storiografia italiana', pp. 155–6; Tabacco, 'Latinità e germanesimo nella tradizione medievistica italiana', pp. 699–700.

the Lombards had initially caused disruption, after Authari, who ruled from 584 to 590, there was steady assimilation.[36] Following the great seventeenth-century Dutch lawyer Hugo Grotius, Muratori gave a positive assessment of Lombard law.[37] Similar positions were taken by Giannone, Denina, and Fumagalli, all of whom were critical of the power of the Church.[38] Muratori's position on Lombard law, however, was challenged by Maffei and Tiraboschi, although both of them had positive opinions of Authari.[39] Exactly contemporary with Manzoni, Berchet and Romagnosi were debating the nature of the ethnic mixture of Italy, with the latter in particular stressing the extent to which the various peoples had fused into a single nation—a point which would be strongly denied by Manzoni.[40]

Before Manzoni set down his *Discorso* there was, then, a well-established field of debate about the post-Roman period or, rather, about the Lombards—for, perhaps because there was general approval of Theodoric, the Ostrogoths prompted less discussion. In many respects Manzoni's work is a direct attack on Machiavelli, as well as a reply to Giannone, Muratore, Denina, and Fumagalli.[41] The precise context of Manzoni's decision to write about the Lombard occupation, however, was French, not Italian. Just as he cited earlier Italian scholars, so Manzoni cited Du Bos and Montesquieu.[42] But it was not the eighteenth-century French writers who had inspired him. Rather it was the circle of his own contemporaries: of Fauriel and of Augustin Thierry in Paris.[43]

In the opening decades of the nineteenth century Manzoni was a frequent visitor to the French capital. His mother had gone there after her divorce, to join her lover, Carlo Imbonati. By the time that the young Manzoni arrived in Paris in 1805, however, Imbonati was already dead.[44] Despite this setback, Manzoni's mother had a significant circle of acquaintances, being attached to the circle of Mme Condorcet, whose lover, Fauriel, became a close friend of Alessandro. The Frenchman would later translate a number of the Italian's works, including the *Adelchi*, into French. After 1810 the Manzonis moved back to Italy,[45] although Alessandro revisited Paris in 1819.[46] On this occasion Fauriel introduced him to Augustin Thierry, and Thierry in turn introduced him to the novels of Walter Scott, and in particular to *Ivanhoe*, which had just

[36] Scotti, 'Il Medioevo nell'Illuminismo', pp. 145–52; Soldani, 'Il Medioevo del Risorgimento nello specchio della nazione', p. 156.

[37] Falco, 'La questione longobarda e la moderna storiografia italiana', pp. 156–9; Tabacco, 'Latinità e germanesimo nella tradizione medievistica italiana', pp. 700–3.

[38] Falco, 'La questione longobarda e la moderna storiografia italiana', pp. 156–7.

[39] Falco, 'La questione longobarda e la moderna storiografia italiana', p. 160; Artifoni, 'Il Medioevo nel Romanticismo', pp. 210–11.

[40] Thom, *Republics, Nations and Tribes*, p. 281.

[41] Falco, 'La questione longobarda e la moderna storiografia italiana', p. 161; Artifoni, 'Il Medioevo nel Romanticismo', p. 211.

[42] On Montesquieu, Manzoni, *Discorso* (1822), p. 84.

[43] De Lollis *Alessandro Manzoni e gli storici liberali francesi della restaurazione*, pp. 5–64. See now Banti, 'Le invasioni barbariche e l'origine delle nazione'.

[44] Deigan, *Alessandro Manzoni's Count of Carmagnola and Adelchis*, p. 2.

[45] Deigan, *Alessandro Manzoni's Count of Carmagnola and Adelchis*, p. 3.

[46] Deigan, *Alessandro Manzoni's Count of Carmagnola and Adelchis*, pp. 13–14.

appeared.[47] As we have seen, it was Thierry who raised the issue of how to give a voice to the lower classes, which for Manzoni meant the Italian people.[48] Meanwhile, Manzoni also showed an interest in the sources on which Thierry himself was working, commenting in a letter to Fauriel that they were 'indispensible, not only for the immediate connections between the history of Charlemagne and that of the Lombards, but also for catching certain indications about the establishment of the barbarian conquerors, who are all very similar'.[49] The intellectual background to the *Adelchi* and to its accompanying *Discorso* was, then, French at least as much as it was Italian, and if the emphasis on the existence of a race of conquerors and a race of conquered in the two works smacks of French historiography of the eighteenth and early nineteenth centuries, that is because their immediate source of inspiration was Thierry and his current projects. But whereas Thierry was concerned with the class system in France, and the oppression of the *roturiers*, for Manzoni the oppressed were the indigenous Italian population, in much of the North under Austrian control and in the South ruled by a dynasty that traced its origins to Spain, except during a brief period under Napoleon's brother and brother-in-law.

7.3 MANZONI AND SISMONDI

While Manzoni was inspired by one strand in French historiography, he was hostile to another. For a variety of reasons he was not in sympathy with Sismondi. One point of difference was religious. During his first visits to France, Manzoni rediscovered his Catholic faith under the influence of French Jansenists.[50] As a result, in his eyes, the role of the papacy in early medieval Italy is consistently positive. Sismondi, by contrast, was a staunch Protestant, who, in his *History of the Italian Republics*, attributed the moral corruption of the Italians to the papacy, a point vigorously attacked by Manzoni in his *Osservazioni sulla morale cattolica* of 1819, which was explicitly written 'to defend the morality of the Catholic Church from the accusations made in chapter 127 of the *History of the Italian Republics in the Middle Ages*'.[51]

---

[47] Deigan, *Alessandro Manzoni's Count of Carmagnola and Adelchis*, p. 14; Banti, 'Le invasioni barbariche e l'origine delle nazione'; Chandler, *Alessandro Manzoni. The Story of a Spiritual Quest*, p. 79.
[48] De Lollis, *Alessandro Manzoni e gli storici liberali francesi*, p. 10.
[49] Manzoni, ep. 137, *Lettere* I, p. 216. For Manzoni and Fauriel, Chandler, *Alessandro Manzoni*, p. 73; Colquhoun, *Manzoni and his times*, pp. 157–8.
[50] De Lollis, *Alessandro Manzoni e gli storici liberali francesi*, pp. 102–29; Deigan, *Alessandro Manzoni's Count of Carmagnola and Adelchis*, p. 3.
[51] Martelli and Bacchelli (eds), *Manzoni, Tutte le opere*, vol. 2, pp.1335–461, especially at pp. 1335 and 1497; Deigan, *Alessandro Manzoni's Count of Carmagnola and Adelchis*, pp. 13, 89, 94. Sismondi's position is clearly stated in his abridged (English) *History of the Italian Republics—Being a View of the Origin, Progress and Fall of Italian Freedom*, p. 10: 'For more than twenty years the popes or the bishops of Rome had been in the habit of opposing the kings of France to the monarchs of Lombardy, who were odious to them, at first as pagans, and afterwards as heretics.' For Manzoni's response, Carsaniga, 'The Romantic controversy', p. 432. On Sismondi's hostility to Catholicism, Patriaca, 'Indolence and regeneration', pp. 397–9.

Despite this difference of opinion, Sismondi was in many respects the other inspirational figure for Italian historiography in the early part of the nineteenth century. Nor was it simply in the *History of the Italian Republics* that he treated material relating to Italy. His earlier book, the *Tableau de l'agriculture toscane* (1801), reflected the experiences of his family when they decamped from Geneva to carve out a new life in Tuscany, which was where they claimed to have originated. As we have seen, in 1804–5 Sismondi was one of those who escorted Mme de Staël through the peninsula on the visit that would lead to her writing the allegorical novel *Corinne, or Italy*.[52] His magnum opus as regards Italy, however, was his *Repubbliche Italiane*.[53] Unlike Manzoni, he did accept that there was intermarriage between Italians and Lombards,[54] and he thought that the barbarian invaders had a positive role to play, in that they contributed to the development of the Italian city-republics. Not surprisingly, his vision of the Italian city republics was treasured by the Risorgimento:[55] his *Repubbliche* has been called the 'omnipresent *Republics* of Sismondi',[56] and it was described by de Santis as 'our codex, our Gospel'.[57] However, even more than in his writings on the history of France, the core of Sismondi's interpretation of the history of Italy lies in the high Middle Ages, and it was for its high medieval stories that it was most plundered during the course of the Risorgimento.[58]

Manzoni's interpretation of the Lombard invasion and conquest of Italy was, therefore, of greater importance than Sismondi's for the development of Italian scholarship on the early medieval period. The simple fact that one of the leading literary figures of the Risorgimento wrote about the kingdom of the Lombards, and did so in a poetic work of theatre as well as in the *Discorso*, inevitably drew its history to the attention of a wider public than the scholarly confraternity. Significantly, Manzoni was concerned not with the fifth century, nor with the Ostrogothic kingdom, but only with the Lombards and their relations with the indigenous population. The Italian debates about the post-Roman period centred not on Theodoric or Ravenna (although they did not ignore them), but on the establishment of the Lombard State and on its collapse in the eighth century before the forces of Charlemagne.

7.4 CESARE BALBO

Most Italian scholars writing on the early Middle Ages in the decades before the unification of Italy took over the basic line set out by Manzoni—not least because they

---

[52] On the importance of *Corinne*, Bizzocchi, 'Una nuova morale per la donna e la famiglia', pp. 83–4; Soldani, 'Il Risorgimento delle donne', pp. 184, 192; Chiappini, 'La voce della martire', pp. 289–90; Finelli and Fruci, 'Il "momento risorgimentale" nel discorso politico francese (1796–1870)', p. 758; Duggan, 'Gran Bretagna e Italia nel Risorgimento', pp. 777–8, 784.

[53] Duggan, *The Force of Destiny*, pp. 96–8.

[54] Toppan, 'Evolution du concept de "barbare" en Italie', p. 130.

[55] Lyttelton, 'Sismondi's *Histoire des républiques italiennes* and the Risorgimento'.

[56] Porciani, 'Disciplinamento nazionale e modelli domestici', p. 102. Compare Patriarca, 'Indolence and Regeneration', p. 397.

[57] Bizzocchi, 'Una nuova morale per la donna e la famiglia', p. 84.

[58] Duggan, *The Force of Destiny*, p. 98.

shared his dislike of foreign rule, and his hope for a united peninsula. Of these the two most important were Cesare Balbo and Carlo Troya. Balbo, an aristocrat from Turin, provides an interesting counterpart to Sismondi, from just across the Alps in Republican Geneva.[59] Despite his father's disapproval he worked for the Napoleonic government in Florence and Rome, where he was involved in the dismantling of the Papal States, which earned him a period of excommunication. Thereafter he was transferred to Paris, but disillusion with Napoleon had set in by 1814. In 1816, when his father was sent by the Savoy government to Madrid as ambassador, Cesare accompanied him, and there he familiarized himself with Spanish history. Back in Piedmont in 1820 he started to champion liberal reforms, as a result of which he was exiled. He took advantage of his enforced leisure to read widely in current French and German scholarship.[60] He returned to the family estate at Camerano in 1824 and began writing works of history, including the *Storia d'Italia*.[61] His most important political work was *Delle speranze d'Italia* of 1844, with its vision of an independent liberal Italy.[62] Three years later he founded the Turin journal *Il Risorgimento*. He served briefly as premier of Piedmont in 1848. He died in 1853.

Balbo's interpretation of Italian history changed over the years, as he came to accept some, though by no means all, of the arguments put forward by Manzoni and Troya: and indeed on some topics he changed his mind more than once.[63] Even his *Storia d'Italia* went through a number of incarnations in the 1830s and 40s. It was also translated into French. The most widely disseminated version of Balbo's history, the *Sommario della storia d'Italia*, which was originally written for the *Nuova enciclopedia popolare*, provides a notable survey of Italian history from the earliest times down to the end of the Middle Ages. The most substantial section of it deals with the period of the communes, but the Fall of the Roman Empire, and the Ostrogothic and Lombard periods are covered at impressive length. He also wrote a separate account of the period of barbarian rule in Italy.[64]

As one of the leading intellectuals of the Risorgimento, it is not surprising that Balbo regarded the history of Italy as a history of a series of conquests by outsiders, and that he saw this as being something that the Italians had suffered uniquely:

[59] For Balbo's life, see Fubini Leuzzi, ed., *Cesare Balbo, Storia d'Italia e altri scritti editi ed inediti*, pp. 9–70.

[60] Duggan, *The Force of Destiny*, pp. 157–8; Artifoni, 'Il Medioevo nel Romanticismo', pp. 216–17; Fubini Leuzzi, 'Metodi e temi della ricerca storica promossa in Piemonte prima e dopo l'Unità', p. 875.

[61] Balbo, *Storia d'Italia e altri scritti editi ed inediti*, ed. Fubini Leuzzi. For an overview of Balbo's historical work, Fubini Leuzzi, 'Contributi e discussioni su alcuni aspetti del pensiero storiografico di Cesare Balbo'.

[62] On Balbo's view of the state of Italy, see Patriaca, 'Indolence and regeneration'.

[63] On the changes within Balbo's thought in this period, Artifoni, 'Le questioni longobarde', p. 301. A crucial insight into the changes in the thought of Balbo can be found in his correspondence with Troya: Troya and Balbo, *Delle civile condizione dei Romani vinti dai Longobardi e di altre quistioni storichi: lettere inedite*. I am greatly indebted to Enrico Artifoni for providing me with a copy of the Troya-Balbo correspondence.

[64] Balbo, *Storia d'Italia sotto ai barbari*.

Other peoples, who were formerly provincials, ultimately our fellow subjects in the Empire, none of them had to suffer so many conquests as we did: for the others, these had concluded by the end of the fifth century, and as a result from the Roman and German peoples together there could emerge from that, mixed, and assimilated, those Spanish, French, and English populations, which were therefore more easily able to resist the more recent conquests. In Italy, by contrast, we see in succession the barbarians of Odovacer, the Goths, Lombards, Franks, French, and Germans, ancient and modern. And the old invaders, pressed hard on by the new, virtually never had enough time to found a nation. And thus, what is usually said of the other modern European nations, that their servile blood, being Roman provincials, was renewed by free German blood, is not true for Italy. The much-vaunted pure Italian blood (which was not just servile, as can properly be said of them as provincials, but the most servile, as the least warlike and the most humiliated under the immediate imperial tyranny, which was the local reality for them) was renewed by no free and military blood for a long period of time. The northern warriors did not integrate with the Italian slaves, or if they did so, it was much later, when they were also in turn invaded and made fellow slaves.[65]

There are nuances here that are not present in Manzoni. Balbo accepts that outside Italy Germanic blood brought an infusion of freedom. Clearly he is tapping into traditions that emphasized the notion of liberty: his work for the Napoleonic government and his subsequent visits to France had introduced him to a wide range of French scholarship, perhaps most importantly that of Guizot[66]— rather than Thierry, Manzoni's inspiration. Yet Balbo was also drawing on German scholarship, not least on Savigny's *Geschichte des römischen Rechts*.[67] In 1836 he translated Heinrich Leo's *Entwicklung der Verfassung der lombardischen Städte*, which had appeared twelve years earlier.[68] Leo was concerned with Lombardy, and thus with the high Middle Ages, rather than the Lombards, who, he thought, had a negative impact on the development of the Italian city, but he was interested enough in the invaders to provide an account of their history, up to and including their rule in Italy, as well as their organization.[69] Balbo, in his account of the Lombards, is similarly keen to describe their institutions and to provide a discussion of the relevant Germanic terminology.[70] His enthusiasm for the early Germans had led him to translate Tacitus' *Germania*, and to compare the information it contained with what is to be found in the Germanic law codes.[71] Ideas of Germanic liberty and democracy sorted well with his own political views, which led both to his political exile within Piedmont, and also to his own brief premiership in 1848.

---

[65] Balbo, *Sommario della Storia d'Italia*, p. 416.
[66] Balbo, *Storia d'Italia*, p. 876. The page references to the *Storia d'Italia* are to Fubini Leuzzi's edition.
[67] Balbo, *Storia d'Italia*, pp. 20–1.
[68] Leo, *Entwicklung der Verfassung der lombardischen Städte*; trans. Balbo, *Vicende della costituzione delle città lombarde*: see Artifoni, 'Il Medioevo nel Romanticismo', p. 215; Fubini Leuzzi, 'Metodi e temi della ricerca storica promossa in Piemonte prima e dopo l'Unità', p. 875.
[69] Leo, *Geschichte der italienischen Staaten*, vol. 1, pp. 74–203.
[70] Balbo, *Storia d'Italia*, pp. 412–16, 425–6, 439–41.   [71] Balbo, *Storia d'Italia*, pp. 274–6.

Balbo acknowledged the possibility that invaders of Italy could be admirable. He praised the Ostrogoths under Theodoric, and while he noted the persecution in which Boethius and Symmachus died, he pointed to the actions of the emperor Justin as initiating the crisis.[72] When he reached the collapse of the Ostrogothic kingdom, he offered this positive assessment:

> A noble and strong race, to tell the truth, and more than any other barbarian group kind towards the defeated, in Italy as in Spain. Thus, it did not merit the bad name that our history has given it, an evil made and remade for the most part with the prejudices of Roman imperialism. If it had not been for these prejudices, who knows? These Goths might have remained and held out among us, as did their brothers in Spain and the Franks in France. And we could have mingled with them, and we might not have changed our lords so often, nor would we have had to suffer the division of Italy. Instead we can see the beginnings of what we actually see.[73]

The Lombards he viewed very differently from the Ostrogoths. In dealing with their arrival in Italy he quoted Velleius Paterculus' opinion that their savagery was even greater than that of the *Germani*.[74] Not that they were a single *gens* at the time of the invasion of Italy: indeed Balbo went out of his way to describe the mongrel nature of the invading group. Nor were they a large enough force to take over the whole of the peninsula, which was a significant factor in their actions, since it left them open to threats from the Byzantines and from the Franks. Like almost all historians of the Lombards, Balbo illustrates their ferocity with the story, related by Paul the Deacon, of the cup that Alboin had made out of the skull of his defeated opponent, Cunimund, king of the Gepids. Foolishly, the Lombard king asked his wife, daughter of his dead enemy, to serve him a drink in the cup, a demand that prompted her to arrange for her husband's murder.[75] From the point of view of the Italians, matters were no less harsh under Alboin's successor Clef, who caused many of the leading Italians to be killed. Over this early period Balbo agreed with Manzoni.

He also emphasized the barbarism of the Lombards in his account of the interregnum, between the death of Clef and the elevation of Authari. Acting without a king, the dukes continued to oppress the churches and people of Italy, taking a third of the produce of the indigenous population.[76] Yet with the end of the Interregnum and the accession of Authari, the nature of Lombard rule began to change. Balbo pauses on a sentence that had long been a matter of debate, and continues to be problematic, not least, as he notes. because different manuscripts of Paul the Deacon give different readings: 'Populi tamen aggravati pro longobardis hospitia partiuntur' ('the lodgings of the oppressed people, however, were parceled out among the Lombards'), or 'Populi tamen aggravati per longobardos hospites partiuntur' ('the oppressed people, however, were parceled out among the

---

[72] Balbo, *Storia d'Italia*, p. 420.   [73] Balbo, *Storia d'Italia*, p. 423.
[74] Balbo, *Storia d'Italia*, p. 424, 'gente più feroce che non la germanica ferocità'; *Velleius Paterculus*, II 106, 'gens germana feritate ferociore'.
[75] Balbo, *Storia d'Italia*, pp. 424–6; Paul, *Historia Langobardorum*, II 28.
[76] Balbo, *Storia d'Italia*, pp. 427–8, citing Paul, *Historia Langobardorum*, II 32.

Lombard guests'), while 'patiuntur' ('suffered') also appears as an alternative to 'partiuntur'.[77] Unlike Manzoni and, later, Troya, Balbo opted for the first reading, which he felt was more in keeping with the general picture of declining oppression to be found in Paul's account. Like Manzoni, he noted the following sentence, in which Paul claimed that the Lombard kingdom witnessed a period of peace, but unlike him, he accepted its force.[78]

Balbo's picture of the Lombard kingdom grows increasingly positive during the reign of Authari's successor, Agilulf, and his wife Theodelinda. They reigned together for twenty-five glorious years, and as a result 'there was a new and massive mitigation of the conquest'.[79] There was, however, a continuing source of tension, notably the fact that the Lombards had not yet abandoned Arianism. Yet Theodelinda herself was Catholic. Balbo noted her benefactions, above all those to Monza, whose treasure he pauses to discuss. He stressed the importance of the Iron Crown, supposedly containing one of the nails from the True Cross, and he reflected on Napoleon's vanity, for, as he crowned himself with the Iron Crown in the cathedral of Milan in 1805, he repeated the text (in fact part of the ritual), 'Dio me l'ha data, guai a chi la tocca': 'God has given it to me: woe to him that touches it.'[80] Given Balbo's own involvement in the Napoleonic government of Italy this story clearly had a number of different and conflicting resonances.

However, decline set in after the highpoint of the joint reign of Agilulf and Theodelinda. Balbo compared their successors to their Merovingian contemporaries, the 'do-nothing kings', 'rois fainéants', or 'fa nulla'.[81] Here he may have underestimated both the Lombards and the Franks of the mid-seventh century. Curiously he offered no detailed comment on the Edict of king Rothari, issued in 643, which could certainly have been used against those who saw nothing but barbarism in seventh-century Italy. In his view the Lombards of this period provided material for painters and poets, rather than for historians, though—or perhaps therefore—he went on to refer to the story of Gundeperga, and her maltreatment by her two successive husbands.

While Balbo had little good to say about the Lombards of the late seventh century he regarded Liutprand in the early eighth as 'the least worthless, or the closest to greatness among the Lombard kings, after Agilulf and Theudelinda'.[82] He did not, however, go into detail, reserving his discussion of law for a later chapter. Yet in his assessment of the early eighth century it is not the king or even the Lombards that prompt his favourable assessment: this was, in his view, the period of the emergence of the first independent cities, notably Venice and the cities of the Pentapolis, and of the first independent popes.[83] His notion that this was a period of urban

---

[77] Balbo, *Storia d'Italia*, pp. 428–9, citing Paul, *Historia Langobardorum*, III 16. See the discussion of the problems of translating the text, and of the various translations offered, in Foulke, *Paul the Deacon*, pp. 114–16, n. 2, though he does not cite Balbo.

[78] See above n. 32 on Paul, *Historia Langobardorum*, III 16.

[79] Balbo, *Storia d'Italia*, p. 429.   [80] Balbo, *Storia d'Italia*, p. 430.

[81] Balbo, *Storia d'Italia*, p. 430.

[82] Balbo, *Storia d'Italia*, pp. 431–2. Fubini Leuzzi notes, p. 432, that Paul's words are taken from Muratori.

[83] Balbo, *Storia d'Italia*, p. 432.

development was, no doubt, drawn partly from Sismondi, but also from Heinrich Leo, who had pointed to the emergence of the cities of the Veneto after 713.[84]

After Liutprand the decline was swift. Balbo had nothing positive to say about the last Lombard kings. He provided a narrative of their conflict with the papacy and their collapse before the Carolingians, noting in passing what can accurately be said about Desiderius and Adelchis—with a quick glance towards Manzoni, who had made the latter famous. However, the epitaph for the Lombards that he provided is a good deal more measured that that of Manzoni's *Discorso*. Talking of 774 he wrote:

> And thus the Lombard nation fell, with little glory, in keeping with its exercise of power. It had kept itself, as long as it governed, more than had the other barbarians, separate, divided from the Italians, though thenceforth mixed and confused with the latter in their common servitude. Their existence as an independent political power was destroyed, but their families were not destroyed or banished: many of their laws and customs remained for several centuries: as did much blood in the veins, many words in the language and dialects throughout almost the whole of Italy down to today. And the name remains attached to a great, beautiful, good, rich Italian province, which, however, is now subject to the Empire and throne of Austria.[85]

Thus, Balbo followed in the line of Manzoni, seeing the Lombards as one of a succession of invading peoples who failed to integrate properly with the Italians. Indeed, they could be taken as symbols of foreign rule in Italy. Yet he had something to say in their favour. This is largely because he was prepared to acknowledge a change in Lombard rule in the seventh century, and to accept some of the more optimistic statements of Paul the Deacon, especially with regard to Authari, Theodelinda, and Liutprand. His stance also reflects his own liberal politics and his awareness of French and German scholarship—a spin-off, perhaps, of his career in the service of Napoleon—which had led him to see more virtues in the invaders than Manzoni had done.

7.5 CARLO TROYA

Balbo's arguments were taken seriously, not least by Manzoni, who felt he needed to restate his case in the appendices to the revised version of the *Discorso* issued in 1847. Equally significant was the discussion that developed between Balbo and Carlo Troya, both in private correspondence, some of which was published in Milan in 1869, in a small volume that gave the rather misleading impression that Balbo had accepted Troya's arguments, whereas the various editions of the former's *Storia d'Italia* make it clear that he continued to take a less pessimistic view of the Lombard kingdom in the seventh and eighth centuries than did his correspondent.[86]

---

[84] Leo, *Geschichte der italienischen Staaten*, vol. 1, p. 174.

[85] Balbo, *Storia d'Italia*, p. 437.

[86] Troya and Balbo, *Delle civile condizione dei Romani vinti dai Longobardi e di altre quistioni storichi: lettere inedite*. See Artifoni, 'Il Medioevo nel Romanticismo', pp. 126–7. Balbo's side of the correspondence is published in Fubini Leuzzi, ed., Balbo, *Storia d'Italia*, pp. 844–85.

Like Balbo, Troya was an important politician as well as a significant historian. He took part in the Neapolitan revolution of 1820–1, which led to him spending some time in exile. He played a major role in the crisis that engulfed the Kingdom of the Two Sicilies in 1848–9, and despite his neo-Guelf views (favouring papal leadership in Italy) he briefly headed a moderate government in Naples.[87] His contribution to scholarship would be longer lasting, and not just his contribution to the history of the early Middle Ages, for he also published notable work on Dante. Yet it was his *Storia d'Italia* which was his greatest achievement.[88] Of Troya, G.P. Gooch stated in 1913, '[h]e exhibited the Lombards as barbarians and tyrants, and the Popes as the guardians of Roman law, the Latin language and Christian civilization. The book pointed to the resurrection of Italy through the Vatican.'[89] This was, after all, the age of Pius IX (1846–78).

Having dealt with the Lombards before their entry into Italy, Troya set out his view of the relations between the Lombards and the Italians in the last of the first five parts of his *Storia d'Italia*. This was published in 1841 under the title 'On the state of the Romans conquered by the Lombards'. There followed a volume, in three parts, on the Herules and Goths, and another on the Greeks and Lombards. Then there are the six parts of the magisterial *Codice diplomatico longobardo*, a milestone in the publication of Lombard charters.

Sensitive, like Manzoni and Balbo, to the parallels with foreign regimes in Italy in his own day, Troya began by stating that under the Lombards the Romans were deprived of all traces of citizenship, of their own magistrates, and of use of the *Codex Justinianus*, and he added that the proprietors were reduced to servile status. He contrasted this situation with the status of a Germanic warrior. This, he admitted, was not the position of Muratori or the German legal historian Savigny, who had interpreted Paul the Deacon as indicating the continuity of Roman *curiae* and of the *ordines* of the cities.[90]

Having set out his basic position, Troya turned to the evidence for Gaul, beginning with the debates of Boulainvilliers, Du Bos, and Montesquieu.[91] His own concern was largely with institutional issues. He argued that, although the *curiae*[92] and Roman law continued, the Gauls were in a state of political subjection. They had lesser *wergelds* (man- or blood-money) than the Franks, and although some did manage to abandon Roman law to live under *Lex Salica* they could only do so as a matter of royal favour.[93] With this model in mind, Troya turned to the Lombard conquest in Italy, and its initial brutality, offering a direct comparison: 'then in Italy there would have been, as in Gaul, a noble race set over an ignoble one'.[94] Status for the Lombards and the Franks was understood only in terms of a

---

[87] On Troya, see Tabacco, 'Latinità e germanesimo nella tradizione medievistica italiana', pp. 707–10.

[88] Troya, *Storia d'Italia del Medioevo*, 6 vols, in 16 parts.

[89] Gooch, *History and Historians in the Nineteenth Century*, p. 436.

[90] Troya, *Della condizione de' Romani*, pp. iii–iv.

[91] Troya, *Della condizione de' Romani*, p. vi. For Du Bos see also p. xxviii.

[92] Troya, *Della condizione de' Romani*, p. xiv.   [93] Troya, *Della condizione de' Romani*, p. ix.

[94] Troya, *Della condizione de' Romani*, pp. xxv–xxix.

man's *wergeld*, and a Roman did not have one.[95] It was possible for Romans to accumulate wealth, but that conveyed neither citizenship, nor membership of the army.[96] Their condition was, therefore, servile. They were tributary, having been divided up and allocated to the victors.[97] Troya's position here comes close to Manzoni's. As he subsequently remarked:

> Alessandro Manzoni was the first, and he gained great honour therefrom, who dared to express a doubt, judging such principles false, and the hope of establishing our true history vain, if one did not set out first in clear light the civil condition of the conquered Romans.[98]

Yet Troya acknowledged that not all Romans were allocated to Lombard masters, and that there was manumission, particularly in the context of enlisting men into the army to fight the Byzantines.[99] Indeed, he recognized a longstanding tradition among the Lombards of incorporating defeated peoples into their armies, thus admitting, as did Balbo, that the Lombards were a somewhat mongrel people—though this mongrel people was very clearly differentiated from the servile tribute payers.[100]

The Lombards, Troya insisted, hated urban life, regarding towns as prisons[101]—a somewhat fanciful view, derived from a simplistic reading of Germanic custom, albeit one that was similar to the views of Montlosier. They preferred to live in the country. As a result urban life declined—though Troya did admit that Lombards had an impact on towns and on the buildings erected in them.[102] The *curiae* came to an end, and with them the magistracies of the Roman world.[103] There were no Roman judges, nor, in Troya's view, was any use made of Roman law.[104] With regard to religion, Troya maintained, on very dubious grounds, that the pagan Lombards mainly worshipped Wodan. He accepted that there were some Lombard Catholics and speculated that they may have been kinder than their pagan or Arian counterparts.[105] Initially, the Lombards treated Christian clergy with extreme cruelty—here Troya was following the evidence of Gregory I.[106]

Having dealt with the period of conquest and the subsequent interregnum, Troya turned to the question of Authari, and to the awkward sentence which so bothered Balbo. The reading he preferred was 'Populi tamen aggravati per Longobardos hospites patiuntur', with its emphasis on the suffering of the Italians.[107]

---

[95] Troya, *Della condizione de' Romani*, pp. xxix–xxxi, xxxviii, xl.

[96] Troya, *Della condizione de' Romani*, pp. xxxi–xxxii.

[97] Troya, *Della condizione de' Romani*, pp. xxxiv–xxxix, xl–xli.

[98] Troya, *Della condizione de' Romani*, p. lx.

[99] Troya, *Della condizione de' Romani*, pp. lii–liii.

[100] Troya, *Della condizione de' Romani*, pp. liv–lv, lvii.

[101] Troya, *Della condizione de' Romani*, pp. xli–xlii.

[102] Troya, *Della condizione de' Romani*, p. ccccxix.

[103] Troya, *Della condizione de' Romani*, pp. xliii–xliv. On Lombard distaste for city life see also pp. cxxv–cxxvii.

[104] Troya, *Della condizione de' Romani*, p. xlv.

[105] Troya, *Della condizione de' Romani*, p. xlviii.

[106] Troya, *Della condizione de' Romani*, p. lviii.

[107] Troya, *Della condizione de' Romani*, pp. lxiii; see also pp. ccccix–ccccxii.

Like Balbo, however, he did admit an improvement in the status of the tribute-payers on royal lands in Authari's time. Nevertheless, oppression continued. Agilulf initially persecuted Catholics, despite his marriage to Theodelinda. Meanwhile, the wars of the Lombards with the Byzantines continued to cause disruption and devastation.[108]

Troya did see an improvement later in Agilulf's reign, which he linked to the fact that in his eyes the king had converted to Catholicism. He also thought that Agilulf and Theodelinda had conferred citizenship on the bishops, thus making them equal to noble Lombards.[109] He had already noted that because the *Germani* had revered priests they probably did not regard bishops as servile.[110] This new elevation of the senior clergy he linked to the fact that the children of nobles were starting to enter the Church. He used later evidence to show that clergy had *wergelds*.[111] Whereas Savigny thought that the Church was subject to Roman law, as in Francia, Troya argued that the evidence for this largely dates from Charlemagne's time, and that in general the clergy were subject to Lombard law.[112]

Law is much more at the heart of Troya's discussion than it had been either for Manzoni or for Balbo. He was a lawyer by training, and he was the editor of the *Codice diplomatico*. Not surprisingly he discussed the *Edict of Rothari* and Liutprand's laws at some length. Keen to set Lombard developments within a broader European context, he made comparison with legislation in Francia, noting that Rothari (636–52) and Dagobert I (623–39), to whom he attributed the *Lex Ribvaria*, and also a revised version of *Lex Salica*, were contemporaries.[113] In his view, the status of the Romans continued to be servile in both the Lombard and the Frankish codes of the mid-seventh century.[114]

Given the fact that Rothari's *Edict* is in Latin, Troya was prepared to accept that its scribes were Roman in origin,[115] but he also noted that the *Edict* makes no reference to Romans or Roman citizenship. In his view everything hinged on a person's *wergeld*, and Romans did not have the same *wergelds* as Lombards.[116] He also observed that the *Edict of Rothari* explicitly abolished all earlier laws. The *Edict* must, therefore, have applied to all the inhabitants of Lombard Italy.[117] He accepted that there were some borrowings from Roman law, seeing these as the first light of a new dawn—though only the first light. No one as yet was studying Roman law; Rothari's lawyers were merely taking over the bits that they found useful.[118]

[108] Troya, *Della condizione de' Romani*, pp. lxiii–lxvii, lxix, lxxiii–lxxiv.
[109] Troya, *Della condizione de' Romani*, pp. lxxxiv–v.
[110] Troya, *Della condizione de' Romani*, p. lviii.
[111] Troya, *Della condizione de' Romani*, pp. lxxxv–vi.
[112] Troya, *Della condizione de' Romani*, pp. lxxxix–xcii.
[113] Troya, *Della condizione de' Romani*, p. ciii. He also draws comparison with Anglo-Saxon laws: *Della condizione de' Romani*, pp. ccccxiii–ccccxvi, ccccxxiii.
[114] Troya, *Della condizione de' Romani*, pp. ciii–civ.
[115] Troya, *Della condizione de' Romani*, p. cix.
[116] On the *wergeld* of a Roman slave-woman, Troya, *Della condizione de' Romani*, pp. cx–cxii.
[117] Troya, *Della condizione de' Romani*, p. cxxxi, where he also notes the lack of any comparable act in Merovingian legislation. There are, however, parallels in Visigothic Spain.
[118] Troya, *Della condizione de' Romani*, pp. cxxxv–cxxxvi.

Troya detected some growing Roman influence in the eighth century, not least because of Liutprand's temporary acquisition of Ravenna.[119] Even so, whereas in Charlemagne's laws one finds *Theodosiani* (men subject to the Theodosian Code) from Francia and *Justiniani* (men subject to the Code of Justinian) from Rome and the Exarchate, in Lombard Italy there was no equivalent. The Romans of the Lombard kingdom were thus living by Lombard law: they had no citizenship, but they had skills. He made a comparison with the early sixth-century Burgundian kingdom: there are forty references to Romans in the Code attributed to Gundobad, but in Lombard Italy Roman citizenship vanished.[120]

Troya's argument, with its remarkable underpinning of documentary evidence, may look overwhelming. Yet, despite his citation of evidence, the case was still founded on silence: on the absence of any clear reference to Romans in the sources. Silence, however, does not necessarily prove that the indigenous Italians were subject to the level of oppression supposed by Troya, at least after the initial period of the conquest. It was, therefore, possible for Balbo to republish his view that there was some survival of Roman law even after the appearance of Troya's *Della condizione de' Romani vinti da' Longobardi*. Yet while Balbo and Troya disagreed, and did so over more than mere details, they were at one on the importance of the Lombard period for an understanding of Italy. Balbo had placed the Lombard conquest in a long line of invasions to which the peninsula was subjected. Troya, with his legal eye, had placed the question of citizenship at the heart of that subjection. Both men, like Manzoni, found in the history of Lombard Italy an echo of their own day, with the peninsula divided and, at least in part, subject to foreign rule.

7.6 VERDI AND *ATTILA*

Despite the pile of publications on the Lombard and later periods, Balbo felt that the Italians needed more history, though not just academic works: 'poesia storica, filosofia storica, romanzi storici', but based on good documentary evidence.[121] In his *Storia d'Italia* he consigned the seventh century largely to painters and poets. The challenge does not appear to have been picked up, at least not in comparison with the use made of the historic highpoints of the twelfth and thirteenth centuries. Yet the Lombard period had attracted the attention of artists in the past: Rubens had painted the death of Alboin, and Handel had composed *Rodelinda*. If Risorgimento artists made relatively little use of the Lombard period one might guess that it did not provide much opportunity for portraying the themes of the moment: the oppression of the Italians by the Lombards was general; there was no great anecdote of persecution or defiance. In so far as an episode from the early Middle Ages acted as a source of inspiration, it was Attila's invasion of Italy—and

---

[119] Troya, *Della condizione de' Romani*, pp. clxxxvii–cxci.
[120] Troya, *Della condizione de' Romani*, pp. cclix–cclxii.
[121] Soldani, 'Il Medioevo del Risorgimento nello specchio della nazione', p. 174.

here the version of the story was that of Werner, which Mme de Staël had presented as being a critique of Napoleon.

During the 1845–6 season at La Fenice in Venice two settings of the Attila story were presented, Francesco Malipiero's *Ildegonda di Borgogna* and Verdi's *Attila*. Both were based on Werner's drama, Ildegonda being the Italian version of the name given by Werner to Attila's last wife and supposed killer. Nor were these the first such operas: in Italy there was Giuseppe Persiani's *Attila* of 1827, while Verdi's initial librettist Temistocle Solera also composed the music for his own version of *Ildegonda* in 1840, and he provided the libretto for Pascual Juan Emilio Arrieta y Corera's opera of the same name, which, like Verdi's work, was performed in 1846.[122] Of this clutch of works, only Verdi's has survived the test of time.

Verdi's *Attila* came to be seen as a quintessentially Risorgimento work, and in particular words sung by Ezio (the historical Aetius), in which he asks Attila to leave Italy to him—*Avrai tu l'universo, resti l'Italia a me* ('You take the universe, but leave Italy to me')—were turned into a call against rule by foreign powers.[123] Some have been surprised that a libretto with such inflammatory potential passed the Venetian censors. The parallel between Huns and the Austrians, however, was not immediately obvious: the Habsburgs were not, after all, recent invaders. Moreover, despite the fact that Attila and the Huns (like the Lombards, or, as we shall see, the Ostrogoths) could be understood to symbolize the Austrians, Werner's play had been well received in Vienna, where its operatic potential was noted from the start: Beethoven had considered setting it, and it had been performed with music by his friend Ignaz Seyfried.[124] Considered in context, it is easy to see how the work could have slipped past the censors, and indeed its political impact may well have been overestimated.[125]

In fact Attila's invasion of Italy scarcely had the same resonance as the subsequent conquest by the Lombards—or even that by the relatively well-respected Ostrogoths. Nor did the historical research undertaken by Verdi or his librettists compare remotely with that undertaken by Manzoni for the *Adelchi*. Verdi did urge his second librettist, Francesco Maria Piave, to do some homework, but principally on Mme de Staël's *De l'Allemagne*.[126] He also sent his friend Vincenzo Luccardi, to investigate Hunnic costume and hairstyle, though for this he suggested that the Roman artist consult Raphael's fresco in the Vatican depicting the meeting of Attila and pope Leo.[127] Rather more historical research may underlie the scene

---

[122] Carlà, 'Il modello di ogni caduta', p. 85, n. 9.

[123] Martin, 'Verdi and the Risorgimento', p. 22. On the patriotism of Verdi, see Sorba, 'Il Risorgimento in musica: l'opera lirica nei teatri del 1848', pp. 143, 148. On the question of the extent to which the image of Verdi as 'vate del Risorgimento' is an oversimplification, Abbate and Parker, 'Introduction: On Analyzing Opera', pp. 11–12. Also, Parker, *The New Grove Guide to Verdi and his Operas*, p. 30; Wood, ' "Adelchi" and "Attila" '. See most recently Sorba, '*Attila* and Verdi's historical imagination', pp. 241–8.

[124] Porter, 'Verdi's Attila: an ethnomusicological analysis', p. 46.

[125] Stamatov, 'Interpretive activism and the political uses of Verdi's operas in the 1840s', pp. 345–66.

[126] *I Copialettere di Giuseppe Verdi*, pp. 437–8. Also, Wood, ' "Adelchi" and "Attila" ', p. 251.

[127] *I Copialettere di Giuseppe Verdi*, p. 441.

in the opera where the refugees from Aquileia cross the Venetian lagoon to found Venice. Clearly it was added to please the first audiences of the work at La Fenice. Yet it may well reflect the impact of Sismondi's writings, which associate the foundation of the city with Attila's invasion.[128]

Some have seen Verdi's *Attila* as being one of the major examples of the exploitation of early medieval narratives in the Risorgimento. In historiographical terms, it does not compare in importance with Manzoni's *Adelchi* or with his *Discorso*. Certainly it does not constitute the measured consideration of the fifth, sixth, and seventh centuries, that one finds in Manzoni, Troya, or Balbo. Nor, in comparison with Manzoni's *Adelchi* and *Discorso*, does *Attila* sustain the parallel between late Antiquity and the present in any scholarly way. Yet Ezio's demand that the Hun should transfer Italy to him was a powerful one.

7.7 PASQUALE VILLARI

Before returning northwards, we should take note of one further Italian historian, who was active during 1848—although he was a rather younger contemporary, and would live a good deal longer than Manzoni, Balbo, or Troya. Indeed his interpretation both of the Fall of the Roman Empire and of the Lombards did not appear until 1901, when it reflected a very different attitude towards the barbarians than had been dominant before the success of the Risorgimento.

Pasquale Villari, like Carlo Troya a Neapolitan, had been involved in the anti-Bourbon uprisings of 1848, as a result of which he had to flee north to Florence. He became a professor of history at Pisa and subsequently at Florence, concentrating largely on the Renaissance period and writing notable works on Savonarola and Machiavelli. He was also involved in national politics, as a member of the legislative chamber between 1867 and 1882, and as minister for education between 1889–92. It was only towards the end of a long career that he turned his mind to the fall of the Roman Empire, publishing *Le invasioni barbariche in Italia* in 1901, when he was 75. It appeared a year later in English, translated by his English-born wife.

Villari's preface suggests a very different world, both political and intellectual, from that in which Manzoni, Troya, and Balbo had been writing: he noted the improvement in the resources available to historians and in historical method, but went on to state:

> Nevertheless books supplying narratives of past events in a simple, easy, readable style, such as abounded formerly in Italy, and served as models to other countries, are becoming increasingly scarce here…history in general, and the history of Italy in particular, should be not only a means of instruction, but likewise of national education, by serving as a real factor in the formation of the moral and political character of our country. Cesare Balbo, who was always inspired by lofty patriotism, deplored throughout his life the absence of any popular history that all might read with pleasure

---

[128] Sismondi, *Histoire des Républiques italiennes du Moyen Age*, 5th edn, vol. 1, pp. 188–90; Sismondi, *A History of the Fall of the Roman Empire*, vol. 1, pp. 163–4.

and profit…Thus we have sometimes the humiliation of seeing foreigners produce better books than we the Italians can write on ancient, mediæval, or modern Italy; and our rising generation has to learn the history of its own land from foreign sources. Unfortunately, too, in spite of great learning and good method, such works are sometimes written in a hostile key; their authors being naturally moved by patriotism to extol their own country at Italy's expense.[129]

At the end of the preface he noted the works that he has most frequently consulted: the established classics by Gibbon, Tillemont, and Muratori, and more recent works by Bury, Malfatti, Bertolini, Dahn, Mühlbacher, Hartmann, and above all Hodgkin—to Bury, Dahn, and Hodgkin we will return. This is a significant list, both for those included and for those omitted. Although Villari has already mentioned Balbo, his name does not appear here, nor do the names of Manzoni or Troya. Oddly, Sismondi is not mentioned, although Villari wrote about him and his work for Gabriel Monod's *Revue historique*.[130]

Villari's coverage differs from that of most of his predecessors: he dedicated nearly as much space to the background to the invasions, both Roman and barbarian, as he did to each of the periods of barbarian rule: Gothic, Lombard, and Frankish. Thus, no more attention is paid to the Lombards than to the Goths or the Franks. Like other historians he found the space to dwell in some detail on the wars of the sixth century—a simple reflection of the quality of Procopius' narrative. He also had more to say about the Church and particularly the papacy, which reflects not only his own religious position, but also the growth in papal influence since the beginning of the pontificate of Pius IX.

Villari begins his account of the Barbarian invasions with an assessment of the weakness of the Roman Empire. He stresses that 'it was a compound of different races, held together by force',[131] thus presenting a relatively critical view. He notes the military weaknesses: recruitment to the army meant that it depended on discipline rather than patriotism.[132] The absence of patriotism is something that he returns to when he considers the unpopularity of Justinian's rule in Italy[133] and is clearly central to his understanding. His view of the barbarians and the threat they posed falls back on the views of Caesar and Tacitus,[134] though he adds the modish description of them as being Aryan, like the Greeks and Romans.[135] The Huns, however, were quite different, being Turanian central Asiatic nomads.[136]

Having set out background descriptions of the Empire and its barbarian invaders, for the most part Villari provides a straight narrative of events.[137] Inevitably,

---

[129] Villari, *The Barbarian Invasions of Italy*, pp. v–vii.
[130] Villari, 'Une conversation inédite entre Napoléon Ier et Sismondi'; Villari and Monod, 'Lettres inédites de Sismondi écrites pendant les Cent-Jours'; Villari and Monod, 'Notes de Sismondi sur l'empire et les cent jours'; Villari, 'La storia dei centi Giorni narrata del S. (epistolario inedito)'.
[131] Villari, *The Barbarian Invasions of Italy*, vol. 1, p. 3.
[132] Villari, *The Barbarian Invasions of Italy*, vol. 1, p. 4.
[133] Villari, *The Barbarian Invasions of Italy*, vol. 2, p. 270.
[134] Villari, *The Barbarian Invasions of Italy*, vol. 1, pp. 14–17.
[135] Villari, *The Barbarian Invasions of Italy*, vol. 1, p. 13.
[136] Villari, *The Barbarian Invasions of Italy*, vol. 1, p. 45.
[137] Villari, *The Barbarian Invasions of Italy*, vol. 1, p. ix.

however, he makes choices: he accepts Salvian's view that the barbarians were less oppressive than was generally thought, and he even notes that the Vandals did not cause much hardship for the majority of the population.[138] On reaching the Hunnic invasion, like others before him, he pauses to discuss the foundation of Venice, though he does so with reference to Hodgkin rather than Sismondi.[139] He discusses Attila's meeting with pope Leo, who is described at some length and presented as a key figure in the development of the notion of the Universal Church.[140] Having recounted the deposition of Romulus Augustulus by Odovacer, Villari announces that 'The Empire of the West had fallen, the history of Italy had begun'.[141]

Odovacer's rule attracts Villari's attention: he it was who first settled significant numbers of barbarians in Italy, though according to Villari this settlement must have been a modification of an imperial system, and it must have been less of a burden than it may appear: after all, the army had always been a burden. Moreover, the settlement must have been geographically limited. The only novelty was that retired barbarians and their families had to be catered for.[142]

Odovacer was soon challenged by Theodoric, with his followers, who Villari thought may have amounted to 200–300,000 people, of whom perhaps 40,000 were armed men. Like Odovacer's following, they were a mixed lot.[143] They had also lost most of their Germanic traditions: they did not hold property in common, nor were there any popular institutions. Their king, Theodoric, effectively ruled as a tyrant.[144] There was a clear distinction between the Goths, who were essentially a military group, and the Romans, who were essentially civilian. Civil government remained in Roman hands, while military government was Gothic. Yet Villari did allow movement between the two races. Citing Cassiodorus, he noted that Romans could undertake military training and become soldiers: there was, as yet, no ban on them bearing arms. He also assumed that Goths could become civilian administrators.[145] Even so, despite an attempt at fusion, there was apparently lasting antagonism between the two groups,[146] and in the last years of Theodoric's rule the alliance between the two peoples started to fade.[147]

Justinian's reconquest of Italy brought its own problems. The length of the war alienated many. At the same time the taxes raised on the newly conquered territory by the emperor, as well as his religious policies, were unpopular.[148] For Villari the crisis of the Three Chapters marked the start of the alienation of the Church from the Empire: the religious controversy revealed that the papacy could not be independent under Byzantine rule.[149] Justinian's intervention provided the background

[138] Villari, *The Barbarian Invasions of Italy*, vol. 1, pp. 100–1.
[139] Villari, *The Barbarian Invasions of Italy*, vol. 1, p. 116.
[140] Villari, *The Barbarian Invasions of Italy*, vol. 1, pp. 116–18, 125.
[141] Villari, *The Barbarian Invasions of Italy*, vol. 1, p. 138.
[142] Villari, *The Barbarian Invasions of Italy*, vol. 1, pp. 142–3.
[143] Villari, *The Barbarian Invasions of Italy*, vol. 1, pp. 154, 159.
[144] Villari, *The Barbarian Invasions of Italy*, vol. 1, pp. 160–1.
[145] Villari, *The Barbarian Invasions of Italy*, vol. 1, p. 163.
[146] Villari, *The Barbarian Invasions of Italy*, vol. 1, pp. 164, 168.
[147] Villari, *The Barbarian Invasions of Italy*, vol. 1, p. 180.
[148] Villari, *The Barbarian Invasions of Italy*, vol. 1, p. 216, vol. 2, p. 269.
[149] Villari, *The Barbarian Invasions of Italy*, vol. 2, p. 254.

for other developments. Villari set the popularity of monasticism in the context of the desolation of the peninsula: Benedict at Subiacio and Monte Cassino provided a focus for men to turn to God.[150] Cassiodorus realized that welding Goths and Romans into a single nation would not work, and the monastery he founded at the Vivarium turned, like Benedict, to the promotion of monasticism.[151]

By comparison with the Ostrogoths, the Lombards learnt little from either the Empire or the Church.[152] Like Manzoni, Balbo, and Troya, Villari saw the conquest and the succeeding interregnum as a period of great oppression for the indigenous population of Italy: the fact that the dukes demanded a third of the income of the Italians was a disaster, worse than giving up a proportion of land, for it implied there was no free ownership.[153] Like Balbo, he saw a change during the reign of Authari, and he insisted that the infamous sentence of Paul the Deacon on Lombard oppression had to be read in the light of the very positive sentence that follows. However, he went further: he rejected fully the notion of the semi-enslavement of the Romans, arguing that the absence of any reference to Roman *wergeld* meant nothing, and that there was no evidence to suggest that servitude was the norm. Sensibly he concluded that the gaps in Paul's account may reflect the slightness of his knowledge.[154]

Yet while his assessment of the position of the Romans under Lombard rule is more positive than that given by most of his Italian predecessors (though not by the German scholar, Sybel),[155] he was still critical of Lombard government. If Roman traditions were ever broken, it was under the Lombards. As mercenaries who had long been on the move, they had lost their 'primitive Germanic institutions', but they were not a coherent group, remaining 'a congeries of separate bodies', whose disunity ultimately ensured the failure of the kingdom. The monarchy was neither exclusively hereditary nor elective. As for the monarch, he was in charge of the army and of justice, and while the Lombards did have their own legal traditions, the kings increasingly issued their own laws. Nevertheless, the dukes were largely able to act as independent viceroys. Even so, having 'failed to make Italy German', the Lombards ended up by being Romanized and virtually merged into the nation they had conquered. Moreover, although the Germanic peoples preferred life in the country, many of the Lombards, and especially their dukes, must have lived in towns.[156]

Villari presents this remarkably moderate picture, despite devoting a good deal of time to the pontificate of Gregory I.[157] For him, Gregory 'was recognised by the whole population as their true and legitimate head'.[158] His correspondent and ally,

---

[150] Villari, *The Barbarian Invasions of Italy*, vol. 1, pp. 225–30. Incorrectly Villari saw Benedict as establishing the Benedictine Order—something that would not emerge for centuries.
[151] Villari, *The Barbarian Invasions of Italy*, vol. 1, pp. 230–1.
[152] Villari, *The Barbarian Invasions of Italy*, vol. 2, p. 281.
[153] Villari, *The Barbarian Invasions of Italy*, vol. 2, p. 285.
[154] Villari, *The Barbarian Invasions of Italy*, vol. 2, pp. 296–9. On *wergelds* see also p. 346.
[155] Villari, *The Barbarian Invasions of Italy*, vol. 2, p. 296.
[156] Villari, *The Barbarian Invasions of Italy*, vol. 2, pp. 300–2.
[157] Villari, *The Barbarian Invasions of Italy*, vol. 2, pp. 310–29.
[158] Villari, *The Barbarian Invasions of Italy*, vol. 2, p. 322; see also p. 320.

the Lombard queen Theodelinda, also gets a good press, particularly for her promotion of Catholicism among her people: 'Thus the way was smoothed for their complete fusion with the Romans.'[159] When he came to discuss her gifts to Monza, Villari (like Balbo) noted Napoleon's taking of the supposed crown of Agilulf.[160]

In his discussion of the seventh century, Villari looked outside Italy, to the problems faced by Byzantium and especially to the expansion of Islam.[161] As a result Rothari did not have to worry about any Byzantine threat. Unlike Balbo, Villari paused at length to consider Rothari's laws. In his opinion, they were the first legislation in Italy issued without any regard for the Empire or for earlier Roman law, but they were still one of the finest legal compilations issued by the barbarians.[162] While maintaining that barbarian codes were usually directed only to the Germanic population, Villari thought that Rothari's edict was addressed to all his subjects, although he acknowledged that at the same time Roman law must have survived as custom, and he accepted Savigny's argument on its persistence.[163]

In tune with his emphasis on the Church, his discussion of the second half of the seventh century is largely dominated by the relations of the papacy with Byzantium and with the Lombards. With Liutprand, however, he reached the man he considered the greatest of the Lombard kings, above all, because of his legislative achievement.[164] Villari offered his positive assessment despite the threats posed to the papacy by Liutprand's expansionist policies.[165] Yet for all, the king's greatness as a legislator, he was not a statesman, and he failed to unite Italy, which he might just have succeeded in doing at the end of his reign.[166]

Before recounting the fall of Lombard Italy, Villari provided a brief (and, even for its time, rather old-fashioned) account of Frankish history. His discussion of Charles Martel depended largely on his reading of the early development of feudalism, which was heavily infected by his understanding of Italian *latifundia* (slave estates), rather than by then-current French scholarship.[167] As for the collapse of the Lombard kingdom itself, Villari largely resorted to narrative, but he used revolts against Charlemagne to argue that the Lombards and Romans had finally been welded into a single nation.[168] It would be difficult to be further from Manzoni. It is Charlemagne, rather than the last Lombard rulers, who comes across as brutal.[169]

No one could claim that Villari's account has the historiographical importance of those of Manzoni or Troya. Yet, like Balbo's reading, it is for the most part more

---

[159] Villari, *The Barbarian Invasions of Italy*, vol. 2, p. 327.
[160] Villari, *The Barbarian Invasions of Italy*, vol. 2, p. 328.
[161] Villari, *The Barbarian Invasions of Italy*, vol. 2, pp. 330–7.
[162] Villari, *The Barbarian Invasions of Italy*, vol. 2, pp. 339–40.
[163] Villari, *The Barbarian Invasions of Italy*, vol. 2, pp. 340–1, 343.
[164] Villari, *The Barbarian Invasions of Italy*, vol. 2, pp. 361–2.
[165] Villari, *The Barbarian Invasions of Italy*, vol. 2, p. 370.
[166] Villari, *The Barbarian Invasions of Italy*, vol. 2, p. 374.
[167] Villari, *The Barbarian Invasions of Italy*, vol. 2, pp. 382–95. For the opinions of Fustel de Coulanges, see below.
[168] Villari, *The Barbarian Invasions of Italy*, vol. 2, p. 437.
[169] Villari, *The Barbarian Invasions of Italy*, vol. 2, p. 440.

balanced than theirs. Villari did not share their harsh views of the Lombards. Despite his early involvement in the Risorgimento this is scarcely surprising. He wrote his account of the barbarian invasions of Italy a full half century after his involvement in the Neapolitan uprising of 1848, and thus after the success of Italian Unification. Foreign occupation did not trouble him as much as it had Manzoni or his immediate followers. The question of racial distinction, which had been so crucial to them, did interest Villari, but he thought, on the whole, that the differences between Romans and barbarians had eventually been overcome, and he reformulated the issue in terms of national spirit, and of patriotism. There had been other developments as well. Among the issues that most attracted Villari was the history of the Church (though he was not entirely in sympathy with the Church of his own day, comparing the sixteenth-century St Peter's in Rome unfavourably to its Constantinian predecessor: the new one was far too like an art gallery).[170] So far we have touched on Church History only in passing. It is, however, necessary to examine it head on.

[170] Villari, *The Barbarian Invasions of Italy*, vol. 2, pp. 429–30.

8

Heirs of the Martyrs

8.1 CHATEAUBRIAND AND *LES MARTYRS*

As we have seen, the history of the Fall of Rome and of the establishment of the Merovingians was caught up in debates about politics, society, and the economy in the first half of the nineteenth century. In addition, it was deeply affected by the religious changes of the period: above all by the Catholic revival which began in France, but which also had its reverberations in Italy, as well as Germany and England, even reaching some strands of Protestantism.[1] It would lead to a reading of the role of the Church which was very different from that proposed by Gibbon. On more than one occasion we have met the idea that Christianity saved Western Europe—not least in Guizot's reading of the history of Civilization. It is this argument, as propounded by Chateaubriand, Ozanam, and Montalembert, that is the central concern of this chapter. All three men both wrote about early Christianity, while at the same time being deeply engaged in the work of the Church: their scholarship and their commitment fed off each other. They were not unique, nor was such religious engagement confined to France. Manzoni was involved in Church polemic. Moreover, a number of English Catholics, including cardinals Newman and Wiseman, also looked to the Age of the Persecutions for inspiration. So did the Anglican Charles Kingsley, another figure who (like Ozanam in particular) was deeply involved in the social mission of the Church. While he wrote no major historical work on the Fall of Rome, his novel *Hypatia* provides a counterpoint to the history written by French Catholic evangelicals.

Central to the renewal of interest in the religious history of the later Roman Empire, and to the growing appreciation of its relevance to nineteenth-century Christianity, were the writings of François-René de Chateaubriand. Born in 1768, he had initially been sympathetic to the Revolution, but as it turned more bloodthirsty he decided on self-imposed exile and lived for two years in America. On his return he joined the royalist forces of the Prince de Condé in Coblenz, only to be wounded at the siege of Thionville in 1792. He escaped to England, where he remained until Napoleon offered an amnesty to French émigrés in 1800, returning to France shortly before Montlosier. During his English exile he was reconverted to the Catholicism in which he had been brought up, and as a result wrote his justification of Catholic Christianity, *Génie du christianisme ou beautés de la religion*

---

[1] For the position of the Catholic Church within French society, see Tombs, *France 1814–1914*, pp. 132–8.

chrétienne, which was published in 1802. This was a sharp riposte to Enlightenment and Revolutionary views of Christianity. It attracted Napoleon's attention, and Chateaubriand was appointed secretary to the legation to the Holy See. He soon fell out, however, with cardinal Fesch, the French ambassador to the papacy, and resigned his post. In 1804 he also resigned from being Napoleon's minister to the Valais. He would subsequently make his living by writing.

Although *Génie du christianisme* is not primarily a historical work, but rather a religious apologia, many of its illustrative details are drawn from history, not least from that of late-Roman and early-medieval Christianity: thus, the Germanic invaders are presented as providential figures.[2] For Chateaubriand, as for de Staël in *De la littérature*, though from rather different viewpoints, the barbarians and Christianity were positive forces. More important as a presentation of the end of Antiquity was Chateaubriand's novel, *Les Martyrs*, begun at the time he was finishing *Génie du christianisme*, and published in 1809.

Les Martyrs is set at the end of the Great Persecution: it tells the story of Eudore, a young Christian, and Cymodocée, daughter of a pagan priest, who as a descendant of Homer was responsible for the upkeep of the shrine of the great poet. Most of the first half of the novel is taken up with the exploits of Eudore. He had been a soldier, whose postings had taken him through much of the Empire. He spent time in Rome, where he had been educated with Ambrose and Augustine (a chronological impossibility, like much that follows). Then in the Rhineland he was captured and was given as a slave to Clothilde, the wife of Pharamond, before he escaped to become commander in Armorica, where the druidess Velleda fell for him—the episode would be the basis for the play by Chateaubriand's protégé Alexandre Soumet, which was to form the libretto of Bellini's opera *Norma*.[3] In the course of his wanderings Eudore ended up excommunicated, and as a result was subject to a long period of penance. It was while he was a penitent that Cymodocée first saw him and fell in love with him. She, however, had attracted the attentions of the governor Hiéroclès. Eudore saved her from the governor, and instructed her to go to Jerusalem, where she entered service with Helena, the mother of Constantine. He meanwhile went to Rome where he represented the Christians before Diocletian, who is presented as wise but weak, and as a result was persuaded by Galerius and Hiéroclès to sign the edict of persecution and then to abdicate. Eudore warned Constantine to flee to Britain. He himself remained in Rome and was tried, condemned, and imprisoned with just about every other martyr who ever existed. The outbreak of persecution meant that Helena could not protect Cymodocée, who headed into the Judaean desert and was baptized in the Jordan by Jerome. She then made her way to Rome to join Eudore in the Colosseum, where he managed to place a ring on her finger before they were eaten by wild beasts.

It is difficult to do justice to the narrative of *Les Martyrs*, and not just because of its narrative hokum and chronological impossibilities, not least because alongside its worldly narrative there are scenes in Heaven and Hell, and even a brief trip to

---

[2] Chateaubriand, *Génie du christianisme*, ed. Regard, Pt. III, bk III, ch. 6, p. 842.
[3] On the indebtedness of Soumet to Chateaubriand, Beffort, *Alexandre Soumet*, pp. 74–5.

Purgatory. The earthly scenes are heavily footnoted: they are underpinned with a barrage of citations of classical and early Christian sources, as well as references to objects and sites that Chateaubriand knew or had read about. In the preface he insists that there is a factual basis for what he has to say. He does, however, admit, disarmingly, that there is a certain amount of apparent anachronism (which is a massive understatement, seeing that the material he draws on stretches from Greece in the Archaic Age to the fifth century AD), but he urges the reader not to be disturbed by any apparent discrepancy, arguing that Augustine and Jerome behave as they would have done had they been around at the beginning of the fourth century, and that if one thinks that a figure like Pharamond, Clodion, or Mérovée, is out of place, one should just imagine that it was another person of the same name as the individual known from Fredegar: there were, he claimed, lots of Pharamonds, Clodions, and Mérovées in history.[4]

For the modern reader the historical anachronisms may seem easier to stomach than the scenes in Heaven and Hell, which are unfootnoted, but which are partly dependent on Milton's *Paradise Lost*, as Chateaubriand states in the preface. Indeed the whole work is conceived as a confrontation between Homer and Milton.[5] Heaven and Hell are every bit as real as the Roman Empire in the novel: effectively the world conjured up by Chateaubriand is that of religious art, which in precisely the same decade was being revived with, for instance, plans for the decoration of the dome of the Panthéon, which, as we have seen, was to have represented Napoleon and Josephine in Heaven with, among others, Clovis, Clothilde, and Charlemagne.[6] There were those whose religious understanding meant that their reading of history was cosmic. And if *Les Martyrs* lacks historical truth for us, for Chateaubriand it was concerned with eternal truth: the work represented an attempt to put the arguments of the *Génie du christianisme* into a novel, so as to reach a wider audience.

Within the French tradition *Les Martyrs* would be as significant as Scott's historical novels, and far more influential than Sismondi's *Julia Sévéra*. Well written and furiously paced, it conjures up a vivid picture of the past. Even so, the initial reviews were mixed, though Guizot was among those who praised it.[7] Equally important, the young Augustin Thierry was enthralled when he came across the work in 1810, a year after its publication.[8] Above all, however, it appealed to committed Catholics. Essentially it was an allegory of de-Christianization during the Terror, while the character of the persecuting emperor Diocletian, clear-sighted but weak-minded, was intended as a portrait of Napoleon.[9] Alongside *Génie*, *Les Martyrs* amounted to a manifesto for a Catholic revival. The novel in particular presented the late Roman Church as a model to be emulated. Committed Catholics were to look back to the martyrs and their immediate successors for inspiration.

---

[4] Chateaubriand, *Les Martyrs*, p. 7. I have used the edition published in Paris in 1873.
[5] Chateaubriand, *Les Martyrs*, p. 3.
[6] Lépinay, *Peintures et sculptures du Panthéon*, pp. 26–8.
[7] For an account of the initial reaction to Chateaubriand's work and of Guizot's review, see de Broglie, *Guizot*, pp. 30–1.
[8] Thierry, 'Preface to the Narratives', pp. 111–12.
[9] Thom, *Republics, Nations and Tribes*, pp. 211, 247–54.

8.2 FRÉDÉRIC OZANAM

Just as the third and fourth centuries provided inspiration for a Catholic revival, so too the revival itself was to have a major impact on interpretations of the End of Antiquity and the early Middle Ages. Hitherto, interpretations of the period had been largely influenced by the political and social debates of the *Ancien Régime* and its aftermath, and in Italy by the opening salvos of Risorgimento argument. The issue of religion had largely been left to one side. Gibbon had addressed it only in order to denounce the influence of Christianity and its superstitions. The notion that the Church was central to the developments of the centuries from the fourth to the seventh would be one of the major contributions of French scholarship in the mid-nineteenth. Here the central figures were Antoine Frédéric Ozanam, closely followed by Charles Forbes René de Montalembert and Albert duc de Broglie. Ozanam, like Chateaubriand, put the image of the early Church at the heart of his call for religious renewal.

Frédéric Ozanam was born in Milan, in 1813, of French parents. Three years after his birth the family returned to Lyons, where his father was appointed to a chair of medicine.[10] Although Frédéric was perhaps more influenced by his mother, who played a central role in forming his (and his siblings') religious outlook,[11] his rather more secular father also had an impact on his son's development.[12] As Professor of Medicine in Lyons, Jean-Antoine Ozanam was associated with a hospital founded in the sixth century by the Merovingian king Childebert, a fact of which he was intensely aware.[13] While practising as a doctor he also wrote historical studies, including a history of Christianity in Lyons,[14] as well as an *Histoire des épidémies*.[15] Equally important for his son's development was Jean-Antoine's social conscience: he treated the silk workers who were wounded in the first of the riots known as the Révoltes des Canuts in Lyons in 1831, and publicly denounced the comparison between the rioters and the Carlists in Spain.[16] Piety, social conscience, and history were at the heart of his son's career: Frédéric could find all three in his family background.

The young Ozanam was intended to become a lawyer and was sent to Paris to gain the necessary education.[17] There he lodged initially at the house of the mathematician André-Marie Ampère, becoming a friend of his son, the philologist Jean-Jacques.[18] However, he found himself increasingly attracted to the study of religious and literary

---

[10] Cholvy, *Frédéric Ozanam*, pp. 32–40.   [11] Cholvy, *Frédéric Ozanam*, pp. 62, 64.
[12] Cholvy, *Frédéric Ozanam*, p. 347, on his father's return to the fold shortly before his death in 1837.
[13] Ozanam, *Comte rendu du service médical et des observations faites au Grand Hôtel-Dieu de Lyon*: Cholvy, *Frédéric Ozanam*, p. 48.
[14] Ozanam, *Mémoire statistique pour servir à l'histoire de l'établissement du christianisme à Lyon*: Cholvy, *Frédéric Ozanam*, p. 41.
[15] Cholvy, *Frédéric Ozanam*, p. 345.   [16] Cholvy, *Frédéric Ozanam*, p. 162.
[17] Cholvy, *Frédéric Ozanam*, pp. 184–8.   [18] Cholvy, *Frédéric Ozanam*, pp. 146, 174, 193.

history. At the same time, while still a student he played a major role in the establishment of the *Société de Saint-Vincent-de-Paul*, a religious organization aimed at helping the poor[19]—a key factor in his canonization in 1997.

Having become a lawyer, Ozanam was appointed to the Chair of Commercial Law in Lyons in 1839.[20] Fully aware of the silk-workers' riots of 1831 and 1834 he began to develop a notion of the just price of work, arguing the case on Christian principles (unlike Sismondi and Marx).[21] His interests, however, were turning increasingly towards literature, and in 1840 he sat the *agrégation* in Literature at the Sorbonne.[22] In Paris he impressed Claude Fauriel despite their religious differences.[23] Fauriel, who we have met as a friend of Mme de Staël and of Augustin Thierry, had recently published his *Histoire de la Gaule méridionale sous la domination des conquérants Germains*. On Fauriel's death in 1844 Ozanam was elected to his chair.[24]

As Professor of Foreign Literature, Ozanam lectured over a wide field. As early as 1840 he had written a book on Dante,[25] by which time he had already sketched out his idea for a comparative history of 'Rome et les Barbares, le Sacerdoce et l'Empire, Dante et les Nibelungen, S. Thomas d'Aquin et Albert le Grand, Galilée et Leibnitz'.[26] Among the lectures he delivered was a series on civilization from the Fall of the Roman Empire to the death of Dante. These he intended to turn into a book, but he died in 1853 before doing so. He was only 40. The most complete of his lectures, versions of which had already appeared as articles in the *Le Correspondant*, were, however, worked up into two volumes which were given the title *La Civilisation au cinquième siècle*.[27]

Ozanam explained that his intention in the lectures was above all 'to show how Christianity availed to evoke from the ruins of Rome, and the hordes encamped thereupon, a new society which was capable of holding truth, doing good, and finding the true idea of beauty'.[28] This interpretation he explicitly set against Gibbon's:

> We know how Gibbon, the historian, visited Rome in his youth, and how one day, as, full of its associations, he was wandering over the Capitol, he beheld a long procession of Franciscans issuing from the doors of the *Ara Coeli* basilica, and brushing with their sandals the pavement which had been traversed by so many triumphs. It was then that,

---

[19] Ozanam, *History of Civilization in the Fifth Century*, p. vi; Cholvy, *Frédéric Ozanam*, pp. 241–68.

[20] Cholvy, *Frédéric Ozanam*, p. 313.

[21] Cholvy, *Frédéric Ozanam*, p. 320.

[22] Cholvy, *Frédéric Ozanam*, p. 368–71.

[23] Cholvy, *Frédéric Ozanam*, p. 380, 395–8.

[24] Cholvy, *Frédéric Ozanam*, p. 475–7.

[25] Cholvy, *Frédéric Ozanam*, p. 373.

[26] Cholvy, *Frédéric Ozanam*, p. 366.

[27] Ozanam, *La Civilisation au cinquième siècle*. The origins of the work, in articles in *Le Correspondant*, are described by O'Meara, *Frédéric Ozanam*, pp. 382–6. O'Meara, who provides a far more detailed account of Ozanam's historical writings than does Cholvy, offers a clear discussion of the work's argument on pp. 386–94.

[28] Ozanam, *History of Civilization in the Fifth Century*, vol. 1, p. xi.

indignation giving him inspiration, he formed the plan of avenging the antiquity which had been outraged by Christian barbarism, and conceived the idea of a history of the decline of the Roman Empire. And I have also seen the monks of *Ara Coeli* crowding the old pavement of the Capitolian Jove. I rejoiced therein as in a victory of love over force, and resolved to describe the history of progress in that epoch where the English philosopher saw only decay, the history of civilization in the period of barbarism, the history of thought as it escaped from the shipwreck of the empire of letters, and traversed at length those stormy waves of invasion, as the Hebrews passed the Red Sea, and under a similar guidance, *forti tegente brachio*. I know of no fact which is more supernatural, or more plainly proves that divinity of Christianity, than that of its having saved the human intellect.[29]

Against Gibbon's thesis, which he denounced as old, but claimed was still fashionable in Germany, Ozanam set out to show how much Christianity salvaged from the Roman Empire.

What Ozanam actually provided in these lectures is primarily a study of the Christianization of literature, which reflects the field in which he was professor. His considerable knowledge of the Church Fathers also reflects the fact that he was an acquaintance of the abbé Migne, the great publisher of patristic texts, who was a member of the same socially-aware group of Catholic intellectuals.[30]

Pagan Roman culture is explored in some detail, before its transformation at the hands of the leading Christian writers is set out. Augustine is perhaps Ozanam's protagonist, being used to illustrate the nature of Christian philosophy, and the development of Christian eloquence. The Frenchman argues strongly that the version of Latin that played a central role in the development of language in Western Europe was the Latin of the Bible and not that of Cicero.[31] Indeed the civilization of Spain, Italy, and Gaul was essentially Roman, but it was the Roman civilization of the Church and not of the Empire.[32] Unusually in a work of history of the period, Ozanam dedicated a complete chapter to the 'Women of Christendom'.[33]

La Civilisation au cinquième siècle looks largely at Rome and the development of a Latin Christian culture. Ozanam had already provided his view of the Germanic side of the story in the two volumes of his *Études germaniques*, published in 1847 and 1849, the first of which was devoted to the barbarians before their Christianization, and the second to the Christian civilization of the Franks.[34] Again, Ozanam's knowledge of comparative literature is to the fore. In certain respects his argument looks back to Mme de Staël's account of the post-Roman period in seeing the barbarians as bringing an infusion of new blood to a tired civilization, but it goes far beyond it in sophistication and learning. Ozanam's extremely elaborate reconstruction of the Germanic thought-world drew heavily on the *Edda*

[29] Ozanam, *History of Civilization in the Fifth Century*, vol. 1, pp. xi–xii.
[30] Cholvy, *Frédéric Ozanam*, pp. 219, 334.
[31] Ozanam, *History of Civilization in the Fifth Century*, vol. 1, p. 115.
[32] Ozanam, *History of Civilization in the Fifth Century*, vol. 1, p. 274.
[33] The recognition of the importance of women, however, is not new. It was a strand in Enlightenment thought and is present in the writings of Saint-Simon.
[34] See the discussion in O'Meara, *Frédéric Ozanam*, pp. 394–401.

and on Middle High German poetry. It even includes a chapter devoted to the Germanic languages.[35] Ozanam was well acquainted with the writings of the brothers Grimm as well as Herder. He himself would be read, alongside Gobineau, by Victor Courtet, the so-called 'premier théoricien de la hiérarchie des races'.[36]

The argument in the *Études germaniques* was that French society was made up of a combination of Roman, Germanic, and Christian elements.[37] Ozanam admitted the underlying significance of Roman civilization, but saw it as being decadent, certainly by the time of the later Empire. Germanic civilization by contrast was vigorous, but untamed. For him, however, the two cultures were very much more compatible than had usually been thought: Ozanam made a great deal of the relatively new idea that both were Indo-European,[38] looking as far afield as Persia and India to point to common cultural traits. This was a reading of the past that would find its fullest expression in the writings of Georges Dumézil in the twentieth century. Germanic literature might be less polished than Roman, but it nevertheless shared a common ancestry and was worthy of respect.

Although the conquest of Western Europe by the Germanic peoples saw a mixing of Roman and Germanic civilization, the immediate result was not entirely happy: essentially it amounted to decadence combined with disorder. What gradually transformed matters was the Church. The emphasis on the role played by the Church in the salvation of civilization, which was at the heart of Ozanam's historical writing, was not new: it had been a central idea for Chateaubriand in the *Génie du christianisme*, and had subsequently been expressed by Guizot among others.[39] For Ozanam and Montalembert, however, it was not so much the Church of the Fathers, but that of the Irish and Anglo-Saxon missionaries, that transformed post-Roman society, and for the two Frenchmen these holy men provided a parallel for the missionaries of their own day, working to revive the Catholicism of the distant past. The Church of the fourth, fifth, sixth, and seventh centuries was to be regarded as a model for evangelicals in the nineteenth.

Ozanam was among the first to see insular influence as fundamental to the development of Western Europe. The work of Columbanus had, of course, been noted by earlier scholars. Generations of Irishmen had argued over whether he should be seen as Catholic or Protestant, though they had rarely extended their horizons enough to consider his impact on the wider world of European history. Mabillon had already edited Jonas of Bobbio's *Vita Columbani*, along with the Lives of other Irish saints.[40] Yet these *vitae* had not received much attention in histories of early

---

[35] Ozanam, *Les Germains avant le christianisme*, ch. 4.

[36] Cholvy, *Frédéric Ozanam*, pp. 109, 336, 396, 531.

[37] Ozanam, *Les Germains avant le christianisme*, p. i.

[38] Ozanam, *Les Germains avant le christianisme*, p. 151. The term Indo-European was first used in 1813. The concept received its major academic support from Franz Bopp, whose comparative grammar appeared in 1833, a mere fourteen years before Ozanam's publication.

[39] Graceffa, *Les Historiens et la question franque*, pp. 67–8.

[40] Mabillon, *Acta Sanctorum ordinis sancti Benedicti*, 3rd edn, vol. 2, pp. 5–55 (Columbanus), 102–16 (Deicolus), 116–23 (Eustasius), 123–9 (Athala), 160–7 (Bertulf), 227–68 (Gallus), 299–315 (Fursey), 438–49 (Burgundofara), as well as 129–35 (Amatus), 187–227 (Richarius), 315–34 (Agilus), 415–20 (Romaric), 421–32 (Sadalberga), 432–8 (Sigiramnus).

medieval Europe. Gibbon had done no more than take three swipes at Columbanus in his footnotes,[41] and even Chateaubriand had only mentioned him in passing in the *Génie du christianisme*.[42] The importance of the Irish in the post-Roman period was only to be spelled out in the following decades. In Ozanam's words they were 'a people whose sufferings are better known to us than their services, and whose magnificent vocation we have not sufficiently studied'.[43] For Montalembert, no one better appreciated the Irish contribution to history than did Ozanam.[44] The interpretation that envisaged a decadent Rome conquered by the more vigorous Germans, and the subsequent Christian transformation of the new social order at the hands of insular holymen, was one that would be followed from the mid-nineteenth century onwards by generations of Catholic, and not just Catholic, historians.

A number of contemporary factors weighed on Ozanam's reading. He saw parallels between the Fall of Rome and its aftermath and the situation of his own day. The decadence of the eighteenth century had been overthrown by the barbarism of revolution. The underclass of the nineteenth century could be seen as the barbarians. In the aftermath of the 1848 Revolution he wrote,

> I persist in comparing the February Revolution to the Fall of the Roman Empire, and I cannot forget that the barbarians, the proletarians of those days, forced the old inhabitants of the Empire to divide their lands, and that history still today praises the moderation of the Goths of Italy who only took a third.[45]

What was needed was a religious revival equivalent to that of the triumph of the Church in the post-Roman period. He saw glimmers of this in the Catholic movement in which he was involved, and, initially, in the election of Pius IX. Famously, having visited the new pope after his appointment, he exclaimed in print 'Passons aux barbares et suivons Pie IX.' ('Let's turn our attention to the barbarians and follow Pius IX.')[46] He thought that the pope would address the needs of the people: 'We perhaps won't convert Attila and Gaiseric, but God and we will perhaps get to the fringes of the Huns and Vandals.'[47] His hopes would be sadly dashed after the Roman uprising against Pius in 1848 and the pope's return to the Holy See backed by French arms in 1851.[48]

8.3 OZANAM, MONTALEMBERT, AND *LE LIBÉRATEUR*

There was perhaps another reason for Ozanam's emphasis on the role of the Irish: the recent history of Catholic Emancipation in Great Britain and Ireland, and above all the achievements of Daniel O'Connell, the 'martyre de la perfide Albion'. For many French Catholics, the emancipation of their co-religionists in Ireland

---

[41] The notes appear in chapter 37 of *Decline and Fall*.
[42] Chateaubriand, *Génie du christianisme*, Pt. IV, bk VI, ch. 7, p. 1055.
[43] O'Meara, *Frédéric Ozanam*, p. 399.
[44] Montalembert, *Les Moines d'Occident*, vol. 2, p. 454. See Coccia, 'La cultura irlandese precarolingia: miracola o mito?', pp. 414–15.
[45] Cholvy, *Frédéric Ozanam*, p. 615.   [46] Cholvy, *Frédéric Ozanam*, p. 591.
[47] Cholvy, *Frédéric Ozanam*, p. 592.   [48] Cholvy, *Frédéric Ozanam*, p. 597.

was of great significance. It was an inspiration for those looking to a spiritual revival in France. One possible indication of the significance of O'Connell to Ozanam's ideas in 1849 may be found in the development of his interpretation of the origins of Christianity among the Franks. This was first sketched in a series of four articles by Ozanam in *Le Correspondant*, which a German redactor translated and transformed into a book in 1845, under the title *Die Begründung des Christenthums in Deutschland und die sittliche und geistige Erziehung der Germanen.*[49] These articles were effectively a preliminary sketch for the second volume of the *Études franques*, although there are certain differences in emphasis. In particular, while the German work devotes eight pages to the Irish Church—admittedly rather more than can be found in the writings of Ozanam's contemporaries—in the French volume the subject is allocated a full forty-six page chapter, and discussions of Irish religious and intellectual influence also appear elsewhere in the book.[50] Something would appear to have struck Ozanam between 1845 and 1849, leading him to give enhanced emphasis to the role of the Irish. One possible explanation might lie in his reaction to the death of O'Connell in 1847, midway between the German and French publications of Ozanam's views. Montalembert saw the demise of the man he and many French Catholics called *le Libérateur* as an opportunity to encourage his fellow citizens to respond to a papal encyclical issued as a call to help the Irish, caught up as they were in the Potato Famine. He, therefore, persuaded Henri-Dominique Lacordaire, the re-founder of the Dominican Order in France, to deliver a eulogy on O'Connell in Notre Dame de Paris, which he did in 1848.[51] Lacordaire placed *le Libérateur* at the heart of the revival of Catholicism. Ozanam, too, was a close friend of Lacordaire. Here, perhaps, is part of the context for Ozanam's growing sense that the Irish *peregrini*—those monks who abandoned their homeland to live the ascetic life on the continent—provided a model for the spiritual revival he worked to achieve in his own day.

In claiming that Ozanam more than anyone understood the role of the Irish, Montalembert left unstated his own contribution to historical awareness of the issue. As Ashley Glyn, the English translator of *La Civilisation au cinquième siècle* pointed out, the overall argument of the work has a great deal in common with that of Montalembert, whose *Les moines d'Occident* appeared in 1860.[52] Here again it was the Church, and more specifically the monks of the early Middle Ages, that played a key role in the survival of civilization. Ozanam and Montalembert were offering a firm retort to Gibbon. Yet while Montalembert's magnum opus only appeared seven years after Ozanam's death, it is arguable that he had been aware of the significance of the Irish since the late 1820s.

---

[49] Ozanam, *Die Begründung des Christenthums in Deutschland und die sittliche und geistige Erziehung der Germanen*, pp. iv–v. On pp. iii–iv the translator explains that hitherto Ozanam had been little read in Germany, and he sets out to correct this.

[50] Ozanam, *La Civilisation chrétienne chez les francs*, pp. 96–142, 472–92.

[51] Montalembert, Letter to Lacordaire, 23rd May 1847; Lacordaire, Letter to Montalembert, 26th May 1847: *La Liberté de la parole évangélique*, <http://worksoflacordaire.com/.../Funeral_Oration_of_Daniel_O_Connell>; Cholvy, *Frédéric Ozanam*, p. 586.

[52] Ozanam, *History of Civilization in the Fifth Century*, vol. 1, p. v.

Charles Forbes René de Montalembert (1810–70) was the son of a Catholic French aristocrat and a Protestant Scot who converted to Catholicism. More than a historian, he was a polemicist, who strenuously defended the position of the Catholic Church in France. Like Ozanam he argued against the state monopoly of education, claiming that 'we don't want to be little islands in the middle of a free people: we are the successors of the martyrs; we don't tremble before the successors of Julian the Apostate. We are the sons of the Crusaders, we don't shrink before the sons of Voltaire.'[53] For the most part he revered the papacy, although the liberal Catholicism that he shared with Ozanam did not always find favour with Pius IX or his predecessors.

His concern with the state of the Church was already apparent when at the age of twenty he travelled to Ireland to visit Daniel O'Connell, whom he, along with other French Catholics, called 'le Libérateur'.[54] Only a year earlier emancipation had been secured with the Roman Catholic Relief Act of 1829. Trying to work out what he himself might do to further promote the Catholic cause, he concluded that he could write a history of Ireland.[55] The idea was an ambitious one given his youth, and to some extent it had already been pre-empted. John Lanigan's *Ecclesiastical History*, published in 1822, had clearly been written as an apologia for the Irish Catholics—and indeed the history of the early Irish Church had been picked over by Protestants and Catholics in Britain and Ireland since the Reformation. It may, however, not be too fanciful to think that it was Montalembert's visit to O'Connell, in the course of which he saw several of the early monastic sites of Ireland, including Kilkenny and Glendalough,[56] that the seeds of his presentation of Columbanus in *Les Moines d'Occident* were sown.

The six volumes of Montalembert's study of the monks of the West cover the history of monasticism from St Benedict to St Bernard. They include strikingly lengthy discussions of Benedict and of Columbanus. Particularly remarkable is the emphasis placed on the Irishman: lengthy discussion of Benedict's Rule could be expected, since it was, after all, the key text in western monasticism. For an appreciation of Montalembert's interest in Columbanus a mere page count is illuminating. Whereas St Benedict and his Rule take up just short of a hundred pages of *Les moines d'Occident*, Columbanus and his disciples occupy twice that number.[57] In addition to providing support for Ozanam's reading of the post-Roman period, this emphasis can perhaps be seen as a left-over from Montalembert's youthful proposal to write a history of Ireland: that the position of the Irish Catholics had continued to be a matter of interest is clear from his involvement in the organization of Lacordaire's *éloge funèbre* for O'Connell in 1848. Yet there were certainly other issues involving the early Middle Ages that were at the forefront of Montalembert's

---

[53] Cholvy, *Frédéric Ozanam*, pp. 509–10.
[54] Montalembert, *Journal intime inédit*, vol. 2, pp. 58–109.
[55] Lecanuet, *Montalembert*, vol. 1, p. 102.
[56] Montalembert, *Journal intime inédit*, p. 75.
[57] Montalembert, *Les Moines d'Occident*, vol. 2, bk 9, pp. 3–92 on Benedict, pp. 451–640 on Columbanus.

mind. Above all, there was the matter of the re-establishment of the monastic orders in France: of the Benedictines by the abbé Prosper Guéranger in 1837, and of the Dominicans by Lacordaire himself in 1850. Obviously *Les Moines d'Occident* belonged to the monastic revival.

8.4 GUÉRANGER AND DE BROGLIE

As the man who re-established the Benedictine Order in France, the abbé Guéranger inevitably had an interest in the early history of the Church. Moreover, monks from his community of Solesmes re-founded the monastery of Ligugé, the site of Martin's first monastic foundation. They thus presented themselves as heirs of one of the leading ascetics of the fourth century. Guéranger's chief contribution to debates about the late Roman period, however, revolves around a series of attacks that he launched on the Duc de Broglie's *L'Église et l'Empire au quatrième siècle*. Jacques-Victor-Albert, fourth duc de Broglie was the grandson of Mme de Staël. Born in 1821, he had an early career as a diplomat of the government of Louis-Philippe. This came to an end with the Revolution of 1848, and he retired to write, contributing to various journals, including the Catholic *Le Correspondant*, which had been revived by Montalembert in 1855, and to which Ozanam and Lacordaire contributed. In 1856 he published *L'Église et l'Empire au quatrième siècle* in six substantial volumes.

De Broglie's argument was simple. The Roman Empire and the Church had been founded on the same day (the idea had been enshrined in tradition by the Church Fathers): with the conversion of Constantine it looked as if their histories would intertwine. But this was not to be. De Broglie followed the history of the Church in the fourth century: Constantine's conversion was a major act, but he himself was neither big enough, nor pure enough, for the task he set himself.[58] What followed was a period dominated by adherents of the Arian heresy and the persecution of the orthodox, notably of Athanasius, under the emperor Constantius, and thereafter by the pagan revival under Julian. Under Julian's successors there was a return to Arian dominance, although the flame of orthodoxy was upheld by the likes of Basil of Caesarea. Only with the elevation of Theodosius as emperor, working together with Ambrose of Milan, did Church and State come together, despite the former's shortcomings. In his funeral oration for the emperor, Ambrose envisaged a rosy future for the Christian Empire. This, however, was not to be: Divine Providence had other plans.[59]

This was Providential history of a kind that Bossuet would have understood, and indeed de Broglie cited the seventeenth-century bishop in his *discours préliminaire*.[60] Although the interpretation was simple, it was underpinned with a massive amount of detail: numerous documents are quoted in translation. Moreover, the

---

[58] De Broglie, *L'Église et l'Empire au quatrième siècle*, 7th edn, vol. 2, p. 382.
[59] De Broglie, *L'Église et l'Empire au quatrième siècle*, vol. 6, pp. 415–27.
[60] De Broglie, *L'Église et l'Empire au quatrième siècle*, vol. 1, p. 1.

chief secular characters are presented in a notably even-handed manner: the failures of Constantine and Theodosius are not concealed, nor are the virtues of Julian. Why should one hide them?, asks de Broglie.[61] As Charles Maurras noted in the obituary notice he wrote for the duc in 1901, 'Avec quelle vive amitié M. de Broglie, pourtant sévère, traite Julien!'[62]

While not of equal historiographical importance, *L'Église et l'Empire* can reasonably be set alongside Ozanam's *La Civilisation au cinquième siècle*. Although Ozanam's final work had been published posthumously in 1855, de Broglie looked back to the original lectures as they had been delivered at the Sorbonne, before Ozanam's death. As he explained, while they had dealt with the role of the Church in the birth of modern civilization, his own work addressed its role in the survival of classical culture.[63] Clearly he regarded the two projects as complementary.

Despite the pious nature of de Broglie's work, it elicited a hugely critical response from Guéranger: he produced a torrent of articles, which were subsequently collected into a six-hundred page book.[64] Some of the criticisms were nit-picking points of fact, which, as Charles Maurras noted, de Broglie corrected in the second edition.[65] But Guéranger's criticisms went further, suggesting that de Broglie's opinions were heterodox. This intrigued the abbé Louis Marty, resident in Algeria, who read through de Broglie's work, several times, looking for theological error. Admittedly he only read the second edition, where the factual errors had been corrected, but he could find no heterodoxy. As a result he delivered a blistering riposte to Guéranger. He noted that the abbé had understood the book to be an attack on Napoleon III, but wondered why he had objected to a study of the workings of Providence.[66] It is certainly possible that there was an underlying criticism of the French Emperor:[67] given his own early career de Broglie would hardly have approved of Louis-Napoleon's seizure of power in 1851, while, given the emperor's public piety, Guéranger may have found such implied criticism offensive. De Broglie unquestionably saw echoes between the fourth century and the nineteenth, but they were general rather than *ad hominem*: he commented that he had intended to draw a comparison between the triumph of the Church over paganism in the fourth century and its battle with philosophy in his own day.[68] This was a comparison that had already struck Ozanam.[69] Yet the duc went on to note that he had eventually dropped the idea of making any comparison, except at those moments when one forcibly imposed itself.[70] Although one may suspect that some of the imperial portraits, with their stress on the weakness of the individual, might

---

[61] De Broglie, *L'Église et l'Empire au quatrième siècle*, vol. 4, p. 407.
[62] Maurras, *Le Duc Albert de Broglie (1901)*, <http://www.maurras.net>, pp. 8–9.
[63] De Broglie, *L'Église et l'Empire au quatrième siècle*, vol. 1, p. xi.
[64] Guéranger, *Essais sur le naturalisme contemporain*.
[65] Maurras, *Le Duc Albert de Broglie*, p. 8. De Broglie himself alludes to the corrections in the preface to the second edition.
[66] Marty, *Le Prince de Broglie et Dom Guéranger*, p. 12.
[67] I have not been able to see the B.A. thesis of R. Martin, *Albert de Broglie and Dom Guéranger*.
[68] De Broglie, *L'Église et l'Empire au quatrième siècle*, vol. 1, pp. v–vi.
[69] Cholvy, *Frédéric Ozanam*, pp. 592, 615.
[70] De Broglie, *L'Église et l'Empire au quatrième siècle*, vol. 1, p. viii.

have contained a dig at Napoleon III—it would not be the only such comparison[71]—what comes over, above all, is the author's view that the main developments
in history are nothing other than providential.[72]

Guéranger certainly lost the argument. When the second edition of *L'Église et
l'Empire romain* appeared in 1859 it had a preface by none other than Pius IX,
praising its orthodoxy. In France, the establishment threw its weight behind de
Broglie, electing him to a seat in the Académie française on the death of Lacordaire
in 1862. After the fall of Napoleon III in 1870 the duc would be appointed
ambassador to England, and in 1873 and 1877 he would serve as *président* of the
Council.

Unlike Ozanam and Montalembert, de Broglie did not offer a radically new
interpretation. Despite his emphasis on Providence, the strengths of *L'Église et
l'empire* lie in its presentation of detail, and in its wide sympathies. On the other
hand, the fact that the book could become a *cause célèbre*, involving the founder of
Solesmes and the pope, is an indication of the significance with which the early
Christian period was regarded among the upper échelons of French political and
intellectual society in the middle of the nineteenth century.

8.5 *HYPATIA*

While the work of Montalembert and Ozanam can be situated firmly within the
French Catholic revival, it was not just disseminated within France, or indeed
confined to the Catholic community. Montalembert's magnum opus was translated into English as early as 1867.[73] In the same year an Irish Catholic resident in
Paris, Kathleen O'Meara published a biography of Ozanam in English.[74] A year
later the latter's *History of Civilisation in the Fifth Century* appeared in English
translation by the Catholic lawyer Ashley Glyn.[75] The Germans had already been
introduced to Ozanam's work with the appearance of *Die Begründung des Christenthums in Deutschland* in 1845.

Nor was France alone in experiencing a religious revival in the first half of the
nineteenth century. As we have seen, the plight of the Irish Catholics was an issue
that attracted Montalembert as early as the 1820s. A number of them had looked
back to the sixth and seventh centuries in their arguments. So too, some English
Catholics had emphasized the importance of the period of the Christianization of
the Anglo-Saxons, above all John Lingard, in *The History and Antiquities of the
Anglo-Saxon Church* of 1806. The 1830s saw the establishment of the Oxford
Movement in England, and the beginnings of Anglican and Catholic revivals.
Moreover, a number of leading English churchmen turned to the history of the late

---

[71] We will return to Dahn's presentation of Napoleon III as Justinian.
[72] De Broglie, *L'Église et l'Empire au quatrième siècle*, vol. 1, pp. ix–x.
[73] Montalembert, *The Monks of the West from St Benedict to St Bernard*, trans. M. Oliphant.
[74] O'Meara, *Frederick Ozanam*.
[75] Ozanam, *History of Civilization in the Fifth Century*.

Roman Church. Newman, not surprisingly, was attracted to the fourth century. While still an Anglican, and an Oxford academic, he wrote a history of Arianism, and he followed this with an account of the Church Fathers.[76] His study first of Monophysitism, and then of Augustine, were to play a part in his own conversion to Roman Catholicism.[77] While he did not neglect the historical context, Newman was primarily a theologian. At least in terms of his *curriculum vitae* the Anglican cleric Charles Kingley was rather more of a historian.

Kingsley was born in 1819. Having been educated at Cambridge he decided to enter the Anglican Church, becoming rector of Eversley in Hampshire. In addition to his ministry, he devoted himself deeply to social issues, and also to writing: the two combined most famously in *The Water Babies*. In his attempts to involve the Church in social causes Kingsley stands comparison with Ozanam. To general surprise he was appointed Regius Professor of Modern History in Cambridge in 1860, a post that he did not greatly distinguish, and which he resigned in 1869 to become a canon of Chester cathedral.[78]

His appointment to the Regius Chair seems odd: the majority of his publications are either sermon literature or novels, although two of his historical works are of some significance for the student of the late Roman and early Medieval period. We will touch briefly on *The Roman and the Teuton* of 1864 in a later chapter.[79] *Alexandria and her Schools* was published in 1854, and thus before Kingsley's professorial appointment. In fact it is little more than an essay in the history of ideas, discussing the significance of Alexandria as an intellectual and spiritual centre from the Ptolemaic period to early Islam, and is pretty well devoid of factual detail. The key issues of the late fourth and early fifth centuries are covered in much greater depth in a novel that Kingsley published the previous year: *Hypatia: New Foes with an Old Face*.[80]

Hypatia is an account of the last days of the pagan philosopher, lynched at the hands of Christian monks who had been egged on by bishop Cyril of Alexandria. The story is told from the viewpoint of a young Christian ascetic, Philammon, who leaves his monastery in the desert, determined to help in the Christianization of the city, but who falls under the spell of the pagan philosopher Hypatia and is horrified by the behaviour of Cyril's followers, which culminates in the lynching of the heroine. Among the subsidiary characters are a group of Gothic soldiers, who somewhat improbably first appear searching for the legendary city of Asgard by sailing up the Nile, but who turn North, and intervene to help Philammon at various crucial moments in the narrative. While there is no reason to deny that a group of Goths could have been stationed in Alexandria in the early fifth century, their interest in the headwaters of the Nile surely reflects the desire of English explorers

---

[76] Newman, *The Arians of the Fourth Century*; Newman, *The Church of the Fathers*; Goldhill, *Victorian Culture and Classical Antiquity*, p. 203.

[77] Ker, *John Henry Newman*, pp. 177–8, 182–3, with citations from Newman's *Apologia pro vita sua* and his correspondence.

[78] Goldhill, *Victorian Culture and Classical Antiquity*, pp. 39, 163–4.

[79] See below chapter 11.

[80] Goldhill, *Victorian Culture and Classical Antiquity*, pp. 32, 174, 203–7.

to find the river's source in the mid-nineteenth century. Within the scheme of the novel, however, these men essentially symbolize the age to come: summing up the historical period in which the novel is set, Kingsley remarked:

> And thus an age, which to the shallow insight of a sneerer like Gibbon, seems only a rotting and aimless chaos of sensuality and anarchy, fanaticism and hypocrisy, produced a Clement and an Athanase, a Chrysostom and an Augustine...And even for the Western Church, the lofty future which was in store for it would have been impossible, without some infusion of new and healthier blood into the veins of a world drained and tainted by the influence of Rome. And the new blood, at the era of this story, was at hand. The great tide of those Gothic nations...was sweeping onwards...[81]

We will return to Kingsley's Germans. The emphasis on the role of the combined forces of Christianity and the northern peoples in the revival of Western Europe, however, has much in common with the views expressed by Ozanam.

Although Kingsley characterizes Gibbon as a 'sneerer', he had a strong regard for his scholarship, going out of his way to note their agreement on a point of detail.[82] He was not the only Anglican of the period to take such a stance. Henry Hart Milman, the dean of St Paul's, had recently produced his edition of *The Decline and Fall*, which he followed with a biography of Gibbon.[83] Milman, like Kingsley a believer in Christian universalism, was a significant Church historian in his own right. Both men admired Gibbon's scholarship whilst criticizing his view of religion.

As is well known, *Hypatia* provides a fictional critique of a number of leading figures of the time: the novel's subtitle, *New Foes with an Old Face*, draws attention to the book's contemporary resonance. Among Kingsley's targets was the harsh disciplinarian, Henry Phillpotts, bishop of Exeter. More broadly, it was an attack on ecclesiastical extremism and could thus be read as a broadside against the Tractarians and such Catholics as Wiseman and Newman.[84] The novel was to cause intense debate and was thought to have prevented Kingsley from being awarded the degree of Doctor of Civil Law at Oxford.[85] Cardinal Wiseman replied to *Hypatia* with a novel of his own, *Fabiola*, set, like Chateaubriand's *Les Martyrs*, in the Diocletianic persecution. Newman produced a further tale of martyrdom, *Callista*, this time set in the persecution of Decius. Yet there were leading churchmen, both Anglican and Catholic, who were impressed with Kingsley's work: Arthur Stanley, dean of Westminster, thought that he had rightly exposed the hollow Christianity and spurious orthodoxy of Cyril of Alexandria.[86]

Stanley was justified in thinking that the novel had a serious academic core. Even more than Chateaubriand's *Les Martyrs*, *Hypatia* is based on solid historical research. As Kingsley states in the preface,

[81] Kingsley, *Hypatia*, pp. 4–5. I have used the Dodo Press reprint.
[82] Kingsley, *Hypatia*, p. 9.
[83] Gibbon, *Decline and Fall*, ed. H. H. Milman; Milman, *Life of Gibbon*.
[84] Goldhill, *Victorian Culture and Classical Antiquity*, p. 157.
[85] Kingsley, *Charles Kingsley. His letters and memories of his life*, vol. 1, p. 292. References are to the 1891 edition.
[86] Kingsley, *Charles Kingsley*, vol. 1, pp. 292–3.

I have, in my sketch of *Hypatia* and her fate, closely followed authentic history, especially Socrates' account...To Synesius's most charming letters, as well as those of Isidore, the good Abbot of Pelusium, I beg leave to refer those readers who wish for
further information about the private life of the fifth century.[87]

The work, like the novels of Chateaubriand and Sismondi, is footnoted. To footnote a novel was to make it something other than a work of entertainment. Eight
years later, in 1861, Wilkie Collins, would comment in the preface to his novel
Antonina, or the Fall of Rome, that the work was 'free from the fatal displays of
learning which have hopelessly damaged the popularity of the historical romance
in these times'. He nevertheless boasted, 'To the fictitious characters alone is committed the task of representing the spirit of the age...but exact truth in respect to
time, place, and circumstance is observed in every historical event introduced in
the plot...'[88]

Kingsley set out an academic context for his own novel in the series of lectures
on *Alexandria and her Schools* delivered in Edinburgh in 1854. Like *Hypatia*, they
are, above all, a call for civilized toleration. Significantly, while the protagonists of
Les Martyrs are Christians, Hypatia was a pagan philosopher whose virtues were
understood by a young ascetic. Kingsley would return to some of the subject matter of the novel fifteen years later in his study of *The Hermits*. In many ways a book
for beginners, this provided short sketches of early exponents of the eremitical life,
in Egypt, Syria, Noricum, the Celtic fringes of Europe, and finally Northern England. While providing nothing new by way of interpretation, it demonstrated
Kingsley's knowledge of the late Antique East.

Kingsley's impact on the study of the late Roman and early medieval periods is
in no way comparable to that of Ozanam or Montalembert, but there are parallels
to be drawn between the three scholars. Kingsley's critique of Gibbon, expressed in
the preface to *Hypatia*, is no different from that expressed by Ozanam in *La Civilisation au cinquième siècle*. Clearly neither is borrowing from the other, for *Hypatia*
appeared in 1853, the year of Ozanam's death, and nine years before the appearance of his final lectures. Yet Kingsley would seem to have been aware of the cur-
rents of liberal Catholicism in France. Writing in 1892, Moritz Kaufmann noted
the similarities between the Catholic socialism of Ozanam and the muscular Christianity of Kingsley.[89] He placed Kingsley, Ozanam, Chateaubriand, and Lacordaire
in 'the broader school of religious thinkers and workers, who endeavour to attract
by affection rather than to compel by authority.... "Its mission is to bring back
those who have gone astray, and to increase the number of Christians." '[90] The writing of history had a part to play in that mission, which saw the history of the early
Church as providing lessons for the modern age.

Certainly Kingsley had read works by Chateaubriand. While he was courting his
future wife Fanny, a courtship opposed by her parents, he took to illustrating the
Frenchman's *Life of Elizabeth of Hungary*, hoping thereby to show that piety and
sex were compatible.[91] Whether he had read *Les Martyrs* is unclear, although there

---

[87] Kingsley, *Hypatia*, pp. 8–9.   [88] Collins, *Antonina*, pp. v, vii.
[89] Kaufmann, *Charles Kingsley*, pp. 233–8.   [90] Kaufmann, *Charles Kingsley*, p. 236.
[91] Pope-Hennessy, *Canon Charles Kingsley*, p. 25; Chitty, *The Beast and the Monk*, pp. 76–8.

are a number of possible echoes of Chateaubriand's work in *Hypatia*: not least the two male protagonists, Philammon and Eudore, have much in common. More important, however, is the fact that Kingsley, like Chateaubriand, Ozanam, and Montalembert, put the triumph of the Church at the heart of their readings of the end of Rome and the beginnings of the Middle Ages, and they saw that triumph as having a message for their own day. Although a secular reading of the period would remain dominant, there was now in the narrative of European, and not just ecclesiastical, history an alternative interpretation of the role of religion to that offered by Gibbon. The reading was Catholic in origin, but with Kingsley it had become the property of other denominations involved in religious revival.

9
Language, Law, and National Boundaries

9.1 THE EARLY GERMANS AND THE GERMAN NATION

While the religious history of the late Roman and early medieval periods attracted increasing attention during the second and third quarters of the nineteenth century, the same decades also saw a growing emphasis on the importance of language, literature, and law as source material for the historian. We have already encountered this in passing. Fauriel paid great attention to language in his discussion of the Frankish impact on the Midi,[1] as did Ozanam in his study of the early Germanic peoples.[2] As Professors of Foreign Literature at the Sorbonne, both men drew on scholarly traditions outside those of narrative history. In so doing, their intellectual models were German rather than French. It is with the German tradition that this chapter is concerned, and above all the interplay between the idea of Germany itself and scholarship relating to the early Middle Ages. Debates about Germany would place nationalist discourse more firmly at the centre of the study of the distant past.

German scholarship on the late Roman and early medieval periods had followed a rather different trajectory than had French or Italian. Above all, this reflected the fact that most of Germany lay outside the frontiers of the Roman Empire. Moreover, the lands east of the Rhine could boast no early written culture. Before the development of linguistics and archaeology, therefore, they could only be studied through the writings of Latin and Greek authors. Among the earliest of the great scholars who considered the Migration Period there was, of course, Johann Mascov, whose *Geschichte der Teutschen bis zu Anfang der Franckischen Monarchie* has already attracted our attention. Yet Mascov's subject was not Germany, but 'the Ancient Germans', a good proportion of whom came from elsewhere. The Goths, for instance began their migration from Eastern Europe, though the Lombards and the Franks could be claimed as having originated in German territory. For the Germans, in other words, the history of the Migration Period was primarily one of emigration—it was thus a history whose relationship to that of Germany, geographically defined, was in certain respects tangential. Not that this stopped individual Germans from objecting to the denigration of Germanic tribes across the Rhine: Friedrich Meyer, for instance, objected strongly to

---

[1] Espagne, 'Claude Fauriel et l'Allemagne', p. 16.
[2] Ozanam, *Études germaniques*, vol. 1, *Les Germains avant le christianisme*, pp. 154–200.

Grégoire's coinage of the word 'vandalisme'.[3] Moreover, discussion of the 'early Germans' did play a role in German politics, just as the Franks and Lombards were used in French and Italian political debates. As in France and Italy, so the debates in Germany had a profound impact on the way that the Migration Period was understood.

In so far as there was a tradition of studying the history of the early Germans within Germany, this was rooted in the study of local institutions, above all, in the supposed organizational system of *Markgenossenschaft*—that is, the exploitation of common land by a free peasantry, working from independent farmsteads. The basis of this idea (although he did not use the term) was set out by Justus Möser in the second edition of his *History of Osnabrück*, published in 1780.[4] Möser was a jurist from Osnabrück, who studied in Jena and Göttingen. In addition to his work as a legal official, he was also a historian and a poet who wrote a tragedy on the Germanic hero Arminius in 1749. In his *Osnabrückische Geschichte* he presented a picture of communities of free German farmers, who were both independent and jointly involved in the cultivation of common land, which he called the *Mark*. He thought their existence could be traced from Antiquity to the eighteenth century.[5] This idea derived from his political involvement in the liberation of the peasantry, rather than from any early medieval source: indeed there is no evidence for the existence of what Grimm called *Markgenossenschaft* in the early period.[6] The interpretation was, however, widely adopted, and became central to the developing study of *Landesgeschichte*, or regional history. By its very nature such study tended to be directed towards individual regions, rather than Germany as a whole, although Möser's model was also to feed in to the German tradition of constitutional history, or *Verfassungsgeschichte*, through its adoption by Jacob Grimm and Georg Waitz.[7] The latter, however, saw *Markgenossenschaft* as evolving slowly into the system of lordship that characterized the Merovingian period. Nor was Möser's model universally accepted: Heinrich von Sybel, who was concerned primarily with the development of Germanic kingship, denied the importance of egalitarian communities, and stressed instead the role of the king and the influence of Rome on the Germanic family.[8]

When Mme de Staël came to write *De l'Allemagne* she defined Germany in terms of its culture rather than its history or politics. Historians have talked of a *Kulturnation*.[9] There was, of course, a good reason for this. Germany did not exist as a clearly defined political entity, but was made up of a series of principalities: on

---

[3] Merrills, 'The Origins of "Vandalism"', pp. 165–6.

[4] There is a convenient analysis of Möser's ideas and their impact in Dopsch, *The Economic and Social Foundations of European Civilization*, pp. 5–6.

[5] Dopsch, *The Economic and Social Foundations of European Civilization*, p. 123.

[6] Dopsch, *The Economic and Social Foundations of European Civilization*, p. 11, citing Sybel, *Die Enstehung des deutschen Königtums*.

[7] See the comments in Graceffa, *Les Historiens et la question franque*, pp. 94–8.

[8] Dopsch, *The Economic and Social Foundations of European Civilization*, pp. 11–12; Graceffa, *Les Historiens et la question franque*, pp. 93–9.

[9] Leerssen, *National Thought in Europe*, p. 146.

the other hand by the end of the eighteenth century it boasted significant works of literature and philosophy, which could be seen as defining what it was to be German: this was central to de Staël's argument. Equally important was linguistic unity, which had been stressed by a number of luminaries in the late eighteenth century, not least Goethe. Perhaps even more important for the association of language and nationality was Johann Gottfried Herder. His views were stated in *Auch eine Philosophie der Geschichte*, which itself drew on the use made of Tacitus by Mascov and Montesquieu.[10]

The question of how to define Germany became all the more acute as a result of Napoleon's eastward expansion. When the emperor Franz II gave up the imperial title in 1806, the notion of an overarching Habsburg Empire also collapsed. One result of this was to turn the spotlight on the numerous kingdoms and principalities that made up the German nation. Unification was still a long way in the future, but, while Napoleon had broken the power of the Habsburgs, his very intervention in Germany had also helped further a sense of German unity in the reaction it stimulated.[11] Among those most keenly inspired to promote the notion of *Deutschland* were a number of scholars, who would contribute greatly to the study of late Antiquity and the early Middle Ages.

9.2 *THE MONUMENTS OF THE HISTORY OF GERMANY*

Karl Freiherr vom Stein was to play a major role in the development of historical scholarship although he himself was not a historian—beyond the fact that he studied history at the University of Göttingen in the 1770s. His early career was in the Prussian administration, although he lost his post in 1807, only to be installed as chief minister almost immediately afterwards, at the behest of Napoleon. A year later he fell foul of the French emperor: a major event in the eyes of Stein's biographer Georg Heinrich Pertz.[12] Stein fled first to Austria, and then to Russia. From 1812 onwards he threw himself into persuading the Russians to collaborate in driving Napoleon out of Germany. His hope that the defeat of France would lead to German unification was dashed at the Congress of Vienna. In the aftermath of the Congress he turned his mind to the promotion of German history, and in 1819 he founded the *Gesellschaft für Deutschlands ältere Geschichtskunde*, the body that was to produce the great series of editions entitled the *Monumenta Germaniae Historica*.[13] The patriotic inspiration for the *MGH* is proclaimed in its motto:

---

[10] Herder, *Auch eine Philosophie der Geschichte*. On Herder's contribution, see Geary, *The Myth of Nations*, pp. 22–4, 29; Leerssen, *National Thought in Europe*, pp. 97–101.

[11] For the hostility to Napoleonic rule even among the young, Pertz, *Autobiography*, pp. 3–7.

[12] Pertz, *Autobiography*, p. 4.

[13] Fuhrmann, '*Sind eben alles Menschen gewesen*', p. 13; id., 'Die *Monumenta Germaniae Historica* und die Frage einer textkritischen Methode', pp. 18–19. The fullest account of the origins of the *MGH* remains Bresslau, *Geschichte der Monumenta Germaniae Historica*. There is a useful account in Knowles, *Great Historical Enterprises*, pp. 63–97. See also Artifoni, 'Il Medioevo nel Romanticismo. Forme della storiografia tra Sette e Ottocento', pp. 201–2.

Sanctus amor patriae dat animum ('the holy love of the Fatherland gives soul').[14] Writing three-quarters of a century later the French historian, Fustel de Coulanges, only too aware of the outcome of the Franco-Prussian war, wrote:

> German erudition has also had its prejudices: German patriotism has put its stamp on it. One knows that the motto of the *Monumenta Germaniae* is *Sanctus amor patriæ dat animum*. The motto is beautiful, but it is not, perhaps, appropriate for science... Patriotism is a virtue: history is a science: one should not confuse them.[15]

Despite the underlying patriotism of his venture, Stein had difficulty raising the money for the project: indeed a considerable proportion of the early finances came from his own pocket.[16] Neither the King of Prussia nor any of the German princes initially provided money, although Tsar Alexander, who had employed Stein during his exile in Russia, did.[17] Even when the first volume of the *Monumenta* appeared, its list of subscribers was dominated by a man who might be described as a foreigner: for while the King of Prussia did put his name down for twelve copies, George IV, admittedly as King of Hannover rather than of England, signed up for twice that number. The Austrian Kaiser, Franz II, only subscribed for one.[18] The simple point was that, although Pertz thought the first volume of the *Monumenta* 'was favourably received throughout Germany',[19] the German establishment was deeply suspicious of what Stein was doing. So too were the Austrians. As Pertz recorded in his *Autobiography*,

> Herr von Gentz told me that the Emperor did not approve of any societies, since he believed that such meetings were dangerous, and when I explained that the object of our Society [the *Verein von Freunden und Kennern der Deutschen Geschichte*, which Stein founded alongside the *Monumenta*] was to spread the knowledge of German history, he replied it was impossible to foretell to what uses German history might be diverted.[20]

Metternich, however, was willing to join the *Verein*[21] and made sure that rather more copies of the first volume of the *Monumenta* were acquired by the Austrians.[22] But he, like the Kaiser, was worried about the possibility of revolution, and among likely revolutionaries he included university students—exactly the group of people that Stein was employing to transcribe manuscripts[23]—as well as Ernst

---

[14] See Fuhrmann, *'Sind eben alles Menschen gewesen'*, p. 12. In Giesebrecht's words, from the obituary of Pertz, reprinted in Pertz, *Autobiography*, p. 220: 'It is well known that Stein at that period meditated forming an extensive collection of documents relating to early German history, by which he indulged the hope of restoring a patriotic feeling in Germany; and in order to carry out this plan, which at first was traced in the broadest outlines, he founded a society for the purpose of spreading a knowledge of early German history.'

[15] Fustel de Coulanges, *La Monarchie Franque*, 6th edn, p. 31. The work was originally published in 1888. Unlike some other volumes of Fustel's *Histoire des Institutions Politiques*, this was not substantially edited after the author's death by Camille Jullian.

[16] Fuhrmann, *'Sind eben alles Menschen gewesen'*, p. 33.

[17] Fuhrmann, *'Sind eben alles Menschen gewesen'*, p. 14.

[18] Fuhrmann, *'Sind eben alles Menschen gewesen'*, p. 16.

[19] Pertz, *Autobiography*, p. 55. [20] Pertz, *Autobiography*, p. 25.

[21] Pertz, *Autobiography*, p. 18. [22] Pertz, *Autobiography*, p. 55.

[23] Fuhrmann, *'Sind eben alles Menschen gewesen'*, pp. 15, 17.

Moritz Arndt, a friend of Stein, and also a vociferous patriot.[24] Arndt had openly denounced Napoleon, before fleeing to Sweden, and thence to St. Petersburg, which was where he met the exiled Stein.[25] Following his return to Germany, he was appointed to the Chair of History in the newly founded university of Bonn in 1818, but was arrested in 1819, and although he was promptly freed, he was forbidden to teach, only being fully reinstated in 1840.

To a large extent the suspicion of Stein's project was misplaced: it did not necessarily imply a rejection of the old *Reich*. One of the key figures in the enterprise, and the secretary of the *Monumenta* from 1824, was Johann Friedrich Böhmer, a private scholar from Frankfurt, where he also held the posts of city archivist from 1825 and *Stadtbibliothekar* from 1830.[26] His patriotism was firmly old-fashioned: the *patria* that he looked back to was that of the Habsburg Empire.[27] Nevertheless, the seeds of an association with the future Germany were already present. Böhmer's chief collaborator and Stein's biographer, Pertz, was to become *Oberbibliothekar* and *Leiter* of the Prussian royal library in 1842 and insisted on moving the *Monumenta* to Berlin, despite the opposition of Böhmer.[28] Not that he had originally wanted to remove it from its earlier home in Hannover. However, although he was on good terms with King Wilhelm and his government, he found his successor Ernst August (1837–51) impossible to deal with.[29] The new monarch was extremely autocratic: it was he who had seven Göttingen professors, including Dahlmann and the two Grimms, dismissed for their liberal views—something which weighed heavily on Pertz.[30] In addition, however, Ernst August's ministers could see little value in the *Monumenta*: Pertz noted in a letter to Böhmer that one of them claimed

> that the "Monumenta" contains nothing but what is already printed, and even if some Imperial documents had not yet been made known, it would have perhaps been better if the whole work had not been printed.

That a Hannoverian minister could claim as much in 1841 is a salutary reminder that the value of the *Monumenta* was not yet obvious. Nor was it only bureaucrats who held such views: as Pertz discovered in 1843, there were four members of the Prussian Academy of Sciences who thought that the *Monumenta* 'contained only reprints'.[31] Given the lack of interest at the court of Hannover the enterprise came to depend increasingly on Frederick Wilhelm IV of Prussia.[32] Equally approving was Ludwig II of Bavaria.[33] In his *Autobiography*, Pertz talks as much about the support of the German princes as about the response of scholars. Governmental recognition was crucial to the survival of the *MGH*.

---

[24] Fuhrmann, '*Sind eben alles Menschen gewesen*', pp. 17, 47. For Arndt's friendship with Stein, Arndt, *Wanderungen und Wandelungen mit der Reichsfreiherrn Heinrich Karl Friedrich vom Stein*. See also Leerssen, *National Thought in Europe*, p. 130.

[25] Leerssen, *National Thought in Europe*, pp. 107–9.

[26] Fuhrmann, '*Sind eben alles Menschen gewesen*', pp. 34–5.

[27] de Jong, 'Johann Friedrich Böhmer (1795–1863)', pp. 63–72.

[28] Fuhrmann, '*Sind eben alles Menschen gewesen*', p. 37.

[29] Pertz, *Autobiography*, pp. 89, 95–101.   [30] Pertz, *Autobiography*, pp. 100–4.

[31] Pertz, *Autobiography*, pp. 100, 107.   [32] Pertz, *Autobiography*, pp. 115, 119.

[33] Pertz, *Autobiography*, p. 161, 164.

Pertz in many respects laid the foundations of the later greatness of the *Monumenta*, and he himself was largely responsible for the first twenty or twenty-five volumes, which are of great historiographical importance.[34] Not the least significant is his 1826 edition of Carolingian annals, the very first volume of the *Monumenta*, which is still in print.[35] Indeed, Pertz is often seen as setting new standards for the editing of historical texts. Yet one should also beware of attributing too much to the *MGH* in its early stages. Although Pertz's editions are still available, they are not without their flaws. The truly golden age of *Monumenta* editions only really began in the 1870s, with the work of the likes of Theodor Mommsen and of Bruno Krusch—and even their editions, depending as they do on the establishment of an *Urtext*, are open to criticism. In attempting to establish what the original author wrote, Mommsen and his like were both attempting something that was well-nigh impossible—we can rarely be certain about authorial intentions—and at the same time they were ignoring the very exciting possibilities of establishing what the scribe of an individual manuscript was intent on doing.

Yet it is not just that many of the earlier *MGH* editions have been overvalued. It is also that excessive emphasis has been placed on Stein's creation as marking a radical change in the collection and editing of historic texts—as Pertz's Prussian critics noted. Although it is true that Pertz and his helpers had higher standards of source-criticism than many of their predecessors, there was already a long tradition of editorial work, stretching back at least as far as Sirmond in seventeenth-century France. Pertz himself greatly admired his French contemporary Benjamin Guérard, the editor of the Carolingian polyptych of Irminon, the introduction to which offers a magisterial interpretation of the development of land-tenure from the Roman period to the Carolingian.[36] Fustel de Coulanges, in the 1870s, would criticize those of his French colleagues who went overboard in their enthusiasm for the practices of the *Monumenta*, and ignored the great achievements of such Frenchmen as Mabillon and Pardessus[37]—not to mention Bouquet, who had attempted to recruit Du Bos to help in his great *Recueil des historiens des Gaules et de la France* of 1737–86. Nor was France the only country to boast a significant series of editions predating the *Monumenta*. In Italy there were the *Rerum italicarum scriptores*, edited by Ludovico Antonio Muratori and published in twenty-eight volumes between 1723 and 1751.[38] Perhaps a more immediate source of inspiration for the *Monumenta* was J. Langebek's *Scriptores rerum Danicarum medii aevi*, the first volume of which appeared in 1772—a collection whose name seems to prefigure that of the series of *Scriptores* inaugurated by Stein, as does its motto: *Gloria et*

---

[34] See the assessment of Giesebrecht in Pertz, *Autobiography*, p. 220. Waitz, who was perhaps closer to the truth, claimed twenty: Pertz, *Autobiography*, p. 225.

[35] Fuhrmann, '*Sind eben alles Menschen gewesen*', pp. 30–3.

[36] Pertz, *Autobiography*, pp. 59–60, 92, 203; Gooch, *History and Historians in the nineteenth century*, pp. 206–7.

[37] Hartog, *Le XIXe siècle et l'histoire*, pp. 134–5.

[38] On the relation between Muratori and the *MGH*, Arnaldi, 'L'Istituto storico italiano per il medio evo e la ristampa dei RIS', pp. 2–3.

amor patriae,[39] which is not so far from the *Monumenta*'s *Sanctus amor patriae dat animum.*

In the late nineteenth century the *Monumenta* would raise standards of editing and textual criticism, but at the time of its foundation the series did not mark an immediate break with earlier scholarship. This is not to deny the achievement of Pertz, or indeed the significance of his assistant and successor, Georg Waitz. The latter came from Schleswig, which at the time was subject to the Danish crown. This region of southern Jutland was ruled over by the King of Denmark, but as a German fief, and not as part of the Danish kingdom. Not surprisingly, a succession of Danish kings wished to integrate the region into Denmark proper: the local population, and especially the intellectuals of Schleswig, however, largely saw themselves as German. This was the case with Waitz. He attended first the then Danish university of Kiel, and subsequently that of Berlin, where he was persuaded by Ranke to concentrate on history rather than law.

Just as one should not exaggerate the initial significance of the *Monumenta*, so too one should beware of attributing too much to Ranke's influence. His seminars, which he began in 1833 and which Waitz attended, did have a profound effect on the teaching of history in general,[40] but his emphasis on the study of texts was scarcely a revelation to ancient historians or specialists in the early Middle Ages. The *Monumenta* had been founded before Ranke himself was appointed to his Chair in Berlin: in 1819 he was still a classics teacher at the Friedrichs Gymnasium in Frankfurt. To some extent his subsequent emphasis on source criticism was the application to the early modern and modern periods of what he had learnt from the classicists. Pertz, who was Ranke's exact contemporary (they were both born in 1795), had been told by the ancient historian Arnold Hermann Ludwig Heeren in 1813: 'Do not occupy yourself with modern books, but go to the contemporary sources of history, and a light will dawn upon you.'[41] Pertz knew Ranke well, having moved to Berlin from a Chair in Hannover.[42] In his *Autobiography*, however, he does not pay any great attention to him as a scholar.

The main influences on Waitz were Pertz himself, who regarded him as the finest assistant he ever had,[43] and Dahlmann, to whom we will return. Waitz would subsequently become professor at Kiel in 1842. Four years later he represented the university at the provincial diet. His stance, however, was strongly pro-German, and since Kiel was still subject to the Danish Crown he was happy to move to Göttingen in 1847. In addition to contributing to the *Monumenta*, he was the author of a notable work on the constitutional history of medieval Germany[44]—the main emphasis of which lay in the High Middle Ages. At the same time he continued to cultivate links with his homeland: in 1848 he represented Kiel (despite its links

---

[39] Bjork, 'Nineteenth-century Scandinavia and the Birth of Anglo-Saxon Studies', p. 117. On Langebek, see also Shippey and Haarder, *Beowulf*, pp. 4–6.
[40] Gooch, *History and Historians in the nineteenth century*, pp. 113–14.
[41] Pertz, *Autobiography*, p. 8.   [42] Pertz, *Autobiography*, pp. 101–2.
[43] Pertz, *Autobiography*, p. 147.   [44] Pertz, *Autobiography*, pp. 110–11.

with Denmark) in the Frankfurt Parliament. He also wrote a very pro-German history of Schleswig-Holstein.[45]

9.3 *BEOWULF* AND THE SCHLESWIG-HOLSTEIN QUESTION

Denmark and Schleswig-Holstein played a pivotal role in the North European debates about the early Middle Ages of the first three-quarters of the nineteenth century. Of particular importance were the developing science of philology and the study of poetry, and here a key moment came with the publication of Thorkelín's edition of *Beowulf*. It ought to have appeared in 1807, but the proofs were destroyed in the course of the English bombardment of Copenhagen in that year.[46] As a result it did not appear until 1815, although Thorkelín had originally been attracted to the text some thirty years earlier, having had a transcription made as early as 1787.[47]

The solitary manuscript containing the text of *Beowulf* was first described in Humphrey Wanley's catalogue of 1705, but for a century thereafter the poem continued to languish in obscurity.[48] This changed in 1799 with the publication of the first of what would be a much-revised four-volume *History of the Anglo-Saxons* by the lawyer Sharon Turner.[49] He subsequently claimed, with a little exaggeration, that before the publication of this work 'the subject of the Anglo-Saxon antiquities had been nearly forgotten by the British public'.[50] His history was certainly one of the main sources for Walter Scott's construction of the Anglo-Saxons in *Ivanhoe*. Given Turner's own legal training, his study of the Anglo-Saxons is perhaps inevitably rather inclined to present a history of constitutional continuity, and thus to deal with institutions and the periods which provide evidence for them.[51] Nevertheless, the opening chapters provide a reasonably up-to-date account of late Roman Britain and the pre-migration Germans: not surprisingly for a well-read Englishman he knew his Gibbon, but also his Du Bos and his Mascov. Once he reached the Anglo-Saxon migration and the early history of the Anglo-Saxon kingdoms, however, he was much less sure-footed, despite a good deal of common sense—shown, for instance, in cutting the figure of Arthur down to size.[52] His

---

[45] Pertz, *Autobiography*, p. 147.

[46] Frantzen, *Desire for Origins*, pp. 193–4; Bjork. 'Nineteenth-century Scandinavia and the Birth of Anglo-Saxon Studies', p. 112; Shippey and Haarder, *Beowulf*, pp. 6, 13.

[47] Shippey and Haarder, *Beowulf*, p. 6; see Kiernan, *The Thorkelín Transcripts of Beowulf*.

[48] Frantzen, *Desire for Origins*, pp. 192–3; Kiernan, 'The Legacy of Wiglaf', p. 196; Shippey and Harder, *Beowulf*, pp. 1–3.

[49] For an assessment of Turner's impact, Horsman, 'Origins of racial Anglo-Saxonism in Great Britain before 1850', p. 394.

[50] Shippey and Haarder, *Beowulf*, pp. 6–7.

[51] Burrow, *A liberal descent. Victorian historians and the English past*, pp. 116–19; Horsman, 'Origins of racial Anglo-Saxonism', p. 394.

[52] Turner, *The History of the Manners, Landed Property, Laws, Poetry, Literature, Religion, and Language of the Anglo-Saxons*, vol. 1, pp. 224–52.

problem in dealing with fifth- and sixth-century Britain was his lack of any great sense of source criticism—and here he was not alone. He used twelfth-century writers as liberally as he did Bede. What his contemporary critics picked up on, however, was his use of early Welsh poetry, which was dismissed as 'gross credulity'.[53] Turner's world, it should be remembered, was still in the grips of the debate over Ossian, the supposed Scottish bard, whose works were forged by William Macpherson. Given the problems of using the early Welsh material—not least those relating to the dates of the poems and the extent to which they reflect real events, questions that are still matters of disagreement[54]—one should beware of being excessively harsh. German scholars who are still highly regarded (not least Jacob Grimm) would soon be as uncritical in their use of some of the Germanic literary material.

Old English poetry is notably absent from the first volume of Turner's history. The lacuna, however, was remedied in the fourth volume, published in 1805, which includes a translation of part of *Beowulf*. This essentially marks the entrance of the Old English epic into historical scholarship.[55] The reason for this late entry is simply that there was no earlier edition of the poem. The first was Thorkelín's of 1815. The title of his publication points immediately to what would become a central issue: *De Danorum Rebus Gestis Seculis III et IV: Poema Danicum Dialecto Anglosaxonico* ('Concerning the deeds of the Danes in the fourth and fifth centuries: a Danish poem in the Anglo-Saxon dialect'). For Thorkelín the poem was Danish, and it shed light on events of the third and fourth centuries. The date was determined by his identification of Beowulf with Bous, who appears in the work of the medieval Danish historian Saxo Grammaticus: Suhm had calculated that Bous died AD 340.[56] In Thorkelín's view, the poem had originally been recited at the death of the hero and had subsequently been translated into English, at the court of king Alfred.[57] It was, therefore, a text of great historical importance, illustrative of the world of the Danes in the fourth century. In the course of arguing his case, Thorkelín denounced George Hickes, Wanley's collaborator: 'I am therefore completely amazed that Hickes should attribute to the Anglo-Saxons a song which the Danish seer poured out, burning with the fire of a Nordic Apollo.'[58]

Thorkelín's view reflected the fact that for him Old English was really a dialect of Danish: the peoples from the North 'spoke the same language although in different dialects.' 'For this epic, as we now have it, evidently shows that the Anglo-Saxon language is really Danish.'[59] This question of language was important, and would become more so, as it was increasingly presented as an ethnic marker.

[53] Shippey and Haarder, *Beowulf*, pp. 7, 77.

[54] See, for instance, Rowland, *Early Welsh Saga Poetry*.

[55] Turner, *The History of the Manners, Landed Property, Laws, Poetry, Literature, Religion, and Language of the Anglo-Saxons*, vol. 4, pp. 398–408. The passage is reprinted in Shippey and Haarder, *Beowulf*, pp. 78–91.

[56] Suhm, *Geschichte der Dänen*, p. 232; Shippey and Haarder, *Beowulf*, p. 11, 92.

[57] Bjork, 'Nineteenth-century Scandinavia and the Birth of Anglo-Saxon Studies', p. 118.

[58] Shippey and Haarder, *Beowulf*, p. 92. For the attack on Hickes also Bjork, 'Nineteenth-century Scandinavia and the Birth of Anglo-Saxon Studies', p. 118.

[59] Shippey and Haarder, *Beowulf*, p. 92.

In addition to the questions of history and of language, there was another underlying issue: modern politics weighed heavily on Thorkelín in his reading of *Beowulf*.
His comments on the characters Hrothgar and Hygelac are 'statements about the
virtues of monarchy—obviously relevant as Europe was trying to settle down once
more in the very last year of the Napoleonic wars—and about the unity of Denmark, island Danes and peninsular Jutes combined.'[60] Given the problematic relationship between the island Danes and the inhabitants of Jutland, and particularly
of the southern part of the peninsula, many of whom saw themselves as German
rather than Danish, Thorkelín's view of Hrothgar granting 'citizenship' to the people of Jutland, had special significance. It clearly echoed Frederik VI of Denmark's
dealings with the population of Schleswig-Holstein.

Thorkelín's edition immediately attracted attention. Within Denmark it was
favourably reviewed by his friend Peter Erasmus Müller,[61] although he took a
slightly different view of the poem's Danish-ness. He accepted that it had originally
been recited at Beowulf's funeral, and that its form was Old Norse, but insisted
that the work that we have is Anglo-Saxon.[62] Grundtvig was more critical, arguing
in his review that 'the scald was of Anglian stock',[63] but his language was what he
would later classify as Old-Nordisk, or Old Northern.[64] Shortly thereafter, in
another article on the poem, he moved further from Thorkelín's position, rejecting
the date of 340. Instead, he argued for a sixth-century date, having concluded that
the Hygelac of the poem was the same man as Chochilaicus, who appears in book
III of Gregory of Tours' *Histories*.[65] This case would be argued at yet greater length
twenty-two years later by Heinrich Leo,[66] the German historian who we have
already met in the context of Balbo's interpretation of Italian history.[67] The identification of Hygelac with Chochilaicus is still generally accepted[68]—although few
would think any longer that we can extract historical information about him from
Beowulf. If one accepts (as no one would now, but as most did after 1815) that the
poem was a record of real historical events, this would mean that it was a crucial
source for the Migration Period. As for Grundtvig, he would go on to publish a
translation of *Beowulf* into Danish,[69] arguing once again that it should be seen as
an Anglo-Saxon poem: 'The language is ingenuous, without having the German

---

[60] Shippey and Haarder, *Beowulf*, p. 12.

[61] Shippey and Haarder, *Beowulf*, pp. 98–107.

[62] Shippey and Haarder, *Beowulf*, pp. 101, 104; Osborn, 'Translations, versions, illustrations',
p. 341.

[63] Grundtvig, 'Et Par Ord om det nys udkomne angelsaksiske Digt', in Shippey and Haarder,
Beowulf, pp. 108–13, at p. 111.

[64] Shippey and Haarder, *Beowulf*, p. 11; Bjork, 'Nineteenth-century Scandinavia and the birth of
Anglo-Saxon studies', p. 116.

[65] Gundtvig, 'Om *Beovulfs Drape* eller det af Hr. Etatsraad Thorkelín 1815 udgivne angelsachsiske
Digt', trans. Shippey and Haarder, *Beowulf*, pp. 143–52, at p. 150.

[66] Leo, *Beowulf, dasz älteste deutsche, in angelsächsischer mundart erhaltene, Heldengedicht*, trans.
Shippey and Haarder; *Beowulf*, pp. 227–31.

[67] See above, chapter 7.

[68] There is no doubt that Hygelac and Chochilaicus represent the same name.

[69] Grundtvig, '*Om Bjowulfs Drape*', trans. Shippey and Haarder, *Beowulf*, pp. 158–61.

long-windedness, and without remaining obscure in its brevity as so often in the Eddic poems.'[70]

The debate did not long remain confined to Scandinavia. Moreover, the central question shifted from whether the poem was Anglo-Saxon to whether it was German. With this went not only a question about language, but also about whether or not the landscapes in which the events of the poem supposedly occurred were German rather than Danish. The poem, in other words, played into the Schleswig-Holstein question. In the debate over the relevance of *Beowulf* to the determination of whether the two provinces were German or Danish, the opening salvo was fired by Nicholaus Outzen in his review of Thorkelín entitled 'The Anglo-Saxon poem of Beowulf, as the most valuable document about the very great age of our fatherland'.[71] The crucial words here are 'our fatherland' ('unserm Vaterlande'), which for Outzen meant Angeln and North Schleswig. Outzen himself had been born in southern Jutland, just north of the present Danish-German border, and thus well inside the fiefdom of Schleswig. He was one of those south Jutlanders who would play a major role in the Prussian take-over of Schleswig-Holstein, seeing themselves as German rather than Danish. Significantly, he published his review of Thorkelín in the *Kieler Blätter*, a pro-German journal, which would be closed down in 1819 on account of its political leanings.[72] In his view, when the *Beowulf* poet spoke of Danes, he meant Angles.[73] In other words, far from providing evidence on the Danes, the poem was an account of the Angle (that is, Germanic) population of south Jutland at the start of the historic period. In the words of Tom Shippey, '[w]ith this review... *Beowulf* finds itself almost immediately close to the heart of European politics'.[74]

Outzen's position was modified by Dahlmann, who argued that the *Hetware* of the poem are the Angles, and that their power once stretched to Schleswig.[75] Friedrich Christoph Dahlmann had been born in Wismar, a city on the south coast of the Baltic, which was then under Swedish rule. Despite this, and although he took his degree at the University of Copenhagen, he saw Schleswig as *urdeutsch*.[76] He championed the German-ness of Schleswig-Holstein, both as an academic, in his early writings on *Beowulf*, written as Professor of History at Kiel from 1813, and also in his position as secretary to the *Ritterschaft* of Schleswig, which he held from 1815. Not surprisingly, he would fail to obtain a full professorship in Danish Kiel, and moved to Göttingen in 1829, where he became involved in other major political issues. He was one of the Göttingen Seven, along with the brothers Grimm, who lost their posts in 1837 as a result of their opposition to the arbitrary power of the King of Hannover,[77] but he was appointed professor in Bonn in 1842. In

---

[70] Shippey and Haarder, *Beowulf: The Critical Heritage*, p. 161.
[71] Outzen, excerpted in Shippey and Haarder, *Beowulf*, pp. 123–31.
[72] Shippey and Haarder, *Beowulf*, p. 18.
[73] Shippey and Haarder, *Beowulf*, pp. 17–19, 30–1, 126.
[74] Shippey and Haarder, *Beowulf*, p. 123.
[75] Dahlmann, *Forschungen auf den Gebiete der Geschichte*, vol. 1, pp. 439–41, trans. Shippey and Haarder, *Beowulf*, pp. 166–8.
[76] Shippey and Haarder, *Beowulf*, pp. 17–18.
[77] Boockmann, *Göttingen. Vergangenheit und Gegenwart einer europäischen Universität*, pp. 42–8.

1848 he was sent to the Frankfurt *Bundestag*, where he played a leading role in drawing up a draft constitution:[78] he was also a member of the *Gothaer Nachparlament*, and the Erfurt Parliament of 1850.

The German take-over of *Beowulf* was furthered by Jacob Grimm. From early in his career he had pitched into the conflict between German and Danish scholars: in 1812 in his review of Rasmus Rask's Icelandic/Old Norse Grammar he took the opportunity to proclaim the superiority of German over Danish literature.[79] In 1823 he reviewed Gruntvig's translation of *Beowulf*,[80] taking the Dane to task for seeing the poem as Danish. He pointed out that the Danes only play a minor role in the narrative. And, with his philological cap on, he simply dismissed the assertion that 'this epic evidently shows the Anglo-Saxon language to be really Danish'.[81] He did not, here, however, stress the German-ness of the Anglo-Saxons, although, of course, he regarded both the Angles and the Saxons as German peoples.

Grimm's position was extended by his English acolyte, John Mitchell Kemble, in his edition of *Beowulf*.[82] Kemble belonged to one of the great dynasties of the English theatre, being the son of the actor Charles Kemble, the nephew of Mrs Siddons, and the father-in-law of the baritone Charles Santley.[83] Although he studied law at Cambridge, he was primarily interested in the Anglo-Saxon past, and in 1833 he produced his own edition of *Beowulf*, dedicating it to Jacob Grimm, who taught him 'all the knowledge I possess, such as it is', and whom he described as 'the founder of that school of philology which has converted etymological researches, once a chaos of accidents, into a logical and scientific system'.[84] His dependence on Grimm was not limited to matters philological, for he also borrowed Möser's model of *Markgenossenschaft* from him and applied it to early medieval England.[85] Although Kemble produced what was possibly the most groundbreaking study of the Anglo-Saxons to be published in England in the nineteenth century,[86] he was never accepted within the English academic establishment, partly because of his political views, and partly because of the failure of his marriage.[87] As a result he abandoned England in 1849, moving to Hannover, where

---

[78] Leerssen, *National Thought in Europe*, pp. 147–8.

[79] Grimm, *Kleinere Schriften*, vol. 4, p. 73; Leerssen, *National Thought in Europe*, p. 181.

[80] Grimm, *Göttingische gelehrte Anzeigen* (2 January 1823), pp. 1–12, trans. Shippey and Haarder, *Beowulf*, pp. 170–3.

[81] Shippey and Haarder, *Beowulf*, p. 170.

[82] Kemble, *The Anglo-Saxon Poems of Beowulf, The Traveller's Song and the Battle of Finnes-burh*. On Kemble, Dickens, 'John Mitchell Kemble and Old English Scholarship', pp. 51–84; Wiley, 'Anglo-Saxon Kemble: the life and works of John Mitchell Kemble, 1807–57'; Ackerman, 'J. M. Kemble and Sir Frederic Madden'.

[83] Ackerman, 'J. M. Kemble and Sir Frederic Madden', p. 168.

[84] Ackerman, 'J. M. Kemble and Sir Frederic Madden', p. 169.

[85] On the exten t to which Kemble was applying Grimm's ideas to Anglo-Saxon material, Dopsch, *The Economic and Social Foundations of European Civilization*, p. 13. See also Horsman, 'Origins of Racial Anglo-Saxonism in Great Britain before 1850', p. 403, on Kemble's emphasis on the Germanic origins of English institutions.

[86] Kemble, *History of the Saxons in England*. See the assessment in Horsman, 'Origins of racial Anglo-Saxonism', p. 403.

[87] Ackerman, 'J. M. Kemble and Sir Frederic Madden', pp. 175–7.

he turned his attention to early medieval archaeology for the remaining eight years of his life.

In his assessment of the historical value of *Beowulf* Kemble ignored Gruntvig's identification of Hygelac with Chochilaicus—Heinrich Leo's work on the subject had not yet appeared—and turned instead to Migration Period Anglo-Saxon history:

> I infer that *Beowulf* records the exploits of one of our own forefathers, not far removed in point of time from the coming of Hengest and Hors into Britain: and that the poem was probably brought hither by some of those Anglo-Saxons who, in A.D. 495 accompanied Cerdic and Cyneric.[88]

And

> It is more than probable that the tongue spoken by Hengest in Sleswic, was that of Ælfred the king, four centuries later, such provincial variations only being disregarded as always subsist in every stage of a language. To suppose the Anglo-Saxon derived from a mixture of Old Saxon and Danish, is at once to stamp oneself ignorant both of Old Saxon, Old Norse and Anglo-Saxon, and to declare one's incompetency to pass a judgment upon the subject. I do not say that the poem which is now published was not written in England; but I say that the older poem, of which this is a modernized form, was shaped upon Angle legends, celebrates an Angle hero, and was in all probability both written in Angeln, and brought hither by some of the earliest Anglo-Saxon chieftains who settled upon our shores.[89]

Kemble, in other words, like Grundtvig, saw *Beowulf* as a source of information on the Migration Period, but like Grimm, he placed it in a Germanic and not a Scandinavian context. Grundtvig, in his reply to all these arguments, noted the acquisitive sense that went with them.[90] Yet there was no chance that his attempt to place the poem in a pan-Scandinavian context would slow down the juggernaut of pro-German opinion. The position set out by Outzen and Dahlmann was further elaborated by yet another scholar from south Jutland: Karl Victor Müllenhoff. He was a Holsteiner by birth, coming from Marne in Ditmarschen.[91] Like Outzen he stressed the importance of southern Jutland for the poem, going so far as to link *Beowulf* with the area in which he himself had been born.[92] In considering Hygelac and his dynasty he insisted (at this stage of his career) that 'one can confidently accept them as history just as much as any report from Gregory of Tours, Jordanes or Paul the Deacon'. He also argued that the Geats of the poem were presented elsewhere, by Bede and Alfred, as being clearly German[93]—a point with which the editor of the journal in which his article was published, Gregor Wilhelm Nitzsch,

---

[88] Shippey and Haarder, *Beowulf*, p. 193.

[89] Shippey and Haarder, *Beowulf*, p. 194.

[90] Grundtvig, 'Bjovulfs Drape eller det Oldnordiske Heltedigt', trans. Shippey and Haarder, *Beowulf*, pp. 241–5.

[91] Shippey and Haarder, *Beowulf*, p. 38.

[92] Müllenhoff, 'Die deutschen Völker an Nord- und Ostsee in ältester Zeit', trans. Shippey and Haarder, *Beowulf*, pp. 38–41, 252–8.

[93] Shippey and Haarder, *Beowulf*, p. 253–4.

immediately disagreed, claiming that they really were Jutes.[94] Müllenhoff would further push his territorial claims for *Beowulf* the following year, when he included the story in his collection of folktales and songs from the region of Schleswig-Holstein and Lauenburg.[95]

Grundtvig was not alone among Scandinavian scholars in drawing *Beowulf* into a northern orbit. Gísli Brynjúlfsson asserted that Old English (not Anglo-Saxon—he chose his terms carefully) was a South Scandinavian language, not West Germanic, and that the story told by the poem belongs to the Scandinavian legendary cycle.[96] Nor was it only Scandinavians and Icelanders who argued for a Scandinavian origin. The Englishman Benjamin Thorpe, like Kemble an outsider in England, studied philology in Copenhagen with Rasmus Rask, whose *Anglo-Saxon Grammar* he translated into English.[97] In his edition of the poem he argued that it was

> a metrical paraphrase of an heroic Saga composed in the south-west of Sweden in the old common language of the North, and probably brought to this country during the sway of the Danish dynasty.[98]

And he went on to claim that it presented 'a vivid and faithful picture of old Northern manners and usages, as they existed in the halls of the kingly and the noble at the remote period to which it relates'. He also held that the characters were not mythical, but 'real kings and chieftains of the North'.[99]

The fullest German claim, however, had yet to come: it appears in Karl Joseph Simrock's translation,[100] which was explicitly intended to 'win a new naturalisation among us for this poem, emigrated with the Angles and Saxons'. Simrock claimed that 'The myth is a German one.'

> Besides us Germans, the English, Danes and Swedes also have claims to the *Beowulf*. They have however been asserted only by Danes and Englishmen; the Germans have too often let valid claims lie. They do that with their provinces the other side of the Rhine, etc. What does a province matter anyway? And now a poem, even? Every market-fair brings new ones, and they are forgotten before the next. How is a thousand-year glory of our people supposed to depend on an epic? How were the Homeric poems of the Germans, once they had finally been dragged out of the rubble, supposed to be able to contribute to strengthening our self-awareness and making us in the end into a nation?

He went on to define the Anglo-Saxons in no uncertain terms:

> The poem of *Beowulf* has been transmitted in the Anglo-Saxon language and as heirs of the Anglo-Saxons the English are entitled to proclaim it as their property. But the

---

[94] His footnote is published in Shippey and Haarder, *Beowulf*, pp. 257–8.

[95] Müllenhoff, *Sagen Märchen und Lieder der Herzogthümer Schleswig Holstein und Lauenburg* (Kiel, 1845). See Shippey and Haarder, *Beowulf*, p. 261.

[96] Brynjúlfsson, 'Oldengelsk of Oldnorsk', trans. Shippey and Haarder, *Beowulf*, pp. 291–6.

[97] Murphy, 'Antiquary to Academic: the progress of Anglo-Saxon scholarship', pp. 13–14.

[98] Thorpe, *The Anglo-Saxon Poems of Beowulf, The Scop or Gleeman's tale, and the Fight at Finnesburg*. The preface, pp. viii–xii, is excerpted in Shippey and Haarder, *Beowulf*, pp. 297–9, at p. 297.

[99] Shippey and Haarder, *Beowulf*, p. 298.

[100] Simrock, *Beowulf*, trans. Shippey and Haarder, *Beowulf*, pp. 306–17.

Angles and Saxons were German peoples, and the setting of the poem lies on this side of the North Sea, near the old seats of these peoples before the conquest of Britain, and seems from its basis to be of older origin than the Anglo-Saxon people; it is accordingly an Anglian or a Saxon, not an Anglo-Saxon poem.

Nor was it only the language of the poem that was Germanic. Because Tacitus counted the German coasts of the North Sea and both sides of the Baltic as Ingvaeonic, the setting of the poem was itself necessarily *Germania*.[101]

The arguments about *Beowulf*, and its importance for understanding the early histories of Jutland and England of course rumbled on: but by the 1860s the chief historical points relating to the text had been made. Moreover, the Schleswig-Holstein question was concluded (albeit temporarily) with the second Schleswig War of 1864, and Christian IX's renunciation of the provinces to Wilhelm I of Prussia and Franz Josef I of Austria. As a result, discussions of the early population of the region fell into abeyance, and this aspect of debate about *Beowulf* declined. Yet there were some diehards, like the 'the fiery anti-German old northernist George Stephens, and a passionate supporter of the Slesvig-Holsten cause (not Schleswig Holstein—to use the German spelling was to accept the verdict of the 1864 war)'.[102]

In another respect the argument between the Danes and the Germans was not yet over. In 1863 the Danish archaeologist Conrad Engelhardt discovered two boats in the Nydam bog. One of these was fully excavated. The second was left for subsequent excavation—but was unfortunately destroyed in the course of the war of 1864. The finds, which had been added to the Flensburg collection, were claimed jointly by the Prussians and Austrians in the treaty that concluded the war. Initially, the Danes were successful in hiding the collection, but in 1867, after the Austrians abandoned their claims, the Prussians, who by this time had come to realize the importance of the objects, insisted on its being handed over.[103] The Nydam boat, in particular, which is now known to have been built in the mid-fourth century, was a precious survival from the days of the Germanic migrations—indeed it could be presented as the only surviving vessel of the type which took the Angles, Saxons, and Jutes from Germany and Jutland to their new homes in England. It was thus a key piece of evidence of the Migration Period. The story of the Nydam boat, however, did not end with the transfer of the objects to Kiel. Following the conclusion of the First World War, when two plebiscites were held in Schleswig-Holstein to determine whether the territory should remain in Germany or not, North Schleswig, which included the Nydam bog, opted to rejoin Denmark, and the Danes therefore pushed, unsuccessfully as it happened, to have the finds returned to them. They repeated their claims after the Second World War.[104]

---

[101] Shippey and Haarder, *Beowulf*, pp. 307–9.
[102] Wawn, *The Vikings and the Victorians*, pp. 63–4.
[103] Wiell, 'Denmark's bog find pioneer: the archaeologist Conrad Engelhardt and his work', pp. 74–6.
[104] Wiell, 'Denmark's bog find pioneer', pp. 82–3.

9.4 GRIMM AND THE GERMAN FATHERLAND

While *Beowulf* provided the focus for a particular debate about Germany and its provinces, it was part of a much wider set of discussions about borders and about language. As we have seen, Simrock in the introduction to his translation of *Beowulf* referred not just to Schleswig-Holstein, but also to the Rhine frontier.[105] The question of frontiers had been at the heart of discussions about Germany for a long time, but Napoleon's conquests had led to a renewed debate. One of the key figures here was a man we have already met, Ernst Moritz Arndt, friend of both Stein and Grimm. Engels, writing in 1840, looked back on Arndt's early career:

> With the year 1800 Arndt enters the profession allotted to him. Napoleon's armies flood Europe, and as the French Emperor's power increases Arndt's hatred of him grows; the Greifswald professor protests in the name of Germany against the oppression and has to flee. At last the German nation rises up and Arndt returns.[106]

Arndt's patriotic views were expressed in a string of writings: notably the 1813 poem *Was ist des Deutschen Vaterland?* The Fatherland, in his opinion, most certainly did not stop at the Rhine.[107] Engels associated Arndt firmly with the cry 'Give back Alsace and Lorraine.'[108] Arndt could look back to the boundaries of the old Holy Roman Empire, but his arguments for extending the frontiers of Germany across the Rhine and into Jutland were also based on 'his linguistic-historical-ethnologic claims' about language as evidence of early settlement of Germanic peoples[109]—it was an argument which would have frightening repercussions in the twentieth century.

Arndt was a key figure in the transformation of Germany from (in Mme de Staël's terms) a *Kulturnation* to a *Staatsnation*,[110] the development that came to a head with the unification of Germany in 1871. Equally central, and with a good deal more to say about the early Middle Ages, was Jacob Grimm. His contribution to scholarship was considerably greater, and his contribution to politics not much less, than that of Dahlmann. Both were members of the Göttingen Seven, dismissed from their university posts for opposing the autocracy of Ernst August, and both (along with Arndt) played important roles at the Frankfurt Parliament of 1848, which constituted a crucial but politically premature expression of German unity.[111]

---

[105] Shippey and Haarder, *Beowulf*, p. 308.

[106] Engels, *Telegraph für Deutschland* 2 (January, 1841), Marx and Engels Internet archive, <http://www.marx.org/archive/marx/index.htm>.

[107] Leerssen, *National Thought in Europe*, pp. 178–9. See also Arndt, *Der Rhein, Teutschlands Strom, nicht aber Teutschlands Gränze*; Arndt, *Die Frage über die Niederlande*.

[108] Engels, *Telegraph für Deutschland* 5 (January, 1841), Marx and Engels Internet archive, <http://www.marx.org/archive/marx/index.htm>.

[109] Leerssen, *National Thought in Europe*, pp. 178–9.

[110] Leerssen, *National Thought in Europe*, p. 146.

[111] Leerssen, *National Thought in Europe*, pp. 146–50, 177–8, 182–3. In general see Feldman, *Jacob Grimm und die Politik*.

His contribution to early medieval studies was primarily philological, but because of the association of language and individual tribal groups—an association already expressed by Leibniz and Mascov in the eighteenth century—his comments on the language or dialect spoken in a particular region often carried with them implications for the earlier presence of Germanic tribes. This is clearly apparent in his contributions to the Schleswig-Holstein question in the 1840s. Thus, in 1848, he argued,

> No, Schleswig is not an original Danish region, in which the Germans are guests, as is ignominiously pretended here, but an original German one, which conversely the Danes have penetrated uninvited. The entire Cimbric peninsula was formerly inhabited by Germans, not by Scandinavians, and the Jutes themselves, as I have proved, in my *History of the German Language*, were not Scandinavian. One may scarcely think that the Germans had lived patiently under foreigners; it appears unbelievable that the Saxons, Angles and Jutes, who Bede, the oldest guarantor to mention them, called collectively Germans, had not become a people. The foolish champions of the Danish case only have knowledge as far back as Adam of Bremen, in whose time the Danish territory stretched to the Eider. But right up to today, the Jutish language includes German, non-Danish elements, which show the true relationship. The Jutes have now gradually become comfortable with the Danish language, and allowed their flesh and blood to become Danish, but the majority of the Schleswigers do not wish, have not done, and never will do so. They feel themselves bound fast through hallowed contracts and traditions to Holstein and Germany.[112]

In the *Geschichte der deutschen Sprache* to which he refers, he worked his way through the narrative sources for late Antiquity to provide a description of the peoples of the period.[113] He had already done something similar for the Goths in his 'Jornandes [*sic*] und die Geten', where he examined the writing of the *Getica*, the names of individual Goths, and the names applied to supposedly Gothic peoples, working his way through a vast range of classical and medieval sources.[114] He did not, however, extend this into attempting a history of the Goths.

Grimm, or at least both brothers Grimm, had come rather closer to providing a narrative of the early Middle Ages in their collection of *Deutsche Sagen* of 1816–18, much of which is essentially a retelling of episodes from historical narratives. In a letter written to Robert Jamieson in 1818, Wilhelm Grimm described the second volume as containing 'a collection of material related to German legends, found in the works of historians, such as Tacitus, Jornandes, Paulus Diaconus, Gregory of Tours etc...'.[115] To this list of authors one can add others, including Procopius.

---

[112] Grimm, 'Schleswig', in *Kleinere Schriften*, vol. 8, pp. 432–3. See also his 'Adresse an den König für Schleswig-Holstein, 1846', ibid. pp. 430–1 and his 'Vortrag in der nationalversammlung zu Frankfurt a. M., 1848', 'Über Schleswig-Holstein', ibid. pp. 437–8.

[113] Grimm, *Geschichte der deutschen Sprache*, vol. 1, chs 8, 18–20. I have consulted the 1880 Leipzig edition, pp. 113–32, 305–37, which can be found at <www.archive.org/stream/geschichtederdeu01grimuoft>.

[114] Grimm, 'Ueber Jornandes und die Geten', in *Kleinere Schriften*, vol. 3, pp. 171–235.

[115] Michaelis-Jena, 'Early exchanges on oral traditions: two unpublished letters by Robert Jamieson and Wilhelm Grimm', p. 46.

The Grimms claimed that the anecdotes that they translated contained the material of early Germanic sagas: they include many of the most famous episodes of Gothic, Frankish, and Lombard history. But the collection also demonstrates the same acquisitiveness that one finds in German attitudes towards *Beowulf*. Stories that can scarcely be called German tales are annexed, sometimes with a sleight of hand. Thus, a famous story from Gregory of Tours which recounts the escape of his relative Attalus from the house of a Frank where he had been enslaved, following an outbreak of hostility between two Merovingian kings, is presented as a German saga.[116] It is nothing of the sort: Attalus was the nephew of bishop Gregory of Langres, and a relative of Gregory of Tours, and was therefore a Gallo-Roman. The quick-witted cook Leo, who devises the plan of escape, is nowhere described as being a Frank, and his name suggests that he too was a Gallo-Roman. The story is, in other words, a Gallo-Roman story: indeed it is a family tale, concerned with a member of one of the leading Gallo-Roman families of early Merovingian Gaul, and told by a relative. Yet the brothers Grimm omitted to point out that the protagonists were in no sense German.

The success of the retelling of this story can be seen in its use by the Austrian playwright Franz Grillparzer, in his *Weh dem der lügt* of 1838. Grillparzer first thought the tale would make a good subject in 1820/1, shortly after the appearance of the *Deutsche Sagen*.[117] By the time he wrote the play he had also read Jacob Grimm's *Deutsche Rechtsalterthümer* of 1828 and his *Deutsche Mythologie* of 1835—a work in which, unlike de Staël, Guizot, and later Ozanam, Grimm argued that Europe had been reinvigorated after the Fall of Rome not by Christianity, but by the Germanic peoples.[118] Grillparzer followed the essentials of the story, but he did add some love interest, as well as a moral on truth-telling, implicit in Gregory of Tours' original, although perhaps strengthened through reading Montaigne.[119] More important from the historical point of view, he subtly changed the context. Here Attalus and Leo are firmly Frankish, while the household in which they are enslaved belongs to barbarians who are at war with the Franks.

9.5 *RECHTSGESCHICHTE* AND THE SETTLEMENT OF THE BARBARIANS

The editing of medieval texts and their philological analysis were two aspects of the study of the early Middle Ages to which German scholars contributed most during the nineteenth century. A third aspect was that of law. Here too Jacob Grimm was an influential figure, although his contribution to the subject in *Deutsche Rechtsaltertümer* has long been superseded. His general thesis was that law reflected the

---

[116] Grimm, *Deutsche Sagen*, vol. 2, n. 427, pp. 69–73. The same appropriation takes place in Freytag, *Bilder aus der deutschen Vergangenheit*, vol. 1, pp. 308–13. See Wood, 'Ethnicity and language in medieval and modern versions of the Attalus-saga'.

[117] Grillparzer, *Weh dem, der lügt*, ed. Sternelle, pp. 74–5.

[118] Grillparzer, *Weh dem, der lügt*, ed. Sternelle, p. 79, commenting on lines 1406 and 1478.

[119] Grillparzer, *Weh dem, der lügt*, ed. Sternelle, p. 75.

spirit of a people in much the same way as did folktales. This may now look like a 'dusty relic of nineteenth-century German mentalities',[120] but it reflected a serious attempt to understand society. Grimm also provided an introduction to Johannes Merkel's edition of *Lex Salica*, where he commented on the language of the early codes.[121] Merkel's edition has not stood the test of time, although it was to be well into the twentieth century before anyone produced a generally respected edition of the main Frankish lawcode.[122]

Much more important than Grimm in legal studies was his teacher, Friedrich Carl von Savigny, whose lectures he attended at Marburg,[123] and for whom he briefly worked in Paris in 1805. Savigny was also a friend of the Freiherr vom Stein. Moreover, like that of Stein and Grimm, and indeed that of the great Romanist, Barthold Georg Niebuhr,[124] his work was in certain respects a reaction against the Napoleonic period in Germany, and especially against the attempt to impose the *Code Napoléon*.[125] Nevertheless, Savigny's great contribution was not to the understanding of the barbarian codes, but to the study of Roman law in the Middle Ages, though this, of course, included the great compendia of Theodosius and Justinian.[126]

In the course of his *History of Roman Law* he did comment on certain matters of central importance to the history of the early Middle Ages, not least the question of the settlement of the Germanic peoples within the Empire, which he saw as a straightforward act of partition.[127] This line of approach was challenged by the Prussian scholar Ernst Theodor Gaupp in 1844. He proposed instead that the settlement of the barbarians was preceded by an initial period of military quartering.[128] Gaupp's argument has been seen as the point of departure for all later work on the subject, and played a particularly important role in debates of the late twentieth century,[129] although it scarcely impacted upon the nationalist arguments that dominated the nineteenth.

While one may see Gaupp as ultimately having contributed more to the study of the early Germanic peoples than did Savigny, the latter's emphasis on the need to understand law in its historical context was fundamental to the study of all

---

[120] On Grimm, *Deutsche Rechtsaltertümer*, see Wormald, *The Making of English Law*, p. 11.

[121] *Lex Salica*, ed. Merkel with a foreword by Grimm. The 'Vorrede' is reprinted in Grimm, *Kleinere Schriften*, vol. 8, pp. 228–303.

[122] Essentially one has to wait for the editions by Eckhardt for the *Monumenta Germaniae Historica*.

[123] On Grimm and Savigny, see Wyss, *Die wilde Philologie. Jacob Grimm und der Historismus*, pp. 60–4.

[124] Thom, *Republics, Nations and Tribes*, p. 268.

[125] Mollnau, 'The contributions of Savigny to the Theory of Legislation', pp. 84–6; M. Rowe, 'The Napoleonic Legacy in the Rhineland and the Politics of Reform in Restoration Prussia', p. 139.

[126] Savigny, *Das Recht des Besitzes*.

[127] Savigny, *Geschichte des römischen Rechts im Mittelalter*, vol. 1, p. 296.

[128] Gaupp, *Die germanischen Ansiedlungen und Landtheilungen in den Provinzen des römischen Westreiches*.

[129] See, especially, Goffart, *Barbarians and Romans*, pp. xiii, 37, 50, 159–60, 171, 207–9, 216. Also Dopsch, *The Economic and Social Foundations of European Civilization*, pp. 12–13; Graceffa, *Les Historiens et la question franque*, pp. 83–8.

medieval law. The approach was central to the *Zeitschrift für geschichtliche Rechts-wissenschaft*, a journal founded by Savigny, together with Karl Friedrich Eichhorn and Johann Friedrich Ludwig Göschen, in 1815. It would develop into the still continuing *Zeitschrift der Savigny-Stiftung für Rechtsgeschichte*. More generally, however, Savigny's approach (rather than his own research) provided the founda-tion for the German *Rechtsschule*, which would be the dominant school of the historical study of early medieval law through the late nineteenth and early twen-tieth centuries. This tradition, which attempted to present Germanic law as being as worthy of study as Roman, was most fully expressed by Heinrich Brunner in his *Deutsche Rechtsgeschichte*, the first volume of which appeared in 1887.

By this time the *MGH* was producing significant editions of the early codes. Pertz himself had edited a volume of Frankish royal capitularies in 1835. The Bavarian, Burgundian, and Frisian codes appeared in 1863, and five years after them the *Leges Langobardorum*. A final volume of the series of laws that was pub-lished in folio appeared between 1875 and 1889. A new series began in 1888 with Karl Lehmann's edition of the *Leges alamannorum*. At much the same time other new series were being produced by the *Monumenta*: there were the volumes of *Auctores Antiquissimi*, covering the Late Antique texts of Roman authors, the first of which appeared in 1877, and, equally important, the *Scriptores Rerum Merov-ingicarum*. The 1870s and 1880s were in many respects the point at which the initiatives of the German scholars of the first part of the century came to fruition. Despite the importance of the work of Pertz, Grimm, and Savigny, Germany before unification did not produce a major narrative account of the early Middle Ages. The great achievements had been in the study of language and law, rather that in history itself. This would change in the last decades of the century, but not before the study of history had been affected by the crises of 1870 and 1871, much as it had by the Napoleonic wars and the conflicts between Germany and Denmark.

10

Romans, Barbarians, and Prussians

10.1 THEODOR MOMMSEN

Just as the early debates over German unification, and the conflict between the Germans and Denmark had a major impact on the interpretation of the early Middle Ages, so too did the second and third Italian Wars of Independence of 1859 and 1866, as well as the subsequent, and related, Franco-Prussian war of 1870–1 and the German annexation of Alsace. After 1871 any comparison between the Germanic invasions of the fourth and fifth centuries inevitably took on new significance, as did any proclamation of Roman continuity. Exactly how some of the leading French and German scholars reacted to the Italian Wars of Independence and the conflict between Prussia and France will concern us in what follows.

Two of the most significant figures in the study of the late Roman and early medieval periods, Theodor Mommsen (1817–1903) and Numa Denis Fustel de Coulanges (1830–89) involved themselves directly in the debates leading up to the Franco-Prussian war. Mommsen wrote an open letter to the Italian people, encouraging them not to intervene on the French side.[1] In his view, the policies of Napoleon III were a repetition of those of his imperial namesake and predecessor—Mommsen was thinking not only of the immediate conflict, but also of Napoleon III's intervention in Italy in 1859. This interpretation, that the French were the warmongers, was rejected by Fustel, who saw the Prussians as the clear aggressors.[2] A third specialist in the early Middle Ages, Felix Dahn, would also involve himself in the debate over the war—quite apart from volunteering and thus fighting and being slightly wounded at Sedan.[3] He published a pamphlet in 1870 entitled *Das Kriegsrecht: kurze, volksthümliche Darstellung für Jedermann zumal für den deutschen Soldaten*: in 1872 it was translated into French as *Le Droit de la guerre: exposé succintement et mis à la portée des masses*. It is worth noting the change of address from 'everyman and especially the German soldiers', to the French 'masses'.

---

[1] Mommsen's letters are to be found edited by Liberati, 'Agli Italiani', pp. 197–247. For an important recent discussion, Geary, *Historians as Public Individuals*. For a detailed analysis, particularly of the German side of the debate, see Haubrichs, 'Der Krieg der Professoren'.

[2] Fustel's attack on Mommsen is to be found in Hartog, *Le XIXe siècle et l'histoire*, pp. 398–404. On changing attitudes towards Mommsen in France, Nicolet, *La Fabrique d'une nation*, pp. 185–96.

[3] Wahl, *Die Religion des deutschen Nationalismus*, pp. 51–2. Neuhaus, *Literatur und nationale Einheit in Deutschland*, p. 233.

The vitriolic exchanges of Mommsen and Fustel did not, in fact, make reference to the period of the Germanic invasions.[4] Yet the war did impact upon the study of the early Middle Ages in a number of ways. Foreshadowing what would happen in the late 1930s, there was an outpouring of toponymic studies on Alsace-Lorraine from Strasbourg[5]—the subtext of such studies was no doubt to prove the essential German-ness of the region, and to show that this originated in the Migration Period. On the French side, it is not hard to find a simmering sense of resentment. For both Mommsen and Fustel, however, the use of early medieval history and the impact of the Franco-Prussian war on its interpretation was more complex and less explicit.

Mommsen was born in 1817 in Garding, Schleswig, which was at the time still part of Denmark. Most of his career was devoted to the study of Roman history, and his magnum opus, the *Römische Geschichte*, which initially appeared in three volumes, published between 1854 and 1856, though it was subsequently expanded, would ultimately lead to his being awarded the Nobel prize for literature in 1902. He turned to the immediately post-Roman period in the years after the Franco-Prussian war, and largely in the context of his involvement with the *Monumenta Germaniae Historica*, of which he was appointed *Mitglied der Central-direction*. In 1875 he was also put in charge of the *Monumenta*'s new series of *Auctores Antiquissimi*—authors one might place rather more within the classical tradition than as belonging to the early Middle Ages.[6] His involvement was to have a dramatic impact on the *Monumenta*, which at the time was in the doldrums. It was to lead to the publication between 1877 and 1898 of thirteen volumes of Latin sources, of which Mommsen himself edited five, including the *Getica* of Jordanes, the *Variae* of Cassiodorus, and three volumes of chronicles. During the same period he edited the first part of the *Liber Pontificalis*, covering the years up to 715. When he died he left unfinished an edition of the *Codex Theodosianus*, which would appear posthumously. Although in the case of the fifth- and sixth-century chronicles his determination to establish the authentic original text rather obscured the purpose of the compilations in which they are to be found, Mommsen's editions constitute one of the greatest contributions to early medieval studies.

Before the outbreak of the Franco-Prussian war, his *Roman History* had been well received in France, and indeed it was soon translated by Charles-Alfred Alexandre, the first volume of whose translation came out in 1863.[7] In his preface the translator heaped praise on both Mommsen and on the German scholarly tradition. When the final volume came out in 1872, however, the situation had changed. Alexandre went out of his way to draw attention to the events of the previous years, and to Mommsen's role in them:

---

[4] See Geary, *Historians as Public Intellectuals*, pp. 17–21.
[5] Graceffa, *Les Historiens et la question franque*, p. 167, though the importance of Strasbourg is not stressed.
[6] *Phönix aus der Asche: Katalog zur Austellung der Monumenta Germaniae Historica*.
[7] Geary, *Historians as Public Intellectuals*, p. 4, n. 4 and 5.

In this period our author, M. Mommsen, also shouted *haro*, along with all the other German professors. M. Mommsen, who once and so many times made use of our country's liberal and open hospitality, insulted us in his *Letters to the Italians*, in a language unworthy of a guest, unworthy of a noble enemy.[8]

Other scholars felt likewise. Gaston Boissier, professor of Latin at the Collège de France, even found elements intended to stir up hatred in Mommsen's *Roman History*.[9]

10.2 NUMA DENIS FUSTEL DE COULANGES AND FRENCH SCHOLARSHIP AT THE TIME OF THE FRANCO-PRUSSIAN WAR

The response of Fustel, despite his attack on Mommsen's appeal to the Italians, was very different from that of many of his French contemporaries, although in certain respects he can be seen as fulfilling one aspect of Alexandre's hopes, expressed in the last volume of his translation of the *Römische Geschichte*:

> Let us avenge ourselves by crossing the Rhine to reconquer both French scholarship of the sixteenth century, which has been taken prisoner there, and these arms which have helped to conquer us: let us take back from the Germans the education that they have vulgarised, the institutions which accustom peoples to personal dignity and discipline, to the spirit of duty and sacrifice, to faith in all pure dogmas of religion and the fatherland.[10]

Fustel was born in Paris in 1830. His early scholarly work concentrated on the eastern Mediterranean, where he both studied the literary evidence and directed an archaeological excavation. The result was *La Cité antique*, published in 1864, four years after he had been appointed to the Chair of History at the University of Strasbourg. In February 1870 he moved to the *École Normale Supérieure* in Paris. This meant that he had already left Strasbourg before the Prussian take-over, and also that he was in Paris for the duration of the Prussian siege. Five years later he was appointed to a professorship, and in 1878 he became the first Professor of Medieval History at the Sorbonne. The change in Fustel's area of research, from the Ancient World to the Middle Ages, which justified his final appointment is marked, above all, by the appearance in 1875 of the first volume of his *Histoire des institutions politiques de l'ancienne France*. This he almost immediately expanded into three volumes which appeared between 1877 and 1888, on Roman Gaul, the Germanic Invasions, and the Frankish Monarchy.[11] Three more volumes, on land and

---

[8] Mommsen, *Histoire romaine* vol. 8 trans. Alexandre, p. vii, cited by Geary, *Historians as Public Intellectuals*, p. 7.

[9] See Geary *Historians as Public Intellectuals*, pp. 10–14, on Gaston Boissier.

[10] Mommsen, *Histoire romaine* vol. 8 trans. Alexandre, p. vii, cited by Geary, *Historians as Public Intellectuals*, p. 8.

[11] Fustel de Coulanges, 'L'invasion germanique au Ve siècle'. See Hartog, *Le XIXe siècle et l'histoire*, p. 94.

land-tenure, patronage, and Carolingian kingship, were published after his death in 1889, the last two having been substantially edited by Camille Jullian (1859–1933), who also revised some of the earlier volumes—Jullian, himself, it should be noted, had a distinguished career as an Ancient Historian: his own multi-volume *Histoire de la Gaule* was to appear between 1907 and 1928. In addition, he would write a number of patriotic books in the course of the 1914–18 War,[12] and he was a member of the *Comité d'Études* whose work fed in to the Treaty of Versailles.[13]

Volume one of the *Institutions politiques* highlights Fustel's switch of interest from the classical to the early medieval worlds. That the switch occured in the early 1870s becomes more apparent when one includes his articles alongside his books. Most important are a series of pieces published in the *Revue des deux mondes*, especially 'De la manière d'écrire l'histoire en France et en Allemagne' and 'L'invasion germanique au Ve siècle, son caractère et ses effets', both of which appeared in 1872.[14] The first of these pieces makes clear Fustel's hostility to the Germans and to German scholarship, promoting instead French scholarly traditions.[15] Here he not only had the Germans in his sights, but also his colleague in Paris, Gabriel Monod, who had been trained at Göttingen and Berlin.[16] Although German methodology and training would come to outshine its rivals, in the early 1870s Fustel had some justification: the *Auctores Antiquissimi* had not yet begun to appear from the press of the *Monumenta*, nor had the equally important *Scriptores Rerum Merovingicarum*, whose first volume was not published until 1885. Yet, despite his personal hostility to the Prussians, Fustel is notable for not letting it get in the way of his study of the sources, which, as he frequently stressed, a historian had to read scientifically.[17]

Fustel began his study of French institutions in the pre-Roman period, and with the structure of Gaulish society, especially of the *clientelae*. Like Vico, Niebuhr, and Waitz before him, and like Mommsen, he placed the development of patronage at the heart of his discussion.[18] With the coming of the Romans the established social structures changed, and Gaulish language and culture collapsed, though the Gauls remained free and actually liked the Empire, finding that it largely acted in

---

[12] e.g. *Le Rhin gaulois: le Rhin français: L'Alsace française. À un ami du front: la guerre pour la patrie: Aimons la France, conférences: 1914–1919*. For a contrast between the views of Fustel and Jullian on Alsace, see Boswell, 'From liberation to purge trials in the "Mythic Provinces"', p. 139.

[13] Heffernan, 'History, geography and the French national space: the question of Alsace-Lorraine, 1914–18', pp. 37, 41, 43.

[14] Fustel de Coulanges, 'De la manière d'écrire l'histoire en France et en Allemagne'; Fustel de Coulanges, 'L'invasion germanique au Ve siècle, son caractère et ses effets'.

[15] Hartog, *Le XIXe siècle et l'histoire*, pp. 131–5.

[16] Hartog, *Le XIXe siècle et l'histoire*, pp. 103–11; Geary, 'Gabriel Monod, Fustel de Coulanges et les aventures de Sichaire', pp. 87–99.

[17] Fustel de Coulanges (and Jullian) on scientific reading (see the bibliography for the date of the editions cited): *La Monarchie Franque*, pp. 1, 69, 303, 305; Fustel de Coulanges, *L'Alleu et le Domaine Rural pendant l'époque mérovingienne*, p. iv; Fustel de Coulanges, *Les Transformations de la royauté pendant l'époque carolingienne*, p. vii. On some of the problems of Fustel's scientific view: Hartog, *Le XIXe siècle et l'histoire*, pp. 103, 140, 147–9, 168–70.

[18] Thom, *Republics, Nations and Tribes*, p. 75. For Waitz's interpretation of feudalism see Stephenson, 'The origins and significance of feudalism', pp. 791–2.

their interest.[19] Here Fustel was deliberately replying to the view established in the eighteenth century, that the oppression of the people of Gaul began during the Roman period. He noted the changes in involvement with the army—initially the landowners were obliged to supply men to serve as soldiers: this, however, changed to a tax requirement. Service in the army became hereditary for the sons of veterans, but at the same time there was enrolment of barbarians.[20] All this lessened the burden of military service on the majority of the population, but it had the unfortunate side effect of demilitarizing the population at large, while making the army more dangerous.[21]

When he reached the period of the Germanic invasions Fustel criticized the notion that there was a major conquest, insisting that that is not what the sources said. Dismissing much earlier scholarship, he proclaimed,

> I have not spoken of the spirit of liberty of the Frankish warriors, nor of elective royalty, nor of national assemblies, nor of popular juries, nor of the confiscation of the lands of the defeated, nor of allods distributed to the victors. I have looked for all these things in the documents and have not found them there at all.[22]

Instead he stressed continuity, insisting that the invasions were not a single event, and thus that their impact was more subtle and complex. Although the general impression given by the sources may be of a large body of incomers taking over the land and establishing a new regime, precise analysis reveals that the change took place over a long time, and that numerous factors were involved.[23] Equally importantly, he challenged new ethnographic interpretations:

> The modern spirit is entirely preoccupied with ethnographic theories and carries this prejudice into the study of history. Other thoughts enlivened men of the sixth century, and they breathe still in the texts that have come down to us from that period.[24]

This is not a call for a return to old-fashioned scholarship. Fustel himself can be placed in the forefront of the development of sociology: Durkheim was one of his pupils. Yet, although his criticism is very much to the point, as it turned out, the dominant attitudes of the first half of the twentieth century were firmly against him.

Just as he began his study of the Gallo-Romans way back in the Gaulish past, so Fustel looked at the evidence for the early Germanic peoples before their migration, stressing the lack of literary evidence produced by the barbarians themselves, and the weakness or irrelevance of Caesar and Tacitus on the one hand, and Carolingian and Icelandic material on the other, for understanding the fourth and fifth centuries.[25] In so doing he effectively destroyed the interpretations of the early

---

[19] Fustel de Coulanges, *La Gaule romaine*, pp. 65, 71, 173–4.
[20] Fustel de Coulanges, *La Gaule romaine*, pp. 292–4.
[21] Fustel de Coulanges, *La Gaule romaine*, pp. 294–5.
[22] Fustel de Coulanges, *L'Invasion germanique*, p. xi.
[23] Fustel de Coulanges, *L'Invasion germanique*, p. 225.
[24] Fustel de Coulanges, *L'Invasion germanique*, p. xii.
[25] Fustel de Coulanges, *L'Invasion germanique*, pp. 226–47.

Germanic peoples given by the likes of Boulainvilliers, Montesquieu, Mably, even Ozanam, and indeed by German scholars of his own day. He concluded his discussion of the source material by estimating that there are two pages of value for understanding the Germanic peoples in Caesar, two or three in Strabo and Pliny, twenty in Tacitus, some lines in Dio Cassius and Ammianus, and the *Getica* by Jordanes—this, it should be said, underestimated the value of Ammianus, whose account of the Germanic wars of Julian and Valentinian I has more than a few lines of value. In Fustel's view, whilst the Germanists liked to talk of ancient Germans, and the Romanists liked to talk of the Gauls (he is thinking here of Amédée Thierry and his disciples), we know little of either group and cannot attempt a complete reconstruction of their social system.[26]

Despite this pessimism, Fustel did go on to consider class distinctions in the Germanic world,[27] dismissing the vision of an egalitarian society held by some of the Germanists:

> The Germanic spirit of independence has been much acclaimed. However, the majority of these men were caught up in bonds of personal subjection.[28]

The Germanic state of the pre-Migration Period (and he used the word *état*) he saw as relatively sophisticated.[29] He envisaged a set of confederations made up of cantons and villages ruled over by kings, whose power, however, was limited.[30]

When considering the Migration Period, Fustel noted that there had been some changes from what one can see in Tacitus. Old tribal groups had vanished, and there were now others in their place. The Germanic peoples had apparently undergone the same pattern of decline that one finds with other nations: a weakening of institutions and a decrease in population.[31] The power of warrior chiefs had increased, while there was a concomitant decline in liberty.[32] There was also steady interaction with the Roman world. Some fought the Romans, some fought alongside Romans against other Germanic peoples. They tended to copy Roman vices.[33] Above all, there was no sense of Germanic patriotism and no overwhelming hatred of Rome. This idea, Fustel claimed, was a creation of the sixteenth century and found its fullest expression in La Fontaine's poem *Le paysan du Danube*.[34] Of course, Fustel had more immediate concerns in mind here, and he admitted them:

> These violent and blind hatreds which fill the heart of the German [Fustel uses the word *germain* and not *allemand*] nowadays were unknown to these ancestors. For the Germans of those days 'the hereditary enemy' was the German.[35]

---

[26] Fustel de Coulanges, *L'Invasion germanique*, p. 247.
[27] Fustel de Coulanges, *L'Invasion germanique*, pp. 247–68.
[28] Fustel de Coulanges, *L'Invasion germanique*, p. 290.
[29] Fustel de Coulanges, *L'Invasion germanique*, p. 272.
[30] Fustel de Coulanges, *L'Invasion germanique*, p. 290.
[31] Fustel de Coulanges, *L'Invasion germanique*, pp. 297–8.
[32] Fustel de Coulanges, *L'Invasion germanique*, p. 300.
[33] Fustel de Coulanges, *L'Invasion germanique*, pp. 291–3, 313.
[34] Fustel de Coulanges, *L'Invasion germanique*, pp. 313–14.
[35] Fustel de Coulanges, *L'Invasion germanique*, p. 322.

In trying to explain the Germanic invasions, having dismissed the notion of ancestral hatred of the Romans, and also the notion that there could be overpopulation in the German landscape,[36] Fustel suggested that the real cause was internal conflict and social revolution. Germanic peoples left *Germania* out of fear of their neighbours, and they left behind a relatively empty landscape through which the Huns and the Slavs could move with ease.[37] Yet, as the Frenchman went on to admit, if fear were the real cause it was not the only one. He then listed a number of ways in which *Germani* entered the Empire: as invaders and enemies, as subjects of Rome, as slaves or *coloni*, and as faithful or as unfaithful soldiers. In describing each category in turn he effectively provided a discussion of all the invasions of the fifth century.[38] His emphasis is on the extent to which each group, and especially the Goths, Franks, and Burgundians, even if they were invaders, ended up actually serving the Empire. Yet, as Fustel noted, in so doing they destroyed it.[39]

Not surprisingly, he paused at greatest length over the Franks. At the beginning of his discussion he signalled his interest in an overarching question:

> Let us look to see if their establishment in Gaul was carried out in such a way as to be able to change the whole social and political state and give birth to the feudal regime.[40]

The question of the origins of feudalism, however, he temporarily left on one side. Instead, he turned to the emergence of the Franks, insisting that their name is not ethnic. They were made up of a number of smaller groups, many of whom had long been in the service of the Empire.[41] When he reached Childeric, he set the Frankish king's conflict with the Roman general Ægidius firmly within the context of late Roman politics. As for Clovis, he is treated with the same 'scientific' caution that is applied to every other aspect of Frankish history. His reign is extremely obscure, because no contemporary wrote about it[42]—a sharp put-down for anyone over-reliant on Gregory of Tours, though it rather neglects the value of such letter-writers as Avitus, Remigius, and Cassiodorus. Fustel emphasized the fact that Clovis was a Roman functionary as well as a Germanic king, but he would not say, 'as the abbé Du Bos did, that we are dealing here with an office given by the emperor'.[43] It is one of the few places in the earlier volumes of the *Institutions Politiques* where Fustel names Du Bos, although it is clear that he knows his work and largely agrees with it.[44]

[36] Fustel de Coulanges, *L'Invasion germanique*, p. 323.
[37] Fustel de Coulanges, *L'Invasion germanique*, p. 326.
[38] Fustel de Coulanges, *L'Invasion germanique*, pp. 329–64.
[39] Fustel de Coulanges, *L'Invasion germanique*, p. 391.
[40] Fustel de Coulanges, *L'Invasion germanique*, p. 460.
[41] Fustel de Coulanges, *L'Invasion germanique*, pp. 460–76.
[42] Fustel de Coulanges, *L'Invasion germanique*, p. 476.
[43] Fustel de Coulanges, *L'Invasion germanique*, pp. 486–7.
[44] But see Hartog, *Le XIXe siècle et l'histoire*, pp. 95, 106. Hartog here follows the critique of Monod, that Fustel had not read the secondary literature. But see below, n. 132, on Jullian's comment in Fustel de Coulanges, *Les Transformations de la royauté*, p. vii, which directly contradicts this position.

Despite the evidence for the sieges of Paris and Nantes, and the revolt of Verdun, Fustel could find little to suggest a conquest by the Franks.[45] And in coming to that conclusion, he had very present memories of the Franco-Prussian War:

> It is when we judge with our modern ideas that we have been led to construct a violent conquest here, not being able to conceive that a country could be occupied by strangers, other than in the aftermath of obstinate resistance or unbelievable cowardice.[46]

In Fustel's view, there was no real conquest, nor was there racial conflict, and he even played down the religious differences between the Visigoths and the Gallo-Romans, noting that this was the impression that Gregory of Tours wished to give, but that it was not fact.[47] What change there was he described as a shift in the relations between individual cities and the superior powers. As for the relations between the Franks and the emperor, it took a long time before there was any clear break, though Fustel did note that, while the *Vita Trevirii* describes the year 524 as 'that time in which Gaul was under the rule of the emperor Justin', it goes on to say of 539, that it was 'when the kings of the Gauls and the Franks, having been subject to imperial law, threw off the domination of the republic'.[48] It is, one might note, a chronology that Du Bos would have found totally acceptable.

While there was no conquest and no immediate break with the Empire, there was, of course, the question of the settlement of the barbarians. Unlike some of his contemporaries and some modern scholars, Fustel accepted that they received land, interpreting the evidence in the light of the imperial practice of *hospitalitas*: soldiers stationed in a region received lodgings and food. In so far as they held property, it was, in Roman legal terms, as *possessio* rather than *dominium*—in other words, they had temporary control of it. The barbarian was therefore not the actual master of the house.[49] There was, inevitably, some conflict, as Fustel noted.[50] It was, however, limited. The barbarians may have been brutal, greedy, and capricious, but they were accepted as soldiers of the Empire.[51]

Looking back over the scholarship of the previous two centuries Fustel remarked:

> It is usually said that there was a great irruption of Germans at the start of the history of France. Gaul is seen as flooded, crushed, enslaved...It seems that the face of the country was changed, and that its destinies were pointed in a direction that it would otherwise not have had. This conquest is for many historians, and for the man in the street, the origin of the *Ancien Régime*. Feudal lords have claimed to be the descendents of conquerors; the bourgeois and the peasants thought that their being tied to the

---

[45] Fustel de Coulanges, *L'Invasion germanique*, pp. 492, 495.
[46] Fustel de Coulanges, *L'Invasion germanique*, p. 492.
[47] Fustel de Coulanges, *L'Invasion germanique*, pp. 494–7.
[48] Fustel de Coulanges, *L'Invasion germanique*, p. 511. The passage was also noted by Bury, *A History of the Later Roman Empire: From Arcadius to Irene*, vol. 1, p. 397.
[49] Fustel de Coulanges, *L'Invasion germanique*, pp. 521–6. The question of *hospitalitas* and its historiography is set out in Goffart, *Barbarians and Romans*.
[50] Fustel de Coulanges, *L'Invasion germanique*, pp. 524–6, 529–30.
[51] Fustel de Coulanges, *L'Invasion germanique*, pp. 528–9.

land was something imposed on them by a conqueror...Feudalism has been presented as the reign of conquerors, the freeing of the communes as the waking up of the
conquered, and the Revolution of 1789 as their revenge.[52]

Fustel could find little to support this interpretation, which is essentially derived
from that of Boulainvilliers, Montesquieu, Mably, Montlosier, and Thierry. There
is not much to suggest hatred between Gallo-Romans on the one hand and Franks
and Burgundians on the other.

> The opinion that puts a great invasion at the beginning of our history, and which
> thereafter divides the population into two unequal races, only began in the sixteenth
> century, and above all came to be favoured in the eighteenth. It was born of class
> hatred and grew in line with it. It still weighs on our present society...[53]

Indeed, Fustel saw nothing to suggest that the settlement of the Franks constituted
an act of conquest: it merely had the effect of increasing the pace of social
evolution.[54]

In *La Monarchie franque*, Fustel turned to the question of *ordre publique*. This
he described in terms that stretch beyond the immediately Frankish world, which
he regarded as still being linked to the Roman Empire.[55] He noted that Gregory of
Tours called his history *Decem Libri Historiarum*, not *Historia Francorum*—an
observation that was missed by the first *MGH* editors of the text[56] and not properly
appreciated for a century.[57] Nor, as Fustel notes, did Gregory or any other source
of the period concentrate on what more recent historians have wanted to hear:

> Old scholars wanted to find the titles of the monarchy there: Boulainvilliers wanted to
> see those of the nobility, and Montesquieu those of liberty. The friends of the parlia-
> mentary regime sincerely thought they found there a system of national assemblies,
> and almost the whole range of parliamentary practice. Others have wanted to see there
> the origins of the modern jury or yet some other aspect of democracy.[58]

His scorn was not just directed at French historiography: as we have already seen,
he was critical of the way in which German patriotism had infected its scholarship,
even down to the choice of a motto for the *MGH*. Patriotism was a virtue, history
a science: they should not be mixed.[59]

Turning to the Frankish monarchy, he noted that the sources assumed that it was
hereditary rather than elective, but also that kings might bequeath their title to a specific relative of the younger generation.[60] As important as the position of the monarchy in earlier debates was the role of the popular assembly. Fustel cited the views of the

---

[52] Fustel de Coulanges, *L'Invasion germanique*, p. 531.
[53] Fustel de Coulanges, *L'Invasion germanique et la fin de l'Empire*, p. 533.
[54] Fustel de Coulanges, *L'Invasion germanique et la fin de l'Empire*, p. 567.
[55] Fustel de Coulanges, *La Monarchie franque*, p. 2.
[56] See the edition of Arndt and Krusch, *MGH, Scriptores Rerum Merovingicarum* 1, 1.
[57] Goffart, 'From *Historiae* to *Historia Francorum* and back again'.
[58] Fustel de Coulanges, *La Monarchie franque*, p. 30.
[59] Fustel de Coulanges, *La Monarchie franque*, p. 31.
[60] Fustel de Coulanges, *La Monarchie franque*, pp. 33–50.

German scholar Junghans, whose work had just been translated into French by Gabriel Monod under the title *Histoire de Childérich et de Chlodovech*. He had argued that 'at the time of Clovis the Frankish people played a major role in political affairs, and that they exercised this right in the popular assemblies'.[61] Having quoted Junghans, Fustel worked steadily through the evidence, being careful to establish whether an individual assembly could reasonably be classified as national. The setting of the dénouement of the vase of Soissons story is categorized as nothing more than a gathering of soldiers, where the troops were essentially submissive—a quick put-down for all those who saw the episode as evidence for the exercise of Germanic liberty.[62] Fustel worked through the possible examples of a meeting of the Marchfield (*Champ de Mars*), and, after the reign of Clovis, found no evidence until the late seventh century.[63] As for the question of the existence of a Frankish nobility, which has never been fully solved,[64] Fustel could find no evidence of a Frankish hereditary aristocracy in the early Merovingian period, which, as he noted, has implications for the origins of the *régime féodale*.[65] Nevertheless, the king was always surrounded by his counsellors,[66] even if his exercise of power was, in theory, absolute.[67] There was no major conflict between the monarchy and the aristocracy in the late sixth or early seventh century, despite previous readings of the Treaty of Andelot of 587 and the Edict of Paris of 614.[68]

Beyond the royal court, at the provincial level, administration essentially functioned as it had in the late Roman period. Fustel denied the importance of the Germanic units of the *Gau* and the *Hundertschaft* (here he has Waitz and the successors of Möser in his sights), pointing out that there was no evidence for either in Tacitus. In fact, both the *Gau* and *huntari* do appear in early medieval glosses. For Fustel, however, the basic administrative unit of the Merovingian kingdom was the Roman city with its dependent countryside, the *civitas*, and later the sometimes synonymous *pagus* and *comitatus*.[69] The chief administrator was the *comes*, or *graphio*—a word which Fustel thought had exactly the same meaning: 'companion'.[70] He saw similar continuity from Roman practice when he turned to taxation, though he noted that some taxes survived, while others are not mentioned.[71] The basic land tax, or, as he preferred to see it, tax on cultivators, can be traced down to the late seventh century.[72] On the question of whether Franks were liable to pay

[61] Fustel de Coulanges, *La Monarchie franque*, p. 64, with n. 1, citing Junghans, *Histoire de Childérich et de Chlodovech*, trans. Monod, p, 124. See also Fustel, *La Monarchie franque*, p. 68.

[62] Fustel de Coulanges, *La Monarchie franque*, pp. 64–5, 69.

[63] Fustel de Coulanges, *La Monarchie franque*, pp. 63–75; see also pp. 598–601.

[64] See Irsigler, *Untersuchungen zur Geschichte des frühfränkischen Adels*, and Grahn-Hoek, *Die fränkische Oberschicht im 6. Jahrhundert*.

[65] Fustel de Coulanges, *La Monarchie franque*, p. 86.

[66] Fustel de Coulanges, *La Monarchie franque*, p. 88.

[67] Fustel de Coulanges, *La Monarchie franque*, p. 116.

[68] Fustel de Coulanges, *La Monarchie franque*, pp. 610–16.

[69] Fustel de Coulanges, *La Monarchie franque*, pp. 194–5.

[70] Fustel de Coulanges, *La Monarchie franque*, pp. 203–6. For a recent study, which comes to many of the same conclusions as Fustel, Murray, 'The position of the *graphio* in the constitution of Merovingian Gaul'.

[71] Fustel de Coulanges, *La Monarchie franque*, p. 260.

[72] Fustel de Coulanges, *La Monarchie franque*, p. 266. The most recent survey of post-Roman taxation is by Wickham, *Framing the Early Middle Ages, Europe and the Mediterranean, 400–800*, pp. 56–124.

it, Fustel noted that some were exempt just as some churches were exempt, but doubted whether the exemption was general. He found no indication that the Franks were treated as a superior race.[73] Thus, by implication, Fustel rejected the interpretation of Boulainvilliers and those who followed him.

Fustel acknowledged greater evidence for change as regards military service. Here he contrasted the fact that the Romans had a permanent army with the absence of such a force by the late sixth century, though he thought that there was an intermediate period, under Clovis and perhaps his sons, when something of the Roman system survived. Despite the lack of a permanent army, he pointed to the frequency of wars. There were any number of causes for war, and they might last for any length of time. Wars between neighbouring *civitates* would be fought by local armies, summoned for the purpose. Anyone, whether Frank or Gallo-Roman, might be called up[74]—a point which implicitly undermined Boulainvilliers' view of the Franks as a superior military caste. As yet, no clear system had emerged to replace the Roman army: a military structure based on benefices had yet to develop.[75]

The question of popular assemblies returns in Fustel's discussion of the legal system. He pointed to the argument of German scholars (led by Savigny, Waitz, Sohm, Fahlbeck, and Schulte), that judicial power was invested in the people,[76] and noted the extent to which their arguments coincide with those who had emphasized the role of Germanic liberty in the origins of France. Yet, as he insisted, the *mallus*, or legal gathering, was never a popular assembly, but was instead a tribunal, which could be ecclesiastical as well as secular.[77] The man who presided over the *mallus* was the count, and while *rachimburgi* or *boni homines* might act with him, these were not simple members of the community, but men whose status was guaranteed by wealth and honour. The notion of a freely elected panel, as propounded by German legal scholars, thus falls to the ground.[78]

Having dealt with 'the institutions of public order and everything relating to public life', Fustel turned in his fourth volume to 'private institutions'—even though he admitted that the two types of institution overlap, and that to divide them up was no more than a matter of convenience.[79] It was in the private sphere, rather than in the public, that he found the origins of feudalism.[80] It is here, also, that the sociological nature of his approach is most apparent:

> History is not the accumulation of events of every kind, which have been produced in the past. It is the science of human societies... Several years ago the word 'sociology'

---

[73] Fustel de Coulanges, *La Monarchie franque*, pp. 277–87.
[74] Fustel de Coulanges, *La Monarchie franque*, pp. 289–93.
[75] Fustel de Coulanges, *La Monarchie franque*, p. 302.
[76] Fustel de Coulanges, *La Monarchie franque*, p. 305. In his list he also includes the Frenchman Pardessus and the Belgian Thonissen; see also pp. 360–1.
[77] Fustel de Coulanges, *La Monarchie franque*, pp. 307–12.
[78] Fustel de Coulanges, *La Monarchie franque*, pp. 357–71.
[79] Fustel de Coulanges, *La Monarchie franque*, p. i.
[80] Fustel de Coulanges, *L'Alleu et le domaine rural*, p. iii.

was invented. The word 'history' had the same meaning and said the same thing, at least for those who understood it properly.[81]

Fustel began his study of land and land-holding by asking whether they were different in Roman and early medieval law.[82] He allowed that the arrival of numerous Germanic incomers could have changed the laws of possession, but he could find no evidence for communal landholding, even in the forests: private property was everywhere.[83] On these issues Germanic law was the same as Roman.[84] 'To suppose that the Germans introduced a new type of possession of land would be to contradict all the documents.'[85]

He then addressed the question of the nature and origins of the 'allod'. People had argued that such private estates had been allotted to the Franks after the conquest.[86] Yet while the term is not obviously Roman, nor is it obviously Germanic[87]—in fact, here etymology appears to prove him wrong.[88] On the other hand, it is to be found in the Angers formulary, in a document of either 514 or 530,[89] and something very like allodial tenure is already apparent in the *Codex Theodosianus*.[90] Thus, while it is possible that the Germanic incomers could have divided up the land creating a world of small proprietors, it is equally possible that land-holding could have stayed much as it was in the Roman period.[91] This last idea is perhaps supported by the evidence of *-villa* names.[92]

Turning to the inhabitants of the *villas*, Fustel speedily dismissed the idea, derived ultimately from Boulainvilliers, that the servile population was Gallo-Roman and the masters Germanic.[93] Although there were different categories of slaves, there is nothing to show that some categories were exclusively Roman and some Germanic. Moreover, different types of slave can be found on one and the same *villa*.[94] As for the methods of manumission of slaves, and their subsequent

---

[81] Fustel de Coulanges, *L'Alleu et le domaine rural*, p. iv.

[82] Fustel de Coulanges, *L'Alleu et le domaine rural*, pp. 9–10.

[83] Fustel de Coulanges, *L'Alleu et le domaine rural*, pp. 97–113. The issue of communal rights appears again at pp. 424–32.

[84] Fustel de Coulanges, *L'Alleu et le domaine rural*, p. 113.

[85] Fustel de Coulanges, *L'Alleu et le domaine rural*, p. 130.

[86] Fustel de Coulanges, *L'Alleu et le domaine rural*, p. 149.

[87] Fustel de Coulanges, *L'Alleu et le domaine rural*, p. 161.

[88] I am indebted to Wolfgang Haubrichs for the following correction to Fustel's statement: 'Das etymologische Problem von "alodium" ist seit langem gelöst. Es ist etymologisch ein Kompositum (compound) aus germ. *al(l)a- "ganz, vollständig" und germ. *auda "Besitz" > mit Monophthongierung ôd. Die Bedeutung ist ursprünglich *wohl*: "ganzer, uneingeschränkter Besitz". Ähnliche Bildungen gibt es viele in germanischen Sprachen. Es ist im Althochdeutschen belegt (9. Jh.), aber noch früher als lateinisches Lehnwort, die Verbreitung dort in Rechtstexten klar merowingisch seit 6./7. Jahrhundert, d. h. es ist wohl eine frühe fränkische Bildung der Rechtssprache. In anderen Sprachen kommt diese Komposition nicht vor. Ganz sicher ist es aber früh nicht nur in der Volkssprache, sondern auch im Latein der Zeit etabliert.'

[89] Fustel de Coulanges, *L'Alleu et le domaine rural*, pp. 163–4, also 165 on the use of the term in the Auvergne.

[90] Fustel de Coulanges, *L'Alleu et le domaine rural*, p. 159.

[91] Fustel de Coulanges, *L'Alleu et le domaine rural*, p. 199.

[92] Fustel de Coulanges, *L'Alleu et le domaine rural*, p. 225. Such names, however, seem to be Merovingian rather than Roman coinages.

[93] Fustel de Coulanges, *L'Alleu et le domaine rural*, p. 276.

[94] Fustel de Coulanges, *L'Alleu et le domaine rural*, pp. 379–81.

position as freedmen, they appear to have been as much Roman as Germanic in origin.[95] After manumission, a one-time slave still needed the *patrocinium, defensio*, or *mondeburdium* of a patron.[96]

Summing up his views on landholding from the fourth to the ninth century Fustel concluded that the Germanic invasions brought no major change. The Franks introduced neither the allod nor the *villa*—and all land was allodial. Nor could one describe the set-up as feudal. Feudalism developed on top of what was a pattern of land-holding that stretched back to Late Antiquity.[97] Few would accept this argument in its entirely, and detailed local studies have modified our understanding of the *villa*, suggesting that there were changes between the fourth century and the ninth.[98] At the same time, Fustel's basic argument that the fifth and sixth centuries saw little change, at least in the regions away from the north-east of Gaul, probably still holds true.

Book five of the *Institutions politiques* was left unfinished at the time of Fustel's death in 1889. The first fourteen chapters had already been written, but Camille Jullian had to construct the concluding sections from earlier publications of Fustel.[99] The volume begins by addressing the question of whether there had been military benefices in the Roman world. Fustel countered the idea by noting that, while the term *beneficium* does appear in Late Roman sources, it refers not to the land itself, but to the goodwill of the prince who granted it.[100] As an institution the benefice was, therefore, not Roman. He next considered the possibility that Germanic institutions provided the background to feudalism, by examining the *comitatus*. His conclusion was that the Tacitean *comitatus* was entirely military, and that there was, in any case, no reason to think that it was introduced as an institution into late Roman Gaul.[101]

Having considered and dismissed suggested Roman and Germanic origins for feudalism, he turned to the situation after the barbarian invasions. He restated his view that the arrival of the Franks did not lead to the dispossession of Romans.[102] Landholding continued to be hereditary,[103] and there was no evidence for the existence of benefices before the eighth century.[104] From all this he concluded that feudalism was not born of a political system, but that the new *régime* emerged from a set of customs and practices (*usages* and *pratiques*).[105]

He then turned to different types of property-holding: he noted the distinction in Roman law between *dominium* (ultimate ownership), *possessio* (immediate

[95] Fustel de Coulanges, *L'Alleu et le domaine rural*, p. 304.
[96] Fustel de Coulanges, *L'Alleu et le domaine rural*, p. 326.
[97] Fustel de Coulanges, *L'Alleu et le domaine rural*, pp. 462–4.
[98] E.g. Devroey, *Économie rurale et société dans l'Europe franque*, vol. 1.
[99] Fustel de Coulanges, *Le Bénéfice et le patronat*, pp. v–vii.
[100] Fustel de Coulanges, *Le Bénéfice et le patronat*, p. 10; pp. 151–92 follows up with a discussion of Merovingian *beneficia*.
[101] Fustel de Coulanges, *Le Bénéfice et le patronat*, pp. 15, 27–9.
[102] Fustel de Coulanges, *Le Bénéfice et le patronat*, p. 31.
[103] Fustel de Coulanges, *Le Bénéfice et le patronat*, pp. 47, 50.
[104] Fustel de Coulanges, *Le Bénéfice et le patronat*, pp. 43, 45–6.
[105] Fustel de Coulanges, *Le Bénéfice et le patronat*, p. 64.

control), and usufruct (the right to use something belonging to another—which he saw as an element in the feudal benefice).[106] *Precaria*, grants that conveyed a life-interest, he presented as instruments of patronage, which put one man into the debt of another. Initially, however, they were not military.[107] Fustel had already discussed patronage in the first two volumes of his *Institutions politiques*, and he restated his views on the system among both Gauls and the Germanic tribes.[108] What he emphasized was the practice of voluntary subjection by free men, though he insisted that because this was a matter of social rather than political organization, it did not lead directly to feudalism. There were similar patterns of patronage among the Romans.[109] The Roman vocabulary of subordination continued into the Merovingian period,[110] alongside Germanic equivalents. It is these ideas of subordination that, in Fustel's view, lead to feudalism. Yet, he continued to insist that this had nothing to do with military service until later.[111] For him it was in the civil structures of dependence that one could find the origins of feudalism, for military organization was based on the structures of civil society. All men carried arms, so that the *populus* and *exercitus* could be the same. Civil magistrates were military leaders, and landowners followed suit.[112]

In his preface to the last volume of the *Institutions politiques* Camille Jullian placed Fustel's work clearly in its historiographical context. Although he is talking specifically about Fustel's interpretation of the Carolingians, his comments effectively deal with the development of the older scholar's ideas on French institutions over his whole career. Jullian is at pains to note that Fustel had read everything, both sources and more recent scholarship: 'He took the same care [as he did in looking as sources] in studying such secondary authors as Du Bos and Guérard, or Waitz and Roth, the political writings of the eighteenth century and the German theses of our own day.'[113] He then states, more specifically, that initially Fustel was reacting to 'le mouvement historique de la Restauration', and he names Thierry, Michelet, Guizot, and Henri Martin.[114] Michelet's history was born of the July Revolution of 1830. Guizot wanted history to be useful for his government and to be a preparation for his own work as a minister. Henri Martin saw history as the development of national unity—his most notable achievement, however, was not as a historian, but as the man whose speech to the *sénat* in 1870 ensured that 14th July became a national holiday.[115] Thierry saw his work within the development of

---

[106] Fustel de Coulanges, *Le Bénéfice et le patronat*, pp. 65–9.

[107] Fustel de Coulanges, *Le Bénéfice et le patronat*, pp. 70, 74–5, 82, 99, 101, 109. For a recent discussion of *precaria* that failed to take account of Fustel's argument, Wood, 'Teutsind, Witlaic and the history of Merovingian *precaria*'.

[108] Fustel de Coulanges, *Le Bénéfice et le patronat*, pp. 193–204.

[109] Fustel de Coulanges, *Le Bénéfice et le patronat*, pp. 216–18.

[110] Fustel de Coulanges, *Le Bénéfice et le patronat*, pp. 248–9.

[111] Fustel de Coulanges, *Le Bénéfice et le patronat*, p. 274, 294–5, 298–9.

[112] Fustel de Coulanges, *Le Bénéfice et le patronat*, pp. 427–30.

[113] Fustel de Coulanges, *Les Transformations de la royauté*, p. vii. This is surely directed against the arguments of Monod: see Hartog, *Le XIXe siècle et l'histoire*, p. 95.

[114] Jullian, in Fustel de Coulanges, *Les Transformations de la royauté*, pp. viii–xii.

[115] See <http://14juillet.senat.fr/toutsavoir/> for his speech to the Sénat.

the constitutional regimes of 1814 and 1830, and was devastated by the events of 1848. Yet, as Jullian acknowledges, Fustel was not reacting simply to French scholarship: 'The modern German historians willingly present their country as marching for fifteen centuries in the path laid down by Providence to arrive at the Prussian hegemony and the coronation of 1871.'[116] It was not, however, against them that he initially developed his determination to concentrate on the sources, and what could and could not be said, but rather he developed his approach in opposition to the politically committed writings of the period leading up to 1848: it was in response to these earlier writers that he determined to discover the truth, and turned historical science into a religion.[117] In this, Jullian compares him to Zola. What he has in mind here is Fustel's reiterated claim that good history was scientific.

10.3 FUSTEL, PUVIS DE CHAVANNES, AND PATRIOTISM

Fustel had turned back to a vision of the end of Roman Gaul that was remarkably similar to that of Du Bos. It marked a radical rejection of that to be found in the line of argument developed by Mably, and then by Thierry. The two visions can be seen side by side in the decorations of the Panthéon commissioned by Philippe, marquis de Chennevières, directeur des Beaux Arts in 1874.[118] The cycle of paintings depict the histories of Saints Denis and Geneviève, as well as those of Clovis, Charlemagne, St Louis, and Jeanne d'Arc. The early medieval scenes include the childhood of Geneviève, her meeting with Germanus of Auxerre, Attila's siege of Paris, Geneviève watching over the besieged city, her death, and the baptism of Clovis. A number of the images hark back to the dramatic presentation of the early Middle Ages to be found in Thierry's *Récits*, which is scarcely surprising given that the artist of the painting of the death of Geneviève, Jean-Paul Laurens, also illustrated deluxe editions of Thierry's work in 1882 and 1887.[119] This sense of the savagery of the past had been enhanced by the recent experience of the Franco-Prussian War. Jules-Élie Delaunay's depiction of Geneviève calming the people of Paris during Attila's siege, was painted in 1874,[120] and his portrait of the Hunnic king is especially barbarous. At the same time, Clovis, in Paul-Joseph Blanc's depiction, with his long blond moustache is self-evidently a noble Gaul (while among his retinue one can find Antonin Proust, Léon Gambetta, and Georges Clemenceau). Contrasting with these theatrical images are the much more sober scenes painted by Puvis de Chavannes: the childhood of Geneviève, her meeting with Germanus of Auxerre, and her watching over Paris during a second siege, probably

[116] Jullian, in Fustel de Coulanges, *Les Transformations de la royauté*, p. x.
[117] Jullian, in Fustel de Coulanges, *Les Transformations de la royauté*, p. xiii.
[118] Wood, 'The Panthéon in Paris'.
[119] Murray, *Gregory of Tours: The Merovingians*, pp. xxvii–xxviii. A number of Laurens' illustrations are reproduced in the volume.
[120] Lépinay, *Peintures et sculptures du Panthéon*, p. 42.

to be identified as that conducted by the Franks. Here one is faced not with the hectic past of Thierry, but a much more idealized image. In the 1880s Puvis was regarded by many as a symbolist painter.[121] The image he presents would seem to echo the approach of Fustel—though the extraordinary light of the scene of Geneviève's vigil may be a reminiscence of Paris without street lights, as it had been during the Prussian siege.[122]

It is not possible to tie the inspiration of Puvis' vision of the early Middle Ages to Fustel in the same way that can link that of Laurens to Thierry. Yet Fustel had been concerned to encourage painters to depict the past. He had called for artists of his day to paint 'the Gallo-Roman race at work, weaving, building towns, erecting temples, studying law, pursuing head-on the labours and pleasures of peace'.[123] Puvis had done exactly that, notably in a painting of 'Marseille colonie grecque' for the town hall of the great southern city. It would appear that in his paintings for the Panthéon, he was responding to the new reading of the early Merovingian period put forward by Fustel.

For all his insistence on science, and on the need to separate patriotism and scholarship, Fustel was deeply patriotic, and he associated patriotism with history: 'true patriotism isn't the love of the soil, it is the love of the past; it is respect for the generations who have preceded us.'[124] Despite the fact that he did not cite the early medieval past in his exchange with Mommsen, and despite his determination to keep modern hatreds out of his reading of the fifth and sixth centuries, there is more than a touch of xenophobia in his writing, both in his dismissal of German scholarship, and more especially in his criticism of Monod, who had trained with Waitz. Fustel's attitude toward German methodology may have mellowed a little in time, for his pupil Camille Jullian trained with Mommsen in 1883, as a 'boursier-espion' ('scholarship-holder-spy'), in Jullian's coinage[125]—by which time the *Monumenta* was beginning to produce editions of real quality.

Fustel's patriotism was to have unfortunate consequences, for it was to be picked up by the right-wing Charles Maurras, who regarded him as a hero for his opposition to German historiography and liberalism.[126] Fustel died in 1889 at the relatively young age of 59. In 1905, a few months after the establishment of the reactionary monarchist movement *L'action française*, Maurras, who claimed that Fustel was being forgotten (hardly likely given the string of posthumous publications edited by Jullian), decided that what would have been the great man's seventy-fifth birthday should be the occasion of a national celebration.[127] This hijacking of Fustel's memory was to mean that he became a problematic figure in French historical discourse, and he was rarely cited by the intellectual left, although

---

[121] *French Symbolist Painters: Moreau, Puvis de Chavannes, Redon and their Followers*, p. 101.

[122] Wood, 'The Panthéon in Paris', p. 100.

[123] Cited in Brown Price, *Pierre Puvis de Chavannes, Catalogue*, Van Gogh Museum, Amsterdam, p. 17 (with notes p. 26).

[124] Cited in Hartog, *Le XIXe siècle et l'histoire*, p. 131.

[125] Hartog, *Le XIXe siècle et l'histoire*, p. 199; Nicolet, *La Fabrique d'une nation*, p. 228.

[126] For what follows, Hartog, *Le XIXe siècle et l'histoire*, pp. 171–215.

[127] Hartog, *Le XIXe siècle et l'histoire*, pp. 180–5.

Marc Bloch did acknowledge his importance in the creation of the discipline of sociology.[128] After 1945, when Maurras was condemned as a traitor, Fustel's reputation fell further.

Fustel's *Institutions politiques* is a great work by any standards, though inevitably there are passages which have been exposed as wrong or obsolete, not least because of the re-editing of texts and the exposure of some documents (especially charters) as later forgeries, some of which had been exposed in his own lifetime.[129] It was, on the whole, well received at the time of publication, and not just in France or by historians,[130] though right from the start there were those who criticized it, not least Gabriel Monod, who compared Fustel's work unfavourably with that of his own German professor Georg Waitz's *Deutsche Verfassungsgeschichte*.[131] The conflict between Fustel and Monod was to continue at a private[132] as well as a public level. The most obvious public confrontation was over the interpretation of the story of Sichar and Chramnesind, recounted in Gregory of Tours—a violent tale that has been frequently been used in discussion of early medieval feuding.[133] This Monod analysed in an article entitled 'Les Aventures de Sichaire', which he dedicated to Waitz.[134] Fustel's response, tellingly, was entitled 'De l'analyse des textes historiques', and it was largely an attack on Monod's historical methodology, which reflected his training at the hands of Waitz. This, it should be said, did not necessarily conform to the most modern German practice. Waitz was no longer a young man when Monod studied with him. Although Wilhelm Junghans, whose work on *Die fränkische Könige Childerich und Chlodovech* was translated by Monod in 1879, was somewhat younger, the book itself had been published in 1856, and Junghans himself died nine years later, aged 30, before the great developments in German early medieval historiography were really underway. In certain respects, then, Monod was the product of a previous generation of German scholarship.[135]

From the point of view of the French Right, Monod, with his German training, could be presented as the opposite of Fustel. He was further compromised in Maurras' imagination as the author of the *Exposé impartial de l'affaire Dreyfus* in 1899, which he wrote under the pseudonym Pierre Molé, using his paleographical skills to expose the case against Dreyfus.[136] In fact Monod was no less of a French

[128] Hartog, *Le XIXe siècle et l'histoire*, pp. 211–14.

[129] Hartog, *Le XIXe siècle et l'histoire*, pp. 113, 145, 167.

[130] See Fustel de Coulanges, *The Origin of Property in Land*, trans. Ashley. The introduction provides a clear assessment of the position of Fustel's work in contemporary scholarship.

[131] Hartog, *Le XIXe siècle et l'histoire*, pp. 105–6, 113.

[132] Hartog, *Le XIXe siècle et l'histoire*, p. 106; see Lefebve, *Annales* 2 (1954), pp. 149–56.

[133] See Wood, 'The bloodfeud of the Franks'.

[134] Monod, 'Les aventures de Sichaire: commentaire des chapitres xlvii du Livre VII et xix du Livre IX de l'Histoire des Francs de Grégoire de Tours'; Fustel de Coulanges, 'De l'analyse des textes historiques'. See Geary, 'Gabriel Monod, Fustel de Coulanges et les "aventures de Sichaire"'.

[135] His study of Marius of Avenches, and his edition of Fredegar, does, however, continue to have some value: Monod, 'Études critiques sur les sources de l'histoire mérovingienne 1: Grégoire de Tours, Marius d'Avenches'; Monod, 'Études critiques sur les sources de l'histoire mérovingienne 2: la compilation dite de Frédégaire'.

[136] Hartog, *Le XIXe siècle et l'histoire*, pp. 180–1; Molé (alias Monod), *Exposé impartial de l'affaire Dreyfus*. Monod played a particularly important role in exposing some crucial evidence as forged.

patriot than was Fustel, in 1870 going so far as to join two of his cousins in providing an ambulance to support the French army, which he followed from Sedan to Le Mans—an experience that he wrote up in *Allemands et Français, souvenirs de campagne.*[137] As the son of an Alsatian mother he had even more reason than Fustel to regret the loss of Alsace, but he remained remarkably friendly towards the Germans, just as he was even-handed towards Fustel in his assessment of him after his death in 1889.[138]

10.4 FELIX DAHN: THE SCHOLAR AS NOVELIST

While Monod was tending French casualties at Sedan, another early medieval scholar, who was arguably to have more influence on the development of the subject than any of his contemporaries, was wounded while fighting on the German side: Felix Dahn[139]—the author of a multi-volume study of the history, more precisely, the constitutional history, of the early Germanic peoples, and of a work of fiction, *Ein Kampf um Rom*, based on Procopius' account of the Gothic Wars, which would prove to be a long-running best-seller, and would provide generations of readers with their main point of entry into the early Middle Ages.

Dahn (1834–1912) studied law and philosophy at Munich and thereafter took his doctorate in law at Berlin.[140] He subsequently moved back to Munich, before holding academic posts at Würzburg, Königsberg, and, finally Breslau, (now Wrocław in Poland), where apart from holding a chair he was also briefly Rektor. His most significant scholarly publication was a twelve-volume account of the constitutional history of the barbarian kingdoms: *Die Könige der Germanen*, which he began in 1857. The first volume appeared in 1861 and the last in 1909.[141] The contents are largely a sober account of kingship in the early medieval period. Remarkably, Dahn sticks firmly to the sources, avoiding speculation about the Germanic aspects of his subject, even though he felt there must have been some.[142] He also published a significant study of Procopius of Caesarea in 1865, which argued firmly for Procopius as the author of the *Secret Histories (Anekdota).*[143]

Yet Dahn was not simply a highly successful and prolific academic: he was also a literary figure of note. He was born in Hamburg, to a German father and a French mother, both of them actors. After they moved to Munich his parents divorced, and Felix remained with his father, while his siblings stayed with their

---

[137] Monod, *Allemands et Français, souvenirs de campagne.*

[138] See Monod, *Portraits et souvenirs*, pp. 135–54; Hartog, *Le XIXe siècle et l'histoire*, pp. 162, 167.

[139] Wahl, *Die Religion des deutschen Nationalismus*, pp. 51–2; Neuhaus, *Literatur und nationale Einheit in Deutschland*, p. 233; Frech, 'Felix Dahn', p. 686.

[140] For a recent critical evaluation of his career, Wahl, *Die Religion des deutschen Nationalismus*, pp. 56–6. For his legal studies, Frech, 'Felix Dahn', pp. 688–9.

[141] Wahl, *Die Religion des deutschen Nationalismus*, p. 45. See Frech, 'Felix Dahn', p. 689. Others count the number of volumes differently.

[142] Wood, 'Early Medieval History and Nineteenth-Century Politics', p. 546.

[143] Dahn, *Prokopius von Cäsarea.*

mother.[144] Given the theatrical household into which he was born, it is scarcely surprising that in addition to his scholarly work he also wrote plays, opera libretti, poems, and novels, above all his highly successful *Ein Kampf um Rom*, which he first thought of in Ravenna in 1858, began to write in Munich in 1859, continued while travelling round Italy in the years from 1861–3 (during which time he revisited Ravenna),[145] and completed in Königsberg in 1874. It was published two years later.[146] The dates are supremely important.[147] In 1859 Napoleon III joined the Italians in the Second War of Liberation, leading to the crippling of Austrian rule in Italy. The French victories of Magenta and Solferino occurred in June: September saw the establishment of the (*kleindeutsche*) *Deutsche Nationalverein* (an organization committed to the creation of a German federation under the leadership of Prussia) in Frankfurt am Main. There were also rumours of a Franco-Russian entente against Germany, which prompted Dahn to write patriotic poetry.[148] In the event the threat to the new German federation did not materialize, and Dahn felt free to travel in a largely independent Italy—though it would not be until 1866 that Austria lost its toehold in the Veneto. In the late 1860s Dahn put the writing of *Ein Kampf um Rom* on one side, only to pick it up again after the Prussian victory over France in 1870–1.

Ein Kampf um Rom was one of the great publishing successes of the nineteenth and twentieth centuries. Dahn himself was staggered at the sales: 'I often wonder that the Germans, who do not buy directly emotional books, have bought so many volumes of mine every year. For example 84,000 volumes of *Ein Kampf um Rom* in eighteen years.'[149] It is not quite clear what is meant by 84,000 volumes, since the work came out in several parts: this may only indicate between 25 and 30,000 complete sets. Further proof of the scale of the work's success, however, is the number of times it was reprinted. It reached its 30th impression in 1900, its 58th in 1910, and its 92nd in 1918. It has been estimated that by 1938 615,000 copies had been sold, and 750,000 by 1950.[150] It is still in print.

One of the reasons for its huge success, particularly in the period of the two World Wars, was its great sense of the German *Volk*. Indeed, during July and August 1914 it was a regular confirmation present, given to boys to instil in them a sense that '[d]as Höchste ist das Volk, das Vaterland' ('The highest ideal is the People, the Fatherland').[151] The idea recurs on a number of occasions in Dahn's writings.[152] In his own view '[h]eroic enthusiasm for the Nation is perhaps the

[144] On his childhood, Frech, 'Felix Dahn', pp. 686–7, 692.
[145] For visits to Italy: Wahl, *Die Religion des deutschen Nationalismus*, pp. 46, 57.
[146] Neuhaus, *Literatur und nationale Einheit in Deutschland*, p. 233.
[147] Wahl, *Die Religion des deutschen Nationalismus*, pp. 57–9.
[148] Lilie, '*Gens Perfidus* oder Edle Einfalt, Stille Größe?', p. 188.
[149] Dahn, *Erinnerungen*, 2nd edn, vol. 4, p. 183; Wahl, *Die Religion des deutschen Nationalismus*, p. 122; Neuhaus, *Literatur und nationale Einheit in Deutschland*, p. 230; Frech, 'Felix Dahn', p. 685.
[150] Wahl, *Die Religion des deutschen Nationalismus*, pp. 122–7; also Frech, 'Felix Dahn', p. 696.
[151] Neuhaus, *Literatur und nationale Einheit*, p. 232.
[152] Wahl, *Die Religion des deutschen Nationalismus*, pp. 99–100, citing a letter to Dr Otto Braun, 1 April 1891. See also Neuhaus, *Literatur und nationale Einheit*, pp. 230–43.

deepest foundation of my being.'[153] A modern scholar has concluded that 'Dahn's novel is an attempt to write an ideologically motivated prehistory of the German Reich...It is crucial that Dahn's historical novel provides a further building block for the construction of a national past and with it a national identity.'[154]

Dahn essentially retells the story of the final years of the Ostrogothic state in Italy. The work begins in the last years of Theoderich (I here follow Dahn's spelling of personal names to convey something of the flavour he intended). It covers the reigns of Athalarich, Amalaswintha, Theodohad, Witichis, Totila, and Teja. The basic story follows Procopius, and subsequently Agathias.[155] In almost every part of the story, however, a love—or hate—interest is introduced.[156] Athalarich falls for Kamilla, the daughter of the murdered Boethius; Amalaswintha is killed by Theo-dohad's vengeful wife Gothlindis; Witichis has to give up his beloved Rauthgundis to marry the Amal Mataswintha, who turns out to be as full of bile as Theodohad's wife had been; and Totila, who is adored by the highly sympathetic Jewess Miriam,[157] is betrothed to the Roman Valeria, which leads his rival Furius Ahala to betray him at the battle of Taginä. Identification of the site would excite Himmler in 1942.[158] For Byzantium Dahn could follow the picture of Theodora and Antonina presented by Procopius in the *Secret History*. In addition he creates an Italian nationalist anti-hero, Cethegus, whose strategies are woven through the whole book.[159] The book ends in a near-apocalpytic scene, which one might assume was influenced by Wagner's *Götterdammerung*, until one realizes that both works were completed in the same year: Teja's last stand, which also ends in the destruc-tion of Cethegus, takes place on the side of Vesuvius—though in the event his body, that of Theoderich (who is by now transformed into the legendary hero Dietrich von Bern), together with the remnant of the Gothic people are taken to safety in the North, to the *Urheimat* of Thule, as a result of a rather surprising intervention by the Vikings.

By the time *Ein Kampf um Rom* was published, Dahn had already explored the legendary pre-history of Dietrich von Bern in his drama *Markgraf Rüdiger von Bechelaren*, which dealt with an episode from the *Nibelungenlied* in which the Goth appears.[160] He saw the defeat of the Goths as one episode in pan-German history

[153] Dahn, *Erinnerungen*, vol. 3, p. 364, cited in Lilie, '*Gens Perfidus* oder Edle Einfalt, Stille Größe?', p. 200.
[154] Neuhaus, *Literatur und nationale Einheit*, p. 243.
[155] Neuhaus, *Literatur und nationale Einheit*, p. 233.
[156] Lilie, '*Gens Perfidus* oder Edle Einfalt, Stille Größe?', pp. 197–9; Wahl, *Die Religion des deutschen Nationalismus*, pp. 89–94.
[157] Miriam can be compared with Rebecca in *Ivanhoe*, and also with Mirah in George Eliot's *Daniel Deronda* (published at exactly the same time as *Ein Kampf um Rom*). On the question of the presenta-tion of Jews in *Ein Kampf um Rom*, see Wahl, *Die Religion des deutschen Nationalismus*, p. 108, and also Frech, 'Felix Dahn', p. 696, who notes Dahn's medical treatment by a Jewish doctor.
[158] Maischberger, 'German archaeology during the Third Reich, 1933–45', p. 214.
[159] It should, however, be noted that there is a Cethegus, leader of the senate, who is suspected of treachery in Procopius, *History of the Wars*, VII, 13, 12, and who also spent time at Constantinople, see Martindale, *Prosopography of the Later Roman Empire*, vol. 2, pp. 281–2, 'Cethegus'.
[160] Dahn, *Markgraf Rüdiger von Bechelaren*; Lilie, '*Gens Perfidus* oder Edle Einfalt, Stille Größe?', pp. 188–90.

and legend, which stretched from the world of *Beowulf*, through the continental epic tales *Walthari* and the *Nibelungenlied*, to Viking Scandinavia.

It has been noted that the novel is effectively a *roman à clef*.[161] That this is an accurate reading is clear from a comment made by Dahn himself:

> I actually saw clearly the great philosophical, national, world-historical problems of *Ein Kampf um Rom*, only transplanted from the sixth to the nineteenth century. The Holy Father [Pius IX], above all concerned with personal power; the Italians, morally justified, themselves violating agreements, and frequently involved in crimes, conspiracies, betrayal, assassination of Austrian guardians, historically breaking out in their national uprising; the Austrians, certainly in many respects no Goths, but formally entirely in the right, for long years vainly attempting assiduously to win over seething Milan and spiteful Venice by pampering them, and certainly brave as bears; and finally, like Justinian in Byzantium, the cunning emperor on the Seine [Napoleon III], who with beautiful words of freedom in his mouth, himself spinning intrigues, enslaved his Frenchmen, sent them to Cayenne (as Justinian sent his 'Romans' to the mines), and proclaimed the principle of Nationality to the Italians, while he of course did not hand over or begrudged Alsace-Lorraine or Switzerland to Germany, indeed he sought for overlordship in Italy and soon raked in Savoy and Nice. That was *Ein Kampf um Rom* 'all over again'.[162]

The Goths are the Austrians—a point that is made clear in their association with the Alps, as exemplified by Rauthgund and Witichis;[163] the emperor Justinian is Napoleon III; and the scheming Theodora is the empress Eugénie. Cethegus would appear to have been pope Pius IX—it helps to remember that Dahn, a north German Protestant, was a firm critic of the Catholic Church in the struggle over the influence of religion in German society known as the *Kulturkampf* that erupted in the 1870s.[164] A straightforward reading of the novel in this way, however, presents problems, and here the political changes between the late 1850s and the early 1870s are relevant.[165] Whereas Napoleon might be thought of as Justinian in 1859, in 1870 the French government was a good deal closer to the image, wrongly and surely deliberately, given by Dahn of the sixth-century Merovingians as puppet kings.[166] Cethegus's prophecy, that 'one day there will be a dawn, my Rome, when no foreigner rules on Italy's sacred soil' was effectively fulfilled with the Third Italian War of Independence of 1866.[167]

---

[161] Lilie, '*Gens Perfidus* oder Edle Einfalt, Stille Größe?', p. 187; Wahl, *Die Religion des deutschen Nationalismus*, pp. 75–6.

[162] Dahn, *Erinnerungen*, vol. 3, p. 368, quoted in Frech, 'Felix Dahn', p. 694.

[163] Dahn, *Ein Kampf um Rom*, bk 3, ch. 5; trans. Parker, *A Struggle for Rome*, pp. 117–18. I have deliberately cited the German version by book and chapter number, since there are so many editions available. The page references are always to the English translation.

[164] Wahl, *Die Religion des deutschen Nationalismus*, pp. 75–88. See also Lilie, '*Gens Perfidus* oder Edle Einfalt, Stille Größe?', p. 188; Neuhaus, *Literatur und nationale Einheit in Deutschland*, p. 233.

[165] Wahl, *Die Religion des deutschen Nationalismus*, p. 31, 75–6; Lilie, '*Gens Perfidus* oder Edle Einfalt, Stille Größe?', p. 190; Frech, 'Felix Dahn', p. 695.

[166] Dahn, *Ein Kampf um Rom/A Struggle for Rome*, bk 6, ch. 14, p. 426. Compare Dahn, *Procopius von Cäsarea*, pp. 413–15.

[167] Dahn, *Ein Kampf um Rom/A Struggle for Rome*, bk 9, ch. 14, p. 736.

Modern criticism of Dahn's novel has concentrated on its production and reception, on its literary merits (or lack of them), and its contribution to a German sense of its past. It has paid relatively little attention to the extent to which Dahn was engaged in historical debate, even in *Ein Kampf um Rom*.[168] Yet in the book's foreword, Dahn is very explicit about the scholarly foundations of the work, specifically sending the reader to the three relevant volumes of his *Könige der Germanen* and to his study of Procopius.[169] *Ein Kampf um Rom* can, in fact, be seen as introducing Germans to the history of the sixth century. In the words of the mid-twentieth-century German writer Eduard Rothemund:

> In the years from 1861 to 1909 he laboured away at his twenty-volume masterpiece, *Könige der Germanen*, and in addition a string of other works over the early history of the Germanic and Roman peoples and the *Völkerwanderung*. Through these works Dahn became the historian of that great Germanic era, and he excited the people of our blood throughout Europe. But Felix Dahn realized that his findings only influenced a few scholars. He wanted to spread knowledge of Germanic history, joy at its great events and deeds, pride in its pagan world, to the wider circle of the German people and above all to its youth. And for this reason he reworked the same material into numerous historical tales, novellas, and then above all in his mighty novel *Ein Kampf um Rom*.[170]

Thus, while *Ein Kampf um Rom* is a novel, it was intended from the start to introduce a new readership to a historical period in which Dahn himself was an expert.

In fact, the novel offers a sustained argument about the failure of the Goths in Italy, although Dahn presents it through the various viewpoints of his characters, and in so doing offers a remarkably complex reading of the problem. By giving voice to the Goths themselves, he fills what he regarded as a lacuna in the sources, which presented a purely Roman reading of events. He was thus offering what he regarded as a more accurate image from that to be found in his own *Die Könige der Germanen*.[171] Essentially he takes the arguments that Manzoni had put forward in his interpretation of the Lombards in Italy, but offers a mirror image of it. That he has Manzoni in mind may be indicated by the comment of Cethegus when he sees Narses using Lombard troops: they 'will die as foreigners on Italian soil'.[172]

Dahn knew full well that the Ostrogoths entered Italy as an invading force, but, in his view, having taken control of the peninsula their regime was not oppressive. Rather, they pursued a 'well-meaning but hopeless policy of conciliation'.[173] Although, as presented in *Ein Kampf um Rom*, the Goths had a keen sense of

[168] Lilie, '*Gens Perfidus* oder Edle Einfalt, Stille Größe?', is unusual in its emphasis on Dahn's concern with sixth-century history in the novel; Frech, 'Felix Dahn', p. 685, n. 2. See now Wood, 'Early Medieval History and Nineteenth-Century Politics'.
[169] See Wahl, *Die Religion des deutschen Nationalismus*, p. 60. See also Frech, 'Felix Dahn', p. 686.
[170] Cited in Wahl, *Die Religion des deutschen Nationalismus*, p. 145. See also Frech, 'Felix Dahn', p. 686.
[171] Wood, 'Early Medieval History and Nineteenth-Century Politics', p. 546.
[172] Dahn, *Ein Kampf um Rom/A Struggle for Rome*, bk 8, ch. 21, p. 618.
[173] Dahn, *Ein Kampf um Rom/A Struggle for Rome*, bk 1, ch. 5, p. 54.

belonging to a pan-Germanic culture (which meant, remarkably, that they were well versed in the legends of *Beowulf* and *Walthari*),[174] some of them are keenly appreciative of Roman civilization. Dahn says of Totila, that 'he knew the Italian language and both Italian and Greek literature better than most Italians, and he loved and respected the culture of the old world, however he loved his own Goths at the same time.'[175] This, it must be admitted, comes rather closer to describing the attitude of German professors of the late nineteenth century,[176] than to an assessment of the Gothic king.

Not that Dahn ignored the reality of the Ostrogothic settlement. As a legal historian he was well aware that the Goths had been given a third of the land and slaves of the Romans, and he went out of his way to include a discussion of the matter in his depiction of the *bürgerlich* (middle-class)[177] estate of Witichis and Rauthgundis, presenting the division from both a Roman and a Gothic viewpoint. For the Romans it was a matter of theft. Yet as Rauthgundis explains to her son: 'Your father did not steal it. But he did take it openly from our Roman neighbours, because he was better and stronger than they were. Strong men and brave warriors have done this for thousands of years.'[178]

Dahn also claims, in one of the occasional, and short, academic interventions that punctuate the narrative that 'Theodoric had wisely excluded the Italian populace from military service'.[179] Yet the apartheid that this implies is challenged by Dahn's Totila. After their success against Witichis, the Byzantines proceeded to alienate the Italians by their heavy-handed administration and especially their high taxation. As a result, according to Dahn, many Italians looked back to 'the mild and benevolent rule of the Goths', and turned back to them. In this context Dahn gives Totila a reflective speech: 'Could it really be that it is impossible...to maintain this harmony...? Must two peoples always remain in conflict?...We treated them with suspicion instead of trust and we demanded their obedience but never sought their love.'[180] This has strong echoes of the speech in Manzoni's *Adelchi* where the hero analyses what has gone wrong with Lombard rule, but whereas the Lombards had no time to institute their policies, Dahn's Totila does for a short time succeed in turning the 'bitterness on the part of the Italians against their Byzantine oppressors into gratefulness for his own Gothic benevolence' and reestablishes 'the Gothic empire, mightier and more glorious than it had ever been'.[181]

---

[174] Dahn, *Ein Kampf um Rom/A Struggle for Rome*, bk 6, ch. 4, p. 422. Compare also the references to Gothic poetry in bk 8, ch. 1, p. 540, and ch. 15, p. 595.

[175] Dahn, *Ein Kampf um Rom/A Struggle for Rome*, bk 4, p. 228.

[176] But see the discussion of increasing hostility to Rome in Marchand, *Down from Olympus*, pp. 159–60.

[177] I deliberately use an anachronism, to reflect the fact that Witichis and Rauthgundis epitomize late nineteenth-century virtues.

[178] Dahn, *Ein Kampf um Rom/A Struggle for Rome*, bk 3, ch. 4, p. 112; see also ch. 5, pp. 114–15, bk 7, ch. 3, p. 496. See Neuhaus, *Literatur und nationale Einheit in Deutschland*, p. 240.

[179] Dahn, *Ein Kampf um Rom/A Struggle for Rome*, bk 2, ch. 2, p. 59.

[180] Dahn, *Ein Kampf um Rom/A Struggle for Rome*, bk 7, ch. 1, p. 489.

[181] Dahn, *Ein Kampf um Rom/A Struggle for Rome*, bk 7, ch. 2, p. 491.

As he explains to the Viking Harald, on his first unexpected appearance in the book, he wants to combine North and South.[182]

One of his policies is to encourage intermarriage.[183] Here a number of issues impinge on Dahn. First, he would seem to have in mind the Visigothic law banning intermarriage—he was, after all, an authority on the Visigothic Code.[184] Given the extent to which he presents Totila as a hero, one must conclude that Dahn approved of intermarriage in the abstract. On the other hand, none of the possible marriages between Goth and Roman mooted in the book actually work out:[185] Athalarich and Kamilla die before they can be married, and although Totila is betrothed to Valeria events overtake them. These betrothals, of course, are Dahn's inventions: the one high status marriage between a Goth and a Roman which did actually take place in the course of the Gothic Wars, that of Germanus to Mataswintha, Dahn excises by having the princess commit suicide before she can be betrothed. This problem of intermarriage, which would seem largely to exist in Dahn's imagination, one might ascribe to his own personal experience: his father was German and his mother French, or in the polarities of the book Goth and *Wälsch*—one wonders whether the scar of their divorce had a part to play in Dahn's interpretation.

The failure of the Gothic regime, in Dahn's narrative, is not so much a result of Byzantine power, but of treachery (by Gothic women as well as Italian men, and even by the Italians in general),[186] and above all because of the scheming of the Roman Prefect, Cethegus. He is easily the most complex character in the book, a military hero (indeed one of the few on the Roman side), but devious, resorting frequently to lies and to murder. His complexity may well reflect Dahn's own reaction to Italian liberation. Even in *Ein Kampf um Rom* the historian notes that 'the Italians, not that one could blame them, felt the reign of foreigners to be a disgrace to their national pride'.[187] The nineteenth-century context for this he made clear in a comment on his own reactions to 1859:

> And we did not begrudge the Italians freedom and unity so much, if they could gain it themselves on their own, but as the emperor on the Seine [Napoleon III] became involved, we wanted to know that German military assistance should not fail the Austrians, 'the German brothers', against France, which we deeply hated and feared yet more.[188]

Dahn's model, therefore, unlike Manzoni's, saw the Germanic rulers of Italy as benevolent, but, like Manzoni's it could appreciate that the incomers were not welcome. Indeed, some of his characters at least accept that there was a general

---

[182] Dahn, *Ein Kampf um Rom/A Struggle for Rome*, bk 8, ch. 19, p. 610.
[183] Dahn, *Ein Kampf um Rom/A Struggle for Rome*, bk 7, ch. 2, p. 493.
[184] Lilie, '*Gens Perfidus* oder Edle Einfalt, Stille Größe?', p. 198. The law continues to be debated, see Sivan, 'The appropriation of Roman law in barbarian hands'.
[185] Neuhaus, *Literatur und nationale Einheit in Deutschland*, p. 239.
[186] Dahn, *Ein Kampf um Rom/A Struggle for Rome*, bk 9, ch. 1, p. 682.
[187] Dahn, *Ein Kampf um Rom/A Struggle for Rome*, bk 2, ch. 1, p. 47.
[188] Quoted in Wahl, *Die Religion des deutschen Nationalismus*, pp. 53 and 87.

hatred of the invader.[189] There is nothing here of Fustel's sense of integration in the post-Roman period, As a result, the Goths remain foreigners in Italy, however much they wished to integrate.[190] Already right at the start of the book the elderly choric figure Hildebrand remarks: 'We are foreigners here, just as we were forty years ago when we first came down from the Alps, and a thousand years from now we will still be foreign.'[191] So too, the visionary Viking Harald remarks: 'It will never be your home, but it may become your tomb. You are foreign here, and foreign you always will be. Or you will go under, and become southerners like them. But you will not remain here in this land as the sons of Odin.'[192]

Unfortunately, future generations took from Dahn not the image of moderation presented by his Totila, nor indeed Totila's ideal of intermarriage—which the book presents as doomed to failure—but rather the sense of the Gothic and more generally of the German *Volk*. Other Germanic groups are presented as not being as noble as the Goths, though as warriors they are superior to the Greeks and Romans. As Narses says, 'These Germanic peoples will only be defeated by other Germanic peoples.'[193] In fact, some thought that Dahn did not present a pure enough picture of the Goths: while his Totila is the classic blond, blue-eyed hero, Teja is dark-haired, and thus baleful as befits his role as leader in the ultimate crisis.[194]

Despite the fact that in some respects his view of the Goths did not quite fit the ideal German of the twentieth century, Dahn provided a view of the past that was central to National Socialism. It has been remarked that '[t]he philosophies of Fichte, Hegel, or Nietzsche did not contribute as much to Germany's pre-Hitlerian intellectual background for National Socialism as commemorations of the victory at Sedan (in the Franco-Prussian War), Bismarckian "blood and iron" quotations, the historical novels of Felix Dahn...'[195] *Ein Kampf um Rom* was read by Rudolf Hess and probably by Hitler.[196] Ominously, it looks beyond the failure of the Goths in Italy to a period of Germanic world-domination:

> We are of the Hammer-god's people,
> And we are going to inherit his World-kingdom.[197]

We are a long way from the rigorous textual editing of Mommsen, or the 'scientific' reading of the sources, pursued by Fustel, but it would be Dahn's vision of the early Middle Ages, researched with some care in his *Könige der Germanen*, but transmitted to the general public in the pages of *Ein Kampf um Rom*, that would have the greatest impact.

[189] Dahn, *Ein Kampf um Rom/A Struggle for Rome*, bk 3, ch. 1, p. 97.
[190] Neuhaus, *Literatur und nationale Einheit in Deutschland*, p. 240.
[191] Dahn, *Ein Kampf um Rom/A Struggle for Rome*, bk 1, ch. 1, p. 16.
[192] Dahn, *Ein Kampf um Rom/A Struggle for Rome*, bk 8, ch. 19, p. 609.
[193] Dahn, *Ein Kampf um Rom/A Struggle for Rome*, bk 5, ch. 5, p. 270, and bk 8, ch. 25, p. 635.
[194] Wahl, *Die Religion des deutschen Nationalismus*, pp. 63–4.
[195] Housden, *Resistance and Conformity in the Third Reich*, p. 3.
[196] Frech, 'Felix Dahn', pp. 696–7.
[197] Dahn, *Ein Kampf um Rom/A Struggle for Rome*, bk 8, ch. 19. The translation is my adaptation of Parker's (p. 610), which misses some of the nuance. See Wahl, *Die Religion des deutschen Nationalismus*, p. 102.

11

Teutons, Romans, and 'Scientific' History

11.1 ROMANS, TEUTONS, AND 1870–1

Italian Unification, the Franco-Prussian War, and the subsequent unification of Germany impacted upon scholars working on the period of the Fall of Rome more obviously than any subsequent event until 1914. Naturally, the annexation of Alsace-Lorraine in 1871 affected French and German scholars rather more than it did their British counterparts. Yet Insular scholars did observe events across the Channel, and their observations affected their reading of the distant past.[1] One effect of the fall of Napoleon III was to liberate the notion of Empire. Hitherto it had been associated primarily with Austria, or more recently with France. With the power of France broken, British historians were rather more inclined to look favourably on the Roman Empire, and also to see it as a point of comparison for understanding the current, and increasingly imperial, position of Britain in the world.[2]

Meanwhile, new scientific ideas were transforming concepts of race, so that the Teutons who overthrew Roman civilization came to be presented not just through the prism of eighteenth- and early nineteenth-century notions of liberty, or indeed of Providence, but also through an increasingly 'scientific' understanding of racial difference, the origins of which we have already seen in the writings of Amédée Thierry, Edwards, and Gobineau. This racial reading of the barbarians, coupled with the changing view of Empire, led to a new discourse that fed directly into British imperial ideology.[3]

Not surprisingly, the reappraisal of Empire also led to a greater appreciation of Gibbon, not least in the great edition of *Decline and Fall* edited by John Bagnell Bury and in Thomas Hodgkin's *Italy and her invaders*. Not that the works of Bury or Hodgkin can be fitted simply into the new imperial orthodoxy. For Bury, science pointed in a rather more sceptical direction. Hodgkin and Bury belong to the last decades of the nineteenth century and the first of the twentieth: to understand the intellectual world from which they emerged we need to turn back to the period before the fall of Napoleon III.

---

[1] The comments on the absence of English studies of the continent in Bentley, 'The Age of Prothero', pp. 187–8, do not hold good for scholarship on Rome or on the early Middle Ages.

[2] Hingley, *Roman Officers and English Gentlemen*, pp. 19–22.

[3] Hingley, *Roman Officers and English Gentlemen*; Hingley, *The Recovery of Roman Britain 1586–1906*.

11.2 ROMAN DESPOTISM AND ENGLISH FREEDOM

In 1861 John Sheppard published *The Fall of Rome and the Rise of the New Nationalities. A Series of Lectures on the Connection between Ancient and Modern History*. Sheppard was scarcely a major scholar, although he held a fellowship at Wadham College, Oxford, before becoming second master at Repton, and then headmaster of Kidderminster School. He wrote his history 'in the context of the expansion of the university History curriculum'.[4] It shows a man who was well read, and knew his Gibbon, Milman, Sismondi, Michelet, Guizot, and Thierry (certainly Amédée, if not Augustin).[5] In certain respects he admired *Decline and Fall*, though he had his reservations: 'The gorgeous magnificence of Gibbon's style is, after all, but the pomp of a funeral procession. It celebrates the obsequies of a dying world...'[6] Gibbon was more or less correct in seeing the decline of Rome as deriving from 'the dissolution of domestic manners, and the consequent demoralization of society'.[7] What he left out was the hand of God.

> The signs of her coming fate were inscribed in a language which all might read upon the social aspects of the world. The fingers of a hand came forth and wrote upon the wall: 'God hath numbered thy kingdom, and finished it. Thou art weighed in the balances, and found wanting. Thy kingdom is divided, and given to another race.[8]

The barbarian races themselves Sheppard traced to 'the generations of the sons of Noah'.[9] Although *The Origin of the Species* had been published in 1859, this is Providential history uninfluenced by Darwin.

Among the new nationalities were the Anglo-Saxons. Sheppard saw their arrival in Britain as 'the true birthdate of English history'.[10] This was a view shared by a number of other historians, among them Thomas Arnold and Charles Kingsley, who we have already met as the author of *Hypatia*.[11] In his work on the barbarian migrations Kingsley also made much of the providential nature of the coming of the Teutons, and their regeneration of the degenerate peoples of the Roman Empire,[12] despite his sympathy for Darwin. So too, in his inaugural lecture of 1841 Thomas Arnold explained that the Christian Teutons having established their preeminence in Europe, had gone on to do God's work in the rest of the world.[13] With regard to the Migration Period he argued that

---

[4] Sheppard, *The Fall of Rome and the Rise of the New Nationalities*, p. iii.
[5] Sheppard, *The Fall of Rome and the Rise of the New Nationalities*, pp. iv, x, 688–75, 741–5.
[6] Sheppard, *The Fall of Rome and the Rise of the New Nationalities*, p. ix.
[7] Sheppard, *The Fall of Rome and the Rise of the New Nationalities*, p. 103; Hingley, *Roman Officers and English Gentlemen*, p. 20.
[8] Sheppard, *The Fall of Rome and the Rise of the New Nationalities*, p. 104.
[9] Sheppard, *The Fall of Rome and the Rise of the New Nationalities*, p. 106.
[10] Sheppard, *The Fall of Rome and the Rise of the New Nationalities*, p. 131; Hingley, *Roman Officers and English Gentlemen*, p. 64.
[11] See chapter 8, above.
[12] Kingsley, *The Roman and the Teuton*. For a comment see Horsman, 'Origins of Racial Anglo-Saxonism in Great Britain before 1850', pp. 408–10.
[13] Arnold, *An Inaugural Lecture*, esp. p. 41.

[w]e, this great English nation, whose race and language are now overrunning the earth from one end of it to the other—we were born when the white horse of the Saxons had established his dominion from the Tweed to the Tamar. So far we can trace our blood, our language, the name and actual divisions of our country, the beginnings of some of our institutions. So far our national identity extends....[14]

Arnold was by no means the only historian to see a connection between the Saxon conquest of England and the expansion of the British Empire: William Barnes, writing in 1869, thought the Saxon invasions helped towards an understanding of the British success in India.[15]

It is worth noting that Arnold, like Sheppard and Kingsley, did not consider early Anglo-Saxon history in isolation from its continental context, for he went on:

And if we cross the Channel, what is the case of our great neighbour nation of France?... France and Frenchmen came into being when the Franks established themselves west of the Rhine... the Franks were numerically few.... But Clovis and his Germans struck root so deeply and their institutions wrought such changes, that the identity of France cannot be carried back beyond their invasion...[16]

So much, one might say, for 'nos ancêtres les Gaulois'.

Arnold then returned to the English: 'We derive scarcely one drop of our blood from Roman fathers.... Our English race is the German race.'[17] For him the Greeks and the Romans had 'nourished the intellect',[18] but by the fourth century they were in a state of decline. The arrival of the German and Sclavonic peoples, and the impact of Christianity, however, initiated the shift from Ancient to Modern History,[19] and now the influence of the 'Germans' (among whom he included the English) was spread throughout the world, where they were carrying out God's work.[20] A more extreme version of the Teutons as the force that regenerated the degenerate peoples of the Roman Empire at the start of their providential Christian mission would be set out by Charles Kingsley in his lectures on *The Roman and the Teuton*, published in 1864.[21]

The success of the barbarians was not just a matter of brute force: it was also dependent on the moral purity of the incomers. Although the rhetoric was that of Protestant evangelicals, the interpretation was not so different from what was put forward by the likes of de Staël and Ozanam. This was a rephrasing of the theory

[14] Arnold, *An Inaugural Lecture*, p. 32; Parker, 'The failure of liberal racialism: the racial ideas of E. A. Freeman', p. 828, citing the passage from Arnold, *Introductory Lectures on Modern History*, 2nd edn, pp. 23–30.

[15] Barnes, *Early England and the Saxon-English*, p. 7. There was, of course, a more common assertion of parallels between the British and Roman Empires: Hingley, *Roman Officers and British Gentlemen*.

[16] Arnold, *An Inaugural Lecture*, pp. 32–3.   [17] Arnold, *An Inaugural Lecture*, p. 35.

[18] Arnold, *An Inaugural Lecture*, p. 38.   [19] Arnold, *An Inaugural Lecture*, pp. 38–9.

[20] Arnold, *An Inaugural Lecture*, pp. 37, 41.

[21] Horsman, 'Origins of Racial Anglo-Saxonism in Great Britain before 1850', pp. 408–10.

of barbarian liberty, which paid rather more attention to the notion of their supposed moral superiority, which it linked to Providence.

11.3 THE SCIENCE OF RACE

Sheppard, with his reference to the hand of God, presented an essentially Biblical reading of the Fall of Rome. Others were more inclined to stress the impact of new scientific ideas, relating to biology and to race. Darwin's evolutionary theories came to be seen as having something to contribute to the understanding of the past,[22] as did new theories of language. The Indo-European language family had already been identified in the eighteenth century by William Jones, whose work had been elaborated in turn by, among others, Friedrich Schlegel.[23] Their insights were extended by Max Müller, who, although born in Dessau in 1823 and educated at Leipzig, was Taylorian Professor of Modern Languages (1854–68) and subsequently Professor of Comparative Philology (1868–1900) at the University of Oxford. Müller's work was central to the development of the notion of an Aryan group of languages, although, one should note, he distanced himself from the idea of an Aryan race.[24]

Among the historians most keenly influenced by Müller was his exact contemporary Edward Augustus Freeman (1823–92).[25] Yet, while the issue of race is a marked feature of Freeman's historical writing, one should not forget the extent to which he was aware of, and influenced by, other factors. He had a strong geographical sense and was indeed one of the first historians to promote the idea of historical geography.[26] Equally significant for him were current affairs. In the years immediately before his appointment to the Regius Chair of Modern History in Oxford in1884, Freeman worked as an independent scholar from his home in Somerleaze in Somerset, having had to resign a fellowship at Trinity College when he married. Yet he remained fully integrated into the world of scholarship and, also, of politics. A Gladstonian liberal, he stood, unsuccessfully, for Parliament in 1857, 1858, and 1868.[27] His political interests, however, were not limited to Britain. As Regius Professor he delivered two lectures in 1887 to mark the queen's Jubilee. These

---

[22] Kingsley was a champion of *The Origin of the Species*.

[23] On the Schlegels and their development of Jones' ideas, Thom, *Republics, Nations and Tribes*, pp. 221–5.

[24] Müller, *Biographies of Words and the Home of the Aryas*, p. 204: 'An ethnologist who speaks of Aryan race, Aryan blood, Aryan eyes and hair is as great a sinner as a linguist who speaks of a dolichocephalic dictionary or a brachycephalic grammar'. On Müller and Anglo-Saxon studies, MacDougall, *Racial Myth in English History*, pp. 120–1; Parker, 'The failure of liberal racialism: the racial ideas of E. A. Freeman', p. 835; Leerssen, *National Thought in Europe*, p. 208.

[25] For Freeman, see Stephens, *The Life and Letters of Edward A. Freeman*; Barlow, 'Edward Augustus Freeman'; Bryce, *Studies in Contemporary Biography*, pp. 262–92; Burrow, *A Liberal Descent*, pp. 155–228; Momigliano, 'Two types of universal history: the cases of E. A. Freeman and Max Weber'. For Freeman's dependence on Müller, Parker, 'The failure of liberal racialism: the racial ideas of E. A. Freeman', pp. 834–5.

[26] Freeman, *The Historical Geography of Europe*, 2 volumes. Vol. 2 is a collection of maps.

[27] Harvie, *The Lights of Liberalism*, pp. 177, 180–2, 267.

constitute a clear analysis of the developments which had taken place in Europe during the first fifty years of Victoria's reign, from 1837 to 1887.[28] In the course of the lectures he singled out a number of relatively recent dates which he regarded as being of crucial importance for European History: 1830 (Belgian independence), 1848, 1859–60 (the unification of Italy), 1866 (the Prussian annexation of Schleswig-Holstein and Hannover), 1870–1, and 1878 (the independence of Serbia, Montenegro, and Romania). He also noted the establishment of an independent Greece in 1832 and the Crimean War in 1854, which he described as an alliance of the English and French to defend 'the last home of the free Greek and the free Goth'![29] For Freeman, Greece was always a matter of concern[30]—as, more generally, was the Eastern Question: he has recently been seen as a significant commentator on south-eastern Europe.[31] In the words of James Bryce, 'By far the strongest political interest—indeed it rose to a passion—of his later years was his hatred of the Turk.'[32] His attitude towards what had been and what still was the Ottoman world was dominated by his racial and religious anti-Mahometanism[33]—for he was very much a committed High Anglican.

Despite his own concerns over foreign politics, which prompted him to resign from the *Saturday Review*, and thus to lose a substantial annual stipend,[34] he recognized that there were limits to the commitment shown by other English academics. Talking of professors who pronounced on current affairs, he asked: 'How many of us here are ready, if need be, to share the confessorship of Ewald, Dahlmann, Gervinus, and the brothers Grimm?'[35] The reference is to the so-called Göttingen Seven and their removal from their academic posts by Ernst August of Hannover. Some of the most interesting observations in the Jubilee Lectures concern the English failure to react to the end of the House of Hannover and the annexation of the kingdom by Prussia in 1866.[36]

Alongside events in Greece, Freeman was excited by both Italian and German unification. In his Jubilee Lectures he remarked that 'To-day we have to look on the recovery of Rome by Italy as giving the world the sight of such an Italy as has not been since the days of Theodoric, since those thirty years of peace and happiness when the "humanity" of the Roman was so well guarded by the "savagery" of the Goth.'[37] However, he felt a greater attachment to what he regarded as homelands

---

[28] Freeman, *Four Oxford Lectures 1887*, pp. 3–58.

[29] Freeman, *Four Oxford Lectures 1887*, pp. 16, 26–7. For his views on the Crimea, Stephenson, 'E. A. Freeman (1823–1892), a neglected commentator on Byzantium and Modern Greece', pp. 128–9.

[30] Freeman, *Four Oxford Lectures 1887*, p. 81.

[31] Stephenson, 'E. A. Freeman (1823–1892): a neglected commentator on Byzantium and Modern Greece'.

[32] Bryce, *Studies in Contemporary Biography*, p. 275.

[33] Parker, 'The failure of liberal racialism: the racial ideas of E. A. Freeman', pp. 829, 832.

[34] Stephenson, 'E. A. Freeman (1823–1892), a neglected commentator on Byzantium and Modern Greece', p. 129. For his commitment, see also Parker, 'The failure of liberal racialism: the racial ideas of E. A. Freeman', p. 835.

[35] Freeman, *Four Oxford Lectures 1887*, p. 4.

[36] Freeman, *Four Oxford Lectures 1887*, pp. 5–8.

[37] Freeman, *Four Oxford Lectures 1887*, pp. 54–5.

of the Teutons. In the course of his first visit to Germany in 1865 he was inspired at having seen 'the original home of our Teutonic ancestors'.[38] This enthusiasm did not prevent him from being critical of Prussia over its seizure of Schleswig-Holstein, feeling himself to be 'Eider-Danish to the backbone'.[39] His emotion reflects his view of the origins of the English: but he was also sharp-eyed enough to see that the question of North Schleswig would need to be reopened,[40] as indeed it was after 1918.

Much easier for Freeman to stomach was Prussian aggression in the Rhineland. Like Müller, he was delighted with the German seizure of Alsace-Lorraine,[41]—a subject that surfaces in a number of his letters from the period.[42] Immediately after the war he and the younger historian J. R. Green embarked on a tour which took them to Aachen, Cologne, Mainz, Würzburg, Innsbruck, Trent, Verona, Padua, Bologna, Ravenna, and Pisa, before Freeman continued on to Modena, Parma, Piacenza, Pistoia, Pavia, and Milan, alone.[43] The events of 1870–1 prompted him to write an article on the 'Early sieges of Paris', covering those of the ninth and tenth centuries, for the *British Quarterly Review*—like many of his essays, which appeared in such journals, this was not simply for an English academic audience. It would be republished almost immediately in his first volume of *Historical Essays*, and then reissued in Leipzig, in a collection of his (untranslated) papers made for an apparently avid German audience.[44] The opening sentence of the essay makes clear its relation to the present:

> The events of the last four months have in a special way drawn the thoughts of men towards two cities which stand out among European capitals as witnesses of the way in which the history of remote times still has a direct bearing on things which are passing before our eyes. Rome and Paris now stand out, as they have stood out in so many earlier ages, as the historic centres of a period, which, there can be no doubt, will live to all time as one of the marked periods of world history.

The reference to Paris is, of course, to the Franco-Prussian War: that to Rome is to Pius IX's declaration of papal infallibility. Looking back on the events of 1870–1 from the vantage point of Victoria's jubilee, Freeman expressed the view that Paris had become, albeit briefly, 'a little town in Germany', as it had been in the days of Charlemagne![45] He had, however, also come to realize that the French of Alsace

---

[38] Parker, 'The failure of liberal racialism: the racial ideas of E. A. Freeman', p. 834. See also the comments of Barlow, 'Edward Augustus Freeman'.

[39] Quoted by Parker, 'The failure of liberal racialism: the racial ideas of E. A. Freeman', p. 831. See also Stephens, *Freeman*, vol. 1, pp. 289, 291.

[40] Freeman, *Four Oxford Lectures 1887*, pp. 42–4.

[41] Parker, 'The failure of liberal racialism: the racial ideas of E. A. Freeman', pp. 827, 832–4.

[42] Stephens, *The Life and Letters of Edward A. Freeman*, vol. 2, pp. 2–10.

[43] Stephens, *The Life and Letters of Edward A. Freeman*, vol. 2, pp. 10–11.

[44] E. A. Freeman, 'The early sieges of Paris', *British Quarterly Review* 1871, reprinted in Freeman, *Historical Essays*, First Series (London, 1871), 2nd edn, pp. 212–56, and in Freeman, *Select Historical Essays*, pp. 103–50. Freeman's works are frequently cited in German works which refer to the Anglo-Saxons.

[45] Freeman, *Four Oxford Lectures 1887*, p. 54.

had a rather better case than he originally conceded: 'The lands given up by the French people were lands which the French people looked on, and in some ways truly looked on, as having become wholly French.'[46]

While generally a Francophobe,[47] Freeman's animus was directed above all against Napoleon III, whom he saw as a despot and a tyrant.[48] He was certainly not anti-Norman: indeed he came increasingly to stress the ethnic ties which bound the English and the Normans of Normandy.[49] Moreover, for all his hostility to Paris, 'French was the only [foreign] language he could speak with ease'.[50] And indeed he was, from the start, deeply influenced by French scholarship, not least by the writings of Augustin Thierry and by Guizot.[51]

As a historian Freeman is most usually thought of as a specialist in the later Anglo-Saxon period and, especially, in the Norman Conquest, not least because of his conflict with John Horace Round. He did, nevertheless, have an interest in early Anglo-Saxon history, and this is clear not just from the few pages on the subject that begin his *History of the Norman Conquest of England.*[52] He wrote about the Anglo-Saxon conquest, for he regarded the English settlement as an act of conquest, on a number of occasions, and significantly, it was a subject that he thought could not be understood except by contrast with the continent. This is abundantly clear in his rather cantankerous lectures on 'Teutonic conquest in Gaul and Britain', which constituted the third and fourth of his Jubilee pieces.[53] Here his central point was that the Teutonic settlement in Britain must have been different in kind from that on the continent, because of the extent to which the Celtic or Latin language was wiped out. For him the Britons in the eastern part of the country were exterminated—though as he went on to explain, this did not mean that all the Britons were annihilated, and he objected vigorously to any who had attributed such an interpretation to him.[54] What he believed was that there was an initial pagan period, when the Saxons killed, drove out, or enslaved all those in the territory they settled: but that this was followed, after their conversion, by a rather milder expansion. It is possible to find an element of internal contradiction in the argument.

It has recently been noted that Freeman was a not-insignificant Byzantinist—an interest entirely in keeping with his concern for the modern Balkans.[55] In fact, he

---

[46] Freeman, *Four Oxford Lectures 1887*, p. 53.   [47] Barlow, 'Edward Augustus Freeman'.

[48] Parker, 'The failure of liberal racialism: the racial ideas of E. A. Freeman', pp. 831, 832–3.

[49] Parker, 'The failure of liberal racialism: the racial ideas of E. A. Freeman', pp. 830–1.

[50] Stephenson, 'E. A. Freeman (1823–1892), a neglected commentator on Byzantium and Modern Greece', p. 131.

[51] Parker, 'The failure of liberal racialism: the racial ideas of E. A. Freeman', p. 826.

[52] Freeman, *The History of the Norman Conquest of England: Its Causes and its Results*, vol. 1, pp. 19–21.

[53] Freeman, *Four Oxford Lectures 1887*, pp. 59–112. Freeman's tone towards those who dared to disagree with him was often sharp: 'Good but a little "tart"' is the comment inscribed in the Leeds copy of his *Select Historical Essays*.

[54] Freeman, *Four Oxford Lectures 1887*, pp. 76, 83.

[55] Stephenson, 'E. A. Freeman (1823–1892), a neglected commentator on Byzantium and Modern Greece', pp. 120–6.

wrote widely about the Classical World and about the continental early Middle Ages, just as he did about the Anglo-Saxon and Norman worlds. His comparison of the Saxon conquest of England and the Frankish take-over of Gaul is by no means his only excursion into the Migration Period on the other side of the Channel. Among his papers is a piece on 'The Goths at Ravenna'—like much of his work written for the British *Quarterly Review*—in which he indulges his enthusiasm not only for the Teutons, and in particular for Theodoric, but also for architecture, and as a result provides a remarkably early appreciation of the glories of the Ravenna mosaics.[56]

It was not only in articles that he wrote about the last years of the Roman Empire and of the decades that followed. At the time of his death in 1892 he was working on a history of *Western Europe in the Fifth Century*, which was published posthumously in 1904[57]—something that has been curiously overlooked by recent commentators.[58] This last work essentially forms a historical prologomenon to the arguments expressed in the Jubilee Lectures on 'Teutonic conquest in Gaul and Britain'. For Freeman the barbarian invasion of Gaul might have been brutal, but ultimately it was not destructive. In Britain the coming of the Teutons marked a completely new beginning. Freeman offered an equivalent interpretation of the end of the West Roman Empire, where the Teutons, lead by the likes of Atawulf [*sic*] the Goth ('one of the noblest forms in the whole history of our race')[59] revivified a world dogged by tyranny, and prepared Europe for its subsequent struggles against the Saracen 'and the younger power of the Turk'.[60]

More important than the stance adopted by Freeman were some of the theories that underpinned it, most notably those derived from the evolving philological and ethnological sciences. Freeman, in presenting a supposedly scientific concept of race in his interpretation of the early Middle Ages, was picking up on a line of thought that had developed steadily since Pinkerton's *Dissertation on the Origin and Progress of the Scythians or Goths* of 1787, which had not only clarified the distinction between Teuton and Celt, but also argued for the superiority of the former.[61] The notion that this explained the victory of the Saxons over the Britons had been firmly set out by Thomas Carlyle in his lectures *On Heroes, Hero-worship and the Heroic in History*, where, like many contemporary Germans, he drew heavily on the ideas of Herder and Fichte. Carlyle's first lecture, which deals most directly with the early Middle Ages, also revived the theory, dismissed by Grimm, that Odin had been a real hero who was subsequently worshipped.[62] The idea that

---

[56] Freeman, 'The Goths at Ravenna'.   [57] Freeman, *Western Europe in the Fifth Century*.

[58] See, for instance, Burrow, *A Liberal Descent*, p. 192, which states that his *History of Sicily* was his last book. Scott Holmes in his preface to Freeman, *Western Europe in the Fifth Century*, pp. v–vi, provides an account of how the drafts of the work were prepared for publication after Freeman's death.

[59] Freeman, *Western Europe in the Fifth Century*, p. 170.

[60] Freeman, *Western Europe in the Fifth Century*, p. 224.

[61] Pinkerton, *Dissertation on the Origin and Progress of the Scythians or Goths*, pp. 24–31, 51, 67; Horsman, 'Origins of racial Anglo-Saxonism', pp. 391–2.

[62] Carlyle, *On Heroes, Hero-Worship and the Heroic in History*, pp. 28–9.

the Teutons were a superior race was additionally elaborated by I. A. Blackwell in the introduction to his 1847 reissue of Percy's translation of Mallet.[63] Freeman likewise saw the Teutons as superior to the Celts, and especially the Gaels: in Bryce's words, '[h]e was intensely English and Teutonic, and wished the Gael to be left to settle, or fight over, their own affairs in their own island, as they had done eight centuries ago.'[64]

Freeman's main inspiration in his reading of the early Middle Ages was one of his predecessors in the Regius Chair, Thomas Arnold, whose lectures he heard as a student in Oxford in 1841.[65] Freeman, who was deeply influenced by Arnold's reading, refined the latter's definition of nationality as a result of the influence of Max Müller and of his notion of Aryanism—or rather of the Aryan family of languages. Despite Müller's argument that one should only talk of Aryan languages and not of Aryan races, Freeman, while sometimes paying lipservice to the distinction, essentially placed the notion of Aryanism at the centre of his understanding of race.[66] And his sense of the racial superiority of the Aryan races was enhanced by his reading of current events, especially in the Balkans and Greece, which in his view could be read largely as a conflict between Aryans and such non-Aryan races as the Turks.[67]

Freeman set out his ideas on race most fully in his paper on 'Race and language', originally published in successive issues of the *Contemporary* and the *Fortnightly Review* in the early months of January 1877.[68] Some aspects of his thought would change thereafter. Indeed, his attitudes would become more openly racist in the last fifteen years of his life, especially with regard to non-Aryan peoples. Thus, he wrote about the Jews with some sensitivity in 1877,[69] but appears increasingly anti-Semitic thereafter. Equally, he was openly racist in his comments on Negroes after his 1881 visit to the United States.[70] Nevertheless, 'Race and language' provides a useful insight into Freeman's basic ideas, which prove to be a disconcerting mixture of careful observation and argument on the one hand and unthinking prejudice on the other.

Freeman noted that in the past a person's attachment to a particular political community was usually determined by his place of birth, but, in his view,

[63] Horsman, 'Origins of racial Anglo-Saxonism', p. 402, on the revised edition of Percy's Mallet, edited by Blackwell.

[64] Bryce, *Studies in Contemporary Biography*, p. 272.

[65] Parker, 'The failure of liberal racialism: the racial ideas of E. A. Freeman', p. 828; Horsman, 'Origins of racial Anglo-Saxonism', provides a useful background to Freeman, but, since 1850 marks the limits of his enquiry he has little to say about Freeman himself. Arnold's lectures of the period are published as Arnold, *Introductory Lectures on Modern History*.

[66] Parker, 'The failure of liberal racialism: the racial ideas of E. A. Freeman', pp. 826–7, 834–6.

[67] Parker, 'The failure of liberal racialism: the racial ideas of E. A. Freeman', pp. 832, 835, 840–1. Freeman was not alone in drawing parallels with the Ottoman Empire: for similar comparisons drawn by Kingsley, see Hingley, *Roman Officers and English Gentlemen*, pp. 20–1.

[68] Freeman, 'Race and language'.

[69] Freeman, 'The Jews in Europe'.

[70] Parker, 'The failure of liberal racialism: the racial ideas of E. A. Freeman', pp. 839–46, on his increasing anti-Semitism, and, following his visit to the United States in 1881, his denigration of negroes. On Freeman's racism see also Momigliano, 'Two types of universal history: the cases of E. A. Freeman and Max Weber', and Stephenson, 'E. A. Freeman (1823–1892), a neglected commentator on Byzantium and Modern Greece', pp. 127–8.

developments in science and in national feeling meant that a new definition was needed.[71] For him: 'The doctrine of race is essentially an artificial doctrine, a learned doctrine.'[72] And: 'The doctrine of race, in its popular form, is the direct offspring of the science of scientific philology.'[73] He then turned to the problem of the association of race and language, noting—and here he had Müller in mind— that 'scientific philologers' objected to the confusion of the two.[74] He acknowledged Müller's insistence that one could not talk of a Celtic skull—in other words categories evolved for defining language should not be used to define skeletal types: there was, therefore, no fixed relationship between linguistic and physiological groups.[75] Having admitted as much, he tried to square the circle. He continued to assert that: 'Language is no certain test of race; but it is a presumption of race.' In order to hang on to this thesis he proceeded to redefine race: 'we may say that language has a great deal to do with race, as race is commonly understood, and that race has a great deal to do with community of blood. If we once admit the Roman doctrine of adoption our whole course is clear.'[76] While natural or biological kinship was the norm, adoption could be equally strong. This meant that skull shapes were no reliable guide to a man's race[77]—and here (and elsewhere)[78] Freeman was reacting against the current claims of physiological and genetic research.[79] He went on to elaborate his notion of adoption or assimilation. It was common in the Roman Empire, where Romans assimilated those they conquered, and it occurred in Gaul, where it was the conquerors who were assimilated into the conquered population.[80] All groups, in his opinion, contained foreign elements. Races and nations are, thus, artificial, but at the same time they are real. How then are they differentiated? There is no absolute coincidence between a nation and a government: the main badge, rather, is language.[81] Of course there are exceptions, most notably the Swiss, with their three languages.[82] Freeman admitted the influence of other factors in the creation of a race: peoples have memories, grievances, and hopes.[83] Grievances might divide what ought, for linguistic reasons, to be a community, as in the case of Russia and Poland.[84] And where language and nation do not coincide, as in much of south-eastern Europe, religion and nation do.[85] Despite all the exceptions it is language that is 'the rough practical test of nationality'.[86]

One might conclude that all the exceptions render the basic model untenable. Yet, for all the unsatisfactory nature of Freeman's overall conclusions, he made a

---

[71] Freeman, 'Race and language', p. 180.   [72] Freeman, 'Race and language', p. 184.
[73] Freeman, 'Race and language', p. 185.   [74] Freeman, 'Race and language', p. 186.
[75] Freeman, 'Race and language', p. 192.   [76] Freeman, 'Race and language', p. 197.
[77] Freeman, 'Race and language', pp. 198–9.
[78] Freeman, *Four Oxford Lectures 1887*, p. 40, 71, 79, 81–2.
[79] For the importance of phrenology in debates about race, Horsman, 'Origins of racial Anglo-Saxonism in Great Britain before 1850', p. 398.
[80] Freeman, 'Race and language', p. 201.
[81] Freeman, 'Race and language', pp. 202–3, 205. 206.
[82] Freeman, 'Race and language', p. 215.   [83] Freeman, 'Race and language', p. 221.
[84] Freeman, 'Race and language', p. 229.   [85] Freeman, 'Race and language', p. 227.
[86] Freeman, 'Race and language', p. 228.

number of important individual points, not least in his rejection of skull-types and simple biological kinship as providing adequate grounds on which to define race and nation. His notion of adoption and assimilation, his emphasis on choice, on the role of language, and of religion, as well as memories, grievances, and hopes, all point to a much more sophisticated model than is admitted by his final equation.

It was his model of adoption or assimilation that underpinned Freeman's interpretation of the barbarian settlements in both England and Gaul, and which led him to claim that those who accused him of thinking that the Anglo-Saxons exterminated the Britons had misunderstood his argument.

> Though the literal extirpation of a nation is an impossibility, there is every reason to believe that the Celtic inhabitants of those parts of Britain which had become English at the end of the sixth century had been as nearly extirpated as can be. The women would doubtless be often spared; but, as far as the male sex is concerned, we may feel sure that death, emigration, or personal slavery were the only alternatives which the vanquished found at the hands of our fathers.[87]

This situation, he insisted, only related to the early pagan period: he thought that there was a change, especially after the conversion, which led to greater assimilation.[88] What he was sure about, however, was that throughout England it was the Teutonic element and not the British that was dominant, whereas in France it was the Gauls rather the Teutons who dominated. As he explained:

> We are as pure as the High-Germans; we are far purer than the French. We are not a *Mischvolk*, drawing its blood mainly from one source, while it draws its language from another source, and its national name from a third.[89]

The *Mischvolk*, of course, are the French: Gauls by blood, Latin by language, and Frank by name. And he went on to elaborate:

> What we have always held has been that in such a nation there commonly is a certain element which is more than an element, something which is its real kernel, its real essence, something which attracts and absorbs all other elements, so that the other elements are not co-ordinated elements but mere infusions into a whole which is already in being.[90]

The word 'kernel' is worth noting: its German equivalent, 'Kern', would emerge as a keyword after 1961. This real kernel in England was Teutonic, whereas in France it was Celtic or, to use Freeman's terminology, Welsh.[91]

Scholars have noted the racism in Freeman's interpretation of the Anglo-Saxon conquest and settlement.[92] In fact, however, he had some reason for thinking that

---

[87] Freeman, *Four Oxford Lectures 1887*, p. 74, reiterating words from *The Norman Conquest of England*.

[88] Freeman, *Four Oxford Lectures 1887*, p. 84.

[89] Freeman, *Four Oxford Lectures 1887*, p. 77; see also p. 112.

[90] Freeman, *Four Oxford Lectures 1887*, p. 80.

[91] On his general use of Welsh for Celt: Parker, 'The failure of liberal racialism: the racial ideas of E. A. Freeman', p. 833, n. 34. On his non-inclusion of the Principality among those he denigrated as 'Celts', ibid. p. 834; see also p. 840: 'There was a certain arbitrariness in Freeman's bestowal of his favours.'

[92] Parker, 'The failure of liberal racialism: the racial ideas of E. A. Freeman', pp. 839, 840.

his arguments about the settlement of England were seen as being more Celtophobic than they actually were.[93] Certainly he saw the Teutons as the dominant race, and he noted the greatness and purity of the Anglo-Saxons[94]—though the word 'purity' needs to be read in the light of his notion of adoption.[95] The Teutons, in his definition, could have British or Iberian skulls.[96] Yet, alongside his sense of the greatness of the Anglo-Saxons, he also came to stress the valour of the Britons in resisting them.[97] In other words, he acknowledged all the elements that contributed to Englishness (and in so doing effectively contradicted his own denial that the English were a *Mischvolk*):

> No nation is wholly pure; no language is wholly unmixed. The English nation, the English language, are mixed as all others are, but our blood is not more mixed than the blood of every nation must be which has played an equally great part in the history of the world.[98]

He included a British element in his definition of Englishness, and indeed he treasured the survival of Celtic elements in Somerset where he lived.[99]

Blood, then, or rather skull-type, was not significant in Freeman's definition of race. What mattered was identification, and chief among the pointers was language. But with the Teutons he also associated a tradition of democracy. Here, of course, he was looking back to the Tacitean image of the *Germania*. He thought that old Teutonic democracy could be still found in the *Landesgemeinde* of the Swiss cantons of Uri and Appenzell, much to his delight. And it was in these cantons that he felt he could see the origins of the English constitution.[100] The emphasis on Anglo-Saxon democracy was naturally welcome on the other side of the Atlantic, and Freeman was revered in the United States, especially following his lecture tour of 1881.[101] His ideas achieved further currency in the immensely popular historical works of his pupil, his travelling companion of 1871, J. R. Green.

11.4 BURY AND THE SCIENCE OF HISTORY

Although he was certain that England had to be understood with reference to what took place across the Channel, Freeman was ultimately a specialist in English history. The same could not be said of the much younger John Bagnell Bury

---

[93] On his Celtophobia, Parker, 'The failure of liberal racialism: the racial ideas of E. A. Freeman', pp. 825, 833, 834, 839. He, of course, distinguished between Britons and Gaels.

[94] Barlow, 'Edward Augustus Freeman'.

[95] Freeman, *Four Oxford Lectures 1887*, pp. 74, 78.

[96] Parker, 'The failure of liberal racialism: the racial ideas of E. A. Freeman', p. 826.

[97] Freeman, *Western Europe in the Fifth Century*, pp. 146–70.

[98] Freeman, *Four Oxford Lectures 1887*, p. 111.

[99] Freeman, *Four Oxford Lectures 1887*, pp. 83–4.

[100] Parker, 'The failure of liberal racialism: the racial ideas of E. A. Freeman', pp. 831–2. See Freeman, *The Growth of the English Constitution from the Earliest Times*, 3rd edn, pp. 1–20.

[101] Parker, 'The failure of liberal racialism: the racial ideas of E. A. Freeman', pp. 843, 845. On his son who had emigrated to Virginia, ibid. pp. 844–5.

(1861–1927), who was appointed to the Regius Chair of Modern History in Cambridge in 1902. Despite the age-gap, and despite the fact that he was never a colleague of Freeman, Bury nevertheless had a high regard for him. F. J. C. Hearnshaw, who was responsible for the posthumous publication of Bury's *The Invasion of Europe by the Barbarians*, called Freeman 'his friend and master'.[102] Bury himself wrote in the preface to his own first monograph: 'Speaking of Mr Freeman, I am impelled to add that his brilliant and stimulating essays first taught me in all its bearings the truth that the Roman Empire is the key to European History.'[103] Bury's admiration for Freemen went as far as to lead him to prepare the third edition of the older scholar's *Historical Geography of Europe*, and its attendant *Atlas*, for the press.

One of the points for which Bury appreciated Freeman was his sense of the unity of medieval and modern history.[104] Although he is rightly remembered as a Classicist and Byzantinist,[105] like Freeman he had wide ranging interests, and he felt particularly attracted to Modern History because it was more obviously linked to the present.[106] Yet he insisted on the value of all history and on the particular need to study periods other than the modern. His works on the early Middle Ages, like those of Freeman, are injected with references to recent events: the rival Hungarian and Romanian claims in Transylvania, for instance, surface in his discussion of the Roman settlement of Dacia.[107] He also, like Freeman, threw himself into modern debates, writing a notable pamphlet attacking the historical justifications for the outbreak of war put forward by German historians in 1914.[108]

Unlike Freeman, however, Bury was not a proud Englishman. Born in Ireland, where his father was an Anglican Rector, his initial training was at Trinity College Dublin, where he was appointed professor, first of Modern History in 1893, and then of Greek in 1898, before moving to Cambridge in 1902. In addition to being a student in Dublin, he also studied at Göttingen and Leipzig.[109] Not surprisingly, he was fully aware of developments in German scholarship, but as a hugely gifted linguist he was well appraised of publications in other West European, and, indeed, Slavonic languages. He had a particular interest in Slav affairs, and his 1914 pamphlet was dedicated to showing that the current conflict was not a simple one 'between Teutonic and Slavonic civilisation', as claimed by some Germans.[110] In addition he had a love for Italy, and after 1918 he spent his winters in Rome, dying there in 1927.

---

[102] Bury, *The Invasion of Europe by the Barbarians*, p. v.
[103] Bury, *A History of the Later Roman Empire from Arcadius to Irene*, vol. 1, p. xii.
[104] Bury, 'The Science of History (1903)', p. 12.
[105] Cameron, 'Bury, Baynes and Toynbee'.
[106] Temperley, 'The historical ideas of J. B. Bury', p. xxii.
[107] Bury, *The Invasion of Europe by the Barbarians*, p. 23.
[108] Bury, *Germany and Slavonic Civilisation*. Versions in (at least) Dutch, Italian, French, and Danish followed in 1915.
[109] On Bury see Whitby, 'John Bagnell Bury', *Oxford Dictionary of National Biography*. Also Baynes, *A Bibliography of the Works of J. B. Bury, with a Memoir by Norman H. Baynes*.
[110] Bury, *Germany and Slavonic Civilisation*, p. 1.

Bury, not being an Englishman, did not share Freeman's prejudices, or at least he did not share all of them: for he was not without bias, despite his reputation for 'objectivity and precision'.[111] Although his views on historical detachment are ambiguous, he finally came out in clear opposition to impartiality in a letter on the writing of history, addressed to a newspaper in 1926: 'I do not think that freedom from bias is possible, and I do not think it is desirable. Whoever writes completely free from bias will produce a colourless and dull work.'[112] He himself had the obvious biases of his age: he lamented the lack of trade in the Roman Empire, which he thought might have been saved by a good dose of Adam Smith.[113] More important for a historian of Late Antiquity was his religious scepticism (despite his father's calling)—much like that of his hero Gibbon, whose *Decline and Fall* he edited, adding significant notation. This scepticism is most obvious in his *Life of St Patrick*,[114] in which Bury blazed a new trail in attempting to portray the saint as a late Roman figure and to remove him from the context in which he had been placed by Irish hagiography. At the same time, however, his agnosticism led him to overlook the spiritual side of his subject.

While Bury came to acknowledge the positive side to bias in a historian, he also had a keen sense of history as a discipline. For him history was a science, as his inaugural lecture in the Cambridge Chair proclaimed—though here used the word in the sense of *scientia* or *Wissenschaft*.[115] In his view, history as a discipline was in the process of radical change.[116] Up until the mid-nineteenth century it had been an art, dominated by moral philosophy and rhetoric.[117] It had shaken itself free as a result of the development of the scientific movement in Germany, which had begun at the same time as 'the spirit of resurgent nationality'[118]— though this association he saw as dangerous.[119] Dahlmann had rightly stressed that all history, and not just the Golden Past of the nation, should be studied.[120] At the same time Ranke's dictum, 'Ich will nur sagen wie es eigentlich gewesen' ('I wish only to present it as it really was'), was important because it pointed to the need not to transgress the province of facts.[121] Whether that does complete justice to Ranke's dictum might be doubted. When Philip Ashworth, the translator of his *History of the Latin and Teutonic Nations from 1494 to 1514*, went to visit him, Ranke remarked:

---

[111] Whitby, 'John Bagnell Bury'; Goldstein, 'J. B. Bury's Philosophy of History: a reappraisal', p. 897.

[112] Bury, 'A letter on the writing of history (1926)'.

[113] Bury, 'Appendix. Causes of the survival of the Roman Empire in the East (1900)', p. 238.

[114] Bury, *The Life of St Patrick and his Place in History*. Another sceptical Irishman, Thompson, in *Who was Saint Patrick?*, p. xv, said of this 'epoch-making biography', that 'for the first time [it] applied modern methods to the study of Patrick', as a result of which 'the right questions can more and more be formulated...'

[115] Goldstein, 'J. B. Bury's Philosophy of History', p. 906.

[116] Bury, 'The Science of History', p. 4.

[117] Bury, 'The Science of History', p. 11.

[118] Bury, 'The Science of History', p. 7.

[119] Temperley, 'The historical ideas of J. B. Bury', pp. iii–iv.

[120] Bury, 'The Science of History', p. 8.   [121] Bury, 'The Science of History', p. 10.

Great as is the respect and veneration in which I hold Sir Walter Scott, I cannot help regretting he was not more available for the purposes of a historian than he is. If fiction must be built upon facts, facts should never be contorted to meet the ends of the novelist. What valuable lessons were not to be drawn from facts to which the great English novelist had the key; yet, by reason of the fault to which I have referred, I have been unable to illustrate many of my assertions by reference to him.[122]

'Wie es eigenlich gewesen' would seem to indicate a need to capture the true spirit of a period. Not that Bury ignored the English tradition of history as an art: but that pertained to matters of presentation rather than to the establishment of facts or the interpretation based on them.[123]

Bury returned to the question of science six years after his Cambridge inaugural, in a paper on 'Darwinism and history'.[124] This time he was self-evidently thinking about the natural sciences—for, as Arnaldo Momigliano remarked, he had a 'restless and fertile mind'.[125] He described history as 'genetic':

The present condition of the human race is simply and...strictly the result of a causal series (or set of causal series)—a continuous succession of changes, where each state arises causally out of the preceding; and...the business of historians is to trace this genetic process, to explain each change, and ultimately to grasp the complete development of the life of humanity.[126]

He did not, however, see the Modern Age as '"the last step" in the story of man'. He had already dismissed Thomas Arnold's notion that '[i]t appears to bear marks of the fullness of time, as if there would be no future history beyond it'.[127] Rather than progress, Bury preferred to talk of a Darwinian notion of development:[128] 'the Darwinian theory made it tempting to explain the development of civilisation in terms of "adaptation to environment", "struggle for existence", "natural selection", "survival of the fittest", etc.' And this was an approach that he thought the German historian Otto Seeck had already applied to the study of decline of Graeco-Roman civilization in his *Untergang der antiken Welt*.[129] But whereas the biologist might talk of natural selection, civilization was to be explained in the psychical sphere.[130] For the historian '[t]he problem is psychical, but it is analogous to the main problem of the biologist'.[131] And here he looked to the work of Karl Lamprecht with his notion of *Kulturgeschichte* and of sciences of the mind, *Geisteswissenschaften*.[132] Despite the reference to the 'psychical sphere', he seems not to have been thinking

[122] Ranke, *History of the Latin and Teutonic Nations from 1494 to 1514*, trans. Ashworth, p. vi.
[123] Goldstein, 'J. B. Bury's Philosophy of History', pp. 906, 909.
[124] Bury, 'Darwinism and History (1909)'.
[125] Cited by Goldstein, 'J. B. Bury's Philosophy of History', p. 904.
[126] Bury, 'Darwinism and History', pp. 25–6. There is a useful discussion in Goldstein, 'J. B. Bury's Philosophy of History', pp. 898–900.
[127] Bury, 'The Science of History', p. 14. On Bury's distinction between evolution and moral progress, Goldstein, 'J. B. Bury's Philosophy of History', pp. 913–15.
[128] Bury, 'Darwinism and History', p. 32.
[129] Bury, 'Darwinism and History', p. 34, with n. 1, citing Seeck, *Untergang der antiken Welt*.
[130] Bury, 'Darwinism and History', p. 35.
[131] Bury, 'Darwinism and History', p. 42.   [132] Bury, 'Darwinism and History', pp. 38–9.

of Freud: and when he raised the same issue towards the end of his life in his study of *The Idea of Progress*, he referred to the views of the now largely-forgotten Herbert Spencer, together with Eduard von Hartmann's *Philosophy of the Unconscious*.[133]

Alongside any general lines of development Bury also insisted on the importance of the haphazard, or, in Temperley's definition, contingency:[134] 'The collision of two unconnected sequences may be fraught with great results. The sudden death of a leader or a marriage without issue, to take simple cases, has again and again led to permanent political consequences.'[135] As Temperley noted, it is in the early sections of his second study of the Later Roman Empire, dealing with the period from the death of Theodosius to that of Justinian, that one can best see the application of Bury's notions of Darwinian development and contingency[136]—though Doris Goldstein has rather modified Temperley's contrast between the interpretation in his 1923 account, and the 1889 version which dealt with the period from Arcadius to Irene, where there is slightly more emphasis on general causes.[137] Barbarians had begun entering the Empire from early in its history, but it was not until the Huns put pressure on the Goths in the late fourth century that they presented any major problem. This was made worse by the defeat and death of Valens at the battle of Adrianople, and by Theodosius' subsequent settlement of the Visigoths. A further misfortune was the death of Theodosius, leaving two young sons, neither of whom was competent. Stilicho, and after him Aetius, managed to stave off disaster, but Stilicho in particular suffered from being of Germanic descent.

Bury looked once again at the Fall of Rome, with greater emphasis on the barbarians, in his *Invasion of Europe*. Here he began with the Germanic peoples and their long-established relations with the Empire, which meant that they had been influenced by Rome well before they settled within the Empire's borders. He was keen to cut the barbarians down to size, arguing that, before the fourth century, they were not particularly numerous, and thus did not present a great threat to Rome: 'The enormous figures for the German armies given by many of the chroniclers of the time are absolutely untrustworthy: not only are they on a priori grounds impossible, but they are inconsistent among themselves and inconsistent with the statements of those who were most likely to know.'[138] Matters changed dramatically with the arrival of the Huns. The failure of the Empire to deal with the Visigoths as they fled southwards, was to prove fatal. Stilicho's position, a German leading a Germanized army against other Germanic peoples, and at the same time in conflict with rivals in both parts of the Empire, was impossible.[139]

---

[133] Bury, *The Idea of Progress*, pp. 335–46.

[134] Temperley, 'The historical ideas of J. B. Bury', pp. xxiv–v.

[135] Bury, 'Darwinism and History', p. 36.

[136] Temperley, 'The historical ideas of J. B. Bury', pp. xxv–vii; Bury, *History of the Later Roman Empire from the Death of Theodosius I to the death of Justinian*.

[137] Goldstein, 'J. B. Bury's Philosophy of History', pp. 901–2.

[138] Bury, *The Invasion of Europe by the Barbarians*, pp. 42–3. Unfortunately, he does not explain who he thought ought to have known.

[139] Bury, *The Invasion of Europe by the Barbarians*, pp. 64–5, 70, 82–7.

Despite the presence of the Visigoths in Italy, Spain, and then Gaul, and also despite the collapse of the Rhine frontier and the ravaging of Gaul and Spain by the Vandals and Sueves, Bury stressed 'the gradual nature of the process by which Western Europe passed from the power of the Roman to that of the Teuton'.[140] He emphasized the fact that the process by which the barbarians were settled was a Roman one. The Roman system of *hospitalitas*, which he (arguably wrongly)[141] thought involved the transfer of a third of the produce of an estate to a billeted 'guest', was, in his view, transformed into a policy of a land allocation: in the Visigothic case the barbarian soldier received two thirds of an estate, elsewhere a third. 'The change [from Roman to Teutonic rule] was not accomplished without much violence and even continuous warfare; but it was not cataclysmic.'[142]

For Bury the establishment of the Visigoths and Burgundians, as well as the initial settlement of the Salian Franks, in Gaul, and that of the Sueves and Vandals in Spain marked the end of the first phase of the dismemberment of the Western Empire. The Vandal take-over of Africa and the maritime activities of the resulting kingdom dominated the second phase.[143] The Vandals, who were a relatively small group, with perhaps 15,000 fighting men,[144] were able to establish themselves in Africa because of Gaiseric's cunning and the rivalry between Boniface and Aetius. They also benefitted from the emergence of Attila's Huns. Bury does not paint the Huns as a completely alien group. Indeed, he stresses the fact that they had already been partially Germanized: witness the Germanic names of a number of members of the royal family, Attila included.[145] He also plays down the significance of the battle of the Catalaunian Plains: it was not a surprising victory. Attila was retreating from Orleans, and it is inconceivable that Aetius would have risked battle had he expected to lose. Even if Attila had won, the effect would have been short-lived, because in his kingdom everything depended on his own personality.[146] The battle of the Nedao, following Attila's death, when the Germanic subjects of the Huns overthrew their masters, was far more significant.[147] In a way, the most important point about Attila's empire was that it had actually held back a number of Germanic groups, and thus delayed their entry into the Roman Empire, making it more gradual and less disruptive than it might have been.[148]

Far more important for Bury than the Huns, were the Vandals:

The very existence of their kingdom in Africa, and of their naval power in the Mediterranean, acted as a powerful protection for the growth of the new German kingdoms in Gaul and Spain, and ultimately helped the founding of a German kingdom in Italy, by dividing, diverting, and weakening the forces of the Empire. The Vandals had got

---

[140] Bury, *The Invasion of Europe by the Barbarians*, p. 110.
[141] See Goffart, *Barbarians and Romans*, p. 41.
[142] Bury, *The Invasion of Europe by the Barbarians*, pp. 110–11.
[143] Bury, *The Invasion of Europe by the Barbarians*, p. 114.
[144] Bury, *The Invasion of Europe by the Barbarians*, p. 118.
[145] Bury, *The Invasion of Europe by the Barbarians*, pp. 141–2.
[146] Bury, *The Invasion of Europe by the Barbarians*, pp. 150–1.
[147] Bury, *The Invasion of Europe by the Barbarians*, p. 154.
[148] Bury, *The Invasion of Europe by the Barbarians*, p. 156.

round, as it were, to the rear of the Empire; and the effect of their powerful presence there was enhanced by the hostile and aggressive attitude which they continuously adopted.[149]

The effect of the Vandals, however, was all the greater, because the Roman government itself was falling to pieces.

Ricimer's position was impossible, because of the collapse of the House of Theodosius, and the absence of a universally accepted Western Emperor.[150] After his death the intrigues of Julius Nepos and Orestes led to the revolt of Odovacer, and the settlement of his troops in Italy. Yet with no major tribal following, his position was weak, and he was soon overthrown by the Ostrogoth Theodoric. With the Ostrogoths, Bury turned his attention to constitutional matters, following in the wake of the Germans, Mommsen and Sybel.[151] As in his discussion of the initial barbarian settlements, he stressed the extent to which government was largely Roman: the constitution of Theodoric's Italy was essentially that of Odovacer's, which in turn was a direct continuation of the Empire. There was change, but it was slow.

In Gaul he similarly stressed the slow rate of change, insisting that the Frankish expansion took place over generations.[152] And at least in the territory which Clovis took from Syagrius, Roman government must have still been in place.[153] Bury, nevertheless, attributed a great deal to Clovis, seeing him as a cunning politician: his conversion to Catholicism he presented as a deliberate choice.[154] Perhaps surprisingly, given his sceptical attitude towards Christianity, he followed Gregory of Tours in seeing the Arianism of other Germanic kingdoms as being a crucial element in their failure:

> I think it is not too much to lay down the general proposition that the Arian heresy was one main cause of the striking fact that the East German peoples who had begun so brilliantly, sweeping, as it were, all before them, ended their career in failure. The three leading cases are the Vandals, the Visigoths, and the Ostrogoths.[155]

Turning to the Lombards Bury presented a rather different picture.[156]. Once again he noted their contacts with Rome, for which they acted as federates before their entry into the Empire.[157] When he reached the Lombard settlement, however, he paused to address what had been the great historiographical issues raised by Manzoni and Troya—and he most certainly knew the latter's work.[158] Did the Romans

---

[149] Bury, *The Invasion of Europe by the Barbarians*, p. 161.
[150] Bury, *The Invasion of Europe by the Barbarians*, pp. 162–4.
[151] Bury, *The Invasion of Europe by the Barbarians*, pp. 186–202.
[152] Bury, *The Invasion of Europe by the Barbarians*, p. 220.
[153] Bury, *The Invasion of Europe by the Barbarians*, p. 247.
[154] Bury, *The Invasion of Europe by the Barbarians*, p. 240.
[155] Bury, *The Invasion of Europe by the Barbarians*, pp. 214–15.
[156] Bury, *The Invasion of Europe by the Barbarians*, p. 257.
[157] Bury, *The Invasion of Europe by the Barbarians*, p. 262.
[158] Bury, *The Invasion of Europe by the Barbarians*, p. 269. Bury cites Troya by name. Other historians mentioned in the course of the work include Dahn, Gibbon, Grimm, Kossinna, Kurth, Lamprecht, Mommsen, Sybel, and Vinogradov.

of Italy under the Lombards keep their own law as had their counterparts under the Ostrogoths, and the Gauls under the Franks? He noted that there was no evidence for separate Roman courts, and assumed uniformity of government for Lombards and Italians, but reckoned that in civil cases involving Romans alone, they would have kept their own law.[159] On the vexed question of the status of the Italians, and of their land, he turned to an article by Vinogradov, which, however, had appeared in Russian, and had therefore been missed by other scholars. In the Russian's view, the Lombards resorted to the allocation not of land, but of produce, thus conforming to the older Roman version of *hospitalitas*. As a result, free Italians were tributary to the Lombards. They were thus dependent, but they were not enslaved.[160]

Bury concluded his consideration of the barbarians with a chapter on Lombard law, which ends with a brief comparison between Italy and England, which turns, perhaps rather unexpectedly, into a traditional assertion of the virtues of English democracy. While the Anglo-Saxon assemblies had genuine influence, those of the Lombards did nothing except witness donations, leaving justice entirely in the hands of the king.[161] One seems to be back in the patriotic world of Freeman. Yet for the most part, despite his appreciation of the older scholar, Bury's work is markedly different. Although they were both influenced by scientific developments, Freeman's personal use of the science of language led him further and further into racialism, while Bury saw one requirement of scientific history as being the rejection of nationalism.

11.5 HODGKIN AND ITALY

If the closing paragraphs of Bury's *Invasion of Europe* seem to look to Freeman, the dominant influence on the last chapters is in fact that of another Englishman: Thomas Hodgkin (1831–1913), from whom he could even have derived the comparison between the Lombard assembly and the Anglo-Saxon *folc-mote*.[162] Unlike Freeman or Bury, Hodgkin held no university post—like Gibbon, or like Freeman in his years at Somerleaze, he wrote as an independent scholar, though he received an honorary Doctorate of Civil Law from Oxford for his translation of Cassiodorus's letters in 1886, and was a founder member of the British Academy in 1902. As a Quaker he had not been able to attend Oxford or Cambridge, but was, instead, a student at University College, London. He intended to become a lawyer, but health problems prompted him to go into banking, first in Whitehaven, and then in Newcastle, where he established a notably caring bank, which would later be

[159] Bury, *The Invasion of Europe by the Barbarians*, pp. 269, 271.
[160] Bury, *The Invasion of Europe by the Barbarians*, pp. 269–72.
[161] Bury, *The Invasion of Europe by the Barbarians*, p. 291.
[162] Brown, 'Gibbon, Hodgkin and the Invaders of Italy', p. 153.

absorbed into Lloyds.[163] Working initially at weekends, before retiring early from the banking industry, between 1880 and 1899 Hodgkin produced, among other works, his eight-volume *Italy and her invaders*—which has reasonably been compared to Gibbon's *Decline and Fall*,[164] and which Bury regarded as one of the few significant contributions to non-English history made by an Englishman in the nineteenth century.[165]

Despite the admiration of both Bury and Freeman, Hodgkin's approach is remarkably different from that of either of them, though like the latter he showed some enthusiasm for 'golden-haired Teutons'.[166] In composing a vast narrative, he was obviously an heir to Gibbon, while his reading owed much to Guizot, though the interpretation he put on his writings were those of an English liberal.[167] While predominantly a narrative history, *Italy and her invaders* does pause occasionally to comment on 'the Life of the People'.[168] Hodgkin's account of the 'Causes of the fall of the western Empire' is, in fact, notable for its emphasis on social and economic issues, rather than on the weaknesses of individual emperors.[169] Having, as a deeply committed Christian, noted that the Roman Empire fell 'because the Lord God willed it so',[170] he went on to analyse a series of socio-economic factors, among them the decline of the army and depopulation. His main emphasis falls on slavery, the pauperization of the proletariat, the oppression of the Middle Class, and on the weaknesses of the Roman taxation system, which he views specifically from the viewpoint of a 'modern scientific financier'—and one who was critical of the British land tax in India.[171] One might also note that Sismondi had advanced similar views.[172]

Alongside these secular factors, Hodgkin does, however, discuss the role of religion in the Fall of the Empire. Here, as a Quaker, who distrusted the institutional Church, he comes relatively close to the position espoused by Gibbon. Writing of the impact of monasticism, he describes the actions of monks as 'selfishness...of a higher kind'.[173] Yet, while he is critical of the Church, both as an institution and as the centre of doctrinal debate, he devotes a good deal of space to ecclesiatical history, and most especially to the history of the papacy.

Although his work has been republished in recent years as a history of the *Barbarian Invasions of the Roman Empire*, Hodgkin saw his *magnum opus* as an Italian history. His enthusiasm for Italy was kindled when, as an undergraduate, he paid

---

[163] For Hodgkin's career, Martin, 'Thomas Hodgkin'. For his scholarship, Bullough, *Italy and her invaders, Inaugural Lecture*; Brown, 'Gibbon, Hodgkin and the Invaders of Italy'. See also the introductions by Peter Heather to the Folio Society reprint of Hodgkin's *Italy and her invaders*, which appears as *The Barbarian Invasions of the Roman Empire*.

[164] Brown, 'Gibbon, Hodgkin and the Invaders of Italy'.

[165] Bullough, *Italy and her invaders*, p. 10.

[166] Heather, 'Introduction', Hodgkin, *The Barbarian Invasions*, vol. 5, p. xvii.

[167] For his indebtedness to Guizot, see Hodgkin, *Italy and her invaders*, vol. 2, ch. 13.

[168] Hodgkin, *Italy and her invaders*, vol. 3, ch. 7: vol. 8, ch. 10.

[169] Hodgkin, *Italy and her invaders*, vol. 2, ch. 9.

[170] Hodgkin, *Italy and her invaders*, vol. 2, ch. 9.

[171] Hodgkin, *Italy and her invaders*, vol. 2, ch. 9, pt. 6.   [172] See above, chapter 5.

[173] Hodgkin, *Italy and her invaders*, vol. 2, ch. 9, pt. 2.

his first visit to the country, in 1846, before unification.[174] Two years later, when he was still only seventeen, he was deeply concerned about its future, but was already thinking of its glorious past under Ostrogothic rule:

> I well remember walking with a friend on a little hill (then silent and lonely, now covered with houses), looking down on London, and discussing European politics with the earnest interest which young debates bring to such a theme. The time was in those dark days which followed the revolutions of 1848, when it seemed as if the life of the European nations would be crushed out under the heel of returned and triumphant despotism. For Italy especially, after the defeat of Novara, there seemed no hope. We talked of Mazzini, Cavour, Garibaldi, and discussed the possibility—which then seemed so infinitely remote—that there might one day be a free and united Italy. We both agreed that the vision was a beautiful one, but was there any hope of it ever becoming a reality? My friend thought there was not, and argued from the fact of Italy's divided condition in the past, that she must always be divided in the future. I, who was on the side of hope, felt the weakness of my position, and was driven backward through the centuries, till at length I took refuge in the reign of Theodoric. Surely, under the Ostrogothic king, Italy had been united, strong, and prosperous.[175]

A second visit to the peninsula, in the rather more optimistic circumstances of 1868, fired him yet further:

> I have been thoroughly bitten with the Italian Tarantula. I can understand now why Kings and Emperors in the Middle Ages flung away whole realms of dim transalpine regions to secure one bright duchy or county on the sunny side of the Great Wall.[176]

By the time that he wrote his biography of Theodoric, published in 1893, he could comment:

> The beautiful land is now united, free, and mighty; and a new generation has arisen, which, though aware of the fact that she was not always thus, has but a faint conception how much blood and how many tears, what thousands of broken hearts and broken lives went to the winning of Italy's freedom.[177]

Since Hodgkin both translated the letters of Cassiodorus, and also wrote a biography of Theodoric, the subtitle of which was 'the barbarian champion of civilisation', it is scarcely surprising that he emphasized the continuities between imperial and Ostrogothic Italy. The *civilitas* and tolerance shown by Theodoric, especially with regard to the Jews, no doubt appealed strongly to Hodgkin's Quakerism.[178] Like Bury, much of whose interpretation of the Lombards was derived from Hodgkin's, he recognized the greater brutality of the Lombards, but he showed some appreciation of their democratic institutions. His view on the much debated issue

---

[174] Heather, 'Introduction', Hodgkin, *The Barbarian Invasions of the Roman Empire*, vol. 1, p. xi.
[175] Hodgkin, *Theodoric the Goth: The Barbarian Champion of Civilisation*, pp. vi–vii.
[176] Creighton, *Life and Letters of Thomas Hodgkin*, p. 81, cited in Bullough, *Italy and her invaders*, p. 11.
[177] Hodgkin, *Theodoric the Goth*, p. vii.
[178] Hodgkin, *Theodoric the Goth*, pp. 261, 281–2.

of the Lombard treatment of the conquered Italians does, however, differ slightly from that of Bury, since, while he was content to admit that the evidence allows no solution, he accepted the tributary position of the Italians, and assumed that they were tied to the soil.[179] He did, nevertheless, accept the likelihood of generally improving conditions, but could not prove it. What had been a crucial issue for Manzoni, Troya, and, to a lesser extent, Balbo, was now something that was insoluble—though, as we have seen, Bury came to think that it had been solved by Vinogradov, albeit in Russian.

Hodgkin knew his Troya well,[180] but his scholarly connections were rather with Villari, a man closer to him in age, and who in turn came to respect his work, for the Italian cited both Hodgkin and Bury with approval.[181] Indeed, during a visit to Rome in 1894 Hodgkin met and made friends with Pasquale Villari and his English wife Linda.[182] Villari would even introduce Hodgkin to Umberto I of Italy, and the king and the Englishman discussed the coins of Charlemagne.[183] It is not, therefore, surprising to find that Hodgkin had consulted Villari by letter on points relating to the history of early medieval Italy.

Italy and her invaders was Hodgkin's *magnum opus*, but it was not only the Italian peninsula that attracted his attention. Based in the North-East of England, and living for a time in Bamburgh castle, the site of a Northumbrian royal palace, 'as an adoptive Northumbrian',[184] he became a stalwart of the region's history society and its publication *Archaeologia Aeliana*. He relished the presence of Hadrian's Wall, and became involved in the interpretation of Northumbrian history. Thus, in addition to writing about Italy, he also wrote a *History of England from the Earliest Times to the Norman Conquest*, which is notable for its northern viewpoint.[185]

11.6 THE LESSONS OF EMPIRE

In their historical writings Hodgkin and Bury do not often draw attention to modern parallels. This, and the quality of their scholarship, has meant that their work has become rather less dated than that of their contemporaries. Others writing about the Fall of Rome were more inclined to see echoes of the Roman Empire in its British counterpart. In the late nineteenth century Rome's expansion and its treatment of its provinces, and above all of *Britannia*, provided something of a blue-print for Britain's colonial administrators, as they headed to distant parts of

[179] Hodgkin, *Italy and her invaders*, vol. 6, ch. 14, pp. 586–92.
[180] Hodgkin does, however, cite Troya on numerous occasions (alongside Sismondi in vol. V, ch. 6, p. 230), just as he cites, among others, Dahn (particularly at the start of his third volume).
[181] Villari, *The Barbarian Invasions of Italy*, vol. 1, p. vi, 116.
[182] Creighton, *Life and Letters of Thomas Hodgkin*, p. 182.
[183] Creighton, *Life and Letters of Thomas Hodgkin*, pp. 226–7.
[184] Bullough, *Italy and her invaders*, p. 12.
[185] Hodgkin, *History of England from the Earliest Times to the Norman Conquest*: see Bullough, *Italy and her invaders*, p. 22.

the Empire.[186] Rome as bringer of order and civilization—in other words Rome in its heyday—was a strong role model. By the beginning of the twentieth century, however, it was not so much the lessons to be learnt from the history of the early years of the Roman Empire, as the dangers to be noted from its decline that attracted attention.

One result was that there was something of a revival of interest in Gibbon, the centenary of whose death fell in 1894, an anniversary which itself provided the cause for reconsideration of his work.[187] Changing religious attitudes over the previous decades meant that his observations on the decline of the Empire in the West could be read more calmly than had once been the case. Two years later Bury published the first volume of his edition of *Decline and Fall*, providing an up-to-date scholarly apparatus that superceded that of 1872 and Milman's of 1838–9. In 1905 Eliot Mills published a bizarre pamphlet entitled *The Decline and Fall of the British Empire: a brief account of those causes which resulted in the destruction of our late ally, together with a comparison between the British and Roman Empire. Appointed for use in the National Schools of Japan. Tokio, 2005.*[188] Pretending to be written in the early twenty-first century, this used the benefit of hindsight to identify what had gone wrong a hundred years earlier. Mills argued that had the British paid more attention to Gibbon's analysis of the Fall of Rome, their own Empire would not have collapsed.

The comparison was picked up in 1908 by Baden-Powell, the founder of the Scout Movement, who was concerned about the decline of manliness, and by Arthur Balfour, while leader of the opposition, who drew attention to the dangers of 'decadence'.[189] In 1911 the archaeologist Francis Haverfield pointed to the lessons one might learn from Rome with regard to the threat of municipal corruption.[190] Not that everyone agreed that the comparisons were instructive: J. C. Stobart, for one, argued against their value.[191]

By 1900 Rome and its Fall fitted very neatly into a British discourse about Empire and its dangers. By the second decade of the twentieth century another Empire was challenging for preeminence in the world. Like the British, the Germans also looked back to the end of Rome when considering the present. For them, however, it was not empire, civilization, and decadence that were central issues, but rather land and race. A rather different discourse would dominate studies of the fourth, fifth, and sixth centuries for the first half of the twentieth.

---

[186] See especially Seeley, *The Expansion of England*; Hingley, *Roman Officers and English Gentlemen*; Hingley, *The Recovery of Roman Britain*, pp. 306–25.

[187] Hingley, *Roman Officers and English Gentlemen*, pp. 28, 30.

[188] Hingley, *Roman Officers and English Gentlemen*, pp. 31–2.

[189] Hingley, *Roman Officers and English Gentlemen*, pp. 32–3.

[190] Hingley, *Roman Officers and English Gentlemen*, p. 36.

[191] Hingley, *Roman Officers and English Gentlemen*, pp. 33–4.

12

About Belgium
The Impact of the Great War

12.1 FRANCOPHONE SCHOLARSHIP BEFORE 1914

At exactly the time that Bury and Hodgkin were contributing to the historiography of the Later Roman Empire and of early medieval Italy and England, a different set of debates were developing in France, Germany, and Belgium. To some extent they were a continuation of the intellectual conflicts that had been sparked by the Franco-Prussian War. They continued up to, influenced, and were transformed by the greater conflict of 1914–18.

Although Fustel de Coulanges can be seen as winning his argument with Gabriel Monod over the Sichar–Chramnesind blood feud, the younger historian was better attuned to the new directions in scholarship. In particular, while Fustel had some reason for thinking that German scholarship was not superior to French in 1872,[1] Monod had a greater appreciation of the strengths of the new developments to be found in Germany. Fustel's pupil, Camille Jullian, appreciated this, as we have seen. when he went to study under Mommsen as a 'boursier-espion' in 1883.[2]

Monod's determination to introduce the best of German practice into France can be seen in a number of ways. In 1875 he founded the *Revue Historique* on the model of the *Historische Zeitschrift*.[3] In 1888 he drew up a bibliography of French history specifically in imitation of that which had been created in Germany by Dahlmann and extended by Waitz.[4] Above all, he appreciated the German seminar method, which had been developed by Ranke, and pursued it in his teaching at the École pratique des hautes études (1869–1905) and the École normale supérieure (1880–1905).[5] Despite his obviously positive impact on the teaching and dissemination of history in France, he became the butt of attacks from the Right, not least because of his crucial role in challenging the fraudulent nature of the allegations against Dreyfus—it was he who first exposed the treasonable letter supposedly written by Dreyfus as a forgery, using the traditional medievalist's skill of paleography.[6] Just as the enthusiasms of Charles Maurras and the Action Française promoted

---

[1] Fustel de Coulanges, 'De la manière d'écrire l'histoire en France et en Allemagne'.
[2] Hartog, *Le XIXe siècle et l'histoire*, p. 199; Nicolet, *La Fabrique d'une nation*, p. 228.
[3] Den Boer, *History as a Profession*, pp. 288, 330–9.
[4] Den Boer, *History as a Profession*, p. 14.
[5] Den Boer, *History as a Profession*, p. 288.   [6] Den Boer, *History as a Profession*, p. 290.

the memory of Fustel, they did nothing for the standing of Monod. In the words of a recent commentator: 'Monod died in 1912, incorruptible and with a sorely tried but unbroken faith in a future in which reason and human solidarity have the final say. He was spared the pain of witnessing the outbreak of the First World War.'[7]

Such a blessing would not be granted to Monod's near contemporary, the Belgian Godefroid Kurth (1847–1916), who held a similarly positive view of German scholarship, and indeed championed it in much the same way as did his French counterpart, although his immediate inspiration was Ranke rather than Waitz. At the University of Liège he too tried to copy Ranke's seminars, though at the same time he was also keen to preserve what he saw as the strengths of French teaching. 'The master who introduced the German interogatory method into the Belgian universities, jealously preserved the French expository method.'[8]

It was not only in his historical methodology that Kurth looked towards Germany. In *Les Origines de la civilisation moderne* he argued that European culture was the result of the combination of Christianity and the 'German spirit'[9]—not that the interpretation was confined to German scholarship, as we have seen. To Kurth's Catholicism we will return.[10] Germanic tradition he emphasized in his *Histoire poétique des Mérovingiens*, where he claimed to have identified evidence of oral tradition underlying some of the tales recounted by Gregory of Tours and by Fredegar—an approach that clearly goes back to Grimm's recounting of the *Deutsche Heldensage*. He himself stressed his dependence on Junghans and on Monod, whose Göttingen training he emphasized.[11]

All this was to have an impact on the interpretation of Merovingian history: perhaps more important, at least in the medium term, was Kurth's concern with Belgian history, and particularly with the linguistic frontier which divided the Flemish from the Walloon parts of the country. It was an issue about which he was deeply concerned,[12] and it would indeed come to be of immense importance in the 1930s and 1940s. In his own view the solution to Belgium's linguistic divide was for the country to be polyglot, as had been the case in the Middle Ages, with the whole population speaking both languages.[13] Between 1896 and 1898 he published his two-volume study of *La Frontière linguistique en Belgique et dans le Nord de la France*.[14] Here he argued that the Germanic settlement of the Flemish-speaking areas of Belgium took place as a result of the invasions of the fifth century, most

---

[7] Den Boer, *History as a Profession*, p. 290.

[8] Hanquet, 'Godefroid Kurth', p. xxxvi: 'Le maître qui introduisit dans les Universités belges la méthode d'investigation allemande, a gardé avec une fidélité jalouse la méthode française d'exposition.' See also Lyon, 'Henri Pirenne's *Réflexions d'un solitaire* and his re-evaluation of history', p. 288.

[9] Kurth, *Les Origines de la civilisation moderne*; see Hanquet, 'Godefroid Kurth', pp. xxxi–xxxv.

[10] See chapter 14.

[11] Kurth, *Histoire Poétique des Mérovingiens*, pp. 18, 21. On the impact of this work at the time of publication, Hanquet, 'Godefroid Kurth', pp. xxv–vi.

[12] Van Zeebroeck, 'L'Âge d'or médiévale', p. 213.

[13] Van Zeebroeck, 'L'Âge d'or médiévale', p. 214. [14] Kurth, *La Frontière linguistique*.

notably that of 406, and he claimed that the expansion of the Franks in this period was checked on the line of the linguistic frontier by the Roman road between Bavai and Cologne and the Charbonnière forest (which he thought an impenetrable barrier that had originally extended from the confluence of the Sambre and the Meuse to the Scheldt). He was not the first to use place names to elucidate relations between Romans and barbarians within the region. In the *Festschrift* presented to Kurth in 1908 Karl Hanquet commented:

> He did not invent toponymic research, and he was happy to acknowledge his debt to Foerstermann and Arnold. But more than anyone else he knew how to apply himself to the scientific study of Belgian place names and to rehabilitate, from previous unfortunate attempts, 'this mysterious reservoir of memories, many of which are contemporary with the first ages of a people, and which all have something to tell us about the men and things of the past'.[15]

Had he thought about Grimm's deployment of language in his justification that Schleswig and Holstein should belong to Germany, Kurth might have treated the subject with more caution.

12.2 HENRI PIRENNE

His most eminent pupil, Henri Pirenne (1862–1935), looking back from 1921, thought that his teacher should have paid more attention to the dangers of Pan-Germanism and to German militarism.[16] Yet Pirenne himself had initially been enthused by German scholarship much as both Kurth and Monod had been. Like Kurth, Pirenne was a Walloon. In the late 1870s and early 1880s he attended Kurth's lectures at the University of Liège, before heading off to Germany in 1883–4, when he studied with Wilhelm Arndt in Leipzig and with Harry Bresslau, the great diplomatist, in Berlin, where he also met Ranke and Waitz.[17] Thereafter he too became a keen promoter of German historical method. He was also deeply influenced by German approaches to economic history, notably as practised by Karl Bücher and Werner Sombart.[18] Yet more important was his contact with Karl Lamprecht (1856–1915), which was to lead to the writing of the *Histoire de Belgique*.[19] Lamprecht's 'total' approach to cultural history, or *Geistesgeschichte*, was extremely attactive to the young Pirenne, who admired his approach to the 'psychological

---

[15] Hanquet, 'Godefroid Kurth', p. xxvi.
[16] Violante, *La fine della 'grande illusione'*, p. 152. On Pirenne and Kurth, Lyon, 'The letters of Henri Pirenne to Karl Lamprecht', pp. 171–2.
[17] For a brief biography of Pirenne, Ganshof, 'Pirenne, Henri'. For his German training, Lyon, 'The letters of Henri Pirenne to Karl Lamprecht', pp. 172–3.
[18] Delogu, 'Reading Pirenne again', pp. 27–8: 'While rejecting many of the specific claims made by the various exponents of economic theory in this period, Pirenne adopted much of their way of thinking and methodology.'
[19] On Pirenne and Lamprecht, Lyon, 'The letters of Henri Pirenne to Karl Lamprecht', with the important modifications to be found in van Werveke, 'Karl Lamprecht et Henri Pirenne'.

fermentation of economic life'.[20] And Pirenne continued to cultivate his contacts with Germany up until 1914. In 1920 he said of himself and his colleague Paul Fredericq, that they were

> the only foreigners who regularly frequented the German *Historikertage* (historical conferences), and that [they] therefore had the opportunity to get to know personally the majority of the German historians.[21]

He admired the Germans and they respected him: in the very different atmosphere of the pre-War years he had been the recipient of various honorary doctorates and was corresponding fellow of a number of academies.[22]

Having spent a short while in Germany, in 1884–5 Pirenne moved on to Paris, where he worked with the great French diplomatist Arthur Giry, who held posts at the École des hautes études and the École des chartes.[23] Giry likewise had been deeply influenced by recent German study of diplomatic. In 1894 he would produce his own *Manuel de diplomatique*. His skills in the study of paleography were to involve him alongside Monod in the Dreyfus affair. He was also a notable urban historian, and his first major work was his *Histoire de la ville de Saint-Omer et de ses institutions jusqu'au XIVe siècle*. Given that Pirenne had already trained with Bresslau, one might guess that the Belgian was more indebted to Giry for his insights into urban history than into diplomatic history.

Shortly after he returned to Belgium Pirenne was appointed to a post at the Flemish university of Ghent, although he always taught in French (which would come to be a significant issue after 1914). Three years later, in 1889, he produced his first major publication, the *Histoire de la constitution de la ville de Dinant*. Pirenne, whose attitudes were very much those of the urban bourgoisie of late nineteenth-century Belgium,[24] would follow up this study of a single town with his massive *Histoire de Belgique*, commissioned originally by Lamprecht,[25] which presents the creation of the state in 1830 as a natural development which began in the Flemish cities of the eleventh century.[26]

Pirenne's most famous interventions in the study of early Medieval history all date to the period after 1914, although he had already set out what would be his basic contentions in an article on 'L'Origine des constitutions urbaines au Moyen Âge', which was published in Monod's *Revue historique* in 1895.[27] Here he argued

---

[20] Lyon, 'The letters of Henri Pirenne to Karl Lamprecht', p. 212. For an assessment of Lamprecht's influence on Pirenne's thought, ibid. pp. 173–9; Lyon, 'Henri Pirenne's Réflexions d'un solitaire and his re-evaluation of history', pp. 288–90; see Delogu, 'Reading Pirenne again', p. 28.

[21] Pirenne, 'Souvenirs de captivité en Allemagne', p. 540. For examples of his attendance at *Historikertage*, Lyon, 'The letters of Henri Pirenne to Karl Lamprecht', pp. 179–80.

[22] Pirenne, 'Souvenirs de captivité', p. 541; Lyon, 'The letters of Henri Pirenne to Karl Lamprecht', p. 180.

[23] For Pirenne's period in Paris, Lyon, 'The letters of Henri Pirenne to Karl Lamprecht', p. 172.

[24] Dhondt, 'Henri Pirenne, historien des institutions urbaines'.

[25] Lyon, 'The letters of Henri Pirenne to Karl Lamprecht', pp. 164–71.

[26] Pirenne, *Histoire de Belgique*.

[27] Pirenne, 'L'Origine des constitutions urbaines au Moyen Âge', p. 57. See Delogu, 'Reading Pirenne again', pp. 17–18.

that Roman city life survived the Germanic invasions, as did the Mediterranean as a functioning economic unit: the decline of the economy was slow, but would culminate in the emergence of the Mediterranean as a 'lac musulman' ('Muslim lake'). But if Pirenne's basic theses—that the Germanic invasions had little effect, and that the end result of the developments of the post-Roman period was the existence of an Islamic sea—were already in mind in the 1890s, their full development needs to be understood against the events of 1914–18, and the Belgian historian's personal experience of those events. Fortunately, his autobiographical account, his *Souvenirs de captivité* of the years from 1916 to 1918, provides a remarkable source for understanding the context in which his ideas developed.[28]

12.3 PIRENNE IN THE GREAT WAR

In the immediate aftermath of the German seizure of Belgium, Pirenne remained in post, along with all his colleagues, in the University of Ghent. He and the early-modern historian Paul Fredericq, however, were openly opposed to the take-over. They refused to teach, and in particular they (along with the majority of their colleagues) refused to teach in Flemish.[29] As a result of their non-compliance with the regime they were attacked by the *Vlaamsche Post* for not recognizing that the Germans had liberated the Flemish from the Latin yoke.[30] Then, on 18th March 1916, Pirenne was arrested.[31] He was, however, treated with the utmost courtesy: the Germans automatically held professors in a high regard.[32] He was assured that the war would not last long: 'It was the first time that I had the opportunity to note the incredible blindness of the "intellectuals" of modern Germany'.[33] But Pirenne himself had also been blind: he suddenly realized that he had no idea of the political views of the German professors he knew so well. As he considered the matter he came to the conclusion that they simply concentrated on their own research:

> Accustomed to absolutism for centuries, it did not strike them that they themselves were the State. They turned it into an independent being, a sort of mystic entity, a power endowed with all the attributes of force and intelligence. At the desired moment all were ready to obey it, not like citizens, but like servants.[34]

The officer charged with looking after Pirenne, a Dr Clausen, explained that Edward VII had encircled Germany, that the Russians in Serbia were plotting, that Kaiser Wilhelm had tried to maintain the peace after Sarajevo, but that the invasion of Belgium had become a military necessity: that the English outcry—to

---

[28] Pirenne, 'Souvenirs de captivité'. On what follows see especially Violante, *La fine della 'grande illusione'*.

[29] Pirenne, 'Souvenirs de captivité', pp. 543–4.   [30] Pirenne, 'Souvenirs de captivité', p. 543.

[31] Pirenne, 'Souvenirs de captivité', p. 544.   [32] Pirenne, 'Souvenirs de captivité', p. 546.

[33] Pirenne, 'Souvenirs de captivité', p. 546.   [34] Pirenne, 'Souvenirs de captivité', p. 547.

which we will return—was hypocrisy and that France was mad to want to control the coast of Flanders:

> But in the face of the conspiracy launched against her, Germany would inevitably be victorious. No army was capable of resisting hers. She alone understood the beauty and holiness of war, and her militarism was nothing other than the most grandiose manifestation of the sublimity of its *Kultur*.[35]

Kultur Pirenne leaves in German, the word implying, as it had for Lamprecht and has done since, civilization in its broadest sense.

Pirenne was quickly moved to a prisoner of war camp in Krefeld, outside Cologne, where he was interned along with English, Belgian, French, and Russian officers. After the atmosphere in occupied Ghent, however, this was a liberation.[36] Meanwhile the arrest of Pirenne and also of Fredericq prompted an outcry among their colleagues. The Germans tried to persuade the two internees to go back to their teaching duties. Having refused, they were moved further into Germany: Pirenne being sent to a camp in Holzminden. This was very much seedier than Krefeld, though committees within the camp did succeed in improving the food, and the students set up a library and 'university' where the professors could teach. Pirenne gave two courses. One on economic history, which would form the basis of his *Histoire de l'Europe*,[37] was given to a group of two to three hundred Russians who had been captured in Liège in 1914. The other concerned the history of Belgium, and was directed to the Belgian inmates.[38] The prison regime could, however, be difficult: a Dominican who wrote 'Cur Germani sint superporci' ('Why the Germans are superpigs') was put into confinement as a lunatic.[39] Pirenne's own lectures were closely monitored, and denounced when he started to lecture before the arrival of those responsible for checking on them.[40]

Meanwhile, the captivity of Pirenne and Fredericq had become an international issue, causing a great deal of embarrassment for the Germans:

> The respect for scientific freedom that Germany has always boasted, and the impossibility in which she found herself of justifying her actions towards us, without being obliged to unveil her designs on Flanders and Belgium prematurely, put her in a difficult position and gave plenty of scope to the protesters.

As a result, Pirenne and Fredericq were transferred to the university city of Jena where they lived under supervision, but despite the greater comfort Pirenne was sad to leave Holzminden, where he felt he had had something valuable to contribute:

> For the first time in my life I felt that I was genuinely useful, because, also for the first time I found myself in contact with the very base of my existence.[41]

---

[35] Pirenne, 'Souvenirs de captivité', pp. 547–8.
[36] Pirenne, 'Souvenirs de captivité', pp. 548–9.
[37] Pirenne, *Histoire de l'Europe des Invasions au XVIe siècle*, 'Avant-propos'.
[38] Pirenne, 'Souvenirs de captivité', p. 555.   [39] Pirenne, 'Souvenirs de captivité', p. 554.
[40] Pirenne, 'Souvenirs de captivité', p. 556.   [41] Pirenne, 'Souvenirs de captivité', p. 560.

The journey to Jena gave Pirenne another example of German subservience: the guard who was to accompany him treated him as no more than prisoner 10,823 inside the camp, but once outside he behaved as the valet of the Herr Professor.[42] Having arrived in Jena he was committed to the care of *Burgermeister* Fuchs. The university itself seemed to be flourishing, yet at the same time no one showed any understanding of social or political reality: everyone was concerned either with their specialism or their title.[43] Perhaps the professors were less blind than Pirenne wished to admit—for to say that they understood what was happening would have made them culpable. And indeed Pirenne singled out an unnamed specialist in the English Middle Ages, who, he said was both blinded by nationalism and deeply influenced by Gobineau. This unnamed medievalist praised Germany as a young country—though he seemed to know little about it in actual fact, having no idea, for instance, about the existence of German socialism: he denounced France as decadent, England as being on the verge of decline, and America as being in love with the dollar.[44]

Observing the Germans day-by-day Pirenne came to the conclusion that their academic liberty, which he had so praised before 1914, was a mirage. The professors, for all their methodological skill, had no contact with the country at large. The Germans had order, competence, and administrative ability, but no spontaneity. Thus they could not understand the failure of their diplomats, or why other nations did not accept their offers of peace.[45] They were insensitive enough to invite Pirenne and Fredericq to collaborate with some Jena professors on a history of Flanders: the two Belgians naturally refused. No one had stopped to think that even the invitation might be construed as an insult (i.e. that the Germans had no sense of others) or that the Belgian population had been reduced to slavery.[46]

Then suddenly, out of the blue, Pirenne and Fredericq were accused of intrigue with the resistance back in Belgium. They were moved to places where they would be rather more isolated. Fredericq was sent to Burgel, and Pirenne to Kreuzburg an der Werra. He was able to move about the village, but all his actions were monitored. He settled down to learn Russian and to write—at this stage he was working on his *Histoire de l'Europe*.[47] He got into the habit of talking to the local aristocrat, whose attitudes he found peculiarly blinkered. The latter thought that liberty was a specifically German virtue, and was astonished to discover that, while slavery was only abolished in Germany in the nineteenth century, elsewhere its abolition had occurred in the thirteenth.[48] Pirenne advised his readers not to forget that Germany was a good deal closer to the *Ancien Régime* than were the Belgians.[49]

As the tide turned militarily against Germany, the people of Kreuzburg became more bewildered. There were those in the village who even wondered if it would have been better to have allied with France rather than Austria, not realizing that Alsace-Lorraine rendered this a completely impossible scenario![50] Pirenne did

[42] Pirenne, 'Souvenirs de captivité', p. 829.
[43] Pirenne, 'Souvenirs de captivité', p. 831.
[44] Pirenne, 'Souvenirs de captivité', p. 833.
[45] Pirenne, 'Souvenirs de captivité', p. 836.
[46] Pirenne, 'Souvenirs de captivité', p. 838.
[47] Pirenne, 'Souvenirs de captivité', p. 841.
[48] Pirenne, 'Souvenirs de captivité', p. 843.
[49] Pirenne, 'Souvenirs de captivité', p. 844.
[50] Pirenne, 'Souvenirs de captivité', p. 846.

manage to persuade his interlocutor that there was no Belgian conspiracy against Germany, but he could not make him understand why the Belgians might want to resist. And the Germans he talked to in 1917 were convinced that Belgium had either to belong to England or to Germany; and England, which they had assumed would remain neutral in 1914, was now the mortal enemy.[51]

The spirits of the people of Kreuzburg were briefly raised by the Treaty of Brest-Litovsk, which ended the threat from Russia,[52] but otherwise there was growing despair, and a collapse in respect for authority, 'this ultimate and supreme framework of Germany'.[53] Even Pirenne was taken by surprise at the speed of the German collapse, which he could now discuss each evening, since his wife and son had been allowed to join him. He was struck by the calmness of the revolution in Germany when it came, and by the assumption made by the Germans that peace would allow an immediate return to the *status quo* of 1914: they had instantly forgotten the horrors of war, and, as important from Pirenne's point of view, the enslavement of Belgium.[54] His return home was efficiently arranged. At Eisenach he and his family were joined by Fredericq. Two days later they crossed into Belgium and felt as if they were waking from a bad dream.[55]

12.4 KARL LAMPRECHT AT THE OUTBREAK OF WAR

Of course, it was not as simple as that. The *Souvenirs de captivité* provide a fascinating picture of Pirenne's immediate circumstances, but his depiction of a people, including the professoriat, simply following orders rings only partially true, and his own subsequent behaviour suggests that he came increasingly to apportion some blame to the German intelligensia. Many leading academics had been vociferous in favour of war. On 4th October 1914 ninety-three German intellectuals, including fifty-six professors, set down an *Aufruf an die Kulturwelt* ('Appeal to the Civilized World') in which they replied to the charge that Germans had 'raped' Belgium.[56] They rejected the identification of Wilhelm II with Attila (inspired by the Kaiser's own encouragement to his troops to act like Huns in crushing the Boxer Rebellion) and denied that atrocities had been committed by Germans, or that their troops had been responsible for the destruction of Louvain town-hall: indeed, they claimed (falsely) that they had tried to save it.[57] In the East, by contrast, the Russian hordes were drinking the blood of women and children,

---

[51] Pirenne, 'Souvenirs de captivité', p. 848–9.   [52] Pirenne, 'Souvenirs de captivité', pp. 850.
[53] Pirenne, 'Souvenirs de captivité', p. 853.   [54] Pirenne, 'Souvenirs de captivité', pp. 855–6.
[55] Pirenne, 'Souvenirs de captivité', pp. 857–8.
[56] *Aufruf an die Kulturwelt*, pp. 47–9. For recent comment on the *Aufruf*, see Whyte, 'Anglo-German Conflict in Popular Fiction 1870–1914', pp. 43, 45, 48. On the involvement of academics in the propaganda arguments, Violante, *La fine della 'grande illusione'*, pp. 99–108.
[57] Lamprecht soon recognized the fallacy of this account: van Werveke, 'Karl Lamprecht et Henri Pirenne', pp. 45–7, 57–8. On the image of the Germans behaving like Huns and Vandals at Louvain, Martin, 'Nietzsche as hate-figure in Britain's Great War', p. 153.

while among the Allies there were Mongols and Negroes. This was a rather less accurate or reasoned piece of propaganda than the pamphlet produced by a group of Oxford historians entitled *Why we are at War*, or than Bury's *Germany and Slavonic Civilisation*, which debunked the argument that what was at issue was a conflict of civilizations, pointing instead to a very concrete set of political developments. Only four German professors openly contradicted the claims of the 93: Wilhelm Foerster, Albert Einstein, Otto Bueck, and Georg Nicolai wrote their own *Aufruf an die Europäer*. None of them were historians. A number of major historians were, however, included in the 93, among them the Church historian Adolf von Harnack, the classicist Eduard Meyer,[58] and—probably most notable from Pirenne's point of view—Karl Lamprecht.

Pirenne had been a friend of Lamprecht from 1894, and the two continued to correspond after the outbreak of war.[59] Surprisingly, they were still corresponding amicably after the *Aufruf an die Kulturwelt*, about which the Belgian scholar must have known—it may later have prompted him to support the erasure of Lamprecht's name from among the associate members of the Académie royale.[60] Pirenne's final letter even postdates his discovery that his old German friend had been sent to Brussels by the Kaiser to facilitate the German reorganization of Belgium—he had sought the cooperation of Guy Des Marez, and had received a forthright rebuff, about which Fredericq told Pirenne.[61]

Lamprecht had from early 1913 been an enthusiastic supporter of the Kaiser's policies.[62] Apart from signing the *Aufruf*, and acting as the Kaiser's agent, he was also delivering patriotic lectures supporting the war, notably his address *Über Belgien* delivered in Dresden on 4th March 1915. The lecture was delivered as part of a great occasion, which began with an organ voluntary followed by two songs, the first was Hoffmann von Fallersleben's poem of 1840, *An den Stamm der Vlamen* ('To the Flemings'): the second by the Flemish poet Emmanuel Heil, was the 1870 poem *Oproep aan de Dietschers*—which Lamprecht mistranslated as 'Aufruf an die Deutschen' ('Appeal to the Germans'), whereas Heil had used the word *Dietscher* in the sense of *Großniederländisch*, that is the Dutch and the Flemings combined, but without the Germans.[63] After briefly discussing the poems as evidence that the Flemings were German, Lamprecht talked about Brussels as a Flemish city, and about the cultural and geographical distinctions between the Flemish north of Belgium and the Walloon south. He noted the borders with the French cultural region, though what he described follows neither the modern political frontier nor

---

[58] He would be the recipient of Robertson's *Britain versus Germany: An Open Letter to Professor Eduard Meyer*.

[59] Lyon, 'The letters of Henri Pirenne to Karl Lamprecht', pp. 230–1; Violante, *La fine della 'grande illusione'*, p. 148.

[60] Van Werveke, 'Karl Lamprecht et Henri Pirenne', p. 53.

[61] Van Werveke, 'Karl Lamprecht et Henri Pirenne', pp. 44–7, with the relevant section of Fredericq's diary on pp. 57–8.

[62] Van Werveke, 'Karl Lamprecht et Henri Pirenne', p. 47.

[63] The text of the full ceremony, with the lecture is available at <http://www.zum.de/psm/1wk/lamprecht.php>.

that of 1914: he presented Lille as a Flemish city (something that the Lilleois would accept). He then pointed out that Beethoven's family was Flemish. Where, he asked, did this distinction between Fleming and Walloon come from? Its origins lay in the Germanic settlement of Flanders, which he traced in terms of place-names (the subject, of course, had been opened up by Kurth, and it would return to prominence in the 1930s and 1940s). It was in Belgium that the *Lex Salica*, 'das älteste aller unserere Volksrechte' ('the oldest of all our tribal laws'[64]), was compiled. Lamprecht then followed the early history of the Salians, their expansion against the Celts, and their role in Merovingian and Carolingian history. Having reached the ninth century, which was for him the great period of nation formation in Western Europe, he pointed to its importance for Belgium, in four sentences which seem to look forward in certain respects to Pirenne's *Mahomet et Charlemagne*:

> The gates of the Orient, which had been more or less closed in the seventh and eighth century, were opened again. As a result a truly international exchange of European and tropical products opened up. For the most part this trade passed through the Pillars of Hercules, thus through the Straits of Gibraltar, then through the Bay of Biscay, and ended up...yes, where did it end up? Not, as one would now think, in London which was not yet powerful enough, but on the coast of Belgium.

From there he traced the rise of Flanders as the economic centre of trade, paralleling Venice. He noted the region's architecture and painting, as well as its developing democracy. With the Burgundian court, of course, the region enters the Habsburg world. Turning to more modern times, Lamprecht looked at the aftermath of the Peace of Paris in 1815, which he read as an English neutralizing of Belgium and Holland, which at the same time left the way open for French influence, especially in Brussels, Liège, and Ghent. And so he turned to his hope for the future: which was the success of current German policy. The lecture was followed by the singing of 'O Deutschland, hoch in Ehren' ('O, Germany, high in Honour') and 'Haltet aus!' ('Endure').

Just over two months later, on 10th May, Lamprecht was dead. The death was unexpected, and Pirenne's friend and colleague Paul Fredericq initially suspected suicide following his meeting with Des Marez in Brussels. Even after discovering that Lamprecht died in a clinic, he suspected the death might have been related in some way to the visit to Belgium.[65]

Lamprecht's lecture may not appear to be anything more than a piece of propaganda, but the argument undoubtedly emerged out of his own approach to cultural history, which had previously impressed Pirenne. To Lamprecht, Flemish Belgium (and indeed French Flanders) was culturally Germanic, and the origins of the culture lay in the Frankish settlement of the early Middle Ages—and again we

---

[64] In this instance it is almost impossible to find an English equivalent of *Volk*, which is obviously not as grandiose as 'Nation', but is rather more elevated than 'Tribe'. The English phrases 'Germanic codes' or 'Barbarian codes' clearly have overtones that are inappropriate.
[65] Van Werveke, 'Karl Lamprecht et Henri Pirenne', pp. 47, 58–9.

are dealing with Lamprecht's all-embracing concept of *Kultur*. This was little different from Grimm's argument for the incorporation of Schleswig-Holstein into
Germany, although it was couched in cultural rather than linguistic terms. Belgium was the home of *Lex Salica*, the first Germanic law code. The Germanic
Franks had set out from the region to overwhelm the Celtic Gauls. In retrospect it
is not difficult to see that Lamprecht, along with other members of the professoriat, had not just been subservient onlookers, but had furnished the Kaiser and the
governing class in general with a set of attitudes that encouraged the take-over
of Belgium. Further, given that Lamprecht was employed by the Kaiser to investigate how best to deal with the reorganization of Belgium, one has to ask whether
he himself had not become part of the government.

For Lamprecht the early Middle Ages were relevant to modern politics. That
the Germanic past was of interest to a far wider group than the intellectuals and
the governing classes in the feverish atmosphere of the summer of 1914 is clear
from sales figures of Dahn's *Ein Kampf um Rom*, which, as we have already seen,
were particularly strong in the months between July and August, apparently
because the book became a favoured confirmation present. In it young boys could
read that 'Das Höchste ist das Volk, das Vaterland', and thus be inspired in their
patriotism.[66]

12.5 AFTER 1918

Although Pirenne presented the German professoriat as meekly following their
political masters, and allowed them no agency in the build-up to the outbreak of
war in 1914, he clearly felt betrayed by them. And this sense of betrayal was central both to his writing and his actions in the years immediately following the
conflict. In February 1919 he supported the further removal of the names of German scholars from the list of associated members of the Académie royale, singling
out Lamprecht, Wilamowitz, and Liszt.[67] Later the same year he published an
article on Pan-Germanism and Belgium ('Le pangermanisme et la Belgique').
This begins with an analysis of the development of German nationalism, taking
as a starting point Arndt's 'Was ist des Deutschen Vaterland?' of 1813: with its
response, 'So weit die Deutsche Zunge klingt/Das soll es sein,/Das, wackrer Deutscher, nenne dein' ('As far as the German tongue sounds, that, worthy German,
call your own').[68] In the middle of the nineteenth century, according to Pirenne,
the philosophical approaches of Fichte and Hegel were replaced by racial attitudes
influenced by Gobineau, whose ideas were introduced to the German public by
Wagner.[69] After 1870 Germany was thought to be superior not just in the field of

[66] Neuhaus, *Literatur und nationale Einheit in Deutschland*, p. 232.
[67] Van Werveke, 'Karl Lamprecht et Henri Pirenne', pp. 53–4.
[68] Pirenne, 'Le pangermanisme et la Belgique', p. 7. See Violante, *La fine della 'grande illusione'*,
p. 198.
[69] Pirenne, 'Le pangermanisme et la Belgique', p. 10.
[70] Pirenne, 'Le pangermanisme et la Belgique', pp. 12–13.

Kultur, but also of warfare.[70] This sense of supremacy was widespread, even among the intelligensia:

> And the most terrible thing is not that the fanatical publicists have spread this poison among the masses, the most terrible is that the philosophers, the historians, the economists, the philologists, and the sociologists have not been immune, and that they infected these German universities that foreigners, nevertheless, continued to admire smugly as serene schools of learning and criticism.[71]

One of his students, who was studying in Heidelberg in 1913, seems to have been a good deal more clearsighted on German militarism than Pirenne himself had been, for he wrote saying, 'If they make war, they will do so like Huns.'[72]

Pirenne then turned to the intellectuals themselves, to their fallacious association of race and language[73] (an association to be found most explicitly, as we have seen, in the writings of the English Freeman). Contrary to what the Germans thought, Pirenne argued that a people did not have a particular genius:

> Truly, there is no such thing as national genius, only national civilizations. And these civilizations are constantly in a state of flux, moving constantly from one idea to another.[74]

Here, of course, he had Lamprecht in his sights.

In the second part of the paper he turned from the development of German nationalism, to the ways in which their attitudes impacted on their neighbours, and above all to the 'martyrdom' of Belgium.[75] The Pan-Germanists, who also had had their eyes on Holland, had a longstanding interest in the Flemish question.[76] But they did not understand the Belgians: in fact they did not understand many of their neighbours. Pirenne drew a comparison between the Czechs, oppressed by the Germans since the days of Rudolph of Habsburg's overthrow of the Bohemian king Ottokar in 1278, and free Belgium.[77] The Germans, however, had a (for Pirenne) bogus vision of the Flemings oppressed by the Walloons (having forgotten the glories of the whole region, when it belonged to Burgundy in the late Middle Ages),[78] and they also threw into the equation the matter of Belgian imperialism in the Congo. They claimed to desire the liberation of the Flemish, but what they really wanted was to conquer the region.[79] What they did not understand was that Belgium was not created by race or language, but by the free choice of its people.[80]

German misuse of the medieval past was something Pirenne addressed again in a lecture on 'L'Allemagne moderne et l'Empire romain du Moyen Âge' delivered in

---

[71] Pirenne, 'Le pangermanisme et la Belgique', p. 13.
[72] Pirenne, 'Le pangermanisme et la Belgique', p. 13.
[73] Pirenne, 'Le pangermanisme et la Belgique', p. 18.
[74] Pirenne, 'Le pangermanisme et la Belgique', p. 19.
[75] Pirenne, 'Le pangermanisme et la Belgique', p. 21.
[76] Pirenne, 'Le pangermanisme et la Belgique', pp. 23, 25.
[77] Pirenne, 'Le pangermanisme et la Belgique', pp. 26–7. The fall of Ottokar is the subject of a play by Grillparzer (*König Ottokars Glück und Ende*), a playwright whose wisdom was much admired by Pirenne ('Le pangermanisme et la Belgique', p. 20).
[78] Pirenne, 'Le pangermanisme et la Belgique', p. 32.
[79] Pirenne, 'Le pangermanisme et la Belgique', p. 29.
[80] Pirenne, 'Le pangermanisme et la Belgique', p. 34.

1920 at the start of the university year at the University of Ghent, where he had been appointed *Rektor*.[81] The weakness of German scholarship was then mercilessly dissected in 1923 in an article 'De l'influence allemande sur le mouvement historique contemporain'. Here he acknowledges the importance of the scholarly contribution made by Niebuhr, Wolff, Grimm, and Ranke—he does not seem to have noticed that Grimm was in the slightest bit culpable in his association of language and national boundaries. Despite that contribution, however, the Germans had done little other than collect material: they had not interpreted it. They had been greatly overvalued:

> It is nevertheless certain that Droysen, von Sybel, Mommsen, and Lamprecht have been placed well below Michelet, Renan, Taine, Fustel de Coulanges, and Macaulay by posterity.[82]

The War had exposed their 'mentalité' for what it was. Chief among the intellectual weaknesses of German scholarship was the emphasis that it placed on race:

> Prejudice is substituted for criticism. And one has arrived at the aberration of thinking of the Germanic barbarians of the first centuries of the Middle Ages as in no way being an obstacle to civilization, as they were, but as the point of departure for modern civilization.[83]

At the same time German academics had opted out of acting as citizens—and here he was returning to views he had expressed in the *Souvenirs de captivité* concerning the supine nature of the professoriat. Their famed objectivity was no more than 'the application of a method incapable of grasping the social collectivity, in its multiple transformations'.[84] As their prestige had grown, so they had become more inward-looking. As a result they exaggerated their past glories, failing to notice that medieval Germany lagged behind its neighbours.[85] In 1870 Sybel wrote an article on 'Was wir von Frankreich lernen können' ('What we can learn from France'): in Pirenne's eyes it was time to ask 'ce que nous devons désapprendre de l'Allemagne' ('what we ought to unlearn from Germany').[86]

It is not difficult to understand the anger that was consuming Pirenne in the years immediately after 1918. Some of it was probably directed at himself, consciously or subconsciously, since he had been as blind in his acceptance of German scholarship as anybody else. Equally important, a considerable number of non-German scholars clearly sympathized with him, to the extent that in 1923 he was chosen to be the president of the Fifth Congrès international des Sciences historiques, which was held in Brussels. The choice of the venue and of the president was, of course symbolic.[87] The previous congress had been held in London in 1913,

---

[81] Pirenne, 'L'Allemagne moderne et l'Empire romain du Moyen Âge'. Violante, *La fine della 'grande illusione'*, p. 198.

[82] Pirenne, 'De l'influence allemande sur le mouvement historique contemporain', pp. 173–4.

[83] Pirenne, 'De l'influence allemande sur le mouvement historique contemporain', p. 175.

[84] Pirenne, 'De l'influence allemande sur le mouvement historique contemporain', p. 176.

[85] Pirenne, 'De l'influence allemande sur le mouvement historique contemporain', p. 177.

[86] Pirenne, 'De l'influence allemande sur le mouvement historique contemporain', p. 178.

[87] For the proceedings, des Marez and Ganshof, *Compte-rendu du cinquième Congrès international des Sciences historiques*. For the history behind the congress, and for commentary on some of the contents, Leland, 'The International Congress of Historical Sciences held at Brussels'. Also Violante, *La fine della 'grande illusione'*, pp. 251–305.

and St Petersburg had been chosen as the venue for the next meeting, to be held in 1918. In the event this had not taken place for obvious reasons. Members of the Royal Historical Society, however, encouraged the Belgians to consider hosting a substitute conference.

The Brussels congress was a hugely important gathering. There were over 700 delegates, from 27 countries, and over 350 communications.[88] Among those who attended, and who gave foretastes of their work in progress were Halphen,[89] Rostovtzeff,[90] and Lot,[91] as well as Lefebvre, Bloch,[92] and Fliche.[93] Pirenne's inaugural, 'De la méthode comparative en histoire', argued for a return to impartial historiography following the propagandist works of wartime.[94] Pirenne also delivered a second lecture, 'Un contraste économique: Mérovingiens et Carolingiens', which was a return to some points which he had recently published in an article entitled 'Mahomet et Charlemagne',[95] but where he elaborated on the distinction between the Merovingian economy, which as he saw it was still largely urban, and the Carolingian, which was rural.

Pirenne's presentation immediately prompted considerable discussion in the conference hall: Louis Halphen thought that the case for economic continuity at the end of the Roman period was compelling, but that Pirenne had underestimated the importance of the change in legal practice. The numismatist Maurice Prou, while accepting the chronology, thought that the change from the Merovingian to the Carolingian economy was more a product of internal developments than the result of the arrival of the Arabs, while the specialist in Byzantine Italy Jules Gay argued that Pirenne had exaggerated the impact of the Arabs on Mediterranean contacts.[96] The first response to Pirenne's lecture, however, came from Ferdinand Lot, who was already engaged in writing *La Fin du monde antique*.[97] He was much taken by the overall argument that the real break at the end of the Ancient World was caused not by the Germanic invaders, but by the Arabs, although he thought that Pirenne had presented this as rather too clear-cut.[98]

It is worth pausing for a moment on this study of the end of the Ancient World. Lot (1866–1952) initially established himself as a paleographer and archivist. In 1899 he succeeded his master Giry in teaching paleography at the École pratique

---

[88] Leland, 'The International Congress of Historical Sciences held at Brussels', p. 640.
[89] Violante, *La fine della 'grande illusione'*, p. 272.
[90] Violante, *La fine della 'grande illusione'*, p. 273.
[91] Violante, *La fine della 'grande illusione'*, p. 275.
[92] Violante, *La fine della 'grande illusione'*, pp. 285–92.
[93] Violante, *La fine della 'grande illusione'*, p. 293.
[94] Pirenne, 'De la méthode comparative en histoire', pp. 19–32; Violante, *La fine della 'grande illusione'*, pp. 251–6.
[95] Pirenne, 'Un contraste économique: Mérovingiens et Carolingiens'; see Pirenne, 'Mahomet et Charlemagne'; Violante, *La fine della 'grande illusione'*, pp. 260–9.
[96] Violante, *La fine della 'grande illusione'*, p. 269.
[97] Violante, *La fine della 'grande illusione'*, p. 268 merely notes the publication date of 1927.
[98] Violante, *La fine della 'grande illusione'*, pp. 268–9.

des hautes études. At this stage he was very conscious of the weaknesses of French higher education, contrasting its standards ruefully with those of Germany.[99] Gradually, however, he turned from the study of diplomatic to broader aspects of late Antique and medieval history. He had already begun work on the subject of the end of the Ancient World in 1913.[100] Although his book was not published until 1927, it may have been well advanced by 1921.[101] As the English Byzantinist Baynes noted in his review of Lot's book, some of the assertions that might have made sense in 1913 read rather strangely a decade or more later. Thus, in arguing that nothing could stop the decline of the Roman economy, Lot paused to comment:

> It is an extremely surprising phenomenon for us, used to ever-increasing prosperity. A commercial crisis, a war, can interrupt this prosperity, but we are assured that after a more or less extended period of stagnation business will pick up again, and the production of wealth with never stop.[102]

Baynes found a good deal to criticize in Lot's work, not least his apparent lack of knowledge of the work of Bury.[103] Yet he was impressed by his reading of the late Roman economy, which the Frenchman saw as already being in decline in the third century.[104] Despite this sense of decline, Lot also took on board Pirenne's view that the Mediterranean economy continued after the arrival of the Germanic peoples—a point that Baynes contested, putting a good deal more emphasis on the impact of the Vandal conquest of Africa.[105] Yet, while accepting Pirenne's reading of the Mediterranean, at the same time Lot saw the barbarian arrival in Gaul as an unmitigated disaster.[106] The various elements in his argument thus seem awkwardly reconciled. Lot would return to the question of the barbarians in the 1930s in a series of works which were perhaps rather more univocal, as we shall see.

12.6 ALFONS DOPSCH AND THE REACTION OF MARC BLOCH

One potential critic of Pirenne, who might have had more to say than any of those who responded to the lecture on the Merovingian and Carolingian economies at the Brussels congress was Alfons Dopsch (1868–1953), the first edition of whose *Wirtschaftliche und soziale Grundlagen der europäischen Kulturentwicklung* had just appeared.[107] Dopsch, however, was not present at the congress, nor was any other

[99] Den Boer, *History as a Profession*, pp. 218–20.

[100] Baynes, review of Lot, p. 224.

[101] Anderson, *Passages from Antiquity to Feudalism*, p 129, argues that Lot's *La Fin du monde antique* was finished by 1921, but this is difficult to square with the overlap between the book and Pirenne's *Revue belge* articles of 1922 and 1923.

[102] Lot, *La Fin du monde antique et le debut du Moyen Âge*, 2nd edn, p. 68; Baynes, review of Lot, p. 224.

[103] Baynes, review of Lot, p. 226.

[104] Baynes, review of Lot, p. 225.

[105] Baynes, review of Lot, pp. 230–3.

[106] Lot, *La Fin du monde antique*, pp. 462–3, 469; Anderson, *Passages from Antiquity to Feudalism*, p. 129.

[107] Dopsch, *Wirtschaftliche und soziale Grundlagen*; there was a second edition 1923–4, and an abridged English translation, *The Economic and Social Foundations of European Civilization*. On Dopsch, Hruza (ed.), *Österreichische Historiker 1900–1945*, pp. 155–90; Nabholz, 'Alfons Dopsch (1868–1953)—Nécrologie'.

Austrian or German. The Belgians in organizing the gathering, together with the French, had excluded the Germans, despite the arguments to the contrary put forward by some Americans and English,[108] and although Pirenne himself had tried to get some of those who did not sign the *Aufruf* of the 93 exempted.[109] In protest at the exclusion of their German colleagues the Austrians stayed away.

While in terms of methodology Dopsch looked to Max Weber,[110] in some respects his arguments can be seen as developing out of those of Fustel, as he himself admitted.[111] Talking of the *Histoire des institutions politiques* he remarked that 'it was a definite refutation of the earlier conceptions of German barbarism and of the destruction of Roman culture'—not that Fustel had really presented his case as being concerned with culture: here Dopsch perhaps had *Kultur* as defined by Lamprecht in mind. The Germanic incomers of the fourth and fifth centuries had already been Romanized, and they changed relatively little. This reading of the insignificance of the end of the Roman Empire was thus more or less compatible with that of Pirenne, though Dopsch also saw the barbarians as purveyors of their own brand of civilization, which was something that Pirenne was less inclined to concede.[112]

Yet while the interpretation put forward by Dopsch was one that had a good deal in common with that of Fustel, it was also very deliberately presented as a rejection of a particular line of German scholarship. The first chapter of *The Economic and Social Foundations of European Civilization* is an extremely perceptive historiographical essay. The earliest writers discussed by Dopsch were Boulainvilliers, Du Bos, and Montesquieu.[113] Having reached Guizot, however, who he presents largely as continuing Montesquieu's emphasis on the destructive nature of the Germanic barbarians, Dopsch turned his attention away from the French tradition to a very specifically German line of argument, which had begun with Justus Möser.[114]

As we have seen, Möser had imagined a world of communities of free German farmers whose existence he thought could be traced back to Antiquity.[115] For him these farmers were involved in the exploitation of common land, which he called the *Mark*. As Dopsch noted, this was an idea that had more to do with Möser's political agenda than with anything in the sources. Nevertheless, Möser's idea was picked up by Eichhorn and then by Grimm, who noted that the evidence for the existence of the *Mark* was only to be found in late medieval sources, but thought that it fitted with what was known about early Germanic freedom and equality. Grimm, therefore, developed Möser's interpretation, which had been based on his

---

[108] Violante, *La fine della 'grande illusione'*, pp. 294–5.

[109] Violante, *La fine della 'grande illusione'*, pp. 294–7.

[110] Mommsen, *The Age of Bureaucracy*, pp. 47–94.

[111] Dopsch, *The Economic and Social Foundations of European Civilization*, pp. 20–2, 25–6, 32. See also Violante, *La fine della 'grande illusione'*, pp. 265–6, 271, 177–9.

[112] Violante, *La fine della 'grande illusione'*, p. 265.

[113] Dopsch, *The Economic and Social Foundations of European Civilization*, pp. 3–4. Montesquieu he presents as surprisingly Germanophobic.

[114] Dopsch, *The Economic and Social Foundations of European Civilization*, pp. 5–6.

[115] Dopsch, *The Economic and Social Foundations of European Civilization*, p. 123.

detailed knowledge of the landscape of the Osnabrück region, into a juridical theory of *Markgenossenschaft*.[116] Although this notion was challenged in Germany by Sybel and Waitz, it was taken up by English scholars, having been championed by Grimm's acolyte Kemble,[117] and by the jurist Sumner Maine (1822–88) in his *Ancient Law* of 1861 and his *Village Communities* of ten years later.[118] In America similar ideas were championed by the ethnologist Lewis Henry Morgan (1818–81) in his work on *Ancient Society* (1877), where he applied Darwinian notions of evolution to social development.[119] This line of approach was challenged by Denman Waldo Ross (a man who was to be more famous as an artist and as the subject of a portrait by John Singer Sargent) in his *Early History of Landholding among the Germans*, where he attacked the notion of communal land-ownership.[120] Despite this critique, and despite the work of Fustel, the notion of communities of free peasants was still widely held, and it was against this background that Dopsch set out his own ideas.

In dealing with the earliest period of Germanic history Dopsch again asserted that in Caesar and Tacitus one could not find *Markgenossenschaft*, but rather a world of private property.[121] He went on to argue that if there was private property, the communal world identified by legal historians in the law codes cannot have been early or Germanic.[122] In turning to the fifth-century Migration Period, he questioned the extent of migration, choosing rather to emphasize the contacts that had long existed between Romans and barbarians in the *limes* (frontier) region.[123] When the barbarians did enter the Empire they were a good deal less destructive than many had argued: Roman literary sources exaggerated the destruction, which was not supported by the archaeological evidence.[124] The settlement of the barbarians was carried out according to Roman administrative practice,[125] and Dopsch even doubted whether there was any evidence to suggest that the Lombard treatment of the Italians was particularly harsh.[126] Turning to the question of the early agrarian economy, he proposed to replace the model of *Markgenossenschaft* with a picture of the development and subsequent breakdown of seigneurial estates in those areas for which we have evidence. Thus, far from there being a shift from freedom to lordship, he suggested that, while there had been many late Roman *vici*, or small village communities, their inhabitants had increasingly turned to the aristocracy for protection, as a result of which the *vici* became appurtenances of the great estates.[127] However, changes in inheritance in the post-Roman period led to

[116] Dopsch, *The Economic and Social Foundations of European Civilization*, pp. 10–11.
[117] Dopsch, *The Economic and Social Foundations of European Civilization*, pp. 14, 20.
[118] Dopsch, *The Economic and Social Foundations of European Civilization*, pp. 22–3.
[119] Dopsch, *The Economic and Social Foundations of European Civilization*, p. 24.
[120] Ross, *Early History of Landholding among the Germans*.
[121] Dopsch, *The Economic and Social Foundations of European Civilization*, pp. 34, 40.
[122] Dopsch, *The Economic and Social Foundations of European Civilization*, pp. 44, 47.
[123] Dopsch, *The Economic and Social Foundations of European Civilization*, pp. 48–57.
[124] Dopsch, *The Economic and Social Foundations of European Civilization*, pp. 61–92.
[125] Dopsch, *The Economic and Social Foundations of European Civilization*, pp. 93–118.
[126] Dopsch, *The Economic and Social Foundations of European Civilization*, p. 95.
[127] Dopsch, *The Economic and Social Foundations of European Civilization*, p. 156.

the gradual break up of seigneurial estates, and thus while there were no free peasant communes, the period did see a growth in communities of free peasant land-
holders.[128] Dopsch allowed that the lot of the peasant landholder might have
improved under Germanic rule,[129] but he also noted that the peasantry needed
protection from enslavement and oppression in the sixth and seventh centuries.[130]
In general he thought that there was little distinction between Germanic and
Roman approaches to the agrarian economy.[131]

Dopsch defined developments in political structure as being the province of
Kulturgeschichte. Essentially the new Germanic lords had to find a *modus vivendi*
with the Roman population, but given the long-standing contacts between the two
groups, this did not present a major problem.[132] There was, of course, variety, and
always had been, in the Germanic and Roman worlds.[133] Dopsch allowed that not
everything could be ascribed to Roman tradition: Germanic military traditions
had to be accommodated.[134] Contrary to what was believed by many who were
influenced by the chimera of Germanic equality, there was plenty of evidence for
the existence of a nobility among all the different tribes, and one could not get
round this by claiming that the nobility was simply a nobility of service.[135]

Dopsch also insisted on the importance of the role of the Church in developments of the post-Roman period, seeing it as playing the role of intermediary
between ancient civilization and the new Germanic states.[136] The idea was not new,
but Fustel had not made anything of it. More important was Dopsch's emphasis on
the growing property holding of the Church, which became one of the great territorial lordships.[137] And he noted its political power, arguing that it acted as a
check on the monarchy.[138] He also stressed its social role, particularly in caring for
the poor, for widows, orphans, foundlings, and prisoners.[139] Some of these concerns went back to the Roman period,[140] and indeed although Dopsch saw a
growth in ecclesiastical activity, especially after the conversion to Catholicism of
the barbarians,[141] he was keen to see the origins of most developments as lying in
the Roman Empire. Thus, he even noted the existence of *Eigenkirchen*, proprietary
churches, on Roman estates before the year 400, although they were generally
regarded as a Germanic institution.[142]

---

[128] Dopsch, *The Economic and Social Foundations of European Civilization*, p. 157.
[129] Dopsch, *The Economic and Social Foundations of European Civilization*, p. 160.
[130] Dopsch, *The Economic and Social Foundations of European Civilization*, pp. 216–17.
[131] Dopsch, *The Economic and Social Foundations of European Civilization*, p. 162.
[132] Dopsch, *The Economic and Social Foundations of European Civilization*, p. 165.
[133] Dopsch, *The Economic and Social Foundations of European Civilization*, pp. 173–5.
[134] Dopsch, *The Economic and Social Foundations of European Civilization*, p. 188.
[135] Dopsch, *The Economic and Social Foundations of European Civilization*, p. 206.
[136] Dopsch, *The Economic and Social Foundations of European Civilization*, p. 241.
[137] Dopsch, *The Economic and Social Foundations of European Civilization*, pp. 246–7.
[138] Dopsch, *The Economic and Social Foundations of European Civilization*, pp. 188–9.
[139] Dopsch, *The Economic and Social Foundations of European Civilization*, pp. 248–54.
[140] Dopsch, *The Economic and Social Foundations of European Civilization*, pp. 249, 254.
[141] Dopsch, *The Economic and Social Foundations of European Civilization*, p. 271.
[142] Dopsch, *The Economic and Social Foundations of European Civilization*, p. 257. For a modern
assessment of the subject, see Wood, *The Proprietary Church in the Medieval West*.

While he acknowledged the importance of a military tradition among the Germanic peoples, Dopsch argued that the origins of feudalism should be sought at least partly in the Roman world: in the development of personal military followings known as the *bucellarii*, who were tied by oaths of fealty to their lords, from whom they received their equipment.[143] Like Fustel, he noted the importance of Roman traditions of patronage (*patrocinium*): a man entering into a relationship of *patrocinium* commended himself to his patron.[144] He stressed the similarities of this system and the Germanic *comitatus*, noting the semantic similarity between the Roman term *bucellarius*, which meant 'bread-eater', and the Anglo-Saxon term for a lord: *hlaford*, or 'bread-giver'.[145] Romans had endowed military followers with estates, *fundi militares*.[146] The *beneficia* and *precaria* granted out by Charles Martel were, therefore, nothing new, although they may have been allocated on an unusually large scale.[147] What Dopsch saw overall was the adaptation of Roman models, on the one hand because of the difference between Germanic and imperial military organization, and on the other hand because of the needs of the Church.[148]

Dopsch then turned to rather more clearly social and economic matters, and first to the towns of Gaul, Spain, and Italy, which he presented as still recognizably Roman, although local power was in the hands of the royal *comes*, and even more of the bishop, rather than under the old urban councils.[149] The Rhineland urban centres, which overlapped with the Germanic local districts (*Gaue*), he saw as little more than places of refuge,[150] though at the same time he ascribed rather more significance to some fortified *civitas*-centres in free Germany than others had done.[151] He also took an optimistic view of the evidence for continuing industry and for trade, heaping up as many scraps of evidence (including allusions to actors and mimes) as he could find. He saw the economy as still being at least partially monetary—and indeed emphasized the extent to which barbarians living near the frontier of the Roman Empire had long become accustomed to the use of coin.[152] He allowed that coin was sometimes only a unit of account, and that this was probably particularly so for the poor who would not have had access to coin.[153] Yet overall he saw coin as a central feature of the late- and post-Roman economy.

For Dopsch, then, the early Germans were not backward. They did not come out of the primeval forest, but rather from a world that was heavily Romanized. When they took over parts of the Empire, far from destroying its institutions they kept them going. What democratic institutions they may once have had, they largely lost, and in their conflicts with the Roman states the institution of kingship

---

[143] Dopsch, *The Economic and Social Foundations of European Civilization*, pp. 285–6.
[144] Dopsch, *The Economic and Social Foundations of European Civilization*, p. 286.
[145] Dopsch, *The Economic and Social Foundations of European Civilization*, p. 218.
[146] Dopsch, *The Economic and Social Foundations of European Civilization*, p. 286.
[147] Dopsch, *The Economic and Social Foundations of European Civilization*, pp. 290–1.
[148] Dopsch, *The Economic and Social Foundations of European Civilization*, pp. 301–2.
[149] Dopsch, *The Economic and Social Foundations of European Civilization*, pp. 303–12.
[150] Dopsch, *The Economic and Social Foundations of European Civilization*, pp. 312–13.
[151] Dopsch, *The Economic and Social Foundations of European Civilization*, pp. 315–17.
[152] Dopsch, *The Economic and Social Foundations of European Civilization*, pp. 327–58.
[153] Dopsch, *The Economic and Social Foundations of European Civilization*, p. 382.

developed.[154] The new kingdoms did, however, see the end of Roman fiscal oppression, and there was greater solicitude for the poor. Meanwhile the Church, itself a champion of the poor, turned to the monarchy for protection, a move which brought it a good deal of wealth.[155] In the towns the bishops gained a considerable amount of power, more so than held by the count.[156] Kings and aristocrats, however, began to exploit the Church because of its wealth, and to make its property yield more value to the state by making military demands.[157] Dopsch's final comment was that the fifth and sixth centuries constituted a vital link between the Roman and Carolingian periods, and that this meant that there was a need to re-evaluate the Carolingian Renaissance.

Dopsch's case is deliberately set up as a reply to the German notion of *Markgenossenschaft*, and indeed to the tradition of German scholarship that championed the notion of the barbarians as democrats living in the wilderness. Not that this idealized view had been held by all Germans: even a scholar with as vital a role to play in the development of the notion of the *Volk* as Dahn had allowed that the Germanic peoples on the edge of and inside the Empire had been deeply Romanized. One should, however, remember that Dopsch was an Austrian, holding a chair in Vienna, a city which had until recently been the capital of an Empire. It was perhaps not surprising that he challenged both the democratic view of the early Germans, and also their supposed barbarism. Although in many respects his position was, as he himself implied, very close to that of Fustel,[158] there were differences. Marc Bloch, in an article which looked at the origins of what he delineated as *la société féodale*, saw quite considerable differences between the two, pointing out that the Austrian presented the barbarians as having rather more to contribute positively to the development of European civilization than Fustel had allowed.[159]

Although Bloch commented relatively rarely on the end of the Roman Empire and the establishment of the barbarian kingdoms which succeeded it, he did write an article on 'La Société du Haut Moyen Âge et ses origines', which is essentially an extended review of Dopsch's *Wirtschaftliche und soziale Grundlagen der europäischen Kulturentwicklung*.[160] For him the book was an interesting sketch, rather hurriedly produced.[161] He noted some issues that Dopsch had left untouched, among them the Celtic substratum to be found in much of Western Europe.[162] Where he really disagreed, however, was over the question of the disruption caused by the incoming barbarians. While he him-

---

[154] Dopsch, *The Economic and Social Foundations of European Civilization*, pp. 384–7. On this see now Dick, *Der Mythos vom 'germanischen' Königtum*.

[155] Dopsch, *The Economic and Social Foundations of European Civilization*, p. 387.

[156] Dopsch, *The Economic and Social Foundations of European Civilization*, p. 389.

[157] Dopsch, *The Economic and Social Foundations of European Civilization*, p. 388.

[158] Dopsch, *The Economic and Social Foundations of European Civilization*, pp. 20–2.

[159] Bloch, 'La société du Haut Moyen Âge et ses origines', p. 63–4.

[160] Bloch, 'La société du Haut Moyen Âge et ses origines'. For his assessment of the work of Dopsch, Fustel, and Pirenne, see also Bloch, 'Sur les grandes invasions: quelques positions de problèmes', pp. 100–2. For Dopsch and Bloch, see Schöttler, 'Die Annales und ihre Beziehungen zu Österreich in den 20er und 30er Jahren'.

[161] Bloch, 'La société du Haut Moyen Âge et ses origines', p. 62.

[162] Bloch, 'La société du Haut Moyen Âge et ses origines', p. 65.

self believed that there were relatively few incoming barbarians,[163] and largely accepted a picture of continuity, he nevertheless thought that the Migration Period was a time of extreme disorder.[164] In more than one article he stressed the value of Eugippius' *Vita Severini* as a model for what must have happened.[165] Clearly this text, with its picture of the collapse of the Roman army on the Danube frontier, struck a chord. Bloch himself had served in the infantry during the First World War,[166] and one may guess that the reality of war coloured his sense of the period of the invasions. Certainly he alludes to the conflict. In talking of the limitations of Gregory of Tours he drew a comparison with his own day:

> Let's imagine a historian who, out of the 1914–18 War, only wanted to know about the battle of the Marne or the final allied offensive: that gives us the rhythm of Gregory's narrative.[167]

One might guess that personal experience underlay his sense that hunger would be a driving force in a period of disruption:

> In politics as in economics, there is the issue of patterns of behaviour imposed by necessity, and above all by the most imperious of needs: hunger.[168]

In stressing the extent to which the Migration Period was a time of disorder he was not just challenging Dopsch, but also Fustel and Pirenne.[169] The latter, although sharing some of Dopsch's views, would not go quite as far in seeing the barbarians as having been Romanized: and above all, because he came to see a major caesura in the seventh century, was not happy with Dopsch's closing comments on continuity from the Roman to the Carolingian periods. Despite this disagreement, Pirenne and Dopsch were seen to be on good personal terms, going off to have a drink together, at the Congrès international held in Oslo in 1928—which, unlike that held in Brussels five years earlier, the Austrian did feel able to attend.[170] Pirenne was clearly a man who was capable of forgetting old enmities. In 1931 he could even claim that his friendship with Lamprecht had lasted until the German's death, despite his awareness of his support for the Kaiser's policies in the opening years of the war.[171] The connections between Dopsch's views and those held by French and Belgian, as opposed to German scholars, did not go unnoticed. As we shall see, at a *Tagung* held at Bad Dürkheim in 1935 Franz Steinbach connected Dopsch with Pirenne.[172]

---

[163] Bloch, 'Observations sur la conquête de la Gaule romaine par les rois francs', p. 84.

[164] Bloch, 'La société du Haut Moyen Âge et ses origines', p. 67.

[165] Bloch, 'Observations sur la conquête de la Gaule romaine par les rois francs', p. 82; Bloch, 'Sur les grandes invasions: quelques positions de problèmes', p. 106.

[166] Perrin, 'Préface', in Bloch, *Mélanges historiques*, vol. 1, pp. vii–xiii, at p. x.

[167] Bloch, 'Observations sur la conquête de la Gaule romaine par les rois francs', p. 76.

[168] Bloch, 'Observations sur la conquête de la Gaule romaine par les rois francs', p. 78.

[169] For his view of Pirenne, see also Bloch, 'Une mise au point: les invasions', p. 122; Perrin, 'Préface', p. viii.

[170] Violante, *La fine della 'grande illusione'*, p. 305.

[171] Van Werveke, 'Karl Lamprecht et Henri Pirenne', p. 55.

[172] Falhbusch, *Wissenschaft im Dienst der nationalsozialistischen Politik?*, pp. 381–3.

12.7 MAHOMET ET CHARLEMAGNE

The Bad Dürkheim conference took place a few months before Pirenne's death. A year later his son Jacques arranged the publication of the incomplete *Histoire de l'Europe des invasions au XVIe siècle*, the manuscript of which he had discovered. Pirenne had worked on the *Histoire* during his period in captivity, first in the lectures he gave to Russian prisoners in the prison camp at Holzminden, and then at Kreuzburg. The preface is dated 31st January 1917.[173] The work was conceived of as a reply to German views of the origins of the *Reich*, in which the power of the Hohenzollern was elided with that of the Habsburgs. Pirenne countered by presenting the origins of the medieval Empire as being almost exclusively Roman, even though the emperors themselves were German.[174] Indeed, he downplayed the positive German contribution to European history as much as he could.

A year after the publication of the *Histoire de l'Europe* Jacques Pirenne and his mother invited Charles Vercauteren to help in preparing another posthumous volume for publication: this was the book-length treatment of *Mahomet et Charlemagne*,[175] which Pirenne had been working at, unknown to anyone, right up to his death. In certain crucial respects *Mahomet et Charlemagne* differs not only from the *Histoire de l'Europe*, but also from the articles published in the *Revue belge* in 1922 and 1923, suggesting a certain tempering of Pirenne's reaction to the events of 1914–18, in part perhaps in response to his debates with Dopsch.[176] Thus, in assessing Carolingian culture he does allow for some Germanic influence, which he had denied in the works written during and immediately after his internment.[177]

Although Pirenne's most famous book is usually read, first and foremost, as a work of economic history, it begins, significantly, with what is essentially a sketch of the political history of the Mediterranean world in the fourth, fifth, and sixth centuries, even though the title of the chapter is 'The continuation of the Mediterranean civilization in the West after the barbarian invasions'—this is 'civilization' in the broadest, almost Lamprechtian, sense.[178] Having sketched a political narrative, he gathered together snippets of evidence (and there was not much else to go on at the time, because of the absence of relevant archaeological finds) to present a picture of continuing trade in the Mediterranean basin. Equally, he provided an account of cultural continuity, though it is a continuity that, as Pirenne fully admitted, depended on the Church.

Having provided what he thought was a convincing demonstration of continuity through the fifth and sixth centuries (although as Paolo Delogu has argued, the impression is a very misleading one),[179] Pirenne then turned to what he regarded as the real turning point between Antiquity and the Middle Ages: the emergence

---

[173] Pirenne, *Histoire de l'Europe des invasions au XVIe siècle*, 'Avant-propos'. Jacques Pirenne supplies an account of the work's genesis, ibid., pp. v–xiii.

[174] See Violante, *La fine della 'grande illusione'*, pp. 223–34, 307–11.

[175] See the preface and note at the start of Pirenne, *Mahomet et Charlemagne*; for the English translation, Pirenne, *Mahommed and Charlemagne*, pp. 9–14.

[176] See Delogu, 'Reading Pirenne again', pp. 36–8 for the novelties in *Mahomet et Charlemagne*.

[177] Delogu, 'Reading Pirenne again', p. 38.

[178] Delogu, 'Reading Pirenne again', p. 38.   [179] Delogu, 'Reading Pirenne again', p. 35.

of Islam, which in his view disrupted the unity of the Mediterranean, and in so doing changed the economy and the power structure of the early medieval West. Again the presentation of evidence is impressionistic, and the arguments about the impact of Islam on the Mediterranean world are scarcely any more secure than those denying any Germanic impact. Having established to his own satisfaction a case that Mediterranean unity had been broken in the seventh century, he addressed the question of change in the Frankish world, putting particular emphasis on the supposed fact that, having been isolated from Byzantium, the papacy turned instead to the Carolingians. It was the rise to dominance of the Carolingians that gave a fillip to the economy of the northern Francia (including, of course, the lands of Flemish Belgium), thus kick-starting the medieval economy.

In tracing the political and economic emergence of north-eastern Francia, Pirenne was effectively answering a question posed by his own earlier work on the history of Belgium. There he had presented the history of his own country largely in terms of that of the great cities of Flanders, which had taken him to the High Middle Ages, but he had not been able to trace their origins back to the Ancient World. *Mahomet et Charlemagne* provided a background for the history of those cities. In many respects he had written a pre-history of his *Histoire de Belgique*.[180]

Pirenne's argument has been picked over so often that it is hard to find anything new to say either in criticism or in defence. *Mahomet et Charlemagne* certainly describes a major change in the political, social, and religious realities of southern and Western Europe: the Roman world was a largely Mediterranean one, the late Carolingian world was not. The stress Pirenne put on the growing influence of the Church in the West also reflects the distribution of the evidence. Whether he was right to attribute change essentially to an outside agency,[181] that is, to the forces of Islam, rather than, as Dopsch, and before him, Fustel, had done, to steady internal development, is very much open to question. If one does put the stress on outside agency, there are those who attribute a good deal more to the Germanic peoples than Pirenne did—at the very least Baynes' argument that Lot had underestimated the importance of the Vandal seizure of Africa can equally be levelled against Pirenne: so too can Bloch's insistence on the reality of the disruption caused by the barbarian invasions. This, of course, impacts upon the chronology of the change observed.

Mahomet et Charlemagne is eye-catching because of the simplicity of the argument. Pirenne himself reduced it to the aphorism that 'without Mahommed Charlemagne would not have existed'. Whether he would have formulated so stark an argument without his experiences of the First World War, and whether he would have started to modify the extreme Germanophobia he adopted both in internment and in the immediately post-War period, without being faced with the extremely civilized responses of the Austrian Dopsch, are interesting questions. Equally important: it was not just the Belgians and French who felt aggrieved in the 1920s and 30s. In some ways the reactions of German historians are historically (if not historiographically) more important than those of Pirenne.

---

[180] Dhondt, 'Henri Pirenne, historien des institutions urbaines'. See Pirenne's own 'L'Origine des constitutions urbaines au Moyen Âge'.

[181] On external pressure, Delogu, 'Reading Pirenne again', p. 34.

13

Past Settlements

Interpretations of the Migration Period
from 1918 to 1945

13.1 AFTER VERSAILLES

Whether or not the Versailles settlement in 1919 was a total humiliation of Germany,[1] many Germans regarded it as such. The loss of territory was thought to be an injustice, and the resulting sense of grievance fed into the geopolitical thought of the Weimar republic.[2] Not surprisingly, the interpretation of the barbarian migrations and settlements was both influenced by, and contributed to, debates about what constituted the appropriate extent of territory for the German *Volk*, and this was already true before the Nazis came to power in 1933. Just as many of the geopolitical ideas of the Third Reich were already in circulation during the Weimar period, so too were the major lines of interpretation of the *Völkerwanderungzeit*—though the exploitation of the Germanic past reached its peak in 1939–45. One might place the symbolic highwater mark of that abuse of history at Himmler's failed attempt in 1943 to secure the earliest manuscript of Tacitus' *Germania*, the iconic classical description of the barbarians east of the Rhine.[3]

The fact that early medieval studies fed into Nazi ideology has meant that the study of the Migration Period in the 1930s has become a particularly delicate subject. Indeed, for a considerable period of time the matter was sidestepped, particularly in West Germany.[4] In the East after 1945 there was less concern to cover up the problems of Nazi historiography, with the result that, until recently, there was a good deal more awareness of political contamination of the *Ostforschung* (studies of the eastern borders of the Reich, and the lands beyond) than there was of the *Westforschung* (studies of the West).[5] The Nazi associations of most of those who retained their academic positions in the West were quietly forgotten, both by the individuals themselves, and by their students. Within the historical and archaeological communities

---

[1] MacMillan, *The Uses and Abuses of History*, pp. 36, 64, 97–100, argues that the humiliation was less than is often assumed.
[2] The Geopolitics of Weimar has been discussed at length by Murphy, *The Heroic Earth*, though (despite the use of a map showing the German Reich in 925), Murphy makes little of the exploitation of medieval history in the debates.
[3] Schama, *Landscape and Memory*, pp. 75–81; Krebs, *A Most Dangerous Book*, pp. 214–44.
[4] An early exception was Werner, *Das NS-Geschichtsbild und die deutsche Geschichtswissenschaft*.
[5] On *Ostforschung*, Burleigh, *Germany Turns Eastwards*.

it was not until the late 1990s, and in particular the 1998 *Historikertag*, the annual gathering of German historians, held that year in Frankfurt, that the subject boiled over.[6] Since then there has been a string of revelations, and a group of younger historians has started to uncover aspects of early medieval historiography during the period from 1918 to 1945 which had been forgotten or only half-suspected.

13.2 GUSTAF KOSSINNA

Much as German and English scholars had debated the outbreak of War in 1914, in 1919 the archaeologist Gustaf Kossinna put forward an archaeological case which he hoped would influence the Versailles conference in its drawing of Germany's post-War boundaries, arguing in *Die deutsche Ostmark* that lands in the East had been German since time immemorial, and therefore that they should not be handed over to Poland. This work would be reprinted almost immediately in Danzig (to use the German place name) as *Das Weichselland, ein uralter Heimatboden der Germanen*.[7] Kossinna's passion was no doubt fanned by the fact that he himself had been born in Tilsit, then in Memmelland, now part of Russia.

Kossinna (1858–1931) had begun life as a philologist, before adding archaeology and anthropology to his armoury.[8] As he himself explained, he was a student of the philologist Karl Müllenhoff, whose work looked back to the study of Indo-Germanic by the likes of Friedrich Schlegel.[9] However, he found what he described as *historisch-philosophischen und sprachwissenschaftlichen Realien* ('historico-philosophical and linguistic facts') inadequate for the questions he wished to ask about the origins of the Germanic peoples: by contrast, in his view, archaeology and anthropology were well-suited to the task.[10] Before Kossinna's day archaeology within the German academic establishment was dominated by the study of classical antiquity.[11] The classicists certainly had no love for Kossinna, who thought that they had prevented him from becoming director of the departments of prehistory in the royal museums.[12] There was, however, a growing interest in non-classical archaeology, which was marked in 1909 by the establishment of a new journal, the *Prähistorische Zeitschrift*. Not having been involved in this, and seeing himself very

---

[6] The *Historikertag* of 1998 is singled out by Dülffer, 'Sammelrez: Review-Symposium "Westforschung"'. The issue had been debated rather earlier among the philologists.

[7] Kossinna, *Die deutsche Ostmark*, reprinted as *Das Weichselland, ein uralter Heimatboden der Germanen*; see Mees, 'Hitler and *Germanentum*', p. 262, n. 49; see also Veit, 'Ethnic concepts in German prehistory', p. 38.

[8] The importance of Kossinna for early medieval archaeology is stressed in Jones, *The Archaeology of Ethnicity*, pp. 2–3, which also provides reference to a broad range of literature; see especially Härke, 'All quiet on the Western Front?' and Härke, ' "The Hun is a methodical chap." Reflections on the German tradition of pre- and proto-history'. Also Veit, 'Ethnic concepts in German prehistory', at pp. 36–9. Marchand, *Down from Olympus*, pp. 181–7.

[9] For his thesis, Graceffa, *Les Historiens et la question franque*, p. 100.

[10] Kossinna, *Die Herkunft der Germanen*, p. 1.

[11] On the relative underfunding of Prehistory, Arnold, 'The past as propaganda', p. 467.

[12] Marchand, *Down from Olympus*, p. 184.

much as an outsider, Kossinna countered by helping set up in the same year the *Deutsche Gesellschaft für Vorgeschichte*, and, four years later, the journal *Mannus*, which was to become a showcase for the publication of a particularly nationalistic brand of Germanic archaeology and anthropology.[13]

Kossinna's major argument was set out in a short, but sharp, work: *Die Herkunft der Germanen* ('The Origins of the Germanic Peoples'), which appeared in 1911. This was not the first time that Kossinna argued his case: indeed, the slim volume was very much a repetition of views he had already published, preceded by a vitriolic condemnation of those who had dared to question him. His basic contention was that if one wished to discover the homeland of the Germanic peoples, one could first turn to the written sources that describe their whereabouts in the early medieval and classical periods.[14] One could then compare that picture with a map of archaeological finds. In Kossinna's view, this allowed one to identify individual archaeological cultures and to associate them with tribes named in the Latin sources.[15] Once an archaeological culture had been identified in the historic period, it was possible to trace its antecedents in the prehistoric period, identifying which cultures had remained in the same region, and which had migrated. Here Kossinna's own work in developing the notion of typologies for classifying objects, and indeed for placing them within chronological sequences, was crucial. This allowed him to conclude that the *Indogermanen* originated in North Germany, and that they expanded from there to Scandinavia.[16] Moreover, since he thought that one could trace Indogermanic culture back through the Bronze to the Stone Age, he believed that the origins of that culture could be dated to the period from 8000–7000 BC.

This argument had all sorts of ramifications. By placing the origins of the *Indogermanen* in Germany, Kossinna was making a claim that they did not originate in the East, which is what philologists had largely been arguing ever since the identification of a relationship between Sanskrit and the Germanic languages.[17] Inevitably Kossinna's argument had racial implications. Even leaving these aside, it was important because of the central premise which was stressed time and again by Kossinna: that archaeological cultures could be equated with tribal groups: *Kulturgebiete sind Völkerstamme.*[18]

Kossinna did not simply address himself to academics and politicians. In 1914 he argued forcefully for the national importance of prehistoric archaeology in *Die deutsche Vorgeschichte: eine hervorragend nationale Wissenschaft* ('German prehistory: an outstanding national science') a work which betrays its basic contention in its title. In the introduction to the seventh edition of the book, which appeared in 1936, the editor, W. Hülle, quoted Adolf Hitler as saying that 'the Germans already

[13] Marchand, *Down from Olympus*, p. 184.
[14] Kossinna, *Die Herkunft der Germanen*, pp. 3–4, 18–19.
[15] Kossinna, *Die Herkunft der Germanen*, pp. 17, 19.
[16] Kossinna, *Die Herkunft der Germanen*, pp. 24–5.
[17] Mees, '*Germanische Sturmflut*', esp. pp. 184–6.
[18] Kossinna, *Die Herkunft der Germanen*, pp. 4, 17.

1000 years before the foundation of Rome had experienced a cultural prime'. Given that the Führer was usually more enthusiastic about classical culture than about Germanic[19]—both could equally be classified as Aryan[20]—this was a significant quotation.[21] Equally important for the dissemination of Kossinna's ideas to the general public, some of the maps that he drew up for his academic work, demonstrating the distribution of Germanic cultures, were reprinted in what was intended to be 'the standard history primer for the Hitler Youth'.[22] Kossinna himself was already 60 by the end of the First World War. While he continued to write until his death in 1931, it was left to his students and disciples to continue his work in the Nazi period.

13.3 RESEARCH INSTITUTES AND THE HISTORY OF THE LANDSCAPE

Perhaps the most significant element in the study of the Migration Period in the territories to the West of the Rhine in the decade and a half which followed the Treaty of Versailles was not the work of individual scholars, or indeed any one publication: rather it was the foundation of research institutes, part of whose remit was with early medieval history and archaeology. These were radically to change the funding for the study of pre- and proto-historical archaeology in Germany. Although archaeology had been dominated by the classical civilizations of Greece and Rome,[23] from now on, not just in the institutes, but also in universities, pre- and protohistory was no longer a Cinderella subject.[24]

A small number of institutes played a crucial role in the study of settlement of Germanic peoples. First there was the *Institut für geschichtliche Landeskunde der Rheinlande an der Universität Bonn*, which was founded in 1920,[25] This was followed a year later by the *Wissenschaftliche Institut der Elsaß-Lothringer im Reich an der Universität Frankfurt*.[26] The government thought it appropriate that there should be a research institute housed in Frankfurt, dedicated to studying Alsace-Lorraine, which though lost in 1918, had been home for many living Germans. 1931 saw the foundation of the *Rheinische Forschungsgemeinschaft*.[27] All three of

---

[19] Arnold, 'The past as propaganda', pp. 467, 469. See also Junker, 'Research under dictatorship', p. 287.

[20] Hitler saw the Greeks as a branch of Germans: Arnold, 'The past as propaganda', p. 467.

[21] Martens, 'The Vandals: myths and facts about a Germanic tribe of the first half of the 1st millenium AD', p. 61. For Hitler's personal historical preferences, Werner, *Das NS-Geschichtsbild*, p. 24. Also Mees, 'Hitler and *Germanentum*', pp. 263–6.

[22] For the use of Kossinna's maps in Brennecke, *Handbuch für die Schulungsarbeit in der HJ* [Hitler Jugend]: *vom deutschen Volk und seinem Lebensraum*, see Mees, 'Hitler and *Germanentum*', p. 260.

[23] Arnold, 'The past as propaganda', p. 467.

[24] The first chair in prehistory was established in 1928: Arnold and Hassmann, 'Archaeology in Nazi Germany', p. 76.

[25] Fahlbusch, *Wissenschaft im Dienst der nationalsozialistischen Politik?*, pp. 354, 368.

[26] Fahlbusch, *Wissenschaft im Dienst der nationalsozialistischen Politik?*, pp. 352, 369.

[27] Fahlbusch, *Wissenschaft im Dienst der nationalsozialistischen Politik?*, p. 353.

these institutes would be drawn into the *Westdeutsche Forschungsgemeinschaft*, which also included the *Alemannisches Institut*, based in Freiburg, and the *Provinzialinstitut für westfälische Landes- und Volkskunde* in Münster.[28] The research of the *Westdeutsche Forschungsgemeinschaft*, and most especially of its Frankfurt institute, looking as it did across the German–French border, owed a good deal to the sense of grievance caused by the Versailles settlement.[29] Where ought the border to be? Should Alsace-Lorraine belong to Germany? What of Flanders? These were questions that had already been broached as far back as the days of Ernst Moritz Arndt, and history had been drawn in to help provide the answer. In particular, there had been an outpouring of toponymic studies in the years following the take-over of Alsace at the end of the Franco-Prussian War.[30] The new institutes helped to ensure that the discussion continued.

Given the concerns of these institutes founded in the period of the Weimar republic, it is no surprise that the advent of Nazi power brought little immediate change. There was some institutional reorganization: the *Historische Reichskommission*, founded in 1928 was reformed as the *Reichsinstitut* in 1935.[31] There is similar continuity at the level of the individual scholar. Although no full professor of History was a member of the Nazi party before 1933, plenty were already expressing ideas that were entirely in tune with Nazi attitudes[32]—and Nazis certainly held chairs in other cognate disciplines.[33]

13.4 THE *AMT ROSENBERG* AND THE *AHNENERBE*

The mid 1930s did, however, see the formation of two new research institutes which were to become particularly influential. The first of these, the *Institut für Ur- und Frühgeschichte*, otherwise known as the *Amt Rosenberg*, was founded by Alfred Rosenberg in 1934.[34] It was led by Kossinna's pupil Hans Reinerth. Rosenberg himself had belonged to the *Studiengruppe für germanisches Altertum* that met in Munich between 1914 and 1918, and that came to be known as the *Thule Gesellschaft* at the end of the First World War. It included a number of men who would be among the founders of the Nazi party, including Rudolf Hess.[35]

---

[28] Fahlbusch, *Wissenschaft im Dienst der nationalsozialistischen Politik?*, pp. 353–4, 367–75.

[29] In addition to Fahlbusch, *Wissenschaft im Dienst der nationalsozialistischen Politik?*, see also Hammerstein, *Die Deutsche Forschungsgemeinschaft in der Weimarer Republik und im Dritten Reich*, though Hammerstein has little to say about early medieval scholarship. On this, see Ditt, 'The idea of German cultural regions in the Third Reich', pp. 241–58.

[30] Graceffa, *Les Historiens et la question franque*, p. 167.

[31] Schulze, 'German Historiography, 1930s to 1950s', p. 26.

[32] Schulze, 'German Historiography, 1930s to 1950s', p. 25. On the extent to which Nazi historiography continued previous lines of thought, Werner, *Das NS-Geschichtsbild*.

[33] See below on Eckhardt.

[34] Schnitzler and Legendre, 'L'organisation de l'archéologie en Allemagne et dans les régions annexées d'Alsace et de Moselle', pp. 22–6. See also Arnold, 'The past as propaganda', pp. 264–78.

[35] Mees, 'Hitler and *Germanentum*', p. 255. On the *Thule Gesellschaft*, see also Gilbhard, *Die Thule-Gesellschaft*; Goodrick-Clarke, *Black Sun: Aryan Cults, Esoteric Nazism, and the Politics of Identity*. See also the recent popular account in Kavanagh, *The Ice Museum*.

The *Amt Rosenberg*, however, would be overshadowed by another foundation, with which it was sometimes in fierce competition, the *Studien Gesellschaft für Geistesurgeschichte, Deutsches Ahnenerbe* ('Study Society for History of Primordial Ancient Ideas, German Ancestral Heritage') created in 1935 by Heinrich Himmler.[36] The *Ahnenerbe* was concerned largely with prehistory and with anthropology, and essentially with that of the Aryans. As such it was charged with pursuing some of the wilder and (because of the genetic implications of its research) more lethal flights of Himmler's fancies in its racial studies. Search for the origins of the Aryans would lead beyond the boundaries of Germany to Sweden, to look at the early rock carvings: it led to Finnland to study the *Kalevala*, the collection of Finnish and Karelian legends first gathered together by Elias Lönnroth in the nineteenth century, in an attempt to discover something of Aryan religion: to the Crimea, as the supposed centre of a Gothic Empire before its destruction by the Huns, and even to Tibet, because of its importance in the history of Sanskrit and of the Indo-Germans.

Among the scholars working on the Early Middle Ages who had strong links with the *Ahnenerbe* was Otto Höfler.[37] Born in Austria in 1901, he joined the NSDAP (the Nazi students' organization) as early as 1922.[38] His interests lay in pan-Germanism, and he took a good deal of his information from Scandinavian sources. Indeed, he had close links with Scandinavia, lecturing for a while at Uppsala University, before holding chairs at Kiel, from 1935 to 1938, Munich, from 1938 to 1945, and at Vienna from 1951 to 1971.[39] His enthusiasm for Scandinavian sources is apparent in his involvement in the translation of Wilhelm Grönbech's *Kultur und Religion der Germanen*, which had originally appeared in Danish between 1909 and 1912, and which came out in a German translation in 1954.[40] A copy of the Danish version of the work was presented to the University of Vienna on the occasion of the *Anschluß*. Höfler's *Habilitationschrift* on *Kultische Geheimbünde der Germanen*, which looked at the evidence for secret (male) societies among the early Germans, drew heavily on saga material. Höfler continued to pursue his somewhat mystical interpretations of early medieval society even after 1945, publishing the first volume of his *Germanisches Sakralkönigtum* in 1952—the second volume, perhaps fortunately, never appeared.

Not surprisingly, with its emphasis on secrecy and on male warrior ritual in the heroic North, Höfler's *Kultische Geheimbünde der Germanen* appealed strongly to Himmler. By drawing on the saga literature Höfler seemed to be looking at the evidence which shed most light on the early Aryans. The approach was thus very much in tune with that of the *Ahnenerbe*, for whose scholars the *Edda* was a key text, especially for the unravelling of Aryan religion.[41]

---

[36] On the history of the *Ahnenerbe*, see Pringle, *The Master Plan*. See also Mees, 'Hitler and *Germanentum*', and Arnold, 'The past as propaganda'.

[37] On Höfler see Mees, '*Germanische Sturmflut*', p. 189; Murray, 'Reinhard Wenskus on "Ethnogenesis"', pp. 55–7.

[38] Mees, '*Germanische Sturmflut*', p. 189.

[39] Beck, 'Otto Höfler'.

[40] The most accessible edition is Grönbech, *Kultur und Religion der Germanen*; see pp. 5–14. In the 1997 reprint the publishers included a slip to apologize that they had not been aware of Höfler's Nazi associations.

[41] Pringle, *The Master Plan*, pp. 78–81, 84.

Outside Germany there were those who were happy with the general line pursued by the *Ahnenerbe*. Indeed, there were a number of Scandinavians who worked for the organization, including the Finn, Yrjö von Grönhagen, who carried out research on the *Kalevala*.[42] There were Flemish nationalists,[43] and in Burgundy the poet and propagandist Johannès Thomasset.[44] Not surprisingly, there were even more scholars who reacted against such work and the uses to which it was being put. Von Grönhagen was criticized by Martti Haavio.[45] The Norwegian Anton Brøgger, who excavated the Oseberg ship, expressed alarm at the uses to which the Germans were putting Swedish material.[46] He would be denounced by Herbert Jankuhn during the Nazi occupation, though the Norwegians would get some revenge when the University of Bergen turned down Jankuhn's offer of a public lecture in 1968.[47]

This esoteric approach to Aryan origins appealed to Himmler a good deal more than it did to Hitler, who remarked in 1933 that '[t]hese professors and mystery-men who want to found Nordic religions merely get in my way'.[48] What interested the Führer was Germans and not Aryans.[49] Hitler was not alone in thinking that the enthusiasms of Himmler and the *Ahnenerbe* were somewhat fantastical. Heinrich Dannenbauer, despite being a party member who would lose his post after the War as being 'politically incriminated',[50] attacked the idea that the *deutsche Volk* was an unchanging entity, arguing that it was historically constructed. He denounced the presentation of German history as the history of a race, stressing, for instance, the importance of the Celtic substratum in southern Germany.[51]

However, alongside their more fantastical projects, both the *Ahnenerbe* and the *Amt Rosenberg* undertook rather more sober excavations.[52] Among the early-medieval archaeologists supported by one or other institution were Hans Zeiss, professor at Munich, and Joachim Werner, professor of pre- and proto-history at the Reichsuniversität of Strasbourg during the Nazi occupation, as well as Jankuhn, who played a major role in the uncovering of the Viking Age emporium of Haithabu.[53]

---

[42] Pringle, *The Master Plan*, pp. 77–89.

[43] On the *Vlaams Verbond van Frankrijk* and its use of Petri's work, see Ditt, 'The idea of German cultural regions in the Third Reich', p. 249.

[44] Rauwel, 'Die Burgunden in Burgund, 1920–1945', pp. 387–91.

[45] Pringle, *The Master Plan*, p. 89.

[46] Pringle, *The Master Plan*, pp. 74–5.

[47] Pringle, *The Master Plan*, p. 312.

[48] Mees, 'Hitler and *Germanentum*', p. 267. See also p. 256 on Hitler's comment on '*deutschvölkisch* wandering scholars' in *Mein Kampf*.

[49] Mees, 'Hitler and *Germanentum*', p. 268.

[50] Schultze, 'German Historiography, 1930s to 1950s', pp. 25, 36.

[51] Dannenbauer, *Indogermanen, Germanen, Deutsche*. See Werner, *Das NS-Geschichtsbild*, pp. 56–9.

[52] Arnold 'The past as propaganda'.

[53] Olivier, 'L'archéologie nationale-socialiste et la France', p. 57; Schnitzler and Legendre, 'L'archéologie en Alsace-Moselle entre 1940 et 1944', p. 141.

13.5 THE *MONUMENTA* AND ITS *MITARBEITER*

It was not only the new research institutes founded under Weimar and in the early years of National Socialism which contributed to a Nazi reading of the Early Middle Ages. The *Monumenta Germaniae Historica* with its built-in concern for German origins inevitably had a contribution to make, above all in the study of early law codes. These could be used to demonstrate the traditional virtues of the Germanic peoples, and the democratic nature of their justice. Law provided a major insight into the Germanic *Volk*. It is not, therefore, surprising to find committed Nazis editing law codes.[54]

The most significant of these editors was Karl August Eckhardt (1901–79), whose post-War editions of the various versions of *Lex Salica* are usually regarded as the most successful attempts so far to edit what is an extremely complex set of recensions of the main Frankish lawbook. Eckhardt was appointed to a chair of Law at the University of Kiel in 1928 at the early age of twenty-seven. In 1930 he moved to Berlin and two years later to Bonn. After holding a number of other academic posts he would return there to a Chair of *Germanische Rechtsgeschichte*. On taking up the chair at Kiel he had delivered a hugely appreciative eulogy of his predecessor, the Jewish legal-historian Max Pappenheim.[55] He was soon, however, to show his true political colours. In May 1932 he became an SS-Mann, and in March the following year a member of the Nazi party: in October 1933 he became yet further committed to the SS, and in January 1935 he rose to the level of *Untersturmführer*. At the same time, between 1934 and 1936 he was *Hauptreferent* for the *Hochschulabteilung* of the *Reichswissenschaftsministerium* (Chief examiner for the High School division of the National Science Ministry). In 1936 he rose to *Obersturmführer* in the SS, and two years later to *Sturmbannführer*. Given his Nazi credentials he was regarded as a potential president of the *Monumenta Germaniae Historica*, though in the event that post would be taken by Edmund Stengel. Eckhardt was close enough to the Nazi leadership to be one of those to contribute to the *Festgabe für Heinrich Himmler* in 1941,[56]—indeed, from 1935 onwards he was a member of Himmler's Schwarzes Korps. After the war he would no longer have a teaching position, though he did become director of the *Historisches Institut des Werralandes*. It was from here that he produced his major editions of Germanic law, although they were published by the *Monumenta*, of which he himself was a *Mitarbeiter* from 1927 to 1979.

More ideologically questionable than his legal editions were his researches into the family origins of the Carolingians, given the inevitable association of descent with blood and biology. This he published as late as 1965 under the title *Merowingerblut* in the *Germanenrechte* series, for which he had produced an earlier edition

---

[54] On legal studies in the Nazi period, Rückert and Willoweit, *Die deutsche Rechtsgeschichte in der NS-Zeit*.

[55] Fuhrmann, *'Sind eben alles Menschen gewesen'*, pp. 58–64. See also Niemann, 'Karl August Eckhardt'.

[56] Eckhardt, 'Das Fuldaer Vasallengeschlecht vom Stein'.

of *Lex Salica*, as well an edition of Anglo-Saxon law.[57] This was the series for which another Nazi-sympathizer, Franz Beyerle,[58] produced editions of the Burgundian Code in 1936 and the Lombard laws in 1947. Together with Rudolf Buchner, Beyerle also edited the Ripuarian code of the Franks for the *Monumenta*.

In the 1930s the *Monumenta* was seen very much as representing the greatness of German history: a set of volumes, with the bookmark *Geschenk des Deutschen Reiches*, was given to the Institute of Historical Research in the University of London in 1938, although student protest opposed the presentation of the books by ambassador Joachim von Ribbentrop.[59] The gift was a rather more distinguished one than the copy of Grönbech's *Kultur und Religion der Germanen*, received by the University of Vienna on the occasion of the *Anschluß*.

Among other *Mitarbeiter* of the *Monumenta* whose views were largely consonant with the party line and who wrote, at least occasionally, about the *Völkerwanderungzeit* was Johannes Haller (1865–1947).[60] As a Prussian, born before the unification of Germany, the ideology to which he subscribed was patriotic, chauvinist, and militaristic, and was thus one that essentially foreshadowed that of the Nazis,[61] indeed Haller would sign an appeal supporting Hitler's election campaign in 1932.[62] On his seventy-fifth birthday in 1940 he was the recipient of a *Festschrift* with the suggestive title *Das Reich—Idee und Gestalt* ('The *Reich*—Idea and Character').[63] His own *Epochen der deutschen Geschichte*, originally published in 1922, and then reprinted in 1934, 1939, and 1941, has been called the most successful German historical work of the twentieth century.[64] Although Haller was primarily interested in the central Middle Ages, he did have views on the Migration Period, and produced a little book on *Der Eintritt der Germanen in die Geschichte*. Printed in a small format, and amounting to just over a hundred pages, this makes no attempt to argue a detailed case; rather it presents a very condensed narrative, stretching from the first century to the ninth. As the foreword explains, however, this was an age of great importance, when for the first time the continent of Europe gained cultural unity, and when the family of West-European states (*eine Familiengemeinschaft abendländischer Staaten*), which would impact on the whole world, was created: it was the period in which the *Germanen* came to stand alongside the Greeks and the Romans. The book was, in other words, a triumphalist Hegelian statement of the contribution of the early Germanic peoples to European and, by implication, world history.[65]

---

[57] Eckhardt, *Die Gesetze des Merowingerreiches, 481–714*; Eckhardt, *Leges Anglo-saxonum, 601–925*.

[58] On Beyerle as a Nazi, Fahlbusch, *Wissenschaft im Dienst der nationalsozialistischen Politik?*, p. 358. Nazi influence on Beyerle's thought is denied in a letter of Hermann Schultze von Lasaulx published in Rückert and Willoweit (eds), *Die Deutsche Rechtsgeschichte in der NS-Zeit*, pp. 345–6.

[59] *Bulletin of the Institute of Historical Research* 15 (1938), p. 32.

[60] Fuhrmann, *'Sind eben alles Menschen gewesen'*, p. 32.

[61] Werner, *Das NS-Geschichtsbild*, pp. 71–4.

[62] Schulze, 'German historiography, 1930s to 1950s', p. 25.

[63] Dannenbauer and Ernst (eds), *Das Reich—Idee und Gestalt*.

[64] Werner, *Das NS-Geschichtsbild*, p. 71.   [65] Haller, *Die Eintritt der Germanen*, p. 11.

13.6 STEINBACH AND PETRI

To return to the world of the new founded institutes of the 1930s: the director, first of the *Rheinische Forschungsgemeinschaft*, and subsequently of the *Westdeutsche Forschungsgemeinschaft* was Franz Steinbach (1895–1964). To some extent he was a scholar in the Lamprecht-mould: his concern was cultural history, and above all the Romano-Germanic *Mischkultur* of the Merovingian kingdom, which he studied principally through the evidence of archaeology and place names.[66] Initially, at least, his approach was relatively open-minded. At the *Tagung* (conference) held at Bad Dürkheim in 1935 on 'Das Wissenschaftsverhältnis zum westlichen Nachbarn Frankreich' ('Scholarly relations with France, our neighbour to the West') he referred to the work of Alfons Dopsch as providing a bridge between German scholarship and the work of Pirenne.[67] Rather less emollient, at the same conference, was Franz Petri, who went out of his way to attack the work of Fustel de Coulanges and of Camille Jullian for being too negative about Germanic settlement in France.[68]

Petri was a pupil of the philologist Dietrich Schäfer. In some ways, however, his work, combining place names and archaeology looked back to other scholars, not least to the work of Kossinna. Despite the differences in tone they adopted at Bad Dürkheim, Steinbach would come to accept Petri's position, especially after the publication of the latter's monumental thesis, *Germanisches Volkserbe in Wallonien und Nordfrankreich* (1937).[69] So impressed with Petri's work was Steinbach that in 1939 the two of them collaborated to produce a volume on the Frankish settlement: *Zur Grundlegung der europäischen Einheit durch die Franken*. This was in fact simply a reprint of two recent articles, one by Steinbach on German and French *Volksgeschichte*,[70] and the other, rather longer, by Petri on Germanic settlement in the Frankish kingdom, and its historiography.[71] Here the two of them spelt out the importance of what they identified as Germanic settlement, using archaeology and linguistics, alongside rather vaguer cultural and legal indicators. Steinbach, like Petri, presented the land between the Rhine and the Loire as the cultural heart of Europe—the *kerneuropäische Block* ('core-European Block')—while arguing that Germanic settlement was a key feature of the region.[72] Detailed argument about the settlement he essentially left to Petri, whose contribution is little more than a

---

[66] Steinbach, *Studien zur westdeutschen Stammes- und Volksgeschichte*; Freund, 'Burgund in den nationalsozialistischen Planungen', p. 399; Fahlbusch, *Wissenschaft im Dienst der nationalsozialistischen Politik?*, p. 355; Ditt, 'The idea of German cultural regions in the Third Reich', pp. 243–4.

[67] Fahlbusch, *Wissenschaft im Dienst der nationalsozialistischen Politik?*, pp. 381–2.

[68] Fahlbusch, *Wissenschaft im Dienst der nationalsozialistischen Politik?*, p. 383.

[69] On Steinbach's acceptance of Petri's ideas, Ditt, 'The idea of German cultural regions in the Third Reich', pp. 246–7. The quality of Petri's work, however, is not high: Haubrichs, '*Germania submersa*'.

[70] Steinbach, 'Gemeinsame Wesenszüge der deutschen und der französischen Volksgeschichte'.

[71] Petri, 'Um die Volksgrundlagen des Frankenreiches'.

[72] Steinbach, 'Gemeinsame Wesenszüge der deutschen und der französischen Volksgeschichte', pp. 3–4. For Petri's description of the region between the Rhine and the Loire as a *Kerngebiet*, see 'Um die Volksgrundlagen des Frankenreiches', p. 22.

very terse restatement of the argument of his *Germanisches Volkserbe*, bolstered by responses to his critics, above all to the Romance philologist Ernst Gamillscheg. Petri was, however, careful to point to those Francophone scholars whose ideas could be presented as sorting well with his own—at least if one was very selective in which arguments one cited. Thus he referred enthusiastically to Lot's description of the establishment of the Frankish state by Clovis as 'miracle historique'[73] and to Des Marez' work on Frankish colonization[74]—a citation that would doubtless not have pleased Des Marez, the man who refused to cooperate with Lamprecht in the division of Belgium in 1915.

Petri's *Germanisches Volkserbe* begins, traditionally enough, with a lengthy survey of scholarship on the Germanic settlement in Belgium and north-eastern France. When did the Frankish settlement take place? Before or during the conquest which led to the establishment of the Merovingian kingdom? Or was it not a conquest? Petri set out the opinions of different German scholars, though he did not trace the arguments through their French origins back to the time of Boulainvilliers.[75] Where was the limit of settlement, and how many Franks were involved?[76] Here Petri listed some of those who had downplayed the issue of conquest, among them Dopsch, Fustel, and Lot,[77] but also noted that Bloch in particular had reopened the question of the nature of the Frankish conquest.[78] He then pointed out the difficulty of squaring the evidence of the linguistic frontier in Belgium with what was known from the historical narrative, and concluded that the real problem was not geographical, but chronological, and that it was caused by an unwarranted assumption that the linguistic boundary was created at the time that the settlement took place.[79] Petri next considered the work of Kurth, who had acknowledged that some settlement lay to the south of the linguistic frontier, but had also argued that the Charbonnière had presented a formidable barrier to the Franks. As Duvivier had pointed out, however, the Charbonnière runs north–south, while the linguistic frontier runs east–west.[80]

Having addressed the linguistic problem, Petri turned to pay more attention to the archaeology. He noted the excavations that had already been undertaken in the 1830s and 40s,[81] before going on to consider the question of the interpretation of cemeterial archaeology. Kurth had insisted that the majority of the cemeteries that had been excavated were those not of Franks, but of Gallo-Romans,[82] a view that has recently come back into fashion.[83] For Petri, Kurth was mistaken: he had not

---

[73] Petri, 'Um die Volksgrundlagen des Frankenreiches', in Steinbach and Petri, *Zur Grundlegung der europäischen Einheit durch die Franken*, p. 18. Steinbach also cites Lot, ibid. p. 15.

[74] Petri, 'Um die Volksgrundlagen des Frankenreiches', pp. 21, 33.

[75] Petri, *Germanisches Volkserbe*, p. 3.

[76] Petri, *Germanisches Volkserbe*, p. 4.

[77] Petri, *Germanisches Volkserbe*, pp. 5–6.

[78] Petri, *Germanisches Volkserbe*, p. 6, citing Bloch, 'La conqête de la Gaule romaine'.

[79] Petri, *Germanisches Volkserbe*, pp. 9–12.

[80] Petri, *Germanisches Volkserbe*, pp. 13–18.

[81] Petri, *Germanisches Volkserbe*, p. 30.

[82] Petri, *Germanisches Volkserbe*, p. 32.

[83] See James, 'Cemeteries and the problem of Frankish settlement in Gaul'.

recognized the Germanic nature of many of the objects found.[84] To his way of thinking this was something that had become clear from new archaeology: that is, from the new methods of dating, of periodization and typology[85] (which in part go back to Kossinna). New methodologies, both archaeological and toponymic, had, in Petri's view, revealed that the archaeology was directly related to the Frankish conquest.[86]

After setting out the historiography of the subject, Petri worked through the place names of Wallonia and Northern France at considerable length—thus looking beyond the confines of Belgium.[87] He then attempted to offer a reconstruction of Frankish settlement in north-eastern Gaul. He noted the variety of settlement to be found in the evidence. He identified what he described as an initial federate culture (*Föderatenkultur*), following the arguments of the Austrian, Alois Riegl, in his *Spätrömische Kunstindustrie*.[88] As for the row graves, the *Reihengräber*, one of the most distinctive features of early medieval archaeology to be found in parts of Belgium, northern France, and the Rhineland, he insisted that anthropology and archaeology proved that they were Germanic.[89] Taken together, toponyms and cemetery archaeology revealed, for Petri, the existence of cultural *Kerngebiete*, core areas, of the Germanic peoples.[90] *Lex Salica*, meanwhile, with its concern for the territory between the *Silva Carbonnaria* and the Loire, clearly indicated the centrality of that part of Francia for the Merovingians.

On the matter of distinctions between different groups of Franks, Petri saw the problem of distinguishing between the Salians and Ripuarians as insoluble.[91] Instead, he stressed the distinction between the culture of the federates and that of the *Reihengräberkultur* ('row-grave culture').[92] The new cultural unity indicated by the row graves he attributed to Clovis.[93] Unlike Fustel and Kurth, Petri argued for a massive invasion by the Germanic peoples. Fustel, he said, had been right to note the existence of *laeti*, but had been wrong to ignore the evidence for a subsequent incursion, which is illustrated by the archaeology.[94] In Petri's view, the archaeology of the *Reihengräber* confirmed Gregory of Tours' picture of the existence of a Frankish overclass. There was a class distinction between Frank and Gaul, which the French had interpreted as discrimination.[95] There may have been some Roman survival in legal practice, as argued by Fustel, Dopsch, and Pirenne, but the basic principles of Frankish law were Germanic. The State was Germanic, and its officials were Germanic.[96] Vocabulary indicated the impact of the Germanic presence on war, on the household, on peasant life, on industry. In so far as there was cultural continuity, as argued by Dopsch, for Petri that continuity depended on the Germanic incomers.[97] For him, Pirenne was quite right to argue the Merovingians were a powerful group in the Mediterranean world. He was wrong, however, in

[84] Petri, *Germanisches Volkserbe*, pp. 37–40.
[85] Petri, *Germanisches Volkserbe*, pp. 43–4.
[86] Petri, *Germanisches Volkserbe*, pp. 46–7.
[87] Petri, *Germanisches Volkserbe*, pp. 49–767.
[88] Petri, *Germanisches Volkserbe*, pp. 783–5.
[89] Petri, *Germanisches Volkserbe*, pp. 797–800, 844–6.
[90] Petri, *Germanisches Volkserbe*, pp. 851–2.
[91] Petri, *Germanisches Volkserbe*, p. 879.
[92] Petri, *Germanisches Volkserbe*, p. 899.
[93] Petri, *Germanisches Volkserbe*, p. 902.
[94] Petri, *Germanisches Volkserbe*, p. 907.
[95] Petri, *Germanisches Volkserbe*, p. 909.
[96] Petri, *Germanisches Volkserbe*, pp. 912–15.
[97] Petri, *Germanisches Volkserbe*, pp. 917–21.

Petri's eyes, to see the Germanic peoples as dependent on Mediterranean culture. The *laeti* had already Germanized Roman culture, and it was from Germanic elements that medieval art developed. Shortly after 500 northern France looked not to the Mediterranean, but to the Rhine, and it was from here that culture would subsequently spread south and southwest.[98]

In Petri's view the Frankish settlement that went hand in hand with the conquest of Gaul, and with the establishment of the Merovingian kingdom, stretched far beyond the current linguistic frontier. This, for him, did not reflect the actual area of Frankish settlement in the fifth and sixth centuries, but was rather the result of an expansion of Romance culture in the late Carolingian period, though he also accepted that this Roman revival began in the Merovingian court of the sixth century.[99] The linguistic frontier, then, was a *völkische Rückzugslinie* ('line to which the people had retreated'). But what of the indigenous population of the region? In Petri's view even in Caesar's day this included a mixture of Germanic and Celtic peoples, some of whom served as Roman auxiliaries.[100] Thus, there was already a significant Germanic element in the region, as had been demonstrated by the German archaeologist, Doppelfeld. This archaeological work showed that Germanic settlement began in the area between the Maas, Mosel, and Rhine as early as 500 BC[101]—shades of Kossinna's style of argumentation.

For Petri the Rhineland had a central role to play in German historiography, even though it was actually less German, *weniger kernhaft deutsch*, than the old centres of Germanic settlement (Kossinna's *Urheimat der Germanen*). It boasted an important Roman heritage, but it was also a dynamic area that had been settled and refashioned by the Germanic peoples.[102] Rather ominously, in describing the territory of the Maas, Mosel and Rhine Petri adds the proverb: 'Was du ererbt von Deinem Vätern hast, erwirb es, um es zu besitzen', with the rider 'das gilt in der Volksgeschichte so gut wie sonst im Leben.' ('What you have inherited from your fathers, appropriate it to make it your own': 'this applies to *Volksgeschichte* as it applies elsewhere in life.')[103] West of the Rhine was a region that, when Petri was writing his *Habilitation*, was largely in Belgian and French hands, but clearly he wished it otherwise.

Petri's *Germanisches Volkserbe* is a work on a massive scale: as a *Habilitationsschrift* it was, of course, addressed entirely to a specialist audience. It was not accepted by all: indeed, it was met by a good deal of criticism, from, for instance, Gamillscheg and Draye.[104] Petri, however, was successful enough in convincing others of the strength of his scholarship to gain the chair at the German-Dutch institute in Cologne in 1938, and the chair in Dutch history in the same city four

[98] Petri, *Germanisches Volkserbe*, pp. 927–8.
[99] Petri, *Germanisches Volkserbe*, pp. 972–84, 988, 997.
[100] Petri, *Germanisches Volkserbe*, pp. 989–91.
[101] Petri, *Germanisches Volkserbe*, pp. 995–6.
[102] Petri, *Germanisches Volkserbe*, p. 999.
[103] Petri, *Germanisches Volkserbe*, p. 998.
[104] See the assessment of Petri in Haubrichs, '*Germania submersa*'.

years later.[105] He also set out his arguments at a more popular level in numerous articles.[106]

Politics clearly played a role in Petri's academic rise, and he certainly attracted attention well outside the academic world. Not only was he closely associated with Himmler's *Ahnenerbe*.[107] His expertise in Belgian culture led to his being appointed officer in occupied Belgium responsible for cultural politics.[108] There is a clear parallel to be drawn with Lamprecht's mission to Brussels in 1915. In addition, his work on the *Germanisches Volkserbe* had a direct political impact. Hitler read it overnight on 4th May 1942, and was delighted to find in it justification for the annexation of large areas of Belgium.[109] Despite the scale of the work, the Führer's claim to have read it in a short space of time is not implausible, given how much of it is made up simply of lists of place names and archaeological finds. Although Petri himself was not involved in making plans for redrawing the western boundary of the *Reich*, his *Habilitationschrift* was consulted. In fact, Petri came to believe that both the German government and the radical Flemish nationalists were failing to note the subtlety of his arguments and were using them beyond what was legitimate.[110] Even so, and not surprisingly, after the War he was deprived of his academic post in Cologne, as a result of the extent of his association with Nazi policy.

13.7 ARCHAEOLOGY AND THE FRONTIERS OF THE *REICH*

Petri's work was not alone, either in its argument or in the use to which it was put. One can find the same issue of Germanic settlement, as exemplified in the archaeological and toponymic evidence, explored for the territories south of Belgium: for Alsace-Lorraine and for Burgundy, including Franche-Comté, the Côte d'Or, Saône-et-Loire, and Ain. The resulting maps of Germanic settlement were also drawn into discussions of the appropriate border for the *Reich*.

Alsace was of especial interest for German scholars: this had been the case for centuries, and following the Franco-Prussian war the region had, indeed, belonged to the *Reich*. Even after 1918, when it was no longer in German hands, it was the focus of research carried out by the *Wissenschaftliche Institut des Elsaß-Lothringer im Reich an der Universität Frankfurt*. Not surprisingly, during the annexation of 1940–1944 it became a hive of German archaeological activity, some of which was

---

[105] Ditt, 'The idea of German cultural regions in the Third Reich', p. 242.

[106] Oberkrone, 'Entwicklungen und Varianten der deutschen Volksgeschichte', p. 83.

[107] Schnitzler and Legendre, 'L'organisation de l'archéologie en Allemagne et dans les régions annexées d'Alsace et de Moselle', p. 21. See also Fahlbusch, review of Derks, *Deutsche Westforschung*.

[108] Ditt, 'The idea of German cultural regions in the Third Reich', p. 242.

[109] Ditt, 'The idea of German cultural regions in the Third Reich', p. 249, citing Picker (ed.) *Hitlers Tischgespräche im Führerhauptquartier 1941–2*, pp. 424–5. See also Freund, 'Burgund in den nationalsozialistischen Planungen', pp. 401, 406.

[110] Ditt, 'The idea of German cultural regions in the Third Reich', p. 249.

of high quality.[111] While adapting the Maginot Line the Germans excavated a number of early medieval cemeteries.[112] Among the other major sites that were dug were the cemetery at Ennery and the early church of Saint-Pierre-aux-Nonnains in Metz.[113] Above all there was the princely grave of Ittenheim, discovered by Joachim Werner, who was then professor of pre- and proto-history at the Reichsuniversität in Strasbourg.[114] Like the areas of Belgium and the far north of France studied by Petri, Alsace could easily be presented as the territory of intensive Germanic settlement, though the Germanic peoples involved were thought to be Alamans rather than Franks,[115] and the warrior grave of Ittenheim was seen to be that of a seventh-century Alaman warrior.[116]

While Alsace had been settled by Alamans, Burgundy overlapped with the kingdom of the Burgundians, even though the two regions were by no means coterminous. Burgundian archaeology attracted a considerable number of scholars: indeed, despite the lack of any centre for Burgundian studies in Germany, it has been estimated that more SS-*Wissenschaftler* worked in Burgundy that in any other region.[117] Not least among these was Hans Zeiss, who already in 1938 had written on Burgundian grave-finds in the Rhône valley[118] and who wrote several papers on Burgundian archaeology after 1939, including 'Germanen in Burgund', which appeared in *Burgund: Das Land zwischen Rhein und Rhone*, edited by Franz Kerber of the Alamannisches Institut in Freiburg in 1942.[119]

Just as the evidence for Frankish settlement in Flanders was used in plans for redrawing the boundaries of the Reich, so too Burgundian settlement was noted in discussions about the boundaries further south. Already in 1940, following the defeat of France, Hitler had thought of including Nord-Pas-de-Calais, most of Picardy and Champagne-Ardenne, together with Lorraine, Doubs, the Langres plateau, and Jura within the *Reich*, while the Netherlands, Flanders, Wallonia, Lorraine, and Burgundy were included within a new buffer zone that year.[120] Goebbels in his *Tagebuch* (diary) talked of the return of Burgundy to the *Reichgebiet*. In 1942 Hitler and Speer both spoke of incorporating Burgundy within the *Reich*.[121] This was also the moment at which the Führer was considering the relevance of Petri's work for the frontier in Belgium. The plans drawn up for the regions of Alsace-Lorraine and Burgundy

[111] Schnitzler and Legendre, 'L'archéologie en Alsace-Moselle entre 1940 et 1944', p. 200.
[112] Schnitzler, 'Fouilles et thèmes de recherche en Alsace'.
[113] Legendre, 'Sites fouillés et thèmes de recherche en Moselle'.
[114] Schnitzler and Legendre, 'L'organisation de l'archéologie en Allemagne et dans les régions annexées d'Alsace et de Moselle', p. 35; Schnitzler, 'Fouilles et thèmes de recherche en Alsace', p. 89. On Werner in Strasbourg, Adam, 'L'enseignement de la Reichsuniversität de Strasbourg'.
[115] Schnitzler, 'Fouilles et thèmes de recherche en Alsace', p. 89.
[116] Schnitzler and Legendre, 'L'organisation de l'archéologie en Allemagne et dans les régions annexées d'Alsace et de Moselle', p. 35.
[117] Freund, 'Burgund in den nationalsozialistischen Planungen', p. 420.
[118] Zeiss, *Studien zu den Grabfunden aus den Burgunderreich an der Rhône*.
[119] Zeiss, 'Germanen in Burgund'. For Zeiss's writings on Burgundy during the War, see Freund, 'Burgund in den nationalsozialistischen Planungen', p. 414.
[120] Freund, 'Burgund in den nationalsozialistischen Planungen', pp. 406–8.
[121] Freund, 'Burgund in den nationalsozialistischen Planungen', p. 409–10.

certainly looked back to the medieval past, in part to the past of the frontiers within the Carolingian Empire, as drawn up in 843,[122] but also to the Germanic past of the Burgundian kingdom, as illustrated by the cemetery archaeology. Even more than the Franks, the Burgundians, with their supposed origins on the Baltic island of Bornholm/Burgundaholm, could be depicted as northern heroes—indeed, as heroes of the *Nibelungenlied*.[123]

The conquests and settlement of the Migration Period could thus be integrated into aggressive patriotism, which went back at least as far as Ernst Moritz Arndt. Archaeology and toponymics could be combined with Lamprecht's sense that Flanders was culturally German. Such attitudes were shared by scholars who regarded the Versailles settlement as an injustice that had reversed the rightful occupation of Alsace-Lorraine following the Battle of Sedan. Similar views were held with regard to the eastern frontiers of Germany, but for most, their medieval origins were to be found in a slightly different period of time, and there the initial historical conflict was not one between the Germanic barbarians and Rome, but rather between the Germans and the Slavs.

Petri was just one of a number of specialists in the early Middle Ages whose work on settlement played a role in the development of Nazi plans. They provided ammunition to justify and refine policies that had already been decided on. As Ditt says,

> The Nazis gratefully accepted the supply of academic theses as a legitimization of German expansion, the propagation of nationalist values, and also the role given to them as the instrument of a German mission. Their plans to re-draw German political boundaries were however hardly oriented on the primacy of academic research. Their decisions and debates on future boundaries in the West and more especially the East were rather based on political and military considerations.[124]

13.8 GERMANIC ITALY, THE DEUTSCHES ARCHÄOLOGISCHES INSTITUT AND SIEGFRIED FUCHS

As with Alsace, Burgundy, and Belgium, the question of whether south Tirol was German or Italian could be seen through the lens of the *Völkerwanderungzeit* of the fifth and sixth centuries, for it had been settled by the Ostrogoths. Indeed, the region is portrayed as a haven of Gothic settlement in Dahn's *Ein Kampf um Rom*: the Alpine region is the homeland of Witichis' virtuous wife. The population of South Tirol has even been described as 'Goths preserved in glacial ice'.[125] The region had been part of Austria before 1918, when it was handed over to Italy. In

[122] Freund, 'Burgund in den nationalsozialistischen Planungen', p. 408.
[123] Freund, 'Burgund in den nationalsozialistischen Planungen', pp. 411, 414.
[124] Ditt, 'The idea of German cultural regions in the Third Reich', p. 251.
[125] Pringle, *The Master Plan*, p. 229, quoting Nußbaumer, *Alfred Quellmalz und seine Südtiroler Feldforschungen*, p. 93.

the late 1930s and early 1940s relations between Germany and Italy were, of course, very different from those between Germany and France or Belgium. Even so, it is remarkable that Hitler persuaded Mussolini in 1939 to allow the South Tirolese a plebiscite on whether they should be part of the Italian state or the German Reich: in 1940 185,000 out of 210,000 of them opted for Germany.[126] Keeping their Gothic origins in mind, Hitler wanted to settle them in the Crimea, which, according to the *Ahnenerbe* scholar Karl Kersten, had been the centre of the Gothic Empire in the fifth century, before the arrival of the Huns. Indeed, Kersten, backed by Himmler, went in search of the site of the Gothic capital, and he was accompanied by Jankuhn.[127]

For most German scholars, however, Italy presented a very different set of issues than did the lands of the western frontier of the Reich, and that was above all because of a longstanding scholarly love of the classical past. Before 1914 German scholarship on the Fall of Rome and on the Migration Period was associated to a large extent with the work of the German Archaeological Institute (*Deutsches Archäologisches Institut*: DAI).[128] This had been founded as a private initiative as far back as 1829, and was thus almost as venerable an institution as the *Monumenta*. Initially it was based in Rome, although after 1832 it gained a headquarters in Berlin. In 1870 it was transformed into a state institute, subject to the Foreign Office, an affiliation that would be changed in 1934, when it was transferred to the Ministry of Science, Education, and the Formation of the *Volk* (*Reichsministerium für Wissenschaft, Erziehung und Volksbildung*). In 1874 it established a branch in Athens, and branches in Cairo and Istanbul followed in 1907 and 1929. Within Germany it founded the *Römisch-Germanische Kommission* in Frankfurt in 1902. To a large extent the DAI concerned itself with Greek and Roman history—and indeed its staff would be derided as *Römlinge* ('baby Romans') by some of the more nationalist archaeologists of the interwar period.[129] Not surprisingly, however, it became increasingly involved in Migration-Period studies.

This was less the case in its Berlin headquarters than it was in the Roman branch of the DAI, since Germany could boast several rival institutions concentrated on the archaeology of the pre- and proto-historic periods. In Rome the dangerously political figure of Siegfried Fuchs was crucial.[130] Already in 1933, while still a student, Fuchs signed up as a member of the *Sturmabteilung* of the Nazi party. In 1936 he joined the party itself, and three years later he became a member of the SS. Given his political leanings, it is no surprise to discover that Fuchs' original

---

[126] Pringle, *The Master Plan*, p. 229; Freund, 'Burgund in den nationalsozialistischen Planungen', p. 418.

[127] Pringle, *The Master Plan*, pp. 230–5.

[128] On the German study of Greece and Rome, see Marchand, *Down from Olympus*. For the *Deutsches Archäologisches Institut* in this period, pp. 173–80. For the DAI see also Junker, 'Research under dictatorship', esp. pp. 282–3.

[129] Junker, 'Research under dictatorship', pp. 286–7.

[130] Junker, 'Research under dictatorship', pp. 286, 290; Maischberger, 'German archaeology during the Third Reich, 1933–45', p. 212–15; Fröhlich, 'The study of the Lombards and the Ostrogoths at the German Archaeological Institute of Rome'.

work on archaic Greece was concerned with supposed Indogermanic settlement in the Bronze Age.[131] His position in the Nazi party no doubt helped in his being appointed first to the directorship of the Institute's photo-library and then to his elevation to second in command of the DAI in Rome in 1937—though it should also be acknowledged that he was a serious scholar. In the same year, being in charge of the Institute's research programme, Fuchs was entrusted with implementing the Ministry's directive, that research should be focused on evidence for Germanic life in Italy.[132] The director of the Institute in Rome, Armin von Gerkan, decided that it would be best to concentrate on the Lombards, rather than the Goths, whom he thought the Italians regarded as 'a horde of Barbarians'—rather the reverse of the nineteenth-century Italian view.[133] Fuchs had already started work analysing the finds from the post-Roman cemeteries of Nocera Umbra and Castel Trosino—sites that had initially been excavated in the last decade of the nineteenth century, and which would dominate interpretation of the Lombard settlement in Italy for much of the twentieth. They would also provide the backbone of the contents of the Museo dell'alto medioevo.[134] A first result of his work was a study of *Die langobardischen Goldblattkreuze*, gold-leaf crosses that were thought to be peculiar to the Lombard and Bavarian region (although this has subsequently proved not to be the case).[135] He gave a copy of the book to Hitler when he visited Rome in 1938.[136] Subsequently the work attracted Himmler's attention, and helped secure his support for the DAI as it tried to negotiate permission to excavate in Italy. As a result, an official collaboration was agreed: Fuchs was to publish articles in the journal of Himmler's *Ahnenerbe*, which would in turn help to secure approval for excavations. Fuchs was close enough to Himmler to deputize for him at the sixth International Congress of Archaeology, which was held in Berlin in 1939.[137]

Following his work on *Goldblattkreuze*, Fuchs considered collaborating with the Norwegian scholar H. P. L'Orange on a study of early medieval architecture. L'Orange had already collaborated with Armin von Gerkan, the first secretary and later temporary director of the DAI, on the arch of Constantine.[138] In so far as anything came out of the proposed collaboration with Fuchs, it was L'Orange's post-War study, *Art Forms and Civic Life in the Late Roman Empire*, where he portrayed the architecture of Late Antiquity as having similarities with that of the Fascists.[139] Instead, despite being called up to fight in Africa in 1941–2, Fuchs

---

[131] Fuchs, *Die griechischen Fundgruppen der frühen Bronzezeit und ihre auswärtigen Beziehungen.*

[132] Maischberger, 'German archaeology during the Third Reich', p. 213; Junker, 'Research under dictatorship', pp. 286, 290.

[133] Junker, 'Research under dictatorship', p. 290.

[134] Arena and Paroli, *Museo dell'alto medioevo Roma*, pp. 17–54.

[135] Fuchs, *Die langobardischen Goldblattkreuze aus der Zone südwärts der Alpen.*

[136] Fröhlich, 'The study of the Lombards and the Ostrogoths at the German Archaeological Institute of Rome', p. 194.

[137] Fröhlich, 'The study of the Lombards and the Ostrogoths at the German Archaeological Institute of Rome', p. 197.

[138] L'Orange and von Gerkan, *Der spätantike Bildschmuck des Konstantinsbogen.*

[139] L'Orange, *Art Forms and Civic Life in the Late Roman Empire.*

turned his attention to the Ostrogoths, producing a work on Ostrogothic art in 1944.[140] Meanwhile, the DAI initiated an excavation at the site of Theodoric's villa of Galeata, which Fuchs and the excavator, Fritz Krischen, interpreted in the light of surviving remains at Aachen and at Naranco, outside Oviedo, thus stressing what they regarded as the Germanic nature of the building.[141] At the same time the surroundings of Theodoric's mausoleum in Ravenna were excavated. Even more redolent of the heroic past that had been conjured up by Felix Dahn in his *Ein Kampf um Rom* were the excavations at *Busta Gallorum/ Taginae*, the site of Totila's final battle against the Byzantines. Fuchs, who by now had been awarded the SS *Totenkopfring* by Himmler, continued the excavation even as the Allies advanced up Italy.[142] He would himself retreat to Brescia, where he was active in the SS and the police, before being captured by the Americans. He was one of the few archaeologists who, having survived the war, did not have a post-War academic career.[143]

The work of the DAI, and especially of Fuchs, in Rome provides an extraordinary illustration of the combination of politics and scholarship, not just between 1918 and 1939, but also after the outbreak of war. Even during a period of hardship, the German government was concerned to show that it was interested in *Kultur*, and to present Germany as a *Kulturnation*, though the financing of the study of the early Germanic peoples in the Mediterranean World was, of course, an exercise in propaganda that had strong racial and national undertones. In many respects, Fuchs' own scholarship was of a high standard, but it was directed towards the demonstration of the significance of Germanic peoples in the history of early medieval Italy[144]—something that Mussolini had publicly denied in a speech delivered in Bari in 1934.[145]

13.9 SPAIN AND THE VISIGOTHS

The German government intended to establish a further branch of the DAI in Spain, again with the aim of presenting Germany as a keen supporter of culture and of investigating the Germanic contribution to the country. But whereas the Italian branch of the DAI was founded in 1829, the Madrid branch was only agreed in 1940, the year in which Hitler and Franco met at Hendaye, albeit without the German persuading the Spaniard to enter the War. The Madrid office of

---

[140] Fuchs, *Kunst der Ostgotenzeit*; Fröhlich, 'The study of the Lombards and the Ostrogoths at the German Archaeological Institute of Rome', pp. 198–202.

[141] Fröhlich, 'The study of the Lombards and the Ostrogoths at the German Archaeological Institute of Rome', p. 201.

[142] Maischberger, 'German archaeology during the Third Reich', p. 214.

[143] Fröhlich, 'The study of the Lombards and the Ostrogoths at the German Archaeological Institute of Rome', p. 184.

[144] Fröhlich, 'The study of the Lombards and the Ostrogoths at the German Archaeological Institute of Rome', p. 198.

[145] Fröhlich, 'The study of the Lombards and the Ostrogoths at the German Archaeological Institute of Rome', p. 203. See also Bandinelli, *Hitler e Mussolini 1938*.

the DAI was properly established as late as 1943, when a single medieval historian, Helmut Schlunk, was put in post.[146] Schlunk would survive the war, and succeed in establishing himself as an authority on early ecclesiastical architecture in Spain. He would also found the *Madrider Mitteilungen* and *Madrider Forschungen*, which were to include some of the most important publications of work on the Visigoths in Spain in the 1960s.[147]

One wartime work on the Visigoths, Hermann Eicke's *Geschichte der westgotischen Könige seit Alarichs Tod*, shows clearly how Visigothic Spain could be viewed through the same nationalist lens as that used to study the Franks, Lombards, and Ostrogoths. In 1936 the *Ahnenerbe* had already published a short study of the Vandal king, Geiseric, by Eicke,[148] which he followed up two years later with a work whose title, *Kämpfe und Helden Germaniens* ('Wars and Heroes of *Germania*'), gives an indication of its line of interpretation: it depicts the *Germanen* as lords of the Ancient World, and does so through the narrative of the migrations of Goths, Vandals, Anglo-Saxons, Franks, and Vikings.[149] In 1944 Eicke published a study of the Visigoths, dedicated to the memory of his son Dieter, killed at Ilmensee a year earlier. This was intended to present the barbarians in Spain to those Germans who knew nothing about them: Eicke certainly had a school audience in mind—a number of his works were read at the Nazi secondary boarding schools, the NAPOLAs[150]—but he also reminded the reader of Dahn's literary treatment of the Ostrogoths in *Ein Kampf um Rom*.[151]

13.10 DOUBTERS AND CRITICS

One other scholar took a rather more Roman view of the Visigoths: in 1937 Karl Friedrich Stroheker published a remarkable study of Euric, in which he argued that the king was a good deal less of a barbarian aggressor than he appears in the pages of Sidonius Apollinaris and Gregory of Tours.[152] This he followed up two years later with an equally nuanced study of the sixth-century king, Leovigild.[153] Even more revealing is his study of the senatorial aristocracy of fifth- and sixth-century Gaul, written in 1939, but only published in 1948.[154] Significantly, this work was dedicated to his teacher Woldemar Graf Uxkel-Gyllenband, the cousin of Berthold Alfred Maria Graf Schenk von Staufenberg and of Claus Schenk Graf von Staufenberg, both executed for their part in the 20th July 1944 plot against Hitler. Uxkel-Gyllenband died in 1941. Thereafter, Stroheker was taught by Joseph Vogt,

---

[146] Junker, 'Research under dictatorship', pp. 290–1.
[147] See the obituary of Schlunk in *El País*, from 17th November 1981.
[148] Eicke, *König Geiserich*. The *Ahnenerbe* also published Eicke's *Wiking im Südland* and his *Herrführer und Könige*.
[149] Eicke, *Kämpfer und Helden Germaniens*.
[150] See Pajak and Simon, 'Der Deutschunterricht in der Napola', p. 18.
[151] Eicke, *Geschichte der westgotischen Könige seit Alarichs Tod*, pp. 8–9.
[152] Stroheker, *Eurich*.   [153] Stroheker, 'Leowigild'.
[154] Stroheker, *Der senatorische Adel im spätantiken Gallien*.

a signed up member of the Nazi Party. Nazi ideology permeated Vogt's work at the time: an ancient historian, he interpreted the conflict between Rome and Carthage as one between Aryan and Semite.[155] After the war he would head a research project on slavery in Antiquity and would also write about Constantine. One of the great German projects to deal with Antiquity and its end—*Aufstieg und Niedergang der römischen Welt*—started as a *Festschrift* for him. Stroheker's study of the senatorial aristocracy of Merovingian Gaul with its dedication to Uxkel-Gyllenband looks all the more deliberate when set against Vogt's wartime enthusiasms.

There were plenty of others who were both critical of the regime and of the lines of interpretation being pursued by the *Ahnenerbe*, the *Amt Rosenberg*, and by those on the fringes of the two organizations. Indeed, it was not necessary to toe a party line on matters of historical interpretation.[156] We have already noted the criticisms levelled against Petri's scholarship, and against its implications, by Ernst Gamillscheg.[157] Some who were convinced that the Germanic peoples significantly affected Roman culture, were nevertheless openly hostile to the use that was being made of the past. Ludwig Schmidt (1862–1944) set out the history of the *Völkerwanderung* in a series of articles and books published from the last years of the nineteenth century onwards: taking the documentation very much at face value, he presented the migrations as involving substantial movements of population. When his works were reprinted in the late 1930s and 1940s, however, he stated categorically that they should not be taken as having relevance for the present age.[158]

The author of one of the finest and most level-headed surveys of the Later Empire, Ernst Stein—who, like Schmidt, took the barbarian migrations seriously—resigned the chair of Ancient History that he held at the university of Berlin when the Nazis came to power in 1933. Initially he remained in Belgium, where he happened to be at the time of his resignation. He subsequently moved to Switzerland, a necessary precaution given that he was Jewish.[159] Another scholar to end up in Switzerland was Fritz Kern, having escaped the clutches of the *Sicherheitsdienst* (Security Services). He managed to survive in Germany until 1945, despite his support for the Marxist Walter Markov in 1936, and despite being a regular critic of the regime.[160] Rather appropriately, his great work of medieval scholarship, which had been published in 1914, was on the early medieval notion

---

[155] Vogt, *Rom und Karthago*.

[156] Schultze, 'German Historiography, 1930s to 1950s', pp. 26–7; Arnold, 'The past as propaganda', pp. 472–3.

[157] Fahlbusch, *Wissenschaft im Dienst der nationalsozialistischen Politik?*, p. 353; Freund, 'Burgund in den Nationalsozialistischen Planungen', pp. 401–3.

[158] See the following works by Schmidt: *Älteste Geschichte der Langobarden*; *Älteste Geschichte der Wandalen*; *Geschichte der Wandalen*; *Allgemeine Geschichte der germanischen Völker bis zur Mitte des sechsten Jahrhunderts*; *Die germanischen Reiche der Völkerwanderung*; *Die Ostgermanen*; *Die Westgermanen*; *Geschichte der Franken*; *Geschichte der germanischen Frühzeit*. See Springer, 'Ludwig Schmidt'.

[159] Stein, *Geschichte des spätrömischen Reiches*. The second volume was translated into French by Palanque, and this translation, with its additional notes is yet finer than the original. On his exile, Goffart, *Barbarian Tides*, p. 40.

[160] Schultze, 'German historiography, 1930s to 1950s', p. 27.

of resistance: *Gottesgnadentum und Widerstandsrecht im früheren Mittelalter* ('Divine Grace and the right of opposition in the early Middle Ages').[161]

13.11 FERDINAND LOT

The Germans, of course, did not monopolize the interpretation of the Migration Period in the years leading to and including the War. In France, Ferdinand Lot responded to events throughout the 1930s and 40s. In 1935 he followed up his account of the end of the Ancient World with a volume on *Les Invasions germaniques*. The new work was reprinted in 1939, with an *avertissement* that indicated both Lot's dislike of Nazism and also his determination that his history writing would stand aloof from current politics. He announced that the text itself remained unchanged. The argument had always been an objective one: France was in many respects Germanic, like much of the rest of north-western Europe, and there was no reason to alter this reading. Then, having expressed his horror of and disgust for the Nazi regime, Lot insisted that the differences between France and Germany were not racial but moral. A further reprinting in 1945, which again saw no alteration to the text, added the information that the book had not met with approval from the Germans, but it had from the Francophones. Given the fact that one son-in-law of Lot, the resistance activist Boris Vildé, had been shot by the Nazis, and another, the monastic historian, J. B. Mahn, had died fighting at Montecassino, the quiet restatement is all the more impressive.[162]

The volume itself presents the history of the Migration Period, beginning in the classical past, with the first appearance of the Germanic peoples in Greek and Roman sources and taking the story down to the days of the Carolingians and of Alfred the Great. Its basic message is clearly stated in the subtitle: *La Pénétration mutuelle du monde barbare et du monde romain*: 'the mutual penetration of the barbarian and Roman worlds'. Lot did not underestimate the Germanic contribution to the history of Western Europe, but he also attributed a good deal to Roman tradition, and he did not entirely ignore the Celts. Indeed, he stressed that, for a while, before they turned against them, the Germans had been the minor partners of the Celts.[163] Their attacks on the Empire Lot saw as being prompted largely by pressure from behind. Even so, it was only in the frontier zones and in Britain that the Germanic peoples conquered territory: elsewhere they acted in the service of the Empire, although they preserved their own customs.[164] They took over Roman culture as far as they could, but in the period after the Fall of Rome only the Ostrogoths showed any concept of state. Lot criticized as too romantic the nineteenth-century notion that the barbarians had been a force for regeneration, stressing instead their brutality. Much depended on the quality of the individual leader, for Lot saw the royal courts as playing a central role in assimilation. National consciousness devel-

---

[161] Kern, *Gottesgnadentum und Widerstandsrecht*.
[162] I am indebted to Stéphane Lebecq for information on Lot and his family.
[163] Lot, *Les Invasions germaniques*, p. 321.
[164] Lot, *Les Invasions germaniques*, pp. 322–3.

oped in the individual kingdoms, which were often in conflict one with another. There was certainly no sense of Germanic consciousness. Germany itself was not a spontaneous creation, but rather developed out of the Carolingian world.[165] This, of course, was a denial of much of what was being stated by students of the German *Volk* inside Germany—though it was not so very different from the view espoused by Karl Hampe,[166] who, like Stein, had resigned his chair in 1933.

In 1937 Lot followed up his account of the Germanic invasions with a two-volume study of subsequent migrations: *Les Invasions barbares et le peuplement de l'Europe*. This revealed a rather different response to current, or recent, events, looking well outside the confines of the debate about Germany and its borders. Again Lot signalled his intentions in the subtitle: these volumes constituted an *introduction à l'intelligence des derniers traités de paix* ('an introduction to the understanding of the recent peace treaties'), that is, the peace treaties of 1919 to 1923. Here Lot was concerned with the historical roots of Eastern Europe. As he remarked in the preface, 'La nationalité virtuelle est à la base de la nouvelle constitution de l'Europe, telle qu'elle résulte des traités de paix qui s'échelonnent de 1919 à 1923.' ('Virtual nationality is at the base of the new constitution of Europe, such as has resulted from the peace treaties which emerged from 1919 to 1923.')[167] For the peoples of Eastern Europe the nineteenth century had been a period which had seen the loss of independence, while the early twentieth century had seen a renewal of national sentiment.[168] For Lot, a man of the left, who saw himself as heir to French eighteenth-century ideals of universalism, neither development was welcome.[169]

The 1920s and 1930s had marked the final development of a position that had its origins in the ideas of Arndt and Grimm, which had been set out in the context of German aspirations for national unity. The patriotic and linguistic arguments of the nineteenth century had been bolstered with more detailed philology, with archaeology, anthropology, and with a sharper, and supposedly more scientific, sense of race. For the early medievalist, the added poison of anti-Semitism rarely featured in the interpretation of the *Völkerwanderungzeit*, but that was only because Jews played a minor role in events: Jewish early medievalists, like Ernst Stein and Wilhelm Levison, inevitably suffered along with their fellows. Levison, a *Mitarbeiter* of the *Monumenta*, and subsequently assistant of Bruno Krusch, lost his academic post in 1935, and fled to England at the last minute in 1939.[170] Yet if the racial and territorial implications of the arguments over the Germanic settlement impinged only indirectly on the Jewish question, they had a direct and devastating impact on millions of Belgians and French. The legacy of the Nazi historiography of the early Middle Ages could not compete with the shadow of the Holocaust: nevertheless, the history of the *Völkerwanderung* had been put to malign use and had thus played its part in the devastation of the 1930s and 40s.

---

[165] Lot, *Les Invasions germaniques*, pp. 324–5, 327, 328.
[166] Werner, *Das NS-Geschichtsbild*, p. 74.
[167] Lot, *Les Invasions barbares et le peuplement de l'Europe*, vol. 1, p. 8.
[168] Lot, *Les Invasions barbares et le peuplement de l'Europe*, vol. 1, p. 9.
[169] See Lot, *Les Invasions barbares et le peuplement de l'Europe*, vol. 2, p. 230.
[170] Furhmann, *'Sind eben alles Menschen gewesen'*, p. 100.

14

Christian Engagement in the Interwar Period

14.1 THE CONTINUING TRADITION

While the Germanists in the 1920s and 30s had been concerned above all with issues of settlement, and their implications, other debates had also continued. The tradition of Catholic historiography that had begun in the mid-nineteenth century may have weakened in intensity a little before the First World War, but it had certainly not dried up. Not least there was Godefroid Kurth, who, like Ozanam before him and Henri Irénée Marrou after, was described as being an *historien engagé*:[1] alongside their work as historians they were active in the religious and social work of the Catholic Church. In the case of all three scholars, their reading of the past was thoroughly infused with their religious and their political beliefs. Not that they were unique. A number of the significant interpreters of the early Middle Ages writing in the first half of the twentieth century were committed and active Christians. Given their religious commitment, it is no surprise that those aspects of the fourth, fifth, and sixth centuries that most attracted them tended to be religious and cultural. Moreover, Augustine often emerges as a central figure, as if he, in his own soul-searching during a time of crisis, had especial resonance. Thus, both Charles Cochrane and Marrou presented him as being pivotal in the development of Europe.

Before turning to Cochrane and Marrou, and also to Christopher Dawson, Kurth, who we have already met in the context of Belgian historiography, deserves a further word, for while he had one foot in the world of national history, the other was planted in a far more pious historical tradition. He looked back to Ozanam not only in his religious commitment, but also in parts of his scholarship. In providing a preface to the second volume of the *Mélanges Godefroid Kurth* Karl Hanquet described the honorand as adding precision to, and expanding, Ozanam's observations on the land of Belgium, and thereby as superseding them.[2] Yet there are perhaps closer parallels with Ozanam's emphasis on the centrality of Christianity in the emergence of Europe. Kurth's overall argument in *Les Origines de la civilisation moderne*, that European culture was the

---

[1] Van Zeebroeck, 'L'Âge d'or médiévale'. The subtitle of Cholvy's biography of Ozanam is 'l'engagement d'un intellectuel catholique au XIXe siècle'. On Kurth's Catholicism see Cauchie, *Godefroid Kurth*.

[2] Hanquet, 'Godefroid Kurth', p. xxviii.

result of the combination of Christianity and the 'German spirit', could certainly have been taken from Ozanam as much as from the Germans themselves, although it was the historical methodology of the German universities that Kurth most respected.[3]

Nor were Kurth's social concerns so very different from Ozanam's. Like the Frenchman before him, his sensitivity to working-class unrest fed back into his history, although he was far less impressed by the arguments of the Left than was his French predecessor. He was much struck by the strikes of 1886, the so-called Walloon Jaquerie, but neither socialism nor liberalism seemed to him to offer a solution to the social and economic problems to which the strikers drew attention. Rather he looked to the Church for the creation of a new model of society, and he found grounds for optimism in Leo XIII's encyclical *Rerum Novarum* of 1891.[4] The pope, who was deeply concerned by the conflicts caused by growing industrialization, had written to the Catholic bishops instructing them on the 'Rights and Duties of Capital and Labour'. Such an intervention could be seen as a return to the good old days. For Kurth the Middle Ages provided a model for a better society: it was a period when, in his view, central authority lay with the Pope and the bishops—and it was the Pope rather than any Tsar or Bismarck who could claim to be a universal sovereign. At a lower level of social and political organization he thought that medieval corporations and Christian communes were institutions well suited to the needs of the workers.[5] The crucial problem of modern times, for Kurth, was the absence of religion: Christianity needed to reconquer society,[6] and here he was certainly at one with the French Catholics of the mid-nineteenth century.

These views were more closely tied to Kurth's reading of the High Middle Ages than they were to his views of the Merovingian period. He did, however, look to the early Middle Ages for models of sanctity and missionary endeavour,[7] and also, more romantically, of constitutional monarchy, which he felt the Germans lacked, but the Belgians possessed.[8] In his view Clovis founded a monarchy that embraced religious unity and political equality, with the result that the Merovingian dynasty created a new type of Christian kingship.[9] In many ways this can be dismissed as idealist, as can Kurth's biography of Clovis' queen, *Sainte Clotilde*, which naturally makes a great deal of her role in her husband's conversion, but also devotes a good deal of space to her sanctity and cult.[10] Yet underneath the pious representations of Clovis and his wife there lay a good deal of scholarly work: the *Histoire poétique des mérovingiens* had attempted what at the time was a sophisticated reading of narrative and legendary material, where Kurth had noted the need to use a variety of

---

[3] Hanquet, 'Godefroid Kurth', p. xxxvi; Lyon, 'Henri Pirenne's *Réflexions d'un solitaire*', p. 288. See above, chapter 12.

[4] Van Zeebroeck, 'L'Âge d'or médiévale', p. 209.

[5] Van Zeebroeck, 'L'Âge d'or médiévale', pp. 207–12.

[6] Van Zeebroeck, 'L'Âge d'or médiévale', pp. 212, 219.

[7] Kurth, *Saint Boniface.*   [8] Van Zeebroeck, 'L'Âge d'or médiévale', p. 214.

[9] Kurth, *Clovis.*   [10] Kurth, *Sainte Clotilde.*

approaches, German and French, and indeed had observed the ignorance of earlier work shown by some of his predecessors.[11]

14.2 CHRISTOPHER DAWSON AND THE ENGLISH CATHOLIC REVIVAL

Kurth died in 1916. A new generation of Catholic scholars would emerge after the First World War. The soul-searching engendered by the horrors of battle certainly influenced those thinking of the Fall of Rome, though in the case of the English-man Christopher Dawson he had already decided before the outbreak of the First World War to write *The Life of Civilizations*, a projected sequence of five volumes, of which the third was to cover the Fall of Rome and the early Middle Ages up to the year 1000.[12] In the event only two of the volumes would be completed, of which one, *The Making of Europe*, published in 1932, covered the centuries from the Roman to the Ottonian Empire. Like Ozanam and Gibbon before him, Dawson resolved on his plan standing on the steps of the *Ara Coeli* in Rome, and he did so while still a student, in 1909. Also like Ozanam he very deliberately wanted to refute Gibbon.[13] Not that he disliked *Decline and Fall*: it was a work for which he had enormous respect. He had read it before going up to Oxford, as he had read Augustine's *City of God*. For him Gibbon and Augustine were crucial figures, along with Dante.[14] He wished, however, to show that the bishop of Hippo provided 'the antidote to Gibbon's pessimism'.[15] In the words of Aidan Nichols, 'Dawson's own work is best thought of as a latter-day *City of God* (his favourite work among Chris-tian sources), which tries to show the special history of Christian revelation con-fronting and transforming the general history of the world, while remaining conditioned by its possibilities and limitations.'[16] Although Dawson's historical works are seen as a high point in English Catholic writing, he actually conceived his grand scheme before his conversion to Catholicism, which happened in 1916. While he tends to be labelled as a Catholic historian, *The Making of Europe* can be seen rather less narrowly as Christian.

As reconstructed by Dawson, the West Roman Empire was already in decline before it was destroyed by the barbarians. The Church, however, was not caught up in the disaster.[17] It, and particularly the monasteries, ensured the survival of learning.[18] Dawson did not underestimate the importance of the classical past, nor did he deny the significance of the barbarians or of their barbaric culture—and

---

[11] Kurth, *Histoire poétique des Mérovingiens*, pp. 26–7.
[12] Murray, 'Introduction' to the 2006 reprint of Dawson, *The Making of Europe*, pp. xiii–xiv. Sub-sequent references are to this edition. Also Scott, *A Historian and his World: A Life of Christopher Dawson*, pp. 48, 83; Scott, 'The Vision and legacy of Christopher Dawson', pp. 12–14.
[13] Scott, *A Historian and his World*, p. 48.
[14] Scott, *A Historian and his World*, pp. 45, 98–100.
[15] Scott, 'The Vision and legacy of Christopher Dawson', p. 14.
[16] Nichols, 'Christopher Dawson's Catholic setting', p. 125.
[17] Dawson, *The Making of Europe*, p. 48.   [18] Dawson, *The Making of Europe*, p. 66.

here he placed as much emphasis on the Celts as on the Germanic peoples.[19] Rome, the Classical Tradition, the Christian Church, and the barbarians constituted the four elements that contributed to the foundation of European unity.[20] It would be a long time, however, before Western Europe saw a reversal of the forces of disintegration: in the sixth century cultural leadership passed first to Byzantium and then to Islam. Dawson associated the first stages of the development of an independent cultural unity in Western Europe with the Christianization of the barbarians, and here he stressed the role of missionaries from the British Isles, and above all, of the Anglo-Saxons.[21] This led directly to the formation of the Carolingian Empire, which in Dawson's eyes was a theocratic power, to be contrasted with the secular state of the Merovingians.[22] While the Carolingian Empire itself was short-lived, the monastic centres that it created carried the flame of culture though the dark period of the ninth and tenth centuries, dominated as they were by anarchy and by the Viking invasions.[23] Moreover, although the Viking period was a time of disaster, it also brought the Northern World into contact with Christianity.[24] Finally, under the Ottonians, the four elements that had already been in place in the fifth century—the Empire, classical culture, the Church, and the Germanic peoples—fused to create a new Western European culture.[25] The Dark Ages had 'witnessed the conversion of the West, the foundation of Christian civilization and the creation of Christian Art and Catholic liturgy.'[26] European history could thus be read in terms of a Providential dispensation, which subsumed the Fall of Rome—yet it was a rather different providential reading than had been espoused by those nineteenth-century historians who had seen the barbarians as rather more benign.

Most of Dawson's argument was not new, although it is often presented as such.[27] Alexander Murray has drawn attention to a number of the works listed in in the bibliography of *The Making of Europe*, among them Tillemont, Bury, Dill, Rostovtzeff, Diehl, Vasiliev, Seeck, Camille Jullian, and Fustel de Coulanges.[28] He could have added Ferdinand Lot, who had a vision of Europe as a whole not dissimilar to Dawson's, albeit without the overriding sense of Providence.[29] The

---

[19] Dawson, *The Making of Europe*, pp. 71–3.

[20] Dawson, *The Making of Europe*, p. 68; Scott, *A Historian and his World*, p. 103.

[21] Dawson, *The Making of Europe*, p. 191.

[22] Dawson, *The Making of Europe*, p. 192.

[23] Dawson, *The Making of Europe*, p. 208.

[24] Dawson, *The Making of Europe*, p. 226.

[25] Dawson, *The Making of Europe*, p. 249; Cervantes, 'Christopher Dawson and Europe', pp. 51–68.

[26] Dawson, *The Making of Europe*, p. 5; Scott, *A Historian and his World*, p. 102.

[27] Despite the assertions of Cervantes, 'Christopher Dawson and Europe', p. 54. See also Murray, 'Introduction', p. xvi. It is surprising how often scholars who are not specialists in either the early Middle Ages or the relevant historiography have made excessive claims for Dawson.

[28] Murray, 'Introduction', p. xi, lists the works that he sees as central to Dawson's reading. The list does not include either Ozanam or Montalembert, nor do they appear in Dawson's own bibliography. It is almost inconceivable that Dawson did not know Montalembert's work, and quite difficult to believe that he had not come across Ozanam. The absence of their names has led scholars to neglect the close similarities between Dawson's thought and that of the French Catholics of the mid-nineteenth century.

[29] On Lot's *La Fin du monde antique*, published in 1927, see above, chapter 12.

influence of these authors is plain enough. More problematic are those authors and works that do not appear in the bibliography. Murray claims that Dawson effectively pre-empted Pirenne in seeing Islam as being more important for the breaking of the Mediterranean than were the Germanic peoples.[30] While it is true that *The Making of Europe* was published before Pirenne's full-length treatment of *Mahomet et Charlemagne*, which only appeared posthumously in 1937, the Belgian scholar had already announced his interpretation in a number of papers, not least in an article in the *Revue Belge de Philologie et d'Histoire* and at the Congrès international des Sciences historiques of 1922.[31] It is scarcely possible that Dawson had failed to notice what Pirenne was saying. In any case, Lot had already picked up on the Belgian's argument, and Dawson had read Lot.

Pirenne does appear in Dawson's bibliography, but only as the author of the *Histoire de Belgique*. On the other hand Ozanam, Montalembert, and Kurth appear nowhere at all. This raises a major problem: did Dawson not know of their work? It is possible that he was not aware of the second volume of Ozanam's *Études germaniques*, which is where the French scholar comes closest to covering the argument of *The Making of Europe*. Yet Dawson read widely, in several languages. In any case, Ozanam's *History of Civilization in the Fifth Century* was easily available in Britain, having been translated into English. So too were Montalembert's six volumes on *The Monks of the West*, which clearly restated Ozanam's argument on the role of the monasteries in the creation of the Christian Middle Ages. Some of Kurth's work had also appeared in English, notably his *Saint Clotilda* and *The Church at the Turning Points of History*. His *Saint Boniface* would be translated in 1935. It would be surprising if Dawson had failed to notice all these examples of Catholic scholarship.

The Making of Europe did not, then, convey a novel interpretation. This is scarcely surprising. Although Dawson was an avid reader of the Church Fathers,[32] he was not a specialist in the post-Roman period. Rather he was a polymath, who wished to write a history of civilization from Prehistory down to his own day. The scale was extraordinary: comparable in certain respects with that of his contemporary Arnold Toynbee. Not everyone appreciated such breadth. Writing about Gibbon in 1946 Alexander Hamilton Thompson commented:

> To-day, no one could dream of writing history on Gibbon's scale except perhaps Mr. Wells and Mr. Belloc, whose observation of mankind from China to Peru and from Eden to Geneva is pursued with an omniscience to which a thousand years is as one day.[33]

The absence of Dawson's name in this list is surely significant: Thompson was Professor of Medieval History at Leeds in 1933, when Dawson was invited to apply for a Chair in the Philosophy and History of Religion, but was then asked to with-

[30] Murray, 'Introduction', p. xxiii.
[31] Pirenne, 'Mahomet et Charlemagne'; Pirenne, 'Un contraste économique: Mérovingiens et Carolingiens'. On these see chapter 12 above.
[32] Scott, *A Historian and his World*, pp. 98–100.   [33] Thompson, *Gibbon*, p. 14.

draw his application.[34] The supposed reason for the university's decision not to consider Dawson's application was his Catholicism. One might wonder if there was also a matter of intellectual difference between Thompson and Dawson. For Thompson what mattered was careful editing of texts. He represented a school of thought in which precision and the steady build-up of detail was far more telling than the broad brush.[35] Minute analysis of texts was not Dawson's forte. Moreover, although Thompson was primarily a specialist in the High and Late Middle Ages, he had worked on Bede and he was an expert on the history of medieval monasticism. He would certainly have been aware of the extent to which Dawson did not break new ground.

Thompson may have doubted the value of *The Making of Europe*, but the book did have a considerable impact. Why it should have been so much more successful than some of the works on which it depended is an interesting question. It seems to have touched a number of nerves at the right moment. It can be seen as belonging to a Catholic revival within England, which stretched well outside the world of academe:[36] this was after all the age of Belloc and Chesterton, both of whom, like Dawson, published with the new Catholic publishing house of Sheed and Ward.[37] Of all the Catholic voices of the time Dawson was seen as the most influential, not least by T. S. Eliot.[38]

The contemporary implications of Dawson's vision of a Christian Europe would become increasingly apparent through the late 1930s and early 1940s, in his editorship of the *Dublin Review*, and in the Sword of the Spirit,[39] an oecumenical group of Christians arguing against totalitarianism from 1940 onwards, in which Dawson was deeply involved. It is a commitment that again recalls Ozanam. The Sword of the Spirit was not a purely Catholic group, for this was also an age of Anglican as well as Catholic revival, under the leadership of Archbishops Cosmo Gordon Lang and William Temple. *The Making of Europe* was well received not just in the Catholic community: despite the silence of Thompson, it was also hailed by Anglicans, notably the influential dean of St Paul's, William Inge, and by the historian H. A. L. Fisher.[40]

In fact the book's appeal was not limited to a Catholic or more generally committed Christian audience. In addition to being a work with a Christian message, *The Making of Europe* can be read as affirmation of the importance of civilization following the horrors of the First World War.[41] Although Dawson's health had meant that he avoided conscription, he had been old enough to serve. In the 1930s his reading of the post-Roman period offered a vision of a united continent to

---

[34] Scott, *A Historian and his World*, pp. 109–11.

[35] See Coulton, *Five Centuries of Religion*, vol. 1, p. xliii.

[36] Scott, *A Historian and his World*, pp. 94–5.

[37] See the comments of Brown, *The Rise of Western Christendom*, 2nd edn, pp. 11, 13–15.

[38] Scott, *A Historian and his world*, p. 210; Hastings, *A History of English Christianity*, p. 281: 'All in all the English Catholic writer with the greatest influence was probably by the late 1930s, Christopher Dawson.'

[39] Hastings, *A History of English Christianity*, pp. 274, 279, 393–4.

[40] Scott, *A Historian and his World*, pp. 104, 109. [41] Murray, 'Introduction', p. xx.

those who thought that Europe was tearing itself apart: in Dawson's view most modern history had been written from a nationalist viewpoint, which had

> undermined and vitiated the whole international life of modern Europe. It found its nemesis in the European War [of 1914–1918], which represented a far deeper schism in European life than all the many wars of the past, and its consequences are to be seen to-day in the frenzied national rivalries which are bringing economic ruin on the whole of Europe.[42]

For Dawson, the rivalries within Europe were obscuring a basic unity. Nobody saw it as his or her business to defend the continent, and yet it was in need of defence, now that Russia and America could 'no longer be regarded as colonial extensions to European culture'. It was, therefore, necessary to 'develop a common European consciousness and a sense of its historic and organic unity'.[43] To give European culture its due it was necessary to 'rewrite our history': the verb was Dawson's own, and he must have convinced himself, rather optimistically, that the reading of the early Middle Ages that he presented was a new one.[44]

After 1945 Dawson's stress on European unity again fitted the mood of reconstruction in the western part of the continent. Not surprisingly, *The Making of Europe*, which had been reprinted throughout the 1930s, was reissued in 1954. The French translation, originally commissioned by Louis Halphen in 1934, was reprinted with a new title and a preface by Jacques Le Goff in 1960. So too the German translation, which first appeared in 1935, was reprinted ten years later and again in 1961. Rather than a radically new reading, Dawson's work was a very eloquent expression of a number of ideas, most of which had been in circulation for almost a century. Yet those ideas reverberated particularly loudly in the 1930s, 40s, and 50s. The success of *The Making of Europe* has perhaps reflected the circumstances in which it has been read more than the originality of its argument. It is a book that has never been totally forgotten.[45]

14.3 COCHRANE: THE CHRISTIAN AND THE STATE

Arguably more original than Dawson's work on the transition from Rome to the Middle Ages was that of the Canadian Classicist and Ancient Historian, Charles Norris Cochrane, whose interests, like Dawson's, stretched way beyond the last years of Rome: his recurrent concern was the philosophical one of the interrelation of thought and action.[46] Yet his *magnum opus* of 1940 on *Christianity and Classical Culture*, which was once highly regarded, has been forgotten to a greater extent than has the *The Making of Europe*, although it is still admired in certain

---

[42] Dawson, *The Making of Europe*, pp. 8–9. See also p. 68.
[43] Dawson, *The Making of Europe*, pp. 9–10.
[44] Scott, *A Historian and his World*, p. 102.
[45] Murray, 'Introduction', p. ix.
[46] See the obituary by 'H. A. I.' (Innis), 'Charles Norris Cochrane'.

circles.[47] Like Dawson, Cochrane put religion at the heart of his reading of European history.

Along with other historians of the early twentieth century, including the Russian Mikhail Rostovtzeff, Cochrane saw the Roman Empire as a peculiarly oppressive institution. His view of the classical world in general was negative: it depended on 'submission to the "virtue and fortune" of a political leader'.[48] The Roman Republic saw the establishment of what Cochrane called a 'class-state', dominated by a caste structure. This was the social basis of the Empire, and it was in no way changed with the conversion of Constantine. Rather, the evils of the class-state intensified: the fourth century saw the 'systematic and unremitting oppression' of 'the wretched *bourgeoisie*'.[49] Julian did no more than Constantine to address the Empire's social problems: his restoration of paganism was nothing other than the reinstatement of 'a religion which was destitute of theological principles, of moral precepts, and of ecclesiastical discipline'.[50] Cochrane is quoting Gibbon, a historian whom he greatly admired, but more for the insights he provided into the eighteenth century than for those on the distant past. Valentinian attempted to revive the old system, but genuine renovation had to wait until the reign of Theodosius.[51] The result of the latter's reforms was a level of regimentation on a scale unparalleled in the history of Rome.[52] Not only did Theodosius tighten up existing structures, but he also integrated Christianity into the state, and here he was abetted by Ambrose.[53] The result was the destruction of some of the valuable features of Roman society, like the classical concept of the family. Instead there was an exact coincidence of Catholicism and citizenship. All in all there was no Christianization of civilization, but rather a civilizing of Christianity.[54]

For Cochrane,

[t]he ultimate consequence of Theodosianism was, of course, to lay the foundation for a new European order. Its immediate result, however, was to precipitate the final destruction of the old.[55]

Without mentioning the barbarians he goes on to talk about 'the destruction of cities, the devastation of the country-side, and the disruption of communications', as well as 'the rape of the Eternal City itself'. A page later he does acknowledge 'the irruption of the barbarians and the barbarization of the services', but he is far more interested in the failure of the state to cope. The municpalities were already

---

[47] Cochrane, *Christianity and Classical Culture*. As the preface shows, it was completed in 1939. There was a revised edition in 1944, and it was reprinted in 1954, 1957, 1968, if not more often. It appeared in the list of reprints issued by the Liberty Fund in the United States in 2003. It was translated into Polish in 1960.

[48] Cochrane, *Christianity and Classical Culture*, p. vi.

[49] Cochrane, *Christianity and Classical Culture*, pp. 199–204.

[50] Cochrane, *Christianity and Classical Culture*, p. 291.

[51] Cochrane, *Christianity and Classical Culture*, pp. 317–18.

[52] Cochrane, *Christianity and Classical Culture*, p. 319.

[53] Cochrane, *Christianity and Classical Culture*, pp. 325, 350–1.

[54] Cochrane, *Christianity and Classical Culture*, pp. 326, 332, 336.

[55] Cochrane, *Christianity and Classical Culture*, p. 351.

bankrupt because of excessive state demands. The emperors responded to the crisis by extending the definition of what constituted a public enemy, but, given the bankruptcy of the municipalities, they had to appeal to self-help by calling on all to exterminate malefactors, brigands, and deserters. '[T]he Roman wolf, which for centuries had waxed fat on the carcasses of its victims, at last perished not of surfeit but of anaemia.' The collapse of authority had occasioned the dissolution of the community. Following Gibbon again, Christianity and barbarism helped to dismember the Empire, but Cochrane read their impact rather differently: 'the barbarians coveted a place in the sun': the real object of Christianity was 'to build the City of God'.[56] In its emphasis on the saving grace of Christianity, Cochrane's interpretation has much in common with the Providential vision of Dawson. What Virgil had prophesied for Rome could only be achieved by the Christian polity raised in Rome's place.[57]

It is with the contribution of Christianity, and above all with Augustine, that the final section of Cochrane's work is concerned. Although there had been an unhappy integration of Church and State, there were elements of Christianity that refused to be drawn into the established structure of Roman society. Athanasius' opposition to the whole Roman world, 'Athansius contra mundum', was one example.[58] More generally, the individual could find emancipation in religion, and many opted to enter the Church or become monks.[59] It was Augustine, however, who best gave expression to what Christianity could offer. Where the classical tradition had been to respect the leader, the bishop of Hippo insisted that one should not put one's trust in princes. He condemned classical materialism, stressing instead the centrality of the Law of Love (of God and of one's neighbour). Above all, in his emphasis on the need for religious self-knowledge, he effectively discovered the notion of individual personality.[60]

Although Cochrane was a Canadian, he fought in the First Tank Battalion in the First World War, before going to Oxford to study, and in the preface to *Christianity and Classical Culture* he singled out R. G. Collingwood and Ronald Syme as influences. He would spend most of his academic life as a professor at the University of Toronto, but in the Second World War he also served on the commission to consider interned aliens.[61] Given his war-time record and his involvement in official administration it would be no surprise to find parallels being drawn between the Late Roman period and 1930s Europe. In the preface, however, Cochrane explicitly denies the value of such comparisons, stating that it is inappropriate

> to hazard any application of issues debated in the first four centuries to the problems of our own distracted age. Nevertheless, to those who are looking for a solution to those problems, it may at least be suggested that the answer will not be found in any

[56] Cochrane, *Christianity and Classical Culture*, pp. 354–7.
[57] I owe the phrase to Mark Vessey.
[58] Cochrane, *Christianity and Classical Culture*, pp. 257, 272.
[59] Cochrane, *Christianity and Classical Culture*, pp. 221, 244, 341, 344.
[60] Cochrane, *Christianity and Classical Culture*, pp. 376–455, 508.
[61] Innis, 'Charles Norris Cochrane'.

attempted revival of obsolete classical conceptions associated with the life of classical antiquity.[62]

One may nevertheless think that his failure to name the barbarians in his account of the destruction of Gaul in the opening decades of the fifth century has some significance—though since the book was completed in 1939, it would have been memories of his service in the First World War that would have weighed on him, rather than Hitler's aggression. Cochrane's vision of Rome as a totalitarian state surely suggests that he had the problems of 1930s totalitarianism firmly in mind, just as Rostovtzeff's vision of the Later Roman Empire seems to echo the rigidity of the Russian State.[63] In his 'Preface' Cochrane seems to deliberately distance himself from any overtly Christian view, claiming that '[i]t is none of my business as an historian to pronounce upon the ultimate validity of Christian claims as opposed to those of Classicism'.[64] His overall message, however, is a religious one, and he takes a much more evangelical stance in the closing paragraph of the book, where he speaks of the need for 'a united effort of hand and heart and head, in order to expose the fictitious character of secular valuations and to vindicate the reality of Christian claims'.[65] It is difficult not to see in Cochrane's elevation of the Christian individual against the State some element of criticism of developments in Germany and Italy.

14.4 MARROU

Cochrane put Augustine at the heart of his reading of the change from Antiquity to the Middle Ages. So too did Henri Irenée Marrou, who unlike both Cochrane and Dawson was primarily a specialist in what he came in the 1970s to call *Antiquité Tardive* (Late Antiquity),[66] although he ranged widely through the whole history of classical education and civilization. Marrou's study of Augustine was much more obviously directed at a scholarly audience than either Dawson's *Making of Europe* or Cochrane's *Christianity and Classical Culture*. Of the three, Dawson's work was the grandest in scope, but the least innovative, adding little to a well-established tradition of interpretation. In recent years Cochrane's contribution has been largely, but not entirely, forgotten. Ultimately it is the specialist Marrou who has had the more profound impact—in the academic community through his monographs, and more broadly through his works of *haute vulgarisation* and a posthumous *livre de poche*.

Like Kurth, Marrou has been compared directly to Ozanam: the two French-men have been presented as model Christians.[67] Both were the sons of a pious

---

[62] Cochrane, *Christianity and Classical Culture*, p. v.

[63] Brown, *Through the Eye of a Needle*, p. 19.

[64] Cochrane, *Christianity and Classical Culture*, p. vi.

[65] Cochrane, *Christianity and Classical Culture*, p. 516.

[66] Marrou, *Décadence ou antiquité tardive?* For the history of the term: Liebeschuetz, 'The birth of Late Antiquity', pp. 253–61.

[67] Riché, *Marrou*, p. 9.

mother and an uncommitted father.[68] Marrou studied at the elite École normale supérieure in Paris, from 1925 to 1929, and there he joined *Tala*, a group of militant Catholic 'normaliens', calling for a 'révolution chrétienne intérieure' to parallel the shift from Antiquity to the Middle Ages.[69] Again there are parallels with Ozanam's student days in Paris. Marrou's enthusiasm for the Middle Ages was prompted by the Christianity of the period.[70] For him culture in the medieval past had been religious and also popular: and to a man with a keen interest in popular culture (he wrote extensively on folk music)[71] this was a matter of significance. There was also a social issue here, for like Ozanam (and to a lesser extent Kurth) he was deeply concerned with the position of the workers, who he felt had participated in the popular culture of the past.[72]

Having concluded his studies as a *normalien*, Marrou went to Italy as a *boursier* (scholarship-holder), based first in Rome, in the École française, and then in Naples. In Italy he wrote two theses. The first, 'La notion de culture intellectuelle chez saint Augustin', would become his most significant work on the late Roman period, *Saint Augustin et la fin de la culture antique*. His second thesis, *Mousikos Aner: étude sur les scènes de la vie intellectuelle figurant sur les monuments funéraires romains*, was a study of depictions of intellectual life in Roman sculpture. It would be published in 1938, but would also provide a basis for his later *Histoire de l'éducation dans l'antiquité*.[73] Work on these two theses did not, however, preclude a continuing involvement in Catholic political and social groups and projects: Marrou was a regular contributor to *L'Esprit*, a journal founded by Emmanuel Mounier, following an idea of the redoubtable Catholic educationalist Mme Daniélou.[74] He would also work closely with her son, Jean, later Cardinal, Daniélou, both within the Church (they were keen supporters of Vatican II), and as historians. Together they wrote the first volume of the *Nouvelle histoire de l'Église*.[75]

The essays that Marrou wrote for *L'Esprit* appeared under the *nom de plume* of Henri Davenson. Initially this was a pseudonym he employed in order to avoid having to get approval for the publication of his work from his academic superiors.[76] Thereafter, he tended to use it for his openly spiritually and politically committed statements, thus creating a certain distance between his more purely academic publications and those in which current concerns are most clearly stated. It was, for instance under the name of Davenson, that he voiced his criticism of Fascism and of the Italian intervention in Ethiopia.[77] Marrou's pseudonymous works, together with his involvement in politics, have significant implications for how one can read his *magnum opus* on Saint Augustine. At first sight it is a work that is

---

[68] Riché, *Marrou*, p. 16.   [69] Riché, *Marrou*, pp. 20–1, 24–6, 45.   [70] Riché, *Marrou*, p. 45.
[71] Riché, *Marrou*, p. 165.   [72] Riché, *Marrou*, pp. 31, 45.
[73] Riché, *Marrou*, pp. 40, 50; Marrou, *Saint Augustin et la fin de la culture antique*; Marrou, *Mousikos Aner: Étude sur les scènes de la vie intellectuelle figurant sur les monuments funéraires romains*; Marrou, *Histoire de l'éducation dans l'antiquité*.
[74] Riché, *Marrou*, pp. 51–3.
[75] Daniélou and Marrou, *Nouvelle histoire de l'Église*, vol. 1, *Des origines à Grégoire le Grand*; Riché, *Marrou*, pp. 143, 145.
[76] Riché, *Marrou*, p. 37.   [77] Riché, *Marrou*, p. 53.

driven solely by Marrou's reading of a set of theological and literary texts. The relation of that reading to the 1930s is nowhere explicit, but there are echoes to be heard.

14.5 LA DÉCADENCE

Marrou's choice of Augustine as a subject for research is hardly surprising. Here was a deeply committed Catholic choosing to write about a Father of the Church. Moreover, he felt a certain fellow-sympathy for his subject: they were both 'boursiers conquérants': scholars who made their way in the world from relatively insignificant family backgrounds.[78] Yet Marrou's approach to his subject was very much less obvious than might have been expected. *Saint Augustin et la fin de la culture antique* is as much about culture as it is about Augustine. What Marrou does is set Augustine, and by implication most of his ecclesiastical contemporaries, firmly within the educational system of the fourth and fifth centuries, and it is a system that he finds deeply flawed—just as he found the educational systems of his own day in need of reform.[79]

Antique culture was dominated by training in the Seven Liberal Arts: what Boethius later described as the *Trivium* of Grammar, Rhetoric, and Logic, together with the *Quadrivium* of Mathematics, Geometry, Music, and Astronomy. The effect of this curriculum, and especially of the dominance of Grammar and Rhetoric was, in Marrou's view, deadening.[80] It has been said that 'Marrou imagines Graeco-Roman culture dying of boredom in advanced old age'.[81] Even Augustine, who was a master rhetor, was constrained by his education. His conversion, which for Marrou was initially a conversion to Philosophy, did not lead to a complete break from his intellectual past. The saint's subsequent study of the Bible was novel, but it followed the rules of his Liberal Arts' training. There was no sudden shift from Roman decadence to a new Christian culture, but rather a slow transformation, in which traces of classical culture survived.[82] Thus, the history of the End of the Ancient World was, for Marrou, a history of cultural change in which the deadening traditions of Classical culture only gradually broke down before the new Christian culture of the Middle Ages emerged. The reading of Augustine himself is surprisingly down-beat: whilst Dawson concentrated on the positive aspects of fifth- and sixth-century Christianity, and Cochrane saw in Augustine the discovery of personality, Marrou mapped a history of the breakdown of *décadence*. Extraordinarily, he had a much greater sense of discontinuity than did Cochrane, Dawson, or indeed the Christian historiographical tradition to which they all belonged.

---

[78] Riché, *Marrou*, p. 41.
[79] For Marrou and the Syndicat général de l'éducation nationale, see Riché, *Marrou*, pp. 318–2.
[80] Marrou, *Saint Augustin*, pp. 3, 10, 15, 18, 47, 49, 94, 110.
[81] Vessey, 'The demise of the Christian writer and the remaking of "Late Antiquity"', p. 386.
[82] Marrou, *Saint Augustin*, p. 541.

Décadence is at the heart of Marrou's reading of the Late Roman period.[83] It was the product of the oratorical culture of the period:[84] Latin decadence was 'classicisme exaspéré'; it was ossified.[85] It even infected the exegesis of the Church Fathers. Christian intellectuals could not get away from it:[86] 'this taste for the arcane, for the allegorical interpretation of texts effectively characterizes the cultural atmosphere of decadence.'[87] The concept of *la décadence* had strong resonances in early twentieth-century France, and Marrou intended that they should be heard. In the *Retractatio* that he appended to his study of Augustine when it was reprinted in 1949 Marrou claimed that in choosing the term, which he had deliberately adopted in place of the more common 'bas empire', he was looking back to a poem of Verlaine, *Langueur*, which had been published in 1883:

> Je suis l'Empire à la fin de la décadence,
> Qui regarde passer les grands Barbares blancs
> En composant des acrostiches indolents.
> (I am the Empire in the last stages of decadence
> Who looks on at the great white barbarians as they pass,
> composing indolent acrostiches.')

This was not just a whimsical citation of a favourite poem. In Marrou's eyes the citation was entirely apposite: he noted that although Verlaine had not read Gibbon, he was aware of the poetry of Ausonius.[88]

Marrou's account of the concept of *décadence* is, however, curious. In presenting it as a creation of the last hundred years he was ignoring the fact (of which he was surely aware) that it had appeared in the title of Montesquieu's *Considérations sur les causes de la grandeur des Romains et de leur décadence*. So too the word had been used by Ozanam.[89] 'Bas empire' might have been the standard phrase for the Late Roman period in the French academic circles in the early 1930s, but the concept of *décadence* had a long and distinguished academic pedigree. Marrou could, therefore, have situated the notion of *décadence* within an established historiographical tradition, but instead he chose to present the word in terms of the Symbolist movement of the late nineteenth century. Here he was thinking more of the steamy Symbolism of Verlaine and of Odilon Redon, rather than the severe symbolism of Puvis de Chavannes that responded to the scholarship of Fustel de Coulanges. Even so Marrou passed over the centrality of the idea in Joris-Karl Huysmans' novel of 1884, *À rebours*, in which the anti-hero, Des Esseintes, delights in reading the works of Sidonius Apollinaris (not that the author seems to have been particularly familiar with them). Marrou's failure to mention Huysmans is all the more interesting in that he

---

[83] Marrou, *Saint Augustin*, pp. iii, ix; Vessey, 'Theory, or the Dream of the Book', pp. 270–2.
[84] Marrou, *Saint Augustin*, pp. 3, 10, 15, 18, 47, 49, 94, 110.
[85] Marrou, *Saint Augustin*, pp. 498, 543.　　　[86] Marrou, *Saint Augustin*, p. 503.
[87] Marrou, *Saint Augustin*, p. 495.　　　[88] Marrou, *Retractatio*, p. 664.
[89] e.g. Ozanam, *Les Germains avant le christianisme*, p. 273.

himself saw Sidonius as the chief exponent of literary decadence.[90] Huysmans had become a Catholic convert shortly after writing *À rebours* and had even been an oblate at Ligugé, before the monastery was dissolved for the second time in 1901.[91] With his connections with Ligugé, the site of the earliest major Gallo-Roman monastery, and his interest in Sidonius, Huysmans could have been a point of departure for understanding late Roman culture. Regardless of the absence of any reference to *À rebours*, Marrou, in looking to Verlaine, had deliberately implied a comparison between the culture of the end of the Roman Empire and that of the late nineteenth and early twentieth centuries.

He was not alone in seeing a comparison. It had already been made by Robert Vallery-Radot in 1921 and by the Russian emigré Nicolas Berdiaev six years later.[92] Marrou himself drew more explicit comparisons between the fourth and fifth centuries on the one hand, and the 1920s and 30s on the other in works published under the name of Davenson. Already in 1934, talking of the fourth and fifth centuries, he wrote that '[o]ur situation is the same. We too live in a pagan world, and we dream of Christianizing it.' Further, he likened contemporary culture to the world of Ausonius and Symmachus, contrasting it to the religious aspirations of Paulinus of Nola.[93] Similar parallels between past and present were also drawn in *Le Christianisme et la fin du monde antique*, published in Lyons in 1943, in which Marrou, again under the name Davenson, joined forces with five other scholars including Palenque and de Plinval.[94]

14.6 PAGANS, BARBARIANS, AND THE INTERWAR PERIOD

Verlaine's *Langueur* refers not just to *l'Empire à la fin de la décadence*, but also to *les grands Barbares blancs*. Having lived in Paris in 1870 the poet may well have had the Empire of Napoleon III and Bismarck's Germans in mind. Neither the Goths nor the modern Germans appear in *Saint Augustin et la fin de la culture antique*. Marrou's subject is *la décadence*, and by implication the civilization of the Later Roman Empire Empire, and there is no trace of the barbarians, as the author himself noted in his *Retractatio*.[95] The silence is again interesting. The 'great white barbarians', the Aryans, would no doubt have meant something different to Marrou in 1949 than they had in 1938, when the study of Augustine first appeared. By the later date Marrou had lived through the German occupation of Lyons. We know from his own poetry that by 1940 he regarded the Germans as barbarians.[96] Yet even before 1939 he knew about German invaders. Born in Marseille in 1904,

[90] Marrou, *Saint Augustin*, p. 95.
[91] See Monnoyeur, *Joris-Karl Huysmans*.
[92] Vallery-Radot, *Devant des idoles*; Berdiaev, *Un nouveau Moyen Âge*; Riché, *Marrou*, p. 44.
[93] Riché, *Marrou*, pp. 41, 43, citing Davenson, *Fondements d'une culture chrétienne*, pp. 62, 153.
[94] Palanque, Davenson, Favre, de Plinval, Championier, and Lauzière, *Le Christianisme et la fin du monde antique*; Riché, *Marrou*, p. 74.
[95] Marrou, *Saint Augustin*, pp. 663, 700–2.   [96] Riché, *Marrou*, p. 64.

he had been fully aware of the First World War: along with his fellow 'normaliens' he had a sense of having lived through 1914–18 without having fought.[97] Equally important, although one might have reservations about applying the phrase 'grands Barbares blancs' to the Italian fascists in Ethiopia, he had been highly critical of Mussolini's African escapade.[98] More generally, he was hostile to colonialism in all forms, not least as it impacted on North Africa, the homeland of Augustine. Marrou would be alarmed at developments in Algeria after 1945, and he did his best to establish good relations with both Algerians and Tunisians after 1959.[99] He noted oppression everywhere, both as a Christian and as a man of the Left.

While Marrou does acknowledge the absence of the Goths and Vandals from his study of Augustine in three pages of the *Retractatio* of 1949, even at the later date he makes next to no attempt to integrate them into the story, although only one year earlier his colleague Pierre Courcelle had made them central to his *Histoire littéraire des grandes invasions germaniques*, which clearly implied a comparison with the present.[100] Marrou's retraction concerns his sense that in applying the word *décadence* he had undervalued a living and developing culture. The absence of any sustained comment on the barbarians in 1949 is all the more surprising in the light of Marrou's career during the Second World War. He joined the army in 1939, but was demobilized a year later. In his non-academic writing he painted the events of 1940 in apocalyptic terms: 'The end of the world is not for tomorrow. In the course of the terrible weeks of June 1940 everything seemed to collapse around us, the order or at least the family structure in which we grew up, the *patrie*, the State and even the values which were dearest to us, Christian civilization itself.'[101] Directly before the outbreak of war he had been teaching in Nancy. A return to his teaching post was clearly impossible, so he went to Montpellier, before being appointed to a Chair in Lyons in 1941.[102] He was to remain there for four years, and during that time he was a key member of the *Résistance*—although he was not as active as Marc Bloch.[103] Having a number of contacts in Geneva, he helped Jews escape to Switzerland.[104] He signalled his ideological stance in 1948 when he dedicated his *Histoire de l'éducation dans l'antiquité* to Gilbert Dru, executed in Place Bellecour on 14th July 1944.[105] Such a stance meant hostility to the Vichy regime.[106] In 1942 Marrou refused the Chair of Ancient History at the Sorbonne when it was offered to him by Jérôme Carcopino, his old teacher and patron, who had, indeed, supported him in his decision to attend the École française in Rome. Since then, however, Carcopino had been appointed Minister for Education under the Vichy government.[107] Instead, Marrou was appointed to the Chair of Christianity in Paris in 1945. Yet while he was firmly a man of the *Résistance*, Marrou did not stand for retribution: immediately after the War he was appointed to the Lyons *comité de Libération de la ville*, but he resigned in protest against the pursuit of

---

[97] Riché, *Marrou*, p. 20.   [98] Riché, *Marrou*, p. 53.   [99] Riché, *Marrou*, p. 249.
[100] Courcelle, *Histoire littéraire des grandes invasions germaniques*.   [101] Riché, *Marrou*, p. 63.
[102] Riché, *Marrou*, pp. 59–61.   [103] For Bloch's views, see Bloch, *L'Étrange défaite*.
[104] Riché, *Marrou*, p. 79.   [105] Riché, *Marrou*, p. 80.
[106] Riché, *Marrou*, p. 53.   [107] Riché, *Marrou*, pp. 23, 36, 87.

collaborators. For once in the work published under his own name he drew a modern parallel: in *Saint Augustin et l'Augustinisme* he compared the hounding of collaborators with attacks on the Donatists.[108] For the most part, however, while the present weighed constantly on Marrou's understanding of the past, he did not draw attention to the fact when writing under his own name. Writing as Henri Davenson he was often far more explicit. While he clearly thought about parallels between his own day and the fifth- and sixth-century, he tended not to express them openly in his more academic work.

14.7 *HISTOIRE DE L'ÉDUCATION*, THE *RETRACTATIO*, AND THE PATH TO *L'ANTIQUITÉ TARDIVE*

Much has been made of the *Retractatio* which Marrou appended to the reprint of *Saint Augustin et la fin de la culture antique*. It has been described as 'one of the landmarks of twentieth-century scholarship on Christianity in the late Roman Empire',[109] and 'as even more significant than the original book'.[110] What Marrou offered in 1949 was a modification of the interpretation he had offered eleven years earlier. Central to that modification was his rejection of the image of decline, *décadence*, that he had previously set out. This he realized, was the opinion of a classicist with an inbred bias against post-classical culture. Far from being the last gasp of a dying tradition, the culture of the age of Augustine was already something new.[111] We are a little closer here to Cochrane's reading, of which Marrou was aware.

Perhaps Marrou's change of view was the result of 'wartime reflection on the *City of God*',[112] but it was also a response to work that had appeared since 1938. In 1942 André Loyen had produced a detailed study of the panegyrics of Sidonius, followed a year later by a sympathetic reading of the Gallo-Roman's florid style and the related 'esprit précieux' that flourished in aristocratic circles in Gaul in the last days of the Empire.[113] Loyen was not the first to offer a positive reading of Sidonius: the English scholar C. E. Stevens had already done so in 1933.[114] In concentrating on the Latin style of the Gallo-Roman, however, Loyen had shown that Marrou's reading of cultural decadence could be too harsh.

A year before the *Retractatio*, Marrou had published his *Histoire de l'éducation dans l'antiquité*. In many respects this was an extension of his earlier work on the *Mousikos Aner*, but its horizons were rather broader, and it was addressed to a larger

---

[108] Marrou, *Saint Augustin et l'augustinisme*, p. 50; Riché, *Marrou*, p. 81.

[109] See, for instance, the comments of Klingshirn and Vessey, *The Limits of Ancient Christianity*, p. 210.

[110] Markus, 'Between Marrou and Brown', p. 2.

[111] Marrou, *Retractatio*, esp. p. 689. For a concise summary, see Vessey, 'The demise of the Christian writer and the remaking of "Late Antiquity"', pp. 386–7.

[112] Klingshirn and Vessey, *The Limits of Ancient Christianity*, p. 210.

[113] Loyen, *Recherches historiques sur les panégyriques de Sidoine Apollinaire*; Loyen, *Sidoine Apollinaire et l'esprit précieux en Gaule aux derniers jours de l'Empire*.

[114] Stevens, *Sidonius Apollinaris and his Age*.

public.[115] The coverage ran from Homer to the Carolingian Renaissance. In terms of the history of the West it begins in the sixth century BC, when Roman education was essentially for *paysans* (the English 'peasants' will not quite do as a translation).[116] This changed when Rome copied the educational traditions of the Greek cities, with the result that the core of its educational syllabus became what would be called the *Trivium* and *Quadrivium*.[117] Initially Christianity had little impact on this scheme of learning: classical education continued much as it had, despite some worries about the taint of polytheism.[118] The detail here is entirely in keeping with Marrou's original picture of culture in the Age of Augustine, but the tone is different: there is no longer any emphasis on *décadence*.

In fact, moving forward into the sixth and seventh centuries he found a new application for the term: now it served to describe the period when classical culture was neglected: it was a product not simply of ignorance or forgetfulness but of degeneration: *dégénérescence*.[119] In place of urban classical schools, with their traditional syllabus, there were new religious schools, attached largely to monasteries, to the households of bishops and of parish priests.[120] This is no longer a world of predominantly urban culture. We find provision for education in the monastic rules of the sixth and seventh centuries, in the canons of Church councils, and in the narratives of hagiography. This education, however, was directed almost entirely to the question of literacy, and more specifically to literacy with an overriding goal: reading the Psalms, and more generally Scripture, and the Law of God. Monks and Nuns were required to read, write, and transcribe manuscripts.[121] The clergy had to perform the Divine Office. Prayer and veneration were central.[122] There was no need for knowledge of the Classics: Gregory the Great criticized bishop Desiderius of Vienne for involving himself in education.[123] Marrou's is an account that leaves out the functional learning of administrators, and indeed the culture of courtiers, whose letters suggest a rather greater knowledge of the Classics than he allowed.

In his reading the beginnings of a revival came from outside the Roman World: from the monasteries of Ireland, which had never known classical culture, and from Anglo-Saxon England, where schools were established following the Gregorian Mission and also the archiepiscopate of Theodore.[124] The picture is essentially an extension to the history of education of Ozanam's reading of the post-Roman period and indeed of Dawson's, though it has its problems. Irish monasteries were not entirely without classical texts, as can be seen from the scholarship they

[115] Marrou, *Histoire de l'éducation dans l'antiquité*.
[116] Marrou, *Histoire de l'éducation dans l'antiquité*, pp. 315–16.
[117] Marrou, *Histoire de l'éducation dans l'antiquité*, pp. 329–44, 359–89.
[118] Marrou, *Histoire de l'éducation dans l'antiquité*, pp. 416–47.
[119] Marrou, *Histoire de l'éducation dans l'antiquité*, pp. 445–6.
[120] Marrou, *Histoire de l'éducation dans l'antiquité*, pp. 435–44.
[121] Marrou, *Histoire de l'éducation dans l'antiquité*, p. 439, citing the Rule of Caesarius of Arles for nuns.
[122] Marrou, *Histoire de l'éducation dans l'antiquité*, p. 446.
[123] Marrou, *Histoire de l'éducation dans l'antiquité*, p. 445.
[124] Marrou, *Histoire de l'éducation dans l'antiquité*, pp. 452, 455–7.

produced.[125] As for the School of Canterbury, since it was created by Augustine and Theodore, it must bear witness to a level of learning in Rome which Marrou leaves unacknowledged.

A more interesting question is why, in his *History of Education*, did Marrou decide to reallocate the concept of *décadence* to the post-Roman period, rather than to the culture of the Roman Empire? Of course, simply by looking beyond the fifth century may have made him aware of the extent to which late Roman culture was intellectually richer than what followed. It may, however, be significant that he couples the term 'décadence' with 'la barbarie ambiante'.[126] Moreover, he does openly acknowledge the role of the barbarians in the collapse of classical education: 'les invasions ont détruit l'école antique'.[127] He states directly that parish schools emerged in the reorganization that followed 'la tourmente des invasions'.[128] Here, as in the *Retractatio* of 1949, Marrou acknowledges, though he does not elaborate on, the impact of the arrival of the Germanic peoples. It is difficult not to read this acknowledgement alongside the dedication that prefaces the *History of Education*:

> Ce livre est dédié à la mémoire de Gilbert Dru, étudiant français condamné à mort comme Résistant chrétien par l'Occupant national-socialiste allemand et barbarement exécuté Place Bellecour, à Lyon, le 27 juillet 1944, à l'âge de vingt-quatre ans.

The *Histoire de l'éducation* and the *Retractatio* were the beginning of a steady shift in Marrou's appreciation of post-Roman culture. Other scholars followed suit: Pierre Riché, who would later be Marrou's biographer, continued his study of education, with a book on *Éducation et culture dans l'Occident barbare*, providing a much more detailed account of the period from the sixth to the eighth centuries, although its argument is essentially the same as Marrou's interpretation of the period. There was, moreover, a stream of editions of patristic and early medieval texts, published by *Sources Chrétiennes*. The series had been founded in Lyons in 1942 by, among others, Jean Daniélou. Marrou was an enthusiastic supporter of the enterprise from soon after its inception.[129]

These editions and the first volume of the *Nouvelle histoire de l'Église* written with Daniélou would prompt Marrou to a further re-evaluation of the fifth and sixth centuries, in which he was much more inclined to see something positive in the culture of the period. His final assessment of the Late Roman World, *Décadence romaine ou antiquité tardive?*, would appear posthumously, shortly after his death in 1977. There, having revisited Verlaine's poem, he commented on the changing evaluation of the post-Roman period, noting the German term *Spätantike* (a term which he had already acknowledged as having some use in his *Retractatio*).[130] Finally he opted for its French equivalent: *antiquité tardive*.[131] That choice, however,

---

[125] Ó Cróinín, 'Hiberno-Latin literature to 1169', pp. 371–404, at pp. 392–3.
[126] Marrou, *Histoire de l'Éducation dans l'antiquité*, p. 446.
[127] Marrou, *Histoire de l'Éducation dans l'antiquité*, pp. 452–4.
[128] Marrou, *Histoire de l'Éducation dans l'antiquité*, p. 442.
[129] Riché, *Marrou*, p. 132.
[130] Marrou, *Retractatio*, p. 694.
[131] Marrou, *Décadence ou antiquité tardive?*, pp. 9, 12, 13.

was a response not just to developments in Francophone and German scholarship, where the concept had become established,[132] but also to Anglophone writing of the 1960s and 70s. This in turn looked back, not to the broad generalizations of Dawson, but rather to the Germans and above all to Marrou himself.

Marrou, like Dawson and Cochrane, had continued a tradition of cultural history which looked back to the nineteenth century. He, like Cochrane, had done something new with it. All three of them wrote explicitly Christian history, as well as history that engaged implicitly with the horrors of war and totalitarianism. Although Marrou did some rethinking after 1945, the Post-War period did not require a complete renunciation of his ideas. For those German contemporaries like Steinbach and Petri who had seen a different type of relevance in the history of the settlement of the Germanic peoples, resort to a carefully nuanced *Retractatio* was not an option: instead an abjuration of the past was a requirement. A new European reading of the late and post-Roman periods would only emerge slowly in the decades after 1945, and it would owe more to the Christian historiography of Marrou than to the Germanists.

---

[132] Liebeschuetz, 'The birth of Late Antiquity'.

15

The Emergence of Late Antiquity

15.1 THE SHADOW OF 1945

Through the eighteenth and nineteenth centuries and the first half of the twentieth it is usually possible to identify a dominant discourse, or dominant discourses, in the debates surrounding the end of the Roman Empire and the beginning of the Middle Ages. There is a steady shift in interest from class to nation and frontier, and there is a parallel discourse concerned with spiritual regeneration. Of course, there have always been discordant voices, or voices involved in totally different debates, and there is, therefore, a strong element of subjectivity in what one does or does not define as dominant. Even so, debates on the Fall of Rome have tended to concentrate on certain issues, and those issues have often reflected the social and political debates of the day.

In the quarter of a century following 1945 there was perhaps a change: not that social and political issues ceased to tie in with interpretations of the fourth, fifth, and sixth centuries, rather that the themes debated seem to have become more disparate. Individual scholars who had lived through the War reacted in different ways, although it demanded a response from each of them. Some drew very clear comparisons between the War and the Fall of Rome. Others stood back from making such comparisons, at times deliberately. Some topics, especially those which had fed neatly into German nationalism and into the claims of the *Reich* were largely avoided, with the result that certain historiographical traditions were almost entirely forgotten.

When a new discourse did emerge as dominant, it was not prompted by any political event or social change. Unlike 1870 or 1914, neither 1956 nor 1968 feature as turning points in the historiography of the early Middle Ages, although, of course, the events of 1968—in Paris perhaps more than the Prague Spring—contributed to a sense of intellectual ferment. 1989, and the end of the Cold War, did have an effect on the historiography of Central Europe, not least because of the establishment of a dialogue between what had been politically opposed blocs, but that impacted little on debates about the end of the Roman Empire, except perhaps in the field of archaeology.[1] Rather than responding to political or social developments, the major historiographical change to have taken place seems to be instigated by the publication of a book, much as changes in the late 1720s and 30s

---

[1] See chapter 16 for a discussion of the exhibition of objects found in central and eastern Europe.

were instigated by the publications of Boulainvilliers and Du Bos, and in 1822 by Manzoni's *Adelchi* and *Discorso*—although unlike them it carried no political message. Peter Brown's *The World of Late Antiquity*, published in 1971, provided a new focus around which much of the discussion of the shift from Antiquity to the Middle Ages came to revolve.[2]

Brown himself, in a number of publications, has given his reading of the origins of *The World of Late Antiquity* and has thus provided a remarkable insight into the development of his own thought.[3] But the origins of one book, or even a series of books by a single scholar, do not necessarily reflect the state of scholarship at the time the work was written. Indeed, a ground-breaking work necessarily looks very different from the intellectual landscape in which it was conceived—in this case it was a landscape that was dominated by generations of scholars who had experienced the War and the build-up to it at first hand.

15.2 HECTOR MONRO CHADWICK

One can come no closer to the closing months of the War than Hector Monro Chadwick's *The Nationalities of Europe and the Growth of National Ideologies*, which was written in 1945, and which boasts a postscript noting the extent to which events at the war's end were overtaking the author's assertions.[4] In many respects Chadwick's work belonged to an earlier age. He was born in 1870 and had published a major work on *The Origin of the English Nation* in 1907.[5] There, in presenting the Anglo-Saxons as one among many Teutonic nations, he had made considerable use of classical evidence, but despite all the references to Tacitus and to Ptolemy, there is little sense of a culture interacting with that of the Roman world, while later Scandinavian (especially literary) evidence weighs far more heavily than do the sources for Late Antiquity. Chadwick's Anglo-Saxons belong to the Heroic Age of North, which was his major field of interest.[6] The connections he saw were between the Germanic peoples, including the Scandinavians and the Celts. He had little to say on the end of the Roman Empire, although his wife, and collaborator in Celtic studies, Nora Kershaw, did work on the culture of Late Antique Gaul.[7]

Written towards the end of his life, *The Nationalities of Europe* is, nevertheless, a remarkable attempt at showing the relationship between early history, its interpretation, and modern patriotism and nationalism. Indeed, nationalism and its evils

---

[2] Brown, *The World of Late Antiquity*.
[3] Brown, 'Report'; Brown, *A Life of Learning*; Brown, 'What's in a name?'; Brown, *The Body and Society*, Twentieth Anniversary Edition, pp. xxi–lxvii.
[4] Chadwick, *Nationalities of Europe*, p. 180; see also p. 175. See the remarkably positive assessment in de Navarro, 'Hector Munro Chadwick', pp. 213–14, where it is presented as a 'war book'.
[5] Chadwick, *The Origin of the English Nation*.
[6] Lapidge, *Interpreters of Early Medieval Britain*, p. 5.
[7] Chadwick, *Poetry and Letters in Early Christian Gaul*. See also Chadwick and Chadwick, *The Growth of Literature*, vol. 1.

are the chief concern of the work. In Chadwick's view nationalism was a force that was new to England:[8] it had rarely (except in certain frontier zones)[9] been of significance anywhere in the Middle Ages—when it was allegiance or religion that mattered.[10] The most important developments in nationalism had come in nineteenth- and twentieth-century Germany.[11]

Much of *The Nationalities of Europe* is an analysis of the pre-historic and early medieval past, and how it had been misused by scholars in recent generations. Unfortunately Chadwick provides few footnotes, and he is rarely explicit in naming those he is attacking. One of the few was the German prehistoric archaeologist Ludwig Lindenschmit,[12] though it is not difficult to guess that some of his arguments were directed against Kossinna and Petri. One might also suspect that Chadwick was replying in part to Freeman, whose essay on 'Race and language' and whose Jubilee lectures of 1887 come closest to addressing the issues that dominate *The Nationalities of Europe*, even though they were written before the English became interested in nationalism, at least in Chadwick's eyes.

After an introductory chapter on nationalism, Chadwick provides a lengthy description of the linguistic map of Europe[13] and its formation.[14] While he goes back into the pre-Christian era and forward to the modern period, he notes that for the most part the picture in Western Europe and west-central Europe was fully established by the end of the sixth century[15]—thus seeing the Migration Period of the fourth and fifth centuries as the culmination of the early linguistic history of the region. Having described the geographical distribution of languages across Europe, Chadwick turns to the relationship between language and nation,[16] picking up directly on one of Freeman's central ideas, though he nowhere names Freeman, and indeed he comes to very different conclusions. For Chadwick, although the linguistic map of Europe coincided largely with the political map as drawn by the treaties of 1919–1920, this coincidence of language and nation was a novelty.[17] In passing, he poses a question that subsequently came to be much discussed by modernists: whether the Nation State was a modern invention.

In forming and sustaining the tribal groupings that threatened Rome, which remained a political force throughout the Middle Ages, what mattered, according to Chadwick, was a ruling family: 'Among the northern peoples in early times there was in each state one family which formed its nucleus and backbone.'[18] In his view, Tacitus had been misread to produce an image of early democracy. Instead,

---

[8] Chadwick, *Nationalities of Europe*, pp. vii–viii, 1.
[9] Chadwick, *Nationalities of Europe*, p. 97.
[10] Chadwick, *Nationalities of Europe*, pp. 4, 97.
[11] Chadwick, *Nationalities of Europe*, pp. 8–9.
[12] Chadwick, *Nationalities of Europe*, pp. 158–9. Lindenschmit might seem a rather strange figure to single out (1809–93). His first major work, on burial mounds, was published in 1848. In 1851 he was appointed director of the Römisch-germanisches Central-Museum in Mainz.
[13] Chadwick, *Nationalities of Europe*, pp. 14–49.
[14] Chadwick, *Nationalities of Europe*, pp. 50–90.
[15] Chadwick, *Nationalities of Europe*, p. 69.
[16] Chadwick, *Nationalities of Europe*, pp. 91–112.
[17] Chadwick, *Nationalities of Europe*, p. 91.   [18] Chadwick, *Nationalities of Europe*, p. 94.

Chadwick promoted the image given of the Croatians and Serbians in the writings of the tenth-century Byzantine emperor Constantine Porphyrogenitus, who speaks of them having no rulers, while, paradoxically, making it equally clear that each of them was subject to hereditary rule.[19] In his insistence on the existence of a core dynasty, whose genealogy might well be fictitious,[20] Chadwick came close to an idea that would later be elaborated by Reinhard Wenskus. As for the tribes themselves, he regarded them as being rather closer to armies than large ethnic groups—something that goes with his emphasis on allegiance rather than any biological, linguistic, or cultural factor as the central bond in the creation of a medieval people:

> I know of no evidence for believing that whole peoples evacuate their old homes except under strong pressure. Examples of something like wholesale evacuation do occur in the history of the fifth and sixth centuries, e.g. in the movements of the Visigoths and the Vandals. But these were armies, rather than peoples; and they had left their old homes long before.[21]

Chadwick also foreshadowed Wenskus in treating Germanic tribes alongside those of other linguistic affiliation. Celtic and Germanic groups could be difficult to distinguish. Indeed the *Germani* themselves were a Celtic tribe, and their name had been misapplied by the Romans as a general label for Teutons,[22] or as Chadwick preferred, following the terminology propounded by the antiquarian bishop George Hickes in 1700, 'Northerners'.[23] The distinction between Teuton and Slav was equally slight, coming down to the degree of Romanization to which each had been subject, rather than to any other cause.[24] Indeed Chadwick asserted that just as Teutons moved into land where Celts were still present, so too Slavs moved into territory where Teutons could still be found.[25] In short, he thought that linguistic and cultural distinctions between the various tribes of western and central Europe were of minor importance in the early Middle Ages.

This historical reality Chadwick contrasted with the claims made by the pan-Slavists, pan-Latinists (essentially fascist Italians) and pan-Germanists of the nineteenth and twentieth centuries.[26] It was they who misinterpreted the past to provide themselves with claims to domination.[27] In 1940–1 the Nazis and Fascists occupied half of Europe: the Fascists presenting themselves as the heirs to the Roman Empire, and the Nazis as the descendents of the Teutonic conquerors of the fifth and sixth centuries.[28] However, in misusing Tacitus, the Germans failed to note that early Germanic literature dealt not in nations but in heroes[29]—and here Chadwick spoke as a specialist in heroic literature.[30] He never showed much sympathy for the traditions of *Rechts-* or *Verfassungsgeschichte* (legal or constitutional history), which had dominated historical study of the early Germanic peoples. For him,

[19] Chadwick, *Nationalities of Europe*, pp. 67–8.　[20] Chadwick, *Nationalities of Europe*, p. 94.
[21] Chadwick, *Nationalities of Europe*, p. 67.　[22] Chadwick, *Nationalities of Europe*, pp. 147–9.
[23] Chadwick, *Nationalities of Europe*, p. 142.　[24] Chadwick, *Nationalities of Europe*, p. 68.
[25] Chadwick, *Nationalities of Europe*, p. 67.　[26] Chadwick, *Nationalities of Europe*, pp. 113–21.
[27] Chadwick, *Nationalities of Europe*, pp. 122–66.　[28] Chadwick, *Nationalities of Europe*, p. 122.
[29] Chadwick, *Nationalities of Europe*, p. 124.
[30] Among his other works were *The Heroic Age*, and the three-volume work written with his wife, *The Growth of Literature*.

German intellectual dominance, established by state funding of universities from as early as the eighteenth century, meant that their misreading of the past had been generally accepted.[31] Unlike Pirenne, Chadwick saw intellectuals as having played a crucial role in the development of German nationalism. It was their ideas that were promoted in schools: 'Indeed, I doubt whether philological and antiquarian learning has ever produced such far-reaching effects.'[32] For him the parallel to be drawn was not between the Germans and the heroic Goths, but between the Gestapo and the Huns and Avars.[33]

In place of the claims made by German scholars, Chadwick returned to offer his own reading of the development of the linguistic map of Europe—and in doing so not only recapitulated his earlier arguments, but also largely reaffirmed the arguments he had put forward in *The Origin of the English Nation*. He stressed once more the mixture of Celt and Teuton,[34] before rounding on the notion that the Teutonic peoples had originated in northern Germany. Here, although he named Lindenschmit, his criticism was clearly aimed as much at Kossinna and his followers, both in archaeology and in philology.[35]

The two final chapters of Chadwick's work on *The Nationalities of Europe* turn away from the distant past, tracing instead the international failure to understand German nationalism,[36] and proposing that a new Institute of Imperial (or Commonwealth) and International Studies be established, to ensure that Britain in particular, and Europe in general, should never be so blind again.[37] This, along with the fact that throughout his book Chadwick was responding to the very precise circumstances in which he was writing, ensured that *The Nationalities of Europe* would very soon be out of date. Not surprisingly, it was not one of the works that attracted attention when his contribution to scholarship came to be re-evaluated from the 1970s. As a response to German misuse of the past, it had very much less impact than did Geoffrey Barraclough's *The Origins of Modern Germany*, originally published in 1946.[38] Unlike Chadwick, Barraclough offered a narrative response to the German exploitation of history which was used by generations of students: he also chose to go no further back in time than 800. Yet Chadwick's last book, for all its inbuilt obsolescence, remains an extraordinary exploration of the interplay between past and present.

15.3 FRANCOPHONE VIEWS

Chadwick, and to a lesser extent Barraclough, were unusual in the immediate post-War years in the way that they addressed the Nazi representation of the early

---

[31] Chadwick, *Nationalities of Europe*, pp. 137–9, 143–4.
[32] Chadwick, *Nationalities of Europe*, pp. 143–4.
[33] Chadwick, *Nationalities of Europe*, p. 140.
[34] Chadwick, *Nationalities of Europe*, p. 157.
[35] Chadwick, *Nationalities of Europe*, pp. 158–9.
[36] Chadwick, *Nationalities of Europe*, pp. 167–80.
[37] Chadwick, *Nationalities of Europe*, pp. 181–204
[38] Barraclough, *The Origins of Modern Germany*.

medieval past. Others, while still tackling questions that had been at the centre of debate in the 1930s, passed over the arguments that had been put forward by the likes of Petri. The Belgian scholar Charles Verlinden, in a paper on 'Frankish colonization: a new approach', delivered to the Royal Historical Society in 1954 (surely a significant invitation in the years after 1945), dismissed Petri's arguments as having been disproved, without giving any hint of the explosive nature of the German's conclusions and their impact on Nazi policy.[39] He commented that 'the very controversial book of Franz Petri' had in no way helped elucidate the subject: 'Different groups of specialists have shown, and continue to show, how much there was that was unsound in Petri's thesis, and Petri himself has recently abandoned a considerable number of the positions he had taken up.' There was no need to say any more.

This calmness contrasts with that of several of the leading French scholars of the post-War period, both at an institutional and at a personal level. In 1950 another meeting of the Congrès international des sciences historiques, the ninth, was held in Paris— a follow-up to those of Brussels in 1922 and Oslo in 1928. There had been further meetings in Warsaw in 1933 and Zurich in 1938. Like their Belgian counterparts in the period after 1918, the French were determined to prevent Germans from attending: this time only those of 'un passé absolument sans reproche' were allowed.[40]

If one turns to the work of an individual, the most famous description of the Fall of the Roman Empire made by a late-antique scholar in the aftermath of 1939–45 was that of André Piganiol, who announced in no uncertain terms at the end of his account of *L'Empire chrétien*, published in 1947, that the Roman Empire had been assassinated: the closing words of the book state baldly:

La civilisation romaine n'est pas morte de sa belle mort. Elle a été assassinée.[41]
('Roman civilization did not die a natural death: it was assassinated.')

The preceding pages, by contrast, present a very much more nuanced view of the various interpretations of the fall of the Empire which had been under discussion in the decades prior to 1939. Piganiol moves methodically though arguments that the catastrophe which ended the Roman World had been caused by climate or demographic change, by political failure and alienation, by financial, economic, social, moral, religious, or intellectual crisis—in each case evaluating the views of earlier scholars.[42] So too, the barbarians had played a rather less destructive role in Piganiol's own views as expressed in the *Histoire de Rome*, written immediately before the war and published in 1939.[43] There he emphasized the points that monotheism had created an internationalist world that knew no frontiers, and that trade had shifted north from the Mediterranean. In so far as he listed the barbarians as being a major factor in this earlier work, it was in the context of the fact that

[39] Verlinden, 'Frankish colonization: a new approach', p. 2.
[40] Schulze, 'German historiography, 1930s to 1950s', p. 35.
[41] Piganiol, *L'Empire chrétien*, p. 422. See also Piganiol, *Le Sac de Rome*.
[42] Piganiol, *L'Empire chrétien*, pp. 411–20.
[43] Piganiol, *Histoire de Rome*, cited in Puech, 'Éloge funèbre de M. André Piganiol', p. 316.

the Romans themselves had given up performing military service, and that their bureaucracy had become too heavy and expensive, leading the population to welcome the Germanic incomers. The volume that followed *L'Empire chrétien* in the *Histoire générale* collection, *Les Destinées de l'empire en Occident de 395 à 888*, jointly authored by Ferdinand Lot, Christian Pfister, and François Ganshof, which had already been published in 1928, contained the equally moderate inter-war views of Lot.[44]

Piganiol had been professor at Strasbourg after the city was transferred back to France in 1919, moving to the Sorbonne in 1928[45]—a move that echoed that of Fustel half a century earlier. In the aftermath of the German aggression of 1939–45 he took a very different line from that pursued by Fustel, who had admittedly lived through a much lesser conflict. One can scarcely doubt that his view that the Roman Empire had been assassinated by the barbarians stemmed directly from his experience of life in France during the War.

While Piganiol was extreme in his emphasis on barbarian destruction, he was not alone in implying modern parallels to the Fall of the Roman Empire, and thus in presenting the period as one of disaster. Ferdinand Lot's pupil Robert Latouche painted a picture of destruction, with obvious echoes of the recent war in *Les Grandes Invasions et la crise de l'Occident au Ve siècle* published in 1946.[46] Equally inclined to see the fifth century in terms that echoed the recent past was the literary historian André Loyen, who had, as we have seen, established himself as the great interpreter of the fifth-century Gallic letter-writer, poet, senator, and bishop, Sidonius Apollinaris. His approach is explicit in the title of one of his articles analysing the events of the mid-fifth century in Gaul: 'Résistants et collaborateurs en Gaule à l'époque des grandes invasions'.[47] Resistance and collaboration were loaded terms in post-1945 France.

Loyen was not alone in presenting the fifth century as a period of *débâcle*, occupation, and collaboration.[48] The idea is present in the post-War writings of Pierre Courcelle. A member of the École française de Rome at the outbreak of the war, he joined the French army, but soon took over direction of the Institut français in Naples. He moved back to France, to the University of Bordeaux in 1941, transferring to the Sorbonne in 1944. He is perhaps best known as an interpreter of Augustine, like Marrou, and of Boethius, but he also gathered together the literary evidence for the barbarians in his study of the *Histoire littéraire des grandes invasions germaniques*, first published in 1948, and subsequently expanded.[49] Courcelle warned the reader from the start that the book would not contain a narrative of events leading up to the fall of the Empire, recommending the works of Bury,

[44] Lot, Pfister, and Ganshof, *Les Destinées de l'empire en occident de 395 à 888*.

[45] Puech, 'Éloge funèbre de M. André Piganiol', pp. 310–11.

[46] Latouche, *Les Grandes Invasions*. On Latouche see Graceffa, *Les Historiens et la question franque*, pp. 230–4.

[47] Loyen, 'Résistants et collaborateurs en Gaule à l'époque des grandes invasions'.

[48] Graceffa, *Les Historiens et la question franque*, p. 230.

[49] Courcelle, *Histoire littéraire des grandes invasions germaniques*. The references that follow are to the third edition.

Stein, Schmidt, Lot, and Halphen[50]—Piganiol's *L'Empire chrétien* is not mentioned, but it had only just appeared. The works cited at this point by Courcelle do
not, for the most part, present an image of total devastation at the hands of the
barbarians. Yet he himself went on to state that while there was assimilation
between Romans and incomers, this was not to happen until after the disaster of
the invasions, and he described the invaders simply as 'hordes germaniques'.[51]
Indeed his choice of language throughout suggests parallels with the invasions
recently experienced by the French.[52] Moreover, he explicitly rejected the interpretations of Fustel and of Christian Courtois, as well as the views of those German
scholars who did not see the period as one of catastrophe.[53] The literary descriptions of the invasions of the fourth and fifth centuries, and of the destruction they
entailed, were depressing enough, and Courcelle was content to present them more
or less as they stood.

There were, of course, scholars who were rather more interested in looking at the
post-Roman period from the barbarian point of view. As early as 1952 French
archaeologists held a conference in Poitiers under the title *Journées mérovingiennes*,[54]
which was to be the first of a long sequence of conferences that provided a showcase for early medieval archaeology in France. There were also historians who were
drawn to work on the barbarians. Courcelle was certainly correct in seeing Courtois as someone who did not interpret the barbarian invasions in a catastrophic
light, although contemporary politics also influenced the latter's work. Born (like
Courcelle) in 1912, he was a student at the Sorbonne, where his most eminent
master was the ancient historian, Jérôme Carcopino, who, as we have seen, was
subsequently minister of education in the Vichy government. In 1935 Courtois
took a post in the *Lycée* in Algiers. During the war he served 'sous les drapeaux',
first in 1939–40, and then again from 1942–1945, when he was attached to the
Service des Œuvres du Commissariat aux Affaires Etrangères: the phrase 'sous les
drapeaux', of course, obscures the changing nature of the regime under which he
served—and although he would end up in liberated Algeria, he had been a protégé
of Carcopino. Courtois' affiliations were thus radically different from those of
Marrou. In 1945 he moved to the University of Algiers, where he taught until his
death in a car crash in 1956.[55]

Working in Algeria, it is perhaps not surprising that he should have concentrated on
the history of North Africa, and most especially of the Vandal kingdom. In addition to
his *magnum opus* on *Les Vandales et l'Afrique*, he wrote a substantial study of the anti-
Arian churchman Victor of Vita.[56] Despite his concentration on Victor, Courtois'
assessment of the Vandal kingdom is remarkably positive, even though he cast the

[50] Courcelle, *Histoire littéraire des grandes invasions germaniques*, p. 11.
[51] Courcelle, *Histoire littéraire des grandes invasions germaniques*, pp. 1–12.
[52] Ward-Perkins, *The Fall of Rome and the End of Civilization*, pp. 173–4. For a study of Courcelle
in context, Vessey, '407 and all that', pp. 42–6.
[53] Courcelle, *Histoire littéraire des grandes invasions germaniques*, pp. 12–13.
[54] Graceffa, *Les Historiens et la question franque*, p. 237.
[55] For the life of Courtois, see Le Tourneau, 'Biographie de Christian Courtois', pp. 433–4. For an
assessment, see also Fourquin, 'Éloge funèbre de Christian Courtois', pp. 63–9.
[56] Courtois, *Les Vandales et l'Afrique*; Courtois, *Victor de Vita et son œuvre*.

Germanic incomers in a somewhat orientalist mould.[57] Perhaps, as a *voltairien mont-martois* rather than a committed French Catholic,[58] he found it easier to excuse Vandal Arianism than did many of his contemporaries, while as someone with lines to the Vichy government he was unlikely to see the Germanic invaders of the fifth century in terms of the barbarity of twentieth-century Germans. Modern politics impinged on Courtois' reading of Vandal Africa in an additional way, for he certainly saw echoes of the Berber threat to the Vandal kingdom and to its Byzantine successor in the growing Algerian insurgency which had been simmering since 1945 and which had already turned violent in 1954: as Guy Fourquin wrote: 'Or Courtois était hanté par la crainte de voir, en notre XXe siècle, la nature sauvage reprendre encore une fois ses droits dans le Maghreb.' ('But Courtois was haunted by the fear of seeing, in our twentieth century, that savage nature could reclaim its rights in the Maghreb once again,')[59]

France's links with the Maghreb would ensure that French scholars of Antiquity and its aftermath paid particular attention to the history of North Africa, even after the establishment of Algerian independence in 1962. When Algeria became rather less accessible, French archaeologists continued to work in Tunisia,[60] and in so doing played a leading role in uncovering the material culture of the region in the fifth and sixth centuries, while Church historians—Marrou, as we have seen, as well as Courcelle and Jacques Fontaine—perhaps inevitably were drawn to the writings of St Augustine.

Fontaine, however, followed a largely different path from his teachers and his contemporaries. Born in 1922, having passed the *agrégation* in occupied Paris, he headed for the Casa Velasquez in Madrid to study Isidore of Seville, and established himself thereafter as the greatest expert on Visigothic culture. In so doing, whether deliberately or not, he largely avoided the dominant French debates concerning the Germanic invasions, looking instead at arguably the most Romanized of the seventh-century successor states. He would also, in time, co-direct what turned out to be 'a doomed project of a new history of post-classical Latin literature with the much younger (but War-tormented) Reinhart Herzog.'[61]

15.4 THE EARLY MIDDLE AGES IN POST-WAR ITALY

While the experience of the Second World War seems to have inclined the majority of French historians to take a negative view of the fifth- and sixth-century barbarians, the same could not be said of the majority of their Italian counterparts.[62]

---

[57] Wood, 'Royal succession and legitimation in the Roman West, 419–536', at p. 59.

[58] Salama, 'Christian Courtois', p. 299.

[59] Fourquin, 'Éloge funèbre de Christian Courtois', p. 68.

[60] Among major contributors, one should list Noël Duval and Claude Lepelley. For the French in the Maghreb, Mattingly, *Imperialism, Power and Identity*, pp. 45–59.

[61] I owe the phrase to Mark Vessey, to whom I am indebted for guidance on Fontaine. Herzog, who was born in 1941, committed suicide in 1994. On Herzog's work, Vessey, 'Patristics and literary history'.

[62] For overviews of the development of Italian historiography on the early Middle Ages in the post-War period, see Gasparri, 'I Germani immaginari e la realità del regno'. For a broader survey, Giarrizzo, 'Il Medioevo tra Otto e Novecento'.

There were, of course, exceptions: notably Gabriele Pepe, although his initial contribution to the study of the barbarians already appeared in 1941. A French translation followed in 1954.[63] In fact, it was in Italy more than anywhere else in Europe that study of the Germanic peoples flourished in the immediately post-War period. The most obvious monument to this is the foundation of the *Centro Italiano di studi sull'alto medioevo* in 1952: its annual *Settimane* (week-long conference) has ever since been a highpoint in the early medievalist's calendar.[64] In 1955 the Italian government voted to establish a museum dedicated entirely to the Early Middle Ages, a decision which was only implemented in 1967 with the foundation of the *Museo dell'alto medioevo*, housed, with a nice touch of irony, in a building of the Piazza Marconi of Mussolini's EUR.[65] While for the French and for the Germans the period of the Germanic invasions had problematic overtones in the period after 1945, the same was less true in Italy, where Mussolini had developed a cult of *romanità* (Chadwick's 'pan-Latinism'), most obviously in the environs of the Foro Romano, with the result that for many Italians it was the Roman Empire rather than its demise and aftermath that was contaminated by the events of the 1930s and early 1940s.[66] By contrast, the Lombards had been of little interest to the pre-War Fascist government, which had not even been excited by the appearance of a (fake) treasure of Agilulf and Theodelinda.[67] To a certain extent the Second World War helped make the Lombards, who had been denounced by Manzoni and his followers over a century earlier, acceptable.

In its early years the centre at Spoleto was dominated by a small group of Italian scholars, notably Gian Piero Bognetti, Ottorino Bertolini, Giorgio Falco,[68] and Enrico Sestan. They would be followed by a line of equally distinguished historians, among them Girolamo Arnaldi, Giovanni Tabacco, and Cinzio Violante. Of the Lombard historians working on either side of the Second World War the most influential was Bognetti (1902–63).[69] He had already established himself as a major interpreter of the Lombards before the war: his first publication had appeared as early as 1918, when he was only sixteen.[70] As a liberal Catholic, to a large extent he accepted the model of Lombard oppression set out by Manzoni in his *Discorso*—and it is no surprise that he wrote a number of studies on the early years of

[63] Pepe, *Il medio evo barbarico d'Italia*; trans. J. Gonnet, *Le Moyen Âge barbare en Italie*.

[64] *Omaggio al medioevo: i primi cinquanta anni del Centro italiano di studi sull'alto medioevo di Spoleto*.

[65] Arena and Paroli, *Museo dell'alto medioevo*, p. 5.

[66] On Mussolini's *romanità*, see Mees, 'Hitler and *Germanentum*', p. 256; Jansen, 'Warum es in Italien keine Volksgeschichte wie im "Dritten Reich" gab'. On Italian *romanità* in Libya, Mattingly, *Imperialism, Power and Identity*, pp. 45–59.

[67] La Rocca and Gasparri, 'Forging an early medieval couple', pp. 277, 279.

[68] For Falco's view of the development of Italian historiography of the early Middle Ages, see Falco, 'La questione longobarda e la moderna storiografia italiana'.

[69] See the assessment in Vismara, 'G. P. Bognetti, storico dei Longobardi'. Also Gasparri, 'I Germani immaginari e la realtà del regno', pp. 7–8, 11–14; Gasparri, 'Gian Piero Bognetti storico dei Longobardi'.

[70] For a bibliography, Bognetti, *L'età longobarda*, vol. 1, pp. xxi–xxxv.

the nineteenth-century writer.[71] His view of the conquest was a gloomy one.[72] Indeed, he saw the early Lombards as truly barbarian and argued that paganism had continued to be a force within the Lombard kingdom during the seventh century.[73] Even so, he was inclined to see the Lombards, particularly the Lombard military, as being more influenced by Roman practice than Manzoni had allowed.[74] At the same time, both before and after the War, he was open to the influence of German scholarship. Indeed, for all his adherence to Manzoni's scheme, he was actually interested in 'Germanic' tradition.[75]

The question of the interpretation of relations between Romans and Lombards was, however, suddenly altered by the discovery in 1944 of a major fresco cycle in the church of Santa Maria foris portas at Castelseprio in the foothills of the Alps, to the north of Milan. Bognetti ascribed the paintings, incorrectly as it would now seem,[76] to the Lombard period. Already in 1931 he had published a short article about the site of Castelseprio, which boasts the remains of a very interesting set of fortifications from the late Roman and early medieval periods.[77] The new discoveries, however, forced him to re-evaluate the religious and cultural history of the Lombards: how could a people he had regarded as barbarous produce such a major work of art?

Bognetti's solution was to look for external influence. He had already argued in an article published in 1940 that there had been Catholic missions to the Lombards.[78] Now he argued that the paintings at Castelseprio were the work of Syrian artists, thus denying that the frescoes shed any light on the artistic capabilities and theological sophistication of the Lombards themselves, whilst at the same time allowing that their kingdom could boast artistic treasures.[79] The Carolingian dating currently assigned to the frescoes effectively undermine Bognetti's arguments about the church of Santa Maria foris portas, but his investigation did a great deal to further the study of Lombard history. Above all, he drew attention to the importance of early medieval archaeology, and the light it shed on Germanic civilization in Italy.[80] It was an area of study that Fuchs had begun to open up in the late 1930s and 1940s, but which he could no longer pursue. Thus, while French scholars after the War for the most part saw the Germanic migrations as something disastrous, which echoed the crisis that they had recently lived through, leading Italian historians, while still largely accepting Manzoni's view of the barbarian conquest,

---

[71] These are collected in Bognetti, *Manzoni giovane*.

[72] Gasparri, 'I Germani immaginari e la realtà del regno', p. 12.

[73] Bognetti, 'Santa Maria foris portas di Castelseprio'. References here are to the 1966 edition.

[74] Vismara, 'G. P. Bognetti, storico dei Longobardi', pp. x–xvi.

[75] Vismara, 'G. P. Bognetti, storico dei Longobardi', pp xiv–xvi; Gasparri, 'I Germani immaginari e la realtà del regno', p. 12.

[76] Current views of the date can be found in Leveto, 'The Marian themes of the frescoes in S. Maria at Castelseprio', p. 393, n. 2.

[77] Bognetti, 'Tra le rovine di Castelseprio'.

[78] Bognetti, 'Le origini della consacrazione del vescovo di Pavia da parte del pontefice romano'. See Vismara, 'G. P. Bognetti, storico dei Longobardi', p. viii.

[79] Bognetti, 'Santa Maria foris portas', pp. 559–636.

[80] Gasparri, 'I Germani immaginari e la realtà del regno', p. 13.

avoided any comparison with the expansionist policies of Nazi Germany—something that was all the easier, not having been on the receiving end of Hitler's aggression. Instead they set about opening the early medieval period up for renewed discussion.

15.5 GERMANY

In contrast to both the French and the Italians, the Germans largely avoided the period. Indeed, Bognetti, in attempting to understand the Germanic culture of the Lombards, was drawing on scholarship that the Germans themselves were skirting round. There was an institutional aspect to German silence on the Germanic migrations and post-Roman period in the years after 1945. A number of historians who had been too closely associated with the policies of the Reich lost their posts, at least temporarily, in the immediate aftermath of the War.[81] Among them were a handful of scholars who had worked on the early Middle Ages. We have already noted that Fuchs in Rome was one of the few German archaeologists to cease academic work. Not surprisingly, Franz Petri was removed from his chair at Cologne. He would, however, secure an equivalent post in Bonn in 1948, with the support of Steinbach. After his retirement in 1960 he was awarded the *Große Verdienstkreuz des Verdienstordens* of the German *Bundesrepublik*, and he would even receive an honorary doctorate from the University of Louvain—a remarkable testament to the extent to which his earlier work had been forgotten. Otto Höfler was also banned from teaching at the university of Munich, although he was to secure a post at the University of Vienna in 1957. In addition, although the editor Karl Eckhardt was identified as a Nazi *Mitläufer* ('supporter'), despite losing his post at the University of Bonn he still moved to the (much less prestigious) directorship of the Historisches Institut des Werralandes in Witzenhausen, where he continued to produce editions of legal texts for the *MGH*. Steinbach retained his professorship, but concentrated on the later Middle Ages.

In fact, most German scholars avoided the potentially contentious field of the Migration Period. Discussion of the German *Volk* largely came to an end. What had been said, and the uses to which it had been put, were carefully ignored,[82] a factor which facilitated the reinstatement of both Petri and Höfler. The involvement of historians in Nazi activities and the exploitation of their scholarship by the Reich were scarcely spoken about until the publication in 1967 of Karl Ferdinand Werner's *Das NS-Geschichtsbild und die deutsche Geschichtswissenschaft*.[83] Even then the issue was only lightly touched upon: it would take a very open confrontation between younger scholars and the old guard (or rather the students of the old guard) at the *Historikertag* held at Frankfurt in 1998 before the matter was widely

---

[81] For a list of those who lost their posts, Schulze, 'German historiography, 1930s to 1950s', p. 36.

[82] Schulze, 'German historiography, 1930s to 1950s', p. 23.

[83] Werner, *Das NS-Geschichtsbild und die deutsche Geschichtswissenschaft*. For the crucial role played by Werner in the acknowledgement of what had happened, see Schulze, 'German historiography, 1930s to 1950s', p. 24.

aired. In fact, the involvement of historians and archaeologists in the policies of the Third Reich had been very much better documented in communist East Germany, where a clear critique of the immediate past suited the political situation, than it had in the West, where more scholars had retained their posts.[84]

There were, of course, German scholars who continued to work on the late- and post-Roman periods. The great tradition of research on the Ancient World, which in Germany had, since the days of Mommsen, included the Fall of the Empire, continued—not least in the series on the *Aufsteig und Untergang der römischen Welt*, which began life as a *Festschrift* for the one-time Nazi Joseph Vogt in 1972.[85] In 1928 Ernst Stein had produced the first volume of his *Geschichte des spätrömischen Reiches*. The second volume written in exile in Switzerland was published after his death, in a French translation, in 1949.[86] Among German specialists of the Merovingian period the most important to emerge in the years immediately after 1945 was Eugen Ewig, a scholar who was as much at home in studying Late Antiquity as in the ensuing centuries. A student of Levison, he had worked as an archivist during the War and had thus avoided the more doctrinaire debates surrounding early Frankish history. Having already studied in France in the 1930s he was well placed, as a Catholic Europeanist, to play a major role in the re-establishment of Franco-German cultural relations, especially after the creation of the Deutsches Historisches Institut in Paris in 1958.[87] In his own research he made much of the Roman background to the Frankish kingdom. His first book, *Trier im Merowingerreich: Civitas, Stadt, Bistum*, was concerned with a city that had a significant Roman past.[88] Ewig was also deeply sympathetic to the city's strong contemporary Catholicism. His subsequent articles, which transformed understanding of the Merovingian kingdom and of its monastic and episcopal history,[89] reflected a detailed study of the Latin source material, and thus had little or no cause to engage with the problematic issue of the Germanic *Volk* or its migration.

15.6 REINHARD WENSKUS, FRANTIŠEK GRAUS, AND HERWIG WOLFRAM

Volksgeschichte, or the history of Germanic peoples, was scarcely addressed by anyone in Germany in the fifteen years after 1945. Then in 1961 Reinhard Wenskus published a major work of interpretation of the Germanic *Volk*: *Stammesbildung*

---

[84] Burleigh, *Germany Turns Eastwards*.

[85] For a brief overview of scholarship on Late Antiquity before 1971 see Dihle, *SO Debate*, pp. 40–3. For a major overview of German research on the Ancient World, see Marchand, *Down from Olympus*.

[86] Goffart, *Barbarian Tides*, p. 40,

[87] *In Memoriam Eugen Ewig* (esp. Paravicini, 'Eugen Ewig und das Deutsche Historische Institut Paris', pp. 19–31). See also Werner, 'Zum Geleit', in Ewig, *Spätantikes und fränkisches Gallien*, vol. 1, pp. ix–xii; Graceffa, *Les Historiens et la question franque*, p. 315.

[88] Ewig, *Trier im Merowingerreich: Civitas, Stadt, Bistum*.

[89] Most of Ewig's articles are collected in his *Spätantikes und fränkisches Gallien: Gesammelte Schriften*.

und Verfassung: das Werden der frühmittelalterlichen Gentes, which can be translated roughly as 'Tribal formation and constitution: the creation of early medieval peoples'. Although it was the first work of Wenskus to attract significant attention, it was not the work of a young man. Born in Saugen, Memelland (now part of Lithuania) in 1916, and educated in Tilsit (the birthplace of Kossinna, now in Russia), Wenskus came from a German community that had long been established within the Slavonic world, though its days were numbered after the end of the War. He was a member of the German armed forces from 1939–45, being taking prisoner by the Americans in 1945. It was only after 1949 that he studied at university, first at Hannover and then at Marburg. His first book, published in 1956, was concerned with Bruno of Querfurt, one of the most sensitive of missionaries to the Slavs in the tenth and eleventh centuries.[90] Unlike Kossinna, whose origins in Memelland seem to have underpinned his extreme German nationalism, Wenskus' association with the same region seem to have sensitized him to the Slav world.

Central to his reading of the early medieval *Volk* was the notion of ethnogenesis, tribal formation, which he saw in cultural rather than biological terms. He argued that a tribe was formed around a small nucleus, the *Traditionskern*, and that tribal groups could easily dissolve; indeed, his model allowed for a good deal of fluidity.[91] This cultural model flew in the face of Nazi concepts of ethnicity, which had been based largely on the question of bloodlines—though Wenskus did draw on views of lordship (*Herrschaft*) that German scholars were developing in the 1930s.[92] He was careful not to limit his discussion to purely Germanic groups. He also analysed the formation of Celtic tribes, noting that in Antiquity they had absorbed and been absorbed by their Germanic neighbours[93]—a point that had already been stressed by Chadwick.[94] The same could be said of the slightly later Slavic tribal groupings with which Wenskus was also familiar.

Wenskus' argument was not entirely new, although it was out of line with much pre-War German thinking.[95] Chadwick made much of the notion of a ruling family, whether genuine or fictitious. Nor was he Wenskus' only non-German precursor. Ferdinand Lot, writing in 1939, and drawing on generations of philological study, had noted the presence of Celtic elements in Germany[96]—which had been stressed by the likes of Johann Caspar Zeuss and Marie Henri d'Arbois de Jubainville in nineteenth-century Germany and France. Already in his Oxford lectures of 1887 Freeman, who had a very strong sense of the natural superiority of the Aryan

[90] Wenskus, *Studien zur historisch-politischen Gedankenwelt Bruns von Querfurt*.
[91] For convenient English-language statements of Wenskus' basic model, see Little and Rosenwein, *Debating the Middle Ages*, pp. 8–9, and Pohl, 'Ethnicity in early medieval studies', pp. 15–16.
[92] Murray, 'Reinhard Wenskus on "Ethnogenesis"', pp. 53–4.
[93] Wenskus, *Stammesbildung und Verfassung*.
[94] On Wenskus as the culmination of a tradition rather than the beginning of a new one, and on the similarity between his ideas and those of Chadwick, see Murray, 'Reinhard Wenskus on "Ethnogenesis"', pp. 53, 67.
[95] The links between Wenskus' thought and that of 1930s German scholarship is, however, stressed by Murray, 'Reinhard Wenskus on "Ethnogenesis"', pp. 53–4.
[96] Lot, *Les Invasions germaniques*, p. 14. See also his bibliographical introduction, pp. 8–9.

races, had emphasized the importance of tradition in the formation of early medieval nations.[97] Yet, while Wenskus' ideas can be shown to have developed out of pre-existing scholarship, in the post-War context they marked a new departure. They contributed significantly to the de-Nazification of the concept of the *Volk*,[98] and they would steadily come to be accepted as a standard model for thinking about early medieval tribal groupings. This, however, would not occur until well into the 1970s and 1980s, twenty years after the initial publication of *Stammesbildung und Verfassung*.

The early medieval *Volk* would appear in a different guise in the work of the Czech writer František Graus (1921–89), whose *Volk, Heiliger und Herrscher* was published in 1965.[99] It was a work that transformed the appreciation of Merovingian hagiography as a body of source material (although it makes little attempt to distinguish between works written in the Merovingian period and later forgeries). Born in Brno in Czechoslavakia, Graus came from a German-speaking family, but as a Jew he was interned in Theresienstadt during the War. After liberation, perhaps not surprisingly, he became an ardent communist. The concept of the *Volk* in his early work was thus largely Marxist: it referred to the ordinary people as much as the national group. In 1968, at the time of the Russian intervention in Prague, however, Graus was in Konstanz on a visiting research fellowship. Despite his commitment to communism, he decided not to return to Czechoslovakia, but instead found academic employment, first in Giessen and Konstanz, and finally, in 1972, in Basel. As time went on, his use of the term *Volk* changed: by 1980, when he published *Die Nationalbildung der Westslawen im Mittelalter*, a work which reflects his continuing interest in Bohemia, he had moved rather closer to Wenskus in his emphasis on national consciousness.

Wenskus' interpretation of the early Germanic *Volk* had little immediate impact, not least because of the paucity of historical research on the early Middle Ages being carried out in Germany in the 1960s. It would only be with the publication of Herwig Wolfram's *Geschichte der Goten* in 1979 that the notion of *Traditionskern* began to attract regular attention. Wolfram, who trained in Vienna, where he was deeply influenced by Heinrich Fichtenau, had established himself primarily as a expert in diplomatics, most notably with the publication of *Intitulatio*, a study of formal titles in early medieval texts.[100] One other scholar at the Institut für Österreichische Geschichtsforschung, Erich Zöllner, did write the history of a Germanic people, when he revised Ludwig Schmidt's account of the Franks, at the request of Joachim Werner.[101] Zöllner, however, was primarily a specialist in Austrian history rather than in the early Middle Ages. Wolfram was, thus, breaking new ground when he turned to the subject of the Goths, and more especially because he took Wenskus' model of ethnogenesis as a point of departure.

---

[97] See above, chapter 11.
[98] For the de-Nazification of the *Volk*, Schulze, 'German historiography, 1930s to 1950s', p. 39.
[99] I am indebted to Pavlina Richterova for guidance on Graus's career and ideas.
[100] Wolfram, *Intitulatio* I, *Lateinische Königs- und Fürstentitel bis zum Ende des 8, Jahrhunderts*.
[101] Zöllner, *Geschichte der Franken*.

A number of factors may have contributed to Wenskus' model of tribal formation being championed in Austria earlier than it was in Germany. In the nineteenth
century many Austrian intellectuals had not been enthusiastic in adopting the
notion of *Germanentum* as advanced by Grimm. Whilst Grimm and his fellows at
the Frankfurt Parliament had retreated to a more geographically restricted view of
what it was to be German (*kleindeutsch*), the Austrians took a more expansive view
(*großdeutsch*).[102] Pirenne, for one, had noted the wisdom of the anti-nationalist
approach of the nineteenth-century Viennese dramatist Franz Grillparzer.[103] Austrian reservations about nationalism were no doubt influenced by the fact that
Austro-Hungary had included peoples that were not Germanic, among them the
Hungarians themselves, and numerous Slavic groups: nationalist sentiments in
Bohemia, Slovakia, or Hungary were a challenge to the unity of the Habsburg
Reich. Whatever they felt about the Frankfurt Parliament in 1848, the Austrian
authorities moved quickly to close a copy-cat Slav Congress held in Prague the
same year.[104] Even the reduced Austria of post 1945 includes the clearly Slavicized
territory of Carinthia. Despite the Cold War, between 1968 and 1989 Austrian
academics retained closer links with the Slav and Magyar worlds than did their
counterparts elsewhere in the West. Equally important, Austria as a centre of the
ancient Hallstadt culture, named after the salt-producing territory south of Salz-
burg, could be seen to have Celtic roots. This heritage could be conceptualized
within Wenskus' recognition of Celtic elements in the Germanic world. It is not
surprising that Austrian scholars should have emerged as the champions of the
concept of ethnogenesis.

15.7 THE VIEW FROM ENGLAND

The notion of ethnogenesis as elaborated by Wolfram would come to be further
developed by a number of scholars, both Austrian and British, in the 1980s and
1990s. In fact, while Wenskus' work was developed in Austria before it was taken
up in Germany, it had been noted even earlier in England, by Michael Wallace-
Hadrill, who had reviewed *Stammesbildung und Verfassung* in the *English Historical
Review* in 1964.[105] Although he himself rarely wrote about issues of tribal formation in the years that followed, Wallace-Hadrill regularly directed his students to
read Wenskus. As one of the very few English scholars who dedicated himself to
the study of the early Middle Ages in the post-War period, but also as a teacher
with a substantial number of research students, this was to ensure that Wenskus'
approach was largely taken for granted among early medieval historians in England
in the last decades of the twentieth century.

---

[102] On the two ideologies, Rapp, *Grossdeutsch-kleindeutsch*.
[103] Pirenne, 'La pangermanisme et la Belgique', p. 20. Grillparzer's König Ottokars Glück und
Ende surely underlies Pirenne's reference to the Bohemian on p. 26.
[104] Chadwick, *Nationalities of Europe*, p. 116.   [105] Wallace-Hadrill, review of Wenskus.

Despite his awareness of Wenskus, Wallace-Hadrill's own concerns were rather different. As early as 1952 he wrote a short introduction to the early Middle Ages, *The Barbarian West*, commissioned by Sir Maurice Powicke to provide an introduction to the period for 'the man in the train'.[106] Unlike Dawson's *The Making of Europe*, which had presented a picture of the continent destroyed by the barbarians and recreated by the Church, Wallace-Hadrill was rather less inclined to see the barbarians as a purely destructive force, looking instead at what survived from the Roman past, and how it was combined with, and transformed by, contact with Germanic tradition. Rather than providing a narrative, *The Barbarian West* is an essay in interpretation, and already it demonstrated Wallace-Hadrill's tendency to concentrate on individuals whom he found congenial—a feature that became more marked in his later work. In a handful of his subsequent articles, most notably in 'The bloodfeud of the Franks', but also in his inaugural lecture as Chichele Professor at Oxford, on 'Early Medieval History',[107] Wallace-Hadrill turned his attention to an exploration of how early medieval society worked. More often, however, he explored the thought-world of men he appreciated, Gregory of Tours, a host of Carolingian churchmen, and, above all, Bede. In these writers he found what he called 'nobility of mind'.[108] He placed them against a frequently violent backdrop of 'communities, societies, groups, and sects bent on the perpetuation of what they were'. His stress on noble minds may look back to the work of such Anglo-Saxonists as Tolkien,[109] but it is also tempting here to see an echo of Wallace-Hadrill's own wartime experience. He hated bloodshed, but as an intelligence office who served as an interrogator he had been compelled to witness the execution of German spies.[110] He had seen enough barbarism, and wanted to concentrate rather on the more admirable side of human nature, while acknowledging the surrounding horrors.

The Barbarian West was a staple for English early-medieval historians for the two decades after 1952. It was not, however, the only reading available, though the alternatives came largely from the ancient historians who looked at Rome rather than at the barbarian incomers. A. H. M. Jones set out his image of a Roman state still functioning through the fourth, fifth, and sixth centuries, based on a meticulous heaping-up of detail.[111] The result was a firm rejection of the gloomy reading of a top-heavy empire, collapsing under its own weight, which had been propagated by the emigré Russian historian Mikhail Rostovtzeff in his *Social and Economic History of the Roman Empire*, published in 1926.[112] Like Wallace-Hadrill,

---

[106] Wallace-Hadrill, *The Barbarian West*. For what follows see Wood, 'John Michael Wallace-Hadrill', esp. p. 337.

[107] Most of Wallace-Hadrill's papers are collected in his *The Long-haired kings and other studies in Frankish History* and *Early Medieval History*.

[108] Wallace-Hadrill, *Early Medieval History*, p. 18.

[109] For Wallace-Hadrill's links with Dorothy Whitelock, Wood, 'The bloodfeud of the Franks: a historiographical legend', pp. 501–2.

[110] Wood, 'John Michael Wallace-Hadrill', pp. 335, 349.

[111] Jones, *The Later Roman Empire, 284–601*. For a very much shorter account, Jones, *The Decline of the Ancient World*.

[112] See Brown, 'Report', p. 14; also Brown, 'The Later Roman Empire'.

Jones had served in the War. According to Peter Brunt, Jones' wartime service impacted on his understanding of the later Roman Empire: 'His experience of wartime direction of labour helped to suggest to him that a shortage of manpower explained the regulations that tied all sorts of men to their occupations in the late Roman empire.'[113]

One ancient historian from Ireland concentrated on the Germanic peoples of the ancient and late-antique worlds. Having produced a study of Ammianus Marcellinus, Edward Thompson turned his attention first to Attila, and then to the early Germans and the Visigoths: at the end of his career he directed his attention to Germanus of Auxerre and finally, like his compatriot J. B. Bury, to St Patrick. As in the cases of Wallace-Hadrill and Jones, personal experience of Germans and Germany—although in this instance pre-War Germany—seems to have been a significant influence. Present in Berlin in 1937–8, Thompson witnessed Nazi brutality towards the Jews at first hand. Although not himself a Jew, indeed he came from an Irish Presbyterian family, Thompson reacted—as did a significant minority of those who were appalled by what they saw of Nazism—by becoming a Marxist, though he left the Communist Party in 1956 in protest at the Russian intervention in Hungary, and he was equally horrified by events in Prague in 1968.[114] Thompson was a meticulous reader of texts. Among the points he saw in them were, on the one hand, Roman exploitation of their barbarian neighbours—something that he described as 'economic warfare'[115]—and on the other a tendency among the barbarians themselves to lose any sense of solidarity when faced with the possibility of gaining wealth of their own, and instead to enter a world of incipient class division and conflict.[116]

This was not to be the only Marxist reading of the end of Rome to come from the pen of a historian writing in England. Geoffrey de Ste Croix concluded his 1982 study of the class stuggle in the ancient world with the argument that excessive dependence on slave labour was a crucial factor in the fall of the Roman Empire.[117] Already in 1974 Perry Anderson in *Passages from Antiquity to Feudalism* had presented the transition from the ancient to the medieval worlds as a clash between two modes of production, leading to the emergence of feudal society.[118] Unlike Thompson or de Ste Croix, however, Anderson was not a specialist in Ancient History, being rather a modern historian and sociologist who was applying a Marxist model to the early period. Nor, being of a younger generation, was he responding to the events of the 1930s and 40s. Rather, he was at the heart of the British debates of the 1970s on the development of Marxism—and was indeed showing the relevance of Antiquity to those debates.

---

[113] Brunt, 'A. H. M. Jones'.

[114] Todd, 'E.A. Thompson (1914–1994)'.

[115] See Thompson, *Romans and Barbarians*, pp. 3–19. For Thompson's interest in warfare see also his edition of the anonymous *De rebus Bellicis*.

[116] See in particular, Thompson, 'The Visigoths from Fritigern to Euric'.

[117] De Ste Croix, *The Class Struggle in the Ancient Greek World*.

[118] Anderson, *Passages from Antiquity to Feudalism*. For an early medievalist's assessment of Anderson, Balzaretti, 'The creation of Europe', pp. 184–6.

Looking back over the historical interpretations of the Fall of Rome and its aftermath produced in the quarter of a century that followed the end of the Second World War, what is perhaps most striking is the absence of any preponderant line or lines of approach. If there is a dominant discourse to be identified, it would appear to be a reaction to the War itself—at least outside Italy. The de-Nazification of the *Volk* in Germany, which involved both silence and also Wenskus' redefinition of what made a barbarian people; the condemnation of Germanic barbarism, which is a marked feature of French scholarship; and the personal, and differing, responses of Wallace-Hadrill, Jones, and Thompson, all in some way or other reflect the impact of 1939–45. Even Courtois in his favourable view of the Vandals was influenced by his experiences, although the conflict that weighed most on his writing was that in 1950s Algeria.

15.8 THE WORLD OF LATE ANTIQUITY

Peter Brown's *The World of Late Antiquity*, published in 1971, was perhaps the first major study of the end of Rome from the post-War period that was not written in the shadow of the war.[119] Brown, who was born in Dublin in 1935, was too young to serve in any army before the War ended—and Ireland was in any case supposedly neutral—although he was old enough to remember seeing, from the vantage point of the number 8 bus from Dun Laoghaire to the city centre, the swastika flying at half mast outside the German embassy when news came of Hitler's death.[120] He himself has traced the origins of his reading of the late and post-Roman period on a number of occasions. In 1997, in his contribution to a volume discussing *The World of Late Antiquity* a quarter of a century after its publication he provided an account of the intellectual origins of his interpretation of the period.[121] As he presents it, the chief views to which he was responding were those of Henri Pirenne's *Mahomet et Charlemagne* (mediated through the more recent reading of the Mediterranean offered by the historian of sixteenth-century France, Fernand Braudel)[122] and Christopher Dawson's *The Making of Europe*—books which, for all their differences, Brown saw as being joined by their attachment to a notion of the unity of (western) Europe, though for Pirenne this was expressed in terms of trade, while for Dawson the dominant feature was Catholicism. Brown also singled out Rostovtzeff, whose sense of an empire in decline was derived from his experiences as a member of the Russian bourgeoisie in the early years of the twentieth century.[123] In addition, there was the work of A. H. M. Jones, who, contrary to Ros-

---

[119] Interestingly, Markus, 'Between Marrou and Brown', p. 3, mentions the War, when citing Brown, 'Report', p. 9, even though Brown makes no such allusion.

[120] Peter Brown has commented that 'my aunt showed it to me and (lest she seem too exultant) whispered to me: "You know where he is, Peds?" I answered: "Indeed I do." It was my first lesson in the Geography of Hell.'

[121] Brown, *The Rise of Western Christendom*, 2nd edn, pp. 1–34. See also Brown, *A Life of Learning*.

[122] Brown, 'Report', p. 16.   [123] Brown, 'Report', pp. 5–7, 12, 14.

tovtzeff, demonstrated that the Roman Empire functioned remarkably well long after the Russian 'had signed its death warrant'.[124] Then there was the influence of a number of ecclesiastical historians, above all Marrou, but also William Frend, with his insistence on the relation between different forms of Christianity and particular societies,[125] as well as the classicist E. R. Dodds, who had written memorably about the irrational in the Classical World.[126]

It is striking that Brown did not see the great discussions of the barbarian migrations of the period before 1945 as having contributed significantly to his understanding of the period. By way of explanation, in 1997 he argued that Pirenne and Edward Thompson had led to his underestimating the barbarians, the former by excluding them, and the latter by making them 'fragile' through his Marxist exposition of their internal weaknesses.[127] The perceived influence of these two is all the more striking in that other scholars had made much of the Germanic peoples, as Brown knew well. He would later regard his downplaying of the barbarians in *The World of Late Antiquity* as a lacuna and would make an *amende honorable* (the phrase is his own)[128] with the publication in 1996 of *The Rise of Western Christendom*.

Perhaps equally important was the fact Brown came to write about the end of Antiquity having already established himself as the biographer of Augustine.[129] The intellectual ferment of Augustine's works rule out any simple assessment of the fourth and early fifth centuries. Moreover, anyone involved in Augustinian studies in the 1960s was almost inevitably deeply indebted to a French tradition of ecclesiastical and religious history, and above all to Marrou, whom Brown readily acknowledged as an influence.[130] Marrou's *Saint Augustin et la fin de la culture antique*, with its remarkable *Retractatio*,[131] was seminal in what it had to say about Augustine, but also by implication raised the issue of the cultural divide between Antiquity and the early Middle Ages. It was a divide that Brown would come to reformulate within the concept of Late Antiquity.[132]

Not that there was an absence of Anglophone scholarship on Augustine. There was already the work of Cochrane, which Brown knew. Among older contemporaries with whom Brown exchanged ideas were Henry Chadwick and Robert Markus.[133] That Augustine should have provided Brown with his point of departure,

---

[124] Brown, 'Report', p. 14. See Brown's assessment in Brown, *The Body and Society*, Twentieth Anniversary Edition, p. lviii.

[125] e.g. Frend, *The Donatist Church*. Brown has also pointed to the importance of Woodward, *Christianity and Nationalism in the Later Roman Empire*.

[126] Brown, 'Report', pp. 10, 12, 19–20.

[127] Brown, 'Report', p. 23.

[128] Brown, 'Report', p. 23.

[129] Vessey, 'The demise of the Christian writer and the remaking of "Late Antiquity"', p. 378.

[130] Brown, 'Report', p. 10. See on the intellectual links between Brown and Marrou, Vessey, 'The demise of the Christian writer', and Markus, 'Between Marrou and Brown'.

[131] On the importance of the *Retractatio*, Markus, 'Between Marrou and Brown', p. 2. See above, chapter 14.

[132] Vessey, 'The demise of the Christian writer'. On Marrou's notion of *décadence*, see also Vessey, 'Theory, or the Dream of the Book', pp. 270–2.

[133] For the contacts between Brown and Markus, Brown, 'Introducing Robert Markus', pp. 181–7; Markus, 'Between Marrou and Brown'; Brown, '*Gloriosus obitus*: the End of the Ancient Other World', p. 290.

however, was of momentous importance. In Britain religious or Church history had largely followed a different path from that which had dealt with the Fall of the Empire, despite, or perhaps because of, Gibbon's *Decline and Fall*. The ecclesiastical matters that were included in the standard narrative of the Fall of Rome and the creation of the successor states, at least as regards the West, were usually those relating to the conversion of Constantine to Christianity, and of kings such as Clovis and Reccared to Catholicism, or, in the case of the Lombards, the impact that their adherence to Arianism had on their relations with the papacy and more generally with the Catholic population of Italy. Within this grand narrative the idea that the history of the Church or religious life might be a central component of a general account of the fifth, sixth, and seventh centuries was rarely expressed. It was, of course, central to Dawson's reading, which itself echoed a French Catholic tradition of the nineteenth century. For the most part, however, Church history had been treated separately:[134] even in France the secular readings of Thierry, Fustel, and Monod (to whom one could add the Swiss Sismondi and the Belgian Pirenne) paid little attention to the more religious account of Ozanam. As an interpreter of Augustine, Brown naturally drew on the resources of the French tradition of ecclesiastical history, not least of Marrou. His account of Late Antiquity combined that French tradition with the Anglophone secular interpretation of the Later Roman Empire as exemplified by Rostovtzeff and Jones. The mixture was further enriched by the addition of intellectual and cultural history, to which Brown had been introduced by Arnaldo Momigliano.[135] Again there was a French tradition to draw on, in the work of Courcelle and of Jacques Fontaine.

This mixing of traditions was foreshadowed by the growing body of work on Byzantium. Despite Montesquieu, Gibbon, and indeed Bury, Byzantine history tended to begin where that of the West Roman Empire ended. At the same time the historiography of Byzantium had evolved rather differently from that of the later Roman West and the barbarian successor states. There was no great division of secular, ecclesiastical, intellectual, and cultural history. Already in the first half of the twentieth century Norman Baynes had made as much of saints and saints' Lives as of chronicles, most accessibly in the translation of Byzantine hagiography undertaken with E. A. S. Dawes in 1948.[136] Baynes, too, one might note, had responded to the events of 1939–45, preparing an edition of Hitler's early speeches, and indeed lampooning them in a lecture on 'Intellectual liberty and totalitarian claims', delivered in Oxford in 1942.[137]

In combining these various traditions Brown effectively transformed the way in which scholars approached what now came to be widely known as Late Antiquity, which in his definition lay between Marcus Aurelius and Mohammad. Looking back on his contribution to scholarship in 2003 the interim president of the American Council of Learned Societies saw Brown as having 'invented a field of study'.[138] As

[134] Vessey, 'The demise of the Christian writer', p. 392.
[135] Brown, 'Reply to Comments', p. 72; Brown, *A Life of Learning*, p. 4.
[136] Baynes and Dawes, *Three Byzantine Saints*. For Brown's own appreciation of Baynes, 'Gloriosus obitus', p. 289.
[137] Hussey, 'Norman Hepburn Baynes'.   [138] Oakley, in Brown, *A Life of Learning*, p. 3.

Brown himself noted elsewhere there was a long-standing German concept of *Spätan-*
tike—one to which he may have been introduced by Geoffrey Barraclough, who commissioned *The World of Late Antiquity*.[139] The notion that there was a distinct era
between Antiquity and the Middle Ages had also been familiar to French scholars.
Indeed, Ferdinand Lot discussed the matter of periodization in the introduction to
La Fin du monde antique, noting that the idea of an intermediate period had been
adumbrated in the seventeenth century, but that it was not until recently that the idea
had been elaborated.[140] In other words, the idea of Late Antiquity, whether or not the
descriptive phrase was used, was not new, though Brown did somewhat expand its
dates. Yet in combining political, cultural, and religious history, by concentrating on
the eastern provinces of the Roman Empire, and indeed, by drawing Sassanian Persia
and Umayyad Islam into the equation he presented it in a new light.

There was also a further question of methodology: one of the great changes in historical writing through the 1960s and 70s was the opening up of the discipline to a
greater range of approaches than had hitherto been drawn upon by historians, and
among the disciplines attracting attention was social anthropology. In his own analysis
of the origins of his thought, Brown pointed to the fact that he came from an Anglo-
Irish family, which sensitized him to the idea of the decline of Empire, and that his
father's work as an engineer took him to Africa, and particularly to Khartoum, which
introduced him to an exotic world beyond the confines of Europe.[141] This exotic world
was more often the subject of anthropological than of historical study. Brown's vision
of Late Antiquity is one that is influenced almost as much by anthropologists as it is by
historians. This is more apparent in the articles that appeared at about the same time as
The World of Late Antiquity than it is in the book itself. 'The rise and function of the
holy man'[142] is perhaps the most eye-catching example, along with two books which
had their origins in lectures delivered in Oxford, but which found their final shape in
the United States: *The Making of Late Antiquity* and *The Cult of the Saints*.[143] Brown's
introduction to anthropology came through his acquaintance with the retired Edward
Evans-Pritchard and with the London-based scholar Mary Douglas, who he was initially encouraged to read by the later medievalist Paul Hyams.[144] What anthropology
added perhaps above all was the sense of small communities in action. Looking through
the eyes of the anthropologists Brown was able to conjure up a vivid picture of Late
Antique Society—and, as he himself has remarked, understanding society in general,
rather than, say, religion in isolation, mattered greatly to him.[145]

---

[139] Brown, 'Report', p. 17. See also Vessey, 'The demise of the Christian writer', p. 388, with n. 27, and
p. 393–4. On the concept of Late Antiquity see Liebeschuetz, 'The Birth of Late Antiquity'.

[140] Lot, *La Fin du monde antique*, 2nd edn, pp. 1–3.

[141] Brown, 'Report', p. 8; Brown, 'A Life of Learning', pp. 6–7. Compare Brown, *The Body and
Society*, Twentieth Anniversary edition, p. xxii.

[142] See J. Howard-Johnston, 'Introduction', in Howard-Johnston and Hayward, *The Cult of Saints
in Late Antiquity and the Early Middle Ages*, pp. 1–24.

[143] Brown, *The Making of Late Antiquity*; Brown, *The Cult of the Saints*.

[144] On the influence of Douglas and Evans-Pritchard, see Brown, *Body and Society*, twentieth anniversary edition, pp. xxvii–xxix.; Brown, 'Report', p. 21; Brown, *A Life of Learning*, p. 5. See also
Hayward, 'Demystifying the role of sanctity in Western Christendom', pp. 120–2 and 130–1.

[145] Brown, *A Life of Learning*, p. 8.

In turning to anthropology Brown was not alone. Alan Macfarlane and Keith Thomas working on the late medieval and early modern periods had done likewise. Already in 1959 Wallace-Hadrill had made use of the ideas of the Manchester anthropologist Max Gluckman, in his 'Bloodfeud of the Franks'. He was also drawing on a tradition of Anglo-Saxon scholarship that had been influenced by anthropology since the early part of the century.[146] Yet, while Anglo-Saxonists such as Bertha Philpotts had made use of anthropology as early as 1913,[147] there can be no doubt that there was a new vogue for so doing in the 1960s. This itself reflected changes within the discipline of anthropology. Having originally developed in the nineteenth and early twentieth centuries in the context of the need of European imperial powers to understand their African and Asian colonies, there was now a wider appreciation of its value for the understanding of alien societies.

The result of Brown's presentation of Late Antiquity in largely religious, social, and cultural terms, and also of his concentration on the eastern Mediterranean, was a strikingly optimistic reading of the period.[148] It marked a decided rejection of the vision of a world engulfed by barbarism, with the arrival of the Germanic tribes, as put forward by Piganiol and others.[149] At the same time, as Brown himself later argued, it largely ignored the Late Roman state, which for the likes of Rostovtzeff had proved top-heavy, and for Jones had seemed to be a remarkably successful organization.[150] The image put forward in *The World of Late Antiquity* was received with immediate enthusiasm, and not just in Britain, or more broadly in the Anglophone world. Marrou's final work, *Décadence ou antiquité tardive?*, is largely an acknowledgement of its significance.[151] Brown may not have created the notion of Late Antiquity, but he had provided the period with a radically new look, and one that was rather easier to accept a generation after the guns of 1939–45 had fallen silent.

[146] Wood, 'The bloodfeud of the Franks: a historiographical legend'.
[147] Philpotts, *Kindred and Clan in the Middle Ages and After*.
[148] Brown, 'Report', p. 15.
[149] Brown, 'Report', p. 9.
[150] Brown, 'Report', p. 24. See now, Brown, *Through the Eye of a Needle*, pp. 18–19.
[151] Marrou, *Décadence ou antiquité tardive?*

16

Presenting a New Europe

16.1 MOVERS AND SHAKERS

The publication of *The World of Late Antiquity* in 1971 marked a caesura: but a caesura implies no permanent break, and old arguments resurfaced. Moreover, in part because of the success of Brown's work, more scholars were drawn to study the period, with the result that there was more argument: so much that it would be impossible to trace all the different strands that emerged. At the same time the period became popular in another way. *The World of Late Antiquity* offered a radical assessment of the transformation of the Roman World, but did so in a format that was accessible and appealing to the wider public. Although debates about the end of Rome had never been confined to an ivory tower, changes in publication, not least in the cost of printing in colour, meant that new scholarly ideas could be attractively presented to a wide audience. Nor was presentation confined to books: other media, including television, were available. One forum that was particularly well suited to the display of the past was the exhibition hall. Exhibitions were places where the newest ideas could be put on show. However, being expensive they needed funding: naturally, the underwriters had a say in the subjects presented, and, because the objects shown included national treasures, that could mean governmental input. While scholars could benefit from the opportunity of showing their work to a growing audience, in order to do so they had to address, directly or indirectly, subjects of general interest. As a result the dominant discourse shifted: the most substantial of the exhibitions, needing European-wide funding, have tended to address the notion of Europe itself. In this final chapter we will, therefore, shift our gaze slowly from the arguments between academics to their presentation to the general public. In so doing we will see how a new discourse has come to take its place alongside those that were initiated by Boulainvilliers and Du Bos in the eighteenth century, and developed through the nineteenth and early twentieth.

The World of Late Antiquity transformed the image of the late and post-Roman periods. Here was an exotic and culturally vibrant world, which could be presented in full colour. This representation of the centuries from Marcus Aurelius to Muhammad, however, scarcely dealt with the barbarian take-over of the West. In the account given by Brown in 1971, the establishment of the successor states, which had been central to much earlier debate, and had been for many the key issue in the Fall of the Roman Empire, was re-envisioned as no more than 'The Western

Revival, 350–450' and 'The Price of Survival: Western Society, 450–600'.[1] It was Byzantium and the eastern Mediterranean that attracted Brown's attention. This geographical emphasis is equally strong in the work of a number of scholars influenced by Brown, not least Averil Cameron.[2] Brown himself came to look at the barbarian world in rather more detail in *The Rise of Western Christendom*—though the focus there was on religion and society rather than on the creation of the successor states. The same social and religious concerns dominate the work of Robert Markus, who earlier in his career, like Brown, had contributed notably to the interpretation of Augustine.[3] In 1990 Markus took Augustine as one of the points of departure in his study of *The End of Ancient Christianity*. This concluded with the pontificate of Gregory the Great, whose world was to provide the subject matter for his next major publication seven years later.[4] Thus, while changing perceptions of the period as a whole, Brown and those closest to him intellectually left plenty of space for old and new debates to flourish.

In a review article that appeared in 1999 Guy Halsall categorized what he regarded as the two main camps in the interpretations of the Fall of Rome published in the closing decades of the twentieth century. 'Movers' were those who placed a great deal of emphasis on the impact of incoming barbarians, while 'Shakers' were those who saw the 'tensions and changes within the Roman Empire' as being the dominant factor in the developments of the fourth to sixth centuries, and who consequently placed little emphasis on any Germanic incomers.[5] In fact, the division between 'Movers' and 'Shakers' has a good deal in common with the well-established distinction between 'Germanist' and 'Romanist'.[6] Halsall made no reference to Brown, although his work could easily be accommodated within the category of 'Shaker'. Among the Shakers Halsall singled out the French scholar Jean Durliat, who had argued for remarkable continuity in public finances from the period of Diocletian to the Carolingians,[7] and the young American Patrick Amory, whose study of Ostrogothic society in Italy questioned the very nature of a barbarian people, replacing the notion of ethnicity with that of constructed identity.[8] The Movers, as presented in Halsall's discussion, are largely represented by Neil Christie and Peter Heather, both of whom had written books on individual peoples: Christie on the Lombards and Heather on the Goths. In addition, the latter had seen through the press a new edition of Edward Thompson's *History of Attila and the Huns*, under the abbreviated title of *The Huns*.[9]

---

[1] Brown, *The World of Late Antiquity*, pp. 115–35.

[2] Cameron, *The Later Roman Empire AD 284–430*; Cameron, *The Mediterranean World in Late Antiquity AD 395–600*.

[3] Markus, *Saeculum*.

[4] Markus, *The End of Ancient Christianity*; Markus, *Gregory the Great and his World*.

[5] Halsall, 'Movers and Shakers', p. 133.

[6] The terms go back to Fustel, though the arguments go back to Du Bos' critique of Boulainvilliers: Nicolet, *La Fabrique d'une nation*, p. 58.

[7] Durliat, *Les Finances publiques de Dioclétien aux Carolingiens*. The most trenchant criticism of this was Wickham, 'La chute de Rome n'aura pas lieu'.

[8] Amory, *People and Identity in Ostrogothic Italy*. Although Amory's statement is the most radical version of this approach, stress on identity rather than ethnicity was not new.

[9] Christie, *The Lombards*; Heather, *The Goths*; Thompson, *The Huns*. For more recent 'Mover' accounts, see Heather, *The Fall of the Roman Empire*, and Heather, *Empires and Barbarians*.

'Movers and Shakers' is one very clear and useful way of categorising debates on the Fall of Rome, although as Halsall noted, it can give too clear-cut an impression: at the end of his article, while noting that there are extreme proponents of each approach, he acknowledged that there are those, including himself, who are not entirely convinced by either reading.[10] Moreover, there are considerable differences within both the 'Mover' and the 'Shaker' parties. Thus, in a work published since Halsall's article, Bryan Ward-Perkins, most certainly a 'Mover', not only placed a great deal of emphasis on barbarian incomers, he also saw them as causing 'the End of Civilization'.[11] By contrast, a number of scholars who have accepted the importance of the barbarians, have seen them as struggling to continue Roman institutions and culture.[12] The most substantial of the numerous volumes on the late and post-Roman period to have been published since Halsall's article, Chris Wickham's *Framing the Early Middle Ages*, which owes something to Brown in its geographical vision, though not in its exclusion of religion, moves judiciously through many of the debates relating to the social and economic structures of late antiquity, presenting a largely 'Shaker' vision in the Mediterranean region, while acknowledging greater disruption in the North.[13]

16.2 DEFINING THE TRIBE

Cutting across Halsall's categories in other ways, although also overlapping with them, is a debate on the nature of the people or tribe. Again, it is an extension of an old discussion, going back through Wenskus to Chadwick, the nineteenth century, and indeed beyond.[14] It has, however, been infused with methodology from other disciplines, not least from the social sciences, above all Benedict Anderson's *Imagined Communities* of 1983 and Anthony D. Smith's subsequent study of *The Ethnic Origins of Nations*.[15] The intensity of the discussion of the nature of barbarian peoples and the extent that it has drawn on the social sciences, perhaps especially in Britain, indicates its position as part of a broader debate within society relating to issues of immigration. This connection is explicitly noted in such studies as Sian Jones' *The Archaeology of Ethnicity: constructing identities past and present*.[16] Debates about the barbarians over the last quarter of a century still have

---

[10] Halsall, 'Movers and Shakers', p. 145. See Halsall's own interpretation: Halsall, *Barbarian Migrations and the Roman West*.

[11] Ward-Perkins, *The Fall of Rome*.

[12] A useful collection of relevant material is Hägermann, Haubrichs, and Jarnut, (eds), *Akkulturation: Probleme einer germanisch-romanischen Kultursynthese in Spätantike und frühem Mittelalter*.

[13] Wickham, *Framing the Early Middle Ages*. For an assessment of the work, Wood, 'Landscapes compared'.

[14] Murray, 'Reinhard Wenskus on "Ethnogenesis"'.

[15] Anderson, *Imagined Communities*. See also Smith, *The Ethnic Origins of Nations*. For a response to Anderson, see Forde, Johnson, and Murray (eds), *Concepts of National Identity in the Middle Ages*, which includes Smith, 'National identities: modern and medieval?'.

[16] Jones, *The Archaeology of Ethnicity*.

modern resonances, albeit those resonances are nowhere nearly as dangerous as their equivalents in the 1930s.

Alongside the use of sociology to define the peoples of the Migration Period has been a greater use of literary theory and of deconstruction in the analysis of source material. Here the most extreme proponent is perhaps Patrick Amory, categorized by Halsall as a 'Shaker', whose study of Ostrogothic society purported largely to deconstruct the Ostrogoths. In so doing, he turned away, as did others, from notions of ethnicity and ethnography, putting emphasis rather on 'imagined community' (although in so doing he did not cite Anderson).

Often placed at the other extreme to Amory is the so-called Vienna School: a phrase used to describe Herwig Wolfram and those influenced by him, most notably Walter Pohl. Yet while there may be those who believe Germanic tribes to be biologically defined groups, they are not obviously to be found in the Vienna School, which has stressed rather Wenskus' notion of 'ethnogenesis'—a malleable term, it must be admitted, but one which is much more concerned with construction than with any biologically defined ethnicity.[17] Pohl in particular has championed the use of sociological and literary models, not least in the use of concepts such as 'Difference' and 'Strategies of Distinction' to discuss the construction of peoples and communities.[18]

Despite the rhetoric within some sections of the debate, rather than clear camps holding distinct views, what has emerged is a body of scholars who have been sharply attuned to developments in other disciplines, although they naturally do not all privilege the same models to the same extent. The fact that we are dealing with a spectrum of opinions rather than two sharply divided camps may be seen in reactions to work on the Burgundians, which has been described by Charles Bowlus as exposing the abuse of the ethnogenesis construct.[19] Certainly, recent interpretation of the Burgundians (as of the Franks and the Ostrogoths) has placed a good deal of emphasis on the perspective of the sources, thus stressing the extent to which barbarian groups are defined subjectively by the beholder.[20] Whether this necessarily undermines the value of 'ethnogenesis' as a concept is, however, a moot point: what it calls into question is the extent to which a people, rather than being a biological unit, is defined by outsiders or insiders. Related to this is the question of whether tradition, which for Wenskus was a central factor, his tribes being held together by a *Traditionskern*, is something orally transmitted and archaic, or written and subject to manipulation by members of the governing elite.[21]

---

[17] One should also note that the term was taken up in Gumilev, *Ethnogenesis and the Biosphere of Earth*.

[18] e.g. Pohl and Reimitz (eds), *Strategies of Distinction*; Pohl and Reimitz (eds), *Grenze und Differenz im frühen Mittelalter*; Corradini, Diesenberger, and Reimitz (eds), *The Construction of Communities in the Early Middle Ages*.

[19] Bowlus, 'Ethnogenesis: the tyranny of a construct', p. 249.

[20] Wood, 'Ethnicity and the ethnogenesis of the Burgundians'; also Wood, 'Defining the Franks'. Compare Amory, *People and Identity in Ostrogothic Italy*; Wood, 'The meaning and purpose of ethnic terminology in the Burgundian laws'.

[21] Gillett, 'Introduction: ethnicity, history, and methodology', p. 8, argues 'that literary analysis of texts and the elucidation of the immediate circumstances of their composition are the keys to understanding

What is most striking about the attack on the Vienna school is that it has come to emphasize what is thought to be traditional about its arguments, rather than what is new, and indeed to portray those arguments as lying within a pre-War German intellectual tradition.[22] Thus Wenskus is now presented as being the heir to 1930s thought (which in certain respects is true),[23] rather than as belonging to a movement that challenged the Nazi use of *Volk* (which is also true). This is then thought to contaminate those who followed after, notably Wolfram and Pohl.[24] Presented in these terms, what might have been largely compatible discussions of group formation[25] have been recast as a conflict between a predominantly transatlantic group of scholars on the one hand and supposed heirs to German traditional scholarship on the other.

The leading figure among the critics of the Vienna school, Walter Goffart,[26] has, however, done more than anyone to draw attention to the virtues of some nineteenth-century scholars (above all Gaupp). In so doing he has reopened questions about Germanic invasion and settlement, offering challenging assessments of the scale of any migration and of the process by which incomers were settled.[27] A Canadian, perhaps significantly of Belgian extraction,[28] he has, like Pirenne in the 1920s and 30s, gone a long way towards denying any great significance to Germanic incomers to the Roman world—he is, indeed, a 'Shaker' par excellence—and indeed among the 'Shakers' he is very much inclined to stress continuity with the Roman past.

At the same time, while not alone in making use of literary theory, Goffart has played a notable role in propounding the value of the theories of Hayden White and Northrop Frye for an understanding early medieval narrative sources.[29] Goffart has unquestionably sharpened awareness of the constructed nature of our written evidence, even among those who have not accepted his conclusions. He has also shed considerable light on the development of historical cartography and of the mapping of the barbarian invasions.[30] Goffart's study of the barbarians is,

their purpose, runs counter to the role of literary texts in *Traditionskern* ethnogenesis theory as windows onto the orally transmitted *Traditionskern*.' This assumes that *Traditionskern* is orally transmitted, which is questionable. In my view some literary texts were written to create or bolster tradition.

[22] Interestingly, Amory, 'The meaning and purpose of ethnic terminology in Burgundian laws', p. 2, n. 6, is much more inclined to acknowledge the novelty of Wolfram's approach.

[23] Murray, 'Reinhard Wenskus on 'Ethnogenesis' ', esp. at pp. 53–4.

[24] Pohl, 'Ethnicity, Theory, and Tradition', p. 222.

[25] One should also note the wise introductory remarks by Noble in Noble (ed.), *From Roman Provinces to Medieval Kingdoms*, which draws together a number of the main articles on the barbarians, and offers a clearheaded assessment of the debate in general.

[26] On Goffart, see Murray, 'Introduction: Walter André Goffart', pp. 3–7. It is difficult to know how important were Goffart's experiences as a Belgian refugee: Wood, 'Barbarians, historians and the construction of national identities' p. 79.

[27] Above all Goffart, *Barbarians and Roman*. His views have been restated on a number of occasions, most notably in his *Barbarian Tides*.

[28] Murray, 'Introduction: Walter André Goffart', pp. 3–4.

[29] Goffart, *The Narrators of Barbarian History*.

[30] Goffart, *Historical Atlases*.

however, avowedly rooted in texts, and indeed a small number of them.[31] He seems very much less happy with the evidence of surviving material culture and with the historical landscape. In Halsall's words, 'the weakness of the ultra-minimalist Shaker position, whatever its intellectual sophistication, is its divorce from concrete realities on (or in) the ground.'[32]

16.3 THE TRANSFORMATION OF THE ROMAN WORLD

The Mover and Shaker debate on the one hand, and consideration of barbarian ethnicity on the other (not that they are entirely separate), have both attracted a good deal of attention over the last quarter century. Arguably, neither constituted the dominant discourse (although they contributed to it), which in many respects has continued to be amorphous. What dominated the nature of the discussion of the late and post-Roman periods from the late 1980s onwards was not, in fact, a set of questions, but rather the existence of a project on 'The Transformation of the Roman World' funded by the European Science Foundation. This dominated discourse, in part, simply because of the scale of what was set up. It was initiated in 1989, when a working group was established to consider the feasibility of the topic. Thereafter a scientific programme was funded from 1992 to 1998. Six research teams were created, though two of them were later subdivided. The teams met twice a year. As a result, a significant proportion of the European scholars (and a small number of Americans) working on the late Roman and early medieval periods were drawn into the programme, though some countries were little represented because they did not subscribe to the project.[33] An idea of the numbers involved may be gleaned from the fact that ninety-two scholars from eighteen countries participated in the second of three plenary conferences.[34] Thirteen volumes came directly from the research teams,[35] and at least one other volume originated in discussions held by participants in the project.[36] In addition, the programme organized exhibitions in Cologne, Leiden, London, Stockholm, and Thessaloniki, and produced a related exhibition catalogue.[37] Two of the exhibitions, those of Cologne and Thessaloniki, concentrated on burial at the end of the Roman period, in the Rhineland and northern Greece. The Leiden exhibition looked at elite life-style at the start of the Merovingian period, again drawing largely on cemeterial evidence. The iconography, part Roman and part Germanic

[31] Goffart, *Barbarian Tides*, p. 121: 'I … made it clear that my book was strictly confined to the few texts that bear narrowly on the settlements in Gaul and Italy … '
[32] Halsall, 'Movers and Shakers', p. 284.
[33] The most notably under-represented country was France, which reflected the decision of the CNRS not to contribute to funding the project.
[34] Wood, 'Report: The European Science Foundation's Programme on the Transformation of the Roman World and Emergence of Early Medieval Europe'. Papers from the second conference can be found in Pohl, Wood, and Reimitz (eds), *The Transformation of Frontiers*.
[35] *The Transformation of the Roman World*, 13 volumes.
[36] Brubaker and Smith (eds), *Gender in the Early Medieval World: East and West*.
[37] Webster and Brown (eds), *The Transformation of the Roman World*.

in origin, of a group of high status golden objects was the focus of the Stockholm exhibition, while the British Museum took a broader look at the continuing influence of Roman ideology in Britain after the end of imperial rule. Given the workshops, the conferences and the exhibitions, to claim that *The Transformation of the Roman World* project was the dominant element in discussion of the period from 300 to 700 in the last decade of the twentieth century and the first years of the twenty-first is a statement about the numbers involved and the speed at which ideas were exchanged, rather than a claim that any one set of ideas dominated.

The title of the programme, involving the word 'Transformation', led Bryan Ward-Perkins (who was actually a member of the project) to see in it a deliberate avoidance of notions of 'decline', 'fall', or 'crisis',[38] which was indeed the case, but for a rather different reason from the one he suspected. One of the coordinators was a Greek, and, while the project concentrated on the Latin West a good deal more than the Greek East, it was agreed that the establishment of Byzantium precluded any terminology involving or implying 'Fall'. Indeed the project rather avoided taking a particular line: in so far as there was any unity, it lay in a common approach—or rather in the need to accommodate a variety of approaches. The European Science Foundation ensured that the gatherings were multinational: the intellectual tradition of no one nation was dominant. At the same time, the numbers involved meant that the project could be truly interdisciplinary: textual scholars, philologists, political, social, and religious historians, and archaeologists worked together in the individual teams, critiquing each other's work on a regular basis. A party line, if such there was, lay in the project's multidisciplinarity, to the particular benefit of those approaches that were most used to crossing disciplinary boundaries. Issues such as 'representation' and 'rhetoric', and questions of ideal as opposed to actual, thus came to the fore.[39] So too, in discussing the peoples that entered the Empire, it was matters of self-identification, distinction, and difference, and the construction of communities that tended to dominate.[40]

Yet while it would be wrong to see the project as deliberately opting for a 'Shaker' dominated view of the End of the Roman World, there was truth in Ward-Perkins' claim that the project should be seen in the light of the need of the European Union 'to forge a spirit of cooperation between the once warring nations of the Continent…'.[41] The European Science Foundation (not, it should be stressed, an arm of the EU, but rather a forum for European research organizations) is interested in scholarship that says something to Europe as a whole. The project was developed out of an initial submission that concentrated on the Lower Rhine, but which was thought to be too narrow in geographical focus. The ESF wanted a project that would appeal to as many of its members as possible. Thus, while the

[38] Ward-Perkins, *The Fall of Rome*, p. 4.
[39] Wood, 'Report', pp. 221–6; see Brogiolo and Ward-Perkins, *The Idea and Ideal of the Town*; Theuws and Nelson (eds), *Rituals of Power*.
[40] e.g. Pohl and Reimitz (eds), *Strategies of Distinction*; Corradini, Diesenberger, and Reimitz (eds), *The Construction of Communities*; Goetz, Jarnut, and Pohl (eds), *Regna and Gentes*.
[41] Ward-Perkins, *The Fall of Rome*, p. 174.

programme was in no sense expected to come up with a vision of the End of the Ancient World in which, to quote Ward-Perkins, 'the Roman empire is not "assassinated" by Germanic invaders; rather, Romans and Germans together carry forward much that was Roman into a new Romano-Germanic world', it was certainly hoped that the project would address the matters that were of interest to a broad range of the European scholarly community. In that sense it was European.

It is not only Europe that can claim to have an interest in the Fall of Rome. Already there are indications that Americans are finding in the subject analogues for the current experiences of the USA. As early as 1976 the American historian and strategist Edward Luttwak turned his attention to *The Grand Strategy of the Roman Empire*.[42] More recently, in 2007, Cullen Murphy published a volume entitled *Are we Rome? The End of an Empire and the Fate of America*.[43] Further echoes are apparent in Adrian Goldsworthy's *How Rome Fell: The Death of a Superpower*.[44] So too, a specialist in late Antiquity, James O'Donnell, has interpreted Byzantine policy of the sixth century so as to draw out lessons for the United States, pausing to note the ways in which the period was already exploited in the nineteenth century, not least by Felix Dahn.[45] It may well be that the changing position of the US will come to be the major prism through which Late Antiquity is read.

Equally a sign of the times is the increased emphasis on climate and natural disaster. Long an issue in debating migration from Frisia, northern Germany, and Denmark to Britain, because of the relation between rising sea-levels and the abandonment of coastal sites on the continent,[46] the question of climate has, of late, been given considerably more widespread significance. Dendrochronology has indicated a spell of bad summers at the start of the 'Dark Ages'.[47] These have been associated with a probable volcanic eruption of massive scale which apparently occured in 535.[48] It would seem that this in turn triggered a major outbreak of plague which has been shown to have played a significant part in economic collapse in the sixth century.[49] Although the environment in Late Antiqutity had already attracted the interest of scholars, initially in response to Braudel's study of the sixteenth-century Mediterranean,[50] it is significant that the topic was picked up outside academic circles (and indeed before it became a major focus of academic research) in the years on either side of 2000 [51]—an indication that this particular reading of the End of the Roman World resonated broadly in the context of growing global concern about climate change.

---

[42] Luttwak, *The Grand Strategy of the Roman Empire*. On this and what follows, see Cameron, 'Better Barbarians', p. 10.

[43] Murphy, *Are we Rome?*

[44] Goldsworthy, *How Rome Fell*.

[45] O'Donnell, *The Ruin of the Roman Empire*, p. 123.

[46] Meier, 'The North Sea Coastal Area'.

[47] Baillie, 'Dark Ages and Dendrochronology'.

[48] Keys, *Catastrophe*.

[49] Rosen, *Justinian's Flea*.

[50] Braudel, *The Mediterranean and the Mediterranean World*. For a study of the Mediterranean which looked firmly back to Antiquity, Horden and Purcell, *The Corrupting Sea*.

[51] The most substantial academic contribution, Little (ed.), *Plague and the End of Antiquity*, was published after the work of Keys (a journalist) and Rosen (a publisher).

16.4 EXHIBITING THE PAST

As yet, however, the European discourse is probably still the dominant one, and not only in the field of published scholarship. In organizing a set of exhibitions, the ESF scientific programme was deliberately taking the subject of the Transformation of the Roman World to an audience well beyond that of academics. The presentation of the early Middle Ages to the wider public through the means of exhibitions is nothing new: museums were already presenting significant displays in the nineteenth century.[52] For the Carolingian period a change of pace occurred with the mounting of a large-scale exhibition on Charlemagne in Aachen in 1965, which was also accompanied by a lengthy scholarly catalogue.[53] There the Frankish ruler was presented as 'the first *Kaiser* who wished to unite Europe',[54] a statement which makes very clear the image that the organizers wished to convey to the general public: the exhibition was funded by the Council of Europe. The political significance of the event was further emphasized by the presence on the title page of the name of the Bundespräsident, Heinrich Lübke.

The Aachen exhibition of 1965 was not the first to make use of the early Middle Ages for political purposes. Two years earlier the Czechs had mounted an exhibition in Prague, but which also toured Europe. Its subject was Great Moravia, the Slav political power that lay to the east of the Carolingian kingdom in the mid-ninth century. This was an unashamedly propagandist show intended to exhibit the ancient origins of modern Czechoslovakia: indeed it claimed that the region had seen 1100 years of political and cultural continuity.[55] Its catalogue, however, was a rather slight affair, running to a mere 54 pages with 64 plates.[56] The Aachen catalogue easily outdid that, coming in at 568 pages of text and 159 pages of plates: in so doing it set a pattern which would be regularly emulated, and indeed frequently exceeded.

Charlemagne has continued to be the focus of exhibitions, most notably as the subject of a cluster around the year 2000 united under the umbrella title *Charlemagne: The Making of Europe*. The role of the Franks in the development of the idea of Europe was a clear subtext. There were major exhibitions in Barcelona, Brescia, Paderborn, and Split, all with sizeable catalogues,[57] as well as a rather smaller one in York.[58] A different image of Charlemagne was presented in 2003, once again in Aachen, where the elephant given as a present to the

---

[52] e.g. Effros, 'Selling archaeology and anthropology'.
[53] Braunfels (ed.), *Karl der Große: Werk und Wirkung*.
[54] Braunfels (ed.), *Karl der Große: Werk und Wirkung*, p. ix.
[55] For a discussion, Curta, 'The history and archaeology of Great Moravia', pp. 239–40.
[56] Filip (ed.), *The Great Moravia Exhibition*.
[57] Camps (ed.), *Cataluña en la epoca carolingia*; Bertelli and Brogiolo (eds), *Il futuro dei Longobardi*; Milosevic (ed.), *Hrvati I Karolinzi*; Stiegemann and Wemhoff (eds), *799*; *Kunst und Kultur der Karolingerzeit*. On the Paderborn exhibition see also Stiegemenn, '"Ein Erlebnis von Gleichzeitigkeit"', pp. 207–30.
[58] Garrison, Nelson and Tweddle (eds), *Alcuin and Charlemagne*. The smaller scale of the York exhibition, by comparison with those in Barcelona, Brescia, Paderborn, and Split, reflected the scale of its funding—a sharp reminder that some European countries are more attuned to the significance of exhibitions than others.

emperor by the Abbasid caliph Harun al-Rashid was the focus of an exhibition entitled *Ex Oriente. Isaak und der weisse Elefant: Bagdad—Jerusalem—Aachen. Eine Reise durch drei Kulturen um 800 und heute*: 'Out of the East: Isaac and the White elephant: Baghdad—Jerusalem—Aachen: A journey through three cultures around the year 800 and today'. The modern relevance was further emphasized on the cover with the words 'Geschichte und Gegenwart christlicher, jüdischer und islamischer Kulturen': 'History and the Present of Christian, Jewish and Islamic cultures'. This was Charlemagne's reign as a model of tolerance and multiculturalism.

The period before Charlemagne had to wait some years after 1965 before it attracted similar attention, but since 1980 there have been well over a dozen international or national exhibitions—on average more than one new one every other year. The most substantial of them, which was mounted in 1997, was dedicated to the Franks and was shown in Mannheim, Paris, and Berlin. Its title, *Die Franken: Wegbereiter Europas*, or *Les Francs: pionniers de l'Europe*, made explicit its political message. The Franks were the pathfinders of Europe: their heirs, of course, were the French and Germans, a point made clear in the official backing given by President Jacques Chirac and Bundespräsident Helmut Kohl. The implication was surely that their two countries should continue to be the driving forces in the European Union, as they had been ever since the creation of the European Economic Community in 1957. The essays contained within the catalogue scarcely pursued the argument, but the name chosen for the exhibition made the point clearly enough for the general public.

On a much smaller scale *Die Franken* was followed up with an exhibition of some of the greatest princely graves of the post-Roman period, displayed in 2000–1 at the Musée des Antiquités nationales of Saint-Germain-en-Laye (founded by Napoléon III)[59] and at the Reiss-Museum, Mannheim.[60] Unlike the earlier exhibition this was unashamedly concerned only with the princely classes, including significant objects from central Europe (notably from the museum in Brno) to demonstrate the wealth and quality of the grave finds. The display of central European material reflected the new political realities of the continent since 1989. Europe no longer ended at the eastern borders of Germany and Austria.

The collaboration between French and German archaeologists and institutions that is illustrated by the exhibitions of 1997 and 2000–2001 had begun long before the last decade of the century. Already in 1980–1, Paris and Mainz had jointly mounted an exhibition entitled, in its French manifestation, *À l'aube de la France: la Gaule de Constantin à Chilpéric* ('At the dawn of France: Gaul from Constantine to Chilperic'). For all the patriotic appeal in the title, this was a show that had originated in the Römisch-Germanisches Museum in Mainz, and to a significant extent it was a presentation of German scholarship to a French public.[61] As

[59] On the foundation see Effros, *Merovingian Mortuary Archaeology*, p. 53.
[60] *L'Or des princes barbares*: see the 'Préface' for the relationship of the exhibition to *Die Franken*.
[61] Böhme, Böhner, Schulze, Weidemann, Waurick, Baratte, and Vallet (eds), *À l'aube de la France*. I have not seen the German version of the catalogue from 1980.

the subtitle suggests, however, this was a view of French origins rooted in the Roman past, with a very compelling picture of imperial administrative, economic, and military organization.

Five years after the Paris exhibition Franco-German cooperation was on display once again, in a presentation of Neustria, the Frankish North-West. Although *La Neustrie: les pays au nord de la Loire de Dagobert à Charles le Chauve* was mounted in Rouen,[62] it was intended to coincide with a conference on the same subject held at the Deutsches Historisches Institut in Paris[63]—an institution which had played a major part in the development of Franco-German cultural relations since the 1950s. The conference very much reflected interests of some of the leading lights of the Institut, the director Karl-Ferdinand Werner, together with Hartmut Atsma and Martin Heinzelmann: all three of them scholars of the Merovingian period as well as Francophiles. *La Neustrie*, in its manifestation as a conference held under the aegis of Werner in Paris, and as an exhibition organized by Patrick Périn in Rouen, was both a reflection of the personal contacts of the organizers and an illustration of German commitment to European, and specifically French, culture and history.

Before moving to Paris, Werner had significantly broken the silence over the contamination of German scholarship in the Nazi period.[64] The impact of the Nazi occupation of Alsace was highlighted in 2001–2 by an exhibition of rather different type. *L'Archéologie en Alsace et en Moselle au temps de l'annexation (1940–1944)* provided visitors in Strasbourg and Metz with a remarkably detailed survey of the impact of German archaeology on the region in the years of the wartime occupation. This not only presented the excavations themselves (many of them executed to a commendably high standard for their time), but also their use in education and in propaganda.[65] This was surely not the image of the past that the organizers of *Die Franken: Wegbereiter Europas* had wished to see disseminated.

Another counter-image to that presented in the large-scale Frankish exhibition of 1997 was on display at exactly the same time, moving from Stuttgart, to Zürich, and then Augsburg.[66] *Die Alamannen* revealed something of one of the groups that challenged the Franks in the late fifth century, tracing their history well back into the Roman period. The exhibition commemorated their defeat at the hands of the Franks, supposedly in 497. The Alamans, a conglomeration made up of a number of peoples including the *Suebi* (the people who gave their name to the German district of Schwaben/Swabia), had been a threat to Rome long before the Franks emerged on the scene.[67] And while they were defeated and absorbed by the Franks, they continued to produce distinctive high-quality metalwork for generations to come. To mount a major exhibition on the Alamans at precisely the same time as that on the Franks was to emphasize that *Die Franken* did not represent the past of

---

[62] Périn and Feffer (eds), *La Neustrie*.   [63] Atsma (ed.), *La Neustrie*.

[64] Werner, *Das NS-Geschichtsbild*.

[65] Adam et al. (eds), *L'Archéologie en Alsace et en Moselle au temps de l'annexation*.

[66] *Die Alamannen*.

[67] Nuber, 'Seitenwende rechts des Rheins'; Frank, 'Vorboten an Main und Tauber'; Geuenich, 'Ein junges Volk macht Geschichte'.

the whole of Europe, and that even within Germany there were groups that had different allegiances. Moreover, while *Die Franken* was a joint Franco-German exhibition, *Die Alamannen* was a joint Germano-Swiss venture. Its catalogue boasted forewords by the Bundespräsident Roman Herzog, and the President of the Swiss confederation, Arnold Koller, along with the Ministerpräsident of the German Land of Baden-Württemberg, Erwin Teufel. Thus, while Helmut Kohl backed a vision of the Franks foreshadowing a Franco-German Europe, Roman Herzog backed a more regional vision in which Baden-Württemberg allied with Switzerland.

In 2008, eleven years after *Die Franken* offered a Franco-German view of European origins, the Palazzo Grassi in Venice produced a different vision in *Roma e i Barbari*.[68] This exhibition put Rome rather more firmly in the forefront—scarcely surprisingly, given the Italian setting for the exhibition. The lower floor of the Palazzo was entirely taken up with sculpture depicting Romans victorious against the barbarians. The upper floors offered an extraordinary compendium of objects from almost every successor state. The catalogue is prefaced with a number of statements which give some indication of the organizers' intentions:[69] the barbarians, described as conquerors and nomads,[70] are presented within a discourse of 'good immigration',[71] though it was hard to square the notion of 'good immigration' with some of the nineteenth-century paintings of the Fall of Rome which hung upstairs alongside the archaeological objects. A rather more historiographical vision is presented in the foreword by Michel Gras, the director of the École française de Rome, who traced the title of the exhibition back to works by his predecessors: to *Rome et les barbares: étude sur la Germanie de Tacite*, by Mathieu Auguste Geffroy in 1874,[72] whose message he compared to that of Claude Nicolet's *La Fabrique d'une nation* of 2003.[73] Finally, the Patriarch of Venice, Cardinal Angelo Scola, saw in the exhibits displayed a demonstration of the Christian origins of Europe.[74] The detailed essays and catalogue entries, of course, offer a much more fragmented view.

In fact, while some of the most substantial exhibitions, notably *Die Franken* and *Roma e i Barbari*, have presented the late and post-Roman periods to the general public as playing a crucial role in the development of Europe, there has also been a steady stream of rather more nationally-conceived shows. In Italy a major exhibition on the Lombards was mounted in 1990 at Cividale del Friuli, one of the centres with the most significant sculptural and architectural remains from the Lombard period—which also gave the exhibition a distinctively regional focus.

---

[68] Aillagon (ed.), *Rome and the Barbarians*.

[69] For a simple description of the coverage of the exhibition, there is Vitali, 'Rome and the Barbarians'.

[70] Pinault, 'Conquerors and other Nomads'.

[71] Veaute, 'On the good use of immigration'.

[72] Geffroy, *Rome et les barbares*: Geffroy's interest in Tacitus was prompted by the Franco-Prussian War.

[73] M. Gras, in Aillagon (ed.), *Rome and the Barbarians*, pp. 34–5.

[74] A. Scola, in Aillagon (ed.), *Rome and the Barbarians*, p. 39.

Indeed, the regional administration of Friuli-Venezia Giulia was very closely involved in setting up the display.[75] Not that the exhibition was limited to objects from the region: indeed, it drew on finds from throughout Italy and from the swath of central Europe through which the Lombards were said to have migrated.

Following its success, a further exhibition dedicated to the Goths was arranged in Milan in 1994.[76] There was a much smaller display a year later in San Marino, where one of the finest tomb assemblages of the Gothic period was reunited and put on display. The fact that the treasure of Domagnano had been discovered within the Sanmarinese territory in the early 1890s was justification enough for such an exhibition in the hilltop republic:[77] interestingly, however, the exhibition was conceived as part of the celebrations to mark the centenary of San Marino's Pubblico Palazzo.[78] Given its low profile as a centre of culture and scholarship, this was clearly intended to demonstrate a desire on the part of the republic to be associated with rather more than cheap tourism.[79]

A yet more significant modern discovery was to lead to a further display of early medieval objects in Italy: indeed to a permanent museum rather than a temporary exhibition. Beginning in 1981 a major excavation was undertaken in the Crypta Balbi (the cellars or *cryptoporticus* of the Roman theatre of Balbus), on the edge of the Largo Argentina in Rome. The most important (and indeed unexpected) aspect of the excavation was the discovery of a vast quantity of material that had been discarded as rubbish up to the end of the eighth century. The importance of the material led to the decision to create a second early medieval museum in Rome (the *Museo dell'alto medioevo* having already been set up in 1967),[80] this time within the building which covered the excavations. The finds themselves probably constitute the most significant contribution to scholarly understanding of seventh- and eighth-century Rome, and of the central Mediterranean more generally, made in recent decades, for they revealed a wealth of economic activity that had hardly been expected. The finds, however, were not a treasure trove of precious metals (unlike, for instance, the Sutton Hoo, Mildenhall, or Hoxne treasures discovered in England). The decision to make them central to a second museum dedicated to the early Middle Ages is a mark of the recognition in Italy of the value of displaying the post-Roman period to the general public.[81]

While French and German exhibitions have largely presented the early Middle Ages as the marking the beginning of Europe (alias the EU), the Netherlands and Britain have been somewhat closer to Italy in emphasizing more local and national

---

[75] *I Longobardi*: see the comments on the origins of the exhibition by Menis, p. 9.

[76] *I Goti*.

[77] For problems in understanding the initial discovery, Bierbrauer, 'Il rinvenimento di Domagnano', p. 42.

[78] Gatti, foreword, *Il tesoro di Domagnano*.

[79] One should also note the series of conferences organized by Ausenda, commencing with *After Empire. Towards and Ethnology of Europe's Barbarians*.

[80] For the foundation in 1955/67 of the *Museo dell'alto medioevo*, see above, chapter 13.

[81] Alongside the massive scholarly catalogue (Arena, Delogu, Paroli, Ricci, Saguì, and Vendittelli (eds), *Roma dall'antichità al medioevo*), see also the guidebook, Manacorda, *Crypta Balbi*.

issues. In 1995 the Dutch mounted an exhibition on the immediately pre-Carolingian period, with the missionary, St Willibrord, as its focus. But the title, *Willibrord en het begin van Nederland* ('Willibrord and the beginning of the Netherlands'), is also indicative of the saint's importance in the story of national origins.[82]

A similar point was made in the 1991 exhibition on *The Making of England; Anglo-Saxon Art and Culture AD 600–900*, jointly organized by the British Museum and the British Library.[83] Rather than engage in any debate on the origins of the English (which would inevitably have looked towards the continent), this was a counterpart to the highly successful *Golden Age of Anglo-Saxon Art 966–1066*, which had been held in the British Museum seven years previously. Its emphasis was on the cultural achievement of the Middle Saxon period. It was also to be the last joint exhibition of Library and Museum before the Library departed to its new premises.

The Making of England was complemented by another exhibition whose catalogue was edited by one of the members of the British Museum staff, Susan Youngs, but which was shown in Edinburgh and Dublin: *The Work of Angels: Masterpieces of Celtic Metalwork 6th–9th Centuries AD*.[84] If there was a political message here, it was in the statement of national cooperation to be found in the forewords contributed by the Prime Minister, Margaret Thatcher, and the Taoiseach, Charles Haughey.[85] A more scholarly trigger for the collaborative display was the discovery of the Derrynaflan hoard, which had been sent to the British Museum for conservation.[86] The collaboration of French and German scholars apparent in the Mainz–Paris exhibitions of 1980–1, was directly echoed by those from England, Scotland, and Ireland in *The Work of Angels*, with the emphasis in the latter instance being on Anglo-Celtic cooperation.

In terms of exhibitions Britain fell somewhat behind many continental countries in exhibiting its post-Roman and Dark Age treasures in the late 1990s and early twenty-first century, although the British Museum's permanent collections, with its Late Roman and early Anglo-Saxon treasures, have consistently been on show. In 2006 York did boast an exhibition on the emperor Constantine to complement those held in Rimini (2005) and Trier (2007).[87] One other presentation of the period to the general public was the creation of a visitor centre at Sutton Hoo, under the aegis of the National Trust, to explain the early Anglo-Saxon cemetery and to display objects from the British Museum's holdings. It was opened in 2002 by Seamus Heaney, Irish poet and translator of the Old English epic *Beowulf*.[88]

---

[82] Van Vlierden (ed.), *Willibrord en het begin van Nederland*.

[83] Webster and Backhouse (eds), *The Making of England*.

[84] Youngs (ed.), *The Work of Angels*.

[85] Youngs (ed.), *The Work of Angels*, pp. 6–7.

[86] Youngs (ed.), *The Work of Angels*, p. 9.

[87] Hartley, Hawkes, Henig, and Mee (eds), *Constantine the Great*; Demandt and Engemann (eds), *Imperator Caesar Flavius Constantinus: Constantino il Grande. La civiltà antica al bivio tra Occidente e Oriente*.

[88] For a guide book, Plunkett, *Sutton Hoo, Suffolk*.

16.5 EAST AND WEST

More significant in indicating possible new areas of study (or rather the reopening of old areas) was the growing accessibility and regular display of finds from eastern Europe. We have already noted the presence of material from Brno at the St. Germain/Mannheim exhibition of princely gold: indeed there were objects on display from Hungary, Romania, and Russia, as well as from the Czech republic. Even more spectacular were the gold finds from Romania shown in Frankfurt in 1994, though as the title *Goldhelm: Reichtümer aus 6000 Jahren rumänischer Vergangenheit* ('Golden helmet: riches from 6,000 years of the Romanian past') indicates, this was not confined to Migration Period treasures. It did, however, include the great princely finds associated with Goths or Gepids from Pietroasa and Apahida.[89]

Collaboration between scholars from western and central Europe has been a particularly pronounced feature of exhibitions mounted in Austria and Hungary. Even before 1989 Austrian scholars, both historians like Herwig Wolfram and also archaeologists like Falko Daim, tried to build contacts between Vienna and Budapest. One reason for this was that a number of the greatest late Roman and Migration Period finds discovered in the eighteenth and nineteenth centuries had been made in what had been the Austro-Hungarian Empire. With the end of the Empire in 1919, objects which had been found together were divided between different countries, and after 1945 it became very hard for western scholars to see the holdings in eastern museums and vice versa. It is, therefore, no surprise to find, in the catalogue for the exhibition mounted to display the reunited Szilágysomlyó treasure in 1999 that Wolfram had been calling for all the material to be shown together since 1990.[90] It was displayed both in Vienna (where it was presented as Germanic) and in Budapest (where it was presented as specifically Gepid).[91] Quite apart from their magnificence, the finds from Szilágysomlyó (in Romanian Transylvania) shed remarkable light both on pagan cult and on the extent to which the owners of the treasure were imitating Roman high-status and even imperial style.[92]

Another great gold treasure found in the Austro-Hungarian Empire is that of Nagyszentmiklós. Here, the apparently Avar hoard itself had been kept together, but displayed in the *Kunsthistorisches Museum* in Vienna rather than in Romania where it had been found. The Hungarians (despite the fact that Nagyszentmiklós is not within the Hungarian borders) have long regarded the Avars as ancestors of the Magyars. They were, therefore, keen to display the material in Budapest, which they were able to do to mark the bicentenary of the Hungarian National Museum[93]—a building, it should be noted, that is of considerable importance in

[89] *Goldhelm.*   [90] Seipel, *Barbarenschmuck und Römergold*, p. 9.
[91] I have not seen the Hungarian catalogue, but see the comment of Seipel, in *The Gold of the Avars*, p. 9.
[92] For imitation, see in particular Schmauder, 'Imperial representation or barbaric imitation?'.
[93] Kovács, in *The Gold of the Avars*, p. 11.

the history of Hungarian nationalism, having been the site of Sándor Petőfi's denunciation of Austria in 1848.

Cooperation between Hungarians and Austrians also lay behind the *Landes-ausstellung* mounted by the region of Burgenland at Schloß Halbturn in 1996.[94] This display of Hunnic and Avar archaeology from Austria and Central Europe marked the culmination of long years of cooperation between the Austrian archaeologist Falko Daim and his Hungarian counterparts, and the result was one of the most substantial exhibitions of archaeology of the steppe peoples who entered central Europe in the fourth to seventh centuries ever to have been presented to the public.

The largest exhibition to open up the history, culture, and archaeology of central Europe in the early Middle Ages, however, concentrated on a rather later period: moving between Budapest, Krakow, Berlin, Mannheim, Prague, and Bratislava, from 2000 to 2002, *Europas Mitte um 1000* presented an extraordinarily full picture of central Europe during the period in which it was Christianized.[95] Unlike the Great Moravia exhibition of 1963 it pushed no single region as central, although the Czechs, Hungarians, Poles, and Slovaks all presented their own pasts within the overall display. Equally important, they collaborated heavily with German colleagues, and indeed *Europas Mitte* was shown in two German cities. This was a demonstration both of the cultural riches of Central Europe and of its ties with Germany.

Thus, alongside the national pasts and the past and present of the European Union, exhibitions since the early 1990s have also marked the reintegration of Central Europe into the Western European tradition, and in so doing they have made accessible material from the Migration Period that had been almost inaccessible for decades. With 1989 not only was a new European future possible, but at the same time opportunities for a re-evaluation of the European past, and not least the distant European past of the centuries including and following the Fall of Rome, were opened up.

One very particular exposition of material that had become inaccessible was mounted in Moscow and St Petersburg in 2007. Admitting that they did hold a large number of archaeological objects as war booty, the Russian authorities put on display a vast number of early medieval artefacts, taken above all from Berlin, in an exhibition entitled *The Merovingian Period: Europe without Borders*. The Russians thus acknowledged that, alongside the Schliemann Treasure from Troy, and indeed a considerable number of other art works, they also had in their hands numerous Migration Period treasures. In addition to the war booty, the exhibition put on show a vast and somewhat bewildering number of archaeological objects which had been found within Russia itself. The various forewords to the catalogue comment on the importance of the exhibition as marking the development of good relations between Germany and Russia, and also the growing collaboration between German

---

[94] *Reitervölker aus dem Osten: Hunnen und Awaren.*
[95] Wieczorek and Hinz (eds), *Europas Mitte um 1000.*

and Russian scholars.[96] This did not, however, go as far as to suggest the return of the objects. The intellectual theme of the exhibition was presented by Wilfried Menghin as being that of the migration of peoples from the edge of the steppes to Western Europe, and the subsequent establishment of the Merovingian kingdom of the Franks.[97] This is a interpretation, it must be admitted, that pays little attention to the fact that the nature and scale of the barbarian migrations has been radically called into question over the course of the last half century. Equally, it glosses over the fact that the Franks, of all the Germanic peoples, can scarcely be seen as migrants. Despite the old-fashioned nature of the conceptual base for the exhibition, the catalogue is likely to survive as a major handbook for anyone wanting access to objects that had long been inaccessible.

16.6 THE END OF THE SCHLESWIG-HOLSTEIN QUESTION

While the St Petersburg/Moscow exhibition demonstrated the possession of archaeological objects, a display of the bog finds from Denmark acknowledged loss. The most famous of all the bog finds is probably the boat from Nydam. Excavated in what was then Denmark in 1859 by Conrad Engelhardt, it was carefully hidden in the course of the Dano-Prussian War of 1863–44. When Schleswig-Holstein was taken over by Prussia the ship was much desired by both the Danes and the Germans, who had recognized it as a symbol of their ancient past—this being the period in which Jacob Grimm was deploying his knowledge of Germanic antiquity in the service of modern nationalism. Although initially the boat was successfully kept from the Germans, its whereabouts was discovered by a spy, and in 1877 it was transferred to Kiel, which was by that time in Prussian hands. In 1920, however, Northern Schleswig rejoined Denmark, following a plebiscite, and, since the Nydam bog lies within the territory that opted out of Germany, there were unsuccessful claims for the boat's repatriation.[98] Since any display of the Danish bog finds would inevitably seem incomplete without the Nydam boat, the organizers of the 2003 exhibition *The Spoils of Victory: The North in the Shadow of the Roman Empire* were naturally concerned to include it. Yet to do so the Danes had to acknowledge that the boat belonged to the archaeological museum in Schleswig. On page 436 of the catalogue there is a brief statement: 'Belongs to the Archäologisches Landesmuseum, Schleswig, Germany'. With that one phrase the Schleswig-Holstein question was finally concluded.

In his account of Engelhardt, which is included in the *Spoils of Victory* catalogue, Stine Wiell remarks that '[i]t is far from a matter of course today either to refrain from banging one another on the head with history during and after wars—or to

---

[96] Menghin (ed.), *The Merovingian Period: Europe without Borders*, pp. 12–23.
[97] Menghin, *The Merovingian Period: Europe without Borders*.
[98] Wiell, 'Denmark's first bog pioneer'.

collect antiquities in one place and unconditionally tell their story.'[99] The Copen-hagen exhibition set out to tell the story of the bog finds unconditionally. How-ever, in other respects Wiell's comment may be unduly pessimistic. Like the curators of a considerable number of other exhibitions in recent years, those organizing *The Spoils of Victory* and writing the catalogue entries succeeded in collaborating with colleagues from other countries. Indeed, a dominant feature of the exhibitions of the last thirty years has been the collaborative involvement of archaeologists from neighbouring countries, who have been concerned to present an image of the origins of European unity.

16.7 POLICING THE DISCOURSE

Yet the Nydam ship, like the treasures of Nagyszentmiklós and Szilágysomlyó, is a reminder that we look at past objects through a host of filters, which include the account of their modern discovery. Much the same is true of the past in general: the early Middle Ages have been interpreted and reinterpreted through various discourses, each of which has embedded narratives of cultural and national creation and change. In the course of this book we have traced the Fall of Rome and the coming of the barbarians through debates of the rights of the French nobility, the origins of democracy, the oppression of indigenous populations by alien rulers, calls for religious revival, the creation of the German nation, the establishment of Germany's frontiers, and finally the new search for European unity. Although some of these discourses have been superseded, others still inform modern interpretations, sometimes unconsciously. The past is always being used and abused—and while it may be true that the majority of the greatest abusers have been politicians, there are many professional historians and archaeologists who are equally complicit in distorting the past to fit present-day agendas. Indeed, one is often left to wonder who has played the greater role in misrepresentation: academics or politicians?

Besides, historical discourse is not simply created by scholars working in a social or cultural vacuum. Questions attract attention because they have contemporary resonance. For a period as distant as the early Middle Ages the evidence is not such as to provide absolute answers to many questions: interpretation involves personal judgment, which will inevitably be informed by current attitudes. In other words, historical discourse grows out of the cultural, social, and political circumstances in which it exists, as Michel Foucault constantly stressed. Equally, historical discourse feeds back into the culture that creates it. Questions about the Fall of Rome in the eighteenth century were conditioned by ideas of civic virtue, despotism, and political degeneracy, and the answers impacted on political debate. Debates about class structure in post-Revolutionary France informed, and were informed by, readings of the Frankish conquest. So too the Lombard invasion of Italy was interpreted in

---

[99] Wiell, 'Denmark's first bog pioneer', p. 83.

the light of the political circumstances prior to the Risorgimento, and the interpretation affected the current understanding of the influence of foreigners on the political and social structure of Italy. The story of the Church was an inspiration to those wishing to see religious revival in France. In nineteenth-century Germany study of the Germanic peoples was integral to the search for nationhood. In the twentieth century the role of those peoples in the development of Europe was debated in the shadow of German military activity, and the debate fed back into modern views of the frontiers of the Reich and of the destruction caused by Nazi action. *Decline and Fall* was thought to have lessons for those pondering the fate of the British Empire. More pious scholars looked to the role of religion in the survival of societies. Current discussions of the barbarians echo debates about immigration, while they are also drawn into the European Union's search for an identity. The past, even the distant past, was a constant presence in twentieth-century Europe—it was often a malign influence on the ideologies of Mark Mazower's 'Dark Continent'. A historian (whether 'professional' or 'amateur') should try to ask questions and give answers that are unbiased, but he or she will still participate in a discourse created by contemporary society and politics, and will often do so without being aware of the fact.

Although individual historical and archaeological arguments have been esoteric, and have been confined to a small group of academics, much historical debate has long been accessible to a wide audience. That audience is now larger than it has ever been. Many of the books published on Late Antiquity in recent years have had a sizeable print run. Exhibitions are often seen by thousands of visitors, as are heritage sites. Television programmes have given millions of viewers an understanding of the past—all of them drawing on, and feeding into, discourses about current political and social issues. Most recently, the development of the Internet has made the past yet more accessible: anyone with access to a computer can find information using a search engine. Greater and speedier access to historical knowledge brings with it the possibility of an increase in critical thought and understanding, both for the academic and for the layman, but democratization carries with it increased danger of abusing the past, either through carelessness or deliberately.

Moreover, the distinction between the professional historian and the amateur is rather less easy to draw than is sometimes assumed.[100] The professionalization of history was largely a development of the nineteenth century, resulting from the creation of university courses.[101] There was, therefore, no division between the professional historian and the amateur in the eighteenth century. Yet even in the nineteenth century some of the most significant historians, among them Thomas Hodgkin, wrote in their leisure time or their retirement. And how should one categorize E. A. Freeman, who spent long years writing for a living, before being elected to the Regius Chair in Oxford? So too, the twentieth century has seen

---

[100] Macmillan, *The Uses and Abuses of History* seems to have a clear concept of 'history professionals', which is nowhere defined.

[101] See the collection of essays in Lambert and Schofield (eds), *Making History*. For France, see den Boer, *History as a Profession*.

plenty of significant work come from the pens of those without university posts: in France in particular there is the honourable tradition of the *historien du diman- che*, in the words of Philippe Ariès.[102] Indeed, if anything the increased provision of university courses at doctoral as well as undergraduate level throughout the Western World has led to a growth in the number of 'amateurs' trained to 'profes- sional standards'.

It is an act of hubris for the scholarly community to demand that self-profess- edly unbiased professionals should police the work of amateurs, allegedly more prone to bias. Yet, for as long as the past attracts the attention of politicians and the general public, there will be a need for critical debate to test what is and what is not supported by the evidence, and it should be as open and as well-informed as pos- sible. At any one time there will always be one or more discourses that dominate the way in which the past is being read. It is, therefore, not just the interpretation of individual events that should constantly be held up to scrutiny: so too should the more general discourse in which the interpretation is situated. What we do with the past and why we are doing it is a question that no one can afford to ignore. Debate about the past is rarely a simple matter of antiquarianism or of factual accuracy (though that may be an issue): rather, historical debate is a major, perhaps *the* major field of discourse, in which we consider the values of our own age.

---

[102] One 'amateur' scholar to play a leading role in the development of research on the post-Roman period was Giorgio Ausenda, who established an institute (CIROSS) in San Marino which regularly hosted mini-conferences, the proceedings of a number of which have appeared in print.

Bibliography

Abbate, C., and Parker, R., 'Introduction: on analyzing opera', in Abbate and Parker (eds), *Analyzing Opera: Verdi and Wagner* (Berkeley, 1989), pp. 1–24.

Ackerman, G. P., ' "J. M. Kemble and Sir Frederic Madden: "Conceit and too much Germanism?" ', in C. T. Berkhout and M. McC. Gatch (eds), *Anglo-Saxon Scholarship: The First Three Centuries*, pp. 167–81.

Adam. A.-M., 'L'enseignement de la Reichsuniversität de Strasbourg', in A. Adam et al. (eds) *L'Archéologie en Alsace et en Moselle au temps de l'annexion (1940–1944)* (Wasselonne, 2001), pp. 137–43.

Adam, A.-M. et al. (eds), *L'archéologie en Alsace et en Moselle au temps de l'annexation (1940–1944)* (Wasselonne, 2001).

Aillagon, J.-J. (ed.), *Rome and the Barbarians: The Birth of a New World* (Milan, 2008).

Airlie, S., 'Strange eventful histories: the Middle Ages in the cinema', in J. L. Nelson and P. Linehan (eds), *The Medieval World* (London, 2001), pp. 163–83.

Al-Andalus/España. Historiografías en contraste: estudios reunidos y presentados por Manuela Marín (Madrid, 2009).

Amory, P., 'The Meaning and purpose of ethnic terminology in the Burgundian laws', *Early Medieval Europe* 2 (1993), pp. 1–28.

Amory, P., *People and Identity in Ostrogothic Italy, 489–554* (Cambridge, 1997).

Anderson, B., *Imagined Communities: Reflections on the Origin and Spread of Nationalism* (London, 1983).

Anderson, P., *Passages from Antiquity to Feudalism* (London, 1974).

Anzulovic, B., *Heavenly Serbia: From Myth to Genocide* (London, 1999).

Arce, J., *El último siglo de la España romana (284–409)* (Madrid, 1982).

Arce, J., *España entre el mundo antiguo y el mundo medieval* (Madrid, 1988).

Arce, J., *Bárbaros y romanos en Hispania (400–507 A.D.)* (Madrid, 2005).

Arena, M. S., Delogu, P., Paroli, L., Ricci, M., Saguì, L,. Vendittelli, L. (eds), *Roma dall'antichità al medioevo. Archeologia e storia, nel Museo nazionale Romano Crypta Balbi*, 2 vols (Milan, 2001–4).

Arena, M. S., and Paroli, L., *Museo dell'alto medioevo Roma* (Rome, 1993).

Arendt, H., *The Origins of Totalitarianism*, 2nd edn (London, 1958).

Arnaldi, G., 'L'Istituto storico italiano per il medio evo e la ristampa dei RIS', *Bulletino dell'Istituto storico italiano* 100 (1997), pp. 1–15.

Arndt, E. M., *Der Rhein, Teutschlands Strom, nicht aber Teutschlands Gränze* (Leipzig, 1813).

Arndt, E. M., *Die Frage über die Niederlande* (Leipzig, 1831).

Arndt, E. M., *Wanderungen und Wanderlungen mit der Reichsfreiherrn Heinrich Karl Friedrich vom Stein* (Berlin, 1858).

Arndt, W., and Krusch, B. (eds), Gregory of Tours, *Historiae, Monumenta Germaniae Historica, Scriptores Rerum Merovingicarum* 1, 1 (Hannover, 1884).

Arnold, B., 'The past as propaganda: totalitarian archaeology in Nazi Germany', *Antiquity* 64 (1990), pp. 464–78.

Arnold, B., and Hassmann, H., 'Archaeology in Nazi Germany: the legacy of the Faustian bargain', in P. L. Kohl and C. Fawcett (eds), *Nationalism, Politics and the Practice of Archaeology* (Cambridge, 1995).

Arnold, T., *An Inaugural Lecture on the Study of Modern History Delivered in the Theatre*, Oxford, 2 December 1841 (Oxford, 1841).

Arnold, T., *Introductory Lectures on Modern History, with the Inaugural Lecture*, 2nd edn (London, 1848).

Artifoni, E., 'Il Medioevo nel romanticismo: forme della storiografia tra sette e ottocento', in G. Cavallo, C. Leonardi, E. Menestò (eds), *Lo Spazio letterario del medioevo*, 1. *Il Medioevo latino*, vol. 4, *L'attualizzazione del testo* (Rome, 1997), pp. 175–221.

Artifoni, E., 'Le questioni longobarde: osservazioni su alcuni testi del primo Ottocento storiografico italiano', *Mélanges de l'École française de Rome* 119/2 (2007), pp. 297–304.

Atsma, H. (ed.), *La Neustrie: les pays au nord de la Loire de 650 à 850: colloque historique international* (Sigmaringen, 1989).

Aufruf an die Kulturwelt, ed. K, Böhme. *Aufrufe und Reden deutscher Professoren in Ersten Weltkrieg* (Stuttgart, 1975).

Ausenda, G. (ed.), *After Empire: Towards an Ethnology of Europe's Barbarians* (Woodbridge, 1995).

Bailey, R. N., 'St Cuthbert's relics: some neglected evidence', in G. Bonner, D. Rollason, and C. Stancliffe (eds), *St Cuthbert: His Cult and His Community, to AD 1200* (Woodbridge, 1989), pp. 231–46.

Baillie, M. G. L., 'Dark Ages and Dendrochronology', *Emania* 11 (1993), pp. 5–12.

Baker, K.M., 'Representation', in K. M. Baker (ed.), *The French Revolution and the Creation of Modern Political Culture* (Oxford, 1987), pp. 472–7.

Balbo, C., *Storia d'Italia sotto ai barbari*, 2 vols (Turin, 1830).

Balbo, C., *Sommario della storia d'Italia*, ed. M. Fubini Leuzzi, *Cesare Balbo, storia d'Italia e altri scritti editi ed inediti* (Turin, 1984): trans, J. Amigues, C. Balbo, *Histoire d'Italie depuis les origines jusqu'à nos jours, traduite… par J. Amigues*, 2 vols (Paris, 1860).

Balcou, J., 'La Tour d'Auvergne, th éoricien breton du mythe gaulois', in P. Viallaneix and J. Ehrard (eds), *Nos ancêtres les Gaulois, Actes du Colloque International de Clermont-Ferrand* (Clermont-Ferrand, 1982), pp. 107–13.

Balzaretti, R., 'The creation of Europe', *History Workshop* 33 (1992), pp. 181–96.

Bandinelli, R. B., *Hitler e Mussolini 1938: il viaggio del Führer in Italia* (Milan, 1995).

Banniard, M., *Viva voce: communication écrite et communication orale du IVe au XIe siècle en occident latin* (Paris, 1992).

Banti, A. M., 'Le invasioni barbariche e l'origine delle nazione', in A. M. Banti and R. Bizzochi (eds), *Immagini della nazione nell'Italia del Risorgimento* (Rome, 2002), pp. 21–44.

Banti, A. M., *La nazione del Risorgimento: parentela, sanità e onore alle origini dell'Italia unita* (Turin, 2006).

Barford, P. M., *The Early Slavs* (London, 2001).

Barlow, F., 'Edward Augustus Freeman', *Oxford Dictionary of National Biography*.

Barnes, W., *Early England and the Saxon-English: With Some Notes on the Father-stock of the Saxon-English, the Frisians* (London, 1869).

Barraclough, G., *The Origins of Modern Germany* (Oxford, 1946).

Bassett, S. (ed.), *The Origins of Anglo-Saxon Kingdoms* (Leicester, 1989).

Baynes, N. H., *A Bibliography of the Works of J. B. Bury, with a Memoir by Norman H. Baynes* (Cambridge, 1929).

Baynes, N. H., review of F. Lot, *La Fin du monde antique et le debut du Moyen Âge, Journal of Roman Studies* 19 (1929), pp. 224–35.

Baynes, N. H., and Dawes, E. A. S., *Three Byzantine Saints: Contemporary Biographies* (Oxford, 1948).

Beck, H., 'Otto Höfler', in *Reallexikon der Germanischen Altertumskunde* 15 (2000), pp. 30–4.

Beck, T. J., *Northern Antiquities in French Learning and Literature (1755–1855): A Study in Preromantic Ideas*, vol. 1, *The 'Vagina Gentium' and the Liberty Legend* (New York, 1934): vol. 2, *The Odin Legend and the Oriental Fascination* (New York, 1935).

Beffort, A., *Alexandre Soumet, 1788–1845* (Luxembourg, 1908).

Bentley, M., 'The Age of Prothero: British historiography in the long fin de siècle, 1870–1920', *Transactions of the Royal Historical Society*, 6th series, 20 (2010), pp. 171–93.

Berdiaev, N., *Un nouveau Moyen Âge* (Paris, 1927).

Berkhout, C.T., and Gatch, M. McC. (eds), *Anglo-Saxon Scholarship: The First Three Centuries* (Boston, Mass., 1982).

Bertelli, C., and Brogiolo, G. P. (eds), *Il futuro dei Longobardi: l'Italia e la costruzione dell'Europa di Carlo Magno*, 2 vols (Milan, 2000).

Beyerle, F., *Gesetze der Burgunden, Germanenrechte* 10 (Weimar, 1936).

Beyerle, F., *Gesetze der Langobarden, Germanenrechte* 3 (Weimar, 1947).

Beyerle, F., and Buchner, R. (eds), *Lex Ribuaria, Monumenta Germaniae Historica, Leges* 1, 3, 2 (Hannover, 1954).

Biddiss, M. D., *Father of Racist Ideology: The Social and Political Thought of Count Gobineau* (London, 1970).

Bierbrauer, V., 'Il rinvenimento di Domagnano, Repubblica di San Marino, I Goti a San Marino', in *Il tesoro di Domagnano* (Milan, 1995), pp. 42–7.

Binns, J. W., (ed), *Latin Literature of the Fourth Century* (London, 1974).

Bizzocchi, R., 'Una nuova morale per la donna e la famiglia', in A. M. Banti and P. Ginsborg (eds), *Storia d'Italia, Annali 22, Il Risorgimento* (Turin, 2007), pp. 69–96.

Bjork, R. E., 'Nineteenth-century Scandinavia and the Birth of Anglo-Saxon Studies', in A. J. Frantzen and J. D. Niles (eds), *Anglo-Saxonism and the Construction of Social Identity* (Gainesville, 1997), pp. 111–32.

Blanckaert, C., 'On the origins of French ethnology: William Edwards and the Doctrine of Race', in G. W. Stocking, Jr., *Bones, Bodies, Behavior, Essays on Biological Anthropology* (Madison, 1988), pp. 18–55.

Bloch, M., 'La conqête de la Gaule romaine', *Revue Historique* 154 (1922), pp. 161–8.

Bloch, M., 'La société du Haut Moyen Âge et ses origines', *Journal des Savants* (1926), pp. 403–20; reprinted in *Mélanges Historiques* (Paris, 1963), vol. 1, pp. 61–74.

Bloch, M. 'Observations sur la conquête de la Gaule romaine par les rois francs', *Revue Historique* 154 (1927), pp. 161–78: reprinted in M. Boch, *Mélanges historiques*, vol. 1 (Paris, 1963), pp. 75–89.

Bloch, M., *La Société féodale*, 2 vols (Paris, 1939–40).

Bloch, M., 'Sur les grandes invasions. Quelques positions de problèmes', *Revue de Synthèse* 60 (1945), pp. 55–81), reprinted in M. Bloch, *Mélanges Historiques* (Paris, 1963), vol. 1, pp. 90–109.

Bloch, M., *L'Étrange défaite* (Paris, 1946).

Bloch, M., *Mélanges Historiques*, 2 vols (Paris, 1963).

Bloch, M., 'Une mise au point: les Invasions', in M. Bloch, *Mélanges historiques* (Paris, 1963), vol. 1, pp. 110–41.

Bluhme, F., and Boretius, A. (eds), *Leges in Folio* 3 (Hannover, 1868).

Boer, P. den, *History as a Profession: The Study of History in France, 1818–1914* (Princeton, 1998).

Bognetti, G. P., 'Tra le rovine di Castelseprio', *Periodico della Società storica Comense* 28 (1931), pp. 5–12: reprinted in *L'età Longobarda*, vol. 2, pp. 3–9.

Bognetti, G. P., 'Le origini della consacrazione del vescovo di Pavia da parte del pontefice romano e la fine dell'arianesimo presso i Longobardi', in *Atti e Memorie del IV Congresso Storico Lombardo* (Pavia, 1939), pp. 91–151, reprinted in *L'età longobarda*, vol. 1, pp. 145–217.

Bognetti, G. P., 'Santa Maria foris portas di Castelseprio e la storia religiosa dei Longobardi', in G. P. Bognetti, G. Chierici, and A. De Capitani d'Arzago, *S. Maria di Castelseprio* (Milan, 1948), pp. 11–511; reprinted as vol. 2 of *L'età Longobarda*.

Bognetti, G. P., *L'età longobarda*, 4 vols (Milan, 1966–8).

Bognetti, G. P., *Manzoni giovane* (Naples, 1972).

Böhme, H. W., Böhner, K., Schulze, M., Weidemann, K., Waurick, G., Baratte, F., and Vallet, F. (eds), *A l'aube de la France* (Paris, 1981).

Boime, A., 'Marmontel's *Bélisaire* and the pre-revolutionary progressivism of David', *Art History* 3 (1980), pp. 81–101.

Boockmann, H., *Göttingen: Vergangenheit und Gegenwart einer europäischen Universität* (Göttingen, 1997).

Borius, R., *Constance de Lyon, Vie de saint Germain d'Auxerre*, Sources Chrétiennes 112 (Paris, 1965).

Boswell, L., 'From liberation to purge trials in the "mythic provinces": recasting French identities in Alsace and Lorraine, 1918–1920', *French Historical Studies* 23, 1 (2003), pp. 129–62.

Boulainvilliers, H. de, *Essais sur la noblesse de France*, ed. J. F. de Tabary (Amsterdam, 1732).

Boulainvilliers, H. de, *Justification de la naissance légitime de Bernard, roy d'Italie, petit-fils de Charlemagne* (N. D.).

Bowersock, G., Clive, J., and Graubard, S. R. (eds), *Edward Gibbon and the Decline and Fall of the Roman Empire* (Cambridge, Mass., 1977).

Bowlus, 'Ethnogenesis: the Tyranny of a Construct', in A. Gillett (ed), *On Barbarian Identity. Critical approaches to Ethnicity in the Early Middle Ages* (Turnhout, 2002), pp. 241–56.

Braudel, F., *The Mediterranean and the Mediterranean World in the Age of Philip II*, English trans., 2 vols (London, 1972–3).

Braunfels, W. (ed), *Karl der Große: Werk und Wirkung* (Aachen, 1965).

Brennecke, F., *Handbuch für die Schulungsarbeit in der HJ: vom deutschen Volk und seinem Lebensraum* (Munich, 1937), trans. H. L. Childs, *The Nazi Primer* (New York, 1938).

Bresslau, H., *Geschichte der Monumenta Germaniae Historica*, Neues Archiv 14 (1921).

Brizard, G. *Eloge historique de l'Abbé de Mably*, in G. Bonnot de Mably, *Collection complete des oeuvres de l'Abbé de Mably* (Paris, An III = 1794/5), vol. 1, pp. 1–120.

Brogiolo, G. P., and Ward-Perkins, B. (eds), *The Idea and Ideal of the Town between Late Antiquity and the Early Middle Ages* (Leiden, 1999).

Broglie, G. de, *Guizot* (Paris, 2002).

Broglie, J.-V.-A. de, *L'Église et l'Empire au IVe siècle*, 6 vols (Paris, 1856).

Brown, P., 'The Later Roman Empire', *Economic History Review, Essays in Bibliography and Criticism*, lvi, 2 ser. 20 (1967), pp. 327–43, reprinted in P. Brown, *Religion and Society in the Age of Saint Augustine* (London, 1972), pp. 46–73.

Brown, P., 'The rise and function of the holy man in Late Antiquity', *Journal of Roman Studies* 61 (1971), pp. 80–101; reprinted in P. Brown, *Society and the Holy in Late Antiquity* (London, 1982), pp. 103–52.

Brown, P., *The World of Late Antiquity* (London, 1971).

Brown, P., *The Making of Late Antiquity* (Boston, Mass., 1978).

Brown, P., *The Cult of the Saints: Its Rise and Function in Latin Christianity* (Chicago, 1981).

Brown, P., *The Rise of Western Christendom: Triumph and Diversity A.D. 200–1000* (Oxford, 1996): 2nd edn (Oxford, 2003).

Brown, P., 'Reply to Comments', *Symbolae Osloenses* 72 (1997), pp. 70–80.

Brown, P., 'Report', *SO Debate: The World of Late Antiquity Revisited*, *Symbolae Osloenses* 72 (1997), pp. 5–30.

Brown, P., '*Gloriosus obitus*: the end of the ancient other world', in W. E. Klingshirn and M. Vessey, *The Limits of Ancient Christianity: Essays in Late Antique Thought and Culture in Honor of R. A. Markus* (Ann Arbor, 1999), pp. 289–314.

Brown, P., 'Introducing Robert Markus', *Augustinian Studies* 32 (2001), pp. 181–7.

Brown, P., *Poverty and Leadership in the Later Roman Empire* (Hanover, NH, 2002).

Brown, P., *A Life of Learning*, Charles Homer Haskins Lecture for 2003, ACLS Occasional Paper 55 (2003).

Brown, P., 'What's in a name?', a talk given at the opening of the Oxford centre for Late Antiquity (2007), <http://www.ocla.ox.ac.uk/pdf/brown_what_in_name.pdf>.

Brown, P., *The Body and Society: Men, Women, and Sexual Renunciation in Early Christianity*, Twentieth Anniversary Edition (New York, 2008).

Brown, P., *Through the Eye of a Needle: Wealth, the Fall of Rome, and the Making of Christianity in the West, 350–550 AD* (Princeton, 2012).

Brown, T. S., 'Gibbon, Hodgkin, and the invaders of Italy', in R. McKitterick and R. Quinault (eds), *Edward Gibbon and Empire* (Cambridge, 1997), pp. 137–61.

Brown Price, A., *Pierre Puvis de Chavannes, Catalogue, Van Gogh Museum, Amsterdam* (Zwolle, 1994).

Brubaker, L., and Smith, J. M. H. (eds), *Gender in the Early Medieval World, East and West* (Cambridge, 2004).

Brugerette, J., *Le Comte de Montlosier et son temps 1755–1838. Étude de psychologie et d'histoire* (Aurillac, 1931).

Brunner, H., *Deutsche Rechtsgeschichte*, 2 vols (Leipzig, 1887–92).

Brunt, P. A., 'A. H. M. Jones', *Oxford Dictionary of National Biography*.

Bryce, J., *Studies in Contemporary Biography* (London, 1903).

Bryer, A., 'Gibbon and the later Byzantine Empire', in R. McKitterick and R. Quinault (eds), *Edward Gibbon and Empire* (Cambridge, 1997)., pp. 101–16.

Buat-Nançay, L-G. du, *Les Origines ou l'ancienne gouvernement de la France, de l'Italie et de l'Allemagne* (The Hague, 1757).

Bullough, D., *Italy and her Invaders* (Nottingham, 1968).

Burleigh, M., *Germany Turns Eastwards: A Study of Ostforschung in the Third Reich* (Cambridge, 1988).

Burrow, J. W., *A Liberal Descent: Victorian Historians and the English Past* (Cambridge, 1981).

Burrow, R., *Gibbon* (London, 1985).

Bury, J. B., *A History of the Later Roman Empire: From Arcadius to Irene (395 A.D. to 800 A.D.)*, 2 vols (London, 1889).

Bury, J. B., *The Life of St Patrick and his Place in History* (London, 1905).

Bury, J. B., *Germany and Slavonic Civilisation* (London, 1914).

Bury, J. B., *History of the Later Roman Empire from the Death of Theodosius I to the Death of Justinian* (London, 1923).

Bury, J. B., *The Idea of Progress* (London, 1924).

Bury, J. B., *The Invasion of Europe by the Barbarians*, ed. F. J. C. Hearnshaw (London, 1928).

Bury, J. B., 'Appendix. Causes of the Survival of the Roman Empire in the East (1900)', in J. B. Bury, *Selected Essays of J. B. Bury*, ed. H. W. V. Temperley (Cambridge, 1930), pp. 231–42.

Bury, J. B., 'Darwinism and History (1909)', in J. B. Bury, *Selected Essays of J. B. Bury*, ed. H. W. V. Temperley (Cambridge, 1930), pp. 23–42.

Bury, J. B., 'A letter on the writing of history (1926)', in J. B. Bury, *Selected Essays of J. B. Bury*, ed. H. W. V. Temperley (Cambridge, 1930), pp. 70–1.

Bury, J. B., 'The Science of History (1903)', in J. B. Bury, *Selected Essays of J. B. Bury*, ed. H. W. V. Temperley (Cambridge, 1930), pp. 3–22.

Butler, K. T. B., 'A "Petty" Professor of Modern History: William Smyth (1765–1849)', *Cambridge Historical Journal* 9 (1948), pp. 217–38.

Callahan, D., Horton, M., Rogers, F., Swain, B., and Williams, G. H., 'Christopher Dawson 12 October 1889–25 May 1970', *Harvard Theological Review*, 66, 2, (1973), pp. 161–76.

Cameron. A., *The Later Roman Empire AD 284–430* (London, 1993).

Cameron. A., *The Mediterranean World in Late Antiquity AD 395–600* (London, 1993).

Cameron, A., 'Bury, Baynes and Toynbee', in R. Cormack and E. Jeffreys (eds), *Through the Looking Glass: Byzantium through British Eyes* (Aldershot, 2002), pp. 163–75.

Cameron, A., 'Better Barbarians', *TLS* 7th August 2009, No. 5549, p. 10.

Campbell, E., *Continental and Mediterranean Imports to Atlantic Britain and Ireland, AD 400–800* (London, 2007).

Camps, J. (ed), *Cataluña en la epoca carolingia: arte y cultura antes de románico (siglos IX y X)* (Barcelona, 1999).

Candaux, J., 'L'hommage de Sismondi à Paul-Henri Mallet (1807)', *Annales Benjamin Constant* 31–32 (2007), pp. 331–8.

Carlà, F., 'Il modello di ogni caduta: il V secolo d. C. nelle sue riduciozi teatrali tra XIX e XX secolo', in P. J. C. Pascual (ed.), '*Imagines': The Reception of Antiquity in Performing and Visual Arts* (Logrono, 2008), pp. 83–104.

Carlyle, T., *On Heroes, Hero-worship and the Heroic in History* (London, 1870).

Carsaniga, G., 'The Romantic controversy', in P. Brand and L. Pertile (eds), *The Cambridge History of Italian Literature* (Cambridge, 1996), pp. 399–439.

Cauchie, A., *Godefroid Kurth (1847–1916): le patriote, le chrétien, l'historien* (Brussels, 1922).

Cervantes, F., 'Christopher Dawson and Europe', in S. Caldecott and J. Morrill (eds), *Eternity in Time. Christopher Dawson and the Catholic Idea of History* (Edinburgh, 1977), pp. 51–68.

Chadwick, H. M., *The Origin of the English Nation* (Cambridge, 1906).

Chadwick, H. M., *The Heroic Age* (Cambridge, 1912).

Chadwick, H. M., *The Nationalities of Europe and the Growth of National Identities* (Cambridge, 1945).

Chadwick, H. M., and N. K., *The Growth of Literature*, 3 vols (Cambridge, 1932–40).

Chadwick, N. K., *Poetry and Letters in Early Christian Gaul* (London, 1955).

Chadwick, O., 'Gibbon and the Church historians', in G. Bowersock, J. Clive, and S. R. Graubard (ed.), *Edward Gibbon and the Decline and Fall of the Roman Empire* (Cambridge, Mass., 1977), pp. 219–31.

Chateaubriand, F. R. de, *Les Martyrs* (Paris, 1873).

Chateaubriand, F. R. de, *Génie du christianisme ou beautés de la religion chrétienne*, ed. M. Regard, *Chateaubriand: essai sur les révolutions, génie du christianisme* (Paris, 1978).

Chandler, S. B., *Alessandro Manzoni: The Story of a Spiritual Quest* (Edinburgh, 1974).

Chennevières, P. de, 'Le Panthéon', in *Inventaire général des richesses artistiques de la France, Paris, Monuments civils* II (Paris, 1889), pp. 335, 340–1.

Chiappini, S., 'La voce della martire: dagli "evirati cantori" all'eroina romantica', in A. M. Banti and P. Ginsborg (eds), *Storia d'Italia, Annali 22, Il Risorgimento* (Turin, 2007), pp. 289–328.

Chitty, S., *The Beast and the Monk: A Life of Charles Kingsley* (London, 1974).

Cholvy, G., *Frédéric Ozanam (1813–1853). L'Engagement d'un intellectuel catholique au XIXe siècle* (Paris, 2003).

Christensen, A. S., *Cassiodorus, Jordanes and the History of the Goths: Studies in a Migration Myth* (Copenhagen, 2002).

Christie, N., *The Lombards* (Oxford, 1994).

Chrysos, E., 'Die Amaler-Herrschaft in Italien und das Imperium Romanum: Der Vertragsentwurf des Jahres 535', *Byzantion* 51 (1981), pp. 430–74.

Claudio Sánchez-Albornoz, Atti dei Convegni Lincei 113 (Rome, 1995).

Clunies Ross, M., and Lönnroth, L., 'The Norse Muse: report from an international research project', *Alvíssmál* 9 (1999), pp. 3–28.

Clüver, P., *Germania Antiqua* (Leiden, 1616).

Coccia, E., 'La cultura irlandese precarolingia: miracola o mito?', *Studi Medievali* 8 (1) 1967, pp. 256–420.

Cochrane, C. N., *Christianity and Classical Culture: A Study of thought and Action from Augustus to Augustine* (Oxford, 1940).

Collins, W., *Antonina: Or the Fall of Rome. A Romance of the Fifth Century*, revised edn (London, 1861).

Constantino il Grande: la civiltà antica al bivio tra Occidente e Oriente (Milan, 2005).

Corradini, R., Diesenberger, M., and Reimitz, H. (eds), *The Construction of Communities in the Early Middle Ages: Texts, Resources, Artefacts* (Leiden, 2003).

Coulton, G. G., *Five Centuries of Religion*, vol. 1, *St Bernard: His Predecessors And Successor, 1000–1200 AD* (Cambridge, 1923).

Courcelle, P., *Histoire littéraire des grandes invasions germaniques* (Paris, 1948); 3rd edn (Paris, 1964).

Courtois, C., *Victor de Vita et son œuvre: étude critique* (Algiers, 1954).

Courtois, C., *Les Vandales et l'Afrique* (Paris, 1955).

Creighton, L., *Life and Letters of Thomas Hodgkin* (London, 1917).

Croisille, C., 'Michelet et les Gaulois ou les séductions de la patrie celtique', in P. Viallaneix and J. Ehrard (eds), *Nos ancêtres les Gaulois, Actes du Colloque International de Clermont-Ferrand* (Clermont-Ferrand, 1982), pp. 211–19.

Crow, T. E., *Painters and Public Life in Eighteenth-Century Paris* (New Haven, 1985).

Curta, F., *The Making of the Slavs: History and Archaeology of the Lower Danube Region c.500–700* (Cambridge, 2001).

Curta, F., 'The history and archaeology of Great Moravia: an introduction', *Early Medieval Europe* 17 (2009), pp. 238–47.

Dahn, F., *Könige der Germanen*, 13 vols (Leipzig, 1861–1911).

Dahn, F., *Prokopius von Cäsarea: Ein Beitrag zur Historiographie der Völkerwanderung und des sinkenden Römerthums* (Berlin, 1865).

Dahn, F., *Das Kriegsrecht: kurze, volksthümliche Darstellung für Jedermann zumal für den deutschen Soldaten* (Würzburg, 1870): trans. *Le Droit de la guerre: exposé succintement et mis à la portée des masses* (Brussels, 1872).

Dahn, F., *Markgraf Rüdiger von Bechelaren* (Leipzig, 1875).

Dahn, F., *Ein Kampf um Rom* (Leipzig, 1876): trans. H. Parker, *A Struggle for Rome* (London, 2005).

Dahn, F., *Erinnerungen*, 4 vols, 2nd edn (Leipzig, 1894–5).

Dam, R. van, *Leadership and Community in Late Antique Gaul* (Berkeley, 1985).

Daniélou, J., and Marrou, H. I., *Nouvelle histoire de l'Église*, vol. 1, *Des origines à Grégoire le Grand* (Paris, 1963).

Dannenbauer, H., *Indogermanen, Germanen, Deutsche: Vom Werden des deutschen Volkes* (Tübingen, 1935).

Dannenbauer, H., and Ernst, F. (eds), *Das Reich: Idee und Gestalt, Festschrift für Johannes Haller zu seinem 75. Geburtstag* (Stuttgart, 1940).

Davenson, H. (H. I. Marrou), *Fondements d'une culture chrétienne* (Paris, 1934).

Dawson, C., *The Making of Europe 400–1000 A.D.* (London, 1932), reprinted with an introduction by A. C. Murray (London, 2006): trans., *Les Origines de l'Europe et de la civilisation européenne* (Paris, 1934); *Le moyen âge et les origines de l'Europe des invasions à l'an 1000* (Paris, 1960); *Die Gestaltung des Abendlandes* (Leipzig and Frankfurt, 1935).

Deigan, F. B., *Alessandro Manzoni's The Count of Carmagnola and Adelchis* (Baltimore, 2004).

Delogu, P., 'Reading Pirenne again', in R. Hodges and R. Bowden (eds), *The Sixth Century* (Leiden, 1998), pp. 15–40.

Demandt, A., and Engemann, J. (eds), *Imperator Caesar Flavius Constantinus: Constantin der Große* (Mainz, 2007).

Déruelle, A., '*Julia Sévéra* ou pour une autre écriture de l'histoire', *Annales Benjamin Constant* 31–32 (2007), pp. 339–50.

Des Marez, G., and Ganshof, F. L. (eds), *Compte-rendu du cinquième Congrès international des Sciences historiques* (Brussels, 1923).

Devroey, J.-P., *Economie rurale et société dans l'Europe franque (VIe-IXe siècles)*, vol. 1, *Fondements matériels, échanges et lien social* (Paris, 2003).

Dick, S., *Der Mythos vom 'germanischen' Königtum* (Berlin, 2008).

Dickens, B., 'John Mitchell Kemble and Old English scholarship', *Proceedings of the British Academy* 25 (1939), pp. 51–84.

Die Alamannen (Stuttgart, 1997).

Die Franken: Wegbereiter Europas (Mannheim, 1997).

Dihle, A., *So Debate*, *Symbolae Osloenses* 72 (1997), pp. 40–3.

Ditt, K., 'The idea of German cultural regions in the Third Reich: the work of Franz Petri', *Journal of Historical Geography* 27, 2 (2001), pp. 241–58.

Dhondt, J., 'Henri Pirenne, historien des institutions urbaines', *Annali della Fondazione Italiana per la Storia Amministrativa* 3 (1996), pp. 81–129.

Dopsch, A., *Wirtschaftliche und soziale Grundlagen der europäischen Kulturentwicklung* (Vienna, 1918–20): 2nd edn (Vienna, 1923–4); abridged English translation *The Economic and Social Foundations of European Civilization* (London, 1937).

Dreßen, W., Minkenberg, G., and Oellers, A. C. (eds), *Ex Oriente. Isaak und der weisse Elefant: Bagdad—Jerusalem—Aachen. Eine Reise durch drei Kulturen um 800 und heute*, 3 vols (Mainz, 2003).

Drinkwater, J. F., *The Alamanni and Rome 213–496, Caracalla to Clovis* (Oxford, 2007).

Drolet, M., 'Industry, class and society: a historiographic reinterpretation of Michel Chevalier', *English Historical Review* 123 (2008), pp. 1229–71.

Du Bos, J. B., *Histoire critique de l'établissement de la monarchie françoise dans les Gaules*, 3 vols (Amsterdam, 1735).

Duckworth, C., 'Louis XVI and English History: a French reaction to Walpole, Hume and Gibbon on Richard III', in H. Mason (ed.), *Studies on Voltaire and the Eighteenth Century*, vol. 176 (Oxford, 1979), pp. 385–401.

Duggan, C., 'Gran Bretagna e Italia nel Risorgimento', in A. M. Banti and P. Ginsborg, *Storia d'Italia, Annali 22, Il Risorgimento* (Turin, 2007), pp. 777–96.

Duggan, C., *The Force of Destiny: A History of Italy since 1796* (London, 2007).

Dülffer J., 'Sammelrez: Review-Symposium "Westforschung"' [review of D. Dietz, H. Gabel, and U. Tiedau, (eds), *Griff nach dem Western: Die 'Westforschung' der völkisch-nationalen Wissenschaften zum nordwesteuropäischen Raum (1919–1960)*, and H. Derks, *Deutsche Westforschung: Ideologie und Praxis im 20. Jahrhundert*], H-Soz-u-Kult, 14.05.2003, <http://hsozkult.geschichte.hu-berlin.de/rezensionen/2003-2-089>].

Durliat, J., *Les Finances publiques de Dioclétien aux Carolingiens (284–888)* (Sigmaringen, 1990).

Eckhardt, K. A., 'Das Fuldaer Vasallengeschlecht vom Stein', *Festgabe für Heinrich Himmler* (Darmstadt, 1941), pp. 175–214.

Eckhardt, K. A. (ed.), *Pactus Legis Salicae, Monumenta Germaniae Historica, Leges* 4, 1 (Hannover, 1962).

Eckhardt, K. A., *Merowingerblut*, 2 vols, *Germanenrechte*, Neue Folge, *Deutschrechtliches Archiv* 10–11 (Witzenhausen, 1965).

Eckhardt, K. A. (ed.), *Lex Salica, Monumenta Germaniae Historica, Leges* 4, 2 (Hannover, 1969).

Eckhardt, K. A., *Studia Merovingica* (Aalen, 1975).

Effros, B., *Merovingian Mortuary Archaeology and the Making of the Early Middle Ages* (Berkeley, 2003).

Effros, B., 'Selling archaeology and anthropology: early medieval artefacts at the Expositions universelles and the *Wien Weltausstellung*, 1867–1900', *Early Medieval Europe* 16 (2008), pp. 23–48.

Eicke, H., *Kämpfer und Helden Germaniens* (Leipzig, 1936).

Eicke, H., *König Geiserich* (Leipzig, 1936).

Eicke, H., *Wiking im Südland* (Leipzig, 1940).

Eicke, H., *Herrführer und Könige* = Band 6, *Die Welt der Germanen* (Berlin, 1942).

Eicke, H., *Geschichte der westgotischen Könige seit Alarichs Tod* (Leipzig, 1944), pp. 8–9.

Ellis, H. A., *Boulainvilliers and the French Monarchy* (Ithaca, 1988).

Engels, F., *Telegraph für Deutschland* 2 (January, 1841), Marx and Engels Internet archive, <http://www.marx.org/archive/marx/index.htm>.

Engels, F., *Telegraph für Deutschland* 5 (January, 1841), Marx and Engels Internet archive, <http://www.marx.org/archive/marx/index.htm>.

Engels, F., 'The origins of the family, private property and the state', in K. Marx and F. Engels, *Selected Works* (London, 1968), pp. 568–76.

Esders, S., *Römische Rechtstradition und merowingisches Königtum* (Göttingen, 1997).

Espagne, M., 'Claude Fauriel et l'Allemagne', *Romantisme* 21 (1991), pp. 7–18.

État de la France, dans lequel on voit tout ce qui regarde le gouvernement etc, 3 vols (London, 1727–8).

Ewig, E., *Trier im Merowingerreich: Civitas, Stadt, Bistum* (Trier, 1954).

Ewig, E., *Spätantikes und fränkisches Gallien, Gesammelte Schriften*, 3 vols (Munich, 1976–9, Sigmaringen, 2009).

Falhbusch, M., *Wissenschaft im Dienst der nationalsozialistischen Politik? Die 'Volksdeutschen Forschungsgemeinschaften' von 1931–45* (Baden-Baden, 1999).

Fahlbusch, M., review of H. Derks, *Deutsche Westforschung. Ideologie und Praxis im 20. Jahrhundert*: H-Soz-u-Kult, 27.06.2002, <http://hsozkult.geschichte.hu-berlin.de/rezensionen/ZG-2002-085>.

Falco, G., 'La questione longobarda e la moderna storiografia italiana', *Atti del 1° Congresso internazionale di Studi longobardi* (Spoleto, 1952), pp. 153–66.

Fauriel, C. C., *Histoire de la Gaule méridionale sous la domination des conquerants germains*, 4 vols (Paris, 1836).

Fehr, H., *Germanen und Romanen im Merowingerreich: Frühgeschichtliche Archäologie zwischen Wissenschaft und Zeitgeschehen* (Berlin, 2010).

Feldman, M., *Opera and Soveignty. Transforming Myths in Eighteenth-Century Italy* (Chicago, 2007).

Feldman, R., *Jacob Grimm und die Politik* (Frankfurt, 1969).

Ferrill, A., *The Fall of the Roman Empire. The Military Explanation* (London, 1983).

Filip, J. (ed.) *The Great Moravia Exhibition: 1100 years of Tradition of State and Cultural Life* (Prague, 1964).

Finelli, P., and Fruci, G. L., 'Il "momento risorgimentale" nel discorso politico francese (1796–1870)', in A. M. Banti and P. Ginsborg (eds), *Storia d'Italia, Annali 22, Il Risorgimento* (Turin, 2007), pp. 747–76.

Foucault, M., *Il faut défendre la société: cours au Collège de France 1975–6* (Paris, 1997); English trans., *Society Must be Defended* (London, 2003).

Fouracre, P., 'The use of the term *beneficium* in Frankish sources: a society based on favours?', in W. Davies and P. Fouracre (eds), *The Languages of Gift in the Early Middle Ages* (Cambridge, 2010), pp. 62–88.

Fourquin, G., 'Éloge funèbre de Christian Courtois', in *Caratteri del secolo VII in occidente*, Settimane di studio del centro italiano di studi sull'alto medioevo 5 (Spoleto, 1958), pp. 63–9.

Frank, K., 'Vorboten an Main und Tauber. Germanen im Taubergebiet vor und nach der Aufgabe des Limes', in *Die Alamannen* (1997), pp. 69–72.

Frantzen, A. J., *Desire for Origins: New Language, Old English, and Teaching the Tradition* (New Brunswick, 1990), pp. 37–42.

Frantzen, A. J., 'Bede and Bawdy Bale: Gregory the Great, angels, and the "Angli"', in A. J. Frantzen and J. D. Niles (eds), *Anglo-Saxonism and the Construction of Social Identity* (Gainesville, 1997), pp. 17–39.

Frech, K., 'Felix Dahn: Die Verbreitung völkischen Gedankenguts durch den historischen Roman', in U. Puschner, W. Schmitz and J. H. Ulbricht (eds), *Handbuch zur 'Völkischen Bewegung' 1871–1918* (Munich, 1996), pp. 685–98.

Freeman, E. A., 'The early sieges of Paris', *British Quarterly Review* 1871, reprinted in E. A. Freeman, *Historical Essays*, First Series (London, 1871), 2nd edn (London, 1886), pp. 212–56, and in Freeman, E. A., *Select Historical Essays* (Leipzig, 1873), pp. 103–50.

Freeman, E.A, 'The Goths at Ravenna', *British Quarterly Review*, October 1872: republished in E. A. Freeman, *Historical Essays*, Third Series (London, 1879), 2nd edn (London, 1892), pp. 123–75.

Freeman, E. A., 'The Franks and the Gauls', *Select Historical Essays* (Leipzig, 1873).

Freeman, E. A., *The Growth of the English Constitution from the Earliest Times*, 3rd edn (London, 1876).

Freeman, E. A., *The History of the Norman Conquest of England: Its Causes and its Results*, vol. 1, *The Preliminary History to the Election of Eadward the Confessor* (Oxford, 1877).

Freeman, E. A., 'The Jews in Europe', *Saturday Review*, 10th February 1877: reprinted in E. A. Freeman, *Historical Essays*, Third Series, 2nd edn, pp. 230–4.

Freeman, E. A., 'Race and Language', first published in the *Contemporary Review*, February 1877, and the *Fortnightly Review*, January 1877, reprinted in E. A. Freeman, *Historical Essays*, Third Series, 2nd edn, pp. 176–230.

Freeman, E. A., *The Historical Geography of Europe*, 2 vols (London, 1881).

Freeman, E. A., *Four Oxford Lectures 1887: Fifty Years of European History, Teutonic Conquest in Gaul and Britain* (London, 1888).

Freeman, E. A., *The Atlas to Freeman's Historical Geography*, 3rd edn, ed. J. B. Bury (London, 1903).

Freeman, E. A., *Freeman's Historical Geography of Europe*, 3rd edn, ed. J. B. Bury (London, 1903).

Freeman, E. A., *Western Europe in the Fifth Century: An Aftermath* (London, 1904).

French Symbolist Painters: Moreau, Puvis de Chavannes, Redon and their Followers (London, 1972).

Frend, W. H. C., *The Donatist Church: A Movement of Protest in Roman North Africa* (Oxford, 1952).

Frend, W. H. C., 'Heresy and schism as social and national movements', *Studies in Church History* 9 (1972)), pp. 37–49.

Frend, W. H. C., *The Rise of the Monophysite Movement* (Cambridge, 1972).

Freund, W., 'Burgund in den nationalsozialistischen Planungen, in V. Gallé, (ed.), *Die Burgunder: Ethnogenese und assimilation eines Volkes* (Worms, 2008), pp. 395–420.

Freytag, G., *Bilder aus der deutschen Vergangenheit* (Leipzig, 1859–67).

Fried, M., *Absorption and Theatricality: Painting and Beholder in the Age of Diderot* (Chicago, 1980).

Fröhlich, T., 'The study of the Lombards and the Ostrogoths at the German Archaeological Institute of Rome, 1937–1943', *Fragmenta* 2 (2008), pp. 183–213.

Fubini Leuzzi, M., 'Contributi e discussioni su alcuni aspetti del pensiero storiografico di Cesare Balbo', *Rivista storica italiana* 90 (1978), pp. 834–54.

Fubini Leuzzi, M. (ed.), *Cesare Balbo, Storia d'Italia e altri scritti editi ed inediti* (Turin, 1984).

Fubini Leuzzi, M., 'Metodi e temi della ricerca storica promossa in Piemonte prima e dopo l'Unità', *Archivi e storia nell'Europa del XIX secolo. Alle radice dell'identità culturale europea*, ed. I. Cotta and R. M. Tolu, *Pubblicazioni degli Archivio di Stato, Saggi* 90, vol. 2 (Rome. 2006), pp. 863–81.

Fuchs, S., *Kunst der Ostgotenzeit* (Berlin, 1934).

Fuchs, S., *Die griechischen Gundgruppen der frühen Bronzezeit und ihre auswärtigen Beziehungen: ein Beitrag zur Frage der Indogermanisierung Griechenlands* (Berlin, 1937).

Fuchs, S., *Die langobardischen Goldblattkreuze aus der Zone südwärts der Alpen* (Berlin, 1938).

Fuhrmann, H., *'Sind eben alles Menschen gewesen': Gelehrtenleben im 19. und 20. Jahrhundert* (Munich, 1996).

Fuhrmann, H., 'Die *Monumenta Germaniae Historica* und die Frage einer textkritischen Methode', *Bulletino dell'Istituto storico italiano* 100 (1997), pp. 17–29.

Fustel de Coulanges, N. D., 'De la manière d'écrire l'histoire en France et en Allemagne', *Revue des deux mondes* 101, 1 september 1872, pp. 241–9.

Fustel de Coulanges, N. D., 'L'invasion germanique au Ve siècle, son caractère et ses effets', 15 May 1872, *Revue des Deux Mondes*, pp. 241–68.

Fustel de Coulanges, N. D., 'De l'analyse des textes historiques', *Revue des Questions Historiques* 41 (1887), pp. 5–35.

Fustel de Coulanges, N. D., *Histoire des institutions politiques de l'ancienne France*, ed. C. Jullian, vol. 2, *L'Invasion germanique et la fin de l'Empire* (Paris, 1891).

Fustel de Coulanges, N. D., *The Origin of Property in Land*, trans. M. Ashley, with an introduction by W. J. Ashley (London, 1891).

Fustel de Coulanges, N. D., *Histoire des institutions politiques de l'ancienne France*, ed. C. Jullian, vol. 6, *Les Transformations de la royauté pendant l'époque carolingienne* (Paris, 1892).

Fustel de Coulanges, N. D., *Histoire des institutions politiques de l'ancienne France*, ed. C. Jullian, vol. 5, *Le Bénéfice et le patronat pendant l'époque mérovingienne*, 6th edn (Paris, 1926).
Fustel de Coulanges, N. D., *Histoire des institutions politiques de l'ancienne France*, ed. C. Jullian, vol. 4, *L'Alleu et le domaine rural pendant l'époque mérovingienne*, 4th edn (Paris, 1927).
Fustel de Coulanges, N. D., *Histoire des institutions politiques de l'ancienne France*, ed. C. Jullian, vol. 1, *La Gaule romaine*, 6th edn (Paris, 1929).
Fustel de Coulanges, N. D., *Histoire des institutions politiques de l'ancienne France*, ed. C. Jullian, vol. 3, *La Monarchie franque*, 6th edn (Paris, 1930).
Ganshof, F. L., 'Pirenne, Henri', in *Biographie nationale*, vol. 30 (Brussels, 1959), col. 678–722.
Garrison, M., Nelson, J. L., and Tweddle, D. (eds), *Alcuin and Charlemagne: The Golden Age of York* (York, 2001).
Gasparri, S., 'Gian Piero Bognetti storico dei Longobardi', *La Cultura* 38/1 (2000), pp. 129–40.
Gasparri, S., 'I Germani immaginari e la realità del regno: cinquant'anni di studi sui Longobardi', *Atti del 16o congresso internazionale di studi sull'alto medioevo* (Spoleto, 2003), vol. 1, pp. 3–28.
Gaupp, E. T., *Die germanischen Ansiedlungen und Landtheilungen in den Provinzen des römischen Westreiches* (Breslau, 1844).
Geary, P., *The Myth of Nations: The Medieval Origins of Europe* (Princeton, 2002).
Geary, P., *Historians as Public Individuals*, The Reuter Lecture 2006 (Southampton, 2007).
Geary, P. J., 'Gabriel Monod, Fustel de Coulanges et les aventures de Sichaire: la naissance de l'histoire scientifique au XIXe siècle', in D. Barthélemy, F. Bougard, and R. Le Jan (eds), *La Vengeance, 400–1200* (Rome 2006), pp. 87–99.
Geuenich, D., 'Ein junges Volk macht Geschichte. Herkunft und "Landnahme" der Alamannen' *Die Alamannen* (1997), pp. 73–8.
Ghosh, P., 'The conception of Gibbon's History', in R. McKitterick and R. Quinault (eds), *Gibbon and Empire* (Cambridge, 1997), pp. 271–316.
Giarrizzo, G., 'Il Medioevo tra Otto e Novecentro', in G. Cavallo, C. Leonardi, and E. Menestò (eds), *Lo Spazio letterario del medioevo, 1. Il Medioevo latino*, vol. 4, *L'attualizzazione del testo* (Rome, 1997), pp. 223–60.
Gibbon, E., *The Decline and Fall of the Roman Empire* (London, 1776–88): ed. H. H. Milman, 12 vols (London, 1838–9): *The Decline and Fall, with Variorum notes Including those of Guizot, Wenck, Schreiter, and Hugo*, 7 vols (London, 1872). French trans. M. Leclerq de Septchênes, *Histoire de la décadence et de la chute de l'Empire romain* (Paris, 1777).
Gibbon, E., 'Du gouvernement féodal, surtout en France', in *Miscellaneous Works*, ed. John, Lord Sheffield, vol. 3, *Historical and Critical* (London, 1814), pp. 183–202.
Gibbon, E., 'An examination of Mallet's Introduction to the History of Denmark (1764)', in *Miscellaneous Works by Edward Gibbon*, ed. John Lord Sheffield, Vol. 3, *Historical and Critical* (London, 1814), pp. 231–8.
Gibbon, E., *Letters: The Letters of Edward Gibbon*, ed. J. R. E. Norton, 3 vols (London, 1956).
Gibbon, E., *Memoirs of my Life*, ed. G. A. Bonnard (London, 1966).
Gibbon, E., *Memoirs of my Life and Writings*, ed. A. O. Cockshut and S. Constantine (Keele, 1994).

Gilbhard, H., *Die Thule-Gesellschaft* (Berlin, 1994).

Gillett, A., 'Introduction: ethnicity, history, and methodology', in Gillett, A. (ed.), *On Barbarian Identity: Critical Approaches to Ethnicity in the Early Middle Ages* (Turnhout, 2002.), pp. 1–18.

Gillett, A., *Envoys and Political Communication in the Late Antique West, 411–533* (Cambridge, 2003).

Giry, A., *Histoire de la ville de Saint-Omer et de ses institutions jusqu'au XIVe siècle* (Paris, 1877).

Giry, A., *Manuel de diplomatique* (Paris, 1894).

Gobineau, J.A. comte de, *Essai sur l'inégalité des races humaines*, 4th edn, 2 vols (Paris, *c.* 1920); trans. *The Moral and Intellectual Diversity of Races*, trans. of book 1 (Philadelphia, 1856); trans. A. Collins, *The Inequality of Human Races* (New York, 1915); trans. L. Schemann, *Versuch über die Ungleichheit der Menschenracen* (Stuttgart, 1902–3).

Gobineau, J. A. comte de, *Mademoiselle Irnois and Other Stories*, trans. and ed. A. and D. Smith (Berkeley, 1988).

Goetz, H.-W., Jarnut, J., and Pohl, W. (eds), *Regna and Gentes: The Relationship between Late Antique and Early Medieval Peoples and Kingdoms in the Transformation of the Roman World* (Leiden, 2003).

Goffart, W., *Barbarians and Romans A.D. 418–584. The Techniques of Accommodation* (Princeton, 1980).

Goffart, W., 'From *Historiae* to *Historia Francorum* and back again: aspects of the textual history of Gregory of Tours', in T. F. X. Noble and J. J. Contreni (eds), *Religion, Culture and Society in the Early Middle Ages: Studies in Honour of Richard E. Sullivan* (Kalamazoo, 1987), pp. 55–76.

Goffart, W., *The Narrators of Barbarian History. Jordanes, Gregory of Tours, Bede, and Paul the Deacon* (Princeton, 1988).

Goffart, W., *Historical Atlases: The First Three Hundred Years* (Chicago, 2003).

Goffart, W., *Barbarian Tides. The Migration Age and the Later Roman Empire* (Philadelphia, 2006).

Goldhelm. Reichtümer aus 6000 Jahren rümanischen Vergangenheit (Frankfurt, 1994).

Goldhill, S., *Victorian Culture and Classical Antiquity: Art, Opera, Fiction and the Proclamation of Modernity* (Princeton, 2011).

Goldstein, D. S., 'J. B. Bury's Philosophy of History: a reappraisal', *The American Historical Review* 82 (1977), pp. 896–919.

Goldsworthy, A., *How Rome Fell: The Death of a Superpower* (Yale, 2009).

Gooch, G. P., *History and Historians in the Nineteenth Century* (London, 1913).

Goodrick-Clarke, N., *Black Sun: Aryan Cults, Esoteric Nazism, and the Politics of Identity* (New York, 2003).

Goody, J., *The Development of the Family and Marriage in Europe* (Cambridge, 1983).

Gråberg di Hemsø, J., *La Scandinavie vengée de l'accusation d'avoir produit les peuples barbares qui détruisirent l'Empire de Rome* (Lyons, 1822).

Graceffa, A., 'Race mérovingienne et nation française: les paradoxes du moment romantique dans l'historiographie française de 1815 à 1860', in H. Reimitz and B. Zeller (eds), *Vergangenheit und Vergegenwärtigung* (Vienna, 2009), pp. 59–69.

Graceffa, A., *Les Historiens et la question franque: le peuplement franc et les Mérovingiens dans l'historiographie française et allemande des XIXe–XXe siècles* (Turnhout, 2010).

Grahn-Hoek, H., *Die fränkische Oberschicht im 6. Jahrhundert: Studien zu ihrer rechtlichen und politischen Stellung* (Sigmaringen, 1976).

Graus, F., *Volk, Heiliger und Herrscher: Studien zur Hagiographie der Merowingerzeit* (Prague, 1965).

Graus, F., *Die Nationalbildung der Westslawen im Mittelalter* (Sigmaringen, 1980).

Grillparzer, F., *Weh dem, der lügt*, ed. K. Sternelle (Husum, 2005).

Grimm, J., *Deutsche Grammatik* (Göttingen, 1819).

Grimm, J., *Deutsche Rechtsaltertümer*, 2 vols (Göttingen, 1828).

Grimm, J., *Geschichte der deutschen Sprache*, 2 vols (Berlin, 1848).

Grimm, J., *Kleinere Schriften*, 8 vols (Berlin, 1864–90).

Grimm, J. and W., *Deutsche Sagen*, 2 vols (Berlin, 1816–18).

Grönbech, W., *Kultur und Religion der Germanen* (Darmstadt, 1961).

Gruner, S. M., 'Political historiography in Restoration France', *History and Theory* 8 (3) (1969), pp. 346–65.

Guéranger, P., *Essais sur le naturalisme contemporain* (Paris, 1858).

Guizot, F. P. G., *Essais sur l'histoire de France (pour servir de complement aux Observations de l'histoire de France de l'abbé de Mably)* (Paris, 1823): 7th edn (Paris, 1847).

Guizot, F. P. G., *Histoire générale de la civilisation en Europe: depuis la chute de l'Empire romain jusqu'à la Revolution* (Paris, 1828).

Guizot, F. P. G., *The History of Civilization from the Fall of the Roman Empire to the French Revolution*, trans. W. Hazlitt, 3 vols (London, 1856).

Guizot, F. P. G., *Mémoires pour servir à l'histoire de mon temps*, 8 vols (Paris, 1858–67).

Gumilev, L., *Ethnogenesis and the Biosphere of Earth* (Moscow, 1978).

Hägermann, D., Haubrichs, W., and Jarnut, J. (eds), *Akkulturation: Probleme einer germanisch-romanischen Kultursynthese in Spätantike und frühem Mittelalter* (Berlin, 2004).

Haller, J., *Der Eintritt der Germanen in die Geschichte* (Berlin, 1939).

Halsall, G., 'Movers and Shakers: the barbarians and the Fall of Rome', *Early Medieval Europe* 8 (1999), pp. 132–45; reprinted in T. F. X. Noble (ed.), *From Roman Provinces to Medieval Kingdoms* (New York, 2006), pp. 277–91.

Halsall, G., *Barbarian Migrations and the Roman West 376–568* (Cambridge, 2007).

Hammerstein, N., *Die Deutsche Forschungsgemeinschaft in der Weimarer Republik und im Dritten Reich. Wissenschaftspolitik in Republik und Diktatur* (Munich, 1999).

Hancock, R. C., and Lambert, L. G. (eds), *The Legacy of the French Revolution* (Lanham MD, 1996).

Hanquet, K., 'Godefroid Kurth', *Mélanges Godefroid Kurth; recueil de mémoires relatifs à l'histoire, à la philologie et à l'archéologie*, vol. 1, *Mémoires historiques* (Liège, 1908), pp. xx–xxxvii.

Härke, H., 'All quiet on the Western Front? Paradigms, methods and approaches in West German archaeology', in I. Hodder (ed.), *Archaeological Theory in Europe* (London, 1991), pp. 187–222.

Härke, H., ' "The Hun is a methodical chap." Reflections on the German tradition of pre- and proto-history', in P. J. Ucko (ed.), *Theory in Archaeology: A World Perspective* (London, 1995), pp. 46–60.

Hartog, F., *Le XIXe siècle et l'histoire: le cas Fustel de Coulanges*, 2nd edn (with new preface) (Paris, 2001).

Harrison, K., 'Woden', in G. Bonner (ed.), *Famulus Christi* (London, 1976), pp. 351–6.

Harrison, R., Jones, A., and Lambert, P., 'The institutionalisation and organisation of history', in P. Lambert and P. Schofield (eds), *Making History: An Introduction to the History and Practices of a Discipline* (London, 2004), pp. 9–25.

Hartley, E., Hawkes, J., Henig, M., and Mee, F. (eds), *Constantine the Great: York's Roman Emperor* (Aldershot, 2006).

Harvie, C., *The Lights of Liberalism: University Liberals and the Challenge of Democracy 1860–86* (London, 1976).

Hastings, A., *A History of English Christianity 1920–1990* (London, 1991).

Haubrichs, W., '*Germania submersa*: Zur Fragen der Quantität und Dauer germanischer Siedlungsinseln im romanischen Lothringen und in Südbelgien', in H. Burger, A. Maas, and P. von Matt (eds), *Verborum Amor: Studien zur Geschichte und Kunst der deutschen Sprache. Festschrift für Stefan Sonderegger zum 65* (Berlin, 1992), pp. 633–66.

Haubrichs, W., 'Der Krieg der Professoren. Sprachhistorische und sprachpolitische Argumentation in der Auseinandersetzung um Elsaß-Lothringen zwischen 1870 und 1914', in R. Marti (ed.), *Sprachenpolitik in Grenzregionen* (Saarbrücken, 1996), pp. 213–49.

Hayward, P. A., 'Demystifying the role of sanctity in Western Christendom', in J. Howard-Johnston and P. A. Hayward (eds), *The Cult of Saints in Late Antiquity and the Early Middle Ages* (Oxford, 1999), pp. 115–42.

Hazlitt, W., 'Biographical notice of M. Augustin Thierry', in A. Thierry, *History of the Conquest of England by the Normans; its causes, and its consequences, in England, Scotland, Ireland, and on the Continent*, trans. W. Hazlitt, 2 vols (London, 1847), vol. 1.

Heather, P., 'The Crossing of the Danube and the Gothic Conversion', *Greek, Roman and Byzantine Studies* 27 (1986), pp. 289–318.

Heather, P., *The Goths* (Oxford, 1996).

Heather, P., *The Fall of the Roman Empire: A New history* (London, 2005).

Heather, P., *Empires and Barbarians: Migration, Development and the Birth of Europe* (London, 2009).

Heffernan, M., 'History, geography and the French national space: the question of Alsace-Lorraine, 1914–18', *Space and Polity* 5, 1 (2001), pp. 27–48.

Herder, J. G., *Auch eine Philosophie der Geschichte* (Göttingen, 1774).

Hidalgo, M. J., Pérez, D., and Gervás, M. J. R. (eds), '*Romanización*' y '*Reconquista*' en la península Ibérica. Nuevas perspectivas* (Salamanca, 1998).

Hillgarth, J. N., 'Spanish historiography and Iberian reality', *History and Theory* 24, 1 (1985), pp. 23–43.

Hingley, R., *Roman Officers and British Gentlemen. The Imperial Origins of Roman Archaeology* (London, 2000).

Hingley, R., *The Recovery of Roman Britain 1586–1906: A Colony so Fertile* (Oxford, 2008).

Hirschi, C., *Wettkampf der Nationen. Konstruktionen einer deutschen Ehrgemeinschaft an der Wende vom Mittelalter zur Neuzeit* (Gottingen, 2005).

Hodgkin, T., *Italy and her Invaders*, 8 vols (Oxford, 1880–99); new edition, ed. P. Heather; T. Hodgkin, *The Barbarian Invasions of the Roman Empire*, 8 vols (London, 2000–2003).

Hodgkin, T., *Theodoric the Goth: The Barbarian Champion of Civilisation* (London, 1893).

Hodgkin, T., *History of England from the Earliest Times to the Norman Conquest* (London, 1906).

Höfler, O., *Kultische Geheimbünde der Germanen* (Frankfurt, 1934).

Höfler, O., *Germanisches Sakralkönigtum* (Tübingen, 1952).

Horden, P., and Purcell, N., *The Corrupting Sea: A Study of Mediterranean History* (Oxford, 2000).

Horsman, R., 'Origins of racial Anglo-Saxonism in Great Britain before 1850', *Journal of the History of Ideas* 37 (1976), pp. 387–410.

Hotman, F., *Franco-Gallia* (Latin) (Geneva, 1573), (French) (Cologne, 1574); English trans., Francis Hotoman (*sic*), *Franco-Gallia or, an Account of the Ancient Free State of France and Most Other Parts of Europe, before the Loss of their Libeties* (London, 1711).

Housden, M., *Resistance and Conformity in the Third Reich* (London, 1997).

Howard-Johnston, J., 'Introduction', in J. Howard-Johnston and P. A. Hayward, *The Cult of Saints in Late Antiquity and the Early Middle Ages* (Oxford, 1999), pp. 1–24.

Hravti I Karolinzi, ed. Milosevic, A. 2 vols (Split, 2000).

Hruza, K., 'Alfons Dopsch (1868–1953), *Österreichische Historiker 1900–1945* (Vienna, 2008), pp. 155–90.

Hume, D., *History of England from the Invasion of Julius Caesar to the Revolution in 1688*, vol. 1 (London, 1754).

Hume, D., 'Of the populousness of Ancient Nations', *Essay XXXIII*, in D. Hume, *Essays Moral, Political and Literary* (London, 1875), pp. 222–69.

Hussey, J. M., 'Norman Hepburn Baynes (1877–1961)', *Oxford Dictionary of National Biography*.

I Goti (Milan, 1994).

I Longobardi (Milan, 1990).

Il tesoro di Domagnano (Milan, 1995).

In Memoriam Eugen Ewig, Alma Mater 101 (Bonn, 2007).

Innis, H. A., 'Charles Norris Cochrane, 1889–1945', *The Canadian Journal of Economics and Political Science* 12 (1946), pp. 95–7.

Irsigler, F., *Untersuchungen zur Geschichte des frühfränkischen Adels* (Bonn, 1969).

Isbell, J. C., *The Birth of European Romanticism: Truth and Propaganda in Staël's 'De l'Allemagne', 1810–1813* (Cambridge, 1994).

Jackson, G., ed. Lady Jackson, *The Bath Archives: a further selection from the diaries and letters of Sir George Jackson, K. C. H. from 1809 to 1816*, 2 vols, (London, 1873).

James, E., 'Cemeteries and the problem of Frankish settlement in Gaul', in P. H. Sawyer (ed.), *Names, Words and Graves* (Leeds, 1979), pp. 55–89.

Jansen, C., 'Warum es in Italien keine Volksgeschichte wie im "Dritten Reich" gab: Zum Verhältnis von Geschichtswissenschaft und faschistischem Regime', in M. Hettling (ed.), *Volksgeschichte im Europa der Zwischenkriegszeit* (Göttingen, 2003), pp. 120–46.

Jedin, H., *Kardinal Caesar Baronius: der Anfang der katholischen Kirchengeschichtsschreibung im 16. Jahrhundert* (Aschendorff, 1978).

Johnson, D., *Guizot, Aspects of French History, 1787–1874* (London, 1963).

Joly, M., *Dialogue aux enfers entre Machiavel et Montesquieu* (Geneva, 1864).

Jones, A. H. M., *The Later Roman Empire, 284–601: A Social, Economic and Administrative Survey*, 3 vols (Oxford, 1964).

Jones, A. H. M., *The Decline of the Ancient World* (London, 1966).

Jones, C., *The Great Nation: France from Louis XV to Napoleon* (London, 2002).

Jones, S., *The Archaeology of Ethnicity* (London, 1997).

Jong, M. de, 'Johann Friedrich Böhmer (1795–1863): romanticus en rijkspatriot', in *De Middeleeuwen in de negentiende eeuw* (Hilversum, 1996), pp. 63–72.

Jullian, C., *Le Rhin gaulois: le Rhin français* (Paris, 1915).

Jullian, C., *L'Alsace française: à un ami du front* (Paris, 1917).

Jullian, C., *La Guerre pour la patrie* (Paris, 1919).

Jullian, C., *Aimons la France, conférences: 1914–1919* (Paris, 1920).

Junghans, W., *Histoire de Childéric et de Chlodovech*, trans. G. Monod (Paris, 1879).

Junker, K., 'Research under dictatorship: the German Archaeological Institute 1929–1945', *Antiquity* 72 (1998), pp. 282–92.

Kaufmann, M., *Charles Kingsley: Christian Socialist and Social Reformer* (London, 1892).

Kavanagh, J., *The Ice Museum* (London, 2005).

Kelly, G., 'Adrien de Valois and the chapter headings in Ammianus Marcellinus', *Classical Philology* 104 (2009), pp. 233–42.

Kemble, J. M., *The Anglo-Saxon Poems of Beowulf, The Traveller's Song and the Battle of Finnes-burh* (London, 1833).

Kemble, J. M. *History of the Saxons in England* (London, 1849).

Kennedy, H., *The Prophet and the Age of the Caliphates*, 2nd edn (London, 2004).

Kennedy, H., *The Great Arab Conquests: How the Spread of Islam Changed the World we Live In* (London, 2007).

Ker, I. T., *John Henry Newman: A Biography* (Oxford, 1988).

Kern, F., *Gottesgnadentum und Widerstandsrecht im früheren Mittelalter: zur Entwicklungsgeschichte der Monarchie* (Leipzig, 1914).

Keys, D., *Catastrophe: An Investigation into the Origins of the Modern World* (London, 1999).

Kiernan, K., *The Thorkelin Transcripts of Beowulf* (Copenhagen, 1986).

Kiernan, K., 'The legacy of Wiglaf: saving a wounded Beowulf', in P. S. Baker (ed.), *Beowulf: Basic Readings* (New York, 1995), pp. 195–218.

King, C., *A History of Italian Unity, Being a Political History of Italy from 1814 to 1871*, 2 vols (London, 1899).

Kingsley, C., *Hypatia or New Foes with an Old Face* (London, 1853).

Kingsley, C., *Alexandria and her Schools* (Cambridge, 1854).

Kingsley, C., *The Roman and the Teuton* (Cambridge, 1864).

Kingsley, C., *The Hermits* (London, 1869).

Kingsley, F. E., *Charles Kingsley. His Letters and Memories of his Life*, 2 vols (London, 1877).

Klingshirn, W. E., and Vessey, M. (eds), *The Limits of Ancient Christianity: Essays on Late Antique Thought and Culture in Honor of R. A. Markus* (Ann Arbor, 1999).

Knowles, D., *Great Historical Enterprises* (London, 1963).

Kossinna, G., *Die Herkunft der Germanen: Zur Methode der Siedlungsarchäologie* (Würzburg, 1911).

Kossinna, G., *Die deutsche Vorgeschichte: eine hervorragend nationale Wissenschaft* (Würzburg, 1914).

Kossinna, G., *Die deutsche Ostmark* (Kattowitz, 1919); reprinted as *Das Weichselland, ein uralter Heimatboden der Germanen* (Danzig, 1919).

Krebs, C. R., *A Most Dangerous Book. Tacitus's Germania from the Roman Empire to the Third Reich* (New York, 2011).

Kurth, G., *Les Origines de la civilisation moderne*, 2 vols (Louvain, 1886).

Kurth, G., *Histoire poétique des Mérovingiens* (Paris, 1893).

Kurth, G., *Clovis, le fondateur*, 2 vols (Tours, 1896).

Kurth, G., *La Frontière linguistique en Belgique et dans le Nord de la France*, 2 vols (Brussels, 1896–8).

Kurth, G., *Saint Boniface (650–755)* (Paris, 1902); trans. V. Day (Milwaukee, 1935).

Kurth, G., *Sainte Clothilde* (Paris, 1912); trans. V. M. Crawford, *Saint Clotilda* (London, 1898).

Kurth, G., *The Church at the Turning Points of History*, trans. V. Day (Helena, Montana, 1918).

Kurth, G., *Études franques*, 2 vols (Paris, 1919).

La Rocca, C., and Gasparri, S., 'Forging an early medieval couple: Agilulf, Theodelinda and the "Lombard Treasure" (1888–1932)', in W. Pohl and M. Mehofer (eds), *Archaeology of Identity: Archäologie der Identität* (Vienna, 2010), pp. 269–87.

Lacoste, C., 'Les Gaulois d'Amédée Thierry', in P. Viallaneix and J. Ehrard (eds), *Nos ancêtres les Gaulois, Actes du Colloque international de Clermont-Ferrand* (Clermont-Ferrand, 1982), pp. 203–9.

La Liberté de la parole évangélique: écrits, conférences, lettres, ed. A. Duval and J.-P. Jossua (Paris, 1996).

Lamargue, P., *Le Sacre de S. M. l'Empereur Napoléon, 2 decembre 1804, dans l'église metropolitaine de Paris le XI Frimaire an XIII* (Paris, 1805).

Lambert, P., and Schofield, P. (eds), *Making History: An Introduction to the History and Practices of a Discipline* (London, 2004).

Lapidge, M. (ed), *Interpreters of Early Medieval Britain* (Oxford, 2002).

Larrere, C., '"La République des Armoriques", une fiction politique de l'abbé Dubos', in P. Viallaneix and J. Ehrard (eds), *Nos ancêtres les Gaulois, Actes du Colloque International de Clermont-Ferrand* (Clermont-Ferrand, 1982), pp. 51–8.

Latouche, R., *Les Grandes Invasions et la crise de l'Occident au Ve siècle* (Paris, 1946).

Le Tourneau, R., 'Biographie de Christian Courtois (1912–1956), *Revue Africaine* 101 (1957), pp. 433–4.

Lecanuet, E., *Montalembert*, 3 vols (Paris, 1903–5).

Leerssen, J., *National Thought in Europe: A Cultural History* (Amsterdam, 2006).

Leffler, P. K., 'French Historians and the challenge to Louis XIV's absolutism', *French Historical Studies* 14 (1985), pp. 1–22.

Legendre, J.-P. 'Sites fouillés et thèmes de recherche en Moselle: les fouilles d'Ennery (1941) et de Saint-Pierre-aux-Nonnains (1942)', in A.-M. Adam et al. (eds), *L'Archéologie en Alsace et en Moselle au temps de l'annexion (1940–1944)* (Wasselonne, 2001), pp. 67–73.

Leland, W. G., 'The International Congress of Historical Sciences held at Brussels', *The American Historical Review* 28 (1923), pp. 639–55.

Leo, H., *Entwicklung der Verfassung der lombardischen Städte* (Hamburg, 1824); trans. C. Balbo, *Vicende della costituzione delle città lombarde fino alla discesa di Federico I imperatore in Italia* (Turin, 1836).

Leo, H., *Geschichte der italienischen Staaten*, vol. 1 (Hamburg, 1829).

Lépinay, F. M. de, *Peintures et sculptures du Panthéon* (Paris, 1997).

Leveto, P. D., 'The Marian themes of the frescoes in S. Maria at Castelseprio', *The Art Bulletin* 72, 3 (1990), pp. 393–413.

Lex Salica, ed. J. Merkel, with a foreword by J. Grimm (Berlin, 1850); ed., K. A. Eckhardt, *Monumenta Germaniae Historica* (Hannover, 1962, 1969).

Liebeschuetz, W., 'The Birth of Late Antiquity', *Antiquité Tardive* 12 (2004), pp. 253–61.

Lilie, R.-J., '*Gens Perfidus* oder Edle Einfalt, Stille Größe? Zum Byzanzbild in Deutschland während des 19. Jahrhunderts am Beispiel Felix Dahns', *Klio* 69 (1987), pp. 181–203.

Lindsay, S. G., 'Mummies and tombs: Turenne, Napoléon, and death ritual', *The Art Bulletin* 82, 3 (2000), pp. 476–502.

Lingard, J., *The Antiquities of the Anglo-Saxon Church*, 2 vols (Newcastle-upon-Tyne, 1806).

Little, L. K. (ed.), *Plague and the End of Antiquity: The Pandemic of 541–750* (Cambridge, 2007).

Little, L.K., and Rosenwein, B.H. (eds), *Debating the Middle Ages, Issues and Readings* (Oxford, 1998).

Liutprand, *Relatio de Legatione Constantinopolitana*, ed. A. Bauer and A. Rau, *Quellen zur Geschichte der sächsischen Kaiserzeit* (Darmstadt, 1971), pp. 524–89; trans. F. A. Wright, ed. J. J. Norwich, *Liudprand of Cremona: The Embassy to Constantinople and other writings* (London, 1993).

Lollis, C. de, *Alessandro Manzoni e gli storici liberali francesi della restaurazione* (Bari, 1926).

L'Or des princes barbares. Du Caucase à la Gaule Ve siècle après J.-C. (Paris, 2000).

L'Orange, H. P., *Art Forms and Civic Life in the Late Roman Empire* (Princeton, 1965).

L'Orange, H. P., and von Gerkan, A., *Der spätantike Bildschmuck des Konstantinsbogen* (Berlin, 1939).

Locas, C., 'Christopher Dawson: A Bibliography', *The Harvard Theological Review* 66, 2 (1973), pp. 177–206.

Lombard, A., *L'Abbé Du Bos: un initiateur de la pensée moderne (1670–1742)* (Paris, 1913).

Lorcin, P. M. E, review of Owen White, *Children of the French Empire: Miscegenation and Colonial Society in French West Africa 1895–1960* (Oxford, 1999), in *The American Historical Review* 106, 4 (2001), pp. 1507–8.

Lot, F., *Les Invasions germaniques: La pénétration mutuelle du monde barbare et du monde romain* (Paris, 1935).

Lot, F., *Les Invasions barbares et le peuplement de l'Europe: introduction à l'intelligence des derniers traités de paix*, vol. 1, *Arabes et Maures—Scandinaves—Slavs du Sud et du Centre*: vol. 2, *Slaves de l'Est.—Finno-Ougriens.—Turcs et Mongols.—États issus de la décomposition des Empire du Centre et de l'Est* (Paris, 1937).

Lot, F., *La Fin du monde antique et le debut du Moyen Âge*, 2nd edn (Paris, 1952).

Lot, F., Pfister, C., and. Ganshof, F. L., *Les Destinées de l'empire en occident de 395 à 888* (Paris, 1928).

Loyen, A., *Recherches historiques sur les panégyriques de Sidoine Apollinaire* (Paris, 1942).

Loyen, A., *Sidoine Apollinaire et l'esprit précieux en Gaule aux derniers jours de l'Empire* (Paris, 1943).

Loyen, A., 'Résistants et collaborateurs en Gaule à l'époque des grandes invasions', *Bulletin de l'Association Guillaume Budé* 22 (1963), pp. 437–50.

Luttwak, E. N., *The Grand Strategy of the Roman Empire* (Baltimore, 1976).

Lyon, B., 'The letters of Henri Pirenne to Karl Lamprecht (1894–1915)', *Bulletin de la Commission Royale d'Histoire* 132 (1966), pp. 161–231.

Lyon, B., 'Henri Pirenne's *Réflexions d'un solitaire* and his re-evaluation of history', *Journal of Medieval History* 23, 3 (1997), pp. 285–99.

Lyttelton, A., 'Creating a national past: history, myth and image in the Risorgimento', in A. R. Ascoli and K. von Henneberg (eds), *Making and Remaking Italy: The Cultivation of National Identity around the Risorgimento* (Oxford, 2001), pp. 27–74.

Lyttelton, A., 'Sismondi's *Histoire des Républiques italiennes* and the Risorgimento', *Annales Benjamin Constant* 31–32 (2007), pp. 351–66.

Mabillon, J., *Acta Sanctorum ordinis sancti Benedicti*, 3rd edn (Mâcon, 1935).

Mably, G. Bonnot de, *Collection complete des oeuvres de l'Abbé de Mably*, 15 vols (Paris, An III = 1794/5).

Mably, G. Bonnot de, *De la manière d'écrire l'Histoire: collection complete des oeuvres de l'Abbé de Mably* (Paris, An III = 1794/5), vol. 12, pp. 367–565; English trans., *Two dialogues, concerning the manner of writing of history* (London, 1783).

Mably, G. Bonnot de, *Observations sur l'histoire de la France*, in *Collection complete des oeuvres de l'Abbé de Mably* (Paris, An III = 1794/5), vol. 1, pp. 129–214.

MacDougall, H. A., *Racial Myth in English History: Trojans, Teutons and Anglo-Saxons* (Montreal, 1982).

Macmillan, M., *The Uses and Abuses of History* (London, 2008).

Magnus, I., *Historia de omnibus Gothorum Sueonumque Regibus* (Rome, 1554).

Magnus, O., *Historia de gentibus septentrionalibus* (Rome, 1555).

Maischberger, M., 'German archaeology during the Third Reich, 1933–45: a case study based on archival evidence', *Antiquity* 76 (2002), pp. 209–18.

Mallet, P. H., *Introduction à l'histoire de Dannemarc, où l'on traite de la religion, des loix des mœurs et des usages des Anciens Danois* (Copenhagen, 1755).

Mallet, P. H., *Monuments de la mythologie et de la poésie des Celtes et particulierement des ancient Scandinaves* (Copenhagen, 1756).

Mallet, P. H., *Northern antiquities: or, A description of the manners, customs, religion and laws of the Ancient Danes, and other northern nations; including those of our own Saxon ancestors. With a translation of the Edda… in two volumes: Translated from Mons. Mallet's Introduction à l'histoire de Dannemarc, &c. with additional notes by the English translator* (Bishop *Thomas Percy of Dromore), and Goranson's Latin version of the Edda* (London, 1770).

Manacorda, D., *Museo Nationale Romano: Crypta Balbi* (Milan, 2000).

Mandler, P., 'Race and nation in mid-Victorian thought', in S. Collini, B. Whatmore, and B. Young (eds), *History, Religion and Culture: British Intellectual History 1750–1950* (Cambridge, 2000), pp. 224–44.

Manzoni, A., *Lettere* I, ed. A. Chiari and F. Ghisalberti, *Tutte le opere di Alessandro Manzoni*, VII, (Milan, 1970).

Manzoni, A., *Adelchi*, ed. M. Martelli (Florence, 1973), vol. 1, pp. 165–227: trans. F. B. Deigan, *Alessandro Manzoni's The Count of Carmagnola and Adelchis* (Baltimore, 2004).

Manzoni, A., *Osservazioni sulla morale cattolica* (1819), ed. M. Martelli and R. Bacchelli, *Manzoni, Tutte le opere*, 2 vols (Florence, 1973), vol. 2, pp. 1335–461.

Manzoni, A. *Discorso sopra alcuni punti della storia longobardica in Italia*, ed. I. Becherucci (Milan, 2005): see also A. Manzoni, *Tutte le Opere*, ed. M. Martelli (Florence, 1973), vol. 2, pp. 1981–2071.

Marcellinus Comes, ed. B. Croke, *The Chronicle of Marcellinus* (Sydney, 1995).

Marchand, S. L., *Down from Olympus: archaeology and philhellenism in Germany, 1750–1970* (Princeton, 1996).

Markus, R. A., *Saeculum: History and Society in the Theology of Saint Augustine* (Cambridge, 1970).

Markus, R. A., 'Christianity and Dissent in Roman North Africa', *Studies in Church History* 9 (1972).

Markus, R. A., *Christianity in the Roman World* (London, 1974).

Markus, R. A., *The End of Ancient Christianity* (Cambridge, 1990).

Markus, R. A., *Gregory the Great and his World* (Cambridge, 1997).

Markus, R. A., 'Between Marrou and Brown: transformations of Late Antique Christianity', in P. Rousseau and M. Papoutsakis (eds), *Transformations of Late Antiquity. Essays for Peter Brown* (Farnham, 2009), pp. 1–13.

Marmontel, J.-F., *Bélisaire* (Paris, 1767); ed. R. Granderout (Paris, 1994).

Marrou, H. I., *Mousikos Aner: étude sur les scènces de la vie intellectuelle figurant sur les monuments funéraires romains* (Grenoble, 1938).

Marrou, H. I., *Saint Augustin et la fin de la culture antique* (Paris, 1938); 2nd edn (Paris, 1949).

Marrou, H. I., *Histoire de l'éducation dans l'antiquité* (Paris, 1948).

Marrou, H. I., *Retractatio*, in id., *Saint Augustin et la fin de la culture*, 2nd edn (Paris, 1949), pp. 623–702.

Marrou, H. I., *Saint Augustin et l'augusstinisme* (Paris, 1955).

Marrou, H. I., *Décadence ou antiquité tardive? IIIe–VIe siècle* (Paris, 1977).

Martens, J., 'The Vandals: myths and facts about a Germanic tribe of the first half of the 1st millenium AD', in S. J. Shennan (ed.), *Archaeological approaches to cultural identity* (London, 1989), pp. 57–65.

Martin, G., 'Verdi and the Risorgimento', in W. Weaver and M. Chusid (ed), *A Verdi Companion* (London, 1980), pp. 13–41.

Martin, G. H., 'Thomas Hodgkin', *Oxford Dictionary of National Biography*.

Martin, N., 'Nietzsche as Hate-Figure in Britain's Great War: "The Execrable Neech"', in F. Bridgham (ed.), *The First World War as a Calsh of Cultures* (Rochester, NY, 200), pp. 147–66.

Martindale, J. R., *Prosopography of the Later Roman Empire*, vol. 2, *A.D. 395–527* (Cambridge, 1980).

Marty L., *Le Prince de Broglie et Dom Guéranger* (Paris, 1859).

Marx, K., and Engels, F., *Karl Marx-Friedrich Engels Gesamtausgabe, Dritte Abteilung, Briefwechsel*, vol. 5 (Berlin, 1987).

Marx, K., and Engels, F., *The Communist Manifesto*, Marxists Internet Archive (2010).

Mascov, J. J., *In Q. Horatii Flacci satiras* (Leipzig, 1714–1716).

Mascov [Mascou], J. J., *Geschichte der Teutschen bis zu Anfang der Fränckischen Monarchie* (Leipzig, 1726–37): *The History of the Ancient Germans, including that of the Cimbri, Celtae, Teutones, Alemanni, Saxons, and other Northern Nations, who overthrew the Roman Empire and established that of the Germans, and most of the Kingdoms of Europe, trans. Thomas Lediard, Late Secretary to his Majesty's Envoy Extraordinary in Lower Germany*, 2 vols (London, 1737/8).

Mattingly, D. J., *Imperialism, Power and Identity: Experiencing the Roman Empire* (Princeton, 2011).

Maurras, C., *Le Duc Albert de Broglie (1901)*, Édition électronique <http://www.maurras.net>.

McKitterick, R., 'Edward Gibbon and the early Middle Ages in eighteenth-century Europe', in R. T. McKitterick and R. Quinault (eds), *Gibbon and Empire* (Cambridge, 1997), pp. 162–89.

McKitterick R., and Quinault, R. (eds), *Edward Gibbon and Empire* (Cambridge, 1997).

Mees, B., 'Hitler and *Germanentum*', *Journal of Contemporary History* 39, 2 (*Understanding Nazi Germany*) (2004), pp. 255–70.

Mees, B., '*Germanische Sturmflut*: from the Old Norse twilight to the Fascist new dawn', *Studia Neophilologica* 78 (2006), pp. 184–98.

Meier, D., 'The North Sea Coastal Area: settlement history from Roman to early medieval times', in D. H. Green and F. Siegmund (eds), *The Continental Saxons from the Migration Period to the Tenth Century* (Woodbridge, 2003), pp. 37–76.

Menghin, W., 'The Merovingian period—Europe without borders: an introductory survey of the exhibition theme', in Menghin, W. (ed.), *The Merovingian Period: Europe without Borders* (Berlin, 2007), pp. 26–54.

Menghin, W. (ed.), *The Merovingian Period: Europe without Borders* (Berlin, 2007).

Merrills, A., 'The Origins of "Vandalism"', *International Journal of the Classical Tradition* 16 (2009), pp. 155–75.

Merrills, A., and Miles, R., *The Vandals* (Oxford, 2010).

Michaelis-Jena, R., 'Early exchanges on oral traditions: two unpublished letters by Robert Jamieson and Wilhelm Grimm', *Folklore* 86 (1975), pp. 42–7.

Michelet, J., *Histoire de France*: new edition, vol. 1, *Les Celtes—les Gaulois—Les Francs—Le monde germanique—Les Mérovingiens—Les Carolingiens* (Paris, 1881).

Mills, E. E., *The Decline and Fall of the British Empire: a brief account of those causes which resulted in the destruction of our late ally, together with a comparison between the British and Roman Empire. Appointed for use in the National Schools of Japan. Tokio, 2005* (Oxford, 1905).

Molesworth, R., *An Account of Denmark as it was in the year 1692* (London, 1694).

Mollnau, K. A., 'The contributions of Savigny to the Theory of Legislation', *The American Journal of Comparative Law* 37, 1 (1989), pp. 81–93.

Momigliano, A., 'Gibbon's contribution to historical method', in A. Momigliano, *Studies in Historiography* (London, 1966), pp. 40–55.

Momigliano, A., 'Gibbon from an Italian point of view', in G. Bowersock, J. Clive, J., and S. R. Graubard (eds), *Edward Gibbon and the Decline and Fall of the Roman Empire* (Cambridge, Mass., 1977), pp. 75–85.

Momigliano, A., 'Two types of universal history: the cases of E. A. Freeman and Max Weber', *Journal of Modern History* 58, 1 (1986), pp. 235–46.

Mommsen, T., *Histoire romaine* vol. 8 trans. C. A. Alexandre (Paris, 1872).

Mommsen, T., 'Agli Italiani', ed. G. Liberati, *Quaderni di Storia* (1976), pp. 197–247.

Mommsen, W., *The Age of Bureaucracy: Perspectives on the Political Sociology of Max Weber* (Oxford, 1974).

Monnoyeur, J.-B., *Joris-Karl Huysmans, converti et oblat de Liguqé* (Liguqé, 1934).

Monod, G., *Allemands et Français, souvenirs de campagne* (Paris, 1871).

Monod, G., 'Études critiques sur les sources de l'histoire mérovingienne 1: Grégoire de Tours, Marius d'Avenches', *Bibliothèque de l'École des hautes études* 8 (1872).

Monod, G., 'Études critiques sur les sources de l'histoire mérovingienne 2: La compilation dite de Frédégaire', *Bibliothèque de l'École des hautes études* 63 (1885).

Monod, G., 'Les aventures de Sichaire: commentaire des chapitres xlvii du Livre VII et xix du Livre IX de l'Histoire des Francs de Grégoire de Tours', *Revue Historique* 1 (1886), pp. 259–90.

Monod, G., *Portraits et souvenirs* (Paris, 1897).

Monod, G. [P. Molé], *Exposé impartial de l'affair Dreyfus* (Paris, 1899).

Montalembert, C. F. R., Comte de, *Les moines d'Occident*, 7 vols (Paris, 1860–77); trans. M. Oliphant, *The Monks of the West from St Benedict to St Bernard*, 6 vols (Edinburgh, 1867).

Montalembert, C. F. R., Comte de, *Journal intime inédit*, ed. L. le Guillou and N. Roger-Taillarde, 2 vols (Paris, 1990).

Montesquieu, C. de Secondat, baron de, *Lettres persanes* (Paris, 1721).

Montesquieu, C. de Secondat, baron de, *Considérations sur la grandeur des romains et de leur décadence* (1734), ed. J. Charvet, *Considérations sur la grandeur des romains et de leur décadence, avec commentaires et notes de Frédéric-le-Grand* (Paris, 1879); trans. D. Lowenthal, *Considerations of the Causes of the Greatness of the Romans and their Decadence* (Ithaca, 1965).

Montesquieu, C. de Secondat, baron de, *De l'esprit des loix* (1748), ed. J. Brethe de la Gressaye, vol. 4 (Paris, 1961).

Montlosier, F. D. de Reynaud, comte de, *De la monarchie française*, 3 vols (Paris, 1814–15).

Möser, J., *Osnabrückische Geschichte*, 2nd edn (Osnabrück, 1780).

Müller, M., *Biographies of Words and the Home of the Aryas* (London, 1888).

Müller, P. E., *Dansk Litteratur-Tidende* (1815), 26, pp. 401–16.

Murphy, C., *Are we Rome? The End of an Empire and the Fate of America* (Boston, 2007).

Murphy, M., 'Antiquary to Academic: the progress of Anglo-Saxon scholarship', in C. T. Berkhout and M. McC. Gatch (eds), *Anglo-Saxon Scholarship: The First Three Centuries* (Boston, Mass., 1982), pp. 1–17.

Murphy, R. T., *The Heroic Earth: Geopolitical Thought in Weimar Germany, 1918–1933* (Kent, Ohio, 1997).

Murray, A. C., 'The position of the *grafio* in the constitutional history of Merovingian Gaul', *Speculum* 64 (1986), pp. 787–805.

Murray, A. C., 'From Roman to Frankish Gaul: "Centenarii" and "Centenae" in the administration of the Frankish kingdom', *Traditio* 44 (1988), pp. 59–100.

Murray, A. C., 'Introduction: Walter André Goffart', in A. C. Murray (ed), *After Rome's Fall. Narrators and sources of early medieval history* (Toronto, 1998), pp. 3–7.

Murray, A. C., 'Reinhard Wenskus on "Ethnogenesis", Ethnicity, and the Origin of the Franks', in A. Gillett, (ed.), *On Barbarian Identity. Critical approaches to Ethnicity in the Early Middle Ages* (Turnhout, 2002), pp. 39–68.

Murray, A. C., *Gregory of Tours: the Merovingians* (Peterborough, Canada, 2006).

Nabholz, H., 'Alfons Dopsch (1868–1953)—Nécrologie', *Revue Suisse d'Histoire* 3 (1955), pp. 383–4.

Navarro, J. M. de, 'Hector Munro Chadwick, 1870–1947', *Proceedings of the British Academy* 33 (1947), pp. 307–30, reprinted in M. Lapidge (ed.), *Interpreters of Early Medieval Britain* (Oxford, 2002), pp. 195–218.

Negri, F., *Viaggio settentrionale* (Padua, 1700).

Nelson, J. L., *Leadership in Society and the Academy*, Queen's Gender Initiative Lectures, 1 (Belfast, 2010).

Neuhaus, S., *Literatur und nationale Einheit in Deutschland* (Tübingen, 2002).

Newman, J. H., *The Arians of the Fourth Century* (London, 1833).

Newman, J. H., *The Church of the Fathers* (London, 1840).

Newman, J. H., *Callista* (London, 1855).

Nichols, A., 'Christopher Dawson's Catholic Setting', in S. Caldecott and J. Morrill (eds), *Eternity in Time: Christopher Dawson and the Catholic Idea of History* (Edinburgh, 1977), pp. 25–49.

Nicolet, C., *La Fabrique d'une nation: la France entre Rome et les Germains* (Paris, 2003).

Niemann, M., 'Karl August Eckhardt', in M. Schmoeckel (ed.), *Die Juristen der Universität Bonn im 'Dritten Reich'* (Bonn, 2004), pp. 160–84.

Noble, T. F. X. (ed.), *From Roman Provinces to Medieval Kingdoms* (New York, 2006).

Noble, T. F. X., *Images, Iconoclasm, and the Carolingians* (Phildalphia, 2009).

Noonkester, M. C., 'Gibbon and the clergy: private virtues, public vices', *Harvard Theological Review* 83 (1990), pp. 399–414.

Nuber, H. U., 'Seitenwende rechts des Rheins: Rom und die Alamamnen', in *Die Alamannen* (1997), pp. 59–68.

Nußbaumer, T., *Alfred Quellmalz und seine Südtiroler Feldforschungen 1940–1942* (Innsbruck, 2001).

Ó Cróinín, D., 'Hiberno-Latin literature to 1169', in D. Ó Cróinín (ed.), *A New History of Ireland*, vol. 1, *Prehistoric and Early Ireland* (Oxford, 2005), pp. 371–404.

O'Donnell, J. J., *The Ruin of the Roman Empire* (London, 2009).

O'Meara, K., *Frédéric Ozanam. Professor at the Sorbonne* (Edinburgh, 1876).

Oberkrone, W., 'Entwicklungen und Varianten der deutschen Volksgeschichte (1900–1960)', in M. Hettling (ed.), *Volksgeschichten im Europa der Zwischenkriegzeit* (Göttingen, 2003), pp. 65–95.

Olivier, L., 'L'archéologie nationale-socialiste et la France (1933–1943)' in A.-M. Adam et al. (eds), *L'Archéologie en Alsace et en Moselle au temps de l'annexion (1940–1944)* (Wasselonne, 2001), pp. 47–65.

Omaggio al medioevo: i primi cinquanta anni del Centro italiano di studi sull'alto medioevo di Spoleto (Spoleto, 2004).

Osborn, M., 'Translations, versions, illustrations', in R. E. Bjork and J. D. Niles (eds), *A Beowulf Handbook* (Exeter, 1997), pp. 341–59.

Ozanam, A. F., *Die Begründung des Christenthums in Deutschland und die sittliche und geistige Erziehung der Germanen* (Munich, 1845).

Ozanam, A. F., *Études Germaniques pour servir à l'histoire des francs*, vol. 1, *Les Germains avant le christianisme: recherches sur les origines, les traditions, les institutions des peuples germaniques, et sur leur établissement dans l'empire romain* (Paris, 1847).

Ozanam, A. F., *Études Germaniques pour servir à l'histoire des francs*, vol. 2, *La Civilisation chrétienne chez les francs* (Paris, 1849).

Ozanam, A. F., *La Civilisation au Cinquième Siècle*, 2 vols (Paris, 1855): trans. A. C. Glyn, *History of Civilization in the Fifth Century*, 2 vols (London, 1868): trans. A. C. Glyn, *History of Civilization in the Fifth Century*, 2 vols (London, 1868).

Ozanam, J.-A., *Mémoire statistique pour servir à l'histoire de l'établissement du christianisme à Lyon, depuis le IIe siècle de l'Église jusqu'à nos jours* (Lyons, 1829).

Ozanam, J.-A., *Comte rendu du service médical et des observations faites au Grand Hôtel-Dieu de Lyon depuis le 1er octobre 1823 jusqu'au 31 décembre 1833.*

Pajak, E., and Simon, G., 'Der Deutschunterricht in der Napola', <http://homepages.uni-tuebingen.de/gerd.simon/schulung1.pdf>.

Palanque, J.-R., Davenson, H., Favre, P., de Plinval, G., Championier, J., and Lauzière, M. E., *Le Christianisme et la fin du monde antique* (Lyon, 1943).

Pappé, H. O., 'Sismondi's system of Liberty', *Journal of the History of Ideas* 40 (2) (1979), pp. 251–6.

Parker, C. J. W., 'The failure of liberal racialism: the racial ideas of E. A. Freeman', *The Historical Journal* 24, 4 (1981), pp. 825–46.

Parker, R., *The New Grove Guide to Verdi and his Operas* (Oxford, 2007).

Patriaca, S., 'Indolence and regeneration: tropes and tensions of Risorgimento patriotism', *American Historical Review* 110 (2005), pp. 380–408.

Paul the Deacon, *Historia Langobardorum*, ed. L. Bethmann and G. Waitz, *Monumenta Germaniae Historica, Scriptores Rerum Langobardicarum* (Hannover, 1878): trans. W. D. Foulke, *Paul the Deacon: History of the Langobards* (Philadelphia, 1907).

Pelloutier, S., *Histoire des Celtes et particulierement les Gaulois et les Germains depuis le temps fabuleux jusqu'à la prise de Rom par les Gaulois* (The Hague, 1740).

Pepe, G., *Il medio evo barbarico d'Italia* (Turin, 1941); trans. J. Gonnet, *Le Moyen Âge barbare en Italie* (Paris, 1956).

Périn, P., 'The undiscovered grave of king Clovis I (d. 511)', in M. Carver (ed.), *The Age of Sutton Hoo* (Woodbridge, 1992), pp. 255–64.

Périn, P., and Feffer, L.-C. (eds), *La Neustrie: les pays au nord de la Loire, de Dagobert à Charles le Chauve* (VIIe-IXe siècle) (Rouen, 1985).

Pertz, G. H., *Autobiography and Letters of G. H. Pertz, Edited by his Wife* (Leonora Pertz) (London, 1894).

Petri, F., *Germanisches Volkserbe in Wallonien und Nordfrankreich*, 2 vols (Bonn, 1937).

Petri, F., 'Um die Volksgrundlagen des Frankenreiches', *Archiv für Landes- und Volksforschung* 2 (1938), pp. (915–62); reprinted in F. Steinbach and F. Petri, *Zur Grundlegung der europäischen Einheit durch die Franken, Deutsche Schriften zur Landes- und Volksforschung*, vol. 1 (Leipzig, 1939), pp. 17–64.

Phönix aus der Asche: Theodor Mommsen und die Monumenta Germaniae Historica: Katalog zur Austellung der Monumenta Germaniae Historica…2005 (Munich 2005).

Philpotts, B., *Kindred and Clan in the Middle Ages and After: A Study in the Sociology of the Teutonic Races* (Cambridge, 1913).

Picker. H. (ed), *Hitlers Tischgespräche im Führerhauptquartier 1941–2. Im Auftrage des Deutschen Instituts für Geschichte der nationalsozialistischen Zeit geordnet, eingeleitet, und veröffentlicht von Gerhard Ritter* (Bonn, 1951).

Piganiol, A., *Histoire de Rome* (Paris, 1939).

Piganiol, A., *L'Empire chrétien (325–395)* (Paris, 1947).

Piguet, M.-F., 'Race chez Amédée Thierry et William F. Edwards', *L'Homme*, 153 (2000), pp. 93–106.

Pinault, F., 'Conquerors and other Nomads', in J.-J. Aillagon (ed.), *Rome and the Barbarians, The Birth of a New World* (Milan, 2008), p. 31.

Pinkerton, J., *Dissertation on the Origin and Progress of the Scythians or Goths* (London, 1787).

Pirenne, H., *Histoire de la constitution de la ville de Dinant* (Ghent, 1889).

Pirenne, H., 'L'Origine des constitutions urbaines au Moyen Âge', *Revue Historique* 57 (1895), pp. 57–98, 293–327.

Pirenne, H., *Histoire de Belgique* 7 vols (Brussels, 1900–32).

Pirenne, H., 'Le pangermanisme et la Belgique', *Bulletin de l'Académie royale de Belgique, Classe des Lettres* 1919, n. 5, pp. 3–35.

Pirenne, H., 'Souvenirs de captivité en Allemagne (Mars 1916–Novembre 1918)', *Revue des Deux Mondes* 55 (1920), pp. 539–60, 829–50; reprinted as a book (Brussels, 1920).

Pirenne, H., 'L'Allemagne moderne et l'Empire romain du moyen âge', *Discours prononcé à l'ouverture des cours de l'Université de Gant* (Ghent, 1921).

Pirenne, H., 'Mahomet et Charlemagne', *Revue Belge de philologie et d'histoire* 1 (1922), pp. 77–86.

Pirenne, H., 'De l'influence allemande sur le mouvement historique contemporain', *Scientia* (1923), pp. 173–8.

Pirenne, H., 'De la méthode comparative en histoire', in G. des Marez and F. L. Ganshof, *Compte-rendu du cinquième Congrès international des Sciences historiques* (Brussels, 1923), pp. 19–32.

Pirenne, H., *Histoire de l'Europe des Invasions au XVIe siècle* (Paris, 1936).

Pirenne, H., *Mahomet et Charlemagne* (Paris, 1937); English trans., *Mohammed and Charlemagne* (London, 1939).

Plunkett, S. J., *Sutton Hoo, Suffolk* (London, 2002).

Pocock, J. G. A., 'Gibbon's *Decline and Fall* and the World View of the Late Enlightenment', *Eighteenth-Century Studies* 10, 3 (1977), pp. 287–303.

Pocock, J. G. A., *Barbarism and Religion*, 5 vols (Cambridge, 1999–2010).

Pohl, W., 'Ethnicity in early medieval studies', in L. K. Little and B. H. Rosenwein (eds), *Debating the Middle Ages: Issues and Readings* (Oxford, 1998), pp. 14–24.

Pohl, W., *Die Germanen* (Munich, 2000).

Pohl, W., 'Ethnicity, theory, and tradition: a response', in A. Gillett, (ed.), *On Barbarian Identity. Critical Approaches to Ethnicity in the Early Middle Ages* (Turnhout, 2002), pp. 221–39.

Pohl, W., and Reimitz, H. (eds), *Strategies of Distinction: The Construction of Ethnic Communities, 300–800* (Leiden, 1998).

Pohl, W., and Reimitz, H. (eds), *Grenze und Differenz im frühen Mittelalter* (Vienna, 2000).

Pohl, W., Wood, I., and Reimitz, H. (eds), *The Transformation of Frontiers: From Late Antiquitiy to the Carolingians* (Leiden, 2001).

Pope-Hennessy, U., *Canon Charles Kingsley. A Biography* (London, 1948).

Porciani, I., 'Disciplinamento nazionale e modelli domestici', in A. M. Banti and P. Ginsborg (eds), *Storia d'Italia, Annali 22, Il Risorgimento* (Turin, 2007), pp. 97–125.

Porter, J.W., 'Verdi's Attila, an Ethnomusicological Analysis', in F. H. Bäuml and M. D. Birnbaum (eds), *Attila: The Man and his Image* (Budapest, 1993), pp. 45–54.

Pringle, H., *The Master Plan. Himmler's Scholars and the Holocaust* (London, 2006).

Procopius, *History of the Wars*, vol. 4 edn, H. B. Dewing (Cambridge, Mass., 1924).

Puech, H.-C., 'Éloge funèbre de M. André Piganiol, membre de l'Académie', *Comptes-rendus des séances de l'Académie des inscriptions et belles-lettres* 112, 3 (1968), pp. 309–20.

Ranke, L. von, *History of the Latin and Teutonic Nations from 1494 to 1514*, trans P. A. Ashworth (London, 1887).

Rapp, A., *Grossdeutsch-kleindeutsch* (Munich, 1922).

Rauwel, A., 'Die Burgunden in Burgund, 1920–1945: von Chaume zu Thomasset', in V. Gallé (ed.), *Die Burgunder: Ethnogenese und Assimilation eines Volkes* (Worms, 2008), pp. 379–93.

Reid, D. M., *Whose Pharoahs? Archaeology, Museums, and Egyptian National Identity from Napoleon to World War I* (Berkeley, 2002).

Reitervölker aus dem Osten. Hunnen und Awaren (Eisenstadt, 1996).

Richard, D. J., 'Arthur de Gobineau', in C. Savage Brosman, *Dictionary of Literary Biography*, vol. 123, *Nineteenth-century French Fiction Writers: Naturalism and Beyond, 1860–1900* (Detroit, 1992), pp. 101–17.

Riché, P., *Éducation et culture dans l'Occident barbare, VIe-VIIIe siècles* (Paris, 1962).

Riché, P., *Henri Irénée Marrou: historien engagé* (Paris, 2005).

Rigney, A., *Imperfect Histories: The Elusive Past and the Legacy of Romantic Historicism* (Ithaca, 2001).

Robertson, J. M., *Britain versus Germany: An Open Letter to Professor Eduard Meyer* (London, 1917).

Roscoe, T., 'Life of M. Simonde de Sismondi', in J. C. L. Simonde de Sismondi, *Historical View of the Literature of the South of Europe*, trans, T. Roscoe 4th edn (London, 1877), pp. 9–24.

Rosen, W., *Justinian's Flea: Plague, Empire and the Birth of Europe* (New York, 2006).

Ross, D. W., *Early History of Landholding among the Germans* (Boston, 1883).

Rostovtzeff, M., *The Social and Economic History of the Roman Empire*, 2 vols (Oxford, 1926).

Rowe, M., 'The Napoleonic legacy in the Rhineland and the politics of reform in Restoration Prussia', in D. Laven and L. Riall (eds), *Napoleon's Legacy* (Oxford, 2000), pp. 129–50.

Rowland, J., *Early Welsh Saga Poetry* (Cambridge, 1990).

Rückert, J., and Willoweit, D., *Die deutsche Rechsgeschichte in der NS-Zeit: ihre Vorgeschichte und ihre Nachwirkungen* (Tübingen, 1995).

Rudbeck, O., *Atland eller Manheim*, 4 vols (Uppsala, 1675–98).

Salama, P., 'Christian Courtois (1912–1956)', in C. Lepelley and X. Dupuis (eds), *Tableaux de maîtres, frontières et limites géographiques de l'Afrique du nord antique: hommage à Pierre Salama* (Paris, 1999), pp. 295–310.

Salis, J.-R. de, *Sismondi 1773–1842. La vie et l'œuvre d'un cosmopolite philosophe* (Paris, 1932).

Salis, J.-R. de, *Sismondi 1773–1842: lettres et documents inédits suivis d'une liste des sources et d'une bibliographie* (Paris, 1932).

Savigny, F. C. von, *Das Recht des Besitzes* (Gießen, 1803).

Savigny, F. C. von, *Geschichte des römischen Rechts im Mittelalter*, 2nd edn, 7 vols (Heidelberg, 1834–51).

Shackleton, R., *Montesquieu: A Critical Biography* (Oxford, 1961).

Schama, S., *Landscape and Memory* (London, 1995).

Scheible, H., *Die Entstehung der Magdeburger Zenturien: ein Beitrag zur Geschichte der historiographischen Methode* (Gütersloh, 1966).

Schemann, L., *Gobineaus Rassenwerk* (Stuttgart, 1910).

Schmauder, M., 'Imperial representation or barbaric imitation? The imperial brooches (Kaiserfibeln)', in W. Pohl and H. Reimitz (eds), *Strategies of Distinction: The Construction of Ethnic Communities, 300–800* (Leiden, 1998), pp. 281–96.

Schmidt, L., *Älteste Geschichte der Langobarden* (Leipzig, 1884).

Schmidt, L., *Älteste Geschichte der Wandalen* (Leipzig, 1888).

Schmidt, L., *Geschichte der Wandalen* (Leipzig, 1901).

Schmidt, L., *Allgemeine Geschichte der germanischen Völker bis zur Mitte des sechsten Jahrhunderts* (Munich, 1909).

Schmidt, L., *Geschichte der deutschen Stämme bis zum Ausgang der Völkerwanderung*, vol. 1, *Die Ostgermanen* (Berlin, 1910: 2nd edn, revised by H. Zeiss, Munich, 1941): vol. 2, *Die Westgermanen* (Berlin, 1918: 2nd edn, Munich, 1938): vol. 3, *Geschichte der Franken bis zur Mitte des sechsten Jahrhunderts* (revised by J. Werner and E. Zöllner, (1970).

Schmidt, L., *Die germanischen Reiche der Völkerwanderung* (Leipzig, 1918).

Schmidt, L., *Geschichte der germanischen Frühzeit: der Entwicklungsgang der Nation bis zur Begründung der fränkischen Universalmonarchie durch Chlodowech* (Köln, 1925).

Schnitzler, B., 'Fouilles et thèmes de recherche en Alsace', in A.-M. Adam et al. (eds), *L'Archéologie en Alsace et en Moselle au temps de l'annexion (1940–1944)* (Wasselonne, 2001), pp. 81–92.

Schnitzler B., and Legendre, J.-P., 'L'archéologie en Alsace-Moselle entre 1940 et 1944: essai de bilan', A.-M. Adam et al. (eds), *L'Archéologie en Alsace et en Moselle au temps de l'annexion (1940–1944)* (Wasselonne, 2001), pp. 195–201.

Schnitzler, B., and Legendre, J.-P., 'L'organisation de l'archéologie en Allemagne et dans les régions annexées d'Alsace et de Moselle', in A.-M. Adam et al. (eds), *L'Archéologie en Alsace et en Moselle au temps de l'annexion (1940–1944)* (Wasselonne, 2001), pp. 19–45.

Schöttler, P., 'Die Annales und ihre Beziehungen zu Österreich in den 20er und 30er Jahren', *Österreichische Zeitschrift für Geschichtswissenschaften* 3 (1992), pp. 74–99.

Schulenburg, S. von der, *Leibniz als Sprachforscher* (Frankfurt am Main, 1973).

Schulze, W., 'German Historiography, 1930s to 1950s', in H. Lehmann and J. Van Horn Melton (eds), *Paths of Continuity: Central European Historiography from the 1930s to the 1950s* (Cambridge, 1994), pp. 19–42.

Scott, C., 'The Vision and legacy of Christopher Dawson', in S. Caldecott and J. Morrill (eds), *Eternity in Time. Christopher Dawson and the Catholic Idea of History* (Edinburgh, 1977), pp. 11–23.

Scott, C., *A Historian and his World: A Life of Christopher Dawson 1889–1970* (London, 1984).

Scotti, M., 'Il Medioevo nell'Illuminismo', in G. Cavallo, C. Leonardi, and E. Menestò (eds), *Lo Spazio letterario del medioevo, 1. Il Medioevo latino*, vol. 4, *L'attualizzazione del testo* (Rome, 1997), pp. 141–74.

See, H., 'The Intendants' Mémoires of 1698 and their value for economic history', *Economic History Review* 1 (1928), pp. 308–13.

Seeck, O., *Untergang der antiken Welt*, 2 vols (Berlin, 1895, 1901).

Seed, J., '"The deadly principles of fanaticism": puritans and dissenters in Gibbon's *Decline and Fall of the Roman Empire*', in J. Moore, I. M. Morris, and A. J. Bayliss (eds), *Reinventing History: The Enlightenment Origins of Ancient History* (London, 2008), pp. 87–112.

Seeley, J. R., *The Expansion of England* (London, 1883).

Ségur, L.-P. comte de, *Histoire du Bas-Empire, comprenant l'histoire des empires d'occident, d'orient, grec, latin, et du second empire grec, depuis Constantin jusqu'à la prise de Constantinople*, 2 vols. (Paris, 1823).

Seipel, W., *Barbarenschmuck und Römergold. Der Schatz von Szilágysomlyó* (Vienna, 1999).

Seipel, W., in *The Gold of the Avars: The Nagyszentmiklós Treasure* (Budapest, 2002), p. 9.

Seliger, M., 'Race-thinking during the Restoration', *Journal of the History of Ideas* 19 (1958), 273–82.

Sheppard, J. G., *The Fall of Rome and the Rise of the New Nationalities: A Series of Lectures on the Connection between Ancient and Modern History* (London, 1861).

Shippey, T. A., and Haarder, A., *Beowulf: The Critical Heritage* (London, 1998).

Sieyès, E. J., *Qu'est-ce que le Tiers-état*, 3rd. edn (Paris, 1789).

Simar, T., *Étude critique sur la formation de la doctrine des races au XVIIIe siècle et son expansion au XIX siècle* (Brussels, 1922).

Simon, R. *Henry de Boulainviller: historien, politicien, philosophe, astrologue, 1658–1722* (Gap. 1940).

Sismondi, J. C. L. Simonde de, *De la vie et des écrits de P.H. Mallet* (Geneva, 1807).

Sismondi, J. C. L. Simonde de, *Julia Sévéra ou l'an quatre cent quatre-vingt-douze*, 3 vols (Paris, 1822); trans., *Julia Sévéra, or, the Year Four Hundred and Ninety-two*, 2 vols (London, 1822).

Sismondi, J. C. L. Simonde de, *A History of the Fall of the Roman Empire, Comprising a View of the Invasion and Settlement of the Barbarians*, 2 vols (London, 1834).

Sismondi, J. C. L. Simonde de, *Histoire des Français*, vol. 1 (Brussels, 1846) (1st edn: 29 vols (Paris, 1821–43)).

Sismondi, J. C. L. Simonde de, *Histoire des Républiques italiennes du Moyen Âge*, 8 vols, 5th edn (Brussels, 1858–9): trans., *History of the Italian Republics—Being a View of the Origin, Progress and Fall of Italian Freedom* (London, 1832).

Sismondi, J. C. L. Simonde de, *Historical View of the Literature of the South of Europe*, trans. T. Roscoe, 4th edn (London, 1877).

Sivan, H., 'The appropriation of Roman law in barbarian hands: Romano-Barbarian marriage in Visigothic Gaul and Spain', in W. Pohl and H. Reimitz (eds), *Strategies of Distinction: The Construction of Ethnic Communities, 300–800* (Leiden, 1998), pp. 189–203.

Sluhovsky, M., *Patroness of Paris: Rituals of Devotion in Early Modern France* (Leiden, 1998).

Smith, A. D., *The Ethnic Origins of Nations* (Oxford, 1986).

Smith, A. D., 'National Identities: Modern and Medieval?', in S. Forde, L. Johnson and A. V. Murray (eds), *Concepts of National Identity in the Middle Ages* (Leeds, 1995), pp. 21–46.

Smith, R. J., *The Gothic Bequest* (Cambridge, 1987).

Smyth, W., *Lectures on Modern History: From the Irruption of the Northern Nations to the Close of the American Revolution*, 5th edn, 2 vols (Cambridge, 1848).

'SO Debate: Peter Brown, *The World of Late Antiquity*', *Symbolae Osloenses* 72 (1997), pp. 5–90.

Soldani, S., 'Il Medioevo del Risorgimento nello specchio della nazione', in E. Castelnuovo and G. Sergi (eds), *Arte e storia nel Medioevo*, vol. 4, *Il Medioevo al passato e al presente* (Turin, 2004), pp. 149–86.

Soldani, S., 'Il Risorgimento delle donne', in A. M. Banti and P. Ginsborg (eds), *Storia d'Italia, Annali 22, Il Risorgimento* (Turin, 2007), pp. 183–224.

Sorba, C., 'Il Risorgimento in musica: l'opera lirica nei teatri del (1848), in A. M. Banti and R. Bizzochi (eds), *Immagini della nazione nell'Italia del Risorgimento* (Rome, 2002), pp. 133–56.

Sorba, C., '*Attila* and Verdi's historical imagination', *Cambridge Opera Journal* 21 (2010), pp. 241–8.

Springer, M., 'Ludwig Schmidt', *Reallexikon der germanischen Altertumskunde*, vol. 27 (Berlin, 2004), pp. 190–3.

Staël, Mme. de [A. L. G. de Staël-Holstein], *De L'Allemagne*, ed. La comtesse J. de Pange and Mlle S. Balayé, 5 vols (Paris, 1959).

Staël, Mme. de [A. L. G. de Staël-Holstein], *De la littérature considérée dans ses rapports avec les institutions sociales*, ed. P. van Tieghem, 2 vols (Paris, 1959).

Stamatov, P., 'Interpretive activism and the political uses of Verdi's operas in the 1840s', *American Sociological Review* 67 (2002), pp. 345–66.

Stanhope, P. H., (Lord Mahon), *The Life of Belisarius* (London, 1829).

Ste Croix, G. E. M. de, *The Class Struggle in the Ancient Greek World from the Archaic Age to the Arab Conquests* (London, 1982).

Stein, E., *Geschichte des spätrömischen Reiches*, 2 vols (Vienna, 1928–9): vol. 2 trans. J.-R. Palanque, *Histoire du Bas-Empire* (Brussels, 1949).

Steinbach, F., *Studien zur westdeutschen Stammes- und Volksgeschichte* (Jena, 1926).

Steinbach, F., 'Gemeinsame Wesenszüge der deutschen und der französischen Volksgeschichte', *Rheinische Vierteljahresblätter* 8 (1938), pp. 193–212; reprinted in Steinbach and Petri, *Zur Grundlegung der europäischen Einheit durch die Franken*, pp. 1–16.

Steinbach, F., and Petri, F., *Zur Grundlegung der europäischen Einheit durch die Franken; Deutsche Schriften zur Landes- und Volksforschung*, vol. 1 (Leipzig, 1939).

Stephens, W. R. W., *The Life and Letters of Edward A. Freeman*, 2 vols (London, 1895).

Stephenson, C., 'The Origins and Significance of Feudalism', *American Historical Review* 46 (1941), pp. 788–812.

Stephenson, P., 'E. A. Freeman (1823–1892), a neglected commentator on Byzantium and Modern Greece', *Historical Review* 4 (2007), pp. 119–56.

Stevens, C. E., *Sidonius Apollinaris and his Age* (Oxford, 1933).

Stewart, R. E., 'Sismondi's forgotten ethical critique of early capitalism', *Journal of Business Ethics* 3 (1984), pp. 227–34.

Stiegemann, C., and Wemhoff, M. (eds), *799: Kunst und Kultur der Karolingerzeit: Karl der Große und Papst Leo III in Paderborn*, 2 vols (Münster, 1999).

Stiegemann, C., '"Ein Erlebnis von Gleichzeitigkeit": die großen kunst- und kulturhistorischen Mittelalteraustellungen in Paderborn seit 1999 zwischen Wissenschaft und Inzenierung', in A. Sohn (ed.), *Wege der Erinnerung im und an das Mittelalter. Festschrift für Joachim Wollasch zum 80. Geburtstag*, vol. 3 (Bochum, 2011), pp. 207–30.

Stocking, R., 'Review article: continuity, culture and the state in late antique and early medieval Iberia', *Early Medieval Europe* 15 (2007), pp. 335–48.

Stowell, T., 'Sismondi: a neglected pioneer', *History of Political Economy* 4 (1972), pp. 62–88.

Stroheker, K. F., *Eurich* (Stuttgart, 1937).

Stroheker, K. F., 'Leowigild: aus einer Wendezeit westgotischer Geschichte', *Die Welt als Geschichte* 5 (1939), pp. 446–85, reprinted in Stroheker, K. F., *Germanentum und Spätantike* (Zürich, 1965), pp. 134–91.

Stroheker, K. F., *Der senatorische Adel im spätantiken Gallien* (Reutlingen, 1948).

Sybel, H. von, *Die Enstehung des deutschen Königtums* (Frankfurt, 1844).

Tabacco, G., 'Latinità e germanesimo nella tradizione medievistica italiana', *Rivista Storica Italiana* 102, fasc. iii (1990), pp. 691–716.

Tacitus, *Germania* (*De origine et situ Germanorum*), ed. J. G. C. Anderson (Oxford, 1938).

Temperley, H. W. V., 'The Historical Ideas of J. B. Bury', in J. B. Bury, *Selected Essays*, ed. H. W. V., Temperley (Cambridge, 1930), pp. xv–xxxii.

Theuws, F., and Nelson, J. L. (eds), *Rituals of Power from Late Antiquity to the Early Middle Ages* (Leiden, 2000).

Thierry, A. [Amédée], *Histoire des Gaulois, depuis les temps les plus reculés jusqu'à l'entière soumission de la Gaule à la dominance romaine*, 3 vols (Paris, 1828–45).

Thierry, A. [Amédée], *Histoire d'Attila et de ses successeurs jusqu'à l'établissement des Hongrois en Europe suivie des légendes et traditions*, 5th edn, 2 vols (Paris, 1874).

Thierry, A. [Augustin], *L'Industrie littéraire et scientifique liguée avec l'industrie commerciale et manufacturière*, vol. 1, pt. 2, *Politique* (Paris, 1817).

Thierry, A. [Augustin], *The Historical Essays and Narratives of the Merovingian Era* (Philadelphia, 1845).

Thierry, A. [Augustin], *History of the Conquest of England by the Normans; Its Causes, and its Consequences, in England, Scotland, Ireland, and on the Continent*, trans. W. Hazlitt, 2 vols (London, 1847).

Thom, M., *Republics, Nations and Tribes* (London, 1995).

Thompson, A. H., *Gibbon*, Historical Association Pamphlets, General Series G3 (London, 1946).

Thompson, E. A., *A Roman Informer and Inventor: Being a New Text of the Treatise De rebus bellicis* (Oxford, 1952).

Thompson, E. A., 'The Visigoths from Fritigern to Euric', *Historia* 12 (1963), pp. 105–26, reprinted in Thompson, E. A., *Romans and Barbarians: The Decline of the Western Empire* (Madison, 1982), pp. 38–57.

Thompson, E. A., 'Economic Warfare', in Thompson, E. A., *Romans and Barbarians: The Decline of the Western Empire* (Madison, 1982), pp. 3–19.

Thompson, E. A., *Romans and Barbarians: The Decline of the Western Empire* (Madison, 1982).

Thompson, E. A., *Who was Saint Patrick?* (Woodbridge, 1985).

Thompson, E. A., *The Huns* (Oxford, 1996).

Thorkelin, G. J., *De Danorum Rebus Gestis Seculis III et IV: Poema Danicum Dialecto Anglosaxonico* (Copenhagen, 1815).

Tillemont, L.-S. Le Nain de,, *Histoire des empereurs et autres princes qui ont regné pendant les six premiers siècles de l'Église*, 6 vols (Brussels, 1690–1738).

Tillemont, L.-S. le Nain de, *Mémoires pour server à l'histoire ecclésiastique des six premiers siècles*, 16 vols (Paris, 1693–1712).

Todd, M., 'E. A. Thompson (1914–1994)', *Oxford Dictionary of National Biography*.

Tombs, R., *France 1814–1914* (Harlow, 1996).

Toppan, B., 'Evolution du concept de "barbare" en Italie de Machiavel à Manzoni', in J. Shillinger and P. Alexandre (eds), *Le barbare* (Bern, 2008), pp. 117–33.

Troya, C., *Storia d'Italia del Medio-evo*, 6 vols, in 16 parts (Naples, 1839–59): vol. 1, pt. v.: *Della condizione de' Romani vinti da'Longobardi e della vera lezione d'alcune parole di Paolo Diacono intorno a tale argomento* (Naples, 1841).

Troya, C. and Balbo, C., *Delle civile condizione dei Romani vinti dai Longobardi e di altre quistioni storichi: lettere inedite*, ed. E. Mandarini (Naples, 1869).

Tulard, J., 'Qui a fait coudre les abeilles de Childéric sur le manteau du sacre de Napoléon?', in M. Rouche (ed.), *Clovis, Histoire et mémoire. Le baptême de Clovis, son echo à travers l'histoire*, vol. 2 (Paris, 1997), pp. 629–35.

Turner, S., *The History of the Anglo-Saxons from their First Appearance above the Elbe, to the Death of Egbert, with a Map of their Ancient Territory* (London, 1799).

Turner, S., *The History of the Manners, Landed Property, Laws, Poetry, Literature, Religion, and Language of the Anglo-Saxons*, 4 vols (London, 1799–1805).

Vallery-Radot, R., *Devant des idoles* (Paris, 1921).

Veaute, M., 'On the good use of immigration', in J.-J. Aillagon (ed.), *Rome and the Barbarians: The Birth of a New World* (Milan, 2008), pp. 32–3.

Veit, U., 'Ethnic concepts in German prehistory: a case study on the relationship between cultural identity and archaeological objectivity', in S. J. Shennan (ed.), *Archaeological Approaches to Cultural Identity* (London, 1989), pp. 35–56.

Verdi, G., *I Copialettere di Giuseppe Verdi*, ed. G. Cesari and A. Luzio (Milan, 1913).

Verlinden, C., 'Frankish colonization: a new approach', *Transactions of the Royal Historical Society*, 5th series, vol. 4 (1954), pp. 1–17.

Vessey, M., 'Patristics and literary history', *Journal of Literature and Theology* 5 (1991), pp. 341–54; reprinted in Thompson, E. A., *Latin Christian Writers in Late Antiquity and their Texts* (Aldershot, 2005).

Vessey, M., 'The demise of the Christian writer and the remaking of "Late Antiquity": from H.-I. Marrou's *Saint Augustine* (1938) to Peter Brown's *Holy Man* (1983)', *Journal of Early Christian Studies* 6 (1998); reprinted in id., *Latin Christian Writers in Late Antiquity and their Texts* (Aldershot, 2005), pp. 377–411.

Vessey, M., 'Theory, or the Dream of the Book (Mallarmé to Blanchot)', in W. E. Klingshirn and L. Safran (eds), *The Early Christian Book* (Washington, DC., 2007), pp. 241–73.

Vessey, M., '407 and all that: insular late Roman historiography and the literary-historical turn', *Journal of Late Antiquity* 2 (2009), pp. 30–48.

Vie de sainte Mélanie, ed. D. Gorce (Paris, 1961).

Villari, P., 'Conversation de Napoléon Ier et de Sismondi', *Revue Historique* 1 (1876), pp. 238–51.

Villari, P., 'La storia dei centi Giorni narrata del S. (epistolario inedito)', *Nuova Antologia* 33 (Rome, 1876), pp. 697–705.

Villari, P., *Le invasioni barbariche in Italia* (Milan, 1901); trans. L. Villari, *The Barbarian Invasions of Italy*, 2 vols (London, 1902).

Villari, P., and Monod, G., 'Lettres inédites de Sismondi écrites pendant les Cent-Jours', *Revue Historique* 3 (1877), pp. 80–114, 319–51; 4 (1877), pp. 139–62, 347–70; 5 (1877), pp. 347–68; 6 (1877), pp. 106–28.

Villari, P., and Monod, G., 'Notes de Sismondi sur l'empire et les cent jours', *Revue Historique* 4 (1879), pp. 360–93.

Violante, C., *La fine della 'grande illusione': uno storico europeo tra guerra e dopoguerra, Henri Pirenne (1914–1923): Per una rilettuta della 'Histoire de l'Europe'* (Bologna, 1997).

Vismara, G., 'G. P. Bognetti, storico dei Longobardi', in G. P. Bognetti, *L'età longobarda*, vol. 1 (Milan, 1966), pp. v–xix.

Vitali, C., 'Rome and the Barbarians: Europe during the migration period', in J.-J. Aillagon (ed.), *Rome and the Barbarians: The Birth of a New World* (Milan, 2008), pp. 36–7.

Vlierden, M. van (ed.), *Willibrord en het begin van Nederland* (Utrecht, 1995).

Vogt, J., *Rom und Karthago: ein Gemeinschaftswerk* (Leipzig, 1943).

Volpilhac, C., 'Les gaulois à l'Académie des inscriptions et belles-lettres de 1701 à 1793', in P. Viallaneix and J. Ehrard (eds), *Nos ancêtres les Gaulois, Actes du Colloque International de Clermont-Ferrand* (Clermont-Ferrand, 1982), pp. 77–83.

Volpilhac-Auger, C., *Tacite et Montesquieu, Studies on Voltaire and the Eighteenth Century* (Oxford, 1985).

Volpilhac-Auger, C., 'Les rois de Prusse sous le regard de Montesquieu', *Revue Montesquieu* 2 (2004), pp. 55–65.

Voltaire, (F.-M. Arouet), 'Lois (Esprit des)', in Voltaire, *Dictionnaire philosophique*, vol. 4 (Paris, 1879), pp. 1–15.

Wagner, F., *Die politische Bedeutung des Childerich-Grabfundes von 1653*, Bayerische Akademie der Wissenschaften, philosophisch-historische Klasse, Sitzungsberichte (Munich, 1973).

Wahl, H. R., *Die Religion des deutschen Nationalismus. Eine mentalitätsgeschichtliche Studie zur Literatur des Kaiserreichs: Felix Dahn, Ernst von Wildenbruch, Walter Flex, Neue Bremer Beiträge* (Heidelberg, 2002).

Wallace-Hadrill, J. M., *The Barbarian West*, (London, 1952); 3rd edn (London, 1967).

Wallace-Hadrill, J. M., 'The Bloodfeud of the Franks', *Bulletin of the John Rylands Library* 41 (1959), pp. 459–87: reprinted in J. M. Wallace-Hadrill, *The Long-haired Kings* (London, 1962), pp. 121–47.

Wallace-Hadrill, J. M., *The Long-haired Kings and Other Studies in Frankish History* (London, 1962).

Wallace-Hadrill, J. M., review of R. Wenskus, *Stammesbildung und Verfassung*, *English Historical Review* 79 (1964), pp. 137–9.

Wallace-Hadrill, J. M., *Early Germanic Kingship and on the Continent* (Oxford, 1971).

Wallace-Hadrill, J. M., *Early Medieval History* (Oxford, 1975).

Ward-Perkins, B., *The Fall of Rome and the End of Civilization* (Oxford, 2005).

Wawn, A., *The Vikings and the Victorians: Inventing the Old North in 19th-century Britain* (Woodbridge, 2000).

Webster, L., and Backhouse, J. (eds), *The Making of England. Anglo-Saxon Art and Culture* AD 600–900 (London, 1991).

Webster, L., and Brown, M. (eds), *The Transformation of the Roman World*, AD 400–900 (London, 1997).

Wenskus, R., *Studien zur historisch-politischen Gedankenwelt Bruns von Querfurt* (Cologne, 1956).

Wenskus, R., *Stammesbildung und Verfassung: das Werden der frühmittelalterlichen Gentes* (Cologne, 1961).

Werner, J., 'Childerichgrab', *Lexikon des Mittelalters* 2 (Munich, 1983), pp. 1819–20.

Werner, K. F., *Das NS-Geschichtsbild und die deutsche Geschichtswissenschaft* (Stuttgart, 1967).

Werner, K. F., 'Zum Geleit', in E. Ewig, *Spätantikes und fränkisches Gallien*, vol. 1 (Munich, 1976), pp. Ix–xii

Werner, Z., *Attila, Dramatische Werke*, vol. 5 (Bern, 1970).

Werveke, H. van, 'Karl Lamprecht et Henri Pirenne', *Bulletin de la Commission Royale d'Histoire* 138 (1972), pp. 39–60.

Whitby, M., 'John Bagnell Bury', *Oxford Dictionary of National Biography*.

Why we are at War (Oxford, 1914).

Whyte, I. B., 'Anglo-German conflict in popular fiction 1870–1914', in F. Bridgham, ed. *The First World War as a Clash of Cultures* (Rochester, NY, 2006), pp. 43–99.

Wickham, C., 'The other transition: from the ancient world to feudalism', *Past and Present* 113 (1984), pp. 3–36, reprinted in Wickham, C., *Land and Power. Studies in Italian and European Social History, 400–1200* (London, 1994), pp. 7–42.

Wickham, C., 'La chute de Rome n'aura pas lieu', *Le Moyen Âge* 99 (1993), pp. 88–119, reprinted in English as 'The fall of Rome will not take place', in L. K. Little and B. H. Rosenwein (eds), *Debating the Middle Ages* (Oxford, 1998), pp. 45–57.

Wickham, C., *Framing the Early Middle Ages: Europe and the Mediterranean, 400–800* (Oxford, 2005).

Wieczorek, A., and Hinz, H.-M. (eds), *Europas Mitte um 1000. Beiträge zur Geschichte und Archäologie*, 3 vols (Darmstadt, 2001).

Wiell, S., 'Denmark's bog find pioneer: the archaeologist Conrad Engelhardt and his work', in L. Jørgensen, B. Storgaard, and L. Gebauer Thomsen (eds), *The Spoils of Victory: The North in the Shadow of the Roman Empire* (Copenhagen, 2003), pp. 66–83.

Wiley, R. A., 'Anglo-Saxon Kemble: the life and works of John Mitchell Kemble, 1807–57', *Anglo-Saxon Studies in Archaeology and History* 1 (1979), pp. 165–273.

Wiseman, N. P., *Fabiola, or, the Church in the Catacombs* (London, 1854).

Wolfram, H., *Intitulatio* I, *Lateinische Königs- und Fürstentitel bis zum Ende des 8, Jahrhunderts* (Graz, 1967).

Wolfram, H., *Geschichte der Goten* (Munich, 1969); trans., *History of the Goths* (Berkeley, 1979).

Wood, I. N., 'Ethnicity and the ethnogenesis of the Burgundians', with an appendix on 'The settlement of the Burgundians', in H. Wolfram and W. Pohl (eds), *Typen der Ethnogenese unter besonderer Berücksichtigung der Bayern* (Vienna, 1990), pp. 53–69.

Wood, I. N., 'Defining the Franks', in S. Forde, L. Johnson and A. V. Murray (eds), *Concepts of National Identity in the Middle Ages* (Leeds, 1995), pp. 47–57; reprinted in T. F. X. Noble (ed.), *From Roman Provinces to Medieval Kingdoms*, pp. 110–19.

Wood. I. N., 'Teutsind, Witlaic and the history of Merovingian *precaria*', in W. Davies and P. Fouracre (eds), *Property and Power in the Early Middle Ages* (Cambridge, 1995), pp. 31–52.

Wood. I. N., 'Gibbon on the Merovingians', in R. McKitterick and R. Quinault (eds), *Gibbon and Empire* (Cambridge, 1997), pp. 117–36.

Wood, I. N., 'Report: The European Science Foundation's Programme on the Transformation of the Roman World and Emergence of Early Medieval Europe', *Early Medieval Europe* 6 (1997), pp. 217–27.

Wood, I. N., 'Culture', in R. McKitterick (ed.), *The Early Middle Ages, Short Oxford History of Europe* (Oxford, 2001), pp. 167–98.

Wood, I. N., 'John Michael Wallace-Hadrill', *Proceedings of the British Academy* 124 (2004), pp. 333–55.

Wood, I. N., 'Art and architecture of Western Europe', in P. Fouracre (ed.), *Cambridge Medieval History*, vol. 1, *c.500–c.700* (Cambridge, 2005), pp. 760–75.

Wood. I. N., 'The bloodfeud of the Franks: a historiographical legend', *Early Medieval Europe* 14 (2006), pp. 489–504.

Wood, I. N., 'Royal succession and legitimation in the Roman West, 419–536', in S. Airlie, W. Pohl and H. Reimitz (eds), *Staat im frühen Mittelalter* (Vienna, 2006), pp. 59–72.

Wood, I. N., 'Landscapes compared', *Early Medieval Europe* 15 (2007), pp. 223–37.

Wood, I. N., 'The use and abuse of the Early Middle Ages, 1750–2000', in M. Costambeys, A. Hamer, and M. Heale (eds), *The Making of the Middle Ages: Liverpool Essays* (Liverpool, 2007), pp. 36–53.

Wood, I. N., ' "Adelchi" and "Attila": the barbarians and the Risorgimento', *Papers of the British School at Rome* 76 (2008), pp. 233–55.

Wood, I. N., 'Barbarians, historians and the construction of national identities', *Journal of Late Antiquity* 1 (2008), pp. 61–82.

Wood, I. N., 'The Fall of the Roman Empire in the eighteenth and nineteenth centuries', in S. Barton and P. Linehan (eds), *Cross, Crescent and Conversion: Studies on Medieval Spain and Christendom in Memory of Richard Fletcher* (Leiden, 2008), pp. 326–47.

Wood, I. N., 'The Panthéon in Paris: *lieu d'oubli*', in H. Reimitz and B. Zeller (eds), *Vergangenheit und Vergegenwärtigung. Frühes Mittelalter und europäische Erinnerungskultur* (Vienna, 2009), pp. 93–102.

Wood, I. N., 'Early Medieval History and Nineteenth-Century Politics in Dahn's "Ein Kampf um Rom" and Manzoni's "Adelchi"', in S. Patzold, A. Rathmann-Lutz, and V. Scior (eds), *Geschichtsvorstellungen. Bilder, Texte und Begriffe aus dem Mittelalter. Festschrift für Hans-Werner Goetz zum 65. Geburtstag* (Vienna, 2012), pp. 535–57.

Wood, I. N., 'Ethnicity and language in medieval and modern versions of the Attalus-saga', in W. Pohl and B. Zeller (eds), *Sprache und Identität im frühen Mittelalter* (Vienna, 2012), pp. 81–91.

Wood, I. N., 'Entrusting Western Europe to the Church, 400–750', *Transactions of the Royal Historical Society* (forthcoming).

Wood, S., *The Proprietary Church in the Medieval West* (Oxford, 2006).

Woodward, E. L., *Christianity and Nationalism in the Later Roman Empire* (London, 1916).

Wootton, D., 'Narrative, Irony, and Faith in Gibbon's Decline and Fall', *History and Theory* 33, 4 (1994), pp. 77–105.

Wormald, P., *The Making of English Law: King Alfred to the Twelfth Century* (Oxford, 1999).

Wright, R., *Late Latin and early Romance in Spain and Carolingian France* (Liverpool, 1982).

Wyss, U., *Die wilde Philologie. Jacob Grimm und der Historismus* (Munich, 1979).

Young, B. W., '"Scepticism in excess": Gibbon and eighteenth-century Christianity', *The Historical Journal* 41 (1998), pp. 179–99,

Youngs, S. (ed.), *The work of Angels: Masterpieces of Celtic Metalwork 6th–9th Centuries AD* (London, 1989).

Zamoyski, A., *Rites of Peace: the Fall of Napoleon and the Congress of Vienna* (London, 2007).

Zeebroeck, A. van, 'L'Âge d'or médiévale, un idéal pour une nouvelle chrétienté? La réponse d'un historien engagé, Godefroid Kurth (1847–1916)', in L. van Ypersele and A.-D. Marcelis (eds), *Rêves de Chrétienté, Réalités du monde. Imaginaires catholiques* (Louvain, 2001), pp. 205–19.

Zeiss, H., *Studien zu den Grabfunden aus den Burgunderreich an der Rhône, Sitzungsberichte der bayerischen Akademie der Wissenschaften, philosophisch-historische Abteilung*, 7 (Munich, 1938).

Zeiss, H., 'Germanen in Burgund', in F. Kerber (ed.), *Burgund: Das Land zwischen Rhein und Rhone* (Strasbourg, 1942), pp. 19–30.

Zöllner, E., *Geschichte der Franken bis zur Mitte des sechsten Jahrhunderts* (Munich, 1970).

Index

Printed and bound by CPI Group (UK) Ltd, Croydon, CR0 4YY